The Law of Messiah

Torah from a New Covenant Perspective

VOLUME 1

by

Michael Rudolph

in collaboration with

Daniel C. Juster

Published by Tikkun International

The Law of Messiah
Torah from a New Covenant Perspective
Volume 1

Copyright © 2019 by Michael Rudolph, D.Min., J.D.

Published by:

Published by Tikkun International, Inc.
P.O. Box 2997 · Montgomery Village, MD 20886

Library of Congress Control Number: 2019905736

ISBN: 978-1-7337112-3-4 (Volume 1)
Printed in the United States of America

Cover and Select Interior Design by Oz Graphics • malkaoz418@gmail.com

Dedication

I am greatly indebted to my life partner, my
wonderful and excellent wife Marie for her loving
and sacrificial support of all my endeavors, to my son
David for his advice, encouragement, and scholarly
example, to my son Brian for modeling how to
love and serve those who are elderly, disabled, and
otherwise in need, to my other children Kevin, Steve,
and Patty who make being their father a joy, and to
my long-time mentor Dr. Daniel C. Juster for his
friendship, collaboration, and his many contributions
to this book.

Mostly, I am eternally grateful to my Father God,
Messiah Yeshua, and the *Ruach HaKodesh*, who
gave me inspiration, life, and energy to complete this
multi-year task. It is their desire, along with
Dr. Juster's and my own, that this book will
contribute to the biblical knowledge, faith, and
spiritual growth of many in the years to come.

Table of Contents

Subject	Mitzvah Number	Pg.

VOLUME 1

Preface 11
Introduction: Michael Rudolph 13
Introduction: Daniel C. Juster 31
Elephants in the Room: Michael Rudolph.. 50
Mitzvah Subject Keys 57
New Covenant Literal Application (NCLA) Code 58

APPENDICES

Appendix A: Subject Index 790
Appendix B: *Tanakh* Scripture Index: English Versification............... 823
Appendix C: *Tanakh* Scripture Index: Hebrew Versification............... 841
Appendix D: *B'rit Chadasha* Scripture Index 859
Appendix E: Maimonides *Mitzvah* Cross-Reference Index................... 876
Appendix F: Meir *Mitzvah* Cross-Reference Index.............................. 890
Appendix G: HaChinuch *Mitzvah* Cross-Reference Index 897
Appendix H: *Mitzvot* of Three Classical Commentators Arranged
       in Order of HaChinuch's *Mitzvah* Numbers and
       Labeled According to Weekly *Parashiyot* 911
Appendix I: Scriptures Cited by Three Classical Commentators
       Arranged According to Weekly *Parashiyot*............................. 928
Appendix J: Maimonides' List of Positive and Negative *Mitzvot* 946
Appendix K: Explicit and Implicit *Mitzvot* in the Book of Matthew .. 960
Appendix L: Explicit Mitzvot of the New Covenant *Shlichim* 963
Appendix M: Hebrew Word Glossary 972

Note: An asterisk (*) preceding a *Mitzvah* number below indicates that it references one or more
    of the classical *mitzvah* compilations. An asterisk (*) following a *Mitzvah* title below
    indicates that its assigned NCLA Code is other than JMm JFm KMm KFm GMm GFm.

GODLINESS AND GODLY LIVING

Being Unequally Yoked in Matters of Godly Importance *A1 60
Walking in God's Ways *A2 63
Being Good Stewards A3 65
Keeping Vows Made to God *A4 70
Swearing Oaths Only in God's Name *A5 73
Using God's Name Lightly or Falsely... *A6 76
Confessing, Repenting, and Making Restitution for Our Sins............... *A7 80
Succumbing to Fear, Worry and Anxiety.. *A8 83
Swearing Falsely *A9 86
Ritual Purification, Cleanness, Separation and Health *A10 88
Wine and Drunkenness *A11 101
Being Born Again from Above A12 103
Being Pure in Heart A13 105
Aspiring to God's Perfection and Holiness A14 107
Doing Religious Things in Order to Be Seen A15 109

Subject	*Mitzvah* Number	Pg.
Seeking to Please Men over God	A16	111
Being Humble and Not Prideful	A17	113
Being Good Stewards of Our Spiritual Gifts According to the Grace Given Us	A18	116
Assembling with the Brethren	A19	119
Living by God's Words and Not by Bread Alone	A20	121
Fleeing from Love of Money and Pursuing Godly Virtues	A21	123
Allowing Worldly Attractions to Ensnare Us	A22	126
Being Subject to Governing Authorities	A23	128
Being Clean of Spirit as Well as of Body	A24	130

BENEVOLENCE

Lending Money without Interest to Our Poor Brother	*B1	133
Returning a Needed Pledged Item	*B2	136
Eating and Otherwise Partaking of the Produce of Our Work	*B3	137
Giving Financial Help to Persons in Need	*B4	139
Setting Aside Part of Our Increase for the Poor	*B5	142
Gleanings and Part of Life-Sustaining Commodities Left for the Poor and Disadvantaged*	*B6	144

COMMERCE

Being Fair and Honest in Business	*C1	147
Paying an Employee His Wages on the Day He Labors or When Due	*C2	150
Cancelling Loans and Not Refusing to Make Loans In and Near the Sabbatical Year*	*C3	151
Dealing Harshly When Lending Money or Collecting Debts	*C4	155

DAYS AND SEASONS

Resting from Work and Assembling on the Weekly Sabbath*	*D1	159
Leaving Our Homes to Work on the Sabbath*	*D2	165
Keeping the Sabbath Day Holy*	*D3	166
Resting from Work and Assembling on God's Annual Sabbaths*	*D4	169
Counting to *Shavuot* and Waving Two Loaves*	*D5	180
Keeping Our Home and Domain Free of Leaven and Chametz, from Passover through the Feast of Unleavened Bread*	*D6	183
Abstaining from Eating *Chametz*, from Passover through the Feast of Unleavened Bread*	*D7	187
Observing Passover with Matzah and Bitter Herbs*	*D8	191
Observing a Late Passover with *Matzah* and Bitter Herbs*	*D9	196
Observing the Feast of Unleavened Bread by Eating *Matzah* on Each of Its Seven Days*	*D10	199
Ceremonially Recounting What God Did for Us When We Left Egypt*	*D11	203
Blowing the Shofar on Special Days and As an Alarm in War*	*D12	206
Afflicting Our Souls and Repenting on *Yom Kippur**	*D13	210
Rejoicing at the Festivals of *Shavuot, Sukkot,* and *Sh'mini Atzeret**	*D14	217
Living in a *Sukkah* during the Feast of *Sukkot**	*D15	220
Taking Up the Four Species on *Sukkot**	*D16	222
Public Reading of the *Torah* during *Sukkot* in the Sabbatical Year*	*D17	224

Subject	*Mitzvah* Number	Pg.
Cancelling Loans and Resting Our Land in the Sabbatical Year*	*D18	226
Resting and Returning Ownership of Our Land in the Jubilee Year*	*D19	230
Determining Occurrence of the New Moon*	*D20	234

COVENANT RESPONSIBILITIES

Preserving, and Disseminating God's Word	*E1	237
Performing and Receiving *B'rit Milah**	*E2	239
Commemorating *Pidyon HaBen**	*E3	244
Being a Kingdom of Priests, a Holy Nation, Proclaimers of the Good News, and a Light to the Gentiles*	*E4	248
Conversion and Receiving Jewish Proselytes and Converts*	*E5	253
*Tzitzit, Tefillin, and Mezuzot**	*E6	258
Tithes, Offerings, and *Tz'dakah*	*E7	262
Being Fruitful and Multiplying in Number and in Fruitfulness	*E8	267

FAMILY

Honoring and Revering Our Father and Mother	*F1	271
The Covenant Laws of Marriage	*F2	274
Divorce, and Remarriage	*F3	281
Withholding Food, Clothing, or Marital Rights from Our Wife*	*F4	294
Treatment of Children*	F5	296

RELATING TO GOD

Believing in God	*G1	299
Acknowledging and Not Denying Belief in God and in Yeshua	*G2	300
Knowing that God Is *Echad* and Triune	*G3	304
Loving God	*G4	308
Testing God's Promises and Warnings	*G5	310
Fearing God	*G6	312
Treating God as Holy by Proclaiming Him Holy and by Not Profaning His Name	*G7	315
Serving, Worshiping, Praising, and Praying to God	*G8	318
Clinging to God	*G9	324
Approaching God While Unrepentant	G10	326
Being Thankful to God and Blessing Him in All Things	*G11	328
Having Faith in God and Trusting Him in All Things	*G12	332
Dedicating Ourselves to God	*G13	342
Knowing God by Observing His Creation	G14	347
Blaspheming God vs. Receiving Messiah and the Holy Spirit	*G15	351
Putting God First	*G16	358
Being Continuous, Persistent, and Fervent in Prayer	G17	360
Waiting on God	G18	362
Praying in Faith and Having Faith for That Which We Pray	G19	364
Knowing God and Who He Is	G20	366

Subject	Mitzvah Number	Pg.

HOLINESS AND GOD'S ORDER
Having Reverence for God's Sanctuary *H1 375
Modeling God's Holiness by Our Appearance and by What We Wear *H2 377
Preserving Things That Belong to God and That Are Holy *H3 380
Using Our Speech, Thoughts, Hearts and Actions for
that which Is Good and Holy H4 383
Conducting Sacrifices Outside of the Holy Temple *H5 387
Appointing a Ruler Whom God Chooses *H6 389
Castration *H7 391
Dying to Self H8 393

IDOLATRY, HEATHENS, AND THE OCCULT
Practicing Idolatry *I1 397
Pursuing the Occult *I2 403
Benefitting from Idolatry *I3 406
Enticing Others to Idolatry *I4 409
Enabling Idolatry *I5 411
Destroying Idolatry *I6 415
Listening to Those Who Would Lead Us toward Idolatry *I7 421
Covenanting with Idolaters and Unbelievers *I8 424
Adopting Heathen Practices *I9 427

JUSTICE
Applying the Mosaic Law in a Manner Consistent with New Covenant Realities J1 431
God's Law of Justice *J2 461
Injury and Damages *J3 473
Law of Inheritance *J4 479
Appointing Elders to Lead, Pray, Teach, Judge, and Make *Halachah* J5 486

VOLUME 2
KASHRUT
Creatures We Are Allowed to Eat and Forbidden to Eat* *K1 504
Boiling a Young Animal in Its Mother's Milk and
Acts of Similar Heathen Perversion *K2 509
Eating Fat, Meat from Strangled Animals, or Food Polluted by Idols* *K3 512
Eating Blood *K4 514
Eating the Sinew of the Thigh* *K5 517
Hunting and Slaughtering for Food* *K6 520

THE JEWISH PEOPLE AND LAND OF ISRAEL
Occupying the Land of Israel* L1 524
Blessing and Not Cursing the Jewish People L2 529
Gentiles Not to Be Excluded from the Jewish Community L3 532

MORALITY AND COMPASSION
Pursuing Righteousness and Doing What Is Right M1 542
Keeping Our Promises *M2 545

Subject	*Mitzvah* Number	Pg.
Telling the Truth	*M3	548
Returning Lost Items to Their Owners	*M4	552
Committing Murder or Other Unjustifiable Homicide	*M5	554
Committing Theft or Robbery	*M6	559
Pursuing Economic Equity through Our Institutions	*M7	562
Being Humane in Our Dominion over God's Creatures	*M8	567
Coveting or Planning to Acquire Another's Property	*M9	571
Biblical Principles of War	*M10	573
Resisting Temptation to Sin	*M11	578

NEIGHBORS AND BROTHERS

Subject	*Mitzvah* Number	Pg.
Loving Our Neighbor, the Stranger, and Even Our Enemy	*N1	583
Wronging One Another through Our Speech	*N2	587
Helping Our Neighbor Who Is in Need	*N3	592
Forgiving Our Neighbor	N4	595
Resolving Disputes, Correcting, Reconciling with, and Bringing Discipline to Brother Believers	*N5	599
Exploiting a Neighbor's Weakness	*N6	611
Taking Reasonable Steps to Keep Ourselves and Others Safe	*N7	613
Giving Respect and Honor to Persons of Advanced Age	*N8	615
Helping a Person Who Needs Rescue	*N9	618
Kidnapping	*N10	620
Being Hospitable	N11	622
Judging Our Neighbor	N12	625
Repenting of Our Own Sin before Seeking to Correct Our Neighbor	N13	636
Serving Our Neighbor	N14	638
Pursuing Peace with Our Neighbor	N15	640
Nursing Anger Toward Our Neighbor	*N16	642
Despising Our Neighbor	N17	644
Being Compassionate and Merciful Toward Our Neighbor	N18	646

OUTREACH, MINISTRY AND SPIRITUAL AUTHORITY

Subject	*Mitzvah* Number	Pg.
Being Salt for the Earth and a Light for the World	O1	649
Acknowledging and Utilizing Our Spiritual Authority	O2	652
Not Preaching the Word of God to Those Who Are Closed to It	O3	658
Implementing the "Great Commission" Proclaimed by Yeshua	O4	660
Casting Demons Out of Persons Unable to Maintain Deliverance	O5	662

PRIESTHOOD

Subject	*Mitzvah* Number	Pg.
The Priesthood of Israel and of Believers in Yeshua	P1	665
Cohanim to Bless God's People	*P2	673
Regarding God's Priests as Holy	*P3	675
The Priesthood of Believers and Entering God's Most Holy Place	*P4	677
Priests Marrying Persons Likely to Compromise Their Holiness	*P5	681
Priests Ministering While Spiritually Unclean	*P6	684
Levitical Priests Being Near a Dead Body	*P7	687

Subject	Mitzvah Number	Pg.

RU'ACH HAKODESH
Listening to and Heeding God's Voice *R1 690
Receiving the Holy Spirit. R2 694
Coming Against the Holy Spirit. R3 709
Testing the Spirits R4 712

SEXUAL CONDUCT
Engaging in Homosexuality. *S1 714
Having Sexual Relations with Family Members *S2 717
Committing Adultery. *S3 719
Fornicating: Engaging in Sexual Intimacy Outside of Marriage. *S4 723
Having Sexual Relations with a Person and Also with a
Close Member of that Person's Family *S5 728
Engaging in Prostitution *S6 729
Engaging in Sexual Contact with Animals *S7 736
Having Sexual Intercourse with a Woman during Her Menstruation *S8 738
Giving Ourselves to Unlawful Sexual Desires *S9 740

WORD OF GOD—TORAH
Studying, Hearing and Teaching Torah and Torah-Obedience *W1 742
Remembering and Walking in Awareness of God's Word. *W2 746
Prophesying Falsely. *W3 750
Testing Everything that is Spoken in God's Name *W4 753
Writing, Teaching, and Learning the Song of Moses. *W5 755
Adding to, or Subtracting from, the Written Word of God *W6 757
Believing or Advocating Unbiblical Doctrines and
Paying Heed to Persons Who Do. *W7 759
Obeying the Mitzvot of Adonai and Yeshua. W8 761
Nullifying the Word of God through Our Rules and Traditions W9 764
Attending to Both the Lesser and the Weightier Matters of Torah W10 770

MESSIAH YESHUA
Seudat Ha-Adon. Y1 772
Abiding in Yeshua in Order to Bear Fruit Y2 774
Trusting in Yeshua and Believing that He is Our Messiah Sent by God Y3 776
Expecting and Accepting Persecution on Account of Our Faith in Yeshua. Y4 778
Denying Yeshua for Fear of Man. Y5 780
Following Yeshua and Putting Him Before All Else Y6 781
Acknowledging God as Our Supreme Father, and Yeshua as
Our Supreme Rabbi, Teacher, and Leader. Y7 783
Coming to Yeshua for Spiritual Rest Y8 784
Obeying the Commandments and Teachings of Yeshua Y9 785

END-TIMES
Believing End-Time False Prophets and Messiahs Z1 787

Preface

Our purpose in writing this book is to codify the *mitzvot* of Scripture without the classical Jewish presumption and constraint that they must total six hundred thirteen, and to discuss their meaning and application from a New Covenant perspective.

In modern times until recently, the New Covenant and the *Kit'vei B'rit Chadashah* (New Testament) were considered solely Christian and, since the First Century, God's Law as an approach to biblical living has been considered exclusively Jewish and limited to the commandments given through Moses. In addition to mainstream Judaism's having rejected Yeshua as Messiah, a chasm of interpretation and application of Scripture developed between Judaism and Christianity such that Judaism's approach to holiness has come to be through obedience to law, while Christianity's approach has been through faith with the assumption of God's grace apart from law.

The resurgence of Jewish belief in Messiah Yeshua in the Twentieth Century has created the need for a fresh look at God's law applied with New Covenant principles and the Holy Spirit's interpretation, taking into account historic Rabbinic interpretations as well. This book seeks to fulfill that need by codifying and commenting on God's *mitzvot* wherever they may be found in Scripture—in the *Torah,* the *Nev'im,* the *Ketuvim,* the *Besorah* (Gospels) or the Apostolic Writings.

> **The resurgence of Jewish belief in Messiah Yeshua in the Twentieth Century has created the need for a fresh look at God's law...**

Introduction by Michael Rudolph

The Bible can be appreciated from many points of view. It may be thought of as the biography of God in His dealings with mankind. It may be read as a treatise on the history of the world and, in particular, the history of Israel and the heathen nations. It may also be studied as a prophetic book, revealing our future here on earth and in eternity. In this work, however, it is mainly presented as a book of *Torah* law, containing God's instructions for holy, moral, and victorious living.

The term "Law of Messiah" appears only once in the Bible, and that is in Galatians 6:2. That notwithstanding, the term is extremely significant in signaling that there exists such a law, that it is related to *"Torah"* and, as we shall see, that both it and *"Torah"* are alive and well under the New Covenant.

Torah and the Law

The *Theological Wordbook of the Old Testament* defines *"Torah"* (תּוֹרָה—Strong's number 8451) as follows: [1]

> "The word tôrâ means basically "teaching" whether it is the wise man instructing his son or God instructing Israel. The wise give insight into all aspects of life so that the young may know how to conduct themselves and to live a long blessed life (Prov 3:1f). So too God, motivated by love, reveals to man basic insight into how to live with each other and how to approach God. Through the law God shows his interest in all aspects of man's life which is to be lived under his direction and care. Law of God stands parallel to word of the Lord to signify that law is the revelation of God's will (e.g. Isa 1:10). In this capacity it becomes the nation's wisdom and understanding so that others will marvel at the quality of Israel's distinctive life style (Deut 4:6). Thus there is a very similar understanding of the role of teaching with its results in the wisdom school, in the priestly instruction, and the role of the law with its results for all the people of the covenant."

> "Specifically law refers to any set of regulations; e.g., Exo 12 contains the law in regard to observing the Passover, Some other specific laws include those for the various offerings (Lev 7:37), for leprosy (Lev 14:57) and for jealousy (Num 5:29). In this light law is often considered to consist of statutes, ordinances, precepts, commandments, and testimonies."

> "The meaning of the word gains further perspective in the light of Deut. According to Deut 1:5 Moses sets about to explain the law; law here would encompass the moral law, both in its apodictic and casuistic formulation, and the ceremonial law. The genius of Deut is that it interprets the external law in the light of its desired effect on man's inner attitudes. In addition, the book of Deut itself shows that the law has a broad meaning to encompass history, regulations and their interpretation, and exhortations. It is not merely the listing of casuistic statements as is the case in Hammurabi's code. Later the word extended to include the first five books of the Bible in all their variety."

In addition, The *New Brown-Driver-Briggs-Gesenius Hebrew and English Lexicon* gives "direction, instruction, law"[2] as the primary definitions of *"Torah,"* and the *Encyclopaedia Judaica* states:[3]

---

1 R. Laird Harris, editor, *Theological Wordbook of the Old Testament*, TWOT No. 910, p. 404, Moody Press (Chicago, Illinois: 1980).

2 Francis Brown, editor, *The New Brown-Driver-Briggs-Gesenius Hebrew and English Lexicon*, "Torah," p. 435-436, Hendrickson Publishers (Peabody, Massachusetts: 1979).

3 Louis Isaac Rabinowitz, *Encyclopaedia Judaica*, "Torah," vol. 15, pp. 1235-36, Keter Publishing House Ltd. (Jerusalem: 1971).

"*Torah* is derived from the root יָרָה which in the *hifil* conjugation means "to teach" (cf. Lev. 10:11). The meaning of the word is therefore "teaching," "doctrine," or "instructions"; the commonly accepted "law" gives a wrong impression. The word is used in different ways but the underlying idea of "teaching" is common to all.

There are basically two ways in which "*Torah*" is used in the *Tanakh*. In one usage, "*Torah*" refers to "the Law"—God's legal code which provides instructions on specific matters. Examples of this usage are:

"This is the *Torah* of the burnt offering..." (Leviticus 6:2(9)ff);[4] "grain offering..." (Leviticus 6:7(14)ff); "sin offering..." (Leviticus 6:18(25)ff); "trespass offering..." (Leviticus 7:1ff); "peace offering..." (Leviticus 7:11ff); "leprous plague..." (Leviticus 13:59ff); "jealousy..." (Numbers 5:29ff).

In most instances, however, "*Torah*" refers broadly to God's teaching—His universal and eternal standard for conduct and life. Where "*Torah*" means "law," it is usually accompanied by other Hebrew words having to do with law, such as:

מִצְוָה *mitzvah* (commandment—Strong's 4687)[5]

חֻקָּה *khukah* (statute or ordinance ("regulation" in the CJB)—Strong's 2708)[6]

מִשְׁפָּט *mishpat* (judgment ("ruling" in the CJB)—Strong's 4941)[7]

The following examples contain the word "*Torah*" in addition to one or more of the above words, showing that "*Torah*" is connected to, but distinguishable from, commandments, statutes, ordinances and judgments:

Numbers 19:2: "*This is the regulation from the Torah which Adonai has commanded.*"
Here, "*Torah*" cannot mean "regulation" or "ordinance."

Numbers 31:21: "*... This is the regulation from the Torah which Adonai has ordered Moshe.*"
Here also, "*Torah*" cannot mean "regulation" or "ordinance."

Deuteronomy 30:10: "*... so that you obey his mitzvot and regulations which are written in this book of the Torah ...*"
Some translations of this verse speak of "statutes" rather than "regulations," so here, "*Torah*" cannot mean "*mitzvot* (commandments)" or "regulations (statutes)."

---

4 Except where otherwise noted or is part of a quotation, the English translation of Scripture used in this book is from David H. Stern's "*Complete Jewish Bible* (CJB)," and the *Tanakh* chapter and verse numbers cited are those of the standard Hebrew Bible (followed by the traditional English citations, in parentheses or brackets, where they are different). The copyright of "The Complete Jewish Bible" and its translation are held by "Jewish New Testament Publications, Inc.," and may not be reproduced without its permission.

5 "A commandment is an order from, and enforceable by, a singular authority such as a king." Francis Brown, editor, *The New Brown-Driver-Briggs-Gesenius Hebrew and English Lexicon*, "*mitzvah*," p. 846, Hendrickson Publishers (Peabody, Massachusetts: 1979).

6 A statute is a legislated directive, generally enforceable by a branch of government. An ordinance is similar, but at a lower level.

7 A judgment is law created by a decision made in a case in controversy or a specific situation.

<u>Psalms 89:31(30)-32(31)</u>: *"If his descendants abandon my Torah and fail to live by my rulings, if they profane my regulations and don't obey my mitzvot, ..."*
Here, *"Torah"* cannot mean "rulings (judgments)," "regulations (statutes)" or *"mitzvot* (commandments)."

Another way of distinguishing *"Torah"* (teaching) from "commandment," "statute," "ordinance," and "judgment" is by its context. The following Scriptures are best understood when *"Torah"* means "teaching":

<u>Exodus 13:9</u>: *"Moreover, it will serve you as a sign on your hand and as a reminder between your eyes, so that Adonai's Torah may be on your lips; because with a strong hand Adonai brought you out of Egypt."*

<u>Exodus 16:4</u>: *"Adonai said to Moshe, 'Here, I will cause bread to rain down from heaven for you. The people are to go out and gather a day's ration every day. By this I will test whether they will observe my Torah or not."*

<u>Psalms 1:2</u>: *"Their delight is in Adonai's Torah; on his Torah they meditate day and night."*

<u>Psalms 37:31</u>: *"The Torah of his God is in his heart; his footsteps do not falter."*

<u>Psalms 40:9(8)</u>: *"Doing your will, my God, is my joy; your Torah is in my inmost being."*

<u>Proverbs 6:23</u>: *"For the mitzvah is a lamp, Torah is light, and reproofs that discipline are a way to life."*

<u>Proverbs 7:2</u>: *"Obey my commandments, and live; guard my teaching like the pupil of your eye."*

<u>Proverbs 13:14</u>: *"The teaching of a wise man is a fountain of life, enabling one to avoid deadly traps."*

Torah in the New Covenant

The New Covenant was prophesied in <u>Jeremiah 31:30(31)-33(34)</u>[8]:

"'Here the days are coming,' says Adonai, 'when I will make a new covenant with the house of Isra'el and with the house of Y'hudah. It will not be like the covenant I made with their fathers on the day I took them by their hand and brought them out of the land of Egypt; because they, for their part, violated my covenant, even though I, for my part, was a husband to them,' says Adonai. For this is the covenant I will make with the house of Isra'el after those days,' says Adonai: 'I will put my Torah within them and write it on their hearts; I will be their God, and they will be my people. No longer will any of them teach his fellow community member or his brother, 'Know Adonai'; for all will know me, from the least of them to the greatest; because I will forgive their wickednesses and remember their sins no more.'"

---

8 The CJB numbering for these verses is not standard; the majority Tanakh Hebrew verse numbering is <u>Jer. 31:31-34</u>.

Since in the Hebrew text of this Scripture, the word for "law" is תּוֹרָה (*Torah*), Jeremiah is quoting God as saying: "I will put My *Torah* in their minds and write it on their hearts." Handily, this Scripture is repeated in the Greek New Covenant Scriptures in <u>Hebrews 8:8-12</u>. There, the Greek word corresponding to "*Torah*" (verse 10) is "*nomos*" (Strong's No. 3551). This word is defined as "*Torah*" by Friberg's *New Testament Lexicon*[9] as follows:

> "νόμος, ου, ὁ w. a basic mng. of what is assigned or proper *law*; (1) gener. any *law* in the judicial sphere (<u>RO 7.1</u>); (2) as rule governing one's conduct *principle, law* (<u>RO 7.23</u>); (3) more specif. in the NT, of the Mosaic system of legislation as revealing the divine will (the *Torah*) *the law (of Moses)* (<u>LU 2.22</u>); in an expanded sense, Jewish relig. laws developed fr. the Mosaic law *(Jewish) law* (<u>JN 18.31</u>; <u>AC 23.29</u>); (4) as the collection of writings considered sacred by the Jews; (a) in a narrower sense, the Pentateuch, the first five books of the Bible, as comprising *the law* (<u>MT 12.5</u>; <u>GA 3.10b</u>); (b) in a wider sense, the OT scriptures as a whole (<u>MT 5.18</u>; <u>RO 3.19</u>); (5) fig. as the Christian Gospel, the New Covenant, as furnishing a new principle to govern spiritual life *law* (<u>RO 8.2a</u>; <u>HE 10.16</u>)."

A word related to "*nomos*," the Greek root word, "*nomotheteo*" (νομοθετέω—Strong's No. 3549), occurs in <u>Hebrews 8:6</u> as νενομοθέτηται. This word is translated "established" in the New King James Version:

> *"But now He has obtained a more excellent ministry, inasmuch as He is also Mediator of a better covenant, which was established on better promises."*

Stern recognizes the equivalence of "*nomotheteo*" and *"Torah"* in his translation of <u>Hebrews 8:6</u> in his "Jewish New Testament":[10]

> *"But now the work Yeshua has been given to do is far superior to theirs, just as the covenant he mediates is better. For this covenant has been given as Torah on the basis of better promises."*

In support of Stern's thesis that the root word "*nomotheteo*" and "*Torah*" are equivalent, consider that νομοθετῆσαι (*nomothetersai* from the root *nomotheteo*) is also found in <u>Exodus 24:12</u> of the Septuagint,[11] and that very same word in the Hebrew text is וְהַתּוֹרָה—"*v'ha-Torah*." Employing these definitions, one may confidently modify <u>Hebrews 8:6</u> in the New King James Version to be rendered:

> *"But now He has obtained a more excellent ministry, inasmuch as He is also Mediator of a better covenant, which was given as Torah (based) on better promises."*

---

9   Timothy and Barbara Friberg, *Analytical Lexicon to the Greek New Testament*, "νόμος," BibleWorks 4.0, Hermeneutica Bible Research Software (Big Fork, Montana: 1999).

10 David H. Stern, *Jewish New Testament*, 1ˢᵗ ed., p. 302, Jewish New Testament Publications (Clarksville, Maryland: 1991).

11 George Morrish, editor, *A Concordance of the Septuagint*, p. 166, Zondervan Publishing House (Grand Rapids, Michigan: 1988).

Since the "better covenant" in <u>Hebrews 8:6</u> is the "New Covenant" which is referred to in <u>Jeremiah 31:31(32)</u> and <u>Hebrews 8:8</u>, one must conclude that the New Covenant was given as *Torah*, and therefore is *Torah*,[12] not referring to the New Covenant Scriptures, but to the covenant itself.

What Makes the Pentateuch *Torah*?

Since "*Torah*" is God's teaching, there is a sense in which all Scripture is "*Torah.*"

> <u>2 Timothy 3:16-17</u>: "*All Scripture is God-breathed and is valuable for teaching the truth, convicting of sin, correcting faults and training in right living; thus anyone who belongs to God may be fully equipped for every good work.*"

Nevertheless, Yeshua himself recognized a distinction between the *Torah* of the *Pentateuch* and other classifications of Scriptures:

> <u>Luke 24:44</u>: "*Yeshua said to them, 'This is what I meant when I was still with you and told you that everything written about me in the Torah of Moshe, the Prophets and the Psalms had to be fulfilled.*"

Why then, are the first five books of the Bible traditionally classified as "*Torah*,"[13] whereas the remaining Hebrew Scriptures are not? It cannot be their inspiration, for by definition, all Scripture is inspired (<u>2 Timothy 3:16</u>). No, the uniqueness of the *Pentateuch* is that it contains God's major covenants prior to Yeshua. The other books of the *Tanakh* expound on these covenants, teach about them, prophesy about them, and present their history, but they do not themselves contain the covenants.

The Gospels as *Torah*

I hope by now the reader is convinced that the New Covenant is a covenant of *Torah*—God's teaching written on our hearts. Now let us see if any of the New Covenant books are *Torah* analogous to the *Pentateuch*. If the test for "*pentateuchal*" *Torah* is whether a New Covenant book of the Bible contains the New Covenant itself—that is, the "*Torah*" put in our minds and written on our hearts—then the Gospel books—Mathew, Mark, Luke and John certainly pass the test. Consider the many similarities between the *Pentateuch* and the Gospels:

> 1. The *Pentateuch* contains the life of Moses who was used by God to deliver the Sinai Covenant to Israel (<u>Exodus 34:27</u>).[14] The Gospels collectively contain the life of Yeshua, who was used by God to deliver the New Covenant to Israel (<u>Hebrews 8:6</u>).

> 2. The *Pentateuch* contains the event in which Moses proclaims the blood of the Sinai Covenant (<u>Exodus 24:8</u>). The Gospels collectively contain the event in which Yeshua proclaims his blood of the New Covenant (<u>Matthew 26:28</u>).

---

12 'According to <u>MJ 8:6&N</u>, the New Covenant itself "has been made *Torah*."' David H. Stern, *Jewish New Testament Commentary*, 1st ed., p. 498, Jewish New Testament Publications (Clarksville, Maryland: 1992). See also, p.220 and p. 466.

13 Joseph Telushkin, *Jewish Literacy*, p. 23, William Morrow and Company, Inc. (New York: 1991).

14 The *Pentateuch* also contains the lives of the patriarchs of earlier covenants.

3. The *Pentateuch* contains the teachings and the commandments of the Sinai Covenant conveyed through Moses (Deuteronomy 4:13). The Gospels collectively contain the teachings and the commandments of the New Covenant conveyed through Yeshua (Matthew 5:1-7:29).

4. The *Pentateuch* contains the means by which men must atone for their sins through animal Sacrifice. The Gospels collectively contain the means by which men must be forgiven for their sins through Yeshua's sacrifice.

5. The *Pentateuch* initiates a priesthood and the appointment of Aaron as High Priest (Exodus 28:1-3). The Gospels collectively initiate a new priesthood and the appointment of Yeshua as High Priest (described in Hebrews 7:20-28).[15]

6. The *Pentateuch* contains shadows of things to come. The Gospels collectively contain the prophetic fulfillment of those shadows.

7. The *Pentateuch* ends with the death of Moses. The Gospels collectively end with the death, resurrection, and ascension of Yeshua.

Yeshua's life and blood are the substance of the New Covenant—its *"Torah"* (John 1:14, 14:6), and Yeshua's sacrificial death and resurrection mark both the New Covenant's beginning (John 19:30) and its fulfillment. It is in the Gospel books that we find this New Covenant substance, and therefore the New Covenant itself.

The Mosaic Law: Rabbinical View

According to Rabbinical understanding, the Holy Scriptures are organized into three parts—the *Torah* (*Pentateuch*, Law), the *Nev'im* (Prophets), and the *Ketuvim* (Holy Writings).[16] Rabbinical Judaism does not acknowledge the current existence of the "New Covenant" prophesied in Jeremiah 31:30(31), or the inspiration of the New Covenant Scriptures. One of the ways that Judaism has historically viewed *"Torah"* has been as synonymous with the Law of Moses—the law to which it considers itself bound today. Its further understanding is that all of the Mosaic Law is contained in "the *Torah*" (Pentateuch), and that all remaining Scriptures of the *Tanakh*, while inspired, merely historicize, exemplify, and embellish. Consequently, Rabbinical Judaism devotes most of its attention to the *"Torah"* and to the oral tradition (*Talmud*), to which it looks for interpretation.

Statutes of the Mosaic Law: Dependent and Transcendent

The Commandments contained in the *Tanakh* are God's explicit directives and are, therefore, divine statutory law.[17] There are two categories of statutes commanded by God under the Mosaic Covenant—those whose literal compliance depends upon the Covenant's continued existence, and those whose literal compliance does not. I call the first of these, "covenant-dependent," and

---

15 Yeshua's priesthood begins with his resurrection.

16 This categorization, to-wit, *Torah, Nev'im* and *Ketuvim*, has resulted in the Rabbinical canon of the Bible being known by the acronym *"Tanakh."* It is noteworthy that Yeshua himself referred to Scripture by these categories (Luke 24:44).

17 The terms "statutory law" and "statutes," as used here, contemplate ordinances as well.

the second of these, "covenant- transcendent." Recognizing these two categories is important, because <u>Hebrews 8:13</u> teaches:

> *"By using the term, 'new,' he has made the first covenant 'old'; and something being made old, something in the process of aging, is on its way to vanishing altogether."*

<u>Hebrews 8:13</u> suggests a diminishing literal role for covenant-dependant statutes; consequently, such statutes are not incorporated into New Covenant law in their original form and application, while statutes that are covenant-transcendent are readily adopted without change.[18] So, for example, the literal application of statutes dealing with the Levitical priesthood, the Temple, and the government of ancient Israel, are in the process of vanishing (or have already vanished)[19] as has the Mosaic Covenant has been vanishing, but the principles they teach remain important,[20] and we must not ignore them.

> <u>Romans 7:6:</u> *"But now we have been released from this aspect of the Torah, because we have died to that which had us in its clutches, so that we are serving in the new way provided by the Spirit and not in the old way of outwardly following the letter of the law."*

It is my opinion that "oldness of the letter," as some translations read, refers to the diminishing role of covenant-dependent statutes as literal law, whereas our need for literal obedience to covenant-transcendent statutes (e.g. <u>Exodus 20:1–17</u>) is timeless.

In the *Tanakh*, statutes are not labeled as "covenant-dependent" or "covenant-transcendent," and so one must exercise judgment in determining which is which. A rule-of-thumb test is to ask: "Can or should this statute be complied with in the New Covenant era exactly and literally as commanded?" If the answer is "yes," it is "transcendent." If "no," it is "dependent."

Sometimes, the answer to the above "test" question is obvious. No one would disagree, for example, that it is as sinful to commit murder today, as in the past. On the other hand, the question of whether Jews in the New Covenant are still required to wear fringes on the corners of their garments (<u>Numbers 15:38-41</u>), may evoke two opinions opposite: (1) Yes, the original reason for doing so still applies—to remind those who see the fringes of the commandments of God, and (2) No, one can comply with the commandment's principle by wearing an alternative item such as a necklace depicting two tablets. In making such decisions for myself I rely on the wisdom of a saying that is not found in Scripture: "If it isn't broken, don't try to fix it." So, if the

---

18 Mosaic statutes are not enforceable as law in the New Covenant; it is their underlying teaching *(Torah)* and not the statutes themselves that carry over (See "*Torah*" infra).

19 Some believe that the Mosaic Covenant has already "vanished" as evidenced by Israel's two thousand-year inability to conduct the Temple sacrifices (The Temple was destroyed in 70 A.D.).

20 The author does not believe that the temple, priesthood, and statutes prophesied in <u>Ezekiel 40-48</u> indicate a revitalization of the Mosaic Covenant. This is because (1) The priests serving in that temple are limited to the sons of Zadock, (2) the High Priest in that temple is "the prince"—not the sons of Aaron—and (3) revitalization of the Mosaic Covenant would contradict <u>Hebrews 8:13</u>. That being the case, the statutes appearing in the Ezekiel chapters are, even where similar to Mosaic statutes, newly enacted and not continuations of those in the Mosaic Covenant.

literal commandment is as appropriately performable today as during the time of Moses, then I do not search for an alternative.

Torah Underlies the Statutes

Underlying each of God's commandments is *Torah*, which we have seen is broadly defined as God's essential teaching.[21, 22] Although not all *Torah* is statutory in origin, all *torah* is God's law because it is essentially His will. Even if a commandment is covenant-dependent, its *torah* transcends the change in covenant because God's values never change (Numbers 23:19; Psalms 102:26(25)-28(27); Hebrews 13:8). You will notice that sometimes I capitalize *"Torah"* and sometimes I do not and write it *"torah."* It is just my way of indicating whether I am speaking of God's teaching generically or more specifically as His law (or do I mean "Law?"). You see? That is why you should not take my capitalizations seriously, and Hebrew is not capitalized anyway.

Torah is not only revealed through Mosaic commandments, but through all Scripture.[23] The apostle Paul expressed this in 2 Timothy 3:16-17:

> *"All Scripture is God-breathed and is valuable for teaching the truth, convicting of sin, correcting faults and training in right living; thus anyone who belongs to God may be fully equipped for every good work."*

And of the *Torah* that underlies covenant-dependent statutes contained in the Law of Moses, Paul wrote in Galatians 3:24-25:

> *"Accordingly, the Torah functioned as a custodian until the Messiah came, so that we might be declared righteous on the ground of trusting and being faithful. But now that the time for this trusting faithfulness has come, we are no longer under a custodian."*

Finally, in Jeremiah 31:30(31)-33(34)[24, 25] Jeremiah prophesied that God would make a New Covenant based upon existing *Torah*:

> *"'Here the days are coming,' says Adonai, 'when I will make a new covenant with the house of Isra'el and with the house of Y'hudah. It will not be like the covenant I made with their fathers on the day I took them by their hand and brought them out of the land of Egypt; because they, for their part, violated my covenant, even though I, for my part, was a husband to them,' says Adonai. For this is the covenant I will make with the house of Isra'el after those days,' says Adonai: 'I will put my Torah within them and write it on their hearts; I will be their God, and they will be my people. No longer will any of them teach his fellow community member or his brother, 'Know Adonai'; for all will know me, from the least of them to the greatest; because I will forgive their wickednesses and remember their sins no more.'"*

---

21 R. Laird Harris, p. 404.
22 Francis Brown, p. 435-436.
23 This includes New Covenant Scripture.
24 Quoted in Hebrews 8:8-12.
25 The CJB numbering for these verses is not standard; the majority *Tanakh* Hebrew verse numbering is Jeremiah. 31:31-34.

Thus, not only does *Torah* pass into the New Covenant, it defines it, and without it there would be no New Covenant.[26]

The Law of Messiah

In Galatians 6:2, Paul instructs us:

> *"Bear one another's burdens—in this way you will be fulfilling the Torah's true meaning, which the Messiah upholds."*

Most English translations of this verse of Scripture employ the expression "the Law of Messiah,"[27] which is from where I derive the title of this book.[28] Although this verse is the only occurrence of the term in Scripture, the Apostolic writings are replete with references to operative law in the New Covenant; for example:

> Acts 1:1-2 : *"Dear Theophilos: In the first book, I wrote about everything Yeshua set out to do and teach, until the day when, after giving instructions through the Ruach HaKodesh to the emissaries whom he had chosen, he was taken up into heaven."*

> 1 John 2:3-4 : *"The way we can be sure we know him is if we are obeying his commands; anyone who says 'I know him,' but isn't obeying his commands is a liar."*

> 1 Thessalonians 4:2 : *"For you know what instructions we gave you on the authority of the Lord Yeshua."*

> Romans 2:14-15: *"For whenever Gentiles, who have no Torah, do naturally what the Torah requires, then these, even though they don't have the Torah, for themselves are Torah! For their lives show that the conduct the Torah dictates is written in their hearts."*

> Romans 8:3-4: *"For what the Torah could not do by itself, because it lacked the power to make the old nature cooperate, God did by sending his own Son as a human being with a nature like our own sinful one [but without sin]. God did this in order to deal with sin, and in doing so he executed the punishment against sin in human nature, so that the just requirement of the Torah might be fulfilled in us who do not run our lives according to what our old nature wants but according to what the Spirit wants."*

We have seen that there are two components of law in the *Tanakh* that are eternal; they are (1) covenant-transcendent statutes, and (2) *Torah* (teaching) that is revealed through all Scripture. Since, by definition, covenant-dependent statutes vanish along with their vanishing covenant, it is the covenant-transcendent statutes, plus all *Torah* contained in the *Tanakh*, plus all law added in the New Covenant Scriptures, which form the "Law of Messiah" to which we are accountable today. Hence, the Law of Messiah is the New Covenant counterpart of the Law of Moses.

---

26 "According to *MJ 8:6&N*, the New Covenant itself 'has been made Torah.'" David H. Stern, *Jewish New Testament Commentary*.
27 Usually rendered "the law of Christ."
28 It is ironic that the CJB translation does not employ the term "law of Messiah" (the title of this book) in its rendering of Galatians 6:2.

Dibeyr, Torah and *Mitzvot*

As used in this book, a *"dibeyr"* is an explicit commandment of God in Scripture—an imperative directive (usually a statute or ordinance of the Mosaic Law) which may be either covenant-dependent or transcendent. *"Torah"* can mean several things but, in the absence of the article "the" (e.g. "the *Torah*"), it most often means God's essential and eternal teaching or instruction. As used in this book, *Torah* underlies all of God's *dibrot*,[29] and is revealed (explicitly or implicitly) by all Scripture—not just the Scriptures of the *Pentateuch*. A *"Mitzvah"* is an interpreted statement of God's will, derived from Scripture, and expressed in the form of a commandment. A Mosaic statute or ordinance does not become a *mitzvah* (as used herein) until it is interpreted and restated.

There have been several attempts in history to codify God's Word into numbered *mitzvot*.[30] The earliest of these was *Hilchot Gedolot*, a work by Simon Kairo published sometime in the 8th Century. By that time, a principle had already been established in the *Talmud*, that the total number of *mitzvot* in the *Torah* was *Taryag* (613);[31] and of these, two hundred forty-eight (248) were positive (*mitzvot aseh*), and three hundred sixty-five (365) were negative (*mitzvot lo ta'aseh*)[32].

Anyone who attempts to enumerate *mitzvot* in the *Torah* soon realizes that there are decisions to be made. What, for example, should one consider to be a *mitzvah*?[33] What level of departure from the plain meaning of the Biblical text is permissible? What level of inference is allowable? How does one count similar expressions of God's will that are stated differently at different places in the Scriptures? Do we count as two *mitzvot* those that are expressed both in the positive and in the negative in different verses of Scripture, or do we count them as one? It is not surprising that those who have attempted this work have sometimes come to different conclusions.

Maimonides and Yisrael Meir HaKohen

To bring consensus, Judaism needed a scholar of such prestige that he could define 613 *mitzvot* that would be acceptable to a majority of the Jewish community. Such a scholar emerged in the person of Moshe ben Maimon (Maimonides, aka "the RAMBAM") who, sometime prior to 1170 c.e., wrote his compilation of *Torah* law in Arabic under the title *Kitab Al-Fara'id* (*The Book of Divine Precepts*). He subsequently revised his work and, by the end of his life, there were two Arabic texts or versions of *Kitab Al-Fara'id* in existence. Unlike his predecessors, Maimonides was careful to follow defined principles (fourteen) to justify his conclusions. This made all the difference, and his work received almost universal acceptance.[34]

Three contemporaries of Maimonides translated his texts into Hebrew, and these translations became known as *Sefer haMitzvot*. Abraham ibn Chasdai made his translation from Maimonides' first version.[35] Maimonides' second text (translated into Hebrew by Solomon ibn Job of Granada

---

29 The plural of *dibeyr*.
30 The plural of *mitzvah*.
31 Shab. 87a.
32 Mak. 23b.
33 I. Brull, *Jewish Encyclopedia*, "Commandments, the 613," vol. 4, p. 181 (ed. Isidore Singer; New York: 1901–1906). Describes the opinions of early Jewish scholars over the selection of commandments that comprise the *taryag*.
34 Some critics remained, notably Moshe ben Nachman Gerondi (Nachmanides).
35 *Sefer HaChinuch* and Nachmanides' criticisms are based upon Maimonides' first version.

and separately by Moses ibn Tibbon) is , however, considered the "standard Arabic text" today. More recently, Dr. Chaim Heller published a "corrected" Hebrew text in which he compared and reconciled Maimonides' Arabic texts with that of ibn Job, and an even more recent translation (Jerusalem Hebrew Text) was made by Rabbi Joseph Kapach.

As an academic achievement, Maimonides' enumeration of *mitzvot* was huge. However, it was too exhaustive to be a convenient tool in the post-Temple era, when many of the *mitzvot* dealing with sacrifices and the Levitical priesthood could no longer be performed.

Enter Rabbi Yisrael Meir haKohen.[36] In 1931, Rabbi Meir published *Sefer haMitzvot haKatzar* ("The Concise Book of *Mitvoth*")[37] in which he extracted from Maimonides' list, Two Hundred Ninety-Seven (297) *mitzvot*—Seventy-seven (77) positive, One Hundred Ninety-four (194) negative, and Twenty-six (26) applicable only in the Land of Israel. Rabbi Meir intended his book to be a compilation of *mitzvot* that could be observed by Jews in the post-Temple era and, particularly in the Diaspora.

Besides listing fewer *mitzvot* than Maimonides, Rabbi Meir differs from him in other ways as well. To begin with, the two compilers number their *mitzvot* differently and present them in a different order. As a consequence, it is not always easy to determine which one of Meir's *mitzvot* corresponds to a given *mitzvah* of Maimonides. Second, while they usually agree on the Scriptures that define a given *mitzvah*, it is not always the case (nor is it the case with other commentators). It is also important to note that, while both Maimonides and Meir quote Hebrew Scripture as proof texts for their respective *mitzvot*, neither of their original writings give supportive chapter and verse numbers,[38, 39] and their quotations are not always of the entire verses as they appear in modern Hebrew Bibles. Translators and editors of both of their works added chapter and verse citations that did not appear in the originals[40] and, in some cases, they quoted entire verses of Scripture where the original writings quoted only parts of verses.[41]

Finally, Maimonides and Meir do not always agree on the statement of the *mitzvah* that they extract from a given Scripture. For example, in response to Exodus 12:18, Maimonides' Positive *Mitzvah* #RP158 states that we are to eat unleavened bread on the evening of the 15th day of *Nisan*, while Meir's Positive *Mitzvah* #MP23 states that we are to eat unleavened bread on the evening of the 14th day of *Nisan*. Presumably, the interpretive difference is in whether "evening" is understood to be before or after sundown. Another example is presented by Deuteronomy 6:13. The Scripture itself states that we are to "fear the LORD your God and serve Him." That

---

36 Known respectfully as "the *Chafetz Chayim*."
37 English adaptation and notes by Charles Wengrove, Feldheim Publishers, Jerusalem / New York, 1990.
38 For Maimonides, this may be confirmed (without consulting *Kitab al Fara'id* in Arabic) by consulting early copies of *Sefer haMitzvot*, all of which lack chapter and verse references.
39 For Meir, see Yisrael Meir haKohen, *Sefer haMitzvot haKatzar (The Concise Book of haMitzvot)*, p. VIII, (Charles Wengrove, trans. and ed.; Jerusalem: Feldheim Publishers, 1990).
40 E.g. see Moshe ben Maimon, *Sefer haMitzvot*, vol. 1 of *Rambam L'am*, (Jerusalem: *Mossad harav kook*, 1957) and ibid. 1971 (both in Hebrew). The former contains chapter and verse references while the latter does not.
41 To see an example of this in English, compare Positive *Mitzvah* #1 appearing in Moshe ben Maimon (Maimonides), *The Commandments*, (Charles B. Chavel, trans. and ed.; London: The Soncino Press, 1967) with Moshe ben Maimon (Maimonides), *Sefer HaMitzvot (The Book of Mitzvot)*, vols. 21 and 22 in the *Mishneh Torah* series, (Shraga Silverstein, trans.; New York: Moznaim Publishing Corporation, 1993). The former contains the entire text of Exodus 20:2 while the latter contains only the few words of the verse quoted by Maimonides.

notwithstanding, Maimonides' Positive *Mitzvah* #RP5 interprets it as "worshipping" God, while Rabbi Meir's Positive *Mitzvah* #MP7 says it means to "pray" to God. Clearly, the ways the two commentators interpret the Scripture and write their respective *mitzvot* reflect both their judgment and their theology.

Other Classical Enumerations

Codifications written after *Sefer haMitzvot* have added to our overall understanding of God's commandments, but no other codifier ever attained the prestige and influence of Maimonides. As already stated, Yisrael Meir haKohen's work *Sefer haMitzvot haKatzar*, was chosen here as a major comparison to Maimonides because he attempted to limit his list of commandments to those he deemed performable in the Twentieth Century. Although a complete listing and in-depth discussion of other codes of law are beyond the scope of this book, several nevertheless deserve special mention:

(a) Mishneh Torah, written by Maimonides, is a fourteen-book compilation of laws gleaned from both Scripture and Talmud. It is reputed to be complete, taking no account of a law's applicability in the post-Temple era. Maimonides built *Mishneh Torah* around his *Sefer haMitzvot*, so he reiterated all the *mitzvot* in an introductory list[42] and the relevant ones again before each of the fourteen books. The relevance of *Mishneh Torah* for the present work is for its expansive commentary and its subject-oriented organization.

(b) Sefer Mitzvot Gadol (Big Book of Commandments), Moses of Coucy (1st half of the 13th Century).

(c) Sefer Mitzvot Katan (Little Book of Commandments), Isaac ben Joseph of Corveil (2nd half of the 13th Century).

(d) Sefer HaChinuch (The Book of Education) is attributed to Aaron haLevi of Barcelona (c. 1257) and is still in common use today. It was most probably based upon Abraham ibn Chasdai's translation of Maimonides' first Arabic edition and, although basically organized according to the chapter and verse sequence of the *Tanakh*,[43] his first manuscript retained some positive and negative commandment groupings as part of its order. In contrast, the *Sefer HaChinuch* version that is in print today contains none of the positive/negative groupings. This is the result (according to Charles Wengrov)[44] of an early printer's decision to reorder the *mitzvot*, causing them to appear in exactly the same sequence as the verses in the *Tanakh;* and so it remains today. The importance of *Sefer HaChinuch* for the present work, besides its order and historical content, is its commentary on Scripture application which is superb.

Most other codifications of Jewish law such as the *Shulchan Aruch* and the *Kitzur Shulchan Aruch* combine Scriptural and rabbinical elements, and are therefore beyond the scope and purpose of this book.

---

42 A few differences exist between this list and *Sefer haMitzvot*, particularly in the Scriptures chosen as proof texts.
43 Alternatively the *Chumash*, which consists of the Pentateuch and selections from the remainder of the *Tanakh*.
44 Aaron haLevi of Barcelona, *Sefer haHinnuch*, vols. 1-5, p. xiii, (Charles Wengrov, trans.; Jerusalem/New York: Feldheim Publishers, 1978-89).

Need for a New Covenant Codification

For Messianic Jews and *Torah*-adherent Gentile believers (followers of Messiah Yeshua), neither Maimonides nor Meir's, nor HaChinuch's works are a sufficient guide for daily conduct and for relating to God.[45] It is because these believers acknowledge the continuing priesthood of Yeshua, look to regular communication with and through the *Ruach Hakodesh* for personal guidance (including for applying Scripture),[46] and seek to be obedient to additional *Torah* contained in the *Kitvey B'rit Chadasha* (the New Testament Scriptures)[47]—all part of a New Covenant between God and the Jewish people.[48] Jews who do not acknowledge New Covenant realities have no sacrifice for sin, no benefits of an interceding priesthood, and therefore their approach to God is necessarily more limiting. That notwithstanding, New Covenant believers (both Jews and Gentiles) have the same need as Rabbinical Jews for a handy compilation of Scripture-based *mitzvot* to assist them in their walk of obedience.

The challenge in writing this book was to provide such a tool—one that parallels the older works in form, but which adds additional Scriptures, and provides interpretation for New Covenant usage. Under-girding this attempt is my conviction, based in Scripture, that the *Torah*, which God gave to the ancient Israelites, is relevant today for both the Jew and the non-Jew, albeit sometimes differently for each:

Exodus 12:49: *"The same teaching is to apply equally to the citizen and to the foreigner living among you."*[49,50]

Romans 15:4: *"For everything written in the past was written to teach us, so that with the encouragement of the Tanakh we might patiently hold on to our hope."*

1 Corinthians 7:19: *"Being circumcised means nothing, and being uncircumcised means nothing; what does mean something is keeping God's commandments."*

Galatians 3:24: *"Accordingly, the Torah functioned as a custodian until the Messiah came, so that we might be declared righteous on the ground of trusting and being faithful."*

2 Timothy 3:16-17: *"All Scripture is God-breathed and is valuable for teaching the truth, convicting of sin, correcting faults and training in right living; thus anyone who belongs to God may be fully equipped for every good work."*

Hebrews 10:1: *"For the Torah has in it a shadow of the good things to come, but not the actual manifestation of the originals. Therefore, it can never, by means of the same sacrifices repeated endlessly year after year, bring to the goal those who approach the Holy Place to offer them."*

---

45 Rabbinical Jews do not believe that Yeshua is the Messiah.

46 Messianic Jews and Gentiles affiliated with them do not look to *Talmud* for authoritative interpretation.

47 Rabbinical Jews do not consider these Apostolic Writings to be Scripture.

48 Rabbinical Jews do not acknowledge the existence of a New Covenant.

49 This verse of Scripture is sometimes wrongly generalized to mean that all the commandments of *Torah* are applicable to Jews and Gentiles in the same way. This is a mistaken view because the context of this Scripture is of the sojourner who desired to eat the *Pesach* and thus needed to be circumcised.

50 Even if one generalizes the verse from its narrow context of *Pesach* and circumcision, the CJB's choice of the word "teaching" rather than "law" suggests that there may be different applications for the Jew and the Gentile.

Considerations in Writing this Book

The matter of proper application of Scripture looms very large. I have approached this work prayerfully, and my interpretations are derived from my sincere attempt to receive the wisdom of God through the *Ruach HaKodesh*. I began with the *mitzvot* promulgated by Rabbi Yisrael Meir HaKohen (the Chafetz Chaiyim) in his *"Sefer haMitzvot haKatzar,*[51] determined which *mitzvot* in Maimonides'[52, 53] and HaChinuch's[54] compilations corresponded, and then compared the Scriptures that each of them purported to interpret. As a final step, I consulted a third translator of Maimonides,[55] as well as New Covenant Scriptures that appeared relevant. Differences in the chapter and verse citations among the various translated sources can be explained by the fact that the translators and editors—not Maimonides, Meir, or HaChinuch—placed them there.[56]

Not being bound by Talmudic authority, I did not attempt to arrive at *Taryag (613) mitzvot,* and I did not follow Maimonides' practice of listing *mitzvot* in categories of positive and negative. *Mitzvot* that addressed the same or similar issues were combined, and I made independent judgments regarding their applications and preferred means of expression. All of this was done in collaboration with Dr. Daniel C. Juster whose comments are liberally included.

After merging the work of Meir and Maimonides and eliminating duplications, I reduced the resulting list by eliminating those *mitzvot* that I judged to be not literally observable in the New Covenant.[57] For example, Meir's Positive *Mitzvah* #MP52 (Deuteronomy 18:4) requires that we give the *kohen* (Levitical priest) the first wool of our sheep. With the Mosaic Covenant in the process of vanishing away or having already vanished (Hebrews 8:13),[58] I conclude that there is no longer a reason to support the Levitical *kohanim* with such gifts.[59]

Although the New Covenant has rendered some of the Mosaic *mitzvot* literally unobservable, it also produced new ones, and changed how some of the Mosaic *mitzvot* are to be applied today.

---

51 Yisrael Meir haKohen, *Sefer haMitzvot haKatzar (The Concise Book of Mitzvot)*, (Charles Wengrove, trans. and ed.; Jerusalem: Feldheim Publishers, 1990).

52 Moshe ben Maimon (Maimonides), *The Commandments*, (Charles B. Chavel, trans. and ed.; London: The Soncino Press, 1967).

53 Moshe ben Maimon (Maimonides), *Sefer HaMitzvot (The Book of Mitzvot)*, vols. 21 and 22 in the *Mishneh Torah* series, (Shraga Silverstein, trans.; New York: Moznaim Publishing Corporation, 1993).

54 Aaron haLevi of Barcelona, *Sefer haHinnuch*, vols. 1-5, p. xiii, (Charles Wengrov, trans.; Jerusalem/New York: Feldheim Publishers, 1978-89).

55 Moshe ben Maimon (Maimonides), *Sefer haMitzvot*, 10ᵗʰ ed., vol. 1 in the *Rambam l'Am* (Yosef Kapach, trans.; Jerusalem: Mossad Harav Kook, 1990).

56 Although most Hebrew and English renderings of *Sefer haMitzvot, Sefer haMitzvot haKatzar* and *Sefer haChinuch* contain parenthetical chapter and verse citations, they were not in Maimonides Meir's, or Chinuch's original works. All three quoted words of Scripture to support their respective *mitzvot*, but they did not identify the chapters and verses from which the words came. This resulted in ambiguities as to which Scriptures were intended where the quoted words occur in more than one place in the *Torah*.

57 Even commandments which are no longer observable have teaching value for our lives (Galatians 3:24; 2 Timothy 3:16-17).

58 The author believes that after Yeshua's death and prior to the 70 c.e. destruction, both the Mosaic and the New Covenant existed simultaneously, but that after the destruction, it is likely that the Mosaic Covenant, already in the process of vanishing away, finally came to an end. Even if the Mosaic Covenant has not yet fully vanished, the author's view is that we are to enthusiastically pursue where God is leading—not dwell on what He is ending.

59 There is reference to what we understand to be a Millennial Temple in Ezekiel, that some think implies a future restoration of a functioning Levitical priesthood.

Consider, for example, Meir's Positive *Mitzvah* #MP38 (<u>Leviticus 25:35-36</u> and <u>Deuteronomy 15:8</u>), in which he states that we are to give charity to the poor in Jewry. This limited interpretation was justified under the Mosaic Covenant because the terms "brethren" and "brother" in <u>Leviticus</u> referred only to fellow Israelites and *gerim*. Under the New Covenant, however, our brethren include non-Jews of the faith grafted to Israel as well (<u>Romans 11:16-19</u>), and so I broadened the *mitzvah* to read: "We are to give *tz'dakah* (charity) to the poor among us."[60]

Matters Left for a Future Volume

Although New Covenant Scriptures (especially *mitzvot* spoken by Yeshua) are liberally referenced in this work, a methodical list and commentary of all the *mitzvot* in the New Testament remains for a future volume. As a foretaste of what is planned to come, I have included an Appendix listing the *mitzvot* that appear in the Book of Matthew, and an Appendix listing *mitzvot* spoken by the *shlichim* in the New Testament.

Organization and References

The organization of this book and the Scripture verses selected to support each *mitzvah* are not necessarily the same as those of the classical commentators and, similar to their respective works, no attempt is made to reference every confirming Scripture. Indeed, some *mitzvot* are included here that were not contemplated by the classical commentators—e.g. *mitzvot* that are derived from parts of the *Tanakh* other than the *Torah*, and *mitzvot* derived from the Apostolic Writings. Also, I list some Scriptures merely because they are relied on by Maimonides or Meir, and not necessarily because I deem them critical (or even logical) for supporting a *mitzvah* under discussion. Finally, when I quote Scripture, I quote entire verses even where Maimonides or Meir quote them only in part, and even when I am only relying on part of a verse to prove or support a *mitzvah*.

Maimonides, Meir and HaChinuch are the principal classical commentators / codifiers referenced in this book. Each *Torah*-derived *mitzvah* that I list includes its Scripture proof texts as well as secondary references where pertinent. I also include comparative comments where I deem them appropriate.

There is a modern work, *The Mitzvot: The Commandments and their Rationale* by Abraham Chill,[61] that I consult from time to time and that deserves special mention because, in addition to his own commentary, he includes extensive references to classical rabbinical literature. Mainly, the order of his *mitzvot* are the same as *HaChinuch's*—organized according to the Scripture order of the *Tanakh*—and, when more than one Scripture is cited, it is the first that governs the order; unfortunately, there are several occasions in which the order of Chill's *mitzvot* depart from this plan, but Chill's reader is alerted where that happens. Chill's Scripture proof texts for the various *mitzvot* he lists are more numerous and diverse than those of either Maimonides or Meir, but his *mitzvot* are not easy to reference because they are not numbered.

---

60 It is interesting to note that Maimonides' positive *Mitzvah* #RP195, the counterpart to Meir's positive *Mitzvah* #MP38, does not so clearly limit the application of charity to fellow Jews.

61 Abraham Chill, *The Mitzvot: The Commandments and their Rationale*, 2nd ed., (Jerusalem: Keter Publishing House, 2000).

There is another modern work *The 613 Mitzvot: A Contemporary Guide to the Commandments of Judaism* by Ronald L. Eisenberg,[62] that I recommend for its clarity of commentary, and its excellent indices that allow one to easily determine Maimonides' *mitzvah* number from its Scripture citation, and vice versa.

In addition to the rabbinical commentaries that focus on the *mitzvot,* there are others of a more general character, and there are also a growing number of Messianic Jewish commentaries such as the "*Jewish New Testament Commentary: A Companion Volume to the Jewish New Testament*" by David H. Stern.[63]

The following list summarizes this book's overall approach and content:
- Cross-references to the *mitzvot* identified by Maimonides, Meir and HaChinuch, and to additional Scriptures not referenced by them.
- *Mitzvot* identified by Maimonides, Meir and HaChinuch that I do not deem observable in the New Covenant.
- *Mitzvot* not traditionally recognized, yet which I deem relevant in the New Covenant.
- Interpretations of Scripture from a New Covenant perspective.
- A Selective commentary that includes (1) differences in Meir's, Maimonides and HaChinuch's perspectives where differences exist; (2) New Covenant interpretation of Scripture and *mitzvot;* and (3) application of *mitzvot* to Jews and Gentiles (including *k'rovei Yisrael)*[64] and men and women.
- *Mitzvot* organized into subject categories.
- A New Covenant Literal Application (NCLA) code designation for each *mitzvah,* assigning one of seven possible New Covenant literal compliance levels to Jewish men, Jewish women, Gentile men, Gentile women, *K'rov Yisrael* men, and *K'rov Yisrael* women.
- A Table of Contents.
- A Preface.
- This Introduction.
- An Introduction by Daniel C. Juster.
- An article on Paul's understanding of the *Torah.*
- A Subject Index.
- An English-versified Scripture Index of Hebrew Scriptures.
- A Hebrew-versified Scripture Index of Hebrew Scriptures.
- A Scripture Index of New Covenant Scriptures.
- A Maimonides *Mitzvah* Cross-Reference Index.
- A Meir *Mitzvah* Cross-Reference Index.
- A Chinuch *Mitzvah* Cross-Reference Index.
- An Index of Three Classical Commentators' *Mitzvot* Arranged in Order of HaChinuch's *Mitzvah* Numbers and Labeled According to Weekly *Parashiyot.*
- An Index of Scriptures Cited by Three Classical Commentators Arranged According to Weekly *Parashiyot.*
- Maimonides' List of Positive and Negative *Mitzvot.*

---

62 Ronald L. Eisenberg, *The 613 Mitzvot: A Contemporary Guide to the Commandments of Judaism,* (Rockville, Maryland: Schreiber Publishing, 2005).
63 David H. Stern, *Jewish New Testament Commentary.*
64 Gentile members of a Jewish community.

- *Mitzvot* in the Book of Matthew
- A List of Explicit *Mitzvot* of the New Covenant *Shlichim.*
- Hebrew Word Glossary.

Finally, I should like to say a word about usage. The writings of Meir, Maimonides, HaChinuch, and my writings as well, are attempts at interpretation, codification, explanation, and application of *mitzvot* that we believe we have found in the Scriptures. Although we did not write or compose (or intend to write or compose) any new commandments, this book follows the common usage of saying that XYZ "wrote" *mitzvot,* or of referring to one of our writings as "XYZ's *mitzvah"* when referring to our compilations and explanations. I follow this convention of usage both for the historical commentators as well as for myself within this book and by doing so, no disrespect to God (from whom these *mitzvot* are derived) is intended.

Two Kinds of *Mitzvot*

The Law of Messiah *Mitzvot* in this book are of two kinds; they are (1) inclusive of one or more of the classical *mitzvot* (those from Maimonides, Meir, or HaChinuch), or (2) completely unrelated to the classical *mitzvot.* The classical *mitzvot* are based only upon Scriptures from the *Torah*, whereas the *Mitzvot* written by the authors herein are based upon Scriptures throughout the Bible. Those containing Scripture references from the classical *mitzvah* compilations are marked by an asterisk in the Table of Contents, and one or more of the referenced Scriptures carry the label "Key Scriptures." In the *Mitzvot* that are unrelated, their "Key Scriptures" are those that appear to the authors as most relevant; these are not necessarily presented in a canonical order.

Choice of Translation

The *mitzvot* which are the subject of this book derive from the original biblical languages and not from any English or other translation. Nevertheless, because this book was written with the English speaker in mind, it was necessary that I select an English translation in which the Scriptures being discussed could be displayed. I chose to use David H. Stern's 1998 translation known as the *Complete Jewish Bible* (CJB)[65] because, when the writing of this book began, more than any other, it brought out the Jewish background and nuances of the Scriptures, and this, despite Dr. Stern himself stating:

> *"So the Tanakh you have in this book is something between a translation and a paraphrase; since it is partly one and partly the other, I refuse to define it as either and instead call it simply a "version." On the other hand, the books of the New Covenant are my translation from the original Greek."*[66] [67]

Collaboration with Daniel C. Juster

This book has been written in collaboration with Dr. Daniel C. Juster. Dr. Juster is a *shaliach* of *Tikkun,* an international network of Messianic Jewish congregations, and he is the author of numerous books and journal articles on Messianic Jewish theology and ministry subjects. In

---

65 Stern, *Complete Jewish Bible (CJB)*, The copyright of *"The Complete Jewish Bible"* and its translation are held by "Jewish New Testament Publications, Inc.," and may not be reproduced without its permission.

66 Stern, *CJB*, p. xiv.

67 Since then, the *Tree of Life* (TLV) version has been published.

some cases Dr. Juster's commentary is labeled as his alone, but in many cases his and mine are integrated seamlessly.

A Work to Build Upon

The uniqueness of this book is not so much in its commentary (although I have prayerfully sought God's wisdom while writing it), but in its utility as a handbook and a framework for others to build upon. I am aware that there are some who might criticize me for publishing my personal views and interpretations of God's commandments, preferring that a work such as this be undertaken by a plurality of scholars and with the authority of a community behind it. In my defense, I will only say that this work is no different than any other commentary on Scripture, most of which have been written by individuals. Indeed, Maimonides himself came under criticism for not citing Talmudic sources to support his application of rules for deciding which *mitzvot* to codify[68] and for not disclosing the identity of scholars that declared rules on which he relied.[69]

---

68 Nahum Rakover, ed., *Maimonides as Codifier of Jewish Law*, p.26, in the Library of Jewish Law, (Jerusalem: The Jewish Legal Heritage Society, 1987).
69 Ibid., p.39.

Introduction by Daniel C. Juster

New Covenant *Torah:* What is the meaning of this phrase? New Covenant *Torah* is a concept that recognizes the continuing place of *Torah* (Law-instruction) of God as given in the Mosaic writings and expanded in the Prophets and the writings of the New Covenant Scriptures. It is a concept that also recognizes that we are in the New Covenant Era of fulfillment. Though not under the Mosaic Covenant *per se,* we are still to be instructed by the Mosaic writings and apply them, as fitting, to the New Covenant order. This meaning will become clearer as I continue.

As Thomas McComiskey argued in his excellent book *Covenants of Promise*, the Abrahamic Covenant is permanent. The Mosaic Covenant is a temporary administration of the Abrahamic Covenant, and the New Covenant is its permanent administration. However, the New Covenant teaches (explicitly in some passages and implicitly throughout) that the Mosaic teaching is of continuing validity; it is Scripture, and is *"profitable for teaching, for reproof, for correction, and for training in righteousness, that the man of God may be complete, equipped for every good work"* (*2Timothy 3:16-17* RSV). This leads us to the unavoidable question of how it trains us; what does its teaching require us to do if anything? This is the question of *halakhah,* the Jewish concept of the way, or the application of the *Torah* to new situations.

It has been common to teach that Judaism is a religion of law and Christianity a religion of grace. This is a distortion of both Judaism (especially Biblical Judaism) and of Christianity. Judaism knows grace and mercy; its prayers constantly appeal to God for forgiveness, not on the basis of our merit, but solely on the basis of God's mercy and grace. Classical Christianity also knows the place of the *Torah* (Law-instruction) and has sought to apply the Law of God according to its understanding of what is fitting to the New Covenant order. This has been so, even where it is not clearly acknowledged that this is what is happening. For example, Christianity has universally endorsed the teaching of Moses from Leviticus concerning forbidden marriages which define incest. These standards are not repeated in the New Testament. Christianity has an ethical tradition of applying the Law which we could call its *halakhah.* The weakness of Christianity in the west today is partly due to the loss of this ethical tradition, and the gross abandonment of duty to train in it.

The Concept of *Halakhah* in Jewish Thought

The word *halakhah* comes from the word *halak,* which means "way." The first followers of Yeshua were called "followers of the way," i.e. *halakhah* from Yeshua! *Halakhah* derives from two motives. One is to apply the *Torah* (Law-instruction) of God to new situations where the application is not obvious. The second is to protect the *Torah* by adding regulations so that one will not get close to breaking the law. The second motive is found in the ancient rabbinic text *Pirke Avot,* the "Ethics of the Fathers." This is called "building a fence around the *Torah.*" At times, this endeavor led to an expanding legalism that was far removed and even opposed to the original instruction of the *Torah.* Sometimes it also gave grounds for violating the intent of the commandment through ingenious ways of getting around it. We can see the controversy of Yeshua and the Pharisees in this light. Pharisaic Judaism evolved into Rabbinical Judaism with all of its pros and cons; perhaps much evolved in opposition to Messianic Judaism and an attempt to gain total government over the Jewish people (see Daniel Gruber's "*Rabbi Akiba's Messiah*)." Yet the basic need for *halakhah* is unavoidable. Just as the United States Constitution has to be applied to new situations by the courts of our land, so the Mosaic Constitution needs to be applied to new situations as well (e.g.: What do we do with all of the laws related to the Temple, now that there is no Temple?).

Halakhah (binding law upon the Jewish community) that was not explicitly written in the *Torah,* was built through consensus that arose out of intense debate in the early rabbinic *yeshivot* or academies. If the academy was important enough and other academies were swayed to its viewpoint, it became the universal practice among the Jewish people. The decision for each academy was either made by the ruling rabbi who was especially revered (and hence the others would concur), or it was made by the majority opinion of all the rabbis of a particular school. The *halakhah* was orally preserved and passed down (in the *Mishnah* first of all) and in the application of the *Mishnah* called the *Gemara.* The *Mishnah* contains the earlier of these decisions and the tradition of law passed on from these. The *Mishnah* and the *Gemara* together make up the *Talmud.* The rules of logic for reaching decisions are sometimes in accord with the normal rules of logic studied today. However, other rules are recipes for subjective conclusions and provide ways to ingeniously defend any position desired by the proponent. Rabbi Ishmael's early 13 rules of logic are simpler and more objective than Akiba's expansive list of rules of interpretation. The amazing thing is the claim that the Oral Law (which was later written down contrary to the Oral Law itself) is from Moses, was handed down from generation to generation, and has equal authority to the written *Torah.* Lawrence H. Shiffman of New York University, an eminent authority on Rabbinic Judaism, argues in his book "*From Text to Tradition,*"[70] that the Oral *Torah,* in traditional Judaism, in fact supersedes and really replaces the written *Torah.*

The claim that the Oral Law is from Moses is really quite indefensible and is certainly an attempt by the rabbinic community in the early centuries after the first century to establish the authority of their traditions and their conclusions. Indeed, two aspects of this claim are within the *Talmud.* One is that the earlier tradition of the elders, perhaps a very small body of material introduced by the phrase "we have a tradition" is seen as accurately passed down. Indeed, the rest is sometimes seen as lost and rediscovered by the application of rabbinic logic to the questions at hand; this is not reasonably believable. That is not to say that rabbinic reflection is not important in our own work in applying the *Torah.* The rabbis' conclusions are sometimes very insightful and helpful to our own application today. God's common grace is at work here.

The rabbis were correct concerning the need for applying the *Torah* to new situations and having sufficient authority vested in some body to unify the Jewish community in its basic practice. The process is akin to legislation and constitutional law in the United States and other constitutional nations. However, the Protestant Reformation position teaches us that every generation must re-think and re-apply what is handed down in every generation. Traditional application must be tested by the bar of the Written Word and adjusted to be true to it. Reformed Churches were fond of saying that they were reformed and always reforming, seeking to be truer to the written word for all new situations. Hence, it is wrong to create a fixed tradition of authoritative *halakhah*

70 Schiffman, Lawrence H., *From Text to Tradition*, (New York: KTAV, 1991).

which so overlays the Written Word that we can never get back to the Written Word to test the Oral *Torah*. As Lawrence Shiffman shows, the appeal to the Written Word to defend the Oral *Halakhah* is often strained and far-fetched, but done to give some reverence to the Written Word.

Messianic Jews seek to apply the *Torah* (Law-instruction) of God to the New Covenant situation and to the particular situation of life in which we find ourselves. We use the words "Law-instruction" as a hyphenated expression because the concept of *Torah* is more than law; it is God's whole instruction or teaching. However, it is a mistake to not recognize that a large part of this instruction consists of laws and commandments. Some in response to Christian criticism of the idea of a cold impersonal law have sought to strip *Torah* of its association with law. However, I want to argue that the idea of law should be a happy and attractive concept. Suffice it to say that all must grapple with the meaning as it applies to the whole Bible and its application to our present lives. This includes the Mosaic writings.

The New Testament and the *Torah*
The New Testament, which Messianic Jews often prefer to call the New Covenant Scriptures, is *Torah*-positive. Unfortunately, there has been a gross misunderstanding of the place of the Law of God in recent Christianity which was not true in most of classical Christianity. This misunderstanding derives from a theology called "dispensationalism" (in its classical form). The problem is, in my opinion, grave but solely from the promise of God, I do believe the Church will get it right before the return of the Lord (John 17:21). Present theological trends are, however, not too encouraging, though there are some glimmers of hope. Despite some significant differences between classical Christianity and dispensationalism (which we will outline later), classical Christianity came to a reasonably correct conclusion concerning the place of the Law and the application of Moses to the New Covenant order. This consensus basically yields a specific theology of the relationship of spirit and law, gospel and law, and law and grace. Perhaps John Calvin's summary in Book II Chapter 7 of his *Institutes of the Christian Religion* is representative.

The Church Consensus
Generally, this consensus taught that the Church was the new Israel and had replaced the old ethnic Israel (There were significant dissenters from this viewpoint, especially among the Puritans, English Anglicans, and Baptists). The Protestant Church divided the Law into two parts—the Moral Law and the Ceremonial Law. The Moral Law continued in the New Covenant order, but the Ceremonial Law was merely for the purpose of pointing forward to the Messiah, and was therefore temporary. When fulfillment came, the Ceremonial Law was made obsolete, and to continue to engage in the Ceremonial Law was understood to be acting as though the Messiah (the law's fulfillment) had not come; hence, practice of the Ceremonial Law was forbidden by the Catholic and Orthodox churches.

The Classical Protestant View
Basically, it is understood that we are under condemnation due to our violation of the universal dimensions of the Law of God as taught in Scripture. However, Yeshua died to pay the penalty due us according to the Law, and the record of our transgressions was cancelled. Not only so, but

when we repent and believe, submitting to Yeshua as Lord, we are transformed within. The old man is crucified, and the body of sin is rendered powerless (Romans 6:6). It is not only that He dies in our place, but we die in Him and are raised to new life. This transformation of the inner man takes place by identification with Messiah crucified and risen. Yeshua does not die for us as separate from us, but He is part of the human race and our corporate representative. In corporate reality, we are in Him, and He in us by faith, just as we were in Adam. Furthermore, we can be filled with the Spirit by faith in Him. Thereby do we enter the Kingdom of God. The Gospel is the Gospel of the Kingdom, the invitation to come under the rule of the King by submitting to His transforming grace rooted in His sacrificial death. Having undergone this transformation, we are now capable of submitting to the Law-instruction of God. Hence the biblical statements that by faith we establish the Law (Romans 3:31) and the righteous requirement of the Law is fulfilled in us who walk by the Spirit and not by the flesh (Romans 8:3-4). The Law is summarized in the commandments to love God with all our hearts and to love our neighbors as ourselves (Deuteronomy 6:4ff; Leviticus 19:18; Mark 12:28-31). Therefore "biblical ethics" is part of the training of ministers and catechumens in Classical Christianity.

Many understood that the Gospel of the Kingdom required that we come under the rule of God. We seek to live out God's righteous order in every realm of life. The righteous order is discerned by the teaching of the whole Bible. It includes the order of God in marriage, in family, in business and government, and in science and art! It, of course, includes His order for the Church. Except for a post millennial minority which saw the Christians taking over the whole world progressively and completely before the return of Yeshua, Classical Christianity taught that we are to live out the Kingdom in every sphere of life. Though we will not come into the fullness of the Kingdom until the return of the Messiah, we are called to do all we can, through the power of His Spirit, to establish the Law of God in every sphere of human life and to thereby show as much of the Kingdom as possible. This was seen as part of the believer's witness and as part of manifesting the Glory of God in human life.

Many saw that the Ten Commandments were, for example, really two-fold. Some of them summarized the requirement to love God exclusively, e.g., all of the commandments against idolatry. All of the other commandments are expressions of love for our fellow human beings created in His image. We love God in rightly loving others. This was seen in the summary of both Yeshua and in the Judaism of the first century (Mark 12:28-31; Luke 10:25-28). The love of our fellows is expressed in seeking justice and in establishing God's righteous order. To pursue justice is therefore equivalent to loving our neighbors, for human beings only find fulfillment in God's order (Micah 6:6-8). Without the Law, love deteriorates into mere humanistic sentiment. However, love motivates us to seek to establish the order of God's righteousness, to maximize the fulfillment of human beings, and more importantly, to show the wisdom and Glory of God in human communities that live according to His ways. Justice is rectifying that which is out of order by applying the blood of Yeshua for forgiveness and establishing community on the basis of God's principles.

The Call for Justice

The degree of lack of understanding God's call for justice (His righteous order as defined in Scripture—not some false humanistic idea of equality) is appalling. God's justice is hardly a topic in the contemporary Church, whereas it ought to be seen as number one. The Gospel is commonly understood as cheap grace (Bonhoeffer) that requires nothing of us. Rather, Scripture puts forth two primary motives for man. The first is to love, glorify and serve God. This is to capture our hearts totally. The second is to pursue justice. We preach the Gospel because unless people are transformed and receive eternal life, they cannot pursue justice motivated by love for others. The Gospel is God's means of establishing justice. Micah summarized it well in his great verse that answers the question, "…what does the LORD require of you but to do justice, and to love kindness, and to walk humbly with your God" (Micah 6:8 RSV)? God has not changed. All of the instruction of God is to be understood as the details of how to live out love for God and our fellows. In the Bible, love and justice are not opposed, but could be seen as a hyphenated word, "love-justice." When the law is broken, justice is satisfied by blood sacrifice or by paying the penalty. Love requires restitution to the one wronged; if the offender is truly repentant, this is his desire. God's love-justice provides the sacrifice of Yeshua so He can be both just and the justifier of those who are in Yeshua. I should note that justice in the Bible is only equality before the law and its requirement. It does not imply economic equality as today's Marxist influenced social justice warriors. It is rather an order of righteousness where each person can fulfill their God intended good destiny. But there can be great disparities of wealth as long as there is good provision for all. Those with much are to expand opportunity and provision for all.

In addition, love is the passionate identification with others that seeks their good guided by law. As such, love seeks the destiny fulfillment of the other. We share much in destiny; to know and love God, to marry and have children, to have adequate provision. But there is a distinct calling for every person.

I believe that the Messianic Jewish perspective is in basic accord with this classical Christian understanding of the relationship of Law and Grace. It is by grace that we are saved, but the saved individual is a Kingdom person who glorifies God in obedience to the Law of God. The point at issue with Messianic Jews is rather the easy distinction between the moral and Ceremonial Law, which eliminates the place of ethnic Israel in the plan of God, and eliminates the distinct practices of the Jewish people which define their "irrevocable" call (Romans 11:29). Having looked at the general consensus of Classical Protestantism, we now need to more closely look at the New Testament.

Yeshua and the *Torah*

The Gospel material implies a context for understanding the coming of the New Covenant order. It is the order of the in-breaking Kingdom which is at hand here. He that is least in the Kingdom of God has a better place that John the Immerser (Mark 1:14-15; Matthew 11:12). The order of the New Covenant Kingdom is seen in the acts and teaching of Yeshua and the disciples. He heals the sick, casts out demons, and raises the dead. These are manifestations of the Age to Come. Yet it is still a transitional time, for the Kingdom will not come in fullness until His return. This is the growing stage of the Kingdom where the Word of the Good News is preached as a farmer scatters seed, and the Kingdom grows from a small beginning until it is a large tree as in the parable of the mustard seed (Matthew 13). Though partial, though "already but not yet" (George Ladd in *The Gospel of the Kingdom*), the Kingdom (God's New Covenant order) has come and manifests itself in many spheres when the people of the New Covenant are submitted to the rule of God. We pray and work to extend this Kingdom and disciple those from the nations to live by its precepts.

In this context, Yeshua teaches that the written *Torah* has not been abolished. Heaven and earth will pass away before "one jot or one tittle" passes from the *Torah* (Matthew 5:18 NKJ). Yeshua has come to fulfill the *Torah*. What does this mean? It is clear from His teaching in Matthew 5-7, but is also reflected in all of the Gospel material. Where the Law of Moses implied a right heart given to obedience to the Law of God, Yeshua made the right heart orientation the key to His whole exposition. From the heart comes evil. Not only must one not commit adultery, but one must not sin by entertaining adultery in one's thought life. Not only are we to not murder, but me must not entertain thoughts of hatred and vengeance. The New Covenant elevates our ability with greater grace, and therefore requires an application of Mosaic teaching that is more exacting. While disagreeing with the Pharisees in some of their applications, Yeshua removes certain accommodations of Moses that were due to the "hardness of their hearts" and the weakness of the people (e.g. divorce). The teaching of Yeshua (and the Apostles) constitutes New Covenant *Halakhah*. Yeshua shows the meaning of the Sabbath, the legitimacy of healing on the Sabbath, eating grain as one walks through the fields, and the non-binding nature of the tradition of the elders (e.g. hand washing, Mark 7; Matthew 15). Yeshua makes authoritative *halakhah*, not by appealing to past tradition (as did the scribes), but by pronouncement according to his own authority (Matthew 7:28).

This role of making authoritative *halakhah* is given to the disciples who will supersede the Jewish Supreme Court, the Sanhedrin. In Matthew 16, Yeshua gives to Peter and the Apostles the keys to the Kingdom of Heaven, which is the authority to bind and loose. This authority is the right to forbid behavior (bind) and permit behavior (loose), and was exercised at the Jerusalem Council concerning the requirements for Gentiles to join the New Covenant Communities of faith. In addition, Matthew 16 and 18 provide the foundation for enjoining congregational discipling for the New Covenant community, a community of righteous order.

In those passages where Yeshua is accused of violating the *Torah,* closer observation shows that He was only violating Pharisaic traditions—not any commandment of *Torah.* Where the teaching of Moses set a standard, sometimes Yeshua would require more. Instead of being truthful in oath taking, we are to fulfill every word we speak. Instead of allowing unlimited revenge, the *Torah* prescribed "an eye for an eye" as the court standard; this is not, however, a standard for personal ethics and retaliation. Yeshua corrects this misapplication, and calls for loving our enemies. All of this is New Covenant *Torah* instruction. Yeshua did not violate the Sabbath, but only Pharisaic interpretation. As Lord of the Sabbath, He established *halakhah* under the principle that the Sabbath was made for man and not man for the Sabbath.

We can see in all of this, that Yeshua taught, enhanced, and applied the *Torah.* While the New Testament and the *Shlichim* (Apostles) are given binding *halakhic* authority, there is no warrant that the authority of later leaders in the New Covenant Community can make *halakhah* of this absolute binding nature. There is, however, authority to interpret and apply, and to govern as is necessary. That notwithstanding, everything can be questioned by the Written Word, and is to be reformed by it. Post New Testament, we seek consensus in practical applications, and the humility to follow this consensus; this never has the status of the *Torah,* or the *halakhic* authority of the New Testament.

The Letters of Sha'ul (Paul)

The letters of Sha'ul (Paul) are the primary source of controversy concerning the place of the *Torah* in the New Covenant. Some have interpreted him as teaching the very thing his accusers claimed, that the Jewish People are to forsake circumcision and Moses. This was denied by Paul in his testimony in Acts 21 where he brought an offering to profess that he lived according to the *Torah* [which *Ya'akov* (James) called orderly]. Paul's continued profession before Felix, Agrippa, and the community of Jews in Rome, was unwavering loyalty to the *Torah* (Acts 28:17). Indeed, the Book of Acts was written in part to show the nature of Jewish and Gentile life together in one Body, where Jewish distinctions of life and calling are maintained.

Gentiles are not generally required to live according to everything that God requires of Jews, but they are called to live out the universal dimensions of the *Torah.* If individual Gentiles and Gentile families have covenanted to draw near to Jews in a special way and live within a Jewish community, they will naturally participate in most of the community's Jewish expressions of *Torah* life and practice. As for Gentiles who are not so called and do not live within a Jewish Community, there is much latitude. However, they become citizens of the Commonwealth of Israel by virtue of their faith in Yeshua (Ephesians 2:11-22), so it would be well for them to seek understanding, and appreciation of Jewish aspects of the *Torah* for their connection to the Jewish people. This includes an understanding and application of the "appointed times" (Leviticus 23). These times give us a sense of the agricultural pattern of life in Israel, foreshadow the work of Yeshua, and show the meaning of his work. They also point to the last days and the Age to Come. As a biblical expression and recognition of their grafted-in Jewish connection (Romans 11) it is wise that Gentiles and all kinds of church communities teach on these matters during the seasons of Jewish celebration, and in cases where it is feasible, to have celebrations of their own connected to these meanings. That notwithstanding, Gentiles are not required to keep specific calendar days as Sabbaths (i.e. no work), whether connected to the Rabbinical Calendar, or to what some scholars now think was the Temple calendar.

The relationship of grace and law, or spirit and law is apparently paradoxical. Too quick an oversimplification, and we are bound for error. The paradox is not really a contradiction, but requires deeper unpacking. This was seen in a correct way by many writers. Calvin largely got it right. So did Wesley, Finney, Abraham Kuyper, and other classical representatives. Today, W. D. Davies in *Paul and Rabbinic Judaism,* Mark Nanos, Michael Wyschogrod, Professor Averbeck of Trinity in Illinois, C. E. B. Cranfield, J. Murray, Rhyne, W. P. Kaiser, and many others have gotten it right. What is Sha'ul saying?

First, he notes that by the law and standard of God, all human beings stand condemned. Those who are not of Israel do have a reflection of the Law of God in their ethical tradition. They know deep down that they are responsible to a Law-giver above themselves. Though Gentile traditions are greatly corrupted, they yet have sufficient knowledge of the standard of God to stand condemned before God. Secondly, the Jewish people who have a clear written revelation of the Law of God stand condemned by its standards. What is the solution? We cannot save ourselves.

Our righteousness is as filthy rags before the perfection of God's standard. Otherwise, why all of the blood sacrifices which show the mercy and forgiveness of God, based on substitution? The answer to this is a free gift which is received by faith, a trusting response to God's provision and a wholehearted turning to Him in submission. It is through identification with the crucified and risen Messiah that we are transformed. We accept that the penalty has been paid by our representative and that we are by faith said to have been crucified with Him (Galatians 3:20; Romans 6). Therefore, we are accepted in Him as righteous.

Before we see this, the Law (this would be true of the Gentile knowledge of the Law of God as well) is our schoolmaster. It teaches us right from wrong and shows us that we need a savior. Therefore, we receive righteousness as a gift apart from the Law, and are justified by faith. However, this does not mean that the Law (God's Law) has been done away with, but it now reappears as a tool of discipleship by the power of the Spirit. Thus Paul can say, *"... there is one God who will justify the circumcised by faith and the uncircumcised through faith. Do we then make void the law through faith? Certainly not! On the contrary, we establish the law"* (Romans 3:30-31 NKJ). The Gospel is God's means of establishing His *Torah* which is the goal of salvation history. *"The 'Torah' will go out from Zion, the word of the LORD from Jerusalem"* (Isaiah 2:3 NIV). Grace in the Pauline writings is not simply unmerited favor as taught by many, but includes the idea of empowerment by the Spirit to do righteousness. Sin is still defined as the transgression of the Law and righteousness is still defined by the Law. So Paul can say that the Hebrew Scriptures train us in righteousness (2 Timothy 3:16-17; 1 John 3:4). However, the focus of the truly righteous man is not prideful self-striving, but rather relational loving passion for the Father, the Messiah, and their glory. In this orientation, we are empowered by Grace via the Spirit, and we fulfill the righteousness of the Law *("... that the righteous requirement of the law might be fulfilled in us who do not walk according to the flesh but according to the Spirit"* (Romans 8:4 NKJ)).

As if this is not enough, Paul rebukes those who say that he teaches antinomianism (anti-*Torah*). Such a claim is slanderous (Romans 3:8, 6:1-2). In addition, Paul makes it clear that the standards of the Law are upheld by the Gospel message and states, concerning the standards of the *Torah*, that their violation is against the Gospel he preaches.

> *"Now we know that the law is good, if any one uses it lawfully, understanding this, that the law is not laid down for the just but for the lawless and disobedient, for the ungodly and sinners, for the unholy and profane, for murderers of fathers and murderers of mothers, for manslayers, immoral persons, sodomites, kidnapers, liars, perjurers, and whatever else is contrary to sound doctrine, in accordance with the glorious gospel of the blessed God with which I have been entrusted."* (1 Timothy 1:8-11 RSV)

In 1 Timothy 1 we find that the Law restrains the godless and, in *chapter 3*, that it instructs and trains in righteousness.

The Book of Galatians

Actually, but for the Book of Galatians, error in interpreting Paul would have been much less. The principles of interpretation should have led us to interpret Galatians through Romans since it is the fuller and more detailed presentation of the law-grace issues. The Book of Acts as well provides both the historical context and interpretation for understanding Galatians. The issue in Galatians was requiring the circumcision of Gentiles for their acceptance into the New Covenant community of faith. It was an issue of understanding that righteousness comes by faith, not by works and the issue of the broadness of fellowship (which John Yoder and Mark Nanos see as more central than the issue of justification by faith). However, Galatians is not against the instruction of the *Torah.* Indeed, its list of the works of the flesh can only be understood in the light of the *Torah.* Those who walk by the Spirit are not under the Law (subject to striving by our own efforts and under the condemnation of its penalty which was paid for us).

"Now the works of the flesh are plain: fornication, impurity, licentiousness, idolatry, sorcery, enmity, strife, jealousy, anger, selfishness, dissension, party spirit, envy, drunkenness, carousing, and the like. I warn you, as I warned you before, that those who do such things shall not inherit the kingdom of God." (Galatians 5:19-21 *RSV*)

What defines these sins? What is immorality? Paul says that, apart from the Law, we would not know what these sins are! Indeed, today we defend as right open marriage, homosexual marriage, abortion, and much more. How shall we argue that these things are wrong? Shall we say that the Spirit told me? Or shall we say that God has revealed His standard in His *Torah* and in the extension of that teaching in the whole Bible? Paul's catalogue of sinful behavior is known to him by the *Torah,* not by the teaching of Hollywood! Faith establishes the *Torah,* but if we by-pass the way of faith, we do not establish it. The whole Bible looks forward to the age of the establishing of God's rule, the *Torah.* The way of faith in the New Covenant is God's way to it, for He writes the *Torah* on our hearts.

The Book of Hebrews

If Paul wrote Hebrews, we see nothing but confirmation. The Mosaic Covenant Order is fading and becoming obsolete. However, in the New Covenant Order, the *Torah* is written on our hearts and every individual may appropriate the power of his co-death with the Messiah, put to death the old man and be filled with the Spirit. In this the *Torah* is not done away with, but is written on our hearts as is applicable to the New Covenant Order. What passes away are not the standards of God, but the pre-New Covenant Temple system which looked forward to His coming and an order in which only a special few could be filled with the Spirit. Now that He has died, He gives the Holy Spirit to all who are born again. Hebrews is speaking about the coming of the greater order of the New Covenant. It is not about abandoning the instruction found within Moses, the Prophet, and the writings and applying it as is fitting to the New Covenant Order. The issue is a better covenant where this transforming work is done in us (Hebrews 8:7-13). Ezekiel notes that the New Covenant offers the Spirit who will move us to obey God's statutes, ordinances, and judgments (Ezekiel 36:24 ff).

Furthermore, Paul teaches that the *Torah* is still part of Jewish calling as it is applicable in the New Covenant. This is shown by his example in completing a Nazirite vow in Acts 18:18, in his profession in Acts 21 and 28, and in his explicit statements in Romans 9:4 ff where he indicates the gifts given to Israel are still of significance. In Romans 11:29 he states that the gifts and call to Israel are irrevocable. More will be stated about this continuing call. However, suffice it to say that the Bible shows us that God is committed to establishing an order of righteous call to *Torah,* justice, etc. This order includes proper relationships between husbands and wives, parents and children, employers and employees, merchants and shoppers, governments and peoples, elders and the flock, and Israel and the nations. The last is an issue of God's right order as well, which He will establish according to His promise to Abraham.

The General Epistles

We will find no evidence against our orientation in the General Epistles. It is our call to pursue justice, even the establishment of God's righteous order through the power of the cross and Spirit. John is clear on this and lets us know that sin is transgression against the Law of God and that the true disciple does not intentionally sin (or violate the *Torah* of God) (1 John 3:4)! He is one who practices righteousness. Peter warns us that some have misunderstood Paul as an antinomian (against the *Torah* and its applicability to the New Covenant). He states that the untaught and unstable have distorted his writings and twisted them to their own destruction. That twisting would most probably be connected with allowing sin because of an anti-law interpretation of Paul. The writings of James could be well seen as a corrective to those who were misunderstanding Paul. Therefore he calls for *mitzvot* (good works) to prove faith and notes that the *Torah* is a *torah* of liberty (James 1:25). His exposition of the *Torah* and warning against being found a transgressor of the *Torah* are clear (James 2:9). In the history of interpretation, those who have tended to antinomianism (anti-law) have had a great struggle with James even to the point of claiming that it was not Scripture.

Enough has been said, I believe, to convince the fair minded that the understanding and application of the teaching of the whole Bible on right and wrong, justice and righteousness, is crucial. It is a key to fighting the ethical laxity in the Body of believers and is crucial to the legitimacy of the Messianic Jewish Movement. When teaching the whole Bible, we begin with Moses and reapply it to the New Covenant Order as did Yeshua and the *Shlichim.*

The Discovery of Hittite Treaties

One of the great archaeological discoveries was the treaties of the Hittites, a large nation at the time of Exodus. The tablets were discovered at the sites of Nuzi and Mari. They prove the existence of the significant nation mentioned in the Bible. Before that time, liberal scholars thought that the Biblical information on this nation was mythological. In the 1950s Professor George Mendenhall of the University of Michigan noted strong parallels between these treaties and the form of Covenant material in the Mosaic writings, especially the Book of Deuteronomy. Meredith Kline expanded this work and showed that not only were the treaties parallel to covenant material in the Mosaic writings, but the order and form of the Hittite treaties were an exact match. His first articles on this were published in the *Westminster Theological Journal* in the mid-1960s and later found in such books as *Treaty of the Great King* and *The Structure of Biblical Authority.* Two great conclusions were asserted by Kline. First, the Mosaic writings were from Moses, from the time period traditionally as understood (15th-13th centuries B.C.). Indeed, only the Hittite treaty forms from that era exactly parallel Deuteronomy. Secondly, Kline asserted that the treaty form proves that the Mosaic material and especially Deuteronomy is fully a covenant of grace. Covenant—not law—is the basic category for understanding this material.

Law is a subsidiary concept. Other leading scholars picked up on this work and now assert the same view as Kline. Samuel Schultz, the esteemed Old Testament professor from Wheaton, in his books *The Gospel of Moses* and *Deuteronomy: The Gospel of God's Love* show his stand by the very titles. Thomas McComiskey in *Covenants of Promise* argues similarly with added insights. Other scholars such as Walter Kaiser, Kenneth Kitchen, Professor Averbech at Trinity in Illinois, and many more have affirmed these views as have Messianic Jewish writers, including myself, John Fischer, Michael Shiffman, and David Stern. I will not repeat in detail what was written in my book *Jewish Roots*. Walter Kaiser has his own attempt at what he might call Christian *halakhah* in *Toward an Old Testament Ethic*. Many of those who argue are Christian scholars with no Messianic Jewish axe to grind. Because I have given an extensive outline of this scholarship in *Jewish Roots*, I will only give a very brief summary.

Deuteronomy is in the form of a covenant of grace whereby God first recounts to Israel that He saved them through no merits of their own. This is asserted explicitly and repeatedly in Deuteronomy 8 through 10, where God says it is not because of her righteousness, largeness, strength, or attractiveness that she has been saved. Hittite kings liked to assert that their rule over a subject people was a grace act which the subjects did not deserve. The historical material is to demonstrate that Israel's history is characterized by being given mercy, grace, and love that is undeserved. In gratitude for this love, Israel is called to be a society in obedience to God's *Torah* in every realm of life, from absolute loyalty to God Himself, to business integrity, to integrity and truth in the court system, to caring for the poor. Obedience is a response to grace and salvation offered as a gift. Therefore, Israel's corporate salvation fits the same pattern as the invitation for individual salvation in the New Covenant. Furthermore, the sacrificial system shows that repentance, forgiveness, and blood substitution is at the heart of the Covenant, forestalling any proud view that salvation is gained by our autonomous attainment of good works. The Sabbath is in the center of the Ten Commandments because it is a covenant sign between God and Israel. It shows forth the meaning of God's creation pattern, and is a perfect symbol for a people delivered from the bondage of slavery, for freedom from work one day in seven is a manifestation of a people set free. This day is given for God, worship, and fellowship.

Once this is understood, we can see that there is greater continuity between the Mosaic Covenant and the New Covenant than even perceived by our *Torah*-positive Puritan brothers of yesteryear. Even the Ten Commandments is really a covenant of grace beginning with the declaration of unearned salvation, 'I am the Lord your God who brought you out of the land of Egypt, out of the house of slavery.' The New Testament looks at us all as in a house of slavery spiritually until we are born again and enter the Kingdom of God.

Continuity and Discontinuity in *Halakhah*

As we stated, the application of the teaching of Moses (and of the whole Bible) to new challenges and situations requires prayer and thinking akin to what Jewish people call *halakhic* thinking. Even the New Testament material requires such thinking. Do women wear head coverings today as specified in 1 Corinthians 11? If so, how much must they cover of the woman's head? Are the coverings only to be worn in the worship service in public? If not, why not? However, our concern will primarily be the application of Mosaic material to the

41

New Covenant order. Much has been written in debate concerning women and head coverings. Different conclusions have been reached by different denominations. This is their *halakhah!*

Consistency is a virtue, but not all followers of Yeshua or theologians are consistent. Consistency is based on the virtue of integrity, honesty, and the trustworthiness of our words; however, sometimes it is better that there are some inconsistencies rather than people following the full logical conclusions of their positions. For example, the most anti-*Torah* theologians usually follow the *Torah* when it comes to its list of forbidden sexual unions that would constitute incest. Christian theologians that are more consistent have put forth theses for what parts of the *Torah* should be followed in the New Covenant era, and what should be rejected. With regard to their varying theses, Protestant streams have differed with regard to the question of the extent to which the Mosaic writings are in continuity with the New Covenant. This continuity-discontinuity question is one of the most foundational issues in theology. Generally, Protestant theology in its classical form distinguished between the ceremonial and moral parts of the Mosaic *Torah*. The former is valuable for study that we might more fully understand the work of Yeshua, but is no longer to be practiced. However, the Moral Law is binding in the New Covenant. Where the lines are drawn between moral and ceremonial varies. I will now briefly outline the continuity-discontinuity pattern in various streams.

Roman Catholic Thought

Roman Catholic and Eastern Orthodox thought did not make a clear distinction between ceremonial and moral law. Instead, the early Church that gave rise to both the Eastern and Western Churches developed patterns that were parallel to Tabernacle-Temple ceremonies. In addition, moral theologians did seek to apply the Mosaic teaching for part of the ethical and social basis of Christian civilization.

Let us take the Roman Catholic Church as an example. There is, first of all, a class of priests provided by the population. These priests are analogous to the Levites and *Kohanim* of ancient Israel. The Levites continued by tribal descent. Roman Catholic Priests serve by entering into training, taking vows of celibacy, and by being ordained by a bishop who is seen in apostolic succession to the original Apostles. Lineage is important in priesthoods—physical lineage in the former, and a spiritual lineage of continuity by the laying on of hands in the latter. The Church parallels the Tabernacle-Temple in offering daily and special sacrifices upon an altar. However, the sacrifice offered is the sacrifice of "Christ" in the Mass. Until recently, the priest turned from the congregation for the elements to be transformed in the liturgy. This was analogous to the High Priest entering the Most Holy Place on Yom Kippur.

In the Eastern Church, the priest actually goes behind the door and leaves the presence of the congregation to enter the "Most Holy Place." The people eat of the sacrifice (the bread); traditionally there was a portion only for the priest (the wine—blood). This was before today's change whereby the people are also offered the wine. There are many symbols reminiscent of the Hebrew Scriptures. There are seven-branched lamps, priestly garments, priestly hats, and an eternal light and incense. Stained glass windows include heroes from ancient Israel as well as New Testament figures. The Roman Catholic Church has created a "New Covenant Temple worship." The Sabbath day is also special, but has been transferred to Sunday when the resurrection is also celebrated. Whatever one might think of the totality of the Roman Catholic orientation, it is clear that there is a large degree of continuity from ancient times. Yet, continued Jewish life among Jewish believers was seen as not entering into the reality of the New Covenant priesthood and Temple realities. Catholic moral theology also developed a Canon Law tradition that is parallel to Rabbinic thought. New rules are added and ways are developed to get around the law in various cases (casuistry). It should also be noted that the Christian calendar is in continuity in some ways, and in discontinuity in other ways, with the biblical calendar. Passover and Easter sometimes coincide, but solar dating makes this happen only periodically; nevertheless, the fact that Easter occurs in the Spring is clearly rooted in Passover. In the Eastern Church, which defended the Bible's lunar calendar, the concordance of its feasts with the Jewish calendar is more obvious. Good Friday before Easter and Passover season is the closest thing on the Christian calendar to Yom Kippur, the Day of Atonement. Protestant tradition largely maintained the same calendar as the Catholic tradition, so we can see that the distinction between moral and Ceremonial Law is not followed through with.

Lutheranism

Martin Luther rejected much of Catholic doctrine. The priesthood of all believers and the identification of the gathered community of saints (as a temple) was asserted. However, the bread and wine of the Messiah's Supper was seen as truly conveying the body and blood of Yeshua spiritually. The liturgy that sets these elements apart, the role of the clergy, and the symbolism of the Church itself still show marks of continuity to ancient Israel. The seven-branch lamp, the eternal light, the priestly robes, and the designation of the table of the Lord's Supper as the altar still show continuity with the Ceremonial Law even if Lutheran theology too-easily adopted the "ceremonial" and "moral" as distinctions. Luther was not consistent in his approach to the Law. At one point he would assert that we should love God and do as we please. He railed against those who held that the Sunday Sabbath should be enforced and wrote that the English that were enjoining sedate quiet and reflection, should be required to have sports and recreation on Sunday. On the other hand, Luther's *Shorter and Larger Catechism* put forth the Ten Commandments, with explanation and application such that they should be obeyed. Luther's associate Philip Melancthon and the great Lutheran systematician Johannes Andreas Quenstedt both moved toward a more consistent position similar to Reform thought. Luther's thought was, therefore, ambivalent to the Mosaic writings and was inconsistent in approach. The relationship of the Law-Gospel dialectic was never resolved; the ambivalence is still present in Lutheran thought today.

Calvinism

Those of the Calvinist tradition projected a very high regard for *Torah*. They accepted the distinction of the Ceremonial and Moral Law. Calvin put forth a clear theology of the Law whereby it brings conviction of sin and leads us to the Messiah; it restrains sin in society by becoming the basis of civil law with its penalties, and it is a tool of discipleship for the believer through the work of the Holy Spirit. This discipling tool dimension for believers was called the "third use of the Law." Calvin found this in 2 Timothy 3:16-17 where all Scripture was said to be valid for training in righteousness. When the grace of God has been received, the Spirit enables us to be obedient to the Law of God. The Sabbath (now switched to Sunday according to their understanding of the New Testament) was considered to be part of the Moral Law since it was in the Ten Commandments, while (for example) *Yom Kippur* was seen as part of the Ceremonial Law. Circumcision, the biblical calendar, and the Temple service have not passed away. Dutch Reform Churches and Presbyterians followed in this tradition.

Puritans in the Calvinist tradition maintained the same basic stance whether they became British Presbyterians or Congregationalist or Calvinist Baptists. We see the same reflected in the writings of Increase Mather in the American Colonies, and of Jonathan Edwards one hundred years later. The Colonial Puritans, especially, wrestled with how to apply the Law of God and, more than any other group, thought to build a society upon the basis of the Law. The Moral Law was seen as including personal, civil, and business law. Puritans exacted civil penalties, including capital punishment, based on the Mosaic Law. They were a prosperous society, seeing themselves as a New Israel, parallel to ancient Israel; yet they had special regard for ancient Israel. Many saw a future purpose for ethnic Israel. Christmas celebration in Puritan New England was forbidden as too pagan in its roots! On the continuity-discontinuity issue, Puritans weighed in heavily on the side of continuity. Applying the Law was not only abstract, but ordered Puritan life for over a century.

Anglicanism
The Anglican Church developed an amazing eclecticism of Catholic, Lutheran, and Reform thought. Puritans were in and out of the Church of England preceding, during, and after the period of Oliver Cromwell in the 17th Century. One can see the Ceremonial Law applied as in the Catholic Church in the ceremony of the High Anglican. The theology of the Eucharist which is given in both kinds (bread and wine) is closer to Luther. The understanding of the general relationship of law to grace is like unto Calvin, and justification by faith is accepted doctrine. A married priesthood by apostolic succession is parallel to but different than the Roman Catholic view. When it came to applying the Mosaic Law, the Anglican orientation was set by Richard Hooker in his *Laws of Ecclesiastical Polity*. Hooker argues against the Puritan position of literally applying the Mosaic Law to order social and civil life (There was no debate between Puritans and Anglicans). Hooker argues that the Mosaic Law, as given, was for ancient Israel. We had to discern more universal principles in the Law and apply them to new circumstances in our society. Reason could as well discover principles for Church, civil and social life as well as helping us apply the Scriptures to new situations. The Puritans responded that the human mind is not given to second-guess the Law of God by looking for principles in the manner of Hooker. One can see from this debate that the question of continuity-discontinuity and the application of the Law is no new issue. My view is that the Anglicans were too quick to dismiss direct application because it offended their human sentiment. However, many laws are based on obvious principle and are not required of us literally. Shall we build a fence on our roof (Deuteronomy 22:8) when it is not used for living space as in ancient flat-roof houses? The principle of taking reasonable steps to protect human life from accident is clear.

The Methodists
John Wesley, the founder of the Methodist movement was an Anglican. He did not emphasize the application of specific Mosaic commandments, but exhibited a high regard for law. After his death, the Methodists were forced to leave the Anglican Church to practice their convictions. A

high regard for moral standards and holiness based on the Law and its exposition in the Sermon on the Mount was a noteworthy part of Methodism.

The Anabaptists

In the 16th Century, several leaders believed that the reformation did not go far enough. These were the Anabaptist, committed to simple life, pacifism, adult baptism, and material sharing. While having a high regard for the Law and seeing obedience as the outworking of grace, they saw the teaching of the New Testament as a sufficient exposition and application of the Law for Christians. The Sermon on the Mount was the center of this understanding. Anabaptists saw continuity and discontinuity, but thought that the New Covenant required a much higher standard than the Mosaic. The Mosaic writings would be studied for ethical guidance, mostly to supplement the New Testament. There was high regard for the principle of law and holiness, but the New Covenant community in its pacifism, communal sharing, openness to all peoples, and love for the enemy, was seen in discontinuity with the "Old Testament." Mennonites, Amish, Church of the Brethren, Brethren in Christ and others come from the Anabaptist traditions. In all of these traditions, we see that the Church has had to wrestle with the issue of continuity and discontinuity. In doing so, the Church produced varieties of Christian *halachah*. Some saw great continuity and others more discontinuity.

The Dispensationalists

The end of the 19th Century spawned a movement that dramatically affected western Evangelical Protestantism. It broke from Classical Christianity and presented a view of radical discontinuity between the Mosaic Covenant and the New Covenant. Others had anticipated these views, but were labeled antinomian heretics. Their movements came to little. An Irish Anglican priest by the name of John Nelson Darby was troubled by the "deadness" in the Anglican Church. In reflecting on the problem, Darby concluded that the basic problem was confusion between law and grace. This problem was rooted in the 39 Articles, the basic doctrinal statement of the Anglican Communion. Darby asserted that the "Old Testament" was a dispensation of law that was in total contrast to the New Testament period, a dispensation of grace. Though having a place for ethnic Israel in the future, all who become Christians are no longer "Jew" or "Gentile," but part of the bride. Continued Jewish life in the New Covenant would confuse law and grace. In Darby, the Mosaic Covenant offered salvation on the basis of keeping the Law, and this was bound to lead to failure and death. However, the sacrifices anticipated the coming of the Messiah so the "Old Testament" saints were not without a grace element, and by believing in the substitute sacrifices, they were preserved for the salvation that would come in Yeshua. Darby radically redefined grace as only unmerited favor. Darby taught that New Testament offers salvation by grace through faith with a specific "Darby-ite" slant. It was that believing or faith in the death and resurrection of Yeshua as one's personal Savior from sin is the only necessary thing required for salvation. Repentance is not necessary. Submitting to His holy lordship is not necessary. One may continue to live in sin without showing life change or gratitude and still be saved. One should not do so, however, but if salvation is by grace, it is a logical possibility in his scheme. In Classical Christianity, however, the grace concept included the content of empowerment and motivation to obedience. This radical redefinition of grace produced a radical discontinuity between the Mosaic Covenant and the New Covenant. Even the Sermon on the Mount was seen as part of the dispensation of law. We are not duty-bound to anything of this dispensation according to Darby and his followers. Even the Ten Commandments do not have claim on us. We are only duty-bound to the teaching of the epistles of the New Testament which do repeat the content of nine of the Ten Commandments.

In this radical discontinuity, Darby asserted the priesthood of all believers and eschewed clergy. Lay ministers working in other professions would be the elder-leaders. Ritual would be at a bare minimum (baptism and the Lord's Supper). How did Darby see this as revitalizing the Church? In his view, many would be grateful for the unmerited salvation, and they would dedicate their entire lives. This is a second (but not required) step. The Church, however, would then be populated by dedicated volunteers, not by people who thought it was required of them for salvation. Carnal Christians would largely be outside. In addition, the Church would enforce spiritual discipline on the flock. Classical Dispensationalism made clear distinctions. Israel has to do with the Law, the Church with grace. The former has an earthly salvation, the latter a heavenly one. Today, neo-dispensationalism is moderating this radical stance. Some teach that repentance is needed and submission to His lordship (John McArthur). Others now see the Sermon on the Mount as instruction for the New Covenant. A few are even saying (from 2 Timothy 3:16-17) that one can discern principles in the Mosaic writings that have application to the dispensation of grace.

The orientation of Dispensational theology has become part of the popular sub-culture of American Evangelism. Many who could not even define the term "Dispensationalism" reflect a popular culture born out of its theology. Statements like "We are no longer under the Law," in a slant that is contrary to Classical Christianity, are rooted in this movement. Those who say a person was saved in a meeting reflect this sub-culture. Classical Christians would only say a person made a profession and would not find confidence in their salvation until the fruit of a changed life was brought forth. Carnal Christianity has some rooting as well, since one may live in sin and still hope for eternal security (contrary to both Calvinism and Arminianism). Looseness and disrespect for the Law of God is a plague that has affected Baptists, Charismatics, Pentecostals, Independent Churches, and many smaller denominations and streams. Because America has been the leading force for world missions, Dispensationalism is also found in many nations, including (to my great chagrin) Israel. Many Israelis link the concept of *Torah* with Rabbinical legalism. They unbiblically react in a negative way to the idea of *Torah*. When some Israelis become believers in Yeshua, they easily buy into the anti-Law dimensions of dispensational theology from the past influence of Christian missions in the Land of Israel. This is done without conscious realization. The Bible is read through glasses without awareness that a Christian sub-culture has placed these glasses upon them.

Messianic Judaism

Messianic Judaism finds itself in a unique position. We oppose the replacement theology of Classical Christianity where ethnic Israel has been fully replaced in the purposes of God by the Church. On the other hand, we oppose the antinomian heresy of Classical Dispensationalism. Messianic Judaism does see discontinuity between the Mosaic Covenant and the New Covenant. However, because Paul says that the gift and call of God to Israel is irrevocable (Romans 11:29), we are oriented to greater continuity than most Christian views. My little book *The Irrevocable Calling* puts forth the idea of why Jewish followers of Yeshua are to live a Jewish life and the essence of what Jewish life is. In summary, Jewish life is a priestly witness and an intercessory activity. Our preservation as a nation, our return to our land, and our celebrations and unique Jewish practices are a witness to the reality of God and the truth of His Word. In addition, the Jewish celebrations of Sabbath and the Feasts are a picture of redemptive meanings that are fulfilled in Yeshua and yet have further fulfillment at the return of Yeshua and in the Age to Come. We can discern in Scripture what is required of the Jewish people and what is required of Gentiles in Yeshua. It is not the same in all regards. Jewish and Gentile believers form a complementary priesthood. The Sabbath proclaims the existence of God, recalls creation, and releases intercession that all people might enter their Sabbath rest through salvation in Yeshua. Passover recalls our deliverance from Egypt through the Passover blood of the lamb, the coming of Yeshua as God's lamb, and releases intercessory power by faith, that all people might "pass over" from sin and death into their promised land in God, and might sit down together and celebrate. As Israel will inherit the Land, the meek will inherit the earth. Jewish life in Yeshua is willed by God; it is the teaching and example of the Apostles.

More on Continuity and Discontinuity

In applying the *Torah,* we recognize a degree of discontinuity between the Mosaic and New Covenants. Just how does the New Covenant differ from the Mosaic? How is it a better covenant? It is not a contrast between one being of law and the other of grace, one where God is harsh and the other where God is forgiving and kind. These are sub-cultural myths. Nor is it that one is for Israel and the other is for the Nations. Both are made with Israel, but the New Covenant explicitly applies the promise of the Abrahamic Covenant to bless all nations by commanding us to bring the message of the Gospel to all. The following are the basic differences. We now have the power of identification with Yeshua's crucifixion to put to death the deeds of the flesh. In addition, all may now be indwelt and filled with the Holy Spirit. Each individual is a Temple of the Holy Spirit. Furthermore, a Temple is formed wherever a New Covenant congregation gathers together in faith. Prophecy is given to all and the gifts of the Holy Spirit are poured out upon us. Jew and Gentile are now one in the Messiah. The Law has been written upon our hearts, and we are moved by the Spirit to obey God. As for the Mosaic writings, its teachings and principles are to be applied to the New Covenant Order. This is the teaching of Yeshua and Paul (Matthew 5:17-18; 2 Timothy 3:16-17) and it is their example to quote from Moses to settle issues.

In addition, the New Covenant enjoins us to share the Gospel with all people and to disciple the nations. Jew and Gentile in the Messiah are now one in fellowship, foreshadowing the day when Israel and the nations will be one under the rule of the Messiah. Thus there is a change in the application of Mosaic *Torah.* The restriction that physically uncircumcised men must not join our Passover *Seder* is changed. Gentiles who are in Yeshua may join us; they have circumcised hearts and are clean. In addition, because of the power of Yeshua's sacrifice and the Spirit, accommodations in the Mosaic Law (such as in Matthew 19:8) are seen as no longer acceptable. Divorce laws are more stringent and slavery and polygamy are forbidden, and so there is both continuity and discontinuity. We are now under the New Covenant, a covenant said to be not like the Covenant given through Moses (Jeremiah 31:31ff). There is now no physical Temple; therefore, we need to think through the meaning of clean and unclean laws whose violation usually required temporary preclusion (until evening or for seven days) from Temple involvement. Also, some of the clean-unclean laws, if intentionally violated, required severe penalties. Today, these are connected to higher moral meanings with contemporary application; an example is the holiness of blood). This gives some sense of where we see the New Covenant as differing from the Mosaic. We should note that the New Covenant replaces the administration of the Mosaic Covenant, but does not replace or alter the Abrahamic Covenant. Rather, as McComiskey taught, the New Covenant is the permanent administration of the Abrahamic Covenant. The New Covenant is based on the fulfillments of the Messiah's crucifixion and resurrection, and the outpouring of the Spirit.

The Messianic Jewish Task

One of the more universal dimensions of the Messianic Jewish task is to reassert the fact that God has not changed in His desire for justice and for establishing His righteous order in every realm of life. Some Classical Christian theology was clear on this (e.g. Calvin and Kuyper). By contrast, "Darby-ite" theology opted out of social responsibility. We pray "Your Kingdom come, your will be done on earth as it is in heaven" (Matthew 6:10). We read in Isaiah 42:4 (RSV) of the Messiah, "He will not fail or be discouraged till he has established justice in the earth; and the coastlands wait for his law." In the Age to Come the Messiah will have established justice. It is now through us that He seeks to establish it. It is part of our witness and calling to exhibit the righteous order of God in every sphere of life we touch to the fullest extent of our Spirit-led influence. This means that in our business life, congregational life (including the standards of congregational discipline), our family order (Ephesians 5), our artistic life and our citizenship responsibility. Scientists also have a Kingdom calling rooted in Genesis 1:26ff. In the Bible, justice and love are not in opposition. Micah says we are to do justice and love mercy (Micah 6:8). Therefore, the pursuit of God's righteous order in every sphere of life is an expression of the second of the two greatest commandments—to love our neighbors as ourselves. To pursue justice from a motive of love for the sake of the Glory of God is to love our neighbors. Everywhere in the Bible exhorts us to this. However, anti-law theology of recent years has influenced many to not pursue the order of God's righteousness for the various spheres of life in which we are involved. Charles Coleson has applied biblical *Torah* teaching to our penal system, and rightly so. We have little to say to the concerns of society without the *Torah*. We could say that love for God and man are expressed by worship and the pursuit of love-justice. Justice (or God's order of righteousness) is defined by His Word or *Torah*—not by the Marxist or socialist deception of absolute equality. It is equality before the Law of God, but includes a place for varieties of talents, gifts, callings and outcomes. In the international scene, justice occurs when Jerusalem is the capital of the world, and Israel and the nations are in proper relationship under the rule of the Messiah.

The goal of God is that the *"Torah* will go forth from Zion, and the Word of the Lord from Jerusalem" (Micah 4:2). The goal of the Gospel (the New Covenant) is the establishment of the *Torah,* the Rule of God, and the Kingdom of God. As we pursue God's righteous order, we move history to its climax which is the return of the Lord. We will only see partial manifestations of the Kingdom now but these manifestations are a crucial part of our witness. When God's Kingdom holds greater sway in a society, conditions for all improve markedly. Indeed, bringing the Gospel to the nations and discipling are the first order of business in pursuing justice because unless people are born again, they cannot submit to the Rule or *Torah* of God.

May I end this section with a heart cry for Israeli Messianic Jews not to give themselves to antinomian theology. Deliver the term *Torah* from the Rabbinical *Talmud* if you are so convicted, but do not abandon the biblical meaning of *Torah* in the New Covenant and the hope of the prophets to establish *Torah* over all the earth. May the word *Torah* be a delight to you.

The Plan of this Book

This book suggests a Messianic Jewish *halakhic* approach to the various commandments and laws (explicit and implied) that are found in the Bible. It does not claim to be *halakhah* because it is not a body of rules that any community has adopted as binding on its members. It nevertheless presents a way of thinking that seeks to apply the Mosaic *Torah* (and also other parts of the Bible) to the New Covenant order and to contemporary life. As such, we have categorized the Law into basic subject divisions for a more coherent presentation. One will see by this that the easy distinction of Ceremonial and Moral Law does not fly, nor was it ever consistently applied in any tradition of Christianity. Categorizing by subject does have the disadvantage of not following the classical listing of 613 laws. In a study of the laws and commandments, one will find that 613 is somewhat arbitrary since some are repeated and not categorized well by subject. However, because this is the classical Jewish way of putting forth the biblical commandments, we will put traditional citations next to each commandment or law being discussed, so that one can find it in Jewish lists and commentaries.

In applying the Law we will discuss the traditional Jewish consensus, applications made in the New Testament, Classical Christian applications, and our concluding position. One will see that most of the *Torah* is not so difficult to understand and apply. Two men are working on this project, so if we do not agree on the final interpretation and application, we will make our differences known. This is a very Jewish way to deal with the issues. We trust that this book will aid in training in personal and social ethics for all believers and will point out specific applications for Jewish calling.

Elephants in the Room

What Paul Really Meant by His Comments on the Law
by Michael Rudolph

Messianic Judaism is similar to other "Judaisms" in seeking to apply the laws of *Torah* that God gave to the Israelites at Mt. Sinai. Since those early days, many changes have occurred that impact our ability to keep the Law as our ancestors did. They include (1) a change in the Covenant, (2) Yeshua's birth, ministry on earth, death, and resurrection, (3) universal accessibility to the Holy Spirit, (4) expansion of the Scriptures to include the New Testament, (5) lack of a functioning Levitical Priesthood, (6) absence of the Temple of God and, most important of all, (7) salvation through faith in Yeshua. These are the New Covenant realities under which we now live. Consequently the way we keep the Law today cannot be solely according to the letter; rather, it must be guided by the Holy Spirit for both wisdom and application.

But as we seek the Holy Spirit for how to keep the Law, we are hindered by ever-present "elephants in the room." The "elephants" of which I speak are the well-known writings of the Apostle Paul which seem to say that obeying the Mosaic Law is no longer profitable and may even cause spiritual harm. I knew it was not so, but because I have had to restudy and rethink Paul's statements every time someone raised them to me in debate, I decided to write this short commentary in order to explain what I believe Paul really meant in his writings.

Each numbered caption that follows is a statement one often hears from opponents of observing Biblical Law. Then following each caption are Scriptures (translated in the New King James), authored by Paul, that are often used to support erroneous views of the Law, and after that comes my commentary. The New King James translation is used (with "Messiah" replacing "Christ" and "Yeshua" replacing "Jesus") because it and the NIV are among the most popular, and the most egregious in misrepresenting Paul.

1. We no longer have to obey the Law because we are now under grace.

> Romans 6:14: *"For sin shall not have dominion over you, for you are not under law but under grace."*

This sounds like Paul is saying that God's "grace" releases us to do anything we want, and from having to obey any of God's laws. Why would the Apostle Paul, a confessed keeper of the Law (Acts 21:17-26), say such a thing? Did Yeshua's appearance on earth and subsequent sacrifice cause God to change into a permissive liberal? I knew that couldn't be the case, but still, what Paul said perplexed me, so I decided to pray and ask God about it.

What I believe I heard prophetically in reply is this: Being "under grace" is not automatically permissive as some would like it to be. Grace does sometimes imply permissive allowance or forgiveness, but being under God's grace does not mean that He always grants it to us. Rather, it means that we are subject to the *operation* of God's grace, and that He (and only He) decides when to extend it and when to withhold it.

Theologians often define "grace" *(kharis)* as "God's unmerited favor" (which is correct) but, in his writings, Paul uses it metaphorically to mean God Himself, whose very person embodies grace. Romans 6:14 is therefore informing us that our accountability is no longer merely to the "statutes" of God's written Word (His *Torah* or Law*)*, but is now directly to God Himself through the living Word, who is Yeshua (John 1:14). Our being "under grace" is Paul's way of saying that, in this direct accountability to God, God may either extend His grace to us or withhold it, on a case by case basis, according to His supreme sense of mercy and justice. Our being "not under law," (the Greek word here for "under" is *hupo,* meaning "underneath") connotes that we are no longer "underneath" the Law's enforcement; that is, we no longer automatically receive the Law's penalties for disobedience, but there is no doubt that we continue to be (and are now *directly*) subject to God's correction and punishment (as well as His praise and reward) when we are deserving of them. Meanwhile, the commandments of *Torah,* as interpreted by the Holy Spirit, retain their relevance in being a main source for our determining God's Will, but our "obedience" relationship with God is now direct rather than indirect. That is why Paul says in Galatians 5:18:

"But if you are led by the Spirit, you are not under the law."

And similarly in Galatians 3:24-25:

"Therefore the law was our tutor to bring us to Messiah, that we might be justified by faith. But after faith [meaning "Messiah"] *has come, we are no longer under a tutor."*

What I have said about "grace" thus far has been in response to Paul's juxtaposing "grace" and "law." I would, however, be remiss were I not to mention another kind of grace that God *never* withholds. It is God's empowerment, through the Holy Spirit, to do as well and as much as God, in His sovereignty, is willing to release us to. So it would seem, for example, that God always extends grace to a person who seeks His power for obedience, and to do good. We depend on God's grace to perform His will.

2. We are justified by faith and not by the Law, so the deeds of the Law no longer have value.

In Romans 3:20 and 28, Paul says:

"Therefore by the deeds of the law no flesh will be justified in His sight, for by the law is the knowledge of sin. ...Therefore we conclude that a man is justified by faith apart from the deeds of the law."

And in Galatians 2:15-16 and 21:

"We who are Jews by nature, and not sinners of the Gentiles, knowing that a man is not justified by the works of the law but by faith in Yeshua the Messiah, even we have believed in Messiah Yeshua, that we might be justified by faith in Messiah and not by the works of the law; for by the works of the law no flesh shall be justified. ... I do not set aside the grace of God; for if righteousness comes through the law, then Messiah died in vain."

These Scriptures and others like them are often quoted to deny the Law's continuing value in the New Covenant. After all (some think), if righteousness cannot be acquired from performing the deeds of the Law, then why do them? The answer is that, with the power and discernment that the Holy Spirit allows us, we perform the deeds of the Law because they are God's will—not in order to become righteous and acquire salvation.

Paul is very clear that no one is justified (i.e. made righteous—saved) through merely obeying commandments. Justification comes only through our reliance on Yeshua's sacrifice that expunges our sins if we receive Him and repent; that's why Galatians 2:16 states:

> "...a man is not justified by the works of the law but by faith in Yeshua the Messiah..."

Romans 3:28 says the same thing but differently; it says:

> "...a man is justified by faith apart from the deeds of the law."

None of this contradicts Paul's contention that God's Law continues to have value in the New Covenant. We can be certain of this because in Romans 3:31 Paul says:

> "Do we then make void the law through faith? Certainly not! On the contrary, we establish the law."

3. We are now dead to the law, having been delivered from it.

In Romans 7:4-6, Paul says:

> "Therefore, my brethren, you also have become dead to the law through the body of Messiah, that you may be married to another-- to Him who was raised from the dead, that we should bear fruit to God. For when we were in the flesh, the sinful passions which were aroused by the law were at work in our members to bear fruit to death. But now we have been delivered from the law, having died to what we were held by, so that we should serve in the newness of the Spirit and not in the oldness of the letter."

Also, in Galatians 2:19-20, Paul says:

> "For I through the law died to the law that I might live to God. I have been crucified with Messiah; it is no longer I who live, but Messiah lives in me; and the life which I now live in the flesh I live by faith in the Son of God, who loved me and gave Himself for me."

The expressions "dead to the law," "died to the law," and "delivered from the law" have led many to believe that God's Law no longer applies to us. That is not at all what Paul is saying.

In Romans 7:4-6, Paul is comparing our relationship with God to the intimate relationship of marriage. Prior to the New Covenant, our "marriage" relationship with God was mostly through our obedience to the statutes of *Torah* because we did not yet have Yeshua's sacrifice or the Holy Spirit to draw us closer. It was a wonderful relationship, but God made it even better by sending Yeshua who sacrificed Himself for us. This brought us into a "marriage" relationship with Yeshua that was more intimate than our marriage relationship through the Law. But because it is not God's will that we be in two marriages at the same time, Paul explains that we died during our marriage to the Law in order to clear the way for our "marriage" to Yeshua. That is what Paul meant when he said:

"you also have become dead to the law through the body of Messiah, that you may be married to another (Romans 7:4) *–"* and his other saying: *"I through the law died to the law that I might live to God"* (Galatians 2:19).

Paul's reference to being "delivered from the Law" and being "held" by the law is a continuation of his metaphor that we have moved from one marriage relationship to another. It is not as some believe—Paul stating that God's Law held us in bondage. I said "God's Law" instead of just "Law" purposely, in order to illustrate how much easier it is to accept that some nondescript "Law" held us in bondage, than to think that "God's Law" held us in bondage, which we know cannot be true. Also, Paul's reference to the "newness of the Spirit" and the "oldness of the letter" is completely consistent with the Scriptures and everything else Paul said because, in the New Covenant, our principal way of relating to God has changed. Paul recognizes our changed relationship to the Law, but at no time infers that the *Torah* has been done away with or has been rendered useless.

4. The Mosaic Law is a curse, and those who seek to obey it are under its curse.

Galatians 3:10-13: *"For as many as are of the works of the law are under the curse; for it is written, "Cursed is everyone who does not continue in all things which are written in the book of the law, to do them. But that no one is justified by the law in the sight of God is evident, for "the just shall live by faith." Yet the law is not of faith, but "the man who does them shall live by them." Messiah has redeemed us from the curse of the law, having become a curse for us (for it is written, "Cursed is everyone who hangs on a tree ")..."*

Once again, the words that Paul uses are often misconstrued—in this case, the word "curse," which some would have us believe means that God's Law is a curse. No, the curse to which Paul is referring originates in Deuteronomy 30:19, which reads:

"I call heaven and earth as witnesses today against you, that I have set before you life and death, blessing and cursing; therefore choose life, that both you and your descendants may live;"

When these words were given by God to Moses under the previous covenant, the context was 'covering over sin' through obedience to the Law and animal sacrifice. Israel's choice to either obey the Law and live, or disobey and not live, was a reference to salvation that, unbeknown to the Israelites at Mt. Sinai, would be granted in the future as a result of Yeshua's sacrifice. Paul's words paralleling Deuteronomy were spoken many centuries after Sinai under the New Covenant, when our path to salvation had been transferred from conducting animal sacrifices to having faith in Yeshua, the ultimate sacrifice. Paul was warning the Galatians not to seek covering over of their sins in the old way of obedience to the Law with attendant animal sacrifices, but rather to seek salvation in the new way which was through Yeshua. Not only was the old way no longer authorized but, under it, even a single violation would result in the cursing referred to in Deuteronomy 30:19 that led to death. But Paul is clear in Galatians 3:11 (NKJ) that in the New Covenant:

"no one is justified by the law…"

…and he quotes <u>Habakkuk 2:4</u> (see also, <u>Romans 1:7</u> and <u>Hebrews 10:38</u>):

> *"the just shall live by his faith."*

Bottom line: It is not a curse to seek to keep the Law; the curse comes from trying to keep it as a means of acquiring salvation.

5. It no longer matters what we eat, or drink, or whether we keep God's special days.

> <u>Colossians 2:16-17</u>: *"So let no one judge you in food or in drink, or regarding a festival or a new moon or sabbaths, which are a shadow of things to come, but the substance is of Messiah."*

This Scripture is sometimes used to assert that God's food laws, appointed times, and other special days commanded in Scripture are no longer in effect, and that those who adhere to them are putting themselves back under the "Law of sin and death," and even denying Yeshua. Now that's a pretty ominous charge for merely resting on the Sabbath and abstaining from pork. To see what is actually being said here, let's widen our search to verses of Scripture that come both before and after:

> **Before:** <u>Colossians 2:8</u>: *"Beware lest anyone cheat you through philosophy and empty deceit, according to the tradition of men, according to the basic principles of the world, and not according to Messiah."*

> **After:** <u>Colossians 2:20-22</u>: *"Therefore, if you died with Messiah from the basic principles of the world, why, as though living in the world, do you subject yourselves to regulations— "Do not touch, do not taste, do not handle," which all concern things which perish with the using—according to the commandments and doctrines of men?"*

Notice that the words in <u>verse 16</u>,

> *"let no one judge you in food or in drink, or regarding a festival or a new moon or sabbaths…"*

are sandwiched between <u>verse 8</u> and <u>verses 20-22</u> that warn against becoming captive to the traditions, commandments, and doctrines of men. But God's *Torah* regarding permissible foods and how to keep His festivals, new moons, and Sabbaths, are not the traditions of men, so Paul was not, therefore, advocating disregard for the *Torah*. Rather, he was warning us against being in bondage to "fences" that some would place around the *Torah*—rules promulgated by men that are beyond and more stringent than those commanded by God.

6. The Mosaic Law was defective and is now obsolete.

> <u>Hebrews 8:6-7 and 13</u>: *"But now He has obtained a more excellent ministry, inasmuch as He is also Mediator of a better covenant, which was established on better promises. For if that first covenant had been faultless, then no place would have been sought for a second.… In that He says, "A new covenant," He has made the first obsolete. Now what is becoming obsolete and growing old is ready to vanish away."*

These verses of Scripture are sometimes used, in conjunction with others, to assert the Mosaic Law's inadequacy, defectiveness, and obsolescence. But if those making the assertion would look at the Scriptures carefully, they would see that what is being spoken of is the Mosaic Covenant—not the Mosaic Law. A covenant is a relationship—an agreement between parties. The Mosaic Covenant was the relationship that was consummated at Mt. Sinai between God and the Israelites, where God gave the Israelites His Laws (the *Torah*), and the Israelites promised to obey. Well, they didn't obey, and they consequently breached the Covenant; the word "breach" and "fault" are the same. The Covenant between God and the Israelites developed a fault that was not intrinsic to the covenant agreement, but rather one that was created by the Israelites' disobedience. We see this clearly in Hebrews 8:8 that says:

> "Because finding fault with **them**, He says: 'Behold, the days are coming, says the LORD, when I will make a new covenant with the house of Israel and with the house of Judah…'"

Notice how the Scripture says *"finding fault with **them**…"* The fault was with the Israelites—not in the design of the covenant. And we read in both Hebrews 8:8 and Jeremiah 31:30(31)-31(32) that, rather than God leaving Israel without a covenant (which He could have done and which they deserved), He graciously gave them a New and different covenant that was based on better promises. In the process of doing that, He allowed the First Covenant to gradually pass into oblivion; that is what Paul means by the First Covenant becoming obsolete.

So, do we need to obey the Mosaic Law? Well, yes and no! Part of the Mosaic Law can no longer be complied with because it has lost its covenantal infrastructure. We have no operative Levitical Priesthood, no Jerusalem Temple in which to conduct animal sacrifices, and no unified leadership of Israel. Yeshua should be recognized by everyone as the King of Israel, and His sacrifice as the reason why many commandments connected to the Temple can no longer be performed. Still, there are many commandments that remain doable, but they have now come under New Covenant administration and are subject to New Covenant enforcement. When added to other mandates of the New Covenant, they collectively become what Galatians 6:2 calls "the Law of Messiah."

7. The Mosaic Law is a ministry of death, so literal observance of it kills.

> 2 Corinthians 3:5-8: *"Not that we are sufficient of ourselves to think of anything as being from ourselves, but our sufficiency is from God, who also made us sufficient as ministers of the new covenant, not of the letter but of the Spirit; for the letter kills, but the Spirit gives life. But if the ministry of death, written and engraved on stones, was glorious, so that the children of Israel could not look steadily at the face of Moses because of the glory of his countenance, which glory was passing away, how will the ministry of the Spirit not be more glorious?"*

> Romans 7:6: *"But now we have been delivered from the law, having died to what we were held by, so that we should serve in the newness of the Spirit and not in the oldness of the letter."*

The 2 Corinthians Scripture refers to the written Law as a "Ministry of Death," and says that "the letter (presumably of the Law) kills." It certainly appears to support the view of those who would preach doing away with the Law, yet the Scripture also says that the written Law was glorious—an apparent contradiction. What then is Paul trying to say? Paul is reflecting about the

Old Covenant, when the Holy Spirit was not accessible to the average Israelite, and when literal obedience to the Law was indeed the prescribed path to life. But it ceased to be the path to life in the New Covenant when Yeshua's sacrifice gave us direct access to God, and the Holy Spirit was given to us to be the Law's interpreter. So Paul is warning us that today our approach to God's Law must be through the Holy Spirit and not through mere literal observance. He is warning us that although literal obedience to the Law led us to life under the Old Covenant, by-passing the Holy Spirit to pursue literal obedience will lead us to death under the New. That is not to say that today the letter of the Law has no application. It does, but it must be the Holy Spirit who gives us the application.

8. The Mosaic Law was done away with by Messiah, so all we need do now is love our neighbor.

> Romans 10:4: *"For Messiah is the end of the law for righteousness to everyone who believes."*

> Galatians 5:14: *"For all the law is fulfilled in one word, even in this: "You shall love your neighbor as yourself.""*

These Scriptures have occasionally been used to teach that, when Messiah came, he brought an end to God's Law because all God ever wanted was for us to love our neighbor, which is the Law's fulfillment.

Romans 10:4 is easy to explain. Put simply, the word "end" in the verse does not mean "termination of existence," it means "purposeful destination" as in the expression "the end justifies the means." It tells us that Messiah is to whom the Law brings us. As for Galatians 5:14, both the Law of Moses and the Gospel of Yeshua stand for selfless sacrifice as against self-interest. When we *"love 'our' neighbor as 'ourself,'"* we fulfill the ultimate of what the Law stands for, but we are not released from obeying God's specific and detailed Commandments. If we were, He would have told us.

Conclusion

I hope this commentary helps to clear the "elephants" from the room. We can criticize Paul's choice of words or the translations of his writings, but what we cannot do is believe that Paul would condone the myriad of anti-law statements that have been attributed to him.

2 Timothy 3:16-17 teaches us:

> *"All Scripture is given by inspiration of God, and is profitable for doctrine, for reproof, for correction, for instruction in righteousness, that the man of God may be complete, thoroughly equipped for every good work."*

Let us keep in mind that the *Torah* (the Pentateuch) that contains the Law of Moses is Scripture, and is therefore profitable for all that 2 Timothy says it is. And by the way—take note of who wrote 2 Timothy—*It was Paul!*

Mitzvah Subject Keys

The following capital letters are prefixed to and made a part of the number of each *mitzvah* developed by the author as a means of indicating its principal subject category.

A	Godliness and Godly Living
B	Benevolence
C	Commerce
D	Days and Seasons
E	Covenant Responsibilities
F	Family
G	Relating to God
H	Holiness and God's Order
I	Idolatry, Heathens, and the Occult
J	Justice
K	*Kashrut*
L	The Jewish People and the Land of Israel
M	Morality and Compassion
N	Neighbors and Brothers
O	Outreach and Spiritual Authority
P	Priesthood
R	*Ru'ach Hakodesh*
S	Sexual Conduct
W	Word of God
Y	Messiah Yeshua
Z	End-Times

New Covenant Literal Application Code (NCLA)

Each *Mitzvah* in this compilation includes a New Covenant Literal Application Code (abbreviated NCLA) that consists of three parts. The first part specifies Jew, *K'rov Yisrael,* or Gentile. The second part specifies Male, or Female. The third part specifies one of seven possible levels of literal compliance that applies to each. The NCLA Code accompanying each *Mitzvah* reflects the author's interpretive opinion and is provided for the reader's prayerful consideration only.

The keys to the **NCLA** Code are as follows:

Person Categories

JM Jewish male
JF Jewish female
KM *K'rov Yisrael* male
KF *K'rovat Yisrael* female
GM Gentile male
GF Gentile female

Literal Application Categories

m Literal compliance **mandated**
r Literal compliance **recommended**
o Literal compliance **optional / allowable**
n Literal compliance **not generally recommended**
u Literal compliance **unauthorized**
p Literal compliance **prohibited**
i Literal compliance **not applicable or impossible**

Example:

A *Mitzvah* followed by **JMm JFm KMo KFo GMn GFn**, means that literal compliance of the *Mitzvah* is mandatory for Jewish males and females, is optional for *K'rov Yisrael* males and females, and is not generally recommended for other Gentiles.

A: Godliness and Godly Living

A1. Being Unequally Yoked in Matters of Godly Importance.

We are not to be unequally yoked in matters of godly importance.

This precept is derived from His Word (blessed is He):

Key Scriptures

Leviticus 19:19 (Maimonides RN215, 216, 217; Meir MN107, 142; Chinuch C244, 245, 548)
Observe my regulations. "'Don't let your livestock mate with those of another kind, don't sow your field with two different kinds of grain, and don't wear a garment of cloth made with two different kinds of thread.

Leviticus 21:2-3 (Maimonides RN158, 159; Meir MN138, 139; Chinuch C266, 267)
A cohen is not to marry a woman who is a prostitute, who has been profaned or who has been divorced; because he is holy for his God.

Numbers 25:1-3
Isra'el stayed at Sheetim, and there the people began whoring with the women of Mo'av. These women invited the people to the sacrifices of their gods, where the people ate and bowed down to their gods. With Isra'el thus joined to Ba'al-P'or, the anger of ADONAI blazed up against Isra'el.

Deuteronomy 7:1-4 (Maimonides RN52; Meir MN19; Chinuch C427)[71]
ADONAI your God is going to bring you into the land you will enter in order to take possession of it, and he will expel many nations ahead of you—the Hitti, Girgashi, Emori, Kena'ani, P'rizi, Hivi and Y'vusi, seven nations bigger and stronger than you. When he does this, when ADONAI your God hands them over ahead of you, and you defeat them, you are to destroy them completely! Do not make any covenant with them. Show them no mercy. Don't intermarry with them—don't give your daughter to his son, and don't take his daughter for your son. For he will turn your children away from following me in order to serve other gods. If this happens, the anger of ADONAI will flare up against you, and he will quickly destroy you.

Deuteronomy 22:9 (Maimonides RN216; Chinuch C548)
You are not to sow two kinds of seed between your rows of vines; if you do, both the two harvested crops and the yield from the vines must be forfeited.

Deuteronomy 22:10 (Maimonides RN218; Meir MN180; Chinuch C550)
You are not to plow with an ox and a donkey together.

Deuteronomy 22:11 (Maimonides RN42; Meir MN181; Chinuch C551)
You are not to wear clothing woven with two kinds of thread, wool and linen together.

---

71   The commentators' *mitzvot* are based on Deuteronomy 7:3.

<u>2 Corinthians 6:14-17</u>
Do not yoke yourselves together in a team with unbelievers. For how can righteousness and lawlessness be partners? What fellowship does light have with darkness? What harmony can there be between the Messiah and B'liya'al? What does a believer have in common with an unbeliever? What agreement can there be between the temple of God and idols? For we are the temple of the living God—as God said, "I will house myself in them, and I will walk among you. I will be their God, and they will be my people." Therefore ADONAI says, "'Go out from their midst; separate yourselves; don't even touch what is unclean. Then I myself will receive you.

Supportive Scriptures

Exodus 23:32-33
Matthew 6:24

Commentary

The Scriptures supporting this *mitzvah* appear to have three dissimilar themes: agriculture, marriage, and idolatry. What they all have in common however, are sets of things that work in opposition to each other, causing a nullification of positive value that one of them alone might otherwise have had.

First, the agricultural examples: (1) that we not yoke an ox and a donkey together to a plow, (2) that we not wear garments with wool and linen woven together, and (3) that we not sow two kinds of seeds in fields and in vineyards. The traditional explanation for not working two kinds of animals together is that it is cruel to the animals since the stronger of the two will drag the weaker one, and the weaker of the two will impede the stronger one. An additional observation offered here is that the work that either of the animals could do alone is impeded by their having to pull against each other.

Maimonides' explanation (echoed by HaChinuch) for not wearing wool and linen woven together is that such a fabric was worn by the heathen priests in Egypt. From a different point of view and the one I offer here is that wool and linen shrink different amounts after they are wet, so if they are woven together, they pull against each other when they dry and weaken the fabric.

HaChinuch's explanation for not sowing two kinds of seed is that it is an extension of the prohibition against mating mixed species. From a different point of view and the one I offer here is that different species of plants absorb nutrients from the soil in different proportions, so when they are planted close together they compete for the nutrients to the detriment of both.

Consider the marriage examples next: <u>2 Corinthians 6:14-17</u> explains it best (although marriage is not mentioned in that Scripture) when it states:

> *"What does a believer have in common with an unbeliever? What agreement can there be between the temple of God and idols?"*

61

Without agreement on spiritual things between husband and wife, the husband cannot lead the wife; they inevitably pull in different directions, and destruction follows, sometimes with the believer compromising his or her faith.

Finally, consider the idolatry examples: Israel was prohibited from making covenants with heathen nations and intermarrying with their sons and daughters for the same reason as was stated between believers and unbelievers. God predicted that if that happened, the Israelites would be lured away from Him and into idol worship; as is stated in Deuteronomy 7:4:

> *"For he will turn your children away from following me in order to serve other gods."*

Whereas, the classical commentators tend to interpret the Scriptures of this *mitzvah* according to the plain meaning of their words and separate from each other, I see them as connected by their common thread of forces pulling against each other. Clearly, the weight of this *mitzvah's* application is that, if we belong to God, we must not yoke ourselves with anything or anyone who is not of God. Marriage is the most obvious example, followed perhaps by other partnerships like business partnerships. People who do not believe similarly about God hold different values, and take different ethical and moral positions on things. This either causes the believer to compromise, or it breaks up the partnership. As Matthew 6:24 states:

> *"No one can be slave to two masters."*

If 2 Corinthians 6:14-17 were the only subject of this *Mitzvah,* I could have given it the more narrow title "Being Unequally Yoked with Unbelievers." I did not, because but even in a partnership between two believers, the partnership is unwise if the partners see things very differently and respond accordingly. In this, the Scriptures have very far-reaching wisdom.

Classical Commentators

None of Maimonides', Meir's, or HaChinuch's *mitzvot* are expressed so as to oppose unequal yoking in general. Rather, their *mitzvot* speak against specific dissimilar combinations; Maimonides' *mitzvot* prohibiting such combinations are as follows:

RN42: Not wearing cloth made from both wool and linen.
RN52: Not marrying an heretic.
RN158: A priest not marrying a harlot.
RN159: A priest not marrying a profaned woman.
RN215: Not sowing two kinds of seeds.
RN216: Not sowing grain or vegetables among grape vines.
RN218: Not working a field with two different kinds of animals.

NCLA: JMm JFm KMm KFm GMm GFm

A2. Walking in God's Ways.

We are to walk in God's ways and adopt them as our own.

This precept is derived from His Word (blessed is He):

Key Scriptures

Deuteronomy 10:12-13 (Maimonides RP8; Chinuch C611)
So now, Isra'el, all that ADONAI your God asks from you is to fear ADONAI your God, follow all his ways, love him and serve ADONAI your God with all your heart and all your being; to obey, for your own good, the mitzvot and regulations of ADONAI which I am giving you today.

Deuteronomy 13:5(4) (Maimonides RP8)
You are to follow ADONAI your God, fear him, obey his mitzvot, listen to what he says, serve him and cling to him;

Deuteronomy 28:9 (Maimonides RP8; Meir MP6; Chinuch C611)
ADONAI will establish you as a people separated out for himself, as he has sworn to you—if you will observe the mitzvot of ADONAI your God and follow his ways.

Psalms 25:4
Make me know your ways, ADONAI, teach me your paths.

Supportive Scriptures

Leviticus 11:44
Luke 9:23
John 10:27
Ephesians 5:1
1 Peter 1:14-16
1 John 2:6

Commentary

"Following" God, "imitating" Him, and "walking" in His ways are different ways of saying the same thing—learning God's ways and adopting them as our own. We see from the above Scriptures that this principle traverses both the Mosaic Covenant and the New Covenant, and that adopting the ways of Yeshua (who is more visible to us than the Father) assures us of adopting the ways of our Father in heaven as well. Yeshua Himself modeled this for us as we read His words in John 5:19:

> *"Therefore, Yeshua said this to them: "Yes, indeed! I tell you that the Son cannot do anything on his own, but only what he sees the Father doing; whatever the Father does, the Son does too."*

There is a common misunderstanding that the Scriptures quoted in this *Mitzvah* should help dispel; the misunderstanding is that only through the indwelling of the *Ru'ach HaKodesh* brought by the New Covenant, can men succeed in obeying God. It is wrong because God never holds us accountable for that which we cannot do, and Scripture teaches that, at Mt. Sinai, God gave us instructions for conduct that He expected of us. On the other hand, to think that man on his own can accomplish God's will is wrong also, so what of the Spirit was available to man before the coming of the New Covenant? Since man in his own strength cannot fully accomplish God's will, it must be that the Holy Spirit was available at Sinai and before, but that the level of the Spirit's availability was limited and was greatly increased with the coming of the New Covenant. Jeremiah 31:32(33)-33(34) partially explains this:

> *"For this is the covenant I will make with the house of Isra'el after those days," says ADONAI: I will put my Torah within them and write it on their hearts; I will be their God, and they will be my people. No longer will any of them teach his fellow community member or his brother, 'Know ADONAI'; for all will know me, from the least of them to the greatest; because I will forgive their wickednesses and remember their sins no more."*

Jeremiah prophesies as to both the Messiah and the *Ru'ach HaKodesh*—the Messiah to provide a just means for God to forgive our sins, and the *Ru'ach* to implant God's nature within us in order to bring Him closer to us and assist us to walk in His ways. Ezekiel 36:24-27 also prophesies a New Covenant in which God would enhance our obedience through the Holy Spirit placed within us, yet God assured us in Deuteronomy 30:11-14, that we were able to obey Him in pre-Yeshua times as well:

> *"For this mitzvah which I am giving you today is not too hard for you, it is not beyond your reach. It isn't in the sky, so that you need to ask, 'Who will go up into the sky for us, bring it to us and make us hear it, so that we can obey it?' Likewise, it isn't beyond the sea, so that you need to ask, 'Who will cross the sea for us, bring it to us and make us hear it, so that we can obey it?' On the contrary, the word is very close to you—in your mouth, even in your heart; therefore, you can do it!"*

Classical Commentators

Meir and Maimonides agree with each other—that we are to model ourselves after God and expect to become like Him in nature. HaChinuch agrees, and references Micah 7:18:

> *"Who is a God like you, pardoning the sin and overlooking the crimes of the remnant of his heritage? He does not retain his anger forever, because he delights in grace."*

NCLA: JMm JFm KMm KFm GMm GFm

A3. Being Good Stewards.

We are to be good stewards of the things and matters that are entrusted to us.

This precept is derived from His Word (blessed be He):

Key Scriptures

Man's Stewardship of God's Creation

Genesis 1:27-30
So God created humankind in his own image; in the image of God he created him: male and female he created them. God blessed them: God said to them, "Be fruitful, multiply, fill the earth and subdue it. Rule over the fish in the sea, the birds in the air and every living creature that crawls on the earth." Then God said, "Here! Throughout the whole earth I am giving you as food every seed-bearing plant and every tree with seed-bearing fruit. And to every wild animal, bird in the air and creature crawling on the earth, in which there is a living soul, I am giving as food every kind of green plant." And that is how it was.

Genesis 2:15-17
ADONAI, God, took the person and put him in the garden of 'Eden to cultivate and care for it. ADONAI, God, gave the person this order: "You may freely eat from every tree in the garden except the tree of the knowledge of good and evil. You are not to eat from it, because on the day that you eat from it, it will become certain that you will die."

Israelites' Stewardship of their Crops

Leviticus 19:9-10
When you harvest the ripe crops produced in your land, don't harvest all the way to corners of your field, and don't gather the ears of grain left by the harvesters. Likewise, don't gather the grapes left on the vine or fallen on the ground after harvest; leave them for the poor and the foreigner; I am ADONAI your God.

Parents' Stewardship of their Children

Proverbs 22:6
Train a child in the way he [should] go; and, even when old, he will not swerve from it.

Israelites' Stewardship of their Money

Mark 12:41-44
Then Yeshua sat down opposite the Temple treasury and watched the crowd as they put money into the offering-boxes. Many rich people put in large sums, but a poor widow came and put in two small coins. He called his talmidim to him and said to them, "Yes! I tell you, this poor widow

has put more in the offering-box than all the others making donations. For all of them, out of their wealth, have contributed money they can easily spare; but she, out of her poverty, has given everything she had to live on."

A Parable of Good and Bad Stewardship

Luke 12:40-48
"You too, be ready! For the Son of Man will come when you are not expecting him." Kefa said, "Sir, are you telling this parable for our benefit only or for everyone's?" The Lord replied, "Nu, who is the faithful and sensible manager whose master puts him in charge of the household staff to give them their share of food at the proper time? It will go well with that servant if he is found doing his job when his master comes. Yes, I tell you he will put him in charge of all he owns. But if that servant says to himself, 'My master is taking his time coming,' and starts bullying the men—and women-servants, and eating and drinking, getting drunk, then his master will come on a day when the servant isn't expecting him, at a time he doesn't know in advance; his master will cut him in two and put him with the disloyal. Now the servant who knew what his master wanted but didn't prepare or act according to his will, will be whipped with many lashes; however, the one who did what deserves a beating, but didn't know, will receive few lashes. From him who has been given much, much will be demanded—from someone to whom people entrust much, they ask still more."

A Manager's Questionable Stewardship of Worldly Wealth as Evidence of His Trustworthiness with Heavenly Wealth

Luke 16:1-13
Speaking to the talmidim, Yeshua said: "There was a wealthy man who employed a general manager. Charges were brought to him that his manager was squandering his resources. So he summoned him and asked him, 'What is this I hear about you? Turn in your accounts, for you can no longer be manager.' 'What am I to do?' said the manager to himself. 'My boss is firing me, I'm not strong enough to dig ditches, and I'm ashamed to go begging. Aha! I know what I'll do—something that will make people welcome me into their homes after I've lost my job here!' So, after making appointments with each of his employer's debtors, he said to the first, 'How much do you owe my boss?' 'Eight hundred gallons of olive oil,' he replied. 'Take your note back,' he told him. 'Now, quickly! Sit down and write one for four hundred!' To the next he said, 'And you, how much do you owe?' 'A thousand bushels of wheat,' he replied. 'Take your note back and write one for eight hundred.' And the employer of this dishonest manager applauded him for acting so shrewdly! For the worldly have more sekhel than those who have received the light—in dealing with their own kind of people! Now what I say to you is this: use worldly wealth to make friends for yourselves, so that when it gives out, you may be welcomed into the eternal home. Someone who is trustworthy in a small matter is also trustworthy in large ones, and someone who is dishonest in a small matter is also dishonest in large ones. So if you haven't been trustworthy in handling worldly wealth, who is going to trust you with the real thing? And if you haven't been trustworthy with what belongs to someone else, who will give you what ought to belong to you? No servant can be slave to two masters, for he will either hate the first and love the second, or scorn the second and be loyal to the first. You can't be a slave to both God and money."

Several Servants' Stewardship of their Masters' Wealth

Matthew 25:13-30 (see also, Luke 19:12-26).
So stay alert, because you know neither the day nor the hour. For it will be like a man about to leave home for a while, who entrusted his possessions to his servants. To one he gave five talents [equivalent to a hundred years' wages]; to another, two talents; and to another, one talent—to each according to his ability. Then he left. The one who had received five talents immediately went out, invested it and earned another five. Similarly, the one given two earned another two. But the one given one talent went off, dug a hole in the ground and hid his master's money. After a long time, the master of those servants returned to settle accounts with them. The one who had received five talents came forward bringing the other five and said, 'Sir, you gave me five talents; here, I have made five more.' His master said to him, 'Excellent! You are a good and trustworthy servant. You have been faithful with a small amount, so I will put you in charge of a large amount. Come and join in your master's happiness!' Also the one who had received two came forward and said, 'Sir, you gave me two talents; here, I have made two more.' His master said to him, 'Excellent! you are a good and trustworthy servant. You have been faithful with a small amount, so I will put you in charge of a large amount. Come and join in your master's happiness!' Now the one who had received one talent came forward and said, 'I knew you were a hard man. You harvest where you didn't plant and gather where you didn't sow seed. I was afraid, so I went and hid your talent in the ground. Here! Take what belongs to you!' 'You wicked, lazy servant!' said his master, 'So you knew, did you, that I harvest where I haven't planted? and that I gather where I didn't sow seed? Then you should have deposited my money with the bankers, so that when I returned, I would at least have gotten back interest with my capital! Take the talent from him and give it to the one who has ten. For everyone who has something will be given more, so that he will have more than enough; but from anyone who has nothing, even what he does have will be taken away. As for this worthless servant, throw him out in the dark, where people will wail and grind their teeth!'

Yeshua's Stewardship of His Manual Labors

Acts 20:34-35
You yourselves know that these hands of mine have provided not only for my own needs, but for the needs of my co-workers as well. In everything I have given you an example of how, by working hard like this, you must help the weak, remembering the words of the Lord Yeshua himself, 'There is more happiness in giving than in receiving.'

Men's Stewardship of Their Bodies

Romans 12:1
I exhort you, therefore, brothers, in view of God's mercies, to offer yourselves as a sacrifice, living and set apart for God. This will please him; it is the logical "Temple worship" for you.

1 Corinthians 6:19-20
Or don't you know that your body is a temple for the Ruach HaKodesh who lives inside you, whom you received from God? The fact is, you don't belong to yourselves; for you were bought at a price. So use your bodies to glorify God.

Disciples' Stewardship of God's Secret Truths

<u>1 Corinthians 4:1-2</u>
So, you should regard us as the Messiah's servants, as trustees of God's secret truths. Now the one thing that is asked of a trustee is that he be found trustworthy.

A Man's Stewardship of His Plantable Seeds

<u>2 Corinthians 9:6</u>
Here's the point: he who plants sparingly also harvests sparingly.

Sha'ul's Stewardship of the Work that God Gave Him

<u>Ephesians 3:1-2</u>
It is a consequence of this that I, Sha'ul, am a prisoner of the Messiah Yeshua on behalf of you Gentiles. I assume that you have heard of the work God in his grace has given me to do for your benefit, ...

A Man's Stewardship of His Time

<u>Ephesians 5:15-16</u>
Therefore, pay careful attention to how you conduct your life—live wisely, not unwisely. Use your time well, for these are evil days.

An Elder's Stewardship of God's Affairs

<u>Titus 1:7</u>
For an overseer, as someone entrusted with God's affairs, must be blameless—he must not be self-willed or quick-tempered, he must not drink excessively, get into fights or be greedy for dishonest gain.

Men's Stewardship of God's Work

<u>1 Timothy 1:3-5</u>
As I counseled you when I was leaving for Macedonia, stay on in Ephesus, so that you may order certain people who are teaching a different doctrine to stop. Have them stop devoting their attention to myths and never-ending genealogies; these divert people to speculating instead of doing God's work, which requires trust. The purpose of this order is to promote love from a clean heart, from a good conscience and from sincere trust.

A Man's Stewardship of His Family's Resources

<u>1 Timothy 5:8</u>
Moreover, anyone who does not provide for his own people, especially for his family, has disowned the faith and is worse than an unbeliever.

A Man's Stewardship of God's Truth

Deuteronomy 29:28(29)
Things which are hidden belong to ADONAI our God. But the things that have been revealed belong to us and our children forever, so that we can observe all the words of this Torah.

2 Timothy 2:15
Do all you can to present yourself to God as someone worthy of his approval, as a worker with no need to be ashamed, because he deals straightforwardly with the Word of the Truth.....

Men's Stewardship of Spiritual Gifts

1 Peter 4:10
As each one has received some spiritual gift, he should use it to serve others, like good managers of God's many-sided grace-

Commentary

A steward is someone who cares for things, and "stewardship" is the conducting, overseeing, or managing of things. The "things" may be tangible property, or intangible items such as time, knowledge, skill, etc. The diverse Scriptures presented are representative of others and make a strong case for God wanting us to be good stewards of the things He has entrusted to us. They may belong to others, to God, or even to ourselves, but whether big or small, God holds us accountable for those things with which we have been entrusted.

Commentary by Daniel C. Juster

Good stewardship is implied by the very idea of being created in the Image of God. We are vice regents, and are called to govern wisely as God's representative rulers.

Classical Commentators

This *Mitzvah* is not addressed by any of the classical commentators.

NCLA: JMm JFm KMm KFm GMm GFm

A4. Keeping Vows Made to God.

We are to keep and not delay our vows that we make to God.

This precept is derived from His Word (blessed be He):

Key Scriptures

Numbers 6:1-21 (Maimonides RN202-209; Chinuch C368-373; 375-376)
ADONAI said to Moshe, "Tell the people of Isra'el, 'When either a man or a woman makes a special kind of vow, the vow of a nazir, consecrating himself to ADONAI; he is to abstain from wine and other intoxicating liquor, he is not to drink vinegar from either source, he is not to drink grape juice, and he is not to eat grapes or raisins. As long as he remains a nazir he is to eat nothing derived from the grapevine, not even the grape-skins or the seeds. Throughout the period of his vow as a nazir, he is not to shave his head. Until the end of the time for which he has consecrated himself to ADONAI he is to be holy: he is to let the hair on his head grow long. Throughout the period for which he has consecrated himself to ADONAI, he is not to approach a corpse. He is not to make himself unclean for his father, mother, brother or sister when they die, since his consecration to God is on his head. Throughout the time of his being a nazir he is holy for ADONAI. If someone next to him dies very suddenly, so that he defiles his consecrated head, then he is to shave his head on the day of his purification; he is to shave it on the seventh day. On the eighth day he is to bring two doves or two young pigeons to the cohen at the entrance to the tent of meeting. The cohen is to prepare one as a sin offering and the other as a burnt offering and thus make atonement for him, inasmuch as he sinned because of the dead person. That same day he is to re-consecrate his head; he is to consecrate to ADONAI the full period of his being a nazir by bringing a male lamb in its first year as a guilt offering. The previous days will not be counted, because his consecration became defiled. This is the law for the nazir when his period of consecration is over: he is to be brought to the entrance of the tent of meeting, where he will present his offering to ADONAI—one male lamb in its first year without defect as a burnt offering, one female lamb in its first year without defect as a sin offering, one ram without defect as peace offerings, a basket of matzah, loaves made of fine flour mixed with olive oil, unleavened wafers spread with olive oil, their grain offering and their drink offerings. The cohen is to bring them before ADONAI, offer his sin offering, his burnt offering, and his ram as a sacrifice of peace offerings to ADONAI, with the basket of matzah. The cohen will also offer the grain offering and drink offering that go with the peace offering. The nazir will shave his consecrated head at the entrance to the tent of meeting, take the hair removed from his consecrated head and put it on the fire under the sacrifice of peace offerings. When the ram has been boiled, the cohen is to take its shoulder, one loaf of matzah from the basket and one unleavened wafer, and place them in the hands of the nazir, after he has shaved his consecrated head. The cohen is to wave them as a wave offering before ADONAI; this is set aside for the cohen, along with the breast for waving and the raised-up thigh. Following that, the nazir may drink wine. This is the law for the nazir who makes a vow and for his offering to ADONAI for his being a nazir—in addition to anything more for which he has sufficient means. In keeping with whatever vow he makes, he must do it according to the law for the nazir.

<u>Numbers 30:2(1)-16(15)</u> (Maimonides RP94, 95, RN157; Meir MP39, 40, MN184; C406, 407, 575)

Then Moshe spoke to the heads of the tribes of the people of Isra'el. He said, "Here is what ADONAI has ordered: when a man makes a vow to ADONAI or formally obligates himself by swearing an oath, he is not to break his word but is to do everything he said he would do. When a woman makes a vow to ADONAI, formally obligating herself, while she is a minor living in her father's house; then, if her father has heard what she vowed or obligated herself to do and holds his peace, then all her vows remain binding—every obligation she has bound herself to will stand. But if on the day her father hears it, he expresses his disapproval, then none of her vows or obligations she has bound herself to will stand; and ADONAI will forgive her, because her father expressed his disapproval. If, having made vows or rashly committed herself to an obligation, she gets married; and her husband hears but holds his peace with her on the day he learns of it, then her vows and obligations she has bound herself to will stand. But if her husband expresses his disapproval on the day he hears it, he will void the vow which is on her and the obligation to which she has bound herself; and ADONAI will forgive her. The vow of a widow, however, or of a divorcee, including everything to which she has obligated herself, will stand against her. If a woman vowed in her husband's house or obligated herself with an oath; and her husband heard it but held his peace with her and did not express disapproval, then all her vows and obligations will stand. But if her husband makes them null and void on the day he hears them, then whatever she said, vows or binding obligation, will not stand; her husband has voided them; and ADONAI will forgive her. Her husband may let every vow and every binding obligation stand, or he may void it. But if her husband entirely holds his peace with her day after day, then he confirms all her vows and obligations; he must let them stand, because he held his peace with her on the day he heard them. If he makes them null and void after he has heard them, then he will bear the consequent guilt."

<u>Deuteronomy 23:22(21)-24(23)</u> (Maimonides RP94, RN155; Meir MP39, MN185; Chinuch C574-5)

When you make a vow to ADONAI your God, you are not to delay in fulfilling it, for ADONAI your God will certainly demand it of you, and your failure to do so will be your sin. If you choose not to make a vow at all, that will not be a sin for you; but if a vow passes your lips, you must take care to perform it according to what you voluntarily vowed to ADONAI your God, what you promised in words spoken aloud.

<u>Psalms 65:2(1)</u>

To you, God, in Tziyon, silence is praise; and vows to you are to be fulfilled.

Supportive Scriptures

Deuteronomy 23:19(18)	Proverbs 20:25
Malachi 1:14	Ecclesiastes 5:5(6)
Psalms 50:14, 56:13(12), 76:12(11)	Matthew 5:33-37

Commentary

A vow is a promise uttered with deliberate solemnity, and it is clear from the Scriptures cited above that vows to God may not be broken. There would be nothing more to say on the matter were it not for the annual musical recitation (in most synagogues) of *Kol Nidre*, rendered just before sundown on the evening of *Yom Kippur. Kol Nidre* (Sephardic pronunciation *Kal Nidre*) means "all vows," and is an ancient Aramaic legal formula that seeks to nullify all vows made to God, by individuals, in the year past and in the year to come. As such, it is a clear and direct violation of the intent of Scripture, and many attempts have been made, over the years, to expunge the tradition from Jewish practice.

Some have sought to justify *Kol Nidre* by inferring that it originated with the "Marranos" during the Spanish Inquisition, in their attempt to nullify vows of conversion to Christianity made under extreme duress. Although the "Marranos" no doubt used the *Kol Nidre* formula for that purpose, the concept originated at least five hundred years earlier. We know this because a similar formula appears in the prayer book of the noted Rabbi Amram Gaon (ca. ninth century).

The controversy persists within Judaism broadly, but is a settled matter in most Messianic Jewish congregations where *Kol Nidre* is either not sung at all, or is replaced by a proclamation of the opposite—a statement affirming all vows made in the year past, and our intention to abide by all vows that we may make in the year to come.

I will say only a few words about Nazirite vows since they are rare today. They are vows of special personal dedication to holiness that incorporate limitations on one's lifestyle (e.g. wine and grapes may not be eaten, and one's hair must not be cut), and have a declared date of expiration. I mention them in connection with this *Mitzvah* because they must, as with other vows, be kept once made notwithstanding our being in the New Covenant.

Classical Commentators

Maimonides, Meir, and HaChinuch each wrote four *mitzvot* related to the keeping of promises (without delay) made with or without vows.

<u>**NCLA**</u>**: JMm JFm KMm KFm GMm GFm**

A5. Swearing Oaths Only in God's Name.

We are to swear oaths only in God's name.

This precept is derived from His Word (blessed is He):

Key Scriptures

Exodus 20:7 (Maimonides RP7; Chinuch C435)
You are not to use lightly the name of ADONAI your God, because ADONAI will not leave unpunished someone who uses his name lightly.

Leviticus 5:21(6:2)-23(6:4) (Maimonides RN249; Chinuch 226)
If someone sins and acts perversely against ADONAI by dealing falsely with his neighbor in regard to a deposit or security entrusted to him, by stealing from him, by extorting him, or by dealing falsely in regard to a lost object he has found, or by swearing to a lie—if a person commits any of these sins, then, if he sinned and is guilty, he is to restore whatever it was he stole or obtained by extortion, or whatever was deposited with him, or the lost object which he found,

Leviticus 19:12 (Maimonides RN249; Meir MN30)
Do not swear by my name falsely, which would be profaning the name of your God; I am ADONAI.

Deuteronomy 6:13-15 (Maimonides RP7)
You are to fear ADONAI your God, serve him and swear by his name. You are not to follow other gods, chosen from the gods of the peoples around you; because ADONAI, your God, who is here with you, is a jealous God. If you do, the anger of ADONAI your God will flare up against you and he will destroy you from the face of the earth.

Deuteronomy 10:20 (Maimonides RP7, Chinuch C435)
You are to fear ADONAI your God, serve him, cling to him and swear by his name.

Supportive Scriptures

Exodus 22:9(10)-10(11)
Leviticus 5:4
Numbers 30:3(2)
Matthew 5:33-37, 23:16-24
Hebrews 6:13-17
James 5:12

Commentary

A vow is a promise uttered with deliberate solemnity. An oath is an utterance added to a vow that invokes an authority capable of enforcing the vow, and punishing the oath-maker if the vow is breached. When a person adds an oath to his vow, he is giving an assurance that is in addition to his personal honor. He is essentially saying that if he reneges on his promise, he invites the invoked authority to enforce his compliance and/or mete out punishment.

It is clear from many Scriptures in the *Tanakh* (e.g. Deuteronomy 10:20) that God endorses the swearing of oaths, but in His Name alone. That makes perfect sense since if a vow is serious enough to require the added assurance of an oath, no authority other than God can be counted upon to enforce it (Deuteronomy 6:13-15). Also, when we swear an oath by God's Name we invoke His Honor; therefore, if we swear falsely we profane His Name (Leviticus 19:12).

The *Tanakh* contains many examples of oaths sworn in ancient times, and even God has been known to swear an oath on occasion (e.g. Hebrews 6:13-17). In more recent times, oaths are most commonly sworn ancillary to giving legal testimony in a court of law. When oaths are sworn outside of a court proceeding they are called "notarizations," and are generally for attesting to the accuracy of a legal document or for affirming the authenticity of a signature.

There are some who refuse to swear oaths based on their interpretation of Matthew 5:34 and James 5:12 that contain the words *"But I tell you not to swear at all ..."* and *"Above all, brothers, stop swearing oaths ..."* respectively. Their explanation for how this can be in light of God's teaching and the many examples in the *Tanakh,* is that Yeshua changed the rules for the New Covenant in order to raise the standard of truth-telling to a higher level. That is not correct for, if one looks at the Matthew and James "statements" that were taken out of context, when each one's entire verse and adjacent verses are returned to them, one sees that there is no contradiction at all. In fact, Matthew 5:33-37 affirms the importance and legitimacy of oaths made in God's Name by warning that we should not swear by "heaven," by "earth," by "Jerusalem," by one's "head" or, by extension, by anything else that is not "God." Similarly, James 5:12 admonishes the reader to stop swearing oaths by "heaven," by "earth," or by "any other formula." These verses of Scripture are apparently intended to stop a common practice of invoking meaningless authorities for their effect in enhancing the oath-taker's appearance that he is telling the truth (when he would never promise the same thing if he was swearing in God's Name). Instead, a man should be able to put forth his reputation that his "yes" and his "no" (i.e. whatever he says) can be relied upon without reinforcement.

The Scriptures prohibit using God's Name lightly (Exodus 20:7), but do not, in any way, prohibit swearing oaths in God's Name in appropriate situations. Matthew 23:16-24 explains this especially well, and infers a warning to the oath-taker that he deludes himself if he thinks that his oath is not binding just because it does not invoke God's Name directly. Yeshua scolds the teachers and Pharisees for using "oath formulas" that create the appearance of enforceability, while their secret intent is to not honor their vows. It is intentional casuistry, and they will be held to their word by God nevertheless.

Commentary by Daniel C. Juster

I do think that, in his "Sermon on the Mount," Yeshua preaches a higher standard for truth-telling and for verbalizing oaths than the one commonly practiced in his day; his exhortation is to return us to the standard that was always implied in the *Torah*. Yeshua is saying that our truthfulness as believers and our commitment to doing what we say we will do should have such integrity, that oaths become unnecessary among us. This would limit our oath-taking to public law contexts where it is required for testifying in court and for entering into certain contracts. As Yeshua-believers, we should become known for our trustworthiness even beyond the New Covenant community.

Classical Commentators:

The corresponding *mitzvot* of Maimonides and HaChinuch are completely consistent with this *Mitzvah*, and emphasize that we must not swear an oath by anything that is created. Maimonides adds to this by saying that if we swear an oath by any created object in the belief that it has, in itself, sufficient truth to support the oath, we have put that created object on an equal footing with the Creator, which is sin. There is no *mitzvah* written on the subject by Meir.

<u>NCLA</u>: JMm JFm KMm KFm GMm GFm

A6. Using God's Name Lightly or Falsely.

We are not to use God's Name lightly or falsely.

This precept is derived from His Word (blessed be He):

Key Scriptures

Exodus 20:7

לֹא תִשָּׂא אֶת־שֵׁם־יְהוָה אֱלֹהֶיךָ לַשָּׁוְא כִּי לֹא יְנַקֶּה יְהוָה אֵת אֲשֶׁר־יִשָּׂא אֶת־שְׁמוֹ לַשָּׁוְא׃

You are not to use lightly the name of ADONAI your God, because ADONAI will not leave unpunished someone who uses his name lightly. (Complete Jewish Bible)

Thou shalt not take the name of the LORD thy God in vain…(King James Version)

You shall not misuse the name of the LORD your God…(New International Version)

You shall not make wrongful use of the name of the LORD your God…(New Revised Standard)

Thou shalt not idly utter the name of Jehovah thy God…(Darby translation)

Do not use the name of the LORD your God profanely…(Revised Berkeley)

Leviticus 19:12 (Maimonides RN63; HaChinuch C295)
Do not swear by my name falsely, which would be profaning the name of your God; I am ADONAI.

Leviticus 22:32 (Maimonides RN63; Meir MN155; Chinuch C295)
You are not to profane my holy name; on the contrary, I am to be regarded as holy among the people of Isra'el; I am ADONAI, who makes you holy…

Deuteronomy 13:2(1)-4(3) (Maimonides RN28; Meir MN22; Chinuch C456)
If a prophet or someone who gets messages while dreaming arises among you and he gives you a sign or wonder, and the sign or wonder comes about as he predicted when he said, 'Let's follow other gods, which you have not known; and let us serve them,' you are not to listen to what that prophet or dreamer says. For ADONAI your God is testing you, in order to find out whether you really do love ADONAI your God with all your heart and being.

Deuteronomy 18:20 (Maimonides RN27; Meier MN175; Chinuch C517)
But if a prophet presumptuously speaks a word in my name which I didn't order him to say, or if he speaks in the name of other gods, then that prophet must die.

<u>Deuteronomy 18:21-22</u> (Maimonides RN29; Chinuch C519)
You may be wondering, 'How are we to know if a word has not been spoken by ADONAI?' When a prophet speaks in the name of ADONAI, and the prediction does not come true—that is, the word is not fulfilled—then ADONAI did not speak that word. The prophet who said it spoke presumptuously; you have nothing to fear from him.

<u>Matthew 6:9</u>
You, therefore, pray like this: 'Our Father in heaven! May your Name be kept holy.

<u>Ephesians 4:29</u>
Let no harmful language come from your mouth, only good words that are helpful in meeting the need, words that will benefit those who hear them.

Supportive Scriptures

Acts 17:11
1 Corinthians 14:29-33
1 Thessalonians 5:19-22
1 John 4:1-3

Commentary

<u>Exodus 20:7</u> is best known for it being the third of the "Ten Commandments," rendered in the King James Version as:

> *"Thou shalt not take the name of the LORD thy God in vain; for the LORD will not hold him guiltless that taketh his name in vain."*

This translation and others like it, causes many to think that the Commandment is only about improperly invoking God's name in the course of communicating verbally (e.g. cussing). That merely would mean not using the word "God" (or one of his proper names), or "Yeshua," or *"Ruach HaKodesh"* in profane, disrespectful, or trivial expressions, either orally or in writing.[72]

Doing so is indeed an obvious prohibition, but one less frequently talked about is profaning God's Name by conducting our lives sinfully while, at the same time, professing to be a believer. Two common sayings (not in the Bible) apply here; "It is not so much what we say as what we do," and "Actions speak louder than words." It is the responsibility of all those who profess belief in God (and Yeshua) to represent God properly by conducting their lives in a holy manner. This responsibility falls especially on Jews (even Jews who do not profess belief in God) because the Jews are widely considered to be "God's chosen people," and are therefore seen as representing God in all that they say and do. Sinful conduct by a Jew or a Gentile believer in God brings discredit, shame, and disgrace to His Name. Virtuous and holy conduct, on the other hand, brings Him honor and glory.

---

72 Orthodox Jewish tradition seeks to respect God's Name by making substitutions when writing or speaking of Him. Examples are substituting "G-d" for "God" in writing, or using substitute words (e.g. *"Hashem,"*) or manufactured words (e.g. *"Adoshem"* and *"Elokeynu,"*) in the course of ordinary speech.

Another and more obvious way of violating this *Mitzvah* is by prophesying in God's Name falsely. The most common way of prophesying falsely is by declaring that God said something that He did not in fact say. A false prophecy can result from an innocent mistake or from an intentional deception, and it is not always preceded by a stylized announcement such as "Thus says the Lord." A prophecy is a serious declaration because anyone who hears it and believes that it originates with God is duty-bound to act on it or to conform his or her life to it. So, if an alleged prophecy is false (i.e. did not originate with God), it is capable of causing considerable damage, including to the reputation of prophetic words in general. That is why we must test all prophecies against Scripture, and exercise spiritual discernment through prayer.

So serious was false prophecy considered under the Mosaic Covenant and Mosaic Law, that prophets who prophesied falsely were put to death (Deuteronomy 18:20). This "zero tolerance" standard was demanded because, in those days, only certain persons called "prophets" were given the *Ruach HaKodesh,* so all of Israel was dependent upon them for their communication with God. That is not the case today in the New Covenant, however, because today the *Ruach HaKodesh* is available to all believers in Yeshua, and therefore, to one extent or another, all believers are able to hear God and prophesy.

Commentary by Daniel C. Juster

I would say in addition, that the most foundational meaning of the Third Commandment is to not swear an oath in God's Name and then fail to perform it (hence "in vain"). However, all Jewish and Christian commentators also see the broader meanings as brought out in their commentaries and in this *Mitzvah.*

Classical Commentators

Maimonides, Meir, and HaChinuch do not cite or refer to the third of the "Ten Commandments" (Exodus 20:7), nor do they write about improperly using God's name lightly.[73] They do, however, cite Leviticus 22:32 that warns against desecrating or profaning the Divine Name which, they say, is a very serious sin—especially if committed in public. HaChinuch echoes Maimonides on this, and Maimonides goes further to give some specific examples, through which it is clear that he agrees with the premise of this *Mitzvah,* that swearing by God's Name falsely or engaging in sinful conduct, even without mentioning God's Name, violates Leviticus 22:32. He says that this is especially so if it is committed by a person of known or presumed piety.

Meir refers to the sin of conspicuously profaning or desecrating the Name of God (including when one is coerced to change his religion) as *chillul Hashem,*[74] and says that a man must even surrender to death rather than commit this sin. He says that even the power of repenting on *Yom Kippur* is not enough to atone for *chillul Hashem,* and therefore the sin remains with the offender for his entire life.[75]

---

73 Although Maimonides, Meir, and HaChinuch do not reference Exodus 20:7 in any of their *mitzvot,* they do warn against speaking God's Name in vain in RP4, MP4, and C432 respectively (See *Mitzvah #G6* of this compilation).

74 Public or conspicuous misbehavior that discredits or disgraces God's Name.

75 Suggestive of Matthew 12:31-32.

Prophesying falsely is another way that God's name can be used wrongfully. Maimonides, Meir, and HaChinuch each wrote *mitzvot* (RN27, MN175, and C517, respectively) codifying Deuteronomy 18:20, that says it is an offense punishable by death for a prophet to prophesy falsely. Maimonides and HaChinuch point out that the offense is not dependent upon whether the prophet's statement is true, but whether God actually told the prophet to speak it. So, for example, if God gave a word of truth to a first prophet, a second prophet to which the word was not given would be in violation were he to invoke God's Name in speaking the same word. All the classical commentators agree that the false prophet should, according to the Mosaic Law, be put to death by strangulation.

Maimonides and HaChinuch (but not Meir) wrote related *mitzvot* (RN29 and C519, respectively) that seek to interpret Deuteronomy 18:22. Maimonides states that we are forbidden to take pity on a false prophet or, out of fear, neglect to put him to death. HaChinuch says the same, and adds that the fear spoken of in the Scripture is fear of our being punished for executing a prophet. That notwithstanding, verse 22 alludes neither to executing false prophets, nor to our being punished for it; it merely says that we have nothing to fear from the false prophet.

NCLA: JMm JFm KMm KFm GMm GFm

A7. Confessing, Repenting, and Making Restitution for Our Sins.

We are to confess and repent of our sins, and make restitution where possible and appropriate.

This precept is derived from His Word (blessed be He):

Key Scriptures

Leviticus 4:27-29 (Maimonides RP69; Chinuch C121)
If an individual among the people commits a sin inadvertently, doing something against any of the mitzvot of ADONAI concerning things which should not be done, he is guilty. If the sin he committed becomes known to him, he is to bring as his offering a female goat without defect for the sin he committed, lay his hand on the head of the sin offering and slaughter the sin offering in the place of burnt offerings.

Leviticus 16:29-31 (Maimonides RP164)
It is to be a permanent regulation for you that on the tenth day of the seventh month you are to deny yourselves and not do any kind of work, both the citizen and the foreigner living with you. For on this day, atonement will be made for you to purify you; you will be clean before ADONAI from all your sins. It is a Shabbat of complete rest for you, and you are to deny yourselves. "This is a permanent regulation.

Leviticus 23:27-29 (Meir MP32; Chinuch C313)
The tenth day of this seventh month is Yom-Kippur; you are to have a holy convocation, you are to deny yourselves, and you are to bring an offering made by fire to ADONAI. You are not to do any kind of work on that day, because it is Yom-Kippur, to make atonement for you before ADONAI your God. Anyone who does not deny himself on that day is to be cut off from his people;

Leviticus 26:40 (Maimonides RP73; Chinuch C364)
Then they will confess their misdeeds and those of their ancestors which they committed against me in their rebellion; they will admit that they went against me.

Numbers 5:6-8 (Maimonides RP73; Meir MP33; Chinuch C364)
Tell the people of Isra'el, 'When a man or woman commits any kind of sin against another person and thus breaks faith with ADONAI, he incurs guilt. He must confess the sin which he has committed; and he must make full restitution for his guilt, add twenty percent and give it to the victim of his sin. But if the person has no relative to whom restitution can be made for the guilt, then what is given in restitution for guilt will belong to ADONAI, that is, to the cohen—in addition to the ram of atonement through which atonement is made for him.

Acts 3:19
Therefore, repent and turn to God, so that your sins may be erased...

<u>Acts 17:30</u>
In the past, God overlooked such ignorance; but now he is commanding all people everywhere to turn to him from their sins.

Supportive Scriptures

Exodus 22:1(2)-14(15)
Leviticus 5:5, 6:2(9)-6(13), 16:11-22
Deuteronomy 4:29-31
Isaiah 55:7
Ezekiel 18:21-23
Psalms 32:1-5
Proverbs 28:13
2 Chronicles 7:14

Matthew 4:17, 5:23-24
Luke 13:3
Acts 2:38
Romans 2:5
2 Corinthians 7:9-10
James 5:16
2 Peter 3:9
1 John 1:9

Commentary

It is the general rule that we are to confess our sins, repent, and make restitution. Confession is always to God but, according to <u>James 5:16</u>, we are also to confess our sins to one another. Confession alone is not adequate, however, and we are commanded to repent as well. Repentance involves regretting that we sinned, and soberly determining to not repeat the sin. A common definition of repentance is "turning away from sin and turning toward God."

Not all sins are of the kind that the making of restitution is wise, reasonable, or even possible. For that reason, we must rely on the *Ru'ach Hakodesh* to know if, when, and how restitution should be made. Regret and repentance, on the other hand, should always occur immediately upon realizing that we have sinned.

<u>Matthew 5:23-24</u> requires that when we sin against a brother in the faith we are to go to him, confess, repent, and attempt to reconcile. Even if we do not think we have sinned but our brother does, we should go to him and try to reconcile. Although Scripture is not explicit on this point, it would seem that we should do so even if the one we sinned against is not a brother, but an unbeliever. When that is not possible or appropriate, Scripture still requires that we confess our sins to God and to one another, meaning to mature brothers and sisters in the faith who will hear us.

Commentary by Daniel C. Juster

Laws of restitution such as referred to in these passages were intended to guide the civil courts in ancient Israel. As such, the idea of paying damages beyond just restoring what was stolen has become part of most Western law systems; the civil laws in the Bible greatly influenced the legal systems of the west. On a personal level, the person who repents should restore what can be restored and, beyond that, should restore even more as the biblical texts suggest. This is so that the pain of the violation is felt by the one who has sinned, and is mitigated somewhat by the one who has been sinned against. The amounts of restitution specified in the Scriptures can guide personal acts of restitution as well as those of the civil courts. When personal restitution takes place, court actions can be avoided, keeping in mind that 1 Corinthians 6:1-8 prohibits a believer from suing a fellow believer in a secular court.

Classical Commentators

Maimonides, Meir, and HaChinuch state that we are to confess our sins and repent, but they do not indicate to whom the confession should be given. Maimonides specifically requires that the confession must be given orally. The others do not specifically say that, but imply it through their use of the word "say" (translated of course). All three commentators reference the fast of repentance on *Yom Kippur*. Maimonides and HaChinuch reference the commandment in Leviticus 4:27-29 to make a sin offering after one sins, while Meir is silent on the matter.

NCLA: JMm JFm KMm KFm GMm GFm

A8. Succumbing to Fear, Worry and Anxiety.

We not to fear, worry or be anxious, but rather put our trust in God.

This precept is derived from His Word (blessed be He):

Key Scriptures

Deuteronomy 1:17 (Maimonides RN276; Meir MN72; Chinuch C415)
You are not to show favoritism when judging, but give equal attention to the small and to the great. No matter how a person presents himself, don't be afraid of him; because the decision is God's. The case that is too hard for you, bring to me and I will hear it.

Deuteronomy 3:19-22 (Maimonides RN58; Chinuch C525)
Your wives, your little ones and your livestock—I know you have much livestock—will stay in your cities which I have given you, until ADONAI allows your brothers to rest, as he has allowed you; and they too take possession of the land ADONAI your God is giving them on the west side of the Yarden. At that point you will return, each man to his own possession which I have given you.' Also at that time I gave this order to Y'hoshua: 'Your eyes have seen everything that ADONAI your God has done to these two kings. ADONAI will do the same to all the kingdoms you encounter when you cross over. Don't be afraid of them, because ADONAI your God will fight on your behalf.

Deuteronomy 7:16-21 (Maimonides RN58; Chinuch C525)
You are to devour all the peoples that ADONAI your God hands over to you—show them no pity, and do not serve their gods, because that will become a trap for you. If you think to yourselves, 'These nations outnumber us; how can we dispossess them?' Nevertheless, you are not to be afraid of them; you are to remember well what ADONAI your God did to Pharaoh and all of Egypt—the great ordeals which you yourself saw, and the signs, wonders, strong hand and outstretched arm by which ADONAI your God brought you out. ADONAI will do the same to all the peoples of whom you are afraid. Moreover, ADONAI your God will send the hornet among them until those who are left and those who hide themselves perish ahead of you. You are not to be frightened of them, because ADONAI your God is there with you, a God great and fearsome.

Deuteronomy 20:2-4 (Chinuch C525)
When you are about to go into battle, the cohen is to come forward and address the people. He should tell them, 'Listen, Isra'el! You are about to do battle against your enemies. Don't be fainthearted or afraid; don't be alarmed or frightened by them; because ADONAI your God is going with you to fight on your behalf against your enemies and give you victory.

Deuteronomy 20:8 (Chinuch C525)
The officials will then add to what they have said to the soldiers: 'Is there a man here who is afraid and fainthearted? He should go back home; otherwise his fear may demoralize his comrades as well.'

Psalms 27:1
ADONAI is my light and salvation; whom do I need to fear? ADONAI is the stronghold of my life; of whom should I be afraid?

Psalms 118:6
With ADONAI on my side, I fear nothing—what can human beings do to me?

Matthew 6:25-34
Therefore, I tell you, don't worry about your life—what you will eat or drink; or about your body—what you will wear. Isn't life more than food and the body more than clothing? Look at the birds flying about! They neither plant nor harvest, nor do they gather food into barns; yet your heavenly Father feeds them. Aren't you worth more than they are? Can any of you by worrying add a single hour to his life? And why be anxious about clothing? Think about the fields of wild irises, and how they grow. They neither work nor spin thread, yet I tell you that not even Shlomo in all his glory was clothed as beautifully as one of these. If this is how God clothes grass in the field—which is here today and gone tomorrow, thrown in an oven—won't he much more clothe you? What little trust you have! So don't be anxious, asking, 'What will we eat?,' 'What will we drink?' or 'How will we be clothed?' For it is the pagans who set their hearts on all these things. Your heavenly Father knows you need them all. But seek first his Kingdom and his righteousness, and all these things will be given to you as well. Don't worry about tomorrow—tomorrow will worry about itself! Today has enough tsuris already!

Luke 12:4-7
My friends, I tell you: don't fear those who kill the body but then have nothing more they can do. I will show you whom to fear: fear him who after killing you has authority to throw you into Gei-Hinnom! Yes, I tell you, this is the one to fear! Aren't sparrows sold for next to nothing, five for two assarions? And not one of them has been forgotten by God. Why, every hair on your head has been counted! Don't be afraid, you are worth more than many sparrows.

Philippians 4:6-7
Don't worry about anything; on the contrary, make your requests known to God by prayer and petition, with thanksgiving. Then God's shalom, passing all understanding, will keep your hearts and minds safe in union with the Messiah Yeshua.

2 Timothy 1:7
For God gave us a Spirit who produces not timidity ["fear" in the NKJV], but power, love and self-discipline.

Hebrews 13:6
Therefore, we say with confidence, "ADONAI is my helper; I will not be afraid—what can a human being do to me?"

Supportive Scriptures

Deuteronomy 31:4-6
Joshua 1:8-9
2 Kings 6:15-17
Isaiah 12:2, 35:4, 41:10-14, 43:1-5
Psalms 23:1-4, 34:5(4), 46:2-3, 55:23(22)-24(23),
    56:3(2)-4(3), 91:1-7, 112:5-8
Proverbs 1:29-33, 12:25, 29:25
Lamentations 3:57

Matthew 8:24-26, 10:25-31
Mark 4:37-40, 5:35-36
Luke 12:22-32
John 14:26-27
Acts 18:9-10
Hebrews 2:14-15
1 Peter 3:12-14, 5:6-7
1 John 4:18

Commentary

There are three kinds of fear that are recognized in the Scriptures. The first kind (exemplified by "fear of God and parents") has to do with having profound respect (reverence), and is appropriate—even commanded in those and similar applications. The second kind (also appropriate) is the kind that is built into us by God, in order to protect us from imminent danger. Examples of this kind of fear are our ducking for cover upon being startled by a loud discharge, and our holding back from touching a hot object after having been previously burned by it. The third kind, the one that the Scriptures command against, is the kind where we seek to protect ourselves in circumstances where we ought instead to be relying on God. This kind is exemplified by fear of man and of unwanted circumstances (e.g. death).

We sometimes think of fear as a feeling, and indeed there is a physiological component to it. However, God does not command us regarding feelings, but rather regarding the choices that we make (in faith) in spite of our feelings. That is the teaching of 2 Corinthians 5:7:

> "... for we live by trust, not by what we see." (rendered in the New King James: "For we walk by faith, not by sight").

The Greek word for "sight" in this Scripture is εἴδους (pronounced *"aye-dos"*), and refers not only to eyesight, but to all of our senses, including those that imbue us with feelings.

Fear, worry, and anxiety are similar in that they are the opposite of trusting God for our welfare and protection. All three are debilitating and open us to spiritual attack, and that is why there are so many Scriptures (in both the *Tanakh* and the *Kitvey B'rit Chadasha*) that warn us against giving in to fear, and exhort us to have faith instead.

Classical Commentators

The *mitzvot* of Maimonides and HaChinuch address only three kinds of fear—the reverent kind (not addressed in this *Mitzvah*), fear of idolaters, and fear (by a judge) of a party to a lawsuit. Meir addresses only reverent fear and a judge's fear.

NCLA: JMm JFm KMm KFm GMm GFm

A9. Swearing Falsely.

We are not to swear to that which we know is not true.

This precept is derived from His Word (blessed be He):

Key Scriptures

Exodus 20:7 (Maimonides RN62; Meir MN29; Chinuch C30)
You are not to use lightly the name of ADONAI your God, because ADONAI will not leave unpunished someone who uses his name lightly.

Leviticus 5:21(6:2)-24(6:5) (Maimonides RN249; Chinuch C226)
If someone sins and acts perversely against ADONAI by dealing falsely with his neighbor in regard to a deposit or security entrusted to him, by stealing from him, by extorting him, or by dealing falsely in regard to a lost object he has found, or by swearing to a lie—if a person commits any of these sins, then, if he sinned and is guilty, he is to restore whatever it was he stole or obtained by extortion, or whatever was deposited with him, or the lost object which he found, or anything about which he has sworn falsely. He is to restore it in full plus an additional one-fifth; he must return it to the person who owns it, on the day when he presents his guilt offering.

Leviticus 19:11-12 (Maimonides RN61, 249; Meir MN30-31; Chinuch C226-227)
Do not steal from, defraud or lie to each other. Do not swear by my name falsely, which would be profaning the name of your God; I am ADONAI.

Numbers 30:2(1)-3(2)
Then Moshe spoke to the heads of the tribes of the people of Isra'el. He said, "Here is what ADONAI has ordered: when a man makes a vow to ADONAI or formally obligates himself by swearing an oath, he is not to break his word but is to do everything he said he would do.

Matthew 5:33-37
Again, you have heard that our fathers were told, 'Do not break your oath,' and 'Keep your vows to ADONAI.' But I tell you not to swear at all—not 'by heaven,' because it is God's throne; not 'by the earth,' because it is his footstool; and not 'by Yerushalayim,' because it is the city of the Great King. And don't swear by your head, because you can't make a single hair white or black. Just let your 'Yes' be a simple 'Yes,' and your 'No' a simple 'No'; anything more than this has its origin in evil.

Supportive Scriptures—Miscellaneous

Exodus 20:13b
Deuteronomy 19:16-20
Zechariah 8:16-17

Supportive Scriptures—Examples of Swearing Falsely

Jeremiah 5:2, 7:9
Hosea 10:4
Zechariah 5:4

Commentary

Swearing, in the context of this *mitzvah*, is invoking the Name of God in order to add a weight of truth to that which is spoken. Swearing can be formal (such as in a court of law), in which case swearing falsely is known as "perjury," and one can be punished by the court for committing it. Swearing can also be informal such as when one makes a comment on the spur of the moment and adds an oath to the comment as a way of attempting to assure its truth. In either case, the Scriptures that underlay this *Mitzvah* make it clear that one must never swear to that which is untrue.

Classical Commentators

Maimonides, Meir, and HaChinuch take great pains to employ three Scriptures (Exodus 20:7, Leviticus 5:22(6:3), and Leviticus 19:11-12) and many words of explanation in order to produce three *mitzvot* from what is essentially the same. Maimonides distinguishes two of them by emphasizing a *shebuat bittui* (verbal oath) from a *shebuat shav* (false oath), from an oath made to repudiate a debt, and the other two commentators do similarly using various indicators of distinction, and they distinguish the third Scripture by its reference to theft.

NCLA: JMm JFm KMm KFm GMm GFm

A10. Ritual Purification, Cleanness, Separation and Health.

We are to guard our physical and spiritual health, and be separate from the heathen nations through ritual purifications and cleanness.

This precept is derived from His Word (blessed be He):

Key Scriptures

Leviticus 11:8 (Maimonides RP96; Chinuch C161)
You are not to eat meat from these or touch their carcasses; they are unclean for you.

Leviticus 11:24 (Maimonides RP96; Chinuch C161)
The following will make you unclean; whoever touches the carcass of them will be unclean until evening,

Leviticus 11:29-30 (Maimonides RP97; Chinuch C159)
The following are unclean for you among the small creatures that swarm on the ground: the weasel, the mouse, the various kinds of lizards, the gecko, the land crocodile, the skink, the sand-lizard and the chameleon.

Leviticus 11:33-34 (Maimonides RP98; Chinuch C160)
If one of them falls into a clay pot, whatever is in it will become unclean, and you are to break the pot. Any food permitted to be eaten that water from such a vessel gets on will become unclean, and any permitted liquid in such a vessel will become unclean.

Leviticus 11:39 (Chinuch C161)
If an animal of a kind that you are permitted to eat dies, whoever touches its carcass will be unclean until evening.

Leviticus 12:2-5 (Maimonides RP100, RN77; Chinuch C166, 363)
Tell the people of Isra'el: 'If a woman conceives and gives birth to a boy, she will be unclean for seven days with the same uncleanness as in niddah, when she is having her menstrual period. On the eighth day, the baby's foreskin is to be circumcised. She is to wait an additional thirty-three days to be purified from her blood; she is not to touch any holy thing or come into the sanctuary until the time of her purification is over. But if she gives birth to a girl, she will be unclean for two weeks, as in her niddah; and she is to wait another sixty-six days to be purified from her blood.

Leviticus 13:1-59 (Maimonides RP101-102, 112, RN307; Chinuch C169; 170-172)
ADONAI said to Moshe and Aharon, "If someone develops on his skin a swelling, scab or bright spot which could develop into the disease tzara'at, he is to be brought to Aharon the cohen or to one of his sons who are cohanim. The cohen is to examine the sore on his skin; if the hair in the sore has turned white, and the sore appears to go deep into the skin, it is tzara'at, and after

examining him the cohen is to declare him unclean. If the bright spot on his skin is white, but it does not appear to go deep into the skin, and its hair has not turned white, then the cohen is to isolate him for seven days. On the seventh day the cohen is to examine him again, and if the sore appears the same as before and has not spread on the skin, then the cohen is to isolate him for seven more days. On the seventh day the cohen is to examine him again, and if the sore has faded and hasn't spread on the skin, then the cohen is to declare him clean—it is only a scab, so he is to wash his clothes and be clean. But if the scab spreads further on the skin after he has been examined by the cohen and declared clean, he is to let himself be examined yet again by the cohen. The cohen will examine him, and if he sees that the scab has spread on his skin, then the cohen will declare him unclean; it is tzara'at. If a person has tzara'at, he is to be brought to the cohen. The cohen is to examine him, and if he sees that there is a white swelling in the skin which has turned the hair white and inflamed flesh in the swelling, then it is chronic tzara'at on his skin, and the cohen is to declare him unclean; he is not to isolate him, because it is already clear that he is unclean. If the tzara'at breaks out all over the skin, so that, as far as the cohen can see, the person with tzara'at has sores everywhere on his body, from his head to his feet; then the cohen is to examine him, and if he sees that the tzara'at has covered his entire body, he is to pronounce the person with the sores clean—it has all turned white, and he is clean. But if one day inflamed flesh appears on him, he will be unclean. The cohen will examine the inflamed flesh and declare him unclean; the inflamed flesh is unclean; it is tzara'at. However, if the inflamed flesh again turns white, he is to come to the cohen. The cohen will examine him, and if he sees that the sores have turned white, then the cohen is to declare clean the person with the sores; he is clean. If a person has on his skin a boil that heals in such a way that in place of the boil there is a white swelling or a reddish-white bright spot, it is to be shown to the cohen. The cohen is to examine it; if he sees that it appears to be more than skin-deep, and its hair has turned white, then the cohen is to pronounce him unclean—the disease of tzara'at has broken out in the boil. But if the cohen looks at it and doesn't see any white hairs in it, and it isn't more than skin-deep but appears faded, the cohen is to isolate him for seven days. If it spreads on the skin, the cohen is to declare him unclean; it is the disease. But if the bright spot stays where it was and has not spread, it is the scar of the boil; and the cohen is to declare him clean. Or if someone has on his skin a burn caused by fire; and the inflamed flesh where it was burned has become a bright spot, reddish-white or white, then the cohen is to examine it; and if he sees that the hair in the bright spot has turned white and that it appears to be deeper than the skin around it, it is tzara'at; it has broken out in the burn, and the cohen is to declare him unclean; it is a sore from tzara'at. But if the cohen examines it and sees no white hair in the bright spot, and it is no lower than the skin around it but looks faded, then the cohen is to isolate him for seven days. On the seventh day the cohen is to examine him; if it has spread on the skin, then the cohen is to declare him unclean; it is a sore from tzara'at. But if the bright spot stays where it was and has not spread on the skin but appears faded, it is a swelling due to the burn; and the cohen is to declare him clean; because it is only a scar from the burn. If a man or woman has a sore on the head or a man in his beard, then the cohen is to examine the sore; if he sees that it appears to be deeper than the skin around it, with yellow, thin hair in it, then the cohen is to declare him unclean; it is a crusted area, a tzara'at of the head or beard. If the cohen examines the diseased crusted area and sees that it appears not to be deeper than the skin around it, and without any black hair in it, then the cohen is to isolate for seven days the person with the diseased crusted area. On the seventh day the cohen is to examine the sore, and if he sees that the crusted area hasn't spread, that it has no yellow hair in it, and that the crusted area is not deeper than the skin around it; then the person is to be shaved, except for the crusted area itself, and the cohen is to isolate him for seven more days. On the seventh day the cohen is to examine the crusted area; and if he sees that the crusted area has not spread on the skin and does not appear to be deeper than the skin around it, then the cohen is to declare him clean; he is to wash his clothes and be clean. But if the crusted area spreads after his purification, then the cohen is to examine him; and if he sees that the crusted area has spread on the skin, the cohen is not to look for yellow hair; he is unclean. But if the crusted area's appearance doesn't change, and black hair grows up in it, then the crusted area is healed; he is clean; and the cohen is to declare him clean. If a man or woman has bright spots on his skin, bright white spots; then the cohen is to examine them. If he sees that the bright spots on the skin are dull white, it is only a rash that has broken out on the skin; he is clean. If a man's hair has fallen from his scalp, he is bald; but he is clean. If his hair has fallen off the front part of his head, he is forehead-bald; but he is clean. But if on the bald scalp or forehead there is a reddish-white sore, it is tzara'at breaking out on his bald scalp or forehead. Then the cohen is to examine him; if he sees that there is a reddish-white swelling on his bald scalp or forehead, appearing like tzara'at on the rest of the body, he is a person with tzara'at; he is unclean; the cohen must declare him unclean; the sore is on his head. Everyone who has tzara'at sores is to wear torn clothes and unbound hair, cover his upper lip and cry, 'Unclean! Unclean!' As long as he has sores, he will be unclean; since he is unclean, he must live in isolation; he must live outside the camp. When tzara'at infects an article of clothing, whether it be a woolen or a linen garment, on the threads or the woven-in parts of either linen or wool, or on a hide or item made of leather; then if the stain on the garment, hide, threads, woven-in parts or leather item is greenish or reddish, it is an infection of tzara'at and is to be shown to the cohen. The cohen is to examine the stain and isolate the article that has the infection for seven days. On the seventh day he is to examine the stain; if the stain has spread on the garment, threads, woven-in parts or leather, whatever its use, the infection is a contagious tzara'at; the garment is unclean. He is to burn the garment, threads, woven-in parts of either wool or linen, or item of leather having the infection; for it is a contagious tzara'at; it must be burned up completely. But if, when the cohen examines it, he sees that the infection has not spread on the garment or in the threads, woven-in parts or leather item, then the cohen is to order that the article having the infection be washed and isolated for seven more days. The cohen is to examine it after the stain has been washed, and if he sees that the stain has not changed color, then, even though the stain has not spread, it is unclean; you are to burn it up completely—it is rotten, no matter whether the spot is on the outside or on the inside. If the cohen examines it and sees that the stain has faded after being washed, then he is to tear the stain out of the garment, leather, threads or woven-in parts. If it appears again in the garment, threads, woven-in parts or leather item, it is contagious, and you are to burn up completely the article that had the stain. But if the infection is gone from the garment, threads, woven-in parts or leather item that you washed, then it is to be washed a second time, and it will be clean. This is the law concerning infections of tzara'at in a garment of wool or linen, or in the threads or the woven-in parts, or in any leather item—when to declare it clean and when to declare it unclean."

Leviticus 14:1-36: (Maimonides RP103, 109-111; Chinuch C173-175, 177)
ADONAI said to Moshe, "This is to be the law concerning the person afflicted with tzara'at on the day of his purification. He is to be brought to the cohen, and the cohen is to go outside

the camp and examine him there. If he sees that the tzara'at sores have been healed in the afflicted person, then the cohen will order that two living clean birds be taken for the one to be purified, along with cedar-wood, scarlet yarn and hyssop leaves. The cohen is to order one of the birds slaughtered in a clay pot over running water. As for the live bird, he is to take it with the cedar-wood, scarlet yarn and hyssop and dip them and the living bird in the blood of the bird slaughtered over running water, and sprinkle the person to be purified from the tzara'at seven times. Next he is to set the live bird free in an open field. He who is to be purified must wash his clothes, shave off all his hair and bathe himself in water. Then he will be clean; and after that, he may enter the camp; but he must live outside his tent for seven days. On the seventh day he is to shave all the hair off his head, also his beard and eyebrows—he must shave off all his hair; and he is to wash his clothes and bathe his body in water; and he will be clean. On the eighth day he is to take two male lambs without defect, one female lamb in its first year without defect and six-and-a-half quarts of fine flour for a grain offering, mixed with olive oil, and two-thirds of a pint of olive oil. The cohen purifying him is to place the person being purified with these items before ADONAI at the entrance to the tent of meeting. The cohen is to take one of the male lambs and offer it as a guilt offering with the two-thirds-pint of olive oil, then wave them as a wave offering before ADONAI. He is to slaughter the male lamb at the place in the sanctuary for slaughtering sin offerings and burnt offerings, because the guilt offering belongs to the cohen, just like the sin offering; it is especially holy. The cohen is to take some of the blood of the guilt offering and put it on the tip of the right ear of the person being purified, on the thumb of his right hand and on the big toe of his right foot. Next, the cohen is to take some of the two-thirds-pint of olive oil and pour it into the palm of his own left hand, dip his right finger in the oil that is in his left hand and sprinkle from the oil with his finger seven times before ADONAI. Then the cohen is to put some of the remaining oil in his hand on the tip of the right ear of the person being purified, on the thumb of his right hand, on the big toe of his right foot and on the blood of the guilt offering. Finally, the cohen is to put the rest of the oil in his hand on the head of the person being purified; and the cohen will make atonement for him before ADONAI. The cohen is to offer the sin offering and make atonement for the person being purified because of his uncleanness; afterwards, he is to slaughter the burnt offering. The cohen is to offer the burnt offering and the grain offering on the altar; thus the cohen will make atonement for him; and he will be clean. If he is poor, so that he can't afford to do otherwise, he is to take one male lamb as a guilt offering to be waved, to make atonement for him; two quarts of fine flour mixed with olive oil for a grain offering; two-thirds of a pint of olive oil; and two doves or two young pigeons, such as he can afford, the one for a sin offering and the other for a burnt offering. On the eighth day, he will bring them to the cohen for his purification, to the entrance of the tent of meeting before ADONAI. The cohen is to take the lamb of the guilt offering and the two-thirds of a pint of olive oil and wave them as a wave offering before ADONAI. He is to slaughter the lamb of the guilt offering; and the cohen is to take some of the blood of the guilt offering and put it on the tip of the right ear of the person being purified, on the thumb of his right hand and on the big toe of his right foot. The cohen is to take some of the olive oil and pour it into the palm of his own left hand, and sprinkle with his right hand some of the oil that is in his left hand seven times before ADONAI. The cohen is to put some of the oil in his hand on the tip of the right ear of the person being purified, on the thumb of his right hand, on the big toe of his right foot—in the same place as the blood of the guilt offering. Finally, the cohen is to put the rest of the oil in his hand on the head of the person being purified, to make atonement for him before ADONAI. He is to offer one of the doves or young pigeons, such as the person can afford, whatever his means suffice for—the one as a sin offering and the other as a burnt offering—with the grain offering; thus the cohen will make atonement before ADONAI for the person being purified. Such is the law for the person who has tzara'at sores if he cannot afford the usual elements used for his purification. ADONAI said to Moshe and Aharon, When you have entered the land of Kena'an which I am giving you as a possession, and I put an infection of tzara'at in a house in the land that you possess, then the owner of the house is to come and tell the cohen, 'It seems to me that there may be an infection in the house. The cohen is to order the house emptied before he goes in to inspect the infection, so that everything in the house won't be made unclean; afterwards, the cohen is to enter and inspect the house."

Leviticus 14:1-32 (Maimonides RP110-111; Chinuch C173-174)

ADONAI said to Moshe, "This is to be the law concerning the person afflicted with tzara'at on the day of his purification. He is to be brought to the cohen, and the cohen is to go outside the camp and examine him there. If he sees that the tzara'at sores have been healed in the afflicted person, then the cohen will order that two living clean birds be taken for the one to be purified, along with cedar-wood, scarlet yarn and hyssop leaves. The cohen is to order one of the birds slaughtered in a clay pot over running water. As for the live bird, he is to take it with the cedar-wood, scarlet yarn and hyssop and dip them and the living bird in the blood of the bird slaughtered over running water, and sprinkle the person to be purified from the tzara'at seven times. Next he is to set the live bird free in an open field. He who is to be purified must wash his clothes, shave off all his hair and bathe himself in water. Then he will be clean; and after that, he may enter the camp; but he must live outside his tent for seven days. On the seventh day he is to shave all the hair off his head, also his beard and eyebrows—he must shave off all his hair; and he is to wash his clothes and bathe his body in water; and he will be clean. On the eighth day he is to take two male lambs without defect, one female lamb in its first year without defect and six-and-a-half quarts of fine flour for a grain offering, mixed with olive oil, and two-thirds of a pint of olive oil. The cohen purifying him is to place the person being purified with these items before ADONAI at the entrance to the tent of meeting. The cohen is to take one of the male lambs and offer it as a guilt offering with the two-thirds-pint of olive oil, then wave them as a wave offering before ADONAI. He is to slaughter the male lamb at the place in the sanctuary for slaughtering sin offerings and burnt offerings, because the guilt offering belongs to the cohen, just like the sin offering; it is especially holy. The cohen is to take some of the blood of the guilt offering and put it on the tip of the right ear of the person being purified, on the thumb of his right hand and on the big toe of his right foot. Next, the cohen is to take some of the two-thirds-pint of olive oil and pour it into the palm of his own left hand, dip his right finger in the oil that is in his left hand and sprinkle from the oil with his finger seven times before ADONAI. Then the cohen is to put some of the remaining oil in his hand on the tip of the right ear of the person being purified, on the thumb of his right hand, on the big toe of his right foot and on the blood of the guilt offering. Finally, the cohen is to put the rest of the oil in his hand on the head of the person being purified; and the cohen will make atonement for him before ADONAI. The cohen is to offer the sin offering and make atonement for the person being purified because of his uncleanness; afterwards, he is to slaughter the burnt offering. The cohen is to offer the burnt offering and the grain offering on the altar; thus the cohen will make atonement for him; and he will be clean. If he is poor, so that he can't afford to do otherwise, he is to take one male lamb as a guilt offering to be waved, to make atonement for him; two quarts of fine flour mixed with olive oil for a grain offering; two thirds of a pint of olive oil; and two doves or two young pigeons, such as he can afford, the one for a sin offering and the other for a burnt offering. On the eighth day, he will bring them to the cohen for his purification, to the entrance of the tent of meeting before ADONAI. The cohen is to take the lamb of the guilt offering and the two-thirds of a pint of olive oil and wave them as a wave offering before ADONAI. He is to slaughter the lamb of the guilt offering; and the cohen is to take some of the blood of the guilt offering and put it on the tip of the right ear of the person being purified, on the thumb of his right hand and on the big toe of his right foot. The cohen is to take some of the olive oil and pour it into the palm of his own left hand, and sprinkle with his right hand some of the oil that is in his left hand seven times before ADONAI. The cohen is to put some of the oil in his hand on the tip of the right ear of the person being purified, on the thumb of his right hand, on the big toe of his right foot—in the same place as the blood of the guilt offering. Finally, the cohen is to put the rest of the oil in his hand on the head of the person being purified, to make atonement for him before ADONAI. He is to offer one of the doves or young pigeons, such as the person can afford, whatever his means suffice for—the one as a sin offering and the other as a burnt offering—with the grain offering; thus the cohen will make atonement before ADONAI for the person being purified. Such is the law for the person who has tzara'at sores if he cannot afford the usual elements used for his purification."

<u>Leviticus 14:34-54</u> (Maimonides RP104)
When you have entered the land of Kena'an which I am giving you as a possession, and I put an infection of tzara'at in a house in the land that you possess, then the owner of the house is to come and tell the cohen, 'It seems to me that there may be an infection in the house. The cohen is to order the house emptied before he goes in to inspect the infection, so that everything in the house won't be made unclean; afterwards, the cohen is to enter and inspect the house. He will examine the infection; and if he sees that the infection is in the walls of the house, with greenish or reddish depressions that seem to go in deeper than the surface of the wall, he is to go out of the house to its door and seal up the house for seven days. The cohen will come again on the seventh day and examine the house; if he sees that the infection has spread over its walls, he is to order them to remove the infected stones and throw them into some unclean place outside the city. Next, he is to have the inside of the house thoroughly scraped, and the scraped-off plaster is to be discarded outside the city in an unclean place. Finally, other stones must be set in the place of the first stones and other plaster used to replaster the house. If the infection returns and breaks out in the house after the stones have been removed and the house scraped and plastered; then the cohen is to enter and examine it. If he sees that the infection has spread in the house, it is a contagious tzara'at in the house; it is unclean. He must break down the house and take its stones, timber and plaster out of the city to an unclean place. Moreover, whoever enters the house at any time while it is sealed up will be unclean until evening. Whoever lies down or eats in the house must wash his clothes. If the cohen enters, examines and sees that the infection has not spread in the house since it was plastered; then he is to declare the house clean; because the infection is cured. To purify the house, he is to take two birds, cedar-wood, scarlet yarn and hyssop leaves. He is to slaughter one of the birds in a clay pot over running water. He is to take the cedar-wood, the hyssop, the scarlet yarn and the live bird and dip them in the blood of the slaughtered bird and in the running water, and sprinkle the house seven times. He will purify the house with the blood of the bird, the running water, the live bird, the cedar-wood, the hyssop and the scarlet yarn. But he is to set the live bird

free outside the city in an open field; thus will he make atonement for the house; and it will be clean. Such is the law for all kinds of tzara'at sores, for a crusted area...

Leviticus 15:1-12 (Maimonides RP104; Chinuch C178)
ADONAI said to Moshe and Aharon, "Tell the people of Isra'el, 'When any man has a discharge from his body, the discharge is unclean. The discharge is unclean no matter whether it continues flowing or has stopped; it is still his uncleanness. Every bed which the person with the discharge lies on is unclean, and everything he sits on is unclean. Whoever touches his bed is to wash his clothes and bathe himself in water; he will be unclean until evening. Whoever sits on anything the person with the discharge sat on is to wash his clothes and bathe himself in water; he will be unclean until evening. Anyone who touches the body of the person with the discharge is to wash his clothes and bathe himself in water; he will be unclean until evening. If the person with the discharge spits on someone who is clean, the latter is to wash his clothes and bathe himself in water; he will be unclean until evening. Any saddle that the person with the discharge rides on will be unclean. Whoever touches anything that was under him will be unclean until evening; he who carries those things is to wash his clothes and bathe himself in water; he will be unclean until evening. If the person with the discharge fails to rinse his hands in water before touching someone, that person is to wash his clothes and bathe himself in water; he will be unclean until evening. If the person with the discharge touches a clay pot, it must be broken; if he touches a wooden utensil, it must be rinsed in water.

Leviticus 15:13 (Maimonides RP109)
When a person with a discharge has become free of it, he is to count seven days for his purification. Then he is to wash his clothes and bathe his body in running water; after that, he will be clean.

Leviticus 15:16-18 (Maimonides RP105, 109; Chinuch C180)
If a man has a seminal emission, he is to bathe his entire body in water; he will be unclean until evening. Any clothing or leather on which there is any semen is to be washed with water; it will be unclean until evening. If a man goes to bed with a woman and has sexual relations, both are to bathe themselves in water; they will be unclean until evening.

Leviticus 15:19-24 (Maimonides RP99; Chinuch C181)
If a woman has a discharge, and the discharge from her body is blood, she will be in her state of niddah for seven days. Whoever touches her will be unclean until evening. Everything she lies on or sits on in her state of niddah will be unclean. Whoever touches her bed is to wash his clothes and bathe himself in water; he will be unclean until evening. Whoever touches anything she sits on is to wash his clothes and bathe himself in water; he will be unclean until evening.
Whether he is on the bed or on something she sits on, when he touches it, he will be unclean until evening. If a man goes to bed with her, and her menstrual flow touches him, he will be unclean seven days; and every bed he lies on will be unclean.

Leviticus 15:25-30 (Maimonides RP106; Chinuch C182)
If a woman has a discharge of blood for many days not during her period, or if her discharge lasts beyond the normal end of her period, then throughout the time she is having an unclean

discharge she will be as when she is in niddah—she is unclean. Every bed she lies on at any time while she is having her discharge will be for her like the bed she uses during her time of niddah; and everything she sits on will be unclean with uncleanness like that of her time of niddah. Whoever touches those things will be unclean; he is to wash his clothes and bathe himself in water; he will be unclean until evening. If she has become free of her discharge, she is to count seven days; after that, she will be clean. On the eighth day, she is to take for herself two doves or two young pigeons and bring them to the cohen at the entrance to the tent of meeting. The cohen is to offer the one as a sin offering and the other as a burnt offering; thus the cohen will make atonement for her before ADONAI on account of her unclean discharge.

Leviticus 21:5-6 (Maimonides RN76; Chinuch C265)
Cohanim are not to make bald spots on their heads, mar the edges of their beards or cut gashes in their flesh. Rather, they are to be holy for their God and not profane the name of their God. For they are the ones who present ADONAI with offerings made by fire, the bread of their God; therefore they must be holy.

Leviticus 22:2-9 (Maimonides RN75; Chinuch C278)
Tell Aharon and his sons to separate themselves from the holy things of the people of Isra'el which they set apart as holy for me, so that they will not profane my holy name; I am ADONAI. Tell them, 'Any descendant of yours through all your generations who approaches the holy things that the people of Isra'el consecrate to ADONAI and is unclean will be cut off from before me; I am ADONAI. Any descendant of Aharon with tzara'at or a discharge is not to eat the holy things until he is clean. Anyone who has touched a person made unclean by a dead body, or who has had a seminal emission, or who has touched a reptile or insect that can make him unclean, or a man who is unclean for any reason and who can transmit to him his uncleanness—the person who touches any of these will be unclean until evening and is not to eat the holy things unless he bathes his body in water. After sunset he will be clean; and afterwards, he may eat the holy things; because they are his food. But he is not to eat anything that dies naturally or is torn to death by wild animals and thereby make himself unclean; I am ADONAI. The cohanim must observe this charge of mine; otherwise, if they profane it, they will bear the consequences of their sin for doing so and die in it; I am ADONAI, who makes them holy.

Numbers 5:2-4 (Maimonides RP31, RN77; Chinuch C362-363)
Order the people of Isra'el to expel from the camp everyone with tzara'at, everyone with a discharge and whoever is unclean because of touching a corpse. Both male and female you must expel; put them outside the camp; so that they won't defile their camp, where I live among you." The people of Isra'el did this and put them outside the camp—the people of Isra'el did what ADONAI had said to Moshe.

Numbers 19:1-22 (Maimonides RP107-108, 113, RN77; Chinuch C363, 397-399)
ADONAI said to Moshe and Aharon, "This is the regulation from the Torah which ADONAI has commanded. Tell the people of Isra'el to bring you a young red female cow without fault or defect and which has never borne a yoke. You are to give it to El'azar the cohen; it is to be brought outside the camp and slaughtered in front of him. El'azar the cohen is to take some of its blood with his finger and sprinkle this blood toward the front of the tent of meeting seven times. The heifer is to be burned to ashes before his eyes—its skin, meat, blood and dung is to be

burned to ashes. The cohen is to take cedar-wood, hyssop and scarlet yarn and throw them onto the heifer as it is burning up. Then the cohen is to wash his clothes and himself in water, after which he may re-enter the camp; but the cohen will remain unclean until evening. The person who burned up the heifer is to wash his clothes and himself in water, but he will remain unclean until evening. A man who is clean is to collect the ashes of the heifer and store them outside the camp in a clean place. They are to be kept for the community of the people of Isra'el to prepare water for purification from sin. The one who collected the ashes of the heifer is to wash his clothes and be unclean until evening. For the people of Isra'el and for the foreigner staying with them this will be a permanent regulation. Anyone who touches a corpse, no matter whose dead body it is, will be unclean for seven days. He must purify himself with [these ashes] on the third and seventh days; then he will be clean. But if he does not purify himself the third and seventh days, he will not be clean. Anyone who touches a corpse, no matter whose dead body it is, and does not purify himself has defiled the tabernacle of ADONAI. That person will be cut off from Isra'el, because the water for purification was not sprinkled on him. He will be unclean; his uncleanness is still on him. This is the law: when a person dies in a tent, everyone who enters the tent and everything in the tent will be unclean for seven days. Every open container without a cover closely attached is unclean. Also whoever is in an open field and touches a corpse, whether of someone killed by a weapon or of someone who died naturally, or the bone of a person, or a grave, will be unclean for seven days. For the unclean person they are to take some of the ashes of the animal burned up as a purification from sin and add them to fresh water in a container. A clean person is to take a bunch of hyssop leaves, dip it in the water and sprinkle it on the tent, on all the containers, on the people who were there, and on the person who touched the bone or the person killed or the one who died naturally or the grave. The clean person will sprinkle the unclean person on the third and seventh days. On the seventh day he will purify him; then he will wash his clothes and himself in water; and he will be clean at evening. The person who remains unclean and does not purify himself will be cut off from the community because he has defiled the sanctuary of ADONAI. The water for purification has not been sprinkled on him; he is unclean. This is to be a permanent regulation for them. The person who sprinkles the water for purification is to wash his clothes. Whoever touches the water for purification will be unclean until evening. Anything the unclean person touches will be unclean, and anyone who touches him will be unclean until evening.

Deuteronomy 23:11(10)-12(11) (Maimonides RP31, RN78; Meir MN193; Chinuch C362, 565)
If there is a man among you who is unclean because of a nocturnal emission, he is to go outside the camp; he is not to enter the camp. When evening arrives he is to bathe himself in water, and after sunset he may enter the camp.

Deuteronomy 23:13(12)-14(13) (Maimonides RP192; Chinuch C566)
Also you are to have an area outside the camp to use as a latrine. You must include a trowel with your equipment, and when you relieve yourself, you are to dig a hole first and afterwards cover your excrement.

Deuteronomy 24:8 (Maimonides RN308; Chinuch C584)
When there is an outbreak of tzara'at, be careful to observe and do just what the cohanim, who are L'vi'im, teach you. Take care to do as I ordered them.

2 Corinthians 6:17-18

Therefore ADONAI says, " 'Go out from their midst; separate yourselves; don't even touch what is unclean. Then I myself will receive you. In fact, I will be your Father, and you will be my sons and daughters.' says ADONAI-Tzva'ot. "

Supportive Scriptures—Ritual Cleanness and Purification

Genesis 7:1-9

Supportive Scriptures—Spiritual Cleanness

Isaiah 1:16-17
Ezekiel 36:25-27
Psalms 51:9(7), 51:12(10)
Matthew 23:26
2 Corinthians 7:1
1 John 1:7-9

Supportive Scriptures—Healthy Living Independent of Ritual Cleanness

Exodus 15:26
Deuteronomy 7:15
Jeremiah 33:4-8
Proverbs 3:7-8, 4:20-22, 17:22
Matthew 8:17
1 Corinthians 10:31
James 5:15
3 John 1:2

Commentary

The concept of ritual cleanness (clean vs. unclean) originates early in the Bible. Most of us have an intuitive sense of what it means to be clean physically, but when something is called "clean" or "unclean" in the Bible, there is usually a spiritual statement being made about it in that only what God declares to be clean is fit to be brought into His presence. So, for example, an unblemished lamb is still considered clean and was suitable for sacrificial worship (under Moses) even if it had recently rolled in mud. A pig, on the other hand, is unclean, and was unfit for sacrificial worship even had it been scrupulously washed down with soap and water. According to the Bible, things are intrinsically clean or unclean and, in addition, things (and persons) that are otherwise ritually clean, can become unclean for a time, according to where they have been, what they have done, or what they have touched. So, for example, a man is intrinsically clean, becomes temporarily unclean by touching a corpse, and returns to being clean at nightfall. A pig, on the other hand, is intrinsically unclean and can never be made clean.

The concept of ritual cleanness is also connected to holiness (spiritual cleanness), and is exemplified by the fate of those who drank alcoholic beverages in the tent of meeting; for we read in Leviticus 10:9-10:

> *"Don't drink any wine or other intoxicating liquor, neither you nor your sons with you, when you enter the tent of meeting, so that you will not die. This is to be a permanent regulation through all your generations, so that you will distinguish between the holy and the common, and between the unclean and the clean;"*

Yeshua considered the distinction between clean and unclean to be important, for he analogized it to holiness and wickedness in Luke 11:37-42:

> *As Yeshua spoke, a Parush asked him to eat dinner with him; so he went in and took his place at the table; and the Parush was surprised that he didn't begin by doing n'tilat yadayim before the meal. However, the Lord said to him, "Now then, you P'rushim, you clean the outside of the cup and plate; but inside, you are full of robbery and wickedness. Fools! Didn't the One who made the outside make the inside too? Rather, give as alms what is inside, and then everything will be clean for you! But woe to you P'rushim! You pay your tithes of mint and rue and every garden herb, but you ignore justice and the love of God. You have an obligation to do these things—but without disregarding the others!*

Animals, objects, food, and even people are either clean or unclean and, apart from their respective acceptability in temple worship, they sometimes have an obvious connection to health as well. For example, Leviticus 13 reads like a medical text on how to diagnose and treat leprosy, and how to protect the population from its contagion. Some also try to make the case that eating non-kosher animals such as pig is unhealthy, but I do not attempt to make that case.

It is clear how all of the ritual cleanness regulations had literal applicability in the time of Moses, but what about now? We have no Tabernacle or Temple today, leprosy (looked at by most scholars today as skin infections that include leprosy) is quickly and easily curable, and there is no functioning Levitical priesthood today to enforce the Mosaic regulations. Nevertheless, the laws of ritual cleanness serve to remind us that maintaining our physical health is a godly value that we must pursue rigorously.

It is impossible to literally obey all of the ritual cleanness laws today. There remains, however, an area of analogy to these laws, and that is to conduct ourselves in such a way that we (both as Jews broadly and as Jewish or Gentile disciples of Yeshua) who are believers are distinguishable from those who are not. God also wants Jews to be distinguishable from non-Jews because He gave Israel a commission to be a "kingdom of priests" to the other nations of the world. God wants disciples of Yeshua to be distinguishable because all disciples of Yeshua (Jewish and non-Jewish disciples alike) have a responsibility to influence those who are not believers by what we say and how we are observed to live our lives.

For those of us that are Jews, we have a plethora of traditional practices to draw from, many of which come directly from the biblical laws of ritual cleanness. One that tops the list is that we do not eat anything that comes from a pig. Two others are that we do not eat any land animal that does not have a split hoof and does not chew its cud, and we do not eat anything from the water that lacks fins and scales. There are, of course, other characteristics that distinguish us as well, such as our keeping of the Sabbath and the Appointed Times, wearing fringes with blue strands, and tacking *m'zuzot* to the doorposts of our houses. Ritual purification ceremonies survive today in the Orthodox Jewish practice of total immersion in *mikvahs* (specially constructed baths of water), and in the washing of the hands and fingers before and after meals (respectively), and at other times prescribed by Rabbinical tradition. Common reasons for total immersion are purification at the end of a woman's menstrual cycle, by a woman prior to her wedding, and as part of conversion to Judaism.

For those of us that are believers but are not Jews, some (but not all) of the Jewish identifying features are appropriate. For most of us, however, it is how we are observed to maintain godly values, in the things we say, and in how we live our lives.

A list of items considered clean and unclean that are given in Leviticus 11 to Leviticus 15, Leviticus 22, and Deuteronomy 23 appear in the appendix to this *Mitzvah* below.

Classical Commentators

Maimonides, Meir, and HaChinuch chose a sampling of Scriptures about which to write their *mitzvot* on ritual (ceremonial) cleanness, leaving many unaddressed. Other than what is obvious when it pertains to leprosy, they did not connect ritual cleanness to health, or separation of the Jewish nation and, in their expositions of immersion, their emphases are more to the physical than to the spiritual.

Addendum

That Which is Ritually Clean

- everything that is not unclean
- land animal that has a divided hoof and chews cud
- creature in the water that has fins and scales
- winged swarming creatures that go on all fours and have jointed legs above their feet
- locusts
- grasshoppers
- katydid
- cricket
- a person with sores all over his body but not deep and no hairs turned white
- a person whose hair has fallen out but no reddish-white sores

That Which Is Ritually Unclean

- pig, vulture, osprey, kite, buzzard, raven, ostrich, owl, seagull, hawk, cormorant, pelican, stork, heron, hoopoe, bat, weasel, mouse, lizard, gecko, land crocodile, skink, sand lizard, chameleon
- land animal that doesn't have a divided hoof and chews cud
- things in the water that do not have fins and scales

- anything or anyone touching the carcass of an unclean land or aquatic animal, or a winged swarming creature on all fours with no leg joints.
- winged swarming creatures that go on all fours except those having jointed legs above their feet
- the carcass of a clean animal that dies of its own accord
- a creature that swarms on the ground, i.e. moves on its stomach, goes on all fours, or has many legs.
- a woman who has given birth
- a woman having her menstrual period
- that which a woman having her menstrual period has touched
- whomever touches a woman or anything she has touched during her menstrual period
- a man who goes to bed with a woman during her menstrual period and touches her blood
- a woman who has a discharge that is not during her menstrual period
- a person with a sore that goes deep into the skin, wherein the hair in the sore has turned white
- a person with a sore wherein its scab has spread, and / or there is white swelling
- a person whose hair has fallen and there are reddish-white sores
- the garments of anyone who is unclean with leprosy
- a house with leprosy in it
- a man with a bodily discharge
- everything that a man with a bodily discharge has touched
- a man with a seminal emission
- a man with a nocturnal emission
- a woman who has recently had sex with a man who has a seminal emission
- any garment that a seminal emission has touched

NCLA: JMm JFm KMm KFm GMm GFm

A11. Wine and Drunkenness.

We may partake of wine but must not become intoxicated.

This precept is derived from His Word (blessed be He):

Key Scripture

Leviticus 10:8-11 (Maimonides RN73; Chinuch C152)
ADONAI said to Aharon, "Don't drink any wine or other intoxicating liquor, neither you nor your sons with you, when you enter the tent of meeting, so that you will not die. This is to be a permanent regulation through all your generations, so that you will distinguish between the holy and the common, and between the unclean and the clean; and so that you will teach the people of Isra'el all the laws ADONAI has told them through Moshe."

Matthew 26:27-29 (see also Mark 14:23-25; Luke 22:17-18; 1 Corinthians 11:25-27)
Also he took a cup of wine, made the b'rakhah, and gave it to them, saying, "All of you, drink from it! For this is my blood, which ratifies the New Covenant, my blood shed on behalf of many, so that they may have their sins forgiven. I tell you, I will not drink this 'fruit of the vine' again until the day I drink new wine with you in my Father's Kingdom."

1 Timothy 3:2-3
A congregation leader [elder] must be above reproach, he must be faithful to his wife, temperate, self-controlled, orderly, hospitable and able to teach. He must not drink excessively or get into fights; rather, he must be kind and gentle. He must not be a lover of money.

1 Timothy 3:8
Likewise, the shammashim must be of good character, people whose word can be trusted. They must not give themselves to excessive drinking or be greedy for dishonest gain.

Ephesians 5:18
Don't get drunk with wine, because it makes you lose control. Instead, keep on being filled with the Spirit...

Supportive Scriptures—Leaders Have a Special Responsibility to Not Become Intoxicated

Proverbs 31:4-5

Supportive Scriptures—Wine in Moderation is Permitted (and Even Recommended) for Suitable Purposes

Genesis 14:18
Psalms 104:14-15
Proverbs 3:9-10, 31:6-7

John 2:1-11
1 Timothy 5:23

Supportive Scriptures—Intoxication with Wine and Other Substances is Prohibited

Isaiah 5:11, 22-23, 28:7
Hosea 4:11
Proverbs 20:1, 23:20-21, 29-35
Romans 13:13
1 Corinthians 5:11
Galatians 5:19-20
1 Peter 4:3

**Supportive Scripture—Neither Wine Nor Grapes Are to be Consumed by
                    Those Who Have Taken a Nazirite Vow**

Numbers 6:2-4

Commentary

The above Scriptures speak for themselves. Drunkenness is prohibited; drinking wine in moderation is not. Wine is used in various ways within Messianic Judaism—as one of the elements in the *Shulchan Adonai* (the Lord's Table), for *Kiddush,* for *Havdalah,* and as a celebratory beverage.

Classical Commentators

Of the numerous Scriptures that command against becoming intoxicated through drinking, Maimonides and HaChinuch quote only <u>Leviticus 10:8-11</u> that prohibits priests from entering the Temple after drinking wine or other intoxicating liquor. Meir does not address the subject at all.

<u>**NCLA**</u>**: JMm JFm KMm KFm GMm GFm**

A12. Being Born Again from Above.

We are to be born again from above.

This precept is derived from His Word (blessed be He):

Key Scripture

John 3:1-16
There was a man among the P'rushim, named Nakdimon, [Nicodemus] who was a ruler of the Judeans. This man came to Yeshua by night and said to him, "Rabbi, we know it is from God that you have come as a teacher; for no one can do these miracles you perform unless God is with him." "Yes, indeed," Yeshua answered him, "I tell you that unless a person is born again from above, he cannot see the Kingdom of God." Nakdimon said to him, "How can a grown man be 'born'? Can he go back into his mother's womb and be born a second time?" Yeshua answered, "Yes, indeed, I tell you that unless a person is born from water and the Spirit, he cannot enter the Kingdom of God. What is born from the flesh is flesh, and what is born from the Spirit is spirit. Stop being amazed at my telling you that you must be born again from above! The wind blows where it wants to, and you hear its sound, but you don't know where it comes from or where it's going. That's how it is with everyone who has been born from the Spirit." Nakdimon replied, "How can this happen?" Yeshua answered him, "You hold the office of teacher in Isra'el, and you don't know this? Yes, indeed! I tell you that what we speak about, we know; and what we give evidence of, we have seen; but you people don't accept our evidence! If you people don't believe me when I tell you about the things of the world, how will you believe me when I tell you about the things of heaven? No one has gone up into heaven; there is only the one who has come down from heaven, the Son of Man. Just as Moshe lifted up the serpent in the desert, so must the Son of Man be lifted up; so that everyone who trusts in him may have eternal life. For God so loved the world that he gave his only and unique Son, so that everyone who trusts in him may have eternal life, instead of being utterly destroyed.

Supportive Scriptures

Mark 16:16
John 5:24
Acts 4:12
Romans 1:16, 5:8, 6:3-5, 10:8-9
2 Corinthians 5:17
Ephesians 2:4-9
Titus 3:4-6
1 Peter 1:3, 23

Commentary

The common understanding of scholars is that Yeshua's exhortation to Nicodemus in John 3:7 that he "must be born again from above" was a reference to his first birth being from the waters of natural childbirth. There is, however, another way to understand this, and that is that man's first birth was also from above—from the waters of creation (Genesis 1:1-2)—and that man's original death due to Adam's disobedience required that he be "born again from above" in order for him to have eternal life, which was God's original intention.

One might argue that being "born again" (while it is God's desire for us all) is not a true *mitzvah* because the power to accomplish it is God's and not ours. True, the supernatural power to cause a man to be born from above is God's alone, but God gave us the key to unleash His power by receiving His son Yeshua—our Messiah—as we read in John 3:14-16:

> *"Just as Moshe lifted up the serpent in the desert, so must the Son of Man be lifted up; so that everyone who trusts in him may have eternal life. For God so loved the world that he gave his only and unique Son, so that everyone who trusts in him may have eternal life, instead of being utterly destroyed."*

Trusting [NKJ: Believing in] Yeshua as our Messiah (savior) means repenting of our former unbelief and accepting his sacrificial death as ours, and our means of receiving God's forgiveness.

> *"Now every cohen stands every day doing his service, offering over and over the same sacrifices, which can never take away sins. But this one, after he had offered for all time a single sacrifice for sins, sat down at the right hand of God, from then on to wait until his enemies be made a footstool for his feet. For by a single offering he has brought to the goal for all time those who are being set apart for God and made holy."* (Hebrews 10:11-14)

As a Messianic Jewish believer in Yeshua I am sometimes confronted with the following question or a variation of it:

> "I consider myself a good person. All the things the Bible teaches I try to do, and all the virtues the Bible teaches I try to have. Are you telling me that just because I do not believe that Yeshua is the Messiah I am destined for Hell?"

My answer to the question is always the same:

> "Your standing with God and your salvation are not for me to judge, nor is it for me to tell God whom he can save and whom He cannot. I can only tell you that Acts 4:12 of the New Covenant Scriptures teaches that *"There is salvation in no one else"* [meaning no one other than Yeshua], and that *"there is no other name under heaven given to mankind by whom we must be saved!"* Notice that the Scripture I quoted is God's promise that if you repent of your sins and receive Yeshua as your Messiah, *you will be saved!* If you want to take your chances and negotiate with God for some other way to heaven, that's up to you. But if you want to be sure of your salvation, I would advise you to do it the way that God guaranteed."

Classical Commentators

This *Mitzvah* is not addressed by any of the Jewish classical commentators.

NCLA: JMm JFm KMm KFm GMm GFm

A13. Being Pure in Heart.

We are to pursue being pure in heart.

This precept is derived from His Word (blessed be He):

Key Scriptures

Psalms 51:12(10)
Create in me a clean heart, God; renew in me a resolute spirit.

Philippians 4:8
In conclusion, brothers, focus your thoughts on what is true, noble, righteous, pure, lovable or admirable, on some virtue or on something praiseworthy.

1 Timothy 1:5
The purpose of this order is to promote love from a clean heart, from a good conscience and from sincere trust.

Supportive Scriptures

Psalms 24:4-5, 73:1, 119:9
Proverbs 16:2, 21:8
Matthew 5:8
2 Corinthians 7:1
Philippians 1:9-10
1 Timothy 5:22
2 Timothy 2:22
Titus 1:15
Hebrews 10:22
1 John 3:3

Commentary

God spoke to Israel through Jeremiah and promised them:

> *"I will put my Torah within them and write it on their hearts; I will be their God, and they will be my people."* (Jeremiah 31:32b; Hebrews 8:10)

Later, God spoke through Ezekiel and said:

> Ezekiel 36:26: *"I will give you a new heart and put a new spirit inside you; I will take the stony heart out of your flesh and give you a heart of flesh."*

This new heart with the *Torah* embedded in it was to be a clean heart with a new Spirit, and it came to fruition as part of the New Covenant and man's "new birth" in Yeshua:

John 3:3: *"Yes, indeed," Yeshua answered him, "I tell you that unless a person is born again from above, he cannot see the Kingdom of God."*

John 3:6: *"What is born from the flesh is flesh, and what is born from the Spirit is spirit."*

2 Corinthians 5:17: *"Therefore, if anyone is united with the Messiah, he is a new creation—the old has passed; look, what has come is fresh and new!"*

1 Peter 1:23: *"You have been born again not from some seed that will decay, but from one that cannot decay, through the living Word of God that lasts forever."*

Classical Commentators

This *Mitzvah* is not addressed by any of the Jewish classical commentators.

NCLA: JMm JFm KMm KFm GMm GFm

A14. Aspiring to God's Perfection and Holiness.

We are to aspire to God's perfection and holiness.

This precept is derived from His Word (blessed be He):

Key Scriptures

Leviticus 11:44-45
For I am ADONAI your God; therefore, consecrate yourselves and be holy, for I am holy; and do not defile yourselves with any kind of swarming creature that moves along the ground. For I am ADONAI, who brought you up out of the land of Egypt to be your God. Therefore you are to be holy, because I am holy.

Leviticus 19:2
Speak to the entire community of Isra'el; tell them, 'You people are to be holy because I, ADONAI your God, am holy.

Leviticus 20:7-8
Therefore consecrate yourselves—you people must be holy, because I am ADONAI your God. Observe my regulations, and obey them; I am ADONAI, who sets you apart to be holy.

1 Peter 1:15-16
On the contrary, following the Holy One who called you, become holy yourselves in your entire way of life; since the Tanakh says, "You are to be holy because I am holy."

Supportive Scriptures

Leviticus 22:32-33
Deuteronomy 7:6
Ecclesiastes 7:20
Matthew 5:48
Romans 6:19b
Ephesians 1:4
Hebrews 12:14

Commentary

At first impression, Matthew 5:48 (*Therefore, be perfect, just as your Father in heaven is perfect*) and Leviticus 11:45 (*Therefore you are to be holy, because I am holy*) seem highly presumptuous and even blasphemous. As God's creation, we are so far below His holiness and perfection—how can we even think of being holy and perfect as He is? Yet, we are commanded to be holy and perfect, so somehow it is possible even though it seems impossible in light of our spiritual imperfections.

The answer is suggested in <u>Leviticus 22:32</u>: *" I am ADONAI, who makes you holy…"* In other words, we cannot aspire to holiness and perfection in our own power; we have to receive it from God Himself, and realize that for us it is a never-ending goal rather than one that we will achieve during our lifetime. In the Mosaic Covenant, the Israelites pursued holiness through repentance and the prescribed Tabernacle (later Temple) sacrifices. In the New Covenant, we are made holy by being one with Yeshua, "the Holy One of Israel." Only through his blood sacrifice can we be made holy and aspire toward perfection, for we read in <u>1 John 1:9</u>:

> *"If we acknowledge our sins, then, since he [Yeshua] is trustworthy and just, he will forgive them and purify us from all wrongdoing."*

Commentary by Dr. Daniel C. Juster

This *Mitzvah* refers to a heart orientation and not literal perfection in this life.

Classical Commentators

This *Mitzvah* is not addressed by any of the Jewish classical commentators.

<u>NCLA</u>: **JMm JFm KMm KFm GMm GFm**

A15. Doing Religious Things in Order to Be Seen.

We are not to do religious things in order to be seen.

This precept is derived from His Word (blessed be He):

Key Scriptures

Matthew 6:1-4
"Be careful not to parade your acts of tzedakah in front of people in order to be seen by them! If you do, you have no reward from your Father in heaven. So, when you do tzedakah, don't announce it with trumpets to win people's praise, like the hypocrites in the synagogues and on the streets. Yes! I tell you, they have their reward already! But you, when you do tzedakah, don't even let your left hand know what your right hand is doing. Then your tzedakah will be in secret; and your Father, who sees what you do in secret, will reward you.

Matthew 6:5-6
When you pray, don't be like the hypocrites, who love to pray standing in the synagogues and on street corners, so that people can see them. Yes! I tell you, they have their reward already! But you, when you pray, go into your room, close the door, and pray to your Father in secret. Your Father, who sees what is done in secret, will reward you.

Matthew 6:16-18
Now when you fast, don't go around looking miserable, like the hypocrites. They make sour faces so that people will know they are fasting. Yes! I tell you, they have their reward already! But you, when you fast, wash your face and groom yourself, so that no one will know you are fasting—except your Father, who is with you in secret. Your Father, who sees what is done in secret, will reward you.

Supportive Scriptures

Matthew 23:5
Mark 12:38-40
Luke 20:45-47

Commentary

This *Mitzvah* exhorts us to not do religious things for the purpose of being seen and receiving the adulation of others. It is the exact opposite of James 1:27 which states:

> *"Pure and undefiled religion before God and the Father is this: to visit orphans and widows in their trouble, and to keep oneself unspotted from the world. "*

Classical Commentators

This *Mitzvah* is not addressed by any of the Jewish classical commentators.

NCLA: **JMm JFm KMm KFm GMm GFm**

A16. Seeking to Please Men over God.

We are not to seek men's approval over God's.

This precept is derived from His Word (blessed be He):

Key Scriptures

Matthew 6:2-4
So, when you do tzedakah, don't announce it with trumpets to win people's praise, like the hypocrites in the synagogues and on the streets. Yes! I tell you, they have their reward already! But you, when you do tzedakah, don't even let your left hand know what your right hand is doing. Then your tzedakah will be in secret; and your Father, who sees what you do in secret, will reward you.

Galatians 1:10
Now does that sound as if I were trying to win human approval? No! I want God's approval! Or that I'm trying to cater to people? If I were still doing that, I would not be a servant of the Messiah.

Supportive Scriptures

Luke 16:15
John 12:42-43
Acts 5:29
Ephesians 6:5-8
Colossians 3:22
1 Thessalonians 2:4-6
Jude 1:16

Commentary

The un-regenerated man seeks man's approval over God's. It is a hold-over from the fall of mankind in the Garden of Eden. But Ephesians 4:22-24 instructs us:

> *"...so far as your former way of life is concerned, you must strip off your old nature, because your old nature is thoroughly rotted by its deceptive desires; and you must let your spirits and minds keep being renewed, and clothe yourselves with the new nature created to be godly, which expresses itself in the righteousness and holiness that flow from the truth."*

It is not wrong to seek men's approval so long as we put God's approval first:

<u>1 Peter 2:13-14</u>: *"For the sake of the Lord, submit yourselves to every human authority—whether to the emperor as being supreme, or to governors as being sent by him to punish wrongdoers and praise those who do what is good."*

Classical Commentators

This *Mitzvah* is not addressed by any of the Jewish classical commentators.

<u>**NCLA**</u>: **JMm JFm KMm KFm GMm GFm**

A17. Being Humble and Not Prideful.

We are to walk in humility and eschew pride.

This precept is derived from His Word (blessed be He):

Key Scriptures

Proverbs 8:13
The fear of ADONAI is hatred of evil. I hate pride and arrogance, evil ways and duplicitous speech.

Proverbs 16:18
Pride goes before destruction, and arrogance before failure.

Matthew 23:11-12
The greatest among you must be your servant, for whoever promotes himself will be humbled, and whoever humbles himself will be promoted.

Ephesians 4:2
Always be humble, gentle and patient, bearing with one another in love…

Philippians 2:5-8
Let your attitude toward one another be governed by your being in union with the Messiah Yeshua: Though he was in the form of God, he did not regard equality with God something to be possessed by force. On the contrary, he emptied himself, in that he took the form of a slave by becoming like human beings are. And when he appeared as a human being, he humbled himself still more by becoming obedient even to death—death on a stake as a criminal!

Colossians 3:12
Therefore, as God's chosen people, holy and dearly loved, clothe yourselves with feelings of compassion and with kindness, humility, gentleness and patience.

James 4:10
Humble yourselves before the Lord, and he will lift you up.

Supportive Scriptures—Yeshua's Humility Prophesied

Isaiah 50:6, 53:7
Zechariah 9:9
Psalms 22:7(6)-8(7)

Supportive Scriptures—Yeshua's Humility Exhibited

Matthew 3:13-15
Matthew 11:29
Matthew 20:28
Matthew 21:5
Luke 22:27
John 6:38
John 13:4-5
Philippians 2:6-8

Supportive Scriptures—Parables and Teachings on Humility

Luke 14:7-11
Luke 18:9-14
Luke 22:24-27

Supportive Scriptures—Humility and the Avoidance of Pride

Isaiah 2:11-12
Isaiah 13:11
Jeremiah 9:22(23)
Micah 6:8
Zephaniah 3:11
Psalms 18:28(27)
Psalms 25:8-9
Psalms 101:5
Psalms 138:6
Psalms 147:6
Proverbs 3:34
Proverbs 11:2
Proverbs 15:33
Proverbs 16:5
Proverbs 16:18-19
Proverbs 18:12
Proverbs 21:4
Proverbs 21:24
Proverbs 22:4
Proverbs 26:12
Proverbs 27:2
Proverbs 29:23
Ecclesiastes 7:8

2 Chronicles 7:14
Matthew 5:3
Matthew 18:2-4
Matthew 20:25-27
Mark 9:35
Mark 10:43-44
Luke 9:48
John 13:14-16
Romans 11:18
Romans 12:3
Romans 12:16
1 Corinthians 13:4-5
2 Corinthians 3:5
Galatians 5:13
Galatians 5:26
Galatians 6:3
Philippians 2:3
James 3:13
James 4:6
James 4:10
1 Peter 3:8
1 Peter 5:5-6

Supportive Scripture—Paul's Thorn in the Flesh

2 Corinthians 12:7

Commentary

There are some words in the Scriptures supporting this *Mitzvah* that are sufficiently similar as to warrant explanation. "Humility" and "humbleness" are the same, and refer to persons who do not elevate themselves in their own eyes. "Pride" is the opposite, in that a prideful person attributes self-value, abilities, qualities, and virtues to himself, whereas, even if they truly exist, they are not something he should be bragging about because they were given to him by God. "Haughtiness" and "arrogance" are similar, except that they refer to one's outward manifestation of pride, whereas pride is largely internal.

The reason that humility is lauded and pride is hated by God, is that pride is essentially a rejection of God, and is the sin that was behind Satan's fall from grace. The sin of pride can manifest in several ways, the most obvious of which results in brash boasting. Motivating such a person is often the delusion that he is a "self-made man," forgetting or denying that God is the one who made him, and made him what he is. The opposite, humility, gives credit to God and also to others that have contributed to who we are, and what we have become.

There is a more subtle way that pride can manifest. We sometimes come across it in a person that has a sour and complaining disposition, even bordering on self-deprecation. When we encounter it, we sometimes conclude that the person has a low opinion of his self-worth, whereas it is exactly the opposite. Instead of being boastful of his self-worth, such a person turns inward and resents that others do not adequately see it. "I deserved to get that job over my competitor" he might say to himself, or "they never give me credit for how valuable I really am." He may withdraw from social interactions by assuming in advance that he will be rejected, and may justify it by saying to himself something like: "I'm worth more than the way they treat me, so I won't give them the benefit and pleasure of what I have to offer them."

Perhaps I should not have to say this, but there is a way that we can experience pride that is not sinful. It is when pleasure is evoked in us by something of quality or by someone doing well, in which we have an interest. An example would be expressing pride in one's son or daughter who is doing well in school, or in one's hometown sports team that is winning most of its games. We need to be careful, however, because even such innocuous excursions into pride can cross the line of holy propriety if we begin thinking that our child's or team's successes are mainly due to us.

Classical Commentators

This *Mitzvah* is not addressed by any of the Jewish classical commentators.

NCLA: JMm JFm KMm KFm GMm GFm

A18. Being Good Stewards of Our Spiritual Gifts According to the Grace Given Us.

We are to be good stewards of our spiritual gifts, using them according to the grace given us.

This precept is derived from His Word (blessed be He):

Key Scriptures

Romans 12:6-8
But we have gifts that differ and which are meant to be used according to the grace that has been given to us. If your gift is prophecy, use it to the extent of your trust; if it is serving, use it to serve; if you are a teacher, use your gift in teaching; if you are a counselor, use your gift to comfort and exhort; if you are someone who gives, do it simply and generously; if you are in a position of leadership, lead with diligence and zeal; if you are one who does acts of mercy, do them cheerfully.

1 Corinthians 12:7-11
Moreover, to each person is given the particular manifestation of the Spirit that will be for the common good. To one, through the Spirit, is given a word of wisdom; to another, a word of knowledge, in accordance with the same Spirit; to another, faith, by the same Spirit; and to another, gifts of healing, by the one Spirit; to another, the working of miracles; to another, prophecy; to another, the ability to judge between spirits; to another, the ability to speak in different kinds of tongues; and to yet another, the ability to interpret tongues. One and the same Spirit is at work in all these things, distributing to each person as he chooses.

Ephesians 4:11-13
Furthermore, he gave some people as emissaries, some as prophets, some as proclaimers of the Good News, and some as shepherds and teachers. Their task is to equip God's people for the work of service that builds the body of the Messiah, until we all arrive at the unity implied by trusting and knowing the Son of God, at full manhood, at the standard of maturity set by the Messiah's perfection.

1 Peter 4:10-11
As each one has received some spiritual gift, he should use it to serve others, like good managers of God's many-sided grace—if someone speaks, let him speak God's words; if someone serves, let him do so out of strength that God supplies; so that in everything God may be glorified through Yeshua the Messiah—to him be glory and power forever and ever. Amen.

Supportive Scriptures—Spiritual Gifts

Psalms 84:12(11)
Ecclesiastes 3:13

Matthew 7:11
Luke 6:38
Romans 5:17, 11:29
1 Corinthians 12:1, 14:1
James 1:17

Supportive Scriptures—God's Grace

Genesis 6:8
Exodus 20:5b-6, 34:6-7
Numbers 6:25
Deuteronomy 5:9b-10, 7:9
Psalms 23:6
1 Chronicles 16:34
Romans 3:24, 6:14
2 Corinthians 12:8-9
Ephesians 2:8
Titus 2:11
Hebrews 4:16
James 4:6

Supportive Scriptures—Examples of Grace Imparted to Men

John 1:14
Acts 6:8
2 Corinthians 8:1-7

Commentary

"Grace," commonly defined as unmerited favor, is both an attribute and a gift that He imparts to us. But for what purpose and how are we to use it? Daniel Juster answers the question this way:

> *"Empowered by the Holy Spirit, we are to use our gifts and talents (from the Spirt) as instruments for the blessing and building up of fellow believers in order to reach others for the Good news. In a large sense then, grace is not only unmerited favor, but includes the idea of power to do things. Hence the grace gifts are gifts of power in that the grace of God changes us and gives us ability to live in a right manner and to bless others."*

One might ask what Scripture means when it says that Yeshua and Stephen were "full of grace and truth." The grace and truth that filled them was not intrinsically their own, but rather that which was placed in them by the Father to benefit others as the Holy Spirit directed.[76] We are to follow their example by being good Stewards of God's grace and other spiritual gifts imparted to us as were they.

---

76 Although in Yeshua dwelt the fullness of God (Colossians 1:19, 2:9), Yeshua became a man like us (Hebrews 2:14-17) and, like us, received his godly attributes (including grace and truth) from His Father in Heaven.

117

Classical Commentators

This *Mitzvah* is not addressed by any of the Jewish classical commentators.

<u>NCLA</u>: JMm JFm KMm KFm GMm GFm

A19. Assembling with the Brethren.

We are not to forsake congregational assembly and fellowship with brother believers.

This precept is derived from His Word (blessed be He):

Key Scripture

<u>Matthew 18:20</u>
For wherever two or three are assembled in my name, I am there with them.

<u>1 Corinthians 14:26</u>
What is our conclusion, brothers? Whenever you come together, let everyone be ready with a psalm or a teaching or a revelation, or ready to use his gift of tongues or give an interpretation; but let everything be for edification.

<u>Hebrews 10:24-25</u>
And let us keep paying attention to one another, in order to spur each other on to love and good deeds, not neglecting our own congregational meetings, as some have made a practice of doing, but, rather, encouraging each other. And let us do this all the more as you see the Day approaching.

<u>1 John 1:7</u>
But if we are walking in the light, as he is in the light, then we have fellowship with each other, and the blood of his Son Yeshua purifies us from all sin.

Supportive Scriptures—Holy Convocations and Festive Assemblies of the Mosaic Law

Exodus 23:14-17, 34:23-24
Leviticus 8:4, 23:1-3, 6-8, 21, 24, 27, 34-36
Numbers 28:18, 25-26,
Numbers 29:1, 7, 12, 35
Deuteronomy 16:16, 31:12-13
Psalms 50:5, 55:15(14), 133:1
John 7:10
Acts 2:1

Supportive Scriptures—Examples of Assembling with Brother Believers in Yeshua

Matthew 12:30
John 7:10
Acts 2:1, 41-42, 44-47, 4:31, 5:12, 42, 14:27, 15:5-6, 20:7
1 Corinthians 5:4
Ephesians 5:19
1 Thessalonians 5:11
2 Thessalonians 2:1
1 John 1:3

Supportive Scriptures—Assembling in the Wrong Way and for the Wrong Reasons

1 Corinthians 11:17-34, 14:22-23

Supportive Scriptures—Assembling in the Right Way and for the Right Reasons

1 Corinthians 14:24-40
Hebrews 3:12-13

Commentary

God's commandments that we assemble with each other and with Him, are initially given during the time of the Mosaic Covenant. Early in the Covenant, the Tabernacle served as the place of assembly for the Israelites to receive communication from God, to pray, and to perform the commanded sacrifices. The Tabernacle and later the Temple also served as places where the Israelites could assemble with each other (e.g. Joshua 18:1), and by the time of Yeshua, the synagogue and individual homes also had become places of communal assembly—mainly for prayer, but also for study and discussion.

With the advent of the New Covenant, Jewish and Gentile followers of Yeshua made increased use of their homes for worship, prayer, and fellowship (Acts 2:46, 5:42), and these home gatherings developed into what eventually became known within Christianity as "home churches," and within Messianic Judaism as "home fellowships," "*chavurot*" or, when they have elder leadership, "congregations."

Scripture enjoins believers[77] to be in regular congregational fellowship with one another (Hebrews 10:24-25) as a means of providing mutual spiritual protection and accountability. Being part of a believing community enables us to observe one another's lives, share our burdens, and rebuke and correct one another (Galatians 6:1) in the event that we observe any of us falling into sin or straying from the faith. Congregational community also provides us with leaders (elders) whose responsibility it is to protect the community from outside evil encroachment (Acts 20:28-29), to stop sin when it is observed (Acts 20:30), to bring correction to members of the community, to judge disputes (Matthew 18:17), and to maintain reconciliation among community members (Luke 17:3; Colossians 3:13).

Classical Commentators

This *Mitzvah* is not addressed by Maimonides, Meir, or HaChinuch. However, in *Pirke Avot* 2:5a, Hillel states: "Do not separate yourself from the community."

NCLA: JMm JFm KMm KFm GMm GFm

---

77 In this *Mitzvah*, the term "brother" (applies to both males and females) means either a believer in God the Father and/or in Yeshua the Messiah, according to the context of its use. To the classical commentators (Maimonides, Meir, and Hachinuch), "brother" means "fellow Jew."

A20. Living by God's Words and Not by Bread Alone.

We are to live by God's Words and Not by Bread Alone.

This precept is derived from His Word (blessed be He):

Key Scriptures

Deuteronomy 8:2-3
You are to remember everything of the way in which ADONAI led you these forty years in the desert, humbling and testing you in order to know what was in your heart—whether you would obey his mitzvot or not. He humbled you, allowing you to become hungry, and then fed you with [manna], which neither you nor your ancestors had ever known, to make you understand that a person does not live on food alone but on everything that comes from the mouth of ADONAI.

Matthew 4:2-4
After Yeshua had fasted forty days and nights, he was hungry. The Tempter came and said to him, "If you are the Son of God, order these stones to become bread." But he answered, "The Tanakh says, 'Man does not live on bread alone, but on every word that comes from the mouth of ADONAI'"

Luke 4:3-4
The Adversary said to him, "If you are the Son of God, order this stone to become bread." Yeshua answered him, "The Tanakh says, 'Man does not live on bread alone.'"

Supportive Scripture—Bread and Hearing the Words of God

Amos 8:11

Supportive Scripture—Yeshua is the Word of God

John 1:1-4, 14

Supportive Scriptures—Yeshua is the Bread of Life

John 6:30-35, 48-51

Supportive Scriptures—Bread Representing Yeshua's Body

Matthew 26:26
Mark 14:22
Luke 22:19
1 Corinthians 10:16, 11:23-24

Commentary

In the Scriptures that underlie this *Mitzvah,* "bread" represents ordinary food, and it also represents God's instructions to us (His words) that are delivered through the Scriptures (the Word of God) and through Messiah Yeshua who is said by Scripture to be God's Word and the "bread of life." Although couched in these symbolisms the plain meaning of this *Mitzvah* is that we are not to live only by that which sustains us physically, but also that which sustains us spiritually and brings us closer to God.

Classical Commentators

This *Mitzvah* is not addressed by any of the Jewish classical commentators.

NCLA: JMm JFm KMm KFm GMm GFm

A21. Fleeing from Love of Money and Pursuing Godly Virtues.

We are to flee from love of money and are to pursue Godly Virtues.

This precept is derived from His Word (blessed be He):

Key Scriptures

Matthew 6:19
Do not store up for yourselves wealth here on earth, where moths and rust destroy, and burglars break in and steal.

1 Timothy 6:10-11
For the love of money is a root of all the evils; because of this craving, some people have wandered away from the faith and pierced themselves to the heart with many pains. But you, as a man of God, flee from these things; and pursue righteousness, godliness, faithfulness, love, steadfastness, gentleness.

Supportive Scriptures—Fleeing from Love of Money

Deuteronomy 7:25
Ecclesiastes 5:12(13)
Matthew 6:24, 19:23-24
1 Timothy 3:2-3
2 Timothy 3:1-2

Supportive Scriptures—Pursuing Righteousness

Isaiah 56:1
Jeremiah 22:3
Hosea 10:12
Zephaniah 2:3
Psalms 34:16(15)
Matthew 6:33
Romans 1:17
2 Corinthians 5:21
2 Timothy 2:22

Supportive Scriptures—Pursuing Godliness

Ephesians 4:22-24
1 Timothy 4:7-8, 6:3-4a, 11
2 Peter 3:11-12a

Supportive Scriptures—Pursuing Faith

Romans 1:17, 10:10
1 Corinthians 16:13
2 Corinthians 5:7
Ephesians 6:16
Galatians 2:15-16

Supportive Scriptures—Pursuing Faithfulness

Exodus 19:5
Deuteronomy 29:8(9)
1 Kings 2:3-4
Ezekiel 18:9
Hosea 2:22(20)
Psalms 78:8, 101:6
Matthew 25:21
Revelation 2:10, 17:14

Supportive Scriptures—Pursuing Love

Leviticus 19:18
Deuteronomy 6:5, 7:9
Proverbs 10:12
Mark 12:29-31
John 13:34-35, 14:23
John 14:23, 15:13
1 Corinthians 13:13, 16:14
Colossians 3:14
1 John 4:7-8, 18_

Supportive Scriptures—Pursuing Steadfastness

Psalms 108:2(1)
1 Corinthians 15:58
Galatians 6:9
2 Timothy 4:7
James 1:4, 12

Supportive Scriptures—Pursuing Gentleness

Proverbs 15:1
Ephesians 4:2
Colossians 3:12
1 Thessalonians 2:7

1 Timothy 3:2-3, 6:11
2 Timothy 2:25
Titus 3:1-2
1 Peter 3:3-4

Supportive Scriptures—Pursuing Eternal Life

John 3:14-16, 4:14
Romans 5:21, 6:23
1 Timothy 1:16, 6:12
1 John 5:11-13

Commentary

"Love of money" is a short way of saying "love of what money can buy." One naturally thinks of money buying goods and services and these alone are enough to ensnare those who are susceptible. However, there is a far greater evil in natural man's quest for money; it is that money can buy the power of men's obedience, and preoccupation with power is the opposite of trusting God and submitting to His power. Wanting to be powerful as God was what brought down Lucifer, and the idolatry of it can bring us down as well. The draw of money and what it can buy is so strong, so seductive, that we are commanded to flee from it. Pursuing godly virtues is the opposite of (and the antidote for) pursuing love of money, and is the reason that these two are linked in <u>1 Timothy 6:10-11</u>.

Commentary by Daniel C. Juster

There are some exceptional people who can buy anything they want, but just love to see their financial worth grow and grow; they are in love with it. The Bible does not say that it is wrong to get rich, but rather that one must not be in love with money; money should primarily be used to advance the Kingdom of God by the leading of the Holy Spirit. In Scripture, the standard for acquiring money seems to favor modesty.

Classical Commentators

This *Mitzvah* is not addressed by any of the Jewish classical commentators.

<u>NCLA</u>: **JMm JFm KMm KFm GMm GFm**

A22. Allowing Worldly Attractions to Ensnare Us.

We are not to allow worldly attractions to ensnare us.

This precept is derived from His Word (blessed be He):

Key Scriptures

Proverbs 6:23-25
For the mitzvah is a lamp, Torah is light, and reproofs that discipline are the way to life. They keep you from an evil woman, from a loose woman's seductive tongue. Don't let your heart lust after her beauty or allow her glance to captivate you.

Matthew 18:7-9
Woe to the world because of snares! For there must be snares, but woe to the person who sets the snare! So if your hand or foot becomes a snare for you, cut it off and throw it away! Better that you should be maimed or crippled and obtain eternal life than keep both hands or both feet and be thrown into everlasting fire! And if your eye is a snare for you, gouge it out and fling it away! Better that you should be one-eyed and obtain eternal life than keep both eyes and be thrown into the fire of Gei-Hinnom.

Mark 9:43-47
If your hand makes you sin, cut it off! Better that you should be maimed but obtain eternal life, rather than keep both hands and go to Gei-Hinnom, to unquenchable fire! And if your foot makes you sin, cut it off! Better that you should be lame but obtain eternal life, rather than keep both feet and be thrown into Gei-Hinnom! And if your eye makes you sin, pluck it out! Better that you should be one-eyed but enter the Kingdom of God, rather than keep both eyes and be thrown into Gei-Hinnom, ...

1 John 2:15-16
Do not love the world or the things of the world. If someone loves the world, then love for the Father is not in him; because all the things of the world—the desires of the old nature, the desires of the eyes, and the pretensions of life—are not from the Father but from the world.

Supportive Scriptures

Exodus 23:32-33, 34:12
Deuteronomy 7:25
Joshua 23:13
Judges 2:3
Isaiah 8:14-15
Psalms 106:36, 119:110, 140:6(5), 141:9
Proverbs 7:25-26, 13:14
Ecclesiastes 7:26

1 Corinthians 6:18
1 Timothy 6:9-10
James 1:14-15
1 John 2:15-17

Commentary

Yeshua prayed to his father in heaven:

> *"But now, I am coming to you; and I say these things while I am still in the world so that they may have my joy made complete in themselves. I have given them your word, and the world hated them, because they do not belong to the world—just as I myself do not belong to the world. I don't ask you to take them out of the world, but to protect them from the Evil One. They do not belong to the world, just as I do not belong to the world. Set them apart for holiness by means of the truth—your word is truth."* (<u>John 17:13-17</u>)

It is God's will that we remain in the world so that we can bear witness to the lost—those who do not know God, and are in need of Messiah. We are nevertheless warned of a danger to us, which is that if we are not on our guard, we can allow ourselves to be ensnared by the things of the world that appeal to our flesh and backslide into sin. The things of which we must beware are numerous—money, power, possessions, and illicit sex are but examples. We are not, however, left to fend for ourselves, for the Holy Spirit is with us, and we assured that:

> *"No temptation has seized you [us] beyond what people normally experience, and God can be trusted not to allow you [us] to be tempted beyond what you [we] can bear. On the contrary, along with the temptation he will also provide the way out, so that you [we] will be able to endure."* (<u>1 Corinthians 10:13-13</u>)

Classical Commentators

This *Mitzvah* is not addressed by any of the Jewish classical commentators.

<u>**NCLA**</u>**: JMm JFm KMm KFm GMm GFm**

A23. Being Subject to Governing Authorities.

We are to be subject to the governing authorities that are established by God.

This precept is derived from His Word (blessed be He):

Key Scripture

Romans 13:1
Let every soul be subject to the governing authorities. For there is no authority except from God, and the authorities that exist are appointed by God. (NKJ)

Supportive Scriptures

Mark 12:14-17
Titus 3:1
Hebrews 13:17
1 Peter 2:13-14

Commentary

This *mitzvah* to be subject to governing authorities is often debated among scholars. We know by the *mitzvah's* date and context that the governing authorities referred to included those of Rome, so the application of Romans 13:1 today undoubtedly contemplates secular governments on all levels.

But how can the Scripture say that all authorities that exist have been established and placed where they are by God, when evil governments such as Natzi Germany are fresh in our minds? Should we have cooperated with Natzi Germany rather than war against her? As absurd as that is, if Romans 13:1 were the only Scripture on the subject, one might come to that conclusion. But let us consider Acts 5:27-29 which seems to say something quite different; it says:

> *"They conducted them to the Sanhedrin, where the cohen hagadol demanded of them, "We gave you strict orders not to teach in this [Yeshua's] name! Look here! you have filled Yerushalayim with your teaching; moreover, you are determined to make us responsible for this man's death!" Kefa and the other emissaries answered, "We must obey God, not men."*

How do we reconcile Romans 13 with Acts 5? Some have attempted to explain Romans 13 by asserting that it refers merely to Rome's authority to assess and collect taxes. That, in my opinion is wrong. No, I suggest that the answer lies rather in the definition of "authority"—that not all persons and governments that claim to be authorities are, in fact, authorities. Stated differently, an alleged "authority" is not an authority if it is not from God. Any government that willfully commits gross sin or that leads persons for which it is responsible into sin is no authority at all and we ought to oppose it. With that understanding, we can unhesitatingly say that "we are to be subject to the governing authorities" because true governing authorities are from God.

Classical Commentators

This *Mitzvah* is not addressed by any of the Jewish classical commentators.

<u>NCLA</u>: JMm JFm KMm KFm GMm GFm

A24. Being Clean of Spirit as Well as of Body.

We are to give as much attention to being clean of spirit as to being clean of body.

This precept is derived from His Word (blessed be He):

Key Scriptures

Matthew 23:25-28
Woe to you hypocritical Torah-teachers and P'rushim! You clean the outside of the cup and the dish, but inside they are full of robbery and self-indulgence. Blind Parush! First clean the inside of the cup, so that the outside may be clean too. Woe to you hypocritical Torah-teachers and P'rushim! You are like whitewashed tombs, which look fine on the outside but inside are full of dead people's bones and all kinds of rottenness. Likewise, you appear to people from the outside to be good and honest, but inwardly you are full of hypocrisy and far from Torah.

Hebrews 10:22
Therefore, let us approach the Holiest Place with a sincere heart, in the full assurance that comes from trusting—with our hearts sprinkled clean from a bad conscience and our bodies washed with pure water.

Supportive Scriptures

Isaiah 1:16
Ezekiel 44:23
Psalms 24:3-4, 51:4(2), 4(2), 9(7), 12(10)
Luke 11:39-41
2 Corinthians 7:1
James 4:8

Commentary

It is a repeated teaching of Scripture that cleanliness of a man's body is analogized to cleanliness of his spirit. Scripture teaches that both are important, but that cleanliness of spirit is weightier in that if a man's spirit is not clean, no amount of washing with water can cleanse him. A man becomes spiritually clean by submitting himself in obedience to God, repenting of his sins, and receiving Messiah Yeshua as his personal savior.

> *"Some of you used to do these things [premarital sex, idol worship, adultery, homosexuality, theft, greed, drunkenness]. But you have cleansed yourselves, you have been set apart for God, you have come to be counted righteous through the power of the Lord Yeshua the Messiah and the Spirit of our God."* (1 Corinthians 6:11)

"If we acknowledge our sins, then, since he is trustworthy and just, he will forgive them and purify us from all wrongdoing." (1 John 1:9)

Classical Commentators

This *Mitzvah* is not addressed by any of the Jewish classical commentators.

<u>**NCLA**</u>: **JMm JFm KMm KFm GMm GFm**

B: Benevolence

B1. Lending Money without Interest to Our Poor Brother.

We are to lend money to our brother sufficient for his need and without regard for the Sabbatical Year. In such a loan, interest must not be charged nor given, and brothers are to take no part whatsoever in interest-bearing loans involving other brothers.

This precept is derived from His Word (blessed is He):

Key Scriptures

Exodus 22:24(25) (Maimonides RP197, RN237; Meir MN53, MP62; Chinuch C66, C68)
If you loan money to one of my people who is poor, you are not to deal with him as would a creditor; and you are not to charge him interest.

Leviticus 19:14 (Maimonides RN299; Meir MN76; Chinuch C232)
Do not speak a curse against a deaf person or place an obstacle in the way of a blind person; rather, fear your God; I am Adonai.

Leviticus 25:35 (Maimonides RP195; Meir MP38; Chinuch C479)
If a member of your people has become poor, so that he can't support himself among you, you are to assist him as you would a foreigner or temporary resident, so that he can continue living with you.

Leviticus 25:36-37 (Maimonides RN235; Meir MN54; Chinuch C343 [only Lev. 25:37])
Do not charge him interest or otherwise profit from him, but fear your God, so that your brother can continue living with you. Do not take interest when you loan him money or take a profit when you sell him food.

Deuteronomy 15:7 (Maimonides RN232; Meir MN62; Chinuch C478)
If someone among you is needy, one of your brothers, in any of your towns in your land which Adonai your God is giving you, you are not to harden your heart or shut your hand from giving to your needy brother.

Deuteronomy 15:8 (Maimonides RP197; Meir MP38; Chinuch C479)
No, you must open your hand to him and lend him enough to meet his need and enable him to obtain what he wants.

Deuteronomy 15:9 (Maimonides RN231; Meir MN56, MP62; Chinuch C480)
Guard yourself against allowing your heart to entertain the mean-spirited thought that because the seventh year, the year of sh'mittah is at hand, you would be stingy toward your needy brother and not give him anything; for then he may cry out to Adonai against you, and it will be your sin.

Deuteronomy 23:20(19) (Maimonides RN236 Meir MN55; Chinuch C572)
You are not to lend at interest to your brother, no matter whether the loan is of money, food or anything else that can earn interest.

<u>Deuteronomy 23:21(20)</u> (Maimonides RP198, RN236; Meir MN55; Chinuch C572, C573)
To an outsider you may lend at interest, but to your brother you are not to lend at interest, so that Adonai your God will prosper you in everything you sent out to do in the land you are entering in order to take possession of it.

<u>Luke 6:34-36</u>
What credit is it to you if you lend only to those who you expect will pay you back?
Even sinners lend to each other, expecting to be repaid in full. But love your enemies, do good, and lend expecting nothing back! Your reward will be great, and you will be children of Ha'Elyon; for he is kind to the ungrateful and the wicked. Show compassion, just as your Father shows compassion.

Commentary

This *Mitzvah* touches a number of principles, as can be seen from the large number of Scriptures and *mitzvot* of Meir, Maimonides, and Chinuch that are involved. It affirmatively requires that we lend money to our brother if he is in need, and to not charge him interest on the loan. Although historically commanded only to Israelites concerning their lending money to other Israelites, strangers, and sojourners who are in need, this *Mitzvah* to lend without interest applies in the New Covenant to all who are our brothers in Yeshua regardless of whether they are Jews or Gentiles. While we have no obligation under this *Mitzvah* to lend money to persons other than brothers, if we do lend money to other poor or needy persons, this *Mitzvah* strongly suggests that, out of compassion for their poverty, we not charge them interest either. Also, this *Mitzvah's* reference to the Sabbatical Year warns us that we must not decline to lend money to needy brothers prior to the Sabbatical Year, even though the debt will be legally discharged and may never be repaid. It should also be noted that <u>Deuteronomy 15:7</u> (referenced above) implies an obligation to give charity *(tz'dakah)* as well as to loan, and <u>Exodus 22:24(25)</u> not only prohibits being a usurer of the needy, but also participating in it as a borrower (even as a needy borrower), a surety, a witness, or in any other way.

<u>Luke 6:34-36</u> tells us that if we loan money to someone (presumably someone in need), we ought not to expect anything in return; rather, our loan should be motivated by compassion and not by the hope of profiting from the transaction either directly or indirectly. In my opinion, several English translations of the Scripture (including the CJB) render <u>verse 34</u> incorrectly by suggesting that the lender should not expect the loan itself to be repaid. Not only is such a notion inconsistent with other Scriptures, it contradicts the very nature and definition of a loan as distinguished from a gift.

<u>Deuteronomy 23:21(20)</u> does not apply to loans made to needy persons; we know this because it allows an Israelite to charge interest to a stranger, whereas <u>Leviticus 25:35</u> prohibits it if the stranger is poor. Nevertheless, it is included here because it indicates that an Israelite brother may not charge interest to another Israelite, even in the case of a general loan, e.g. a business loan. This is in direct conflict with the modern-day practice of charging interest for commercial loans, mortgages, and credit cards. It is possible that, in this anonymous, mixed, and credit-dependant society, this prohibition is no longer applicable because it would prohibit Jews from becoming

134

bankers of any kind, and would prevent Jews from borrowing for business and from acquiring mortgages from banks whose officers were Jewish.

Classical Commentators

Regarding <u>Deuteronomy 23:20(19)</u>, HaChinuch states that, not only are we not to lend money at interest to a brother, but we are not to borrow money at interest from a brother either, thereby making it clear that the lender in such a transaction is not the only guilty party. It is also noteworthy that Meir's *mitzvot* limit this obligation to lending to Jews, while Maimonides' *mitzvah* does not contain this limitation; Meir states that his *mitzvah* (MP62) is greater and more of an obligation than mere charity. It is also noteworthy that other *mitzvot* deal differently with lending money in circumstances that do not involve poverty.

Chill (p 85) references the three-year tithe (<u>Deuteronomy 14:28</u>) because it is used for the needy. He also references <u>Deuteronomy 15:3</u> (Maimonides RP142) that allows an Israelite to charge interest to a Gentile on a loan as well as <u>Exodus 22:24(25)</u> (RN234).

It is noteworthy that this is part of a whole genus of laws that provide a humane and protective society—a society that does not reward laziness, but helps those in genuine need and leads to a gracious caring for one another. It is related to the more clearly social welfare rules to be discussed in other *mitzvot,* such as a planter providing for the poor by not harvesting the corners of his corn field, not double-thrashing olive trees, and not picking up fallen fruit from other trees. A biblically humane society does have a welfare component, though it may not be in redistribution of wealth; that is a big debate. What is clear is that it has rules that foster widespread charity and responsibility for oneself, one's family, and others.

<u>NCLA</u>: JMm JFm KMm KFm GMm GFm

B2. Returning a Needed Pledged Item.

We are to return an item we are holding in pledge when the owner is in need of it.

This precept is derived from His Word (blessed is He):

Key Scriptures

Exodus 22:25(26) (Maimonides RP199; Meir MP63; Chinuch C587)
If you take your neighbor's coat as collateral, you are to restore it to him by sundown,

Deuteronomy 24:12 (Maimonides RN240; Meir MN61; Chinuch C586)
If he is poor, you are not to go to bed with what he gave as collateral in your possession;

Deuteronomy 24:13 (Maimonides RP199; Chinuch C587)
rather, you must restore the pledged item at sunset; then he will go to sleep wearing his garment and bless you. This will be an upright deed of yours before ADONAI *your God.*

Ephesians 4:31-32
Get rid of all bitterness, rage, anger, violent assertiveness and slander, along with all spitefulness. Instead, be kind to each other, tenderhearted; and forgive each other, just as in the Messiah God has also forgiven you.

Colossians 3:12
Therefore, as God's chosen people, holy and dearly loved, clothe yourselves with feelings of compassion and with kindness, humility, gentleness and patience.

Commentary

Although historically commanded to Israelites concerning lending money to (and taking security from) other Israelites, compassion suggests that this *Mitzvah* be applied to everyone. It in fact raises the question of whether it is proper, in the first place, to take possession of any pledged object which is likely to be needed in the future.

In modern times, it is unlikely that a person who is not in the pawn business will take security of chattel for a loan, and it is even less likely that chattel security would involve clothing. Yet, there might be a moral analogy if one takes possession of an item such as a person's tools if the tools are needed by him to earn a living.

Classical Commentators

Maimonides presents a literal interpretation of the relevant Scriptures, requiring the pledged item to be returned during the day or night as needed. "Need," in this context, is on the level of survival, protection, earning capacity, health, and basic comfort. HaChinuch is consistent with Maimonides and Meir.

NCLA: JMm JFm KMm KFm GMm GFm

B3. Limitations on Our Eating and Otherwise Partaking of the Produce of Our Work.

We may eat of crops with which we work, but not take any of it away, nor take to excess. If we lack a basic human need and our work involves providing it, we may partake of the product or service of our labor within the limits of survival but not of luxury.

This precept is derived from His Word (blessed is He):

Key Scriptures

Deuteronomy 23:25(24)-26(25) (Maimonides RP201, RN267, RN268; Meir MP65, MN186; MN187; Chinuch C576, C577, C578)
"When you enter your neighbor's vineyard, you may eat enough grapes to satisfy your appetite; but you are not to put any in your basket. When you enter your neighbor's field of growing grain, you may pluck ears with your hand; but you are not to put a sickle to your neighbor's grain."

1 Corinthians 9:7
Did you ever hear of a soldier paying his own expenses? or of a farmer planting a vineyard without eating its grapes? Who shepherds a flock without drinking some of the milk

1 John 3:17
If someone has worldly possessions and sees his brother in need, yet closes his heart against him, how can he be loving God?

Commentary

This *Mitzvah* is a form of charity known in the Jewish world as *tz'dakah.* It speaks to the worker directly but implies a clear duty on the part of the owner of crops to allow his workers to eat of them while they are at work. One may argue that this also applies to those who work among food items which are not crops. For example, a restaurant worker may eat his fill during his or her work shift but may not take any of it home. Also, because the *Mitzvah* is clearly one of compassion for the poor, in modern times it extends to industries that provide human necessaries other than edibles such as medical care, medicine, clothing basics, and fuel. It seems to me that if one hires an unshod shoe salesman, it is inhumane and a violation of 1 John 3:17 to require that he sell shoes while not equipping him with a pair of his own.

Classical Commentators

In their respective positive *mitzvot,* both Meir and Maimonides emphasize the land-owner's obligation to allow workers to eat, rather than the workers' permission to eat. In contrast, Meir's and Maimonides' *mitzvot* MN186 and RN267 respectively, state that workers are not to eat while performing their work, but only at the end of their work.[78] Meir's *mitzvah* MN187 emphasizes

---

78 Permission to eat at the end of work is a *Talmudic* interpretation.

that the worker is not to take food away and give it to others, while Maimonides' *mitzvah* RN268 states that a laborer is not to pick more crops than he needs for his immediate meal.

HaChinuch says that the root of *mitzvah* C576 is that Israelites are to have good character and exhibit good will. He is in basic agreement with Maimonides and Meir, and all three are very detailed regarding situations and exceptions.

NCLA: JMm JFm KMm KFm GMm GFm

B4. Giving Charitably to Persons in Need.

We are to give tz'dakah to persons in need.

This precept is derived from His Word (blessed is He):

Key Scriptures

<u>Leviticus 25:35-36</u> (Meir MP38; Maimonides RP195; Chinuch C479)
If a member of your people has become poor, so that he can't support himself among you, you are to assist him as you would a foreigner or a temporary resident, so that he can continue living with you. Do not charge him interest or otherwise profit from him, but fear your God, so that your brother can continue living with you.

<u>Deuteronomy 15:7</u> (Maimonides RN232; Meir MN62; Chinuch C478)
If someone among you is needy, one of your brothers, in any of your towns in your land which ADONAI your God is giving you, you are not to harden your heart or shut your hand from giving to your needy brother.

<u>Deuteronomy 15:8</u> (Meir MP38; Chinuch C479)
No, you must open your hand to him and lend him enough to meet his need and enable him to obtain what he wants.

<u>Deuteronomy 15:9-10</u>
Guard yourself against allowing your heart to entertain the mean-spirited thought that because the seventh year, the year of sh'mittah is at hand, you would be stingy toward your needy brother and not give him anything; for then he may cry out to ADONAI against you, and it will be your sin. Rather, you must give to him; and you are not to be grudging when you give to him. If you do this, ADONAI your God will bless you in all your work, in everything you undertake -

<u>Deuteronomy 15:11</u> (Maimonides RP195; Meir MP38)
For there will always be poor people in the land. That is why I am giving you this order, 'You must open your hand to your poor and needy brother in your land.

<u>James 2:14-17</u>
What good is it, my brothers, if someone claims to have faith but has no actions to prove it? Is such "faith" able to save him? Suppose a brother or sister is without clothes and daily food, and someone says to him, "Shalom! Keep warm and eat hearty!" without giving him what he needs, what good does it do? Thus, faith by itself, unaccompanied by actions, is dead.

<u>1 John 3:17</u>
If someone has worldly possessions and sees his brother in need, yet closes his heart against him, how can he be loving God?

Supportive Scriptures

Matthew 6:1-4, 19-21
Luke 6:38, 11:33-34, 12:33, 14:12-14, 16:19-25
Acts 6:1-3
1 Corinthians 16:1-2
2 Corinthians 9:6-9

Commentary

Charity, in the Jewish world, is known as *tz'dakah*. The first thing to notice about the Scriptures that underlie this commandment is that they do not limit *tz'dakah* to giving for, as you can see in Deuteronomy 15:8 and Leviticus 25:36, lending to the poor without charging interest is considered a work of *tz'dakah* as well. Leviticus 25:35 begins by referring to "a member of your people," and charges us with a duty to help our brother Israelite so that he (and presumably his family) can continue to live among us, meaning whatever style of living is par in our community. A charitable burden such as this cannot be complied with by the average person or family, so it is reasonable that the Scripture intends a considerable part of it to be fulfilled communally. Also, although the term "your people" meant fellow Israelites, for us the commandment should be broadened to mean fellow Jews (be we Jewish), and fellow brothers in Messiah, be we Jews or not.

The heart of the commandment is that God wants us to take responsibility for our impoverished brother's welfare and, in order to be able to do so, our communities must establish some level of financial safety net for its members. If we do not, brothers on whom hard times fall will have to move away from the community, and the inevitable result is fractured relationships, which is not God's intent. The possibility of emergency and sometimes long-term needs developing within any congregational community suggests the wisdom of the community establishing a benevolence fund; administering such a fund, as well as coordinating other resources (both congregational and personal), is one of the important functions of a deaconate *(shamashim)*.

Besides the corporate measures I spoke of, the Scriptures I mentioned suggest that we have personal responsibility as well. For that reason, we ought to develop a plan for giving charity that includes setting aside funds, and opening our homes with which *HaShem* has blessed us, to provide emergency sheltering when needed. The degree to which we must divert funds and resources from our own families in order to give to others is not clear from the Scriptures, so we must pray for the Holy Spirit to give us guidance before (and certainly when) the need to give occurs.

Another thing to notice in the Scriptures is that Leviticus 25:35 implies that we are also to give *tz'dakah* to those who we do not count as brothers, for it says "…you are to assist him as you would a foreigner or a temporary resident." The way this is put is interesting because it suggests that we would have no question or hesitation in helping the foreigner, whereas we need a commandment to motivate us to help those closer to us. Could it be that we sometimes have less compassion for our family and peers than we do for strangers?

Our obligation to a give to others in need is carried over to the New Covenant Scriptures with such strength that it might as well have been presented as a commandment there as well. 1 John 3:17 equates withholding *tz'dakah* from our brother with our not loving God, and James 2:14-17 tells us that our charitable acts are an indication of the level of our faith. Luke 6:38 is interesting in its application of sowing and reaping, but I prefer to not think in those terms because I do not want to taint any charitable act on my part with even a fleeting thought of self-interest.

In addition to it being required by *Torah,* giving *tz'dakah* is a time-honored practice in Jewish homes where a *tz'dakah* box for spare coins is often in plain view. It is further my opinion that giving *tz'dakah* should always be over and above other giving that is required of us, including our tithes and other offerings.

Classical Commentators

Maimonides warns us against giving *tz'dakah* as a way of benefiting ourselves and suggests that, where possible, it ought to be given anonymously. Meir has a great deal to say about *tz'dakah* that is very motivating. For starters, he makes the statement: "We are duty-bound to be more careful about the *mitzvah* of charity than about all the other positive commandments.'[79] He goes on to say that "charity is a distinguishing characteristic of the descendants of Abraham,"[80] and that the "faith of truth" and charity are inseparably linked. Maimonides construes the commandment as our being responsible to give *tz'dakah* to humanity broadly, while Meir is more explicit in applying it to Jews. HaChinuch tells us that one of the values of giving *tz'dakah* anonymously is to not embarrass the recipient, and suggests that if a needy person is reluctant to receive it as a gift, he might, nevertheless, receive it as a loan. He also opines that even a poor man is obligated to give *tz'dakah*, and reminds us that even a normally wealthy man can fall on hard times financially due to illness and other causes, and may need temporary help, possibly in the way of a loan.

NCLA: JMm JFm KMm KFm GMm GFm

79 Quoted from C. Chavel, The Commandments *(Sefer Ha-Mitzvoth of Maimonides in two volumes)* (London: *The Soncino Press, Ltd.*, 1967).
80 ibid.

B5. Setting Aside Part of Our Increase for the Poor.

We are to set aside and give a part of our increase to the poor.

This precept is derived from His Word (blessed is He):

Key Scriptures

<u>Leviticus 19:9-10</u> (Maimonides RP120, 123, 124; Meir ML1-4, 8 9; Chinuch 216-223)
When you harvest the ripe crops produced in your land, don't harvest all the way to corners of your field, and don't gather the ears of grain left by the harvesters. Likewise, don't gather the grapes left on the vine or fallen on the ground after harvest; leave them for the poor and the foreigner; I am ADONAI your God.

<u>Leviticus 23:22</u> (Maimonides RP121; Meir ML6, 7)
When you harvest the ripe crops produced in your land, don't harvest all the way to the corners of your field, and don't gather the ears of grain left by the harvesters; leave them for the poor and the foreigner; I am ADONAI your God.

<u>Deuteronomy 24:20-22</u> (Maimonides RN212)
When you beat your olive tree, you are not to go back over the branches again; the olives that are left will be for the foreigner, the orphan and the widow. When you gather the grapes from your vineyard, you are not to return and pick grapes a second time; what is left will be for the foreigner, the orphan and the widow. Remember that you were a slave in the land of Egypt. That is why I am ordering you to do this.

<u>1 Corinthians 16:2</u>
Every week, on Motza'ei-Shabbat, each of you should set some money aside, according to his resources, and save it up; so that when I come I won't have to do fundraising.

Supportive Scriptures

Acts 11:27-30
2 Corinthians 9:7
James 1:27

Commentary

The requirement that God's people give to the poor *(tz'dakah)* is found throughout the Bible. At the time of Moses, Israel was an agrarian society, so a major way of providing for the poor was by leaving a portion of each field and vineyard un-harvested and by not picking up grapes or grain that fell to the ground. By the time of Yeshua, Israel was still agricultural but was already moving toward using money for *tz'dakah*. Today, most of the world's population does not live in a farm environment, and wages paid in money has largely replaced being paid in produce and goods. Nevertheless, the principle of the Mosaic commandments to set aside a part of our increase for the poor is still God's will.

The first Corinthian Scripture cited above makes mention of setting aside money for the Apostle Sha'ul to bring to God's people in Jerusalem. In addition to it being required by *Torah,* giving *tz'dakah* is a time-honored practice in Jewish homes where a *tz'dakah* box for spare coins is often in plain view. It is my opinion that *tz'dakah* should always be in addition to other giving that is required of us such as our tithes and other offerings, and it should be noted that, according to *Torah,* part of the tithe must also be set aside for the poor.

Classical Commentators

Maimonides', Meir's, and HaChinuch's respective *mitzvot* are entirely from the perspective of agriculture in the Land of Israel.

<u>NCLA</u>: JMm JFm KMm KFm GMm GFm

B6. Gleanings and Part of Life-Sustaining Commodities Left for the Poor and Disadvantaged.

(a) The gleanings and part of every harvest and vintage must be left for the poor and disadvantaged.

(b) The gleanings and part of all life-sustaining commodities and services should be reserved for the poor and disadvantaged.

This precept is derived from His Word (blessed be He):

Key Scriptures

Leviticus 19:9-10 (Maimonides RP120-121, 123-124, RN210-213; Meir ML1-4, 7-9; Chinuch C216-223).
When you harvest the ripe crops produced in your land, don't harvest all the way to corners of your field, and don't gather the ears of grain left by the harvesters. Likewise, don't gather the grapes left on the vine or fallen on the ground after harvest; leave them for the poor and the foreigner; I am ADONAI your God.

Leviticus 23:22 (Maimonides RP121; Meir ML6-7)
When you harvest the ripe crops produced in your land, don't harvest all the way to the corners of your field, and don't gather the ears of grain left by the harvesters; leave them for the poor and the foreigner; I am ADONAI your God.

Deuteronomy24:19-22 (Maimonides RP122, RN212, 214; Meir ML5, 8, 10; Chinuch 221, 592-593)
When harvesting the grain in your field, if you forgot a sheaf of grain there, you are not to go back and get it; it will remain there for the foreigner, the orphan and the widow, so that ADONAI your God will bless you in all the work you do. When you beat your olive tree, you are not to go back over the branches again; the olives that are left will be for the foreigner, the orphan and the widow. When you gather the grapes from your vineyard, you are not to return and pick grapes a second time; what is left will be for the foreigner, the orphan and the widow. Remember that you were a slave in the land of Egypt. That is why I am ordering you to do this.

1 Timothy 6:17-19
As for those who do have riches in this present world, charge them not to be proud and not to let their hopes rest on the uncertainties of riches but to rest their hopes on God, who richly provides us with all things for our enjoyment. Charge them to do good, to be rich in good deeds, to be generous and ready to share. In this way they will treasure up for themselves a good foundation for the future, so that they may lay hold of the real life."

Commentary

In ancient Israel, the life-sustaining commodities were foods grown in the soil, typically grains and grapes. God's commandments to leave the gleanings and reserve a part of the fields and vineyards for the poor and the foreigner were part of His larger plan to provide for those who could not otherwise live (e.g. Ruth 2:2). It is instructive that no such commandments were given regarding herds, flocks, manufactured goods, and artisans' services other than the left-over of certain animal offerings to be given to the Levites. My conclusion, therefore, is that these commandments were not intended to impute broad moral responsibility to the owners of all industries and commodities; their purpose was solely *tz'dakah.*

Although the Scriptures heretofore presented have diminished applicability in today's industrial and technical world, they must be complied with literally in agricultural environments where they can be applied. There are also wider applications of the Scriptures that should be considered by those of us who produce or provide life-sustaining (or even life-enhancing) products and services of a non-agricultural nature, and are moved to comply with the spirit of what God sought to achieve in ancient Israel. In such cases, part of our production (be they goods or services) can be identified and set apart as *tz'dakah* (over and above our other requirements to give *tz'dakah*), and the items themselves or profits therefrom can be given to the poor and disadvantaged.[81] Setting aside food and clothing in food banks and humanitarian aid centers is very much in keeping with this concept, and a goodly number of synagogues and churches participate in this kind of charitable giving.

Another opportunity for applying this *Mitzvah* occurs when we inadvertently produce defective but usable products. When that happens, instead of discarding them or selling them at a discount for our own gain, we could donate the irregular items or the proceeds of their sale to the poor and disadvantaged. Examples of such items are blemished fruits, irregularly sewn garments, unevenly cut building materials, discolored fabrics, and dented appliances.

The original agricultural commandments stand unchanged and are mandatory, whereas this broader *mitzvah* is optional but recommended for prayerful resolution.

Classical Commentators

Maimonides, Meir, and HaChinuch interpret the Scriptures of this *Mitzvah* as applying only to agriculture, and Meir (not Maimonides or HaChinuch) considers them applicable only in *Eretz Yisrael.*

Agricultural application:
NCLA: JMm JFm KMm KFm GMr GFr
Non-agricultural application:
NCLA: JMr JFr KMr KFr GMr GFr

---

81 In ancient Israel, foreigners were protected by God's Commandments because they were disadvantaged as were widows and orphans.

C: Commerce

C1. Being Fair and Honest in Business.

We are to deal fairly and honestly in business.

This precept is derived from His Word (blessed is He):

Key Scriptures

Exodus 22:20(21) (Maimonides RN253; Meir MN50; Chinuch C64)
You must neither wrong nor oppress a foreigner living among you, for you yourselves were foreigners in the land of Egypt.

Leviticus 5:21(6:2)-24(6:5) (Maimonides RN248, 249; Chinuch C225, 226)
If someone sins and acts perversely against ADONAI by dealing falsely with his neighbor in regard to a deposit or security entrusted to him, by stealing from him, by extorting him, or by dealing falsely in regard to a lost object he has found, or by swearing to a lie—if a person commits any of these sins, then, if he sinned and is guilty, he is to restore whatever it was he stole or obtained by extortion, or whatever was deposited with him, or the lost object which he found, or anything about which he has sworn falsely. He is to restore it in full plus an additional one-fifth; he must return it to the person who owns it, on the day when he presents his guilt offering.

Leviticus 19:11-12 (Maimonides RN248, 249; Meir MN30, 36; Chinuch C225, 226)
Do not steal from, defraud or lie to each other. Do not swear by my name falsely, which would be profaning the name of your God; I am ADONAI.

Leviticus 19:13 (Maimonides RN247; Meir MN37; Chinuch C228)
Do not oppress or rob your neighbor; specifically, you are not to keep back the wages of a hired worker all night until morning.

Leviticus 19:35 (Maimonides RN271; Meir MN83; Chinuch C258)
Don't be dishonest when measuring length, weight or capacity.

Leviticus 19:36 (Maimonides RP208; Chinuch C259)
Rather, use an honest balance-scale, honest weights, an honest bushel dry-measure and an honest gallon liquid-measure; I am ADONAI your God, who brought you out of the land of Egypt.

Leviticus 25:14 (Maimonides RP245, RN250; Meir MN47, MP67; Chinuch C336, C337)
If you sell anything to your neighbor or buy anything from him, neither of you is to exploit the other.

Deuteronomy 23:20(19) (Maimonides RN272; Chinuch C602)
You are not to lend at interest to your brother, no matter whether the loan is of money, food or anything else that can earn interest.

<u>Deuteronomy 25:13-16</u> (Maimonides RN272; Meir MN84; Chinuch C602)
You are not to have in your pack two sets of weights, one heavy, the other light. You are not to have in your house two sets of measures, one big, the other small. You are to have a correct and fair weight, and you are to have a correct and fair measure, so that you will prolong your days in the land ADONAI your God is giving you. For all who do such things, all who deal dishonestly, are detestable to ADONAI your God.

<u>Proverbs 20:10</u>
False weights and false measures—ADONAI detests them both.

<u>2 Corinthians 8:20-21</u>
Our aim in this is to show that our conduct in dealing with these substantial sums is above reproach; for we take pains to do what is right not only in the sight of God but also in the sight of other people.

<u>Colossians 3:9-10</u>
Never lie to one another; because you have stripped away the old self, with its ways, and have put on the new self, which is continually being renewed in fuller and fuller knowledge, closer and closer to the image of its Creator.

Commentary

This *Mitzvah* consolidates a number of God's *mitzvot* into the single principle that we are to deal fairly and honestly when transacting business with our neighbors; it applies equally to the buyer and to the seller of both goods and services. The buyer must not defraud a seller by purchasing an item which he knows (or suspects) is under-priced in error. Likewise, a seller must not sell an item whose condition and value do not justify its price.

Error in price is only one of several kinds of errors that can be made. It is possible that either the buyer or the seller could err in the identity, condition, or usability of an item. If an error is made and discovered within a reasonable time by either party, it should be called to the other party's attention, and an adjustment should be negotiated to meet Scripture's requirement of fairness.

In an ethical sale, nothing is concealed, there is full disclosure, and both parties act willingly and without coercion. This is in partial contrast with the British and American Common-law which does not countenance fraud, but embraces the principle of *Caveat Emptor*—"Let the buyer beware!"

Intentionally using inaccurate weights and measures in a transaction of buying or selling is, of course, dishonest and sinful. However, it can also be accidental, so Scripture prohibits even possessing weights and measures that are inaccurate. To make the point graphic, Maimonides states that one cannot possess an inaccurate measuring vessel, even if it is only used to collect urine.

Classical Commentators

Maimonides draws on the Oral Tradition to say that one-sixth of the fair price is the amount that an item can be overcharged or undercharged without either side having recourse. It is noteworthy that Maimonides' *Mitzvah* RN253 commands that we are not to wrong a proselyte (convert to Judaism) in matters of business, and derives this from Exodus 22:20(21), which refers neither to conversion nor business. Meir and HaChinuch follow Maimonides' reasoning, but broaden their respective statements to include all matters involving monetary value.

NCLA: JMm JFm KMm KFm GMm GFm

C2. Paying an Employee His Wages on the Day He Labors or When Due.

We are to pay an employee his wages on the same day that he labors or when contractually due.

This precept is derived from His Word (blessed is He):

Key Scriptures

<u>Leviticus 19:13</u> (Maimonides RN238; Meier MN38; Chinuch C230)
Do not oppress or rob your neighbor; specifically, you are not to keep back the wages of a hired worker all night until morning.

<u>Deuteronomy 24:14-15</u> (Maimonides RP200, RN238; Meir MP66, MN38; Chinuch C230, 588)
You are not to exploit a hired worker who is poor and needy, whether one of your brothers or a foreigner living in your land in your town. You are to pay him his wages the day he earns them, before sunset; for he is poor and looks forward to being paid. Otherwise he will cry out against you to ADONAI, and it will be your sin.

<u>Matthew 10:10b</u>
... for a worker is worthy of his food.

Commentary

The essence of this *Mitzvah* is that we must not oppress an employee by withholding or delaying payment of his wages. There are many kinds of employees today in many occupations. Some are day laborers and some are poor and some are not. It is customary to pay a hired man or employee at the end of a specified period of time that may be daily, weekly, bi-weekly, monthly, or at the conclusion of a contract, so this *Mitzvah* should not be interpreted to require that all workers be paid daily. That having been said, <u>Deuteronomy 24:14-15</u> requires that an employer pay a hired man daily if the man's impoverished condition makes it reasonable and compassionate to do so.

The inference of <u>Deuteronomy 14</u> is that not paying wages to a poor worker in a timely manner is akin to exploiting him, and there are undoubtedly unscrupulous employers who would withhold or delay the payment of wages to a poor worker in order to pressure the worker into giving the employer some kind of advantage. This *Mitzvah* can, therefore, be construed to have a broader meaning, which is to not exploit an employee's weakness to gain advantage.

Classical Commentators

Maimonides, Meir, and HaChinuch advocate literal compliance with the referenced Scriptures.

<u>**NCLA: JMm JFm KMm KFm GMm GFm**</u>

C3. Cancelling Loans and Not Refusing to Make Loans In and Near the Sabbatical Year.

We are to cancel all loans (that were made to brothers) in the Sabbatical Year, and we are not to refuse to give a loan to a poor brother on account of the Sabbatical Year being near.[82]

This precept is derived from His Word (blessed be He):

Key Scriptures

Deuteronomy 15:1-4 (Maimonides RP141-142, RN230; Meir MN57, MP64; Chinuch C475-477)
At the end of every seven years you are to have a sh'mittah. Here is how the sh'mittah is to be done: every creditor is to give up what he has loaned to his fellow member of the community—he is not to force his neighbor or relative to repay it, because ADONAI's time of remission has been proclaimed. You may demand that a foreigner repay his debt, but you are to release your claim on whatever your brother owes you. In spite of this, there will be no one needy among you; because ADONAI will certainly bless you in the land which ADONAI your God is giving you as an inheritance to possess -

Deuteronomy 15:7-8
If someone among you is needy, one of your brothers, in any of your towns in your land which ADONAI your God is giving you, you are not to harden your heart or shut your hand from giving to your needy brother. No, you must open your hand to him and lend him enough to meet his need and enable him to obtain what he wants.

Deuteronomy 15:9 (Maimonides RN231; Meir MN56, MP62; Chinuch C480)
Guard yourself against allowing your heart to entertain the mean-spirited thought that because the seventh year, the year of sh'mittah is at hand, you would be stingy toward your needy brother and not give him anything; for then he may cry out to ADONAI against you, and it will be your sin.

Luke 6:34-36
What credit is it to you if you lend only to those who you expect will pay you back? Even sinners lend to each other, expecting to be repaid in full. But love your enemies, do good, and lend expecting nothing back! Your reward will be great, and you will be children of Ha'Elyon; for he is kind to the ungrateful and the wicked. Show compassion, just as your Father shows compassion.

---

82 See *Mitzvah* D18 for a discussion of cancelling loans during the Sabbatical Year from the aspect of days and seasons.

Supportive Scriptures

Proverbs 3:5-6, 11:24-25
Matthew 6:25-31
2 Corinthians 9:10-12

Commentary

The Sabbatical Year is known as the "Year of Release" *(Sh'mittah)* because loans made to Israelites, by Israelites, are cancelled every seventh year. Also, Israelites are prohibited from denying loans to needy brothers when the Sabbatical Year approaches, despite the possibility that the loan will be discharged and not repaid voluntarily. The release of such loans does not (according to Deuteronomy 15:3) apply to—הַנָּכְרִי—foreigners. I believe that one of the reasons God gave Israel the Sabbatical Year was to test well-to-do Israelites' faith and reliance on Him.

A question that naturally comes to mind is how releasing loans in the Sabbatical Year applies today in the New Covenant. I am of the opinion that it continues to apply where the circumstances are similar to those of ancient Israel, and that it applies not only to Jews but also to *K'rov Yisrael* Gentiles; how similar the circumstances need to be will be revealed by the *Ruach HaKodesh* as we pray for guidance. As for other non-Jewish followers of Yeshua, I am inclined to the position that as New Covenant brothers, literal compliance is a blessing for them but not a requirement; I partially draw this conclusion from Isaiah 56:1-7, which promises blessing to the foreigner who keeps Gods Sabbaths, but does not require it of them (although admittedly most Sabbaths do not involve the release of debts). One thing that is certain, however, is that God continues to expect all of us to look to Him for provision rather than to think that we can cause provision to come to us by our own efforts.

This *Mitzvah* has some interesting ramifications in modern times. One of these is that the enforced collection of debts today is generally accomplished through civil courts—not by *batei din.* Therefore, as a practical matter, there is no way to enforce the *Mitzvah* against suing a brother in a secular court if a creditor decides to violate it and sue on a debt. Also, because this *Mitzvah* is so closely connected to Jewish life in *Eretz Yisrael,* it is arguable as to whether it applies among brothers (brother Jews and brothers in Yeshua) in the Diaspora. The weight of rabbinical opinion is that it is valid for Jews everywhere, and it is my opinion that it also applies to Jewish and *K'rov Yisrael* members of Messianic Jewish communities in the Diaspora if the loans are given with the understanding that observing the *Sh'mittah* is part of the community's *halachah.*

It should not be surprising that this *Mitzvah* is unpopular among creditors and that it has encountered much resistance. During the latter years of the Second Temple, the sage Hillel became concerned by the growing number of Jews whose weak faith was such that they were declining to loan money to poor Jewish brothers when the Sabbatical Year was near. To urge them to do so, he invented a legal procedure that, in effect, circumvented God's intent in giving us the *Mitzvah.* The procedure, still used today, is known as a *Pruzbul,* and works this way: Some time before *Sh'mittah,* a lender gives ownership of his uncollected debt to a *bet din* which,

152

in turn, appoints the lender to collect the debt for the *bet din*. The debt is not discharged by *Sh'mittah* because the *bet din* is a corporate entity, not a Jewish brother, so Deuteronomy 15:2 does not apply. When the lender collects the debt and attempts to give the proceeds to the *bet din*, he is told that the *bet din* does not want the money and he is instructed to keep it.

I do not agree with using such casuistic ploys to collect debts or, for that matter, to avoid complying with God's commandments in any other circumstance; I believe it is this kind of thinking to which Yeshua referred when He said to the Pharisees:

> *"Thus, with your tradition which you had handed down to you, you nullify the Word of God! And you do other things like this."* (Mark 7:13).

Nevertheless, I do not believe there is anything wrong with a lender accepting return of his money after the *Sh'mittah* if it is offered voluntarily.

The application of this commandment in modern credit societies requires some adjustment that is legitimate. First of all, commercial loans which are used to increase a person's wealth, to purchase mortgages, to make investments, etc., are not the intended application of this *Mitzvah*, although some of these loans are discharged as well. This *Mitzvah* is meant to apply to loans given by individuals, to individuals, because the borrower (who is a Jewish brother to the lender) is in some kind of personal need. Need-based loans must be given with generosity, and with willingness that the loan will be cancelled on the Sabbatical Year. Modern societies often have something like this in built into their civil laws that is called bankruptcy, where a person who becomes financially insolvent can receive a judicial discharge of his debts; in the United States, this is possible every six years. Bankruptcy laws are the modern alternative to indentured servanthood and Debtor's Prison, and they reflect something of the same spirit as this *Mitzvah* and the Year of Jubilee.

Classical Commentators

Maimonides states that a purpose of the *Sh'mittah* commandment is to teach us to be kind to the poor, and he also puts forth the case that it trains us against coveting what our neighbor owns. The logic is that, by not being allowed to recover money he has lent, how much more must the lender keep from coveting what belongs to the borrower. HaChinuch agrees with this *kal va-chomer* logic.

HaChinuch connects complying with Deuteronomy 15:9 (the requirement to lend even with *Sh'mittah* approaching) with trusting God by citing Proverbs 11:24-25 as God's promise of blessing to those who are generous. The other commentators make no such connection and, in fact, Maimonides exhibits severity toward foreigners by interpreting the permissive language in Deuteronomy 15:3 *("you may demand that a foreigner pay his debt")* into his *mitzvah* RP142 which states that we are required to collect debts from heathen with the same zeal as we forgive the debts of Israelites. Meir does not deal with the issue at all, but HaChinuch, in his *mitzvah* C476, agrees with Maimonides, and says that the reason is so that an idolater will not profit from an Israelite's generosity and possibly entice the sympathetic Israelite to follow after idolatrous practices.

Meir is of the opinion that if a borrower offers return of a loan voluntarily after *Sh'mittah,* the lender should not accept it. However, if it is offered a second time, then he may.

NCLA: **JMm JFm KMm KFm GMr GFr**

C4. Dealing Harshly When Lending Money or Collecting Debts.

We are not to deal harshly when lending or while collecting debts.

This precept is derived from His Word (blessed is He):

Key Scriptures

Exodus 22:24(25) (Maimonides RN234; Meir MN52; Chinuch C67)
If you loan money to one of my people who is poor, you are not to deal with him as would a creditor; and you are not to charge him interest.

Exodus 22:25-26(26-27) (Maimonides RP199, RN240; Meir MN61; Chinuch C586, 587)
If you take your neighbor's coat as collateral, you are to restore it to him by sundown, because it is his only garment—he needs it to wrap his body; what else does he have in which to sleep? Moreover, if he cries out to me, I will listen; because I am compassionate.

Deuteronomy 15:3 (Maimonides RP142; Chinuch C476)
You may demand that a foreigner repay his debt, but you are to release your claim on whatever your brother owes you.

Deuteronomy 15:9 (Maimonides RN231; Meir MN56, MP62; Chinuch C480)
Guard yourself against allowing your heart to entertain the mean-spirited thought that because the seventh year, the year of sh'mittah is at hand, you would be stingy toward your needy brother and not give him anything; for then he may cry out to Adonai against you, and it will be your sin.

Deuteronomy 23:21(20) (Maimonides RP198; Chinuch C573)
To an outsider you may lend at interest, but to your brother you are not to lend at interest, so that ADONAI your God will prosper you in everything you set out to do in the land you are entering in order to take possession of it.

Deuteronomy 24:6 (Maimonides RN242; Meir MN58; Chinuch C583)
No one may take a mill or even an upper millstone as collateral for a loan, because that would be taking as collateral the debtor's very means of sustenance.

Deuteronomy 24:10-13 (Maimonides RP199, RN239, RN240; Meir MN59, MP63; Chinuch C585, C586, C587)
When you make any kind of loan to your neighbor, you are not to enter his house to take his collateral. You must stand outside, and the borrower will bring the collateral outside to you. If he is poor, you are not to go to bed with what he gave as collateral in your possession; rather, you must restore the pledged item at sunset; then he will go to sleep wearing his garment and bless you. This will be an upright deed of yours before ADONAI your God.

Deuteronomy 24:17 (Maimonides RN241; Meir MN60; Chinuch C591)
You are not to deprive the foreigner or the orphan of the justice which is his due, and you are not to take a widow's clothing as collateral for a loan.

Commentary

The first thing to notice is that one should not consider himself a creditor when one lends money to a poor brother (Exodus 24(25)). Scripture establishes a different standard when the loan is to a brother Jew and especially if it is for compassionate reasons. This is clear in the Scriptures that deny interest to the lender and limit his collection options. Notice also that the lender is to treat the borrower so as to preserve both his safety and dignity, as we see in Deuteronomy 24:10-13 which prohibits the lender from entering the borrower's house to remove collateral, and requires that the lender return needed collateral to him at night. Notice also that importance is given to maintaining the borrower's good relationship with the lender and his having gratitude for the lender's compassion in having concern for his welfare.

The lender has no recourse of collection against a brother for a debt which the brother is unable to pay, but such is not the case with a loan made to a foreigner. In making a loan to a foreigner, interest may be charged and collection means employed if the loan is defaulted upon. Nevertheless, compassionate justice is due everyone, including the foreigner, so the overall *torah* of this *Mitzvah* is that we are not to deal harshly or unreasonably when lending money, or collecting debts from anyone.

As with other *mitzvot,* that date back to the Mosaic period, the foreigner or stranger was the Gentile who was not part of the camp of Israel, and was most likely an idol-worshipper. With the New Covenant, Gentile believers in Yeshua become brothers and members of the commonwealth (national life) of Israel through grafting into the olive tree (Romans 11:17; Ephesians 2:12), so this *Mitzvah* and others like it should apply to them as though they are Jews.

It is fairly easy to apply this *Mitzvah* when a loan is made by an individual to an individual. However, in this day and age, many loans are not personal but rather corporate, and in such case the *Mitzvah* is difficult to apply. Consider, for example, the plight of a Jewish bank officer who facilitates his bank's loan to another Jew and, when the loan is defaulted upon, is called to foreclose on the borrower's house in order to collect the loan. Since the bank officer does not own the loan and is duty bound to represent his employer's interest, it is my opinion that he can participate in the foreclosure after making every effort to help the borrower solve his financial difficulty.

Classical Commentators

Interestingly, both Maimonides and HaChinuch, in their respective *mitzvot,* go beyond what Deuteronomy 15:3 and 23:21(20) says. They construe these verses as positive commandments requiring that interest be charged to idol-worshippers and that the collection of their debts be pursued rigorously even if means of pressure are required. This is in contrast to the mercy and compassion that must be shown when dealing with Jews, the logic, expressed by HaChinuch being, that we should not provide idolaters with advantages lest we promote their ways and be drawn into them. Maimonides actually says that it is in order to harm them.

Meir does not deal with <u>Deuteronomy 15:3</u> at all, and I do not believe that following Maimonides' and HaChinuch's emphasis of harshness toward unbelievers or even idolaters is in keeping with the New Covenant's commandments that we attempt to lead them to Messiah and win their souls for God.

<u>NCLA</u>: JMm JFm KMm KFm GMm GFm

D: Days and Seasons

D1. Resting from Work and Assembling on the Weekly Sabbath.

We are to rest, refrain from work, and conduct a holy convocation on the weekly Sabbath.

This precept is derived from His Word (blessed be He):

Key Scriptures

Genesis 2:2-3
On the seventh day God was finished with his work which he had made, so he rested on the seventh day from all his work which he had made. God blessed the seventh day and separated it as holy; because on that day God rested from all his work which he had created, so that it itself could produce.

Exodus 20:8-11 (Maimonides RN320; Meir MN6; Chinuch C32)
Remember the day, Shabbat, to set it apart for God. You have six days to labor and do all your work, but the seventh day is a Shabbat for ADONAI your God. On it, you are not to do any kind of work—not you, your son or your daughter, not your male or female slave, not your livestock, and not the foreigner staying with you inside the gates to your property. For in six days, ADONAI made heaven and earth, the sea and everything in them; but on the seventh day he rested. This is why ADONAI blessed the day, Shabbat, and separated it for himself.

Exodus 23:12 (Meir MP20; Chinuch C85)
For six days, you are to work. But on the seventh day, you are to rest, so that your ox and donkey can rest, and your slave-girl's son and the foreigner be renewed.

Exodus 31:12-17
ADONAI said to Moshe, "Tell the people of Isra'el, 'You are to observe my Shabbats; for this is a sign between me and you through all your generations; so that you will know that I am ADONAI, who sets you apart for me. Therefore you are to keep my Shabbat, because it is set apart for you. Everyone who treats it as ordinary must be put to death; for whoever does any work on it is to be cut off from his people. On six days work will get done; but the seventh day is Shabbat, for complete rest, set apart for ADONAI. Whoever does any work on the day of Shabbat must be put to death. The people of Isra'el are to keep the Shabbat, to observe Shabbat through all their generations as a perpetual covenant. It is a sign between me and the people of Isra'el forever; for in six days ADONAI made heaven and earth, but on the seventh day he stopped working and rested.'

Exodus 34:21 (Maimonides RP154)
Six days you will work, but on the seventh day you are to rest—even in plowing time and harvest season you are to rest.

Exodus 35:1-3 (Maimonides RN322; Chinuch C114)
Moshe assembled the whole community of the people of Isra'el and said to them, "These are the things which ADONAI has ordered you to do. On six days work is to be done, but the seventh day is to be a holy day for you, a Shabbat of complete rest in honor of ADONAI. Whoever does any work on it is to be put to death. You are not to kindle a fire in any of your homes on Shabbat."

Leviticus 19:1-3
ADONAI said to Moshe, "Speak to the entire community of Isra'el; tell them, 'You people are to be holy because I, ADONAI your God, am holy. Every one of you is to revere his father and mother, and you are to keep my Shabbats; I am ADONAI your God." (See also, Leviticus 19:30 and 26:2).

Leviticus 23:3 (Maimonides RP154)
Work is to be done on six days; but the seventh day is a Shabbat of complete rest, a holy convocation; you are not to do any kind of work; it is a Shabbat for ADONAI, even in your homes.

Numbers 28:9-10 (Maimonides RP41; Chinuch C402)
On Shabbat offer two male lambs in their first year and without defect, with one gallon of fine flour as a grain offering, mixed with olive oil, and its drink offering. This is the burnt offering for every Shabbat, in addition to the regular burnt offering and its drink offering.

Deuteronomy 5:12-15
Observe the day of Shabbat, to set it apart as holy, as ADONAI your God ordered you to do. You have six days to labor and do all your work, but the seventh day is a Shabbat for ADONAI your God. On it you are not to do any kind of work—not you, your son or your daughter, not your male or female slave, not your ox, your donkey or any of your other livestock, and not the foreigner staying with you inside the gates to your property—so that your male and female servants can rest just as you do. You are to remember that you were a slave in the land of Egypt, and ADONAI your God brought you out from there with a strong hand and an outstretched arm. Therefore ADONAI your God has ordered you to keep the day of Shabbat.

Isaiah 56:1-7
Here is what ADONAI says: "Observe justice, do what is right, for my salvation is close to coming, my righteousness to being revealed. Happy is the person who does this, anyone who grasps it firmly, who keeps Shabbat and does not profane it, and keeps himself from doing any evil. A foreigner joining ADONAI should not say, "ADONAI will separate me from his people"; likewise the eunuch should not say, "I am only a dried-up tree." For here is what ADONAI says: "As for the eunuchs who keep my Shabbats, who choose what pleases me and hold fast to my covenant: in my house, within my walls, I will give them power and a name greater than sons and daughters; I will give him an everlasting name that will not be cut off. And the foreigners who join themselves to ADONAI to serve him, to love the name of ADONAI, and to be his workers, all who keep Shabbat and do not profane it, and hold fast to my covenant, I will bring them to my holy mountain and make them joyful in my house of prayer; their burnt offerings and sacrifices will be accepted on my altar; for my house will be called a house of prayer for all peoples."

160

Isaiah 58:13-14

If you hold back your foot on Shabbat from pursuing your own interests on my holy day; if you call Shabbat a delight, ADONAI's holy day, worth honoring; then honor it by not doing your usual things or pursuing your interests or speaking about them. If you do, you will find delight in ADONAI—I will make you ride on the heights of the land and feed you with the heritage of your ancestor Ya'akov, for the mouth of ADONAI has spoken.

Matthew 12:1-8

One Shabbat during that time, Yeshua was walking through some wheat fields. His talmidim were hungry, so they began picking heads of grain and eating them. On seeing this, the P'rushim said to him, "Look! Your talmidim are violating Shabbat!" But he said to them, "Haven't you ever read what David did when he and those with him were hungry? He entered the House of God and ate the Bread of the Presence!"—which was prohibited, both to him and to his companions; it is permitted only to the cohanim. Or haven't you read in the Torah that on Shabbat the cohanim profane Shabbat and yet are blameless? I tell you, there is in this place something greater than the Temple! If you knew what 'I want compassion rather than animal-sacrifice' meant, you would not condemn the innocent. For the Son of Man is Lord of Shabbat!"

Hebrews 4:2-11

... for Good News has also been proclaimed to us, just as it was to them. But the message they heard didn't do them any good, because those who heard it did not combine it with trust. For it is we who have trusted who enter the rest. It is just as he said, "And in my anger, I swore that they would not enter my rest." He swore this even though his works have been in existence since the founding of the universe. For there is a place where it is said, concerning the seventh day, "And God rested on the seventh day from all his works." And once more, our present text says, "They will not enter my rest." Therefore, since it still remains for some to enter it, and those who received the Good News earlier did not enter, he again fixes a certain day, "Today," saying through David, so long afterwards, in the text already given, "Today, if you hear God's voice, don't harden your hearts." For if Y'hoshua had given them rest, God would not have spoken later of another "day." So there remains a Shabbat-keeping for God's people. For the one who has entered God's rest has also rested from his own works, as God did from his. Therefore, let us do our best to enter that rest; so that no one will fall short because of the same kind of disobedience.

Supportive Scriptures

Isaiah 66:23-24
Matthew 12:9-13
Mark 2:23-28, 3:1-5
Luke 6:6-10, 13:10-17, 14:1-6
John 5:8-17, 7:22-24

Commentary

The Sabbath was first described in <u>Genesis 2:2-3</u> as the seventh day that God rested and declared holy, following the six days of creation. Later, God commanded the Israelites to keep the Sabbath as a day to rest, refrain from work, and conduct a holy convocation (<u>Leviticus 23:3</u>).[83] He also made the Sabbath applicable to Gentiles—not as a commandment—but as a source of blessing (<u>Isaiah 56:1-7</u>). My belief is, therefore, that keeping the seventh day Sabbath is law for the Jew and a blessing for the Gentile.[84] Conversely, not to keep the Sabbath is sin for the Jew and a blessing lost for the Gentile. In the New Covenant Scriptures, <u>Hebrews 4:1-11</u> compares "Sabbath rest" with "spiritual rest" that is received through having faith in Messiah Yeshua; that, of course, is applicable to Jew and non-Jew alike.

Since rest is the cessation of work, it is important to know the kind of work that is prohibited on the Sabbath. <u>Exodus 23:12</u> provides part of the answer, for if we are to work six days of the week and rest on the seventh, the work referred to must be ordinary work of the kind in which we engage for our livelihood and sustenance.[85] This would seem to mean that, on the Sabbath, carpentry is forbidden for the carpenter and cooking is forbidden for the cook, leaving open the possibility that such activities might be engaged in by persons who do them for pure enjoyment or recreation. Some would say that it is not so, because <u>Isaiah 58:13-14</u> prohibits our pursuing personal interests on the Sabbath. I do not interpret the Scripture that way; I believe it is warning us away from pursuing interests that are at odds with God's interests and from doing usual things that would detract from making the Sabbath day special. So, for example, if immersing ourselves in outdoor nature adds to our *Shabbat shalom,* the fact that we find it interesting and pleasurable should not render it a prohibited activity. On the other hand, we should probably not use the Sabbath to continue our methodical study of birds that we began earlier in the week (restful though it may be) because then we would not be treating the day as special. Such decisions are personal and should be resolved through communion with the Holy Spirit.

I would be remiss were I not to mention that the rabbinical understanding of what constitutes work includes things that are creative, the reason being that when God rested on the seventh day, He rested from "creating." That is why the rabbis forbid Sabbath activities such as writing and composing. It is also why the Pharisees in the First Century objected to Yeshua healing on the Sabbath (see <u>Luke</u> supra); healing and performing miracles was considered creative, and therefore a violation of the Sabbath (healing to save a life has always been permitted as an exception).

Messianic Judaism follows Yeshua's example in desiring to see healings and other miracles occur on the Sabbath, and we therefore have no hesitation in "laying on of hands" and praying for healing. Nor do we hesitate to write down godly inspirations we may receive, or do other things

---

83 See also <u>Isaiah 66:23-24</u> and <u>Hebrews 10:24-25</u>.

84 That notwithstanding, it is my belief that the *k'rov Yisrael* gentile who dwells as a *"ger"* in the midst of Israel is likewise obligated to keep the Sabbath. Evidence of this is that the double portion of Manna given prior to the Sabbath in the wilderness (<u>Exodus 16:10-21</u>) applied to the mixed multitude as well as to Israel (see also, <u>Exodus 20:10</u>; <u>Deuteronomy 5:14</u>).

85 The Orthodox Rabbinical community goes beyond this by adhering to a complex set of rules and a list of prohibited activities that are derived from the Babylonian *Talmud (Shab. 75a).*

to make the Sabbath a delight rather than a burden. When God looked over what He had made, declared it "good" and later rested and gave us a Sabbath of rest as well, He was not supposing that we were engaged in creating things the previous six days and therefore needed to stop. He was summoning us to a day of rest in Him by reflecting on His Creation and affirmatively seeking His power for our restoration. Our position on this is that we may be creative on the Sabbath so long as it is not our usual work, and is an appropriate reflection of Him, and a reminder that we were created in His image.

There is a category of ordinary work that is clearly not forbidden on the Sabbath and that should not be withheld. It is work that is ministerial, because it is analogous to the work of the *cohanim* who were required to conduct Sabbath sacrifices in the Temple as part of their priestly duties.

Modern wider Judaism is split on works of compassion—e.g. works that heal or maintain safety, but there is uniform agreement that working to save a life is permitted. Messianic Judaism, in contrast, follows the example of Yeshua, and considers that works of compassion are not only permitted on the Sabbath, but are encouraged.

A rare category of work that is permitted on the Sabbath is work that must be undertaken so as not to violate another commandment of God. Thus a *mohel* is permitted to circumcise on the eighth day after the birth of a Jewish boy even if it falls on a *Shabbat*. These exceptions to the *Mitzvah* are generally accepted within Messianic Judaism and Judaism broadly; other possible exceptions need to be discerned through prayerfully seeking guidance from the *Ruach HaKodesh*.

Abstaining from work on the Sabbath is not only an act of obedience—it is an act of faith for, by so doing, we are trusting God to provide for us. An example of this is found in Exodus 16:22-30, where the Israelites had to trust God to provide them with food during the *Shabbat* when they were not allowed to gather manna.

Commentary by Daniel C. Juster

The issue of Sabbath is paradoxical for Gentiles:

1. The Sabbath, as a day of rest on the seventh day, is never enjoined upon Gentiles in the New Covenant. Rabbinical Judaism defined it as part of Jewish-specific law, and part of God's Covenant with Israel—not universal law which is required of all people (i.e. the Noachide laws).

2. The Sabbath principle is enjoined upon all, at least as a "rest of faith." (Hebrews 4:2-11).

3. The passages in Isaiah 56 and 66 indicate a more universal observance in the Age to Come than in the Mosaic age. Isaiah 56 may only be referring to Gentiles who are called to live among the Jewish people, but Isaiah 66 may well imply a world-wide Sabbath day.

4. In the light of the passages in Isaiah, it is certainly appropriate for Gentiles to keep one day in seven as unto the Lord when it is practically possible within their cultures (remember that there

was no seven-day week in the Roman world at the time the N.T. was being written). While it is appropriate for Gentiles in Messiah to take the seventh day as their day of rest (and possibly as an eschatological sign of the Age to Come), this does not mean that all Christian Congregations ought to gather for worship on Saturday. Sunday celebrations of the day of Resurrection are certainly appropriate and there is, in this age, a choice to make this the day of rest also, or to add Sabbath rest on the seventh day to the corporate gathering on Sunday, or move the Christian gathering to the seventh day and treat it as a day of rest as well. What is culturally feasible and best is an important factor in the choice, and is within the purview of New Covenant liberty.

Classical Commentators

Maimonides comments very little. HaChinuch states that the underlying meaning of the *mitzvah* to not work on the Sabbath is to refrain from the work of our normal occupations. In our rest, we are to remember each day of God's creation of the world as well as the miracle of Israel's exodus from Egypt. HaChinuch and Meir state that the sages list 39 activities that are prohibited on the Sabbath (Shab. 73a); these are intended as a fence around the *Torah*. Of the three classical commentators, Meir is the only one who states that it is forbidden for a Jew to ask a Gentile to do work in his behalf on the Sabbath, and he also states that doing work on the Sabbath is permitted if it is to save a human life. None of the traditional *mitzvot* addresses the requirement of Leviticus 23:3 that the Sabbath should be a day of "holy convocation."

Special mention is made of Maimonides' RN322 and HaChinuch's C114, in which they profess that we must not inflict punishment on *Shabbat.* the Scripture upon which they rely is Exodus 35:3, which states:

> *"You are not to kindle a fire in any of your homes on Shabbat."*

The logic of relying on this seemingly inapplicable Scripture is that one of the ways of punishing according to the Mosaic Law is burning.

NCLA: JMm JFm KMm KFm GMr GFr

D2. Leaving Our Homes to Work on the Sabbath.

We are not to leave our homes with the intention of doing work on the Sabbath.

This precept is derived from His Word (blessed be He):

Key Scriptures

Exodus 16:29 (Maimonides RN321; Meir MN7; Chinuch C24)
Look, ADONAI has given you the Shabbat. This is why he is providing bread for two days on the sixth day. Each of you, stay where you are; no one is to leave his place on the seventh day.

Hebrews 4:10-11
For the one who has entered God's rest has also rested from his own works, as God did from his. Therefore, let us do our best to enter that rest; so that no one will fall short because of the same kind of disobedience.

Commentary

The commandment in Exodus 16:29 that is reflected in this *Mitzvah* was given to the Israelites after they tried to gather manna on the Sabbath despite God having provided a double portion for them the day before. In today's context, it calls for us to trust that God will provide sufficiently for us six days of the week, so that we should not even contemplate leaving our homes in order to work on the Sabbath. In my opinion, this is not a requirement that we stay in our house or limit the distance that we may travel, but rather it is a requirement that we examine why we are leaving our house, lest it be to go to work.

In addition to other considerations, it is important to remember that God first established the seventh day as holy prior to the Mosaic Covenant, and at a time when there was, as of yet, no Israel (Genesis 2:2-3). Later, speaking through the prophet Isaiah, God said that non-Jews who keep His Sabbaths will receive blessings for doing so (Isaiah 56:1-7). Further confirmation for this is found in Hebrews 4:1-11 which compares Sabbath rest with spiritual rest that comes from faith in Messiah. This is not to say that keeping the seventh day Sabbath is required for Gentile believers in this age. We again note the clearly stated passages in Romans 14, Galatians 5, Colossians 2, and others, that relieve Gentiles of Sabbath responsibility.

Classical Commentators

Maimonides interprets his *mitzvah* so as to prohibit travel on the Sabbath, further than from one's home to across an Israelite's campsite in the desert. Meir's concept in his *mitzvah* is similar, but he describes the maximum permissible travel as the distance across a small town. HaChinuch says the Sabbath limit is three parasangs away from the city, and he explains the prohibition against traveling further by his understanding that, after God created the world, He rested in the vicinity of His creation; HaChinuch's opinion is that we should, therefore, rest in our place as well.

NCLA: **JMm JFm KMm KFm GMr GFr**

D3. Keeping the Sabbath Day Holy.

We are to keep the Sabbath Day holy—set apart for God.

This precept is derived from His Word (blessed be He):

Key Scriptures

Exodus 20:8 (Maimonides RP155; Meir MP19; Chinuch C31)
Remember the day, Shabbat, to set it apart for God.

Exodus 31:14-15
Therefore you are to keep my Shabbat, because it is set apart for you. Everyone who treats it as ordinary must be put to death; for whoever does any work on it is to be cut off from his people. On six days work will get done; but the seventh day is Shabbat, for complete rest, set apart for ADONAI. Whoever does any work on the day of Shabbat must be put to death.

Exodus 35:1-2
Moshe assembled the whole community of the people of Isra'el and said to them, "These are the things which ADONAI has ordered you to do. On six days work is to be done, but the seventh day is to be a holy day for you, a Shabbat of complete rest in honor of ADONAI. Whoever does any work on it is to be put to death.

Deuteronomy 5:12
Observe the day of Shabbat, to set it apart as holy, as ADONAI your God ordered you to do.

Isaiah 56:1-7
Here is what ADONAI says: "Observe justice, do what is right, for my salvation is close to coming, my righteousness to being revealed." Happy is the person who does this, anyone who grasps it firmly, who keeps Shabbat and does not profane it, and keeps himself from doing any evil. A foreigner joining ADONAI should not say, "ADONAI will separate me from his people"; likewise the eunuch should not say, "I am only a dried-up tree." For here is what ADONAI says: "As for the eunuchs who keep my Shabbats, who choose what pleases me and hold fast to my covenant: in my house, within my walls, I will give them power and a name greater than sons and daughters; I will give him an everlasting name that will not be cut off. And the foreigners who join themselves to ADONAI to serve him, to love the name of ADONAI, and to be his workers, all who keep Shabbat and do not profane it, and hold fast to my covenant, I will bring them to my holy mountain and make them joyful in my house of prayer; their burnt offerings and sacrifices will be accepted on my altar; for my house will be called a house of prayer for all peoples.

Mark 1:21-22
They entered K'far-Nachum, and on Shabbat Yeshua went into the synagogue and began teaching. They were amazed at the way he taught, for he did not instruct them like the Torah-teachers but as one who had authority himself.

Mark 2:24-28
The P'rushim said to him, "Look! Why are they violating Shabbat?" He said to them, "Haven't you ever read what David did when he and those with him were hungry and needed food? He entered the House of God when Evyatar was cohen gadol and ate the Bread of the Presence,"—which is forbidden for anyone to eat but the cohanim—"and even gave some to his companions." Then he said to them, "Shabbat was made for mankind, not mankind for Shabbat; So the Son of Man is Lord even of Shabbat."

Luke 4:16-21
Now when he went to Natzeret, where he had been brought up, on Shabbat he went to the synagogue as usual. He stood up to read, and he was given the scroll of the prophet Yesha'yahu. Unrolling the scroll, he found the place where it was written, "The Spirit of ADONAI is upon me; therefore he has anointed me to announce Good News to the poor; he has sent me to proclaim freedom for the imprisoned and renewed sight for the blind, to release those who have been crushed, to proclaim a year of the favor of ADONAI." After closing the scroll and returning it to the shammash, he sat down; and the eyes of everyone in the synagogue were fixed on him. He started to speak to them: "Today, as you heard it read, this passage of the Tanakh was fulfilled!"

Acts 17:1-3
After passing through Amphipolis and Apollonia, Sha'ul and Sila came to Thessalonica, where there was a synagogue. According to his usual practice, Sha'ul went in; and on three Shabbats he gave them drashes from the Tanakh, explaining and proving that the Messiah had to suffer and rise again from the dead, and that "this Yeshua whom I am proclaiming to you is the Messiah.

Commentary

Scripture speaks of keeping the Sabbath Day holy by abstaining from work, resting physically, and assembling for a holy convocation. Beyond those, it is well to remember that keeping the Sabbath Day holy means treating it as special, and setting it apart for God. That does not mean that we cannot engage in some things that are ordinary or recreational, but we need to use good judgment and maintain a Sabbath consciousness.

One way of making the Sabbath special is to keep track of when it begins and when it ends. Jewish practice ushers in the Sabbath on Friday evening (before sundown) with the lighting of candles, *Kiddush,* prayer in either the home or synagogue, and enjoying a festive meal. There are traditionally three daytime services *(Shachrit, Musaf, and Minchah)* held on *Shabbat*, and the *Shabbat* is ended with *Havdalah* at sundown, after which begins the first day of the next work-week (albeit after sundown) with the evening service of *ma'ariv.*

167

Within the wider Jewish community (and especially within the Orthodox community) there are other ways of making the Sabbath special as well. From the original *Torah* command to not light fires, Orthodox tradition has extended the uniqueness of the day to not turning on or off electric appliances including lights, and not driving cars (spark plugs make fire). In the same way, *Torah* is extended to not carrying things on one's person outside of one's home (not even a bible or *siddur* to the synagogue), and not spending money (if one does not carry it, one cannot spend it). In some communities, exceptions are made for those in the military and life-saving services.

We who recognize the New Covenant have an additional appreciation for the Sabbath's holiness because of what Hebrews 4:4-11 says about it:

> *"For there is a place where it is said, concerning the seventh day, "And God rested on the seventh day from all his works." And once more, our present text says, "They will not enter my rest." Therefore, since it still remains for some to enter it, and those who received the Good News earlier did not enter, he again fixes a certain day, "Today," saying through David, so long afterwards, in the text already given, "Today, if you hear God's voice, don't harden your hearts." For if Y'hoshua had given them rest, God would not have spoken later of another "day." So there remains a Shabbat-keeping for God's people. For the one who has entered God's rest has also rested from his own works, as God did from his. Therefore, let us do our best to enter that rest; so that no one will fall short because of the same kind of disobedience."*

Classical Commentators

Maimonides states that the meaning of Exodus 20:8 is that we are to recite words proclaiming the greatness of the Sabbath day—the *Kiddush* at the beginning, and the *Havdalah* at the end. Meir agrees with Maimonides about hallowing the Sabbath with those particular words, and adds that we must recite the *Kiddush* prayer over either wine or bread. He also cites Isaiah 58:13 in calling the Sabbath a delight, and states that we must honor God by washing our hands and face with warm water, dressing in clean clothing, and eating a minimum of three meals. HaChinuch is in agreement about hallowing the Sabbath with words. He states that the *Kiddush* should be said over wine, but that the sages have allowed it to be said over bread if a man delights in bread more than wine. That notwithstanding, HaChinuch maintains that *Havdalah* must be conducted over wine.

NCLA: JMm JFm KMm KFm GMr GFr

D4. Resting from Work and Assembling on God's Annual Sabbaths.

We are to rest, refrain from work, and assemble on God's annual Sabbaths; these are (1) the first (including Pesach) and (2) seventh day of Matzah, (3) Shavuot, (4) Yom T'ruah (Rosh HaShanah), (5) Yom Kippur, (6) the first day of Sukkot, and (7) Sh'mini Atzeret.

This precept is derived from His Word (blessed be He):

Key Scriptures

First Day of Matzah (Unleavened Bread)—Pesach

Exodus 12 :3
Speak to all the assembly of Isra'el and say, 'On the tenth day of this month, each man is to take a lamb or kid for his family, one per household—

Exodus 12:16 (Maimonides RP159, RN323; Meir MP25; Chinuch C297-298)
On the first and seventh days, you are to have an assembly set aside for God. On these days no work is to be done, except what each must do to prepare his food; you may do only that.

Exodus 23:14-17 (Maimonides RP52; Chinuch C88)
Three times a year, you are to observe a festival for me. Keep the festival of matzah: for seven days, as I ordered you, you are to eat matzah at the time determined in the month of Aviv; for it was in that month that you left Egypt. No one is to appear before me empty-handed. Next, the festival of harvest, the firstfruits of your efforts sowing in the field; and last, the festival of ingathering, at the end of the year, when you gather in from the fields the results of your efforts. Three times a year all your men are to appear before the Lord, ADONAI.

Leviticus 23:5-7 (Maimonides RP159, RN323; Meir MP25, MN147; Chinuch C297-298)
In the first month, on the fourteenth day of the month, between sundown and complete darkness, comes Pesach for ADONAI. On the fifteenth day of the same month is the festival of matzah; for seven days you are to eat matzah. On the first day you are to have a holy convocation; don't do any kind of ordinary work.

Numbers 28:17-18
On the fifteenth day of the month is to be a feast. Matzah is to be eaten for seven days. The first day is to be a holy convocation: do not do any kind of ordinary work;

Deuteronomy 16:16a (Maimonides RP53; Chinuch C489)
Three times a year all your men are to appear in the presence of ADONAI your God in the place which he will choose—at the festival of matzah, at the festival of Shavu'ot and at the festival of Sukkot.

Matthew 26:26-28

While they were eating, Yeshua took a piece of matzah, made the b'rakhah, broke it, gave it to the talmidim and said, "Take! Eat! This is my body!" Also he took a cup of wine, made the b'rakhah, and gave it to them, saying, "All of you, drink from it! For this is my blood, which ratifies the New Covenant, my blood shed on behalf of many, so that they may have their sins forgiven.

Mark 14:12-25

On the first day for matzah, when they slaughtered the lamb for Pesach, Yeshua's talmidim asked him, "Where do you want us to go and prepare your Seder?" He sent two of his talmidim with these instructions: "Go into the city, and a man carrying a jar of water will meet you. Follow him; and whichever house he enters, tell him that the Rabbi says, 'Where is the guest room for me, where I am to eat the Pesach meal with my talmidim?' He will show you a large room upstairs, furnished and ready. Make the preparations there." The talmidim went off, came to the city and found things just as he had told them they would be; and they prepared the Seder. When evening came, Yeshua arrived with the Twelve. As they were reclining and eating, Yeshua said, "Yes! I tell you that one of you is going to betray me." They became upset and began asking him, one after the other, "You don't mean me, do you?" "It's one of the Twelve," he said to them, "someone dipping matzah in the dish with me. For the Son of Man will die, just as the Tanakh says he will; but woe to that man by whom the Son of Man is betrayed! It would have been better for him had he never been born!" While they were eating, Yeshua took a piece of matzah, made the b'rakhah, broke it, gave it to them and said, "Take it! This is my body." Also he took a cup of wine, made the b'rakhah, and gave it to them; and they all drank. He said to them, "This is my blood, which ratifies the New Covenant, my blood shed on behalf of many people. Yes! I tell you, I will not drink this 'fruit of the vine' again until the day I drink new wine in the Kingdom of God."

Luke 22:7-20

Then came the day of matzah, on which the Passover lamb had to be killed. Yeshua sent Kefa and Yochanan, instructing them, "Go and prepare our Seder, so we can eat." They asked him, "Where do you want us to prepare it?" He told them, "As you're going into the city, a man carrying a jar of water will meet you. Follow him into the house he enters, and say to its owner, 'The Rabbi says to you, "Where is the guest room, where I am to eat the Pesach meal with my talmidim?"' He will show you a large room upstairs already furnished; make the preparations there." They went and found things just as Yeshua had told them they would be, and they prepared for the Seder. When the time came, Yeshua and the emissaries reclined at the table, and he said to them, "I have really wanted so much to celebrate this Seder with you before I die! For I tell you, it is certain that I will not celebrate it again until it is given its full meaning in the Kingdom of God." Then, taking a cup of wine, he made the b'rakhah and said, "Take this and share it among yourselves. For I tell you that from now on, I will not drink the 'fruit of the vine' until the Kingdom of God comes." Also, taking a piece of matzah, he made the b'rakhah, broke it, gave it to them and said, "This is my body, which is being given for you; do this in memory of me." He did the same with the cup after the meal, saying, "This cup is the New Covenant, ratified by my blood, which is being poured out for you.

170

John 2:13
It was almost time for the festival of Pesach in Y'hudah, so Yeshua went up to Yerushalayim.

1 Corinthians 5:7-8
Get rid of the old hametz, so that you can be a new batch of dough, because in reality you are unleavened. For our Pesach lamb, the Messiah, has been sacrificed. So let us celebrate the Seder not with leftover hametz, the hametz of wickedness and evil, but with the matzah of purity and truth.

Seventh Day of Matzah (Unleavened Bread)

Exodus 12:16 (Maimonides RN324)
On the first and seventh days, you are to have an assembly set aside for God. On these days no work is to be done, except what each must do to prepare his food; you may do only that.

Exodus 23:14-17 (Maimonides RP52; Chinuch C88)
Three times a year, you are to observe a festival for me. Keep the festival of matzah: for seven days, as I ordered you, you are to eat matzah at the time determined in the month of Aviv; for it was in that month that you left Egypt. No one is to appear before me empty-handed. Next, the festival of harvest, the firstfruits of your efforts sowing in the field; and last, the festival of ingathering, at the end of the year, when you gather in from the fields the results of your efforts. Three times a year all your men are to appear before the Lord, ADONAI.

Leviticus 23:8 (Maimonides RP160, RN324; Meir MP27, MN148; Chinuch C300-301)
Bring an offering made by fire to ADONAI for seven days. On the seventh day is a holy convocation; do not do any kind of ordinary work.

Numbers 28:25
On the seventh day you are to have a holy convocation; do not do any kind of ordinary work.

Deuteronomy 16:16a (Maimonides RP53; Chinuch C489)
Three times a year all your men are to appear in the presence of ADONAI your God in the place which he will choose—at the festival of matzah, at the festival of Shavu'ot and at the festival of Sukkot.

1 Corinthians 5:7-8
Get rid of the old hametz, so that you can be a new batch of dough, because in reality you are unleavened. For our Pesach lamb, the Messiah, has been sacrificed. So let us celebrate the Seder not with leftover hametz, the hametz of wickedness and evil, but with the matzah of purity and truth.

Shavuot

Exodus 23:14-17 (Maimonides RP52; Chinuch C88)
Three times a year, you are to observe a festival for me. Keep the festival of matzah: for seven days, as I ordered you, you are to eat matzah at the time determined in the month of Aviv; for it was in that month that you left Egypt. No one is to appear before me empty-handed. Next,

the festival of harvest, the firstfruits of your efforts sowing in the field; and last, the festival of ingathering, at the end of the year, when you gather in from the fields the results of your efforts. Three times a year all your men are to appear before the Lord, ADONAI.

<u>Leviticus 23:10, 15-16</u>
Tell the people of Isra'el, 'After you enter the land I am giving you and harvest its ripe crops, you are to bring a sheaf of the firstfruits of your harvest to the cohen... From the day after the day of rest—that is, from the day you bring the sheaf for waving—you are to count seven full weeks, until the day after the seventh week; you are to count fifty days; and then you are to present a new grain offering to ADONAI.

<u>Leviticus 23:21</u> (Maimonides RP162, RN325; Meir MP28, MN149; Chinuch C308-309)
On the same day, you are to call a holy convocation; do not do any kind of ordinary work; this is a permanent regulation through all your generations, no matter where you live.

<u>Numbers 28:26</u>
On the day of the firstfruits, when you bring a new grain offering to ADONAI in your feast of Shavuot, you are to have a holy convocation; do not do any kind of ordinary work;

<u>Deuteronomy 16:9-10</u>
You are to count seven weeks; you are to begin counting seven weeks from the time you first put your sickle to the standing grain. You are to observe the festival of Shavu'ot [weeks] for ADONAI your God with a voluntary offering, which you are to give in accordance with the degree to which ADONAI your God has prospered you.

<u>Deuteronomy 16:16a</u> (Maimonides RP53; Chinuch C489)
Three times a year all your men are to appear in the presence of ADONAI your God in the place which he will choose—at the festival of matzah, at the festival of Shavu'ot and at the festival of Sukkot.

<u>Luke 24:49</u>
Now I am sending forth upon you what my Father promised, so stay here in the city until you have been equipped with power from above.

<u>Acts 1:3-5</u>
After his death he showed himself to them and gave many convincing proofs that he was alive. During a period of forty days they saw him, and he spoke with them about the Kingdom of God. At one of these gatherings, he instructed them not to leave Yerushalayim but to wait for "what the Father promised, which you heard about from me. For Yochanan used to immerse people in water; but in a few days, you will be immersed in the Ruach HaKodesh!"

<u>Acts 2:1-5</u>
The festival of Shavu'ot arrived, and the believers all gathered together in one place. Suddenly there came a sound from the sky like the roar of a violent wind, and it filled the whole house where they were sitting. Then they saw what looked like tongues of fire, which separated and

came to rest on each one of them. They were all filled with the Ruach HaKodesh and began to talk in different languages, as the Spirit enabled them to speak. Now there were staying in Yerushalayim religious Jews from every nation under heaven.

Yom T'ruah (Rosh Hashanah)

Leviticus 23:24-25 (Maimonides RP163, RN326; Meir MP29, MN150; Chinuch C310-311)
Tell the people of Isra'el, 'In the seventh month, the first of the month is to be for you a day of complete rest for remembering, a holy convocation announced with blasts on the shofar. Do not do any kind of ordinary work, and bring an offering made by fire to ADONAI.'

Numbers 29:1
In the seventh month, on the first day of the month, you are to have a holy convocation; do not do any kind of ordinary work; it is a day of blowing the shofar for you.

Matthew 3:11
It's true that I am immersing you in water so that you might turn from sin to God; but the one coming after me is more powerful than I—I'm not worthy even to carry his sandals—and he will immerse you in the Ruach HaKodesh and in fire.

Matthew 4:17
From that time on, Yeshua began proclaiming, "Turn from your sins to God, for the Kingdom of Heaven is near!"

Mark 1:3-4
The voice of someone crying out: 'In the desert prepare the way for ADONAI! Make straight paths for him!' So it was that Yochanan the Immerser appeared in the desert, proclaiming an immersion involving turning to God from sin in order to be forgiven.

John 1:23
He [John] answered in the words of Yesha'yahu the prophet, "I am The voice of someone crying out: 'In the desert make the way of ADONAI straight!'"

Act 3:19
Therefore, repent and turn to God, so that your sins may be erased;

Yom Kippur

Leviticus 16:1-34 (Maimonides RP49, 165; Chinuch C15)
ADONAI spoke with Moshe after the death of Aharon's two sons, when they tried to sacrifice before ADONAI and died; ADONAI said to Moshe, "Tell your brother Aharon not to come at just any time into the Holy Place beyond the curtain, in front of the ark-cover which is on the ark, so that he will not die; because I appear in the cloud over the ark-cover. Here is how Aharon is to enter the Holy Place: with a young bull as a sin offering and a ram as a burnt offering. He is to put on the holy linen tunic, have the linen shorts next to his bare flesh, have the linen

173

*sash wrapped around him, and be wearing the linen turban—they are the holy garments. He
is to bathe his body in water and put them on. He is to take from the community of the people
of Isra'el two male goats for a sin offering and one ram for a burnt offering. Aharon is to
present the bull for the sin offering which is for himself and make atonement for himself and his
household. He is to take the two goats and place them before ADONAI at the entrance to the tent
of meeting. Then Aharon is to cast lots for the two goats, one lot for ADONAI and the other for
'Az'azel. Aharon is to present the goat whose lot fell to ADONAI and offer it as a sin offering.
But the goat whose lot fell to 'Az'azel is to be presented alive to ADONAI to be used for making
atonement over it by sending it away into the desert for 'Az'azel. Aharon is to present the bull
of the sin offering for himself; he will make atonement for himself and his household; he is to
slaughter the bull of the sin offering which is for himself. He is to take a censer full of burning
coals from the altar before ADONAI and, with his hands full of ground, fragrant incense, bring
it inside the curtain. He is to put the incense on the fire before ADONAI, so that the cloud from
the incense will cover the ark-cover which is over the testimony, in order that he not die. He is
to take some of the bull's blood and sprinkle it with his finger on the ark-cover toward the east;
and in front of the ark-cover he is to sprinkle some of the blood with his finger seven times. Next,
he is to slaughter the goat of the sin offering which is for the people, bring its blood inside the
curtain and do with its blood as he did with the bull's blood, sprinkling it on the ark-cover and in
front of the ark-cover. He will make atonement for the Holy Place because of the uncleannesses
of the people of Isra'el and because of their transgressions—all their sins; and he is to do the
same for the tent of meeting which is there with them right in the middle of their uncleannesses.
No one is to be present in the tent of meeting from the time he enters the Holy Place to make
atonement until the time he comes out, having made atonement for himself, for his household and
for the entire community of Isra'el. Then he is to go out to the altar that is before ADONAI and
make atonement for it; he is to take some of the bull's blood and some of the goat's blood and
put it on all the horns of the altar. He is to sprinkle some of the blood on it with his finger seven
times, thus purifying it and setting it apart from the uncleannesses of the people of Isra'el. When
he has finished atoning for the Holy Place, the tent of meeting and the altar, he is to present the
live goat. Aharon is to lay both his hands on the head of the live goat and confess over it all the
transgressions, crimes and sins of the people of Isra'el; he is to put them on the head of the goat
and then send it away into the desert with a man appointed for the purpose. The goat will bear
all their transgressions away to some isolated place, and he is to let the goat go in the desert.
Aharon is to go back into the tent of meeting, where he is to remove the linen garments he put
on when he entered the Holy Place, and he is to leave them there. Then he is to bathe his body
in water in a holy place, put on his other clothes, come out and offer his burnt offering and the
burnt offering of the people, thus making atonement for himself and for the people. He is to make
the fat of the sin offering go up in smoke on the altar. The man who let go the goat for 'Az'azel
is to wash his clothes and bathe his body in water; afterwards, he may return to the camp.
"The bull for the sin offering and the goat for the sin offering, whose blood was brought in to
make atonement in the Holy Place, is to be carried outside the camp; there they are to burn up
completely their hides, meat and dung. The person burning them is to wash his clothes and bathe
his body in water; afterwards, he may return to the camp. It is to be a permanent regulation
for you that on the tenth day of the seventh month you are to deny yourselves and not do any
kind of work, both the citizen and the foreigner living with you. For on this day, atonement
will be made for you to purify you; you will be clean before ADONAI from all your sins. It*

174

is a Shabbat of complete rest for you, and you are to deny yourselves. "This is a permanent regulation. The cohen anointed and consecrated to be cohen in his father's place will make the atonement; he will put on the linen garments, the holy garments; he will make atonement for the Especially Holy Place; he will make atonement for the tent of meeting and the altar; and he will make atonement for the cohanim and for all the people of the community. This is a permanent regulation for you, to make atonement for the people of Isra'el because of all their sins once a year." Moshe did as ADONAI had ordered him.

Leviticus 23:27-32 (Maimonides RN329; Meir MP31, MN151; Chinuch C315, C317)
The tenth day of this seventh month is Yom-Kippur; you are to have a holy convocation, you are to deny yourselves, and you are to bring an offering made by fire to ADONAI. You are not to do any kind of work on that day, because it is Yom-Kippur, to make atonement for you before ADONAI your God. Anyone who does not deny himself on that day is to be cut off from his people; and anyone who does any kind of work on that day, I will destroy from among his people. You are not to do any kind of work; it is a permanent regulation through all your generations, no matter where you live. It will be for you a Shabbat of complete rest, and you are to deny yourselves; you are to rest on your Shabbat from evening the ninth day of the month until the following evening.

Numbers 29:7
On the tenth day of this seventh month you are to have a holy convocation. You are to deny yourselves, and you are not to do any kind of work;

Romans 12:1
I exhort you, therefore, brothers, in view of God's mercies, to offer yourselves as a sacrifice, living and set apart for God. This will please him; it is the logical "Temple worship" for you.

Hebrews 10:11-14
Now every cohen stands every day doing his service, offering over and over the same sacrifices, which can never take away sins. But this one, after he had offered for all time a single sacrifice for sins, sat down at the right hand of God, from then on to wait until his enemies be made a footstool for his feet. For by a single offering he has brought to the goal for all time those who are being set apart for God and made holy.

First Day of Sukkot

Exodus 23:14-17 (Maimonides RP52; Chinuch C88)
Three times a year, you are to observe a festival for me. Keep the festival of matzah: for seven days, as I ordered you, you are to eat matzah at the time determined in the month of Aviv; for it was in that month that you left Egypt. No one is to appear before me empty-handed. Next, the festival of harvest, the firstfruits of your efforts sowing in the field; and last, the festival of ingathering, at the end of the year, when you gather in from the fields the results of your efforts. Three times a year all your men are to appear before the Lord, ADONAI.

175

<u>Leviticus 23:34-39</u> (Maimonides RP166, RN327; Meir MP34, MN153; Chinuch C318-319)
Tell the people of Isra'el, 'On the fifteenth day of this seventh month is the feast of Sukkot for seven days to ADONAI. On the first day there is to be a holy convocation; do not do any kind of ordinary work. For seven days you are to bring an offering made by fire to ADONAI; on the eighth day you are to have a holy convocation and bring an offering made by fire to ADONAI ; it is a day of public assembly; do not do any kind of ordinary work. These are the designated times of ADONAI that you are to proclaim as holy convocations and bring an offering made by fire to ADONAI—a burnt offering, a grain offering, a sacrifice and drink offerings, each on its own day—besides the Shabbats of ADONAI, your gifts, all your vows and all your voluntary offerings that you give to ADONAI. But on the fifteenth day of the seventh month, when you have gathered the produce of the land, you are to observe the festival of ADONAI seven days; the first day is to be a complete rest and the eighth day is to be a complete rest.

<u>Numbers 29:12</u>
On the fifteenth day of the seventh month you are to have a holy convocation. You are not to do any kind of ordinary work, and you are to observe a feast to ADONAI seven days.

<u>Deuteronomy 16:16a</u> (Maimonides RP53; Chinuch C489)
Three times a year all your men are to appear in the presence of ADONAI your God in the place which he will choose—at the festival of matzah, at the festival of Shavu'ot and at the festival of Sukkot.

<u>John 7:1-3</u>
After this, Yeshua traveled around in the Galil, intentionally avoiding Y'hudah because the Judeans were out to kill him. But the festival of Sukkot in Y'hudah was near; so his brothers said to him, "Leave here and go into Y'hudah, so that your talmidim can see the miracles you do;"

Sh'mini Atzeret

<u>Exodus 23:14-17</u> (Maimonides RP52; Chinuch C88)
Three times a year, you are to observe a festival for me. Keep the festival of matzah: for seven days, as I ordered you, you are to eat matzah at the time determined in the month of Aviv; for it was in that month that you left Egypt. No one is to appear before me empty-handed. Next, the festival of harvest, the firstfruits of your efforts sowing in the field; and last, the festival of ingathering, at the end of the year, when you gather in from the fields the results of your efforts. Three times a year all your men are to appear before the Lord, ADONAI.

<u>Leviticus 23:34-39</u> (Maimonides RP167, RN328; Meir MP37, MN154; Chinuch C321, C323)
Tell the people of Isra'el, 'On the fifteenth day of this seventh month is the feast of Sukkot for seven days to ADONAI. On the first day there is to be a holy convocation; do not do any kind of ordinary work. For seven days you are to bring an offering made by fire to ADONAI; on the eighth day you are to have a holy convocation and bring an offering made by fire to ADONAI; it is a day of public assembly; do not do any kind of ordinary work. These are the designated times of ADONAI that you are to proclaim as holy convocations and bring an offering made by fire to ADONAI—a burnt offering, a grain offering, a sacrifice and drink offerings, each on its

own day—besides the Shabbats of ADONAI, your gifts, all your vows and all your voluntary offerings that you give to ADONAI. But on the fifteenth day of the seventh month, when you have gathered the produce of the land, you are to observe the festival of ADONAI seven days; the first day is to be a complete rest and the eighth day is to be a complete rest.

<u>Numbers 29:35</u>
On the eighth day you are to have a festive assembly: you are not to do any kind of ordinary work;

<u>Deuteronomy 16:16a</u> (Maimonides RP53; Chinuch C489)
Three times a year all your men are to appear in the presence of ADONAI your God in the place which he will choose—at the festival of matzah, at the festival of Shavu'ot and at the festival of Sukkot.

Commentary

This *Mitzvah* bestows the term "Annual Sabbath" on seven of the annually-occurring "designated times" listed in <u>Leviticus 23</u>. This is because, as in the case of the weekly Sabbath, we are commanded to rest on them, refrain from work, and assemble. Of these however, only one of them—*Yom Kippur*—is actually termed a Sabbath in the Scriptures. Each of these days has its unique theme and reason for being, but because they bear a basic similarity to the weekly Sabbath, the related issues of work, rest, and application to Gentiles will be dealt with here only briefly.

The first and seventh days of the Feast of Unleavened Bread remind us of God's provision and our need to purge leaven (analogized to sin) from our lives (<u>1 Corinthians 5:7-8</u>). Of all the feasts, Passover is the one that has most caught the attention of the Christian Church. This is because of the obvious analogy of the Passover lamb sacrifice to Yeshua's sacrifice, where the blood of each of the sacrifices, saved those who applied it.

The next "designated time" listed on the biblical calendar, *Shavuot,* was historically commanded to the Israelites to commemorate the Spring harvest, but it is relevant to Gentile followers of Yeshua as well, both as an identification with the Jewish People, and also as a memorial of the *Shavuot* day that occurred centuries later, when God made the Holy Spirit available to all of mankind (<u>Acts 2:1-21, 10:45</u>). Christian terminology for this day is "Pentecost."[86] *Shavuot* is unique among the Annual Sabbaths in being the only one that Scripture does not assign a particular date on the lunar calendar. Instead, <u>Leviticus 23:10, 15-16</u> states:

> *"Tell the people of Isra'el, 'After you enter the land I am giving you and harvest its ripe crops, you are to bring a sheaf of the firstfruits of your harvest to the cohen... From the day after the day of rest—that is, from the day you bring the sheaf for waving—you are to count seven full weeks, until the day after the seventh week; you are to count fifty days; and then you are to present a new grain offering to ADONAI."*

This fifty-day count from "the day after the day of rest" (or Sabbath) is known in Jewish practice as "counting the *omer*," and determining which one of several possible Sabbaths is "day zero" of the count is a subject of ongoing dispute that involves two different days that Scripture refers

---

86 According to Jewish tradition, the day subsequently defined as *Shavuot* is also the day on which the *Torah* was given at Mt. Sinai.

to as "firstfruits." The first of these is the one in Leviticus 23:10 which, for clarity, I will refer to as *Yom Habikkurim*.[87] The second occurrence is in Numbers 28:26, where the term is again used, but for *Shavuot*.

Yom T'ruah (day of blowing) is also known as the "Day of Trumpets" or *"Shofarot,"* and as *"Rosh Hashanah"* (head of the year, i.e. New Year) by the Rabbinic community. It is followed ten days later by *Yom Kippur* (Day of Atonement). Although these days were historically commanded to the Israelites, Gentile followers of Yeshua may choose to observe them as well, both to identify with the Jewish People, and also to use as times of personal introspection and repentance that may lead to joining with their Jewish brothers in praying for Israel on *Yom Kippur*. This is especially appropriate when one considers the elevated position of New Covenant believers (both Jews and non-Jews) as priests under Messiah Yeshua (1 Peter 2:5-10; Revelation 1:4-7).

Finally, *Sukkot* is particularly significant for Gentiles, because Scripture prophesies the time when all the Gentile nations on earth will be required to join with Israel in keeping the Feast referred to in Zechariah 14:16-19. This appears to be a nation-to-nation mandate and not directed to individuals.

Although "rest" is not specifically mentioned in the supporting Scriptures for the Feast of Unleavened Bread and for *Shavuot*, it is strongly implied by the requirement that we not work. Also, although in Hebrews 4:2-11 it is the weekly Sabbath rest that is analogized to resting in Messiah, its application to all of the annual Sabbaths is unmistakable.

I am of the view that complying with these Annual Sabbaths by resting, abstaining from work, and assembling, is mandatory for Jews and *K'rovei Yisrael* Gentiles but, with the exception of the Feast of *Sukkot*, is not mandatory for Gentiles generally. That notwithstanding, I believe that blessing comes to Gentiles who keep the Annual Sabbaths, analogous to the blessing for keeping the Seventh-day Sabbath that is promised in Isaiah 56:1-7. Keeping the Annual Sabbaths also serves to connect Gentile believers to their Jewish brethren, and enhances understanding of the events in history that led to the Messiah's coming and to the New Covenant.

Commentary by Daniel C. Juster

My view on this is that, without the support of civil law as we have in Israel, it is very difficult for Jews to do all of the Sabbaths (e.g. the seventh day of Passover and the 8th Day of *Sh'mini Atzeret*) because the number of days are just too difficult in a non-Jewish society. I think Messianic Jews should seek to keep them all as an ideal, but there is, in my view, allowance in the Diaspora for some degree of indulgence.

Regarding Gentiles, there is no requirement for them to embrace the Sabbath days, as is made most clear in Colossians 2, Romans 14, and Galatians 5. Also, although there is no evidence in any historical text that this was ever expected of Gentile believers, they are not relieved from understanding and applying these Sabbath days as their communities and they, as individuals, are led by the Holy Spirit. Of course, even when some level of compliance is decided upon, Gentiles

---

87 Hebrew for "Day of Firstfruits."

are not called to add extra-biblical rabbinical practices, although they are not prohibited from them either. The literal partaking of the Annual Sabbaths is covenantal to the Jewish people and would seem to have application to Gentile believers in their communities as follows:

1. There should be teachings regarding the meanings of all the Sabbaths.

2. It would be good and reasonable to teach on the Sabbaths in the seasons of their actual celebrations in Israel and in the Jewish community. This connects the Christian world to the Jewish people with whom they are joined through Yeshua (Romans 11).

3. Whenever Christian communities are led to celebrate these Sabbaths, it would be sufficient for them to do so on the weekends closest to their biblically prescribed dates.

4. Lastly, Christians may choose to abstain from work and rest on these Sabbaths (similar to their Jewish brothers) in identification with the Jewish people.

5. How the Sabbaths are acknowledged and expressed in each Christian community should be led by the Holy Spirit.

Classical Commentators

Maimonides and Meir loosely refer to the "first day of Passover" when they mean the first day of Unleavened Bread. This is a common Jewish practice, but is at odds with the biblical definition which describes Passover as the period from before sundown on the 14th day of the first month (*Nisan* 14), to sometime early the next day (*Nisan* 15), when the Israelites began their exodus from Egypt. HaChinuch specifically refers to *Nisan* 15, and all three commentators recognize the exception from not doing work when food preparation is needed. HaChinuch considers the first and seventh days of "Passover" to be a single festival, unlike the case of *Sh'mini Atzeret*.

In their writings, Maimonides, Meir, and HaChinuch assume the common rabbinical practice in the Diaspora of doubling up on each of the Annual Sabbaths except for *Yom Kippur*. The reason for this duplication is interesting but will not be explored further here.

NCLA: JMm JFm KMm KFm GMo GFo

D5. Counting to *Shavuot* and Waving Two Loaves.

We are to count seven weeks and fifty days from the Day of Firstfruits (following Passover) to Shavuot, at which time we are to waive two loaves of bread to the Lord.

This precept is derived from His Word (blessed be He):

Key Scriptures

Leviticus 23:9-21 (Maimonides RP 46, 161; Meir MP26; Chinuch C306-307)
ADONAI said to Moshe, "Tell the people of Isra'el, 'After you enter the land I am giving you and harvest its ripe crops, you are to bring a sheaf of the firstfruits of your harvest to the cohen. He is to wave the sheaf before ADONAI, so that you will be accepted; the cohen is to wave it on the day after the Shabbat. On the day that you wave the sheaf, you are to offer a male lamb without defect, in its first year, as a burnt offering for ADONAI. Its grain offering is to be one gallon of fine flour mixed with olive oil, an offering made by fire to ADONAI as a fragrant aroma; its drink offering is to be of wine, one quart. You are not to eat bread, dried grain or fresh grain until the day you bring the offering for your God; this is a permanent regulation through all your generations, no matter where you live. From the day after the day of rest—that is, from the day you bring the sheaf for waving—you are to count seven full weeks, until the day after the seventh week; you are to count fifty days; and then you are to present a new grain offering to ADONAI. You must bring bread from your homes for waving—two loaves made with one gallon of fine flour, baked with leaven—as firstfruits for ADONAI. Along with the bread, present seven lambs without defect one year old, one young bull and two rams; these will be a burnt offering for ADONAI, with their grain and drink offerings, an offering made by fire as a fragrant aroma for ADONAI. Offer one male goat as a sin offering and two male lambs one year old as a sacrifice of peace offerings. The cohen will wave them with the bread of the firstfruits as a wave offering before ADONAI, with the two lambs; these will be holy for ADONAI for the cohen. On the same day, you are to call a holy convocation; do not do any kind of ordinary work; this is a permanent regulation through all your generations, no matter where you live.

Numbers 28:26
On the day of the firstfruits, when you bring a new grain offering to ADONAI in your feast of Shavu'ot, you are to have a holy convocation; do not do any kind of ordinary work;

Deuteronomy 16:9-10 (Maimonides RP161; Chinuch C306)
You are to count seven weeks; you are to begin counting seven weeks from the time you first put your sickle to the standing grain. You are to observe the festival of Shavu'ot [weeks] for ADONAI your God with a voluntary offering, which you are to give in accordance with the degree to which ADONAI your God has prospered you.

Acts 2:1-21
The festival of Shavu'ot arrived, and the believers all gathered together in one place. Suddenly there came a sound from the sky like the roar of a violent wind, and it filled the whole house

where they were sitting. Then they saw what looked like tongues of fire, which separated and came to rest on each one of them. They were all filled with the Ruach HaKodesh and began to talk in different languages, as the Spirit enabled them to speak. Now there were staying in Yerushalayim religious Jews from every nation under heaven. When they heard this sound, a crowd gathered; they were confused, because each one heard the believers speaking in his own language. Totally amazed, they asked, "How is this possible? Aren't all these people who are speaking from the Galil? How is it that we hear them speaking in our native languages? We are Parthians, Medes, Elamites; residents of Mesopotamia, Y'hudah, Cappadocia, Pontus, Asia, Phrygia, Pamphylia, Egypt, the parts of Libya near Cyrene; visitors from Rome; Jews by birth and proselytes; Jews from Crete and from Arabia...! How is it that we hear them speaking in our own languages about the great things God has done?" Amazed and confused, they all went on asking each other, "What can this mean?" But others made fun of them and said, "They've just had too much wine!" Then Kefa stood up with the Eleven and raised his voice to address them: "You Judeans, and all of you staying here in Yerushalayim! Let me tell you what this means! Listen carefully to me! "These people aren't drunk, as you suppose—it's only nine in the morning. No, this is what was spoken about through the prophet Yo'el: 'ADONAI says: "In the Last Days, I will pour out from my Spirit upon everyone. Your sons and daughters will prophesy, your young men will see visions, your old men will dream dreams. Even on my slaves, both men and women, will I pour out from my Spirit in those days; and they will prophesy. I will perform miracles in the sky above and signs on the earth below—blood, fire and thick smoke. The sun will become dark and the moon blood before the great and fearful Day of ADONAI comes. And then, whoever calls on the name of ADONAI will be saved."'

Commentary

"From the day after the day of rest—that is, from the day you bring the sheaf for waving" is the day we refer to as *Yom HaBikkurim*—Day of Firstfruits (Leviticus 23:10). It is unique among the "designated times" listed in Leviticus 23, in that it is the only one that is not a Sabbath. The occurrence of the day we call *Shavuot* is determined by counting from *Yom HaBikkurim,* and is unique among the Annual Sabbaths in being the only one to which Scripture does not assign a particular date on the lunar calendar; in that regard, it is similar to the weekly Sabbath. The fifty-day count from "the day after the day of rest" (or Sabbath) in Leviticus 23:15-16 is known in Jewish practice as "counting the *omer,*" and which one of several possible Sabbaths is "day zero" of the count, is a subject of ongoing debate. To add complication, Numbers 28:26 calls *Shavu'ot* "*Yom HaBikkurim*" as well, the reason being that there were two harvests involved.

Jewish orthodoxy has adopted the Pharisaic view that the count should start from *Nissan* 16, the first day of the Feast of Unleavened Bread, thus causing *Shavuot* to always fall on the 6th day of *Sivan.* By contrast, many in Messianic Judaism have adopted the Sadducean view which is that the count should start on the day after the Seventh-Day Sabbath that falls in the midst of the Feast of Unleavened Bread. This causes the count to begin on the first day of the week (a Sunday), on *Yom HaBikkurim,* making this day the probable day of Yeshua's resurrection. A result of this is that *Shavuot* falls on different days of the lunar calendar in adjacent years, a consequence that seems to have been intended in the Leviticus 23 account.

When requiring that there be an animal sacrifice to accompany the grain offering of *Shavuot,* Scripture assumes the existence of a Tabernacle (or Temple) and an operating Levitical priesthood. Since we have neither today, counting to *Shavu'ot* and waiving two loaves of bread in the synagogue are correct adaptations of the Scripture, and are obligatory for both Jews and *K'rov Yisrael* Gentiles. Gentiles of the Nations should also keep track of the count because knowing when *Shavuot* occurs is important for connecting them to the Jewish people, and for commemorating the Holy Spirit's appearance in Jerusalem on the *Shavuot* following Yeshua's resurrection (Acts 2:1-21, 10:45).

Classical Commentators

Maimonides analogizes the individual obligation to count the *omer* to the *San Hedrin's* obligation to count the Years of Jubilee "year by year and Sabbatical cycle by Sabbatical cycle." He also gives much attention to justifying why counting fifty days and seven Sabbaths is one *mitzvah* and not two, but makes no mention of when the count should begin. Meir, in contrast, does not even mention that counting both days and Sabbaths comprises one commandment, but specifically states that we are to start to count the night of the sixteenth of *Nisan,* and that we are to count while standing, and accompany the count with a benediction. HaChinuch states that we must count forty-nine days from the presentation of the sheaf offering, which is the sixteenth of *Nisan,* and we must utter the day count and the week count separately. He agrees that we are to do the count while standing and with an accompanying benediction. Despite the different way that HaChinuch expresses the number of days counted, all three commentators endorse the Pharisaic way of counting—not the Sadducean way.

<u>NCLA</u>: JMm JFm KMm KFm GMo GFo

D6. Keeping Our Home and Domain Free of Leaven and *Chametz*, from Passover through the Feast of Unleavened Bread.

We are to maintain our home and all territory that is under our control completely free of leaven and chametz, from Passover through all seven days of the Feast of Unleavened Bread.

This precept is derived from His Word (blessed be He):

Key Scriptures

Exodus 12:15 (Maimonides RP156; Meir MP22; Chinuch C9)
For seven days you are to eat matzah—on the first day remove the leaven from your houses. For whoever eats hametz [leavened bread] from the first to the seventh day is to be cut off from Isra'el.

Exodus 12:19 (Maimonides RN201; Meir MN3; Chinuch C11)
During those seven days, no leaven is to be found in your houses. Whoever eats food with hametz in it is to be cut off from the community of Isra'el—it doesn't matter whether he is a foreigner or a citizen of the land.

Exodus 12:33-34
The Egyptians pressed to send the people out of the land quickly, because they said, "Otherwise we'll all be dead!" The people took their dough before it had become leavened and wrapped their kneading bowls in their clothes on their shoulders.

Exodus 12:42-49 (Maimonides RN126-128; Chinuch C13-14, 17)
This was a night when ADONAI kept vigil to bring them out of the land of Egypt, and this same night continues to be a night when ADONAI keeps vigil for all the people of Isra'el through all their generations. ADONAI said to Moshe and Aharon, "This is the regulation for the Pesach lamb: no foreigner is to eat it. But if anyone has a slave he bought for money, when you have circumcised him, he may eat it. Neither a traveler nor a hired servant may eat it. It is to be eaten in one house. You are not to take any of the meat outside the house, and you are not to break any of its bones. The whole community of Isra'el is to keep it. If a foreigner staying with you wants to observe ADONAI's Pesach, all his males must be circumcised. Then he may take part and observe it; he will be like a citizen of the land. But no uncircumcised person is to eat it. The same teaching is to apply equally to the citizen and to the foreigner living among you.

Exodus 13:7 (Maimonides RN200; Meir MN2; Chinuch C20)
Matzah is to be eaten throughout the seven days; neither hametz nor leavening agents are to be seen with you throughout your territory.

Matthew 26:17-19

On the first day for matzah, the talmidim came to Yeshua and asked, "Where do you want us to prepare your Seder?" "Go into the city, to so-and-so," he replied, "and tell him that the Rabbi says, 'My time is near, my talmidim and I are celebrating Pesach at your house.'" The talmidim did as Yeshua directed and prepared the Seder.

Mark 14:12-16

On the first day for matzah, when they slaughtered the lamb for Pesach, Yeshua's talmidim asked him, "Where do you want us to go and prepare your Seder?" He sent two of his talmidim with these instructions: "Go into the city, and a man carrying a jar of water will meet you. Follow him; and whichever house he enters, tell him that the Rabbi says, 'Where is the guest room for me, where I am to eat the Pesach meal with my talmidim?' He will show you a large room upstairs, furnished and ready. Make the preparations there." The talmidim went off, came to the city and found things just as he had told them they would be; and they prepared the Seder.

Luke 22:7-13

Then came the day of matzah, on which the Passover lamb had to be killed. Yeshua sent Kefa and Yochanan, instructing them, "Go and prepare our Seder, so we can eat." They asked him, "Where do you want us to prepare it?" He told them, "As you're going into the city, a man carrying a jar of water will meet you. Follow him into the house he enters, and say to its owner, 'The Rabbi says to you, "Where is the guest room, where I am to eat the Pesach meal with my talmidim?"' He will show you a large room upstairs already furnished; make the preparations there." They went and found things just as Yeshua had told them they would be, and they prepared for the Seder.

John 2:23

Now while Yeshua was in Yerushalayim at the Pesach festival, there were many people who "believed in his name" when they saw the miracles he performed.

John 6:4

Now the Judean festival of Pesach was coming up...

John 11:55

The Judean festival of Pesach was near, and many people went up from the country to Yerushalayim to perform the purification ceremony prior to Pesach.

1 Corinthians 5:6-8

Your boasting is not good. Don't you know the saying, "It takes only a little hametz to leaven a whole batch of dough?" Get rid of the old hametz, so that you can be a new batch of dough, because in reality you are unleavened. For our Pesach lamb, the Messiah, has been sacrificed. So let us celebrate the Seder not with leftover hametz, the hametz of wickedness and evil, but with the matzah of purity and truth.

184

Galatians 5:7-9
You were running the race well; who has stopped you from following the truth? Whatever means of persuasion he used was not from the One who calls you. "It takes only a little hametz to leaven the whole batch of dough."

Commentary

This *Mitzvah* requires that no leaven, whether alone or part of food containing leaven *(chametz)*, be in a Jew's possession or within his control during the seven days of the Feast of Unleavened Bread. This implies that he (or she) must, before sundown on the 14th day of *Nisan,* remove it from his house, garage, shed, trash bin, business property, territory domain, or anywhere else where he has proprietary rights of control, and must not let it back in for seven full days. This abstinence commemorates the Jews' hasty departure from Egypt, when they had no time to allow their bread to rise and therefore had to eat unleavened bread on the first leg of their journey. According to Exodus 12:19, obedience to this commandment is not an option for either a Jew or a Gentile who is a *"citizen of the land"* (K'rov Yisrael).

Leaven is analogized to sin in 1 Corinthians 5:6-8 and in Galatians 5:7-9, and its removal from our lives is directly linked to the Passover, and to the Passover lamb—our Messiah. But leaven is not always symbolic of sin, as we can see from Leviticus 23:17, which requires that the firstfruits bread offering of *Shavuot* be made with leaven.

The particulars of what should be considered leaven and *chametz* are controversial within Jewry. *Sephardim* and *Ashkenazim* follow different rules on the subject, and Messianic Jewish congregations are equally diverse. Is leaven anything that can cause food to rise, or must there be fermentation in order for it to qualify? What grains must be removed from the house because they are subject to spontaneous fermentation during storage? Rice? Barley? Beans? Discussions of such particulars are found in the *Talmudic* literature, but not in any of the classical *mitzvah* codifications. I do not think it would be judicious for me to express my opinion of these particulars here. The general idea in the Scriptures is that the Israelites' bread that would otherwise have fermented with yeast did not have time to rise. Therefore, our not keeping casually-stored grains that would have had time to ferment and rise would seem to be the general intent of the biblical text.

The legal fiction, in which people sometimes engage, of keeping ownershup of their *chametz* (whether stored in their house or not) by selling it to a Gentile for a minimum amount of money with the understanding that the Gentile will sell it back to them after the days of Unleavened Bread is not in accord with the spirit of the Scriptures. People should gauge their purchases and production of leavened products so as to minimize their material loss, but they should not engage in subterfuge.

This *Mitzvah* is mandated for Jews and *K'rovei Yisrael,* but not for Gentiles generally; the text of 1 Corinthians 5:6-8 cited above is therefore metaphorical in its application as to them.

Classical Commentators

Maimonides, Meir, and HaChinuch distinguish between not possessing leaven and not finding it in one's house. Meir and HaChinuch require that a Jew search his house for leaven, whereas Maimonides does not mention such a requirement. None of the commentators attempt to define "leaven," but HaChinuch says that yeast is an example of it. Meir states that if a non-Jew places *chametz* in a Jew's house and the Jew has not taken responsibility for it, the *chametz* need not be destroyed; otherwise it must be.

<u>**NCLA**</u>: **JMm JFm KMm KFm GMo GFo**

D7. Abstaining from Eating *Chametz* from Passover through the Feast of Unleavened Bread.

We are not to eat chametz from Passover through the seventh day of the Feast of Unleavened Bread.

This precept is derived from His Word (blessed be He):

Key Scriptures

Exodus 12:19-20 (Maimonides RN198; Meir MN5; Chinuch C12)
During those seven days, no leaven is to be found in your houses. Whoever eats food with hametz in it is to be cut off from the community of Isra'el—it doesn't matter whether he is a foreigner or a citizen of the land. Eat nothing with hametz in it. Wherever you live, eat matzah.

Exodus 12:33-34
The Egyptians pressed to send the people out of the land quickly, because they said, "Otherwise we'll all be dead!" The people took their dough before it had become leavened and wrapped their kneading bowls in their clothes on their shoulders.

Exodus 12:42-49 (Maimonides RN126-128; Chinuch C13-14, 17)
This was a night when ADONAI kept vigil to bring them out of the land of Egypt, and this same night continues to be a night when ADONAI keeps vigil for all the people of Isra'el through all their generations. ADONAI said to Moshe and Aharon, "This is the regulation for the Pesach lamb: no foreigner is to eat it. But if anyone has a slave he bought for money, when you have circumcised him, he may eat it. Neither a traveler nor a hired servant may eat it. It is to be eaten in one house. You are not to take any of the meat outside the house, and you are not to break any of its bones. The whole community of Isra'el is to keep it. If a foreigner staying with you wants to observe ADONAI's Pesach, all his males must be circumcised. Then he may take part and observe it; he will be like a citizen of the land. But no uncircumcised person is to eat it. The same teaching is to apply equally to the citizen and to the foreigner living among you.

Exodus 13:3 (Maimonides RN197; Meir MN4; Chinuch C19)
Moshe said to the people, "Remember this day, on which you left Egypt, the abode of slavery; because ADONAI, by the strength of his hand, has brought you out of this place. Do not eat hametz.

Deuteronomy 16:2-3 (Maimonides RN199; Meir MN104; Chinuch C485)
You are to sacrifice the Pesach offering from flock and herd to ADONAI your God in the place where ADONAI will choose to have his name live. You are not to eat any hametz with it; for seven days you are to eat with it matzah, the bread of affliction; for you came out of the land of Egypt in haste. Thus you will remember the day you left the land of Egypt as long as you live.

<u>Matthew 26:17-19</u>
On the first day for matzah, the talmidim came to Yeshua and asked, "Where do you want us to prepare your Seder?" "Go into the city, to so-and-so," he replied, "and tell him that the Rabbi says, 'My time is near, my talmidim and I are celebrating Pesach at your house.'" The talmidim did as Yeshua directed and prepared the Seder.

<u>Mark 8:15-17</u>
So when Yeshua said to them, "Watch out! Guard yourselves from the hametz of the P'rushim and the hametz of Herod," they thought he had said it because they had no bread. But, aware of this, he said, "Why are you talking with each other about having no bread? Don't you see or understand yet? Have your hearts been made like stone?

<u>Mark 14:12-16</u>
On the first day for matzah, when they slaughtered the lamb for Pesach, Yeshua's talmidim asked him, "Where do you want us to go and prepare your Seder?" He sent two of his talmidim with these instructions: "Go into the city, and a man carrying a jar of water will meet you. Follow him; and whichever house he enters, tell him that the Rabbi says, 'Where is the guest room for me, where I am to eat the Pesach meal with my talmidim?' He will show you a large room upstairs, furnished and ready. Make the preparations there." The talmidim went off, came to the city and found things just as he had told them they would be; and they prepared the Seder.

<u>Luke 22:7-13</u>
Then came the day of matzah, on which the Passover lamb had to be killed. Yeshua sent Kefa and Yochanan, instructing them, "Go and prepare our Seder, so we can eat." They asked him, "Where do you want us to prepare it?" He told them, "As you're going into the city, a man carrying a jar of water will meet you. Follow him into the house he enters, and say to its owner, 'The Rabbi says to you, "Where is the guest room, where I am to eat the Pesach meal with my talmidim?"' He will show you a large room upstairs already furnished; make the preparations there." They went and found things just as Yeshua had told them they would be, and they prepared for the Seder.

<u>John 2:23</u>
Now while Yeshua was in Yerushalayim at the Pesach festival, there were many people who "believed in his name" when they saw the miracles he performed.

<u>John 6:4</u>
Now the Judean festival of Pesach was coming up;

<u>John 11:55</u>
The Judean festival of Pesach was near, and many people went up from the country to Yerushalayim to perform the purification ceremony prior to Pesach.

<u>1 Corinthians 5:6-8</u>
Your boasting is not good. Don't you know the saying, "It takes only a little hametz to leaven a whole batch of dough?" Get rid of the old hametz, so that you can be a new batch of dough,

because in reality you are unleavened. For our Pesach lamb, the Messiah, has been sacrificed. So let us celebrate the Seder not with leftover hametz, the hametz of wickedness and evil, but with the matzah of purity and truth.

Galatians 5:7-9
You were running the race well; who has stopped you from following the truth? Whatever means of persuasion he used was not from the One who calls you. "It takes only a little hametz to leaven the whole batch of dough."

Commentary

Chametz is any food that contains leaven, the quintessential one being bread leavened with yeast. This *Mitzvah* states that we must not eat *chametz,* from Passover through the seventh day of the Feast of Unleavened Bread. Each of the supporting Scriptures above states it a little differently. Exodus 13:3 instructs abstention from *chametz,* Exodus 12:19-20 prohibits eating food that contains *chametz*, and Deuteronomy 16:2-3 prohibits eating *chametz* along with the sacrificed Passover lamb, all of which amount to the same thing which is to not eat *chametz* during the seven days of Unleavened Bread.

The particulars of what should be considered leaven and *chametz* are controversial within Jewry. Sephardic and Ashkenazic communities follow different rules on the subject, and Messianic Jewish congregations are equally diverse. Is leaven anything that can cause food to rise, or must there be fermentation in order for it to qualify? What grains must be removed from the house because they are subject to spontaneous fermentation during storage? Rice? Barley? Beans? Discussions of such particulars are found in the *Talmudic* literature, but not in any of the classical *mitzvah* codifications. I do not think it would be judicious for me to express my opinion of these particulars here. The general idea in the Scriptures is that the Israelites' bread that would otherwise have fermented with yeast did not have time to rise. Therefore, a commonly held view is that our not keeping casually-stored grains which would have had time to ferment and rise is what Scripture intends. An alternative view discounts the effect of airborne yeast and calls for discarding only those items that contain added leaven. The commercially prepared foods found in today's homes pose a special problem of identification in that some contain leaven where you would not expect it. Soups, for example, often contain yeast. My personal practice is to read all of the labels on packaged and canned foods and discard those that contain the words "leaven" or "yeast."

This *Mitzvah* is mandated for Jews and *K'rov Yisrael* Gentiles, but not for Gentiles generally. Exodus 12:19-20 makes this clear in that most Gentiles were not part of the community of Israel in the first place, so their being cut off from it for eating *chametz* is meaningless.

Classical Commentators

The classical commentators' *mitzvot* and this *Mitzvah* are in agreement except for terminology. They use the word *"Pesach"* as inclusive of both Passover and the s even days of the Feast of Unleavened Bread, whereas my use of the word refers only to the evening period from Nisan 14 to 15 when God "passed over" the homes of those Israelite families that applied the blood of the sacrificed lamb to their doorposts. Maimonides, Meir, and HaChinuch agree that chametz is not to be eaten after the middle of the 14th day of Nisan because the Passover lamb was slaughtered at dusk.

<u>NCLA</u>: JMm JFm KMm KFm GMo GFo

D8. Observing Passover with Lamb, *Matzah,* and Bitter Herbs

We are to eat matzah, bitter herbs, and lamb on Passover (Sephardic interpretation).
We are to eat matzah and bitter herbs but not lamb on Passover (Ashkenazic interpretation).

This precept is derived from His Word (blessed be He):

Key Scriptures

Exodus 12:3-8 (Maimonides RP56; Chinuch C6)
Speak to all the assembly of Isra'el and say, 'On the tenth day of this month, each man is to take a lamb or kid for his family, one per household—except that if the household is too small for a whole lamb or kid, then he and his next-door neighbor should share one, dividing it in proportion to the number of people eating it. Your animal must be without defect, a male in its first year, and you may choose it from either the sheep or the goats. You are to keep it until the fourteenth day of the month, and then the entire assembly of the community of Isra'el will slaughter it at dusk. They are to take some of the blood and smear it on the two sides and top of the door-frame at the entrance of the house in which they eat it. That night, they are to eat the meat, roasted in the fire; they are to eat it with matzah and maror.

Exodus 12:18 (Maimonides RP158; Meir MP23; Chinuch C10)
From the evening of the fourteenth day of the first month until the evening of the twenty-first day, you are to eat matzah.

Exodus 12:42-49 (Maimonides RN126-128; Chinuch C13-14, 17)
This was a night when ADONAI kept vigil to bring them out of the land of Egypt, and this same night continues to be a night when ADONAI keeps vigil for all the people of Isra'el through all their generations. ADONAI said to Moshe and Aharon, "This is the regulation for the Pesach lamb: no foreigner is to eat it. But if anyone has a slave he bought for money, when you have circumcised him, he may eat it. Neither a traveler nor a hired servant may eat it. It is to be eaten in one house. You are not to take any of the meat outside the house, and you are not to break any of its bones. The whole community of Isra'el is to keep it. If a foreigner staying with you wants to observe ADONAI's Pesach, all his males must be circumcised. Then he may take part and observe it; he will be like a citizen of the land. But no uncircumcised person is to eat it. The same teaching is to apply equally to the citizen and to the foreigner living among you.

Leviticus 22:21 (Maimonides RP61; Chinuch C286)
Whoever brings a sacrifice of peace offerings to ADONAI in fulfillment of a vow or as a voluntary offering, whether it come from the herd or from the flock, it must be unblemished and without defect in order to be accepted.

Leviticus 23:5-8 (Maimonides RP43; Chinuch C299)
In the first month, on the fourteenth day of the month, between sundown and complete darkness, comes Pesach for ADONAI. On the fifteenth day of the same month is the festival of matzah; for

seven days you are to eat matzah. On the first day you are to have a holy convocation; don't do any kind of ordinary work. Bring an offering made by fire to ADONAI for seven days. On the seventh day is a holy convocation; do not do any kind of ordinary work.

<u>Numbers 28:31</u> (Maimonides RP61; Chinuch C286)
You are to offer these in addition to the regular burnt offering and its grain offering (they are to be without defect for you), with their drink offerings.

<u>Matthew 26:17-19</u>
On the first day for matzah, the talmidim came to Yeshua and asked, "Where do you want us to prepare your Seder?" "Go into the city, to so-and-so," he replied, "and tell him that the Rabbi says, 'My time is near, my talmidim and I are celebrating Pesach at your house.'" The talmidim did as Yeshua directed and prepared the Seder.

<u>Matthew 26:26</u>
While they were eating, Yeshua took a piece of matzah, made the b'rakhah, broke it, gave it to the talmidim and said, "Take! Eat! This is my body!" (see also, <u>Mark 14:22</u> and <u>Luke 22:19</u>).

<u>Mark 14:12-16</u>
On the first day for matzah, when they slaughtered the lamb for Pesach, Yeshua's talmidim asked him, "Where do you want us to go and prepare your Seder?" He sent two of his talmidim with these instructions: "Go into the city, and a man carrying a jar of water will meet you. Follow him; and whichever house he enters, tell him that the Rabbi says, 'Where is the guest room for me, where I am to eat the Pesach meal with my talmidim?' He will show you a large room upstairs, furnished and ready. Make the preparations there." The talmidim went off, came to the city and found things just as he had told them they would be; and they prepared the Seder.

<u>Luke 22:7-13</u>
Then came the day of matzah, on which the Passover lamb had to be killed. Yeshua sent Kefa and Yochanan, instructing them, "Go and prepare our Seder, so we can eat." They asked him, "Where do you want us to prepare it?" He told them, "As you're going into the city, a man carrying a jar of water will meet you. Follow him into the house he enters, and say to its owner, 'The Rabbi says to you, "Where is the guest room, where I am to eat the Pesach meal with my talmidim?"' He will show you a large room upstairs already furnished; make the preparations there." They went and found things just as Yeshua had told them they would be, and they prepared for the Seder.

<u>John 2:23</u>
Now while Yeshua was in Yerushalayim at the Pesach festival, there were many people who "believed in his name" when they saw the miracles he performed.

<u>John 6:4</u>
Now the Judean festival of Pesach was coming up...

John 11:55
The Judean festival of Pesach was near, and many people went up from the country to Yerushalayim to perform the purification ceremony prior to Pesach.

1 Corinthians 5:6-8
Your boasting is not good. Don't you know the saying, "It takes only a little hametz to leaven a whole batch of dough?" Get rid of the old hametz, so that you can be a new batch of dough, because in reality you are unleavened. For our Pesach lamb, the Messiah, has been sacrificed. So let us celebrate the Seder not with leftover hametz, the hametz of wickedness and evil, but with the matzah of purity and truth.

Galatians 5:7-9
You were running the race well; who has stopped you from following the truth? Whatever means of persuasion he used was not from the One who calls you. "It takes only a little hametz to leaven the whole batch of dough."

Hebrews 9:13-14
For if sprinkling ceremonially unclean persons with the blood of goats and bulls and the ashes of a heifer restores their outward purity; then how much more the blood of the Messiah, who, through the eternal Spirit, offered himself to God as a sacrifice without blemish, will purify our conscience from works that lead to death, so that we can serve the living God!

Supportive Scriptures

Exodus 12:33-34
Numbers 9:10-11
Deuteronomy 16:1-2

Commentary

Exodus 12:3-8 gives details of the first Passover that occurred on the 14th day of the first month (on the Jewish lunar calendar), the evening before the Israelites were led out of Egypt. God subsequently commanded the Israelites to keep the Passover as an annual remembrance of their deliverance (Deuteronomy 16:1-2), and Leviticus 23:5 clarifies that Passover is only part of the day, between sundown and complete darkness.

On the original Passover in Egypt, the Israelites were instructed to eat a sacrificed lamb with *matzah* and bitter herbs *(maror)*. Numbers 9:10-11 is significant here because, by commanding Passover observance a month late under certain circumstances, the point is made that Passover is to be kept each year as a lasting ordinance; it was not just a one-time event.

Lambs were sacrificed on Passover until the destruction of the Second Temple, after which, animal sacrifice could no longer be done. Even had the Temple not been destroyed, it is doubtful that the Passover sacrifice would have continued among the Jewish followers of Yeshua because they understood Him to be their "once and for all" sacrificed lamb. On the other hand, they might have partaken of it as part of a memorial to Yeshua, since we see Paul and other disciples engaged in Temple sacrifices long after the time of Yeshua's death (Acts 21). What remains of Passover observance for Jews today, is that we partake of a *seder* meal on the evening of *Nisan* 14, during which we eat lamb if we are Sephardic (we do not if we are Ashkenaz), unleavened bread and *maror* (bitter herbs), and we abstain from eating (or even possessing) leaven. The Sephardim look at the eating of lamb differently from the Ashkenazim. The Sephardim eat it in remembrance of the sacrificed Passover lamb, and the Ashkenazim abstain so that no one can interpret it as comprising a present day sacrifice.

There was one Passover meal (described in Matthew 26:26, Mark 14:22, and Luke 22:19), at which Yeshua picked up a piece of *matzah* from the table, broke it, and gave it to the twelve disciples who were with him, to eat and make a memory they would later use as a memorial of his body that was broken during the sacrifice he was about to endure. This, along with the wine he spoke of as his blood, I consider to be a new commandment to his disciples (present and future—Jew and Gentile).

Observing the Passover (without sacrificing a lamb) is mandatory for Jews and *K'rov Yisrael* Gentiles. It is optional for other Gentiles who may also want to observe it (albeit in some adaptive manner) as a way of identifying with the Jewish People, and also as an acknowledgement of Passover's prophetic significance that points to Yeshua. Over the centuries, various Jewish *halachic* practices have developed that define how Passover is observed in Jewish communities. Gentiles who choose to observe Passover may borrow from these, but are free to depart as well, and to develop their own customs and expressions. It should be noted that the historic churches sometimes call the period from Good Friday to Resurrection Sunday "Passover" *(Pascha)* and do keep it to a degree, but usually without adequate reference to its Exodus roots.

Finally, a word needs to be said about the prohibition to Gentiles recorded in Exodus 12:43-49:

> *"ADONAI said to Moshe and Aharon, "This is the regulation for the Pesach lamb: no foreigner is to eat it. But if anyone has a slave he bought for money, when you have circumcised him, he may eat it. Neither a traveler nor a hired servant may eat it. It is to be eaten in one house. You are not to take any of the meat outside the house, and you are not to break any of its bones. The whole community of Isra'el is to keep it. If a foreigner staying with you wants to observe ADONAI's Pesach, all his males must be circumcised. Then he may take part and observe it; he will be like a citizen of the land. But no uncircumcised person is to eat it. The same teaching is to apply equally to the citizen and to the foreigner living among you."*

This prohibition only applies to eating the sacrificed Passover lamb (which we no longer do). It does not apply to the other aspects of Passover observance, so Gentiles are completely free to attend and even conduct Passover *sedarim*.

Classical Commentators

Maimonides, Meir, and HaChinuch all recognize the requirement to eat *matzah* on Passover. Meir also says that we must eat *matzah, maror,* and *charoset* (a sweet paste-like mixture), and that the *matzah* we eat must be made of wheat, barley, spelt, oats, or rye. He also says that we are prohibited from eating *matzah* the day before Passover, so that our appetite for it will be increased. Maimonides and HaChinuch do not mention eating *maror,* but refer their readers to the Talmud's tractate *Pesachim* for other provisions of their *mitzvot.* Maimonides and HaChinuch state that it is the evening of the 15th day of *Nisan* when we are to eat unleavened bread; Meir says it is on the 1st night of Passover when we must eat it, but does not indicate the date.

NCLA: **JMm JFm KMm KFm GMo GFo**

D9. Observing a Late Passover with *Matzah* and Bitter Herbs.

Anyone who cannot observe Passover on the 14th day of Nisan must make every attempt to do so by eating matzah and maror the following month on the 14th day of Iyar.

This precept is derived from His Word (blessed be He):

Key Scriptures

Exodus 12:42-49 (Maimonides RN126-128; Chinuch C13-14, 17)
This was a night when ADONAI kept vigil to bring them out of the land of Egypt, and this same night continues to be a night when ADONAI keeps vigil for all the people of Isra'el through all their generations. ADONAI said to Moshe and Aharon, "This is the regulation for the Pesach lamb: no foreigner is to eat it. But if anyone has a slave he bought for money, when you have circumcised him, he may eat it. Neither a traveler nor a hired servant may eat it. It is to be eaten in one house. You are not to take any of the meat outside the house, and you are not to break any of its bones. The whole community of Isra'el is to keep it. If a foreigner staying with you wants to observe ADONAI's Pesach, all his males must be circumcised. Then he may take part and observe it; he will be like a citizen of the land. But no uncircumcised person is to eat it. The same teaching is to apply equally to the citizen and to the foreigner living among you.

Numbers 9:10-11
Tell the people of Isra'el, 'If any of you now or in future generations is unclean because of a corpse, or if he is on a trip abroad, nevertheless he is to observe Pesach. But he will observe it in the second month on the fourteenth day at dusk. They are to eat it with matzah and maror...

Numbers 28:31 (Maimonides RP61; Chinuch C286)
You are to offer these in addition to the regular burnt offering and its grain offering (they are to be without defect for you), with their drink offerings.

Matthew 26:17-19
On the first day for matzah, the talmidim came to Yeshua and asked, "Where do you want us to prepare your Seder?" "Go into the city, to so-and-so," he replied, "and tell him that the Rabbi says, 'My time is near, my talmidim and I are celebrating Pesach at your house.'" The talmidim did as Yeshua directed and prepared the Seder.

Mark 14:12-16
On the first day for matzah, when they slaughtered the lamb for Pesach, Yeshua's talmidim asked him, "Where do you want us to go and prepare your Seder?" He sent two of his talmidim with these instructions: "Go into the city, and a man carrying a jar of water will meet you. Follow him; and whichever house he enters, tell him that the Rabbi says, 'Where is the guest room for me, where I am to eat the Pesach meal with my talmidim?' He will show you a large room upstairs, furnished and ready. Make the preparations there." The talmidim went off, came to the city and found things just as he had told them they would be; and they prepared the Seder.

<u>Luke 22:7-13</u>
Then came the day of matzah, on which the Passover lamb had to be killed. Yeshua sent Kefa and Yochanan, instructing them, "Go and prepare our Seder, so we can eat." They asked him, "Where do you want us to prepare it?" He told them, "As you're going into the city, a man carrying a jar of water will meet you. Follow him into the house he enters, and say to its owner, 'The Rabbi says to you, "Where is the guest room, where I am to eat the Pesach meal with my talmidim?"' He will show you a large room upstairs already furnished; make the preparations there." They went and found things just as Yeshua had told them they would be, and they prepared for the Seder.

<u>John 2:23</u>
Now while Yeshua was in Yerushalayim at the Pesach festival, there were many people who "believed in his name" when they saw the miracles he performed.

<u>John 6:4</u>
Now the Judean festival of Pesach was coming up;

<u>John 11:55</u>
The Judean festival of Pesach was near, and many people went up from the country to Yerushalayim to perform the purification ceremony prior to Pesach.

<u>1 Corinthians 5:6-8</u>
Your boasting is not good. Don't you know the saying, "It takes only a little hametz to leaven a whole batch of dough?" Get rid of the old hametz, so that you can be a new batch of dough, because in reality you are unleavened. For our Pesach lamb, the Messiah, has been sacrificed. So let us celebrate the Seder not with leftover hametz, the hametz of wickedness and evil, but with the matzah of purity and truth.

<u>Galatians 5:7-9</u>
You were running the race well; who has stopped you from following the truth? Whatever means of persuasion he used was not from the One who calls you. "It takes only a little hametz to leaven the whole batch of dough."

<u>Hebrews 9:13-14</u>
For if sprinkling ceremonially unclean persons with the blood of goats and bulls and the ashes of a heifer restores their outward purity; then how much more the blood of the Messiah, who, through the eternal Spirit, offered himself to God as a sacrifice without blemish, will purify our conscience from works that lead to death, so that we can serve the living God!

Supportive Scriptures

Exodus 12:33-34
Leviticus 23:5-8

Commentary

I believe the two reasons given in <u>Numbers 9:10</u> for delaying Passover observance are not the only two intended, but are meant to suggest others as well that are equally valid. For example, if a Jewish man or woman cannot observe Passover on the 14th of *Nisan* due to illness, he or she must earnestly seek to do so a month later, on the 14th of *Iyar*.

I consider this *Mitzvah* mandatory for individual Jews and for *K'rov Yisrael* Gentiles who find themselves in the position of not being able to fulfill their Passover observance obligation on the 14th of *Nisan*. Other Gentiles, however, should they undertake this *Mitzvah* would, in my opinion be wrong to state that Passover observance is an obligation as to them. For that reason, I consider literal compliance of this *Mitzvah* to be unauthorized and not recommended for Gentiles who are not *K'rovei Yisrael*.

Classical Commentators

Maimonides, Meir, and HaChinuch do not include a delayed Passover observance among their listed *mitzvot*.

<u>NCLA</u>: **JMm JFm KMm KFm GMn GFn**

D10. Observing the Feast of Unleavened Bread by Eating *Matzah* on Each of Its Seven Days.

We are to observe the Feast of Unleavened Bread by eating matzah on each of its seven days.

This precept is derived from His Word (blessed be He):

Key Scriptures

Exodus 12:15-20
For seven days you are to eat matzah—on the first day remove the leaven from your houses. For whoever eats hametz [leavened bread] from the first to the seventh day is to be cut off from Isra'el. On the first and seventh days, you are to have an assembly set aside for God. On these days no work is to be done, except what each must do to prepare his food; you may do only that. You are to observe the festival of matzah, for on this very day I brought your divisions out of the land of Egypt. Therefore, you are to observe this day from generation to generation by a perpetual regulation. From the evening of the fourteenth day of the first month until the evening of the twenty-first day, you are to eat matzah. During those seven days, no leaven is to be found in your houses. Whoever eats food with hametz in it is to be cut off from the community of Isra'el—it doesn't matter whether he is a foreigner or a citizen of the land. Eat nothing with hametz in it. Wherever you live, eat matzah.

Exodus 12:42-49 (Maimonides RN126-128; Chinuch C13-14, 17)
This was a night when ADONAI kept vigil to bring them out of the land of Egypt, and this same night continues to be a night when ADONAI keeps vigil for all the people of Isra'el through all their generations. ADONAI said to Moshe and Aharon, "This is the regulation for the Pesach lamb: no foreigner is to eat it. But if anyone has a slave he bought for money, when you have circumcised him, he may eat it. Neither a traveler nor a hired servant may eat it. It is to be eaten in one house. You are not to take any of the meat outside the house, and you are not to break any of its bones. The whole community of Isra'el is to keep it. If a foreigner staying with you wants to observe ADONAI's Pesach, all his males must be circumcised. Then he may take part and observe it; he will be like a citizen of the land. But no uncircumcised person is to eat it. The same teaching is to apply equally to the citizen and to the foreigner living among you.

Exodus 13:5-7
When ADONAI brings you into the land of the Kena'ani, Hitti, Emori, Hivi and Y'vusi, which he swore to your ancestors to give you, a land flowing with milk and honey, you are to observe this ceremony in this month. For seven days you are to eat matzah, and the seventh day is to be a festival for ADONAI. Matzah is to be eaten throughout the seven days; neither hametz nor leavening agents are to be seen with you throughout your territory.

Exodus 23:15
Keep the festival of matzah: for seven days, as I ordered you, you are to eat matzah at the time determined in the month of Aviv; for it was in that month that you left Egypt. No one is to appear before me empty-handed.

<u>Leviticus 23:5-6</u>
In the first month, on the fourteenth day of the month, between sundown and complete darkness, comes Pesach for ADONAI. On the fifteenth day of the same month is the festival of matzah; for seven days you are to eat matzah.

<u>Numbers 28:17</u>
On the fifteenth day of the month is to be a feast. Matzah is to be eaten for seven days.

<u>Deuteronomy 16:2-3</u>
You are to sacrifice the Pesach offering from flock and herd to ADONAI your God in the place where ADONAI will choose to have his name live. You are not to eat any hametz with it; for seven days you are to eat with it matzah, the bread of affliction; for you came out of the land of Egypt in haste. Thus you will remember the day you left the land of Egypt as long as you live.

<u>Deuteronomy 16:8</u>
For six days you are to eat matzah; on the seventh day there is to be a festive assembly for ADONAI your God; do not do any kind of work.

<u>Matthew 26:17-19</u>
On the first day for matzah, the talmidim came to Yeshua and asked, "Where do you want us to prepare your Seder?" "Go into the city, to so-and-so," he replied, "and tell him that the Rabbi says, 'My time is near, my talmidim and I are celebrating Pesach at your house.'" The talmidim did as Yeshua directed and prepared the Seder.

<u>Mark 14:12-16</u>
On the first day for matzah, when they slaughtered the lamb for Pesach, Yeshua's talmidim asked him, "Where do you want us to go and prepare your Seder?" He sent two of his talmidim with these instructions: "Go into the city, and a man carrying a jar of water will meet you. Follow him; and whichever house he enters, tell him that the Rabbi says, 'Where is the guest room for me, where I am to eat the Pesach meal with my talmidim?' He will show you a large room upstairs, furnished and ready. Make the preparations there." The talmidim went off, came to the city and found things just as he had told them they would be; and they prepared the Seder.

<u>Luke 22:7-13</u>
Then came the day of matzah, on which the Passover lamb had to be killed. Yeshua sent Kefa and Yochanan, instructing them, "Go and prepare our Seder, so we can eat." They asked him, "Where do you want us to prepare it?" He told them, "As you're going into the city, a man carrying a jar of water will meet you. Follow him into the house he enters, and say to its owner, 'The Rabbi says to you, "Where is the guest room, where I am to eat the Pesach meal with my talmidim?"' He will show you a large room upstairs already furnished; make the preparations there." They went and found things just as Yeshua had told them they would be, and they prepared for the Seder.

John 2:23
Now while Yeshua was in Yerushalayim at the Pesach festival, there were many people who "believed in his name" when they saw the miracles he performed.

John 6:4
Now the Judean festival of Pesach was coming up;

John 11:55
The Judean festival of Pesach was near, and many people went up from the country to Yerushalayim to perform the purification ceremony prior to Pesach.

1 Corinthians 5:6-8
Your boasting is not good. Don't you know the saying, "It takes only a little hametz to leaven a whole batch of dough?" Get rid of the old hametz, so that you can be a new batch of dough, because in reality you are unleavened. For our Pesach lamb, the Messiah, has been sacrificed. So let us celebrate the Seder not with leftover hametz, the hametz of wickedness and evil, but with the matzah of purity and truth.

Galatians 5:7-9
You were running the race well; who has stopped you from following the truth? Whatever means of persuasion he used was not from the One who calls you. "It takes only a little hametz to leaven the whole batch of dough."

Supportive Scripture

Exodus 12:33-34

Commentary

The Scriptures cited herein are unambiguous that God commanded the Israelites to eat *matzah* on each of the seven days of the Feast of unleavened bread that begins on the 15th day of *Nisan*. The rationale for it appears to be to remember the Israelites' hasty departure from Egypt by eating bread similar to the kind they carried with them—bread that did not have time to rise during their travel. This translates to being a mandate today for Jews and *k'rov Yisrael* Gentiles, but not for other Gentiles, although they may do so (if they are so moved) in identification with the Jewish people.

Classical Commentators

Maimonides and HaChinuch state that we must eat *matzah* on the evening of the 15th of *Nisan*, and Maimonides states that doing so after that is optional. On this latter point, Meir and HaChinuch are silent on this latter point, and they offer no *mitzvah* to support eating *matzah* during the Feast of Unleavened Bread. *Pesachim* 120a in the *Talmud* appears to be the source of the commentators' apparent belief that there is no commandment to eat *matzah* after *Pesach*. Perhaps they understand the Scriptures to be saying that if one chooses to eat bread from the 15th

201

to the 21ˢᵗ of *Nisan,* then the bread must be unleavened. I do not know their rationale, but I am of opinion that Scripture commands eating *matzah* on each of the seven days of Unleavened Bread as a daily reminder of God's deliverance of the Israelites from Egypt.

NCLA: **JMm JFm KMm KFm GMo GFo**

D11. Ceremonially Recounting What God Did for Us when We Left Egypt.

On the evening of Passover, we are to ceremonially tell our children that we eat matzah and remove leaven and chametz from our domain as a reminder of what God did for us when we left Egypt.

This precept is derived from His Word (blessed be He):

Key Scriptures

Exodus 12:15-20 (Maimonides RP156, 158, RN198; Meir MP22, 23, MN5; Chinuch C9, 10, 12)
For seven days you are to eat matzah—on the first day remove the leaven from your houses. For whoever eats hametz [leavened bread] from the first to the seventh day is to be cut off from Isra'el. On the first and seventh days, you are to have an assembly set aside for God. On these days no work is to be done, except what each must do to prepare his food; you may do only that. You are to observe the festival of matzah, for on this very day I brought your divisions out of the land of Egypt. Therefore, you are to observe this day from generation to generation by a perpetual regulation. From the evening of the fourteenth day of the first month until the evening of the twenty-first day, you are to eat matzah. During those seven days, no leaven is to be found in your houses. Whoever eats food with hametz in it is to be cut off from the community of Isra'el—it doesn't matter whether he is a foreigner or a citizen of the land. Eat nothing with hametz in it. Wherever you live, eat matzah.

Exodus 12:25-27
When you come to the land which ADONAI will give you, as he has promised, you are to observe this ceremony. When your children ask you, 'What do you mean by this ceremony?' say, 'It is the sacrifice of ADONAI's Pesach [Passover], because [[ADONAI]] passed over the houses of the people of Isra'el in Egypt, when he killed the Egyptians but spared our houses.'" The people of Isra'el bowed their heads and worshipped.

Exodus 12:41-49 (Maimonides RN126-128; Chinuch C13-14, 17)
At the end of 430 years to the day, all the divisions of ADONAI left the land of Egypt. This was a night when ADONAI kept vigil to bring them out of the land of Egypt, and this same night continues to be a night when ADONAI keeps vigil for all the people of Isra'el through all their generations. ADONAI said to Moshe and Aharon, "This is the regulation for the Pesach lamb: no foreigner is to eat it. But if anyone has a slave he bought for money, when you have circumcised him, he may eat it. Neither a traveler nor a hired servant may eat it. It is to be eaten in one house. You are not to take any of the meat outside the house, and you are not to break any of its bones. The whole community of Isra'el is to keep it. If a foreigner staying with you wants to observe ADONAI's Pesach, all his males must be circumcised. Then he may take part and observe it; he will be like a citizen of the land. But no uncircumcised person is to eat it. The same teaching is to apply equally to the citizen and to the foreigner living among you.

Exodus 13:3-8 (Maimonides RP157, RN197, 200; Meir MP24; Chinuch C21)

Moshe said to the people, "Remember this day, on which you left Egypt, the abode of slavery; because ADONAI, by the strength of his hand, has brought you out of this place. Do not eat hametz. You are leaving today, in the month of Aviv. When ADONAI brings you into the land of the Kena'ani, Hitti, Emori, Hivi and Y'vusi, which he swore to your ancestors to give you, a land flowing with milk and honey, you are to observe this ceremony in this month. For seven days you are to eat matzah, and the seventh day is to be a festival for ADONAI. Matzah is to be eaten throughout the seven days; neither hametz nor leavening agents are to be seen with you throughout your territory. On that day you are to tell your son, 'It is because of what ADONAI did for me when I left Egypt.'

Matthew 2:13-15

After they had gone, an angel of ADONAI appeared to Yosef in a dream and said, "Get up, take the child and his mother, and escape to Egypt, and stay there until I tell you to leave. For Herod is going to look for the child in order to kill him." So he got up, took the child and his mother, and left during the night for Egypt, where he stayed until Herod died. This happened in order to fulfill what ADONAI had said through the prophet, "Out of Egypt I called my son."

Hebrews 8:9

It will not be like the covenant which I made with their fathers on the day when I took them by their hand and led them forth out of the land of Egypt; because they, for their part, did not remain faithful to my covenant; so I, for my part, stopped concerning myself with them,' says ADONAI.

Commentary

This ceremony (that we now call a *seder*) was commanded for us (Israelites) to do after we emerged from Egypt and entered the Land that the Lord had promised our ancestors. Although Israel's exodus from Egypt occurred many centuries ago, we retell its events in the first person as though "we" (not "they") left Egypt. I believe it is also applicable to Gentiles who permanently live within the Jewish community *(K'rovei Yisrael)* because those whom God brought out of Egypt were a mixed multitude that consisted, not only of Jews, but of Gentiles as well (Exodus 12:38).

At our modern Passover *seder*, it is customary for a child to ask four questions, and for us to answer the questions by telling him (or her) the story of when we left Egypt. Through this retelling, we are reminded of God's miracles in our behalf, that He brought us out of Egypt "by the strength of His hand," and that we left in such haste that we brought no leaven with us so the bread we had to eat was un-risen. Although our living conditions in the desert were strenuous, God provided for us with *manna*,[88] quail, water, and shoes that did not wear out. His greatest provision for us, however, was His divine presence, for He accompanied us and guided us through the desert in a column of cloud by day and a column of fire by night.

---

88 A flaky sweet-tasting bread sent from heaven—"*man*" in Hebrew.

While this *Mitzvah* to recount Israel's exodus from Egypt is clearly directed to Jews and *K'rov Yisrael* Gentiles, the remembrance of what God did for Israel should be a joy and encouragement for all believers. All Gentile parents who are believers may therefore want to tell the story of the Exodus, and explain about *matzah,* leaven, and *chametz* to their children as well.

Classical Commentators

Maimonides, Meir, and HaChinuch all state that we are to tell about the exodus from Egypt. However, Maimonides and HaChinuch say that we are to tell it on the evening of the 15th of *Nisan,* and Meir says it should be told on the night before the 15th of *Nisan.* These are probably not disagreements, but rather different ways of referring to the Passover *seder* event.

NCLA: **JMm JFm KMm KFm GMr GFr**

D12. Blowing the *Shofar* on Special Days and As an Alarm in War.

We are to blow the shofar on the first day of the seventh month, on the other appointed days, on Rosh Chodesh, in the Jubilee, on days of rejoicing, and as an alarm in war.

This precept is derived from His Word (blessed be He):

Key Scriptures

Leviticus 23:23-5 (Chinuch C312)
ADONAI said to Moshe, "Tell the people of Isra'el, 'In the seventh month, the first of the month is to be for you a day of complete rest for remembering, a holy convocation announced with blasts on the shofar. Do not do any kind of ordinary work, and bring an offering made by fire to ADONAI.

Leviticus 25:8-12
You are to count seven Shabbats of years, seven times seven years, that is, forty-nine years. Then, on the tenth day of the seventh month, on Yom-Kippur, you are to sound a blast on the shofar; you are to sound the shofar all through your land; and you are to consecrate the fiftieth year, proclaiming freedom throughout the land to all its inhabitants. It will be a yovel for you; you will return everyone to the land he owns, and everyone is to return to his family. That fiftieth year will be a yovel for you; in that year you are not to sow, harvest what grows by itself or gather the grapes of untended vines; because it is a yovel. It will be holy for you; whatever the fields produce will be food for all of you.

Numbers 10:1-10 (Maimonides RP59; Chinuch C384)
ADONAI said to Moshe, "Make two trumpets; make them of hammered silver. Use them for summoning the community and for sounding the call to break camp and move on. When they are sounded, the entire community is to assemble before you at the entrance to the tent of meeting. If only one is sounded, then just the leaders, the heads of the clans of Isra'el, are to assemble before you. When you sound an alarm, the camps to the east will commence traveling. When you sound a second alarm, the camps to the south will set out; they will sound alarms to announce when to travel. However, when the community is to be assembled, you are to sound; but don't sound an alarm. It will be the sons of Aharon, the cohanim, who are to sound the trumpets; this will be a permanent regulation for you through all your generations. When you go to war in your land against an adversary who is oppressing you, you are to sound an alarm with the trumpets; then you will be remembered before ADONAI your God, and you will be saved from your enemies. Also on your days of rejoicing, at your designated times and on Rosh-Hodesh, you are to sound the trumpets over your burnt offerings and over the sacrifices of your peace offerings; these will be your reminder before your God. I am ADONAI your God.

Numbers 29:1-5 (Maimonides RP47, 170; Meir MP30; Chinuch C312, 405)
In the seventh month, on the first day of the month, you are to have a holy convocation; do not do any kind of ordinary work; it is a day of blowing the shofar for you. Prepare a burnt offering

to make a fragrant aroma for ADONAI—one young bull, one ram and seven male lambs in their first year and without defect—with their grain offering, consisting of fine flour mixed with olive oil—six quarts for the bull, four quarts for the ram, and two quarts for each of the seven lambs—also one male goat as a sin offering to make atonement for you.

1 Corinthians 14:8
And if the bugle gives an unclear sound, who will get ready for battle?

Revelation 8:1-2
When the Lamb broke the seventh seal, there was silence in heaven for what seemed like half an hour. Then I saw the seven angels who stand before God, and they were given seven shofars.

Supportive Scriptures

Joshua 6:4-20
1 Kings 1:34, 39
Ezekiel 33:1-6
Joel 2:1, 15
Psalms 81:3(2)-5(4), 150:3

Commentary

The Hebrew of Leviticus 23:23:24 says that the first day of the seventh month (*Tishrei* on the lunar calendar) is a remembrance of blowing *(Zich'ron T'ruah)*, and Numbers 29:1 says it is a day of blowing *(Yom T'ruah)*; the CJB translation adds the word *"shofar"* (a trumpet made from an animal horn) because that was what was customarily blown in Moses' time to draw the community's attention, to summon to assembly, and to sound alarms. That is why the first day of *Tishrei* is sometimes referred to as the "Day of Trumpets" *(Yom HaShofar),* and it is a warning to prepare for the Day of Atonement *(Yom Kippur)* that is about to come. It is generally understood that not everyone in the community need blow a *shofar;* it is sufficient that the community cause the *shofar* to be blown in public for all to hear.

In the Jewish world, *Yom T'ruah* is most commonly known as *Rosh HaShanah* (Head of the Year), and considered the "Day of Judgment" *(Yom HaDin)* when the "Books of Life" are opened, and we are called to begin an examination of our lives, with the purpose of repenting of our sins before the "Books" are again closed and sealed, ten days later, on the "Day of Atonement" *(Yom Kippur).* The day is also said, in *Talmud,* to be the anniversary of the creation of the world.

Scripture does not indicate the reason for *Yom T'ruah,* but its placement 10 days prior to *Yom Kippur* strongly suggests that it is intended to begin a count-down of days for personal introspection leading to *Yom Kippur.* This theme is reflected in *Mishna Yoma 1* and its related *Talmudic Gemara*, that explain how the High Priest *(Kohen HaGadol)* was sequestered for purification seven days prior to *Yom Kippur;* that process would have begun three days from when the *shofar* sounded on *Yom T'ruah.*

207

This time of introspection from *Yom T'ruah* to *Yom Kippur* (known as the "Days of Awe" or *Yamim Nora'iym*) should be seen as meaningful to all Jews and all followers of Yeshua because, according to Exodus 19:6, Israel is a kingdom of priests (albeit not all of Israel are Levitical priests) and, according to 1 Peter 2:9 and Revelation 5:10, all New Covenant believers have been made priests as well. Priestly duties require time spent for personal cleansing, so what better use is there of the ten day period from when the trumpets sound to *Yom Kippur?* That notwithstanding, literal compliance with this *Mitzvah*, ie., to blow the *shofar,* is mandatory only for Jews and *K'rov Yisrael Gentiles.* It is optional for Gentiles generally.

It is an interesting side-note that the Babylonian *Talmud (b. Rosh HaShanah 29b)* prohibits the *shofar* from being blown when *Rosh HaShanah* falls on a weekly *Shabbat.* The reason given for this prohibition is to protect the *Shabbat* from being violated by someone who might inadvertently carry his *shofar* beyond the prescribed distance. My position is that the *Talmudic* prohibition is incorrect because it is in direct contradiction of several Scriptures that require that the *shofar* be blown on *Yom T'ruah* (which, by the way, is itself a *Shabbat*).

We have said much about blowing the *shofar* on *Yom T'ruah,* but Scripture commands that the *shofar* be blown at other times as well, such as on the other appointed days, on *Rosh Chodesh,* on days of rejoicing, and as an alarm to war. In this last-mentioned time of blowing we should not limit our understanding of war to just the physical, but also to times of spiritual warfare, especially when declared by our communities' leaders. We are also to blow the *shofar* on days of rejoicing, and the contrast of war and rejoicing is something to consider as we ponder complying with 1 Thessalonians 5:16-18:

> *"Always be joyful. Pray regularly. In everything give thanks, for this is what God wants from you who are united with the Messiah Yeshua."*

Commentary by Daniel C. Juster

I believe that when the New Covenant Scriptures speak of a heavenly *shofar* being sounded upon Yeshua's return, upon the dead being raised and upon His disciples (then alive) being transformed and caught up with Him in the air, they are referring to *Yom T'ruah* (1 Thessalonians 4:16-17; 1 Corinthians 15:51-52). This can also be connected to an eschatological time of universal repentance, including in Israel (Zechariah 12:10), that leads to a world-wide "Day of Atonement." If so, then the days between *Yom T'ruah* and *Yom Kippur* have teaching significance for all followers of Yeshua, and enhanced responsibility for the Jewish People, and for *K'rov Yisrael* Gentiles, who are charged with fulfilling the commandment to blow and hear the sound of the *shofar.*

Classical Commentators

Maimonides, Meir, and HaChinuch all refer to *Yom T'ruah* as *Rosh HaShanah* and state their respective *mitzvot* as our having to hear the *shofar* being blown. This no doubt reflects their view (as it is also mine) that blowing the *shofar* is the responsibility of the community, but going to hear them being blown is the responsibility of each individual.

Of the three, HaChinuch is the most expansive in his discussion of *Rosh HaShanah*. He explains that the *Mishnah* in *Talmud* tractate <u>*Rosh HaShanah 2a*</u> considers the 1st of *Tishrei* to be the beginning of the year (for numbering the years), and that the blowing (or sounding) was determined, by the sages, to be of the *shofar* as distinguished from some other musical instrument. He also speaks of *"t'ruah"* as a broken sound, which he relates to man's need of repentance from sin.

HaChinuch states that any hollow animal horn may be blown on *Rosh HaShanah,* whereas Meir states that only the horn of a sheep is acceptable. They both state that it is obligatory to hear nine sounds of the *shofar,* consisting of *t'kiah* (a single unwavering sound), *t'ruah* (a series of short broken sounds), and *sh'varim* (several short unwavering sounds). They do not refer to a *t'kiah g'dolah.*

<u>NCLA</u>: JMm JFm KMm KFm GMo GFo

D13. Afflicting Our Souls and Repenting on *Yom Kippur.*

We are to afflict our souls, repent of our sins, and adopt Yeshua's death as our atoning sacrifice on Yom Kippur.[89]

This precept is derived from His Word (blessed be He):

Key Scriptures

Leviticus 6:18(25)-23(30) (Maimonides RP64; Chinuch C138)
Tell Aharon and his sons, 'This is the law for the sin offering: the sin offering is to be slaughtered before ADONAI in the place where the burnt offering is slaughtered; it is especially holy. The cohen who offers it for sin is to eat it—it is to be eaten in a holy place, in the courtyard of the tent of meeting. Whatever touches its flesh will become holy; if any of its blood splashes on any item of clothing, you are to wash it in a holy place. The clay pot in which it is cooked must be broken; if it is cooked in a bronze pot, it must be scoured and rinsed in water. Any male from a family of cohanim may eat the sin offering; it is especially holy. But no sin offering which has had any of its blood brought into the tent of meeting to make atonement in the Holy Place is to be eaten; it is to be burned up completely.

Leviticus 16:1-34 (Maimonides RP49, 164-165; Chinuch C15)
ADONAI spoke with Moshe after the death of Aharon's two sons, when they tried to sacrifice before ADONAI and died; ADONAI said to Moshe, "Tell your brother Aharon not to come at just any time into the Holy Place beyond the curtain, in front of the ark-cover which is on the ark, so that he will not die; because I appear in the cloud over the ark-cover. Here is how Aharon is to enter the Holy Place: with a young bull as a sin offering and a ram as a burnt offering. He is to put on the holy linen tunic, have the linen shorts next to his bare flesh, have the linen sash wrapped around him, and be wearing the linen turban—they are the holy garments. He is to bathe his body in water and put them on. He is to take from the community of the people of Isra'el two male goats for a sin offering and one ram for a burnt offering. Aharon is to present the bull for the sin offering which is for himself and make atonement for himself and his household. He is to take the two goats and place them before ADONAI at the entrance to the tent of meeting. Then Aharon is to cast lots for the two goats, one lot for ADONAI and the other for 'Az'azel. Aharon is to present the goat whose lot fell to ADONAI and offer it as a sin offering. But the goat whose lot fell to 'Az'azel is to be presented alive to ADONAI to be used for making atonement over it by sending it away into the desert for 'Az'azel. Aharon is to present the bull of the sin offering for himself; he will make atonement for himself and his household; he is to slaughter the bull of the sin offering which is for himself. He is to take a censer full of burning coals from the altar before ADONAI and, with his hands full of ground, fragrant incense, bring it inside the curtain. He is to put the incense on the fire before ADONAI, so that the cloud from the incense will cover the ark-cover which is over the testimony, in order that he not die. He is to take some of the bull's blood and sprinkle it with his finger on the ark-cover toward the east;

---

89 Our need to repent is not limited to *Yom Kippur,* but is to occur whenever we sin.

and in front of the ark-cover he is to sprinkle some of the blood with his finger seven times. Next, he is to slaughter the goat of the sin offering which is for the people, bring its blood inside the curtain and do with its blood as he did with the bull's blood, sprinkling it on the ark-cover and in front of the ark-cover. He will make atonement for the Holy Place because of the uncleannesses of the people of Isra'el and because of their transgressions—all their sins; and he is to do the same for the tent of meeting which is there with them right in the middle of their uncleannesses. No one is to be present in the tent of meeting from the time he enters the Holy Place to make atonement until the time he comes out, having made atonement for himself, for his household and for the entire community of Isra'el. Then he is to go out to the altar that is before ADONAI and make atonement for it; he is to take some of the bull's blood and some of the goat's blood and put it on all the horns of the altar. He is to sprinkle some of the blood on it with his finger seven times, thus purifying it and setting it apart from the uncleannesses of the people of Isra'el. When he has finished atoning for the Holy Place, the tent of meeting and the altar, he is to present the live goat. Aharon is to lay both his hands on the head of the live goat and confess over it all the transgressions, crimes and sins of the people of Isra'el; he is to put them on the head of the goat and then send it away into the desert with a man appointed for the purpose. The goat will bear all their transgressions away to some isolated place, and he is to let the goat go in the desert. Aharon is to go back into the tent of meeting, where he is to remove the linen garments he put on when he entered the Holy Place, and he is to leave them there. Then he is to bathe his body in water in a holy place, put on his other clothes, come out and offer his burnt offering and the burnt offering of the people, thus making atonement for himself and for the people. He is to make the fat of the sin offering go up in smoke on the altar. The man who let go the goat for 'Az'azel is to wash his clothes and bathe his body in water; afterwards, he may return to the camp. "The bull for the sin offering and the goat for the sin offering, whose blood was brought in to make atonement in the Holy Place, is to be carried outside the camp; there they are to burn up completely their hides, meat and dung. The person burning them is to wash his clothes and bathe his body in water; afterwards, he may return to the camp. It is to be a permanent regulation for you that on the tenth day of the seventh month you are to deny yourselves and not do any kind of work, both the citizen and the foreigner living with you. For on this day, atonement will be made for you to purify you; you will be clean before ADONAI from all your sins. It is a Shabbat of complete rest for you, and you are to deny yourselves. "This is a permanent regulation. The cohen anointed and consecrated to be cohen in his father's place will make the atonement; he will put on the linen garments, the holy garments; he will make atonement for the Especially Holy Place; he will make atonement for the tent of meeting and the altar; and he will make atonement for the cohanim and for all the people of the community. This is a permanent regulation for you, to make atonement for the people of Isra'el because of all their sins once a year." Moshe did as ADONAI had ordered him.

Leviticus 22:21 (Maimonides RP61; Chinuch C286)
Whoever brings a sacrifice of peace offerings to ADONAI in fulfillment of a vow or as a voluntary offering, whether it come from the herd or from the flock, it must be unblemished and without defect in order to be accepted.

Leviticus 23:27-29 (Maimonides RN196; Meir MP32, MN152; Chinuch C313-314 316)
The tenth day of this seventh month is Yom-Kippur; you are to have a holy convocation, you are

211

to deny yourselves (NKJ: "afflict your souls"), and you are to bring an offering made by fire to ADONAI. You are not to do any kind of work on that day, because it is Yom-Kippur, to make atonement for you before ADONAI your God. Anyone who does not deny himself (NKJ: "is not afflicted in soul") on that day is to be cut off from his people;

Numbers 28:31 (Maimonides RP61; Chinuch C286)
You are to offer these in addition to the regular burnt offering and its grain offering (they are to be without defect for you), with their drink offerings.

Numbers 29:7-8 (Maimonides RP48; Chinuch C314)
On the tenth day of this seventh month you are to have a holy convocation. You are to deny yourselves (NKJ: "afflict your souls"), and you are not to do any kind of work; but you are to present a burnt offering to ADONAI to make a fragrant aroma: one young bull, one ram, and seven male lambs in their first year (they are to be without defect for you),

2 Corinthians 5:21
God made this sinless man be a sin offering on our behalf, so that in union with him we might fully share in God's righteousness.

Hebrews 9:6-10:20
With things so arranged, the cohanim go into the outer tent all the time to discharge their duties; but only the cohen hagadol enters the inner one; and he goes in only once a year, and he must always bring blood, which he offers both for himself and for the sins committed in ignorance by the people. By this arrangement, the Ruach HaKodesh showed that so long as the first Tent had standing, the way into the Holiest Place was still closed. This symbolizes the present age and indicates that the conscience of the person performing the service cannot be brought to the goal by the gifts and sacrifices he offers. For they involve only food and drink and various ceremonial washings—regulations concerning the outward life, imposed until the time for God to reshape the whole structure. But when the Messiah appeared as cohen gadol of the good things that are happening already, then, through the greater and more perfect Tent which is not man-made (that is, it is not of this created world), he entered the Holiest Place once and for all. And he entered not by means of the blood of goats and calves, but by means of his own blood, thus setting people free forever. For if sprinkling ceremonially unclean persons with the blood of goats and bulls and the ashes of a heifer restores their outward purity; then how much more the blood of the Messiah, who, through the eternal Spirit, offered himself to God as a sacrifice without blemish, will purify our conscience from works that lead to death, so that we can serve the living God! It is because of this death that he is mediator of a new covenant [or will]. Because a death has occurred which sets people free from the transgressions committed under the first covenant, those who have been called may receive the promised eternal inheritance. For where there is a will, there must necessarily be produced evidence of its maker's death, since a will goes into effect only upon death; it never has force while its maker is still alive. This is why the first covenant too was inaugurated with blood. After Moshe had proclaimed every command of the Torah to all the people, he took the blood of the calves with some water and used scarlet wool and hyssop to sprinkle both the scroll itself and all the people; and he said, "This is the blood of the covenant which God has ordained for you." Likewise, he sprinkled with the blood both the Tent and all the

things used in its ceremonies. In fact, according to the Torah, almost everything is purified with blood; indeed, without the shedding of blood there is no forgiveness of sins. Now this is how the copies of the heavenly things had to be purified, but the heavenly things themselves require better sacrifices than these. For the Messiah has entered a Holiest Place which is not man-made and merely a copy of the true one, but into heaven itself, in order to appear now on our behalf in the very presence of God. Further, he did not enter heaven to offer himself over and over again, like the cohen hagadol who enters the Holiest Place year after year with blood that is not his own; for then he would have had to suffer death many times—from the founding of the universe on. But as it is, he has appeared once at the end of the ages in order to do away with sin through the sacrifice of himself. Just as human beings have to die once, but after this comes judgment, so also the Messiah, having been offered once to bear the sins of many, will appear a second time, not to deal with sin, but to deliver those who are eagerly waiting for him. For the Torah has in it a shadow of the good things to come, but not the actual manifestation of the originals. Therefore, it can never, by means of the same sacrifices repeated endlessly year after year, bring to the goal those who approach the Holy Place to offer them. Otherwise, wouldn't the offering of those sacrifices have ceased? For if the people performing the service had been cleansed once and for all, they would no longer have sins on their conscience. No, it is quite the contrary—in these sacrifices is a reminder of sins, year after year. For it is impossible that the blood of bulls and goats should take away sins. This is why, on coming into the world, he says, "It has not been your will to have an animal sacrifice and a meal offering; rather, you have prepared for me a body. No, you have not been pleased with burnt offerings and sin offerings. Then I said, 'Look! In the scroll of the book it is written about me. I have come to do your will.'" In saying first, "You neither willed nor were pleased with animal sacrifices, meal offerings, burnt offerings and sin offerings," things which are offered in accordance with the Torah; and then, "Look, I have come to do your will"; he takes away the first system in order to set up the second. It is in connection with this will that we have been separated for God and made holy, once and for all, through the offering of Yeshua the Messiah's body. Now every cohen stands every day doing his service, offering over and over the same sacrifices, which can never take away sins. But this one, after he had offered for all time a single sacrifice for sins, sat down at the right hand of God, from then on to wait until his enemies be made a footstool for his feet. For by a single offering he has brought to the goal for all time those who are being set apart for God and made holy. And the Ruach HaKodesh too bears witness to us; for after saying, 'This is the covenant which I will make with them after those days,' says ADONAI: 'I will put my Torah on their hearts, and write it on their minds...,'" he then adds, " 'And their sins and their wickednesses I will remember no more.'" Now where there is forgiveness for these, an offering for sins is no longer needed. So, brothers, we have confidence to use the way into the Holiest Place opened by the blood of Yeshua. He inaugurated it for us as a new and living way through the parokhet, by means of his flesh.

1 Peter 1:18-19

You should be aware that the ransom paid to free you from the worthless way of life which your fathers passed on to you did not consist of anything perishable like silver or gold; on the contrary, it was the costly bloody sacrificial death of the Messiah, as of a lamb without defect or spot.)

He himself bore our sins in his body on the stake, so that we might die to sins and live for righteousness—by his wounds you were healed. For you used to be like sheep gone astray, but now you have turned to the Shepherd, who watches over you

Supportive Scriptures—Yeshua Our Sacrificed Lamb

Isaiah 53:4-12
Matthew 20:28
John 1:29
1 Corinthians 5:7

Commentary

The 10th day of the seventh month is referred to in Leviticus 23:27 and 25:9 as *Yom HaKippurim,* and in Leviticus 23:28 as *Yom Kippurim.* Although the day appears in the plural in Scripture, it is more commonly known as *Yom Kippur,* and is translated "Day of Atonement."

Because the CJB translates the relevant Scriptures differently than do, several other highly regarded English translations, a decision had to be made as to which of them to rely upon in constructing this *Mitzvah.* The five Scripture verses at issue are:

- Leviticus 16:29 תְּעַנּוּ אֶת־נַפְשֹׁתֵיכֶם

- Leviticus 16:31 וְעִנִּיתֶם אֶת־נַפְשֹׁתֵיכֶם

- Leviticus 23:27 וְעִנִּיתֶם אֶת־נַפְשֹׁתֵיכֶם

- Leviticus 23:29 כָל־הַנֶּפֶשׁ אֲשֶׁר לֹא־תְעֻנֶּה

- Numbers 29:7 וְעִנִּיתֶם אֶת־נַפְשֹׁתֵיכֶם

The CJB and NIV translate the first four above as "deny yourselves," and the KJV and NKJ translate them as "afflict your souls." The NAS version differs by translating the first three as "humble your souls," and Numbers 29:7 as "humble yourselves." The CJB and NIV both translate Leviticus 23:29 as "deny himself," the KJV translates it as "not be afflicted," the NKJ version translates it as "not afflicted in soul," and the NAS version translates it as "not humble himself."

The weight of lexical authority appears to favor (and I have adopted) the view that we are commanded to afflict and humble our souls on *Yom Kippur.* The question is "What does that mean, and how are we to accomplish it?" Jewish tradition, based partially upon Scripture (e.g. Psalms 35:13; 69:10; Jeremiah 36:6), interprets "afflict your souls" as meaning that we are to fast from food and drink for twenty-five hours; this fast has become one of *Yom Kippur's* most well-known features.

While fasting on *Yom Kippur* is certainly appropriate and a practice with which I comply, I am of the opinion that the true biblical meaning and intent of afflicting our souls on *Yom Kippur*, is that we repent of our sins.

Consider God's admonition to the Israelites in <u>Isaiah 58:1-8</u>:

> *Shout out loud! Don't hold back! Raise your voice like a shofar! Proclaim to my people what rebels they are, to the house of Ya'akov their sins. Oh yes, they seek me day after day and [claim to] delight in knowing my ways. As if they were an upright nation that had not abandoned the rulings of their God, they ask me for just rulings and [claim] to take pleasure in closeness to God, [asking,] 'Why should we fast, if you don't see? Why mortify ourselves, if you don't notice?' Here is my answer: when you fast, you go about doing whatever you like, while keeping your laborers hard at work. Your fasts lead to quarreling and fighting, to lashing out with violent blows. On a day like today, fasting like yours will not make your voice heard on high. Is this the sort of fast I want, a day when a person mortifies himself? Is the object to hang your head like a reed and spread sackcloth and ashes under yourself? Is this what you call a fast, a day that pleases ADONAI? Here is the sort of fast I want— releasing those unjustly bound, untying the thongs of the yoke, letting the oppressed go free, breaking every yoke, sharing your food with the hungry, taking the homeless poor into your house, clothing the naked when you see them, fulfilling your duty to your kinsmen! Then your light will burst forth like the morning, your new skin will quickly grow over your wound; your righteousness will precede you, and ADONAI's glory will follow you.*

The theme and purpose of *Yom Kippur* is repentance, and the above Scripture eschews any fast (including the *Yom Kippur* fast) that does not include it. We are familiar with the discomfort of not eating, so fasting might seem to be the primary and most logical way that God wants us to afflict our souls on *Yom Kippur*. Consider, however, how much more our souls are afflicted by our having to face the reality of our sins and repent, often with confession and restitution. Although afflicting our souls is called for, what is really sought from us is not bodily discomfort but repentance.

Observance of *Yom Kippur* as a *Shabbat* and time for personal and national repentance is mandatory for Jews and *K'rov Yisrael* Gentiles, and recommended for other Gentile followers of Yeshua as well. Not only is repentance important for us personally, but it is necessary if we are to fulfill the priestly responsibilities that God has given to each of us. According to <u>Exodus 19:6</u>, Israel has been made into a kingdom of priests (albeit not all of Israel are descended from Levitical priests) and, according to <u>1 Peter 2:9</u> and <u>Revelation 5:10</u>, all New Covenant believers have become priests as well. This "priesthood of believers" is not for the purpose of sacrificing animals in an earthly temple, but for serving Yeshua who, as High Priest, entered the heavenly "Holy Place" by means of His own blood sacrifice (<u>Hebrews 9:11-12</u>). So whether we are Jews or Gentiles, all disciples of Yeshua carry priestly responsibilities for which spiritual cleansing through repentance is a prerequisite. Note also that, whereas animal sacrifices (accompanied by repentance) conducted in the Temple merely covered over sins, Yeshua's sacrifice (accompanied by repentance) in the New Covenant completely removes sin.

Classical Commentators

Maimonides, Meir, and HaChinuch express their respective *mitzvot* as our having to fast on *Yom Kippur.* They deduce this from the above Scriptures which they understand to be saying "We must afflict our souls." This *Mitzvah* agrees with them on that latter point, but does not agree that afflicting the soul necessarily equates to fasting. Maimonides and HaChinuch state that on *Yom Kippur,* in addition to resting and fasting, we must refrain from all activities that care for the body; this includes washing, applying oil to the skin, and marital relations. Maimonides and HaChinuch also state that we are not to wear shoes, but Meir limits this to not wearing shoes made of leather. The classical commentators do not connect "afflicting the soul" with "repentance" and, in fact, do not discuss repentance with any depth at all.

<u>NCLA</u>: **JMm JFm KMm KFm GMr GFr**

D14. Rejoicing at the Festivals of *Shavuot, Sukkot,* and *Sh'mini Atzeret.*

We are to rejoice at the festivals of *Shavuot, Sukkot,* and *Sh'mini Atzeret.*

This precept is derived from His Word (blessed be He):

Key Scriptures

Leviticus 23:34-36 (Maimonides RP50-51; Chinuch C320, 322)
Tell the people of Isra'el, 'On the fifteenth day of this seventh month is the feast of Sukkot for seven days to ADONAI. On the first day there is to be a holy convocation; do not do any kind of ordinary work. For seven days you are to bring an offering made by fire to ADONAI; on the eighth day you are to have a holy convocation and bring an offering made by fire to ADONAI; it is a day of public assembly; do not do any kind of ordinary work.

Leviticus 23:39-40
But on the fifteenth day of the seventh month, when you have gathered the produce of the land, you are to observe the festival of ADONAI seven days; the first day is to be a complete rest and the eighth day is to be a complete rest. On the first day you are to take choice fruit, palm fronds, thick branches and river-willows, and celebrate (NKJ: "rejoice") in the presence of ADONAI your God for seven days.

Numbers 28:26-27 (Maimonides RP45; Chinuch C404)
On the day of the firstfruits, when you bring a new grain offering to ADONAI in your feast of Shavu'ot, you are to have a holy convocation; do not do any kind of ordinary work; but present a burnt offering as a fragrant aroma for ADONAI, consisting of two young bulls, one ram, seven male lambs in their first year,

Numbers 29:12-39 (Maimonides RP50-51; Chinuch C320, 322)
On the fifteenth day of the seventh month you are to have a holy convocation. You are not to do any kind of ordinary work, and you are to observe a feast to ADONAI seven days. You are to present a burnt offering, an offering made by fire, bringing a fragrant aroma to ADONAI. It is to consist of thirteen young bulls, two rams, fourteen male lambs in their first year (they are to be without defect), with their grain offering—fine flour mixed with olive oil, six quarts for each of the thirteen bulls, four quarts for each of the two rams, and two quarts for each of the fourteen lambs; also one male goat as a sin offering; in addition to the regular burnt offering with its grain and drink offerings. On the second day you are to present twelve young bulls, two rams, fourteen male lambs in their first year, without defect; with the grain and drink offerings for the bulls, rams and lambs, according to their number, in keeping with the rule; also one male goat as a sin offering; in addition to the regular burnt offering, its grain offering and their drink offerings. On the third day eleven bulls, two rams, fourteen male lambs in their first year, without defect; with the grain and drink offerings for the bulls, rams and lambs, according to their number, in keeping with the rule; also one male goat as a sin offering; in addition to the regular burnt offering with its grain and drink offerings. On the fourth day ten bulls, two rams, fourteen

male lambs in their first year, without defect; with the grain and drink offerings for the bulls, rams and lambs, according to their number, in keeping with the rule; also one male goat as a sin offering; in addition to the regular burnt offering with its grain and drink offerings. On the fifth day nine bulls, two rams, fourteen male lambs in their first year, without defect; with the grain and drink offerings for the bulls, rams and lambs, according to their number, in keeping with the rule; also one male goat as a sin offering; in addition to the regular burnt offering with its grain and drink offerings. On the sixth day eight bulls, two rams, fourteen male lambs in their first year, without defect; with the grain and drink offerings for the bulls, rams and lambs, according to their number, in keeping with the rule; also one male goat as a sin offering; in addition to the regular burnt offering with its grain and drink offerings. On the seventh day seven bulls, two rams, fourteen male lambs in their first year, without defect; with the grain and drink offerings for the bulls, rams and lambs, according to their number, in keeping with the rule; also one male goat as a sin offering; in addition to the regular burnt offering with its grain offering and drink offerings. On the eighth day you are to have a festive assembly: you are not to do any kind of ordinary work; but you are to present a burnt offering, an offering made by fire, giving a fragrant aroma to ADONAI—one bull, one ram, seven male lambs in their first year, without defect; with the grain and drink offerings for the bull, the ram and the lambs, according to their number, in keeping with the rule; also one male goat as a sin offering; in addition to the regular burnt offering with its grain and drink offerings. You are to offer these to ADONAI at your designated times in addition to your vows and voluntary offerings—whether these are your burnt offerings, grain offerings, drink offerings or peace offerings.

Deuteronomy 16:10-11
You are to observe the festival of Shavu'ot [weeks] for ADONAI your God with a voluntary offering, which you are to give in accordance with the degree to which ADONAI your God has prospered you. You are to rejoice in the presence of ADONAI your God—you, your sons and daughters, your male and female slaves, the L'vi'im living in your towns, and the foreigners, orphans and widows living among you—in the place where ADONAI your God will choose to have his name live.

Deuteronomy 16:13-15 (Maimonides RP54; Meir MP21; Chinuch C488)
You are to keep the festival of Sukkot for seven days after you have gathered the produce of your threshing-floor and winepress. Rejoice at your festival—you, your sons and daughters, your male and female slaves, the L'vi'im, and the foreigners, orphans and widows living among you. Seven days you are to keep the festival for ADONAI your God in the place ADONAI your God will choose, because ADONAI your God will bless you in all your crops and in all your work, so you are to be full of joy!

Philippians 4:4
Rejoice in union with the Lord always! I will say it again: rejoice!

1 Thessalonians 5:16
Always be joyful.

218

Commentary

There are many verses in Scripture (e.g. in <u>Psalms</u> and <u>Philippians 4:4</u>) that exhort us to rejoice in the Lord, and <u>1 Thessalonians 5:16</u> that exhorts us to rejoice at all times. That being said, the above Scriptures single out three festivals *(Shavuot, Sukkot,* and *Sh'mini Atzeret*—the eighth day*)* for rejoicing—possibly because they are festivals of harvest.

Most of the appointed times listed in <u>Leviticus 23</u>, while required to be kept by Jews, are only optional for Gentiles who are not *K'rovei Yisrael. Sukkot* is an exception however, because of <u>Zechariah 14:16</u>'s reference to "all the nations." That notwithstanding, its description is of the "Age to Come," so its requirement for Gentile participation in this age cannot be established. However, Gentiles connecting to its meaning is important, however, so the season appears to be a fitting time for Jewish and Gentile congregations to come together for celebration and worship.

Classical Commentators

Maimonides, Meir, and HaChinuch rely on <u>Deuteronomy 16:14</u> (Maimonides and HaChinuch rely additionally on <u>Deuteronomy 27:7</u>) to state that we are to rejoice in (celebrate) all of God's feasts. They do not limit their *mitzvot* of celebration to *Shavuot, Sukkot,* and *Sh'mini Atzeret,* although these are the only festivals in Scripture on which rejoicing or celebrating is specifically commanded.

<u>NCLA</u>: **JMm JFm KMm KFm GMo GFo**

D15. Living in a *Sukkah* During the Feast of *Sukkot*.

We are to live in a sukkah during the seven days of Sukkot.

This precept is derived from His Word (blessed be He):

Key Scriptures

Leviticus 23:42-43 (Maimonides RP168; Meir MP35; Chinuch C325)
You are to live in sukkot for seven days; every citizen of Isra'el is to live in a sukkah, so that generation after generation of you will know that I made the people of Isra'el live in sukkot when I brought them out of the land of Egypt; I am ADONAI your God.

John 7:1-3
After this, Yeshua traveled around in the Galil, intentionally avoiding Y'hudah because the Judeans were out to kill him. But the festival of Sukkot in Y'hudah was near; so his brothers said to him, "Leave here and go into Y'hudah, so that your talmidim can see the miracles you do;

Supportive Scripture

Nehemiah 8:14-17

Commentary

The Leviticus Scripture referenced above commands that all citizens of Israel are to live in *sukkot* for the seven days of the Feast (of *Sukkot*), and it gives the reason—so that each generation of Israel will remember God's provision of shelter for us when He brought us out of Egypt. Although the expression "citizen of Isra'el" might be construed to mean only those Jews who live in the Land, the expression that follows it—"the people of Isra'el"—broadens its meaning to include all Jewish People, wherever in the world they may live. I believe it is also applicable to Gentiles who permanently live within the Jewish community *(K'rovei Yisrael)* because those that God brought out of Egypt were a mixed multitude that consisted of both Jews and Gentiles (Exodus 12:38). That may be part of the explanation for why worshiping God on *Sukkot* is required of all the Gentile nations in Zechariah 14:16-19. Living in a *sukkah* during the Feast is not a requirement for Gentiles who are not *K'rov Yisrael,* but they may do so if they deem it meaningful.

The matter of how often one must physically occupy a *sukkah* during the seven days of the Feast, and what functions one must perform there in order that it be counted as "dwelling" is a matter of interpretation, especially in the Diaspora where climate and other considerations have to be considered. A minimum standard that is common among Diaspora Jews is to eat at least one meal each day in a *sukkah.*

John 7:1-3 references a *Sukkot* Feast that Yeshua attended, but there is no description of the *sukkah* in which he must have lived during the seven days. Nevertheless, the theme of *Sukkot* (which is living under God's provision and protection) is very much a New Covenant theme, with Yeshua, the *Ru'ach HaKodesh,* and the *B'rit Chadashah* Scriptures being the main New Covenant provisions.

Classical Commentators

Maimonides says relatively little in his *mitzvah* ——merely that we are to live in a *sukkah* throughout the seven days of the Feast. Meir is much more detailed, adding that the *sukkah* must have a roof of branches, and that we must eat, drink, and otherwise live in it both day and night to the extent that one must not eat even one regular meal outside of it. HaChinuch expounds on the biblical reason for living in a *sukkah,* speaks a great deal about its structure, and is much more liberal than Meir in how much "living" one must do in it. He states, for example, that on the first night of *Sukkot* one must eat at least an olive's amount of bread in a *sukkah* and, after that, it is voluntary. HaChinuch also focuses on bread by stating that meals other than "regular meals of bread" may be eaten outside of a *sukkah,* but he adds that the early sages would not eat any meal outside of a *sukkah* during the Feast.

NCLA: JMm JFm KMm KFm GMo GFo

D16. Taking Up the Four Species on *Sukkot*.

We are to take up the four species during the Feast of Sukkot.

This precept is derived from His Word (blessed be He):

Key Scriptures

<u>Leviticus 23:39-40</u> (Maimonides RP169; Meir MP36; Chinuch C324)
But on the fifteenth day of the seventh month, when you have gathered the produce of the land, you are to observe the festival of ADONAI seven days; the first day is to be a complete rest and the eighth day is to be a complete rest. On the first day you are to take choice fruit, palm fronds, thick branches and river-willows, and celebrate in the presence of ADONAI your God for seven days.

<u>John 7:1-3</u>
After this, Yeshua traveled around in the Galil, intentionally avoiding Y'hudah because the Judeans were out to kill him. But the festival of Sukkot in Y'hudah was near; so his brothers said to him, "Leave here and go into Y'hudah, so that your talmidim can see the miracles you do;

Commentary

The four species are (1) choice fruit, (2) palm branches, (3) thick branches, and (4) willows of the brook. Traditionally, parts of each are bound together into a bouquet (sometimes referred to as a *lulav,* but literally, *lulav* only refers to a palm branch) and are preserved and waived for each of the seven days of *Sukkot.* The command to take up the four species clearly applies to the first day but, since the Scripture states that we are to celebrate for seven days, we suppose that waving them as part of the celebration is contemplated. Scripture does not specify a particular select fruit, so the tradition developed to use an etrog (citron) that has part of its fragile stem still attached. *Halachically,* therefore, the etrog becomes unusable if the short nub of a stem becomes detached.

We do not know whether, during the time of Yeshua, binding the four species together and waving all four was practiced at celebrations other than *Sukkot.* The practice was probably specific to *Sukkot* because we read in <u>John 12:12</u> (speaking of before Passover) that Yeshua was met with the waving of palm branches only. The question remains, however, "What is the significance of waving the four species at *Sukkot?*" Scripture is silent on this, but its significance was probably agricultural since *Sukkot* is a harvest celebration. The *Talmud* seeks to answer this by suggesting that the four species represent God's creation, and that waving them in all directions signifies that *HaShem* is Lord of all.

It is significant that an expression of worship meant for God (waving palms) was used to recognize and welcome Yeshua, and it is also significant that <u>John 12:15</u> states:

> *"Daughter of Tziyon, don't be afraid! Look! your King is coming, sitting on a donkey's colt."*

What it means to "take up" the four species is open to interpretation, but this *Mitzvah* is unquestionably applicable to Jews and, in my opinion, to *K'rov Yisrael* Gentiles as well. Because we don't know exactly what "taking up" means, the procedure should be done according to the established practice or *halachah* of each community in which the worshiper finds himself. I do not believe that taking up the four species is required of other Gentiles as part of their worship of God during *Sukkot*, but they may do so if they deem it to be meaningful.

Classical Commentators

Maimonides, Meir, and HaChinuch state their respective *mitzvot* somewhat differently as follows: (1) Maimonides: Rejoice with a palm branch for the seven days; (2) Meir: Lift up (or wave) one palm branch, one etrog, three myrtle branches, and two willow branches on each of the seven days (but not on *Shabbat*); (3) HaChinuch: Similar to Meir, but adds considerable content from the "oral tradition," including the analogy of each species to a man's organs. The etrog is said to be like the heart, the *lulav* (palm branch) like the spine, the myrtle like the eyes, and the willow like the lips.

<u>NCLA</u>: JMm JFm KMm KFm GMo GFo

D17. Public Reading of the *Torah* during *Sukkot* in the Sabbatical Year.

We are to assemble to read and to hear read the Torah during the Festival of Sukkot in the Sabbatical Year.

This precept is derived from His Word (blessed be He):

Key Scriptures

Deuteronomy 31:10-13 (Maimonides RP16; Chinuch C612)
Moshe gave them these orders: "At the end of every seven years, during the festival of Sukkot in the year of sh'mittah, when all Isra'el have come to appear in the presence of ADONAI at the place he will choose, you are to read this Torah before all Isra'el, so that they can hear it. Assemble the people—the men, the women, the little ones and the foreigners you have in your towns—so that they can hear, learn, fear ADONAI your God and take care to obey all the words of this Torah; and so that their children, who have not known, can hear and learn to fear ADONAI your God, for as long as you live in the land you are crossing the Yarden to possess."

John 7:1-3
After this, Yeshua traveled around in the Galil, intentionally avoiding Y'hudah because the Judeans were out to kill him. But the festival of Sukkot in Y'hudah was near; so his brothers said to him, "Leave here and go into Y'hudah, so that your talmidim can see the miracles you do;

Commentary

We assume that Moses gave this order in compliance with God's directive, so it should be considered *Torah.* The commandment involves assembling, reading aloud (teaching), hearing, and learning. All of these are good and necessary to do at times other than *Sukkot* and other than in the Sabbatical Year, but the commandment specifies this particular time, so it should be complied with. Since the designated place of assembly was where the Ark of God was, it is especially important to conduct the reading in *Yerushalayim,* at the place where the Temple last stood. Jews everywhere should be encouraged to journey there to hear, read, and otherwise participate but, for those who cannot, similar assemblies and readings can be conducted in synagogues elsewhere and at distant parts of the world.

Complying with this *Mitzvah* today is perhaps more symbolic and ceremonial than actually needed to learn the commandments of God because, unlike in the time of Moses, synagogues the world over read through the entire *Torah* once a year every year, and printed Bibles are generally available to all. That notwithstanding, it is a general principle that blessing follows from literally obeying *Torah* with a heart to please God and wherever possible. Because this *mitzvah* is so closely related to Jewish identity and calling, I consider it to be only optional for non-*k'rov Yisrael* Gentiles.

Classical Commentators

Meir does not include this *Mitzvah* in his compilation, but it is treated by Maimonides and HaChinuch as a requirement for all Jews—including women, even though the commandment appears to be time-dependant.[90] HaChinuch states that the reason this assembly is so important is that possessing the *Torah* is what distinguishes Israel from the other nations.

<u>NCLA</u>: JMm JFm KMm KFm GMo GFo

---

90 According to the *Mishnah (m.Kidd.1:7)*, women are not required to perform positive time-dependant commandments.

D18. Cancelling Loans and Resting Our Land in the Sabbatical Year.

We are to cancel loans and allow our land to lie fallow in the Sabbatical Year.[91]

This precept is derived from His Word (blessed be He):

Key Scriptures

Exodus 23:10-11 (Maimonides RP134; Meir ML20; Chinuch C84)
For six years, you are to sow your land with seed and gather in its harvest. But the seventh year, you are to let it rest and lie fallow, so that the poor among your people can eat; and what they leave, the wild animals in the countryside can eat. Do the same with your vineyard and olive grove.

Exodus 34:21 (Maimonides RP135)
Six days you will work, but on the seventh day you are to rest—even in plowing time and harvest season you are to rest.

Leviticus 25:1-2 (Maimonides RP135; Meir ML21; Chinuch C112)
ADONAI spoke to Moshe on Mount Sinai; he said, "Tell the people of Isra'el, 'When you enter the land I am giving you, the land itself is to observe a Shabbat rest for ADONAI.'"

Leviticus 25:3-4 (Maimonides RN220-221; Meir ML22-23; Chinuch C326-327)
Six years you will sow your field; six years you will prune your grapevines and gather their produce. But in the seventh year is to be a Shabbat of complete rest for the land, a Shabbat for ADONAI; you will neither sow your field nor prune your grapevines.

Leviticus 25:5-7 (Maimonides RP134, RN222-223; Meir ML24-25; Chinuch C84, 328-329)
You are not to harvest what grows by itself from the seeds left by your previous harvest, and you are not to gather the grapes of your untended vine; it is to be a year of complete rest for the land. But what the land produces during the year of Shabbat will be food for all of you—you, your servant, your maid, your employee, anyone living near you, your livestock and the wild animals on your land; everything the land produces may be used for food.

Leviticus 25:20-22
If you ask, "If we aren't allowed to sow seed or harvest what our land produces, what are we going to eat the seventh year?" then I will order my blessing on you during the sixth year, so that the land brings forth enough produce for all three years. The eighth year you will sow seed but eat the old, stored produce until the ninth year; that is, until the produce of the eighth year comes in, you will eat the old, stored food.

---

91 See *Mitzvah* C3 for a discussion of cancelling loans during the Sabbatical Year from the aspect of commercial risk.

Deuteronomy 15:1
At the end of every seven years you are to have a sh'mittah.

Deuteronomy 15:2 (Maimonides RN230; Meir MN57, MP64; Chinuch C475)
Here is how the sh'mittah is to be done: every creditor is to give up what he has loaned to his fellow member of the community—he is not to force his neighbor or relative to repay it, because ADONAI's time of remission has been proclaimed.

Deuteronomy 15:3 (Maimonides RP141-142; Chinuch 476-477)
You may demand that a foreigner repay his debt, but you are to release your claim on whatever your brother owes you.

Deuteronomy 15:4-6
In spite of this [releasing debts owed to you] there will be no one needy among you; because ADONAI will certainly bless you in the land which ADONAI your God is giving you as an inheritance to possess—if only you will listen carefully to what ADONAI your God says and take care to obey all these mitzvot I am giving you today. Yes, ADONAI your God will bless you, as he promised you—you will lend money to many nations without having to borrow, and you will rule over many nations without their ruling over you.

Deuteronomy 15:7-11 (Maimonides RN231; Meir MN56; Chinuch C480)
If someone among you is needy, one of your brothers, in any of your towns in your land which ADONAI your God is giving you, you are not to harden your heart or shut your hand from giving to your needy brother. No, you must open your hand to him and lend him enough to meet his need and enable him to obtain what he wants. Guard yourself against allowing your heart to entertain the mean-spirited thought that because the seventh year, the year of sh'mittah is at hand, you would be stingy toward your needy brother and not give him anything; for then he may cry out to ADONAI against you, and it will be your sin. Rather, you must give to him; and you are not to be grudging when you give to him. If you do this, ADONAI your God will bless you in all your work, in everything you undertake—for there will always be poor people in the land. That is why I am giving you this order, 'You must open your hand to your poor and needy brother in your land.'

Matthew 6:25-31
Therefore I say to you, do not worry about your life, what you will eat or what you will drink; nor about your body, what you will put on. Is not life more than food and the body more than clothing? Look at the birds of the air, for they neither sow nor reap nor gather into barns; yet your heavenly Father feeds them. Are you not of more value than they? Which of you by worrying can add one cubit to his stature? So why do you worry about clothing? Consider the lilies of the field, how they grow: they neither toil nor spin; and yet I say to you that even Solomon in all his glory was not arrayed like one of these. Now if God so clothes the grass of the field, which today is, and tomorrow is thrown into the oven, will He not much more clothe you, O you of little faith? Therefore do not worry, saying, 'What shall we eat?' or 'What shall we drink?' or 'What shall we wear?' For after all these things the Gentiles seek. For your heavenly Father knows that you need all these things.

Supportive Scriptures

Proverbs 11:24-25
Luke 12:22-31
2 Corinthians 9:10-12

Commentary

The Sabbatical Year is characterized by the releasing of debts that are owed to us,[92] and by allowing our land to rest—that is, not cultivating the land or harvesting its crops. On the one hand, this *Mitzvah* can be viewed as one of benevolence (*"so that the poor among your people can eat..."* Exodus 23:11) because (1) crops that grow of their own accord during the *Sh'mittah* are available to the poor for gleaning, and (2) Israelite debtors who cannot repay what they have borrowed can be released from a lifetime of bondage. On the other hand, I believe that the primary reason for the Sabbatical Year is revealed in Deuteronomy 25:20-22, which promises God's supernatural provision to those who will obey Him and trust Him.

A question that naturally comes to mind is how releasing loans and resting our land in the Sabbatical Year applies today. I am of the opinion that it continues to apply where today's circumstances are similar to those under which the ancient Israelites lived. Furthermore, when it does apply, it applies not only to Jews, but also to *K'rov Yisrael* Gentiles. How similar the circumstances need to be are revealed to us by the *Ruach HaKodesh* as we pray for guidance.

As for most Gentiles (not *K'rovei Yisrael*), I believe that their compliance is a blessing but not a requirement; I draw this conclusion (as an analogy) from Isaiah 56:1-7, which promises blessing to the foreigner who keeps Gods Sabbaths, but apparently does not require it of him. One thing that is certain, however, is that God continues to expect all of us to look to Him for provision, rather than to think that we can cause provision to come to us through our own efforts.

We ought to consider the Sabbatical Year (and God's other Sabbaths—both weekly and annual) to be a test of our faith, because our willingness to release loans and to rest our land in the Sabbatical Year (as well as rest ourselves on the other Sabbaths), is an indication that we trust God, and are willing to rely upon Him.

Commentary by Daniel C. Juster

In modern societies that are not primarily agricultural, the *Sh'mittah* command (like the Jubilee command) is difficult to apply. However, there are underlying principles that have been noted by many Bible scholars. First, the command shows the importance of renewing and preserving the land so that it is not worn out. Secondly, the command shows that God does not want people to be forever burdened with debt, but rather to be able to have a new start. So, the command

---

92 There is a rabbinical document called a *pruzbul,* by which a private debt is made public by transferring it to a *beit din,* thus making it redeemable during and after a *Sh'mittah.* It is a legal contrivance to circumvent the discharge of a debt in the *Sh'mittah.*

encompasses a principle of their needing to be a way of release from debts that lead to destruction. Bankruptcy laws are probably the modern social equivalent because the same underlying principle is involved. The Biblical text provides that assistance should be made available for those truly in need, and the Sabbatical year's discharge of debts, coupled with the requirement that we not harvest the corners of our fields (thereby allowing some of our crops to be gleaned) are special applications of God's requirement of us that we care for the poor.

Classical Commentators

Maimonides, Meir, and HaChinuch agree that all debts must be cancelled during the Sabbatical Year, and that loans to needy Jews may not be withheld because an approaching *Sh'mittah* will preclude their collectability. Although <u>Deuteronomy 15:3</u> *permits* the repayment of loans made to foreigners to be demanded during the *Sh'mittah,* Maimonides and HaChinuch interpret the Scripture as *requiring* that loans to idolaters be collected. Meir's compilation does not reference <u>Deuteronomy 15:3</u> at all, and does not promulgate any such requirement. Also, none of the commentators connect trusting God with the *Sh'mittah's* cancellation of debts, or with Scripture's prohibition against our refusing to make uncollectable loans to needy Jews prior to a *Sh'mittah.*

Similarly, neither Maimonides, nor Meir, nor HaChinuch connect our trusting God with Scripture's requirement that we allow our land to rest during the Sabbatical Year. Meir alone asserts that agricultural commandments pertaining to the *Sh'mittah* are only applicable in *Eretz Yisrael,* and he therefore places them in an appendix, and lists them separately from his other *mitzvot.*

<u>NCLA</u>: **JMm JFm KMm KFm GMr GFr**

D19. Resting and Returning Ownership of Our Land in the Jubilee Year.

We are to rest our land, and return it to its prior owner in the Jubilee Year.

This precept is derived from His Word (blessed be He):

Key Scriptures

Exodus 13:12* (Maimonides RP140)
you are to set apart for ADONAI everything that is first from the womb. Every firstborn male animal will belong to ADONAI.

Exodus 34:19* (Maimonides RP140)
Everything that is first from the womb is mine. Of all your livestock, you are to set aside for me the males, the firstborn of cattle and flock.

Leviticus 25:4-5** (Chinuch C334)
But in the seventh year is to be a Shabbat of complete rest for the land, a Shabbat for ADONAI; you will neither sow your field nor prune your grapevines. You are not to harvest what grows by itself from the seeds left by your previous harvest, and you are not to gather the grapes of your untended vine; it is to be a year of complete rest for the land.

Leviticus 25:8 (Maimonides RP140; Chinuch C330)
You are to count seven Shabbats of years, seven times seven years, that is, forty-nine years.

Leviticus 25:9 (Maimonides RP137; Chinuch C331)
Then, on the tenth day of the seventh month, on Yom-Kippur, you are to sound a blast on the shofar; you are to sound the shofar all through your land;

Leviticus 25:10 (Maimonides RP136-137; Chinuch C331-332)
and you are to consecrate the fiftieth year, proclaiming freedom throughout the land to all its inhabitants. It will be a yovel for you; you will return everyone to the land he owns, and everyone is to return to his family.

Leviticus 25:11 (Maimonides RN224-226; Chinuch C333, 335)
That fiftieth year will be a yovel for you; in that year you are not to sow, harvest what grows by itself or gather the grapes of untended vines;

Leviticus 25:12 (Maimonides RP136)
...because it is a yovel. It will be holy for you; whatever the fields produce will be food for all of you.

Leviticus 25:13-17
In this year of yovel, every one of you is to return to the land he owns. If you sell anything to your neighbor or buy anything from him, neither of you is to exploit the other. Rather, you are to

230

take into account the number of years after the yovel when you buy land from your neighbor, and he is to sell to you according to the number of years crops will be raised. If the number of years remaining is large, you will raise the price; if few years remain, you will lower it; because what he is really selling you is the number of crops to be produced. Thus you are not to take advantage of each other, but you are to fear your God; for I am ADONAI your God.

Leviticus 25:23 (Maimonides RN227; Chinuch C339)
The land is not to be sold in perpetuity, because the land belongs to me—you are only foreigners and temporary residents with me.

Leviticus 25:24-28 (Maimonides RP138; Chinuch C340)
Therefore, when you sell your property, you must include the right of redemption. That is, if one of you becomes poor and sells some of his property, his next-of-kin can come and buy back what his relative sold. If the seller has no one to redeem it but becomes rich enough to redeem it himself, he will calculate the number of years the land was sold for, refund the excess to its buyer, and return to his property. If he hasn't sufficient means to get it back himself, then what he sold will remain in the hands of the buyer until the year of yovel; in the yovel the buyer will vacate it and the seller return to his property.

Leviticus 25:29-31 (Maimonides RP139; Chinuch C341)
If someone sells a dwelling in a walled city, he has one year after the date of sale in which to redeem it. For a full year he will have the right of redemption; but if he has not redeemed the dwelling in the walled city within the year, then title in perpetuity passes to the buyer through all his generations; it will not revert in the yovel. However, houses in villages not surrounded by walls are to be dealt with like the fields in the countryside—they may be redeemed [before the yovel], and they revert in the yovel.

Matthew 6:25-31
Therefore I say to you, do not worry about your life, what you will eat or what you will drink; nor about your body, what you will put on. Is not life more than food and the body more than clothing? Look at the birds of the air, for they neither sow nor reap nor gather into barns; yet your heavenly Father feeds them. Are you not of more value than they? Which of you by worrying can add one cubit to his stature? So why do you worry about clothing? Consider the lilies of the field, how they grow: they neither toil nor spin; and yet I say to you that even Solomon in all his glory was not arrayed like one of these. Now if God so clothes the grass of the field, which today is, and tomorrow is thrown into the oven, will He not much more clothe you, O you of little faith? Therefore do not worry, saying, 'What shall we eat?' or 'What shall we drink?' or 'What shall we wear?' For after all these things the Gentiles seek. For your heavenly Father knows that you need all these things.

Supportive Scriptures

Isaiah 61:1-2
Proverbs 11:24-25
Luke 4:16-19, 12:22-31

Commentary

We are to count seven Sabbaths of years (forty-nine years) from each Year of Jubilee to the next. When the Year of Jubilee arrives, we are not to cultivate our land or harvest its crops in the usual way, and we are to return it to its prior owner, the one who sold it to us. When land is sold, it must not be sold in perpetuity, and a right of redemption by the seller must be an inherent part of the sale. In a very real sense, therefore, the sale of land is not of the land itself, but of the value of the crops that the land is likely to produce until the next Jubilee.

The Year of Jubilee, similar to the *Sh'mittah,* can be viewed as a time of faith and benevolence because the crops that grow of their own accord (without cultivation) during the year is available for all to glean, including those who are poor. The Jubilee can also be viewed as a *mitzvah* of social and economic equalization, because Israelites that have become wealthy through land that they have occupied will have to give the source of their wealth up in the Year of Jubilee.

Like the *Sh'mittah,* I believe that the primary reason for God giving the Jubilee Year to the Israelites was to hone their faith and cause them to have to trust Him for their provision. A question that comes to mind, of course, is how resting our land and returning it to its prior owner applies to us today. I am of the opinion that it can only apply literally as in the past, where today's circumstances are similar to those under which the ancient Israelites lived. So far as I am aware it is never the case since the assumption of Scripture regarding the Jubilee is that (1) it is meant to apply only in the Land of Israel, and (2) it is meant to apply by the entire population so that the burden of returning land that one has bought does not unjustly fall on just a few individuals who are willing to comply. Still, all Scripture is inspired by God and is profitable (2 Timothy 3:16-17), so we ought to consider how to use the inspiration when the Year of Jubilee arrives. I propose that we consider it a time to reflect on our faith by considering what our willingness would be to rest our land (should we own land in geographic Israel) and give it up in the Jubilee year as a demonstration of our trust and reliance on God.

Commentary by Daniel C. Juster

In modern societies that are not primarily agricultural, the Jubilee (also the *Sh'mittah*) is difficult to apply. However, there are underlying principles that have been noted by many Bible scholars. First, similar to the *Sh'mittah,* the command shows the importance of renewing and preserving the land so that it is not worn out. Secondly, the command shows that God does not want the ownership of land to create a permanent class of landed gentry. The Jubilee promotes equal economic and social opportunity that is also the goal of our most enlightened and compassionate governmental systems.

The Jubilee restoration of land does not mean socialism since there could be disparities of wealth by other means (e.g. in gold, silver, herds, etc.). However, there is a redistribution of land-wealth in the Jubilee that equalizes opportunity. I think the principle here is not to impose taxes for on-going welfare, but to use taxes (especially inheritance taxes) to provide education and training so that those without financial means have economic opportunity. Perhaps we could call such taxes "equal opportunity taxes."

Classical Commentators

Meir has not constructed any *mitzvot* pertaining to the Jubilee. Maimonides and HaChinuch have, but they do not take into consideration today's changed circumstances as compared to those that existed during the time of Moses. Their *mitzvot* therefore require literal obedience to the Scriptures in a way that is difficult in regard to resting the land, and nearly impossible regarding its return—even in *Eretz Yisrael.*

Similar to their *Sh'mittah mitzvot,* Maimonides and HaChinuch do not connect the Year of Jubilee to man's need to trust God for provision.

<u>**NCLA**</u>**: JMm JFm KMm (not literally); KFm GMo GFo**

*   Scriptures that are discussed in Maimonides' *mitzvot,* but that have no obvious relevance to the Year of Jubilee.

**   Lv25:5 is about the Sabbatical Year—not the Jubilee Year—but it is listed here because it is referred to by HaChinuch in his *mitzvah* C334, which is about the Jubilee Year.

D20. Determining Occurrence of the New Moon.

We are to determine the occurrence of every new moon.

This precept is derived from His Word (blessed be He):

Key Scriptures

Exodus 12:2-3 (Maimonides RP153; Chinuch C4)
You are to begin your calendar with this month; it will be the first month of the year for you. Speak to all the assembly of Isra'el and say, 'On the tenth day of this month, each man is to take a lamb or kid for his family, one per household...'

Exodus 13:10 (Maimonides RP153; Chinuch C4)
Therefore you are to observe this regulation at its proper time, year after year.

Exodus 34:22 (Chinuch C4)
Observe the festival of *Shavu'ot* with the first-gathered produce of the wheat harvest, and the festival of ingathering at the turn of the year.

Leviticus 23:4 (Maimonides RP153; Chinuch C4)
These are the designated times of ADONAI, the holy convocations you are to proclaim at their designated times.

Numbers 11:20 (Maimonides RP15)
...but a whole month!—until it comes out of your nose and you hate it!—because you have rejected ADONAI, who is here with you, and distressed him with your crying and asking, "Why did we ever leave Egypt?"

Numbers 11:21 (Chinuch C4)
But Moshe said, "Here I am with six hundred thousand men on foot, and yet you say, 'I will give them meat to eat for a whole month!'

Numbers 28:11 (Maimonides RP42; Chinuch 403)
At each Rosh-Hodesh of yours, you are to present a burnt offering to ADONAI consisting of two young bulls, one ram and seven male lambs in their first year and without defect;

Deuteronomy 16:1 (Maimonides RP153; Chinuch C4)
"Observe the month of Aviv, and keep Pesach to ADONAI your God; for in the month of Aviv, ADONAI your God brought you out of Egypt at night.

Colossians 2:16
So don't let anyone pass judgment on you in connection with eating and drinking, or in regard to a Jewish festival or Rosh-Hodesh or Shabbat.

Commentary

There is no explicit biblical commandment to determine the occurrence of the New Moon (*Rosh Chodesh*), but the numerous references to the beginning of months and to the New Year makes it a logical imperative to do so. Colossians 2:16 is the only mention of the New Moon in the Apostolic Writings, but there are several references in the New Testament to months and years.

The difficulty of determining the appearance of a New Moon is that there is no appearance of the moon at all. On the night of a New Moon, one sees no moon—similar to nights that are clouded over. During the time of Yeshua, the New Moon was declared by the *San Hedrin* upon its receiving the testimony of two individuals that they observed it. How can one see a moon that one cannot see? The testimony received was that the witnesses saw the last sliver of moon showing from the night previous.

Using modern astronomical methods of determining the New Moon is more precise and is acceptable in most of Judaism today. Explaining these methods is, however, beyond the scope of this *Mitzvah.*

Classical Commentators

Maimonides and HaChinuch reference the above *Torah* Scriptures to support their respective *mitzvot* regarding the New Moon. Meir is silent on the subject.

NCLA: JMm JFm KMm KFm GMo GFo

E: Covenant Responsibilities

E1. Preserving and Disseminating God's Word.

We are to preserve God's Word, and disseminate His Word to the Gentile nations.

This precept is derived from His Word (blessed is He):

Key Scriptures

Exodus 19:5-6
Now if you will pay careful attention to what I say and keep my covenant, then you will be my own treasure from among all the peoples, for all the earth is mine; and you will be a kingdom of cohanim for me, a nation set apart.' These are the words you are to speak to the people of Isra'el.

Deuteronomy 4:9-10 (Meir MP14)
Only be careful, and watch yourselves diligently as long as you live, so that you won't forget what you saw with your own eyes, so that these things won't vanish from your hearts. Rather, make them known to your children and grandchildren—the day you stood before ADONAI your God at Horev, when ADONAI said to me, 'Gather the people to me, and I will make them hear my very words, so that they will learn to hold me in awe as long as they live on earth, and so that they will teach their children.'

Deuteronomy 6:4-9 (Maimonides RP11-13, 15; Meir MP8-9, 12, 14; Chinuch C419, 421-423)
Sh'ma, Yisra'el! ADONAI Eloheinu, ADONAI echad [Hear, Isra'el! ADONAI our God, ADONAI is one]; and you are to love ADONAI your God with all your heart, all your being and all your resources. These words, which I am ordering you today, are to be on your heart; and you are to teach them carefully to your children. You are to talk about them when you sit at home, when you are traveling on the road, when you lie down and when you get up. Tie them on your hand as a sign, put them at the front of a headband around your forehead, and write them on the door-frames of your house and on your gates.

Deuteronomy 11:18-21 (Maimonides RP11, 13, 15; Meir MP12; Chinuch C419, 421, 423)
Therefore, you are to store up these words of mine in your heart and in all your being; tie them on your hand as a sign; put them at the front of a headband around your forehead; teach them carefully to your children, talking about them when you sit at home, when you are traveling on the road, when you lie down and when you get up; and write them on the door-frames of your house and on your gates—so that you and your children will live long on the land ADONAI swore to your ancestors that he would give them for as long as there is sky above the earth.

Deuteronomy 17:18-20 (Maimonides RP17; Chinuch C503)
When he has come to occupy the throne of his kingdom, he is to write a copy of this Torah for himself in a scroll, from the one the cohanim and L'vi'im use. It is to remain with him, and he is to read in it every day, as long as he lives; so that he will learn to fear ADONAI his God and keep all the words of this Torah and these laws and obey them; so that he will not think he is better than his kinsmen; and so that he will not turn aside either to the right or to the left from the mitzvah. In this way he will prolong his own reign and that of his children in Isra'el.

Mark 16:15-20
Then he said to them, "As you go throughout the world, proclaim the Good News to all creation. Whoever trusts and is immersed will be saved; whoever does not trust will be condemned. And these signs will accompany those who do trust: in my name they will drive out demons, speak with new tongues, not be injured if they handle snakes or drink poison, and heal the sick by laying hands on them." So then, after he had spoken to them, the Lord Yeshua was taken up into heaven and sat at the right hand of God. And they went out and proclaimed everywhere, the Lord working with them and confirming the message by the accompanying signs.

Romans 3:1-2
Then what advantage has the Jew? What is the value of being circumcised? Much in every way! In the first place, the Jews were entrusted with the very words of God.

Supportive Scriptures

Isaiah 49:5-9
Matthew 28:16-20
Luke 24:44-48
John 20:19-21
Acts 1:4-8
Ephesians 4:11-12
1 Peter 2:4-5

Commentary

The Jewish People (previously called Israelites and defined as those descended from Abraham, Isaac, and Jacob), are God's original and primary priesthood to the Gentile nations. This priesthood was proclaimed during the time of Moses, and its purpose was (and still is) to bring the Word of God (indeed God Himself) to those in the world who do not know Him.

By virtue of Yeshua's sacrifice and the New Covenant that he brought, all who receive Yeshua as Lord and savior become affiliated with Israel through grafting into a "Jewish" olive tree (Romans 17:11, etc.), not to lose their original intrinsic identities as Jews or non-Jews, but to become members together in a new (co-existing) priesthood that has come to be known as the "priesthood of believers" (1 Peter 2:4-5). This new priesthood has functions and responsibilities that overlap those of the Jewish priesthood, but the latter retains its historic place in preserving and disseminating the Word of God, and now being the host priesthood to the priesthood of believers.

Classical Commentators

Maimonides, Meir, and HaChinuch do not address disseminating God's Word to others directly. They imply it by emphasizing commandments (e.g. *t'fillin, m'zuzot, tzitzit*) that are visible reminders.

NCLA: JMm JFm KMm KFm GMm GFm

E2. Performing and Receiving *B'rit Milah*.

All male Jewish children eight days old must be circumcised.

This precept is derived from His Word (blessed be He):

Key Scriptures

Covenant Made with Abram whose Name Was Changed to Abraham

Genesis 12:1-3
Now ADONAI said to Avram, "Get yourself out of your country, away from your kinsmen and away from your father's house, and go to the land that I will show you. I will make of you a great nation, I will bless you, and I will make your name great; and you are to be a blessing. I will bless those who bless you, but I will curse anyone who curses you; and by you all the families of the earth will be blessed."

Genesis 15:18-21
That day ADONAI made a covenant with Avram: "I have given this land to your descendants— from the Vadi of Egypt to the great river, the Euphrates River—the territory of the Keni, the K'nizi, the Kadmoni, the Hitti, the P'rizi, the Refa'im, the Emori, the Kena'ani, the Girgashi and the Y'vusi."

Genesis 17:1-8 (Maimonides RP215; Meir MP47; Chinuch C2)
When Avram was 99 years old ADONAI appeared to Avram and said to him, "I am El Shaddai [God Almighty]. Walk in my presence and be pure-hearted. I will make my covenant between me and you, and I will increase your numbers greatly." Avram fell on his face, and God continued speaking with him: "As for me, this is my covenant with you: you will be the father of many nations. Your name will no longer be Avram [exalted father], but your name will be Avraham [father of many], because I have made you the father of many nations. I will cause you to be very fruitful. I will make nations of you, kings will descend from you. I am establishing my covenant between me and you, along with your descendants after you, generation after generation, as an everlasting covenant, to be God for you and for your descendants after you.
I will give you and your descendants after you the land in which you are now foreigners, all the land of Kena'an, as a permanent possession; and I will be their God."

Leviticus 12:3 (Meir MP47)
On the eighth day, the [male] baby's foreskin is to be circumcised.

Value and Spiritual Nature of Circumcision

Romans 2:25-3:2
For circumcision is indeed of value if you do what Torah says. But if you are a transgressor of Torah, your circumcision has become uncircumcision! Therefore, if an uncircumcised man keeps

the righteous requirements of the Torah, won't his uncircumcision be counted as circumcision? Indeed, the man who is physically uncircumcised but obeys the Torah will stand as a judgment on you who have had a b'rit-milah and have Torah written out but violate it! For the real Jew is not merely Jewish outwardly: true circumcision is not only external and physical.
On the contrary, the real Jew is one inwardly; and true circumcision is of the heart, spiritual not literal; so that his praise comes not from other people but from God. Then what advantage has the Jew? What is the value of being circumcised? Much in every way! In the first place, the Jews were entrusted with the very words of God.

Colossians 2:8-12
Watch out, so that no one will take you captive by means of philosophy and empty deceit, following human tradition which accords with the elemental spirits of the world but does not accord with the Messiah. For in him, bodily, lives the fullness of all that God is. And it is in union with him that you have been made full—he is the head of every rule and authority. Also it was in union with him that you were circumcised with a circumcision not done by human hands, but accomplished by stripping away the old nature's control over the body. In this circumcision done by the Messiah, you were buried along with him by being immersed; and in union with him, you were also raised up along with him by God's faithfulness that worked when he raised Yeshua from the dead.

Circumcision Required in Order for Gentiles to Eat the Sacrificed Passover Lamb

Exodus 12:41-49 (Maimonides RN126-128; Chinuch C13, 14, 17)
At the end of 430 years to the day, all the divisions of ADONAI left the land of Egypt. This was a night when ADONAI kept vigil to bring them out of the land of Egypt, and this same night continues to be a night when ADONAI keeps vigil for all the people of Isra'el through all their generations. ADONAI said to Moshe and Aharon, "This is the regulation for the Pesach lamb: no foreigner is to eat it. But if anyone has a slave he bought for money, when you have circumcised him, he may eat it. Neither a traveler nor a hired servant may eat it. It is to be eaten in one house. You are not to take any of the meat outside the house, and you are not to break any of its bones. The whole community of Isra'el is to keep it. If a foreigner staying with you wants to observe ADONAI's Pesach, all his males must be circumcised. Then he may take part and observe it; he will be like a citizen of the land. But no uncircumcised person is to eat it. The same teaching is to apply equally to the citizen and to the foreigner living among you. This was a night when ADONAI kept vigil to bring them out of the land of Egypt, and this same night continues to be a night when ADONAI keeps vigil for all the people of Isra'el through all their generations. ADONAI said to Moshe and Aharon, "This is the regulation for the Pesach lamb: no foreigner is to eat it. But if anyone has a slave he bought for money, when you have circumcised him, he may eat it. Neither a traveler nor a hired servant may eat it. It is to be eaten in one house. You are not to take any of the meat outside the house, and you are not to break any of its bones. The whole community of Isra'el is to keep it. If a foreigner staying with you wants to observe ADONAI's Pesach, all his males must be circumcised. Then he may take part and observe it; he will be like a citizen of the land. But no uncircumcised person is to eat it. The same teaching is to apply equally to the citizen and to the foreigner living among you.

240

Supportive Scriptures—Purpose of the Covenant

Genesis 22:14-18
Exodus 19:5-6

Supportive Scripture—Circumcision on the Eighth Day Required in Order to Keep the Covenant

Genesis 17:9-14

Supportive Scripture—Abraham Circumcised along with All in His Household

Genesis 17:22-27

Supportive Scripture—The Abrahamic Covenant is Continued through Isaac

Genesis 17:18-21

Supportive Scripture—The Abrahamic Covenant is Continued through Jacob

Genesis 28:10-15

Supportive Scriptures—Circumcision of Gentiles is Not Required for Salvation in the New Covenant

Acts 15:1-20
Galatians 5 11

Supportive Scriptures—Zipporah Circumcised Her and Moses' Son

Exodus 4:24-26

Supportive Scripture—Paul Circumcised Timothy

Acts 16:1-3

Supportive Scripture—Each Person Should Remain in the State of Circumcision in which He was Called

1 Corinthians 7:18-20

Supportive Scriptures—There is One Body of Law for the Jews and for the Gentile who Joins Himself to the Jewish People through Circumcision

Exodus 12:49
Leviticus 24:22
Numbers 15:14-16, 28-29

Supportive Scriptures—In the New Covenant, Gentiles Connected to the Jewish People through Grafting—Not through Circumcision

Romans 2:25-29, 11:13-18
Colossians 2:11-13

Commentary

It is a common misunderstanding to believe that God's covenant with Abraham (repeated through Isaac and Jacob) applies only to Jews. The Abrahamic Covenant defines the Jewish people generationally, but it is also the framework for Gentiles to willfully connect themselves to the Jewish people, thereby enlarging the "people of God" that comprises both Jews and Gentiles. It is why God told Abraham that he would be the *"father of many nations."* (Genesis 17:4). That notwithstanding, Gentiles (even *K'rovei Yisrael*—those closely connected to a Jewish community) are not themselves Jews because their priestly identity and covenantal responsibilities are not inherited, but are rather, voluntarily derived from their connection to the Jewish People through their covenant with the Jewish Messiah. In the Mosaic Covenant, Gentiles who wanted a special covenantal relationship with God received it by physically moving into the Jewish camp, becoming circumcised, sacrificing at the Tabernacle or Temple, and becoming part of the Jewish community. In the New Covenant, Gentiles who want a special covenantal relationship with God receive it by becoming grafted into the "Jewish" olive tree through faith in Messiah Yeshua—not through circumcision (see Romans 11).[93]

B'rit milah (covenant circumcision) was (and still is) required of all Jewish males who are eight days old lest they be cut off from the covenant they have inherited. In the Mosaic Covenant, circumcision was required of any Gentile male who lived in a Jewish household and wished to covenantally connect to the Jewish people. Such a Gentile became subject to most of the commandments of *Torah,* but it did not result in his becoming a Jew or a Jewish convert,[94] and it is clear from Acts 15:1-20 that circumcision was not required for their salvation.

---

93 Jewish individuals who have been broken off of their olive tree through unbelief have to be re-grafted. Jews that remain unconnected to their tree retain their covenantal responsibilities but not their salvific relationship with God.

94 Uncircumcised Gentiles can participate in today's Passover *seders* because today's *seders* do not include eating a sacrificed Passover animal (see Exodus 12:43-49). In 1 Corinthians 5:7-8, Paul makes it clear that Yeshua is our sacrificed lamb, and he thereby encourages the Gentiles to whom he is speaking to celebrate the *seder.* We do not require that *K'rov Yisrael* Gentiles be ritually circumcised.

Circumcising a Jewish child has historically been considered the duty of the child's father, but an experienced circumciser (a *mohel*) is often employed. The surgery can be performed by a non-Jew, but only a Jew can receive the child into the covenant. The prevailing view is that *b'rit milah* should be done on the eighth day after birth when possible. So important is this eighth day principle, that *halachah* requires that circumcision be performed on that day even if it falls on a Sabbath.

Commentary by Daniel C. Juster

We note that participating at Passover *seders* has special meaning for believers in Yeshua because the fullness of the meaning of Passover is in the death of Yeshua as our Passover Lamb. As such, in the New Covenant order, both Jews and Gentiles commonly participate in the meaning of the Passover sacrifice in its New Covenant fulfilment form. Regarding Gentile participants in particular, since the Passover meal practiced by Jewish people today is a memorial without the sacrificial lamb, it is common for Gentiles to participate, even in traditional Jewish *seders,* without violating the Scriptures.

Classical Commentators

Maimonides, Meir, and HaChinuch are in agreement concerning the requirement that a Jewish baby be circumcised on the eighth day if possible. HaChinuch and Meir state that if a Jewish baby is not circumcised, then there is a continuing obligation on the part of the uncircumcised individual to become circumcised when he is older. It is interesting that Maimonides and HaChinuch state that mothers have no responsibility to circumcise their sons in view of Moses' wife Zipporah having circumcised her son (Exodus 4:24-26). Meir states that circumcision should be done after sunrise.

NCLA: JMm JFm KMo KFo GMu GFu

E3. Commemorating *Pidyon HaBen*.

We are to first sanctify and then ceremonially redeem our firstborn son from priestly service.

This precept is derived from His Word (blessed be He):

Key Scriptures

Exodus 13:1-2 (Maimonides RP79; Meir MP53; Chinuch C18)
ADONAI said to Moshe, "Set aside for me all the firstborn. Whatever is first from the womb among the people of Isra'el, both of humans and of animals, belongs to me."

Exodus 13:10-15 (Maimonides RP81, 82; Chinuch C22, 23)
Therefore you are to observe this regulation at its proper time, year after year. When ADONAI brings you into the land of the Kena'ani, as he swore to you and your ancestors, and gives it to you, you are to set apart for ADONAI everything that is first from the womb. Every firstborn male animal will belong to ADONAI. Every firstborn from a donkey, you are to redeem with a lamb; but if you choose not to redeem it, you must break its neck. But from people, you are to redeem every firstborn son. When, at some future time, your son asks you, 'What is this?' then say to him, 'With a strong hand ADONAI brought us out of Egypt, out of the abode of slavery. When Pharaoh was unwilling to let us go, ADONAI killed all the firstborn males in the land of Egypt, both the firstborn of humans and the firstborn of animals. This is why I sacrifice to ADONAI any male that is first from the womb of an animal, but all the firstborn of my sons I redeem.'

Exodus 22:28(29)-29(30)
You are not to delay offering from your harvest of grain, olive oil or wine. "The firstborn of your sons you are to give to me. You are to do the same with your oxen and your sheep—it is to stay with its mother seven days, and on the eighth day you are to give it to me.

Exodus 34:19-20 (Meir MP55, 56)
Everything that is first from the womb is mine. Of all your livestock, you are to set aside for me the males, the firstborn of cattle and flock. The firstborn of a donkey you must redeem with a lamb; if you won't redeem it, break its neck. All the firstborn of your sons you are to redeem, and no one is to appear before me empty-handed.

Numbers 3:40-51
ADONAI said to Moshe, "Register all the firstborn males of the people of Isra'el a month old and over, and determine how many there are. Then you are to take the L'vi'im for me, ADONAI, in place of all the firstborn among the people of Isra'el, and the cattle of the L'vi'im in place of the firstborn of the cattle belonging to the people of Isra'el." Moshe counted, as ADONAI had ordered him, all the firstborn among the people of Isra'el. The total number of firstborn males registered, a month old and over, of those who were counted, was 22,273. ADONAI said to Moshe, "Take the L'vi'im in place of all the firstborn among the people of Isra'el, and the cattle of the L'vi'im in place of their cattle; the L'vi'im are to belong to me, ADONAI. Since there were

273 more firstborn males from Isra'el than male L'vi'im, in order to redeem them, you are to take five shekels [two ounces] for each of these (use the sanctuary shekel, which is equal to twenty gerahs). Give the redemption money for these extra people to Aharon and his sons." Moshe took the redemption money from those who were over and above those redeemed by the L'vi'im; the amount of money he took from the firstborn of the people of Isra'el was 1,365 shekels, using the sanctuary shekel. Moshe gave the redemption-money to Aharon and his sons, in keeping with what ADONAI had said, as ADONAI had ordered Moshe.

Numbers 18:15-17 (Maimonides RP80, RN108; Meir MP54, 55, MN109; Chinuch C392-393)
Everything that comes first out of the womb, of all living things which they offer to ADONAI, whether human or animal, will be yours. However, the firstborn of a human being you must redeem, and the firstborn of an unclean beast you are to redeem. The sum to be paid for redeeming anyone a month old or over is to be five shekels of silver [two ounces], as you value it, using the sanctuary shekel (this is the same as twenty gerahs). But the firstborn of an ox, sheep or goat you are not to redeem; they are holy—you are to splash their blood against the altar and make their fat go up in smoke as an offering made by fire, as a fragrant aroma for ADONAI.

Deuteronomy 14:22-23 (Maimonides RP79; Chinuch C18)
"Every year you must take one tenth of everything your seed produces in the field, and eat it in the presence of ADONAI your God. In the place where he chooses to have his name live you will eat the tenth of your grain, new wine and olive oil, and the firstborn of your cattle and sheep, so that you will learn to fear ADONAI your God always."

Luke 2:22-32
When the time came for their purification according to the Torah of Moshe, they took him up to Yerushalayim to present him to ADONAI (as it is written in the Torah of ADONAI, "Every firstborn male is to be consecrated to ADONAI") and also to offer a sacrifice of a pair of doves or two young pigeons, as required by the Torah of ADONAI. There was in Yerushalayim a man named Shim'on. This man was a tzaddik, he was devout, he waited eagerly for God to comfort Isra'el, and the Ruach HaKodesh was upon him. It had been revealed to him by the Ruach HaKodesh that he would not die before he had seen the Messiah of ADONAI. Prompted by the Spirit, he went into the Temple courts; and when the parents brought in the child Yeshua to do for him what the Torah required, Shim'on took him in his arms, made a b'rakhah to God, and said, "Now, ADONAI, according to your word, your servant is at peace as you let him go; for I have seen with my own eyes your yeshu'ah, which you prepared in the presence of all peoples- a light that will bring revelation to the Goyim and glory to your people Isra'el."

Commentary

This *Mitzvah* is formulated by joining together two commandments (directed to the Israelites) that were priesthood-related—the second reversing the first. Subsequent to God having saved the firstborn sons of the Israelites when He slew the firstborn males (both sons and cattle) of the Egyptians (Exodus 11:4-6), He declared also, that all firstborn of the womb belonged to Him (Exodus 13:1-2, 34:19; Numbers 3:13). We understand that to mean that each Israelite family was to sanctify its firstborn son (i.e., dedicate him to service in the Tabernacle and later the Temple). After Moses rebuked the Israelites for worshiping the Golden Calf and only the Levites stepped forward to repent (Exodus 32:25-29), God took the priesthood away from the Israelites as a whole, and gave it to the Levites (Numbers 1:49-53, 3:12), appointing the sons of Aaron to serve as *cohanim* in place of the firstborn sons of the Israelites (Numbers 3:10). He did this, not by revoking His previous commandment to sanctify each Israelite firstborn son, but by commanding that each Israelite family redeem their firstborn son from priestly service by paying a Levitical *cohen* five *shekalim* of money (Numbers 3:40-51, 18:15-16).

Because underlying this *Mitzvah* are commandments with which Levites can no longer comply, it could have easily been omitted from this compilation as being obsolete. It has not been, however, because (1) the ceremony of *Pidyon HaBen* (redemption of the firstborn son) is performed among many Jewish people today, and (2) Yeshua's consecration (and possibly His simultaneous *Pidyon HaBen*) is recorded in Luke 2:22-32.

There is no biblically specified ceremony for sanctifying the firstborn son today, although circumcision may be thought of as a sanctification ceremony for all male Jewish children, with the firstborn of them assumed to be specially sanctified. Today, when the firstborn son of a Jewish family (not a *cohen* or a Levite) is 30 days old, he is taken to a Levitical *cohen* who receives the monitary equivalent of five *shekalim* from the father, and then proceeds to bless the child with the *Birkat Cohanim* (the Aaronic Benediction). Since Temple *shekalim* are no longer in use, their equivalent value in silver is substituted—either special coins made for the purpose or, in the U.S., five pre-1936 silver dollars (26.73 grams of 90% silver).

It is obvious that this *Mitzvah* is based upon the assumption of a functioning Temple priesthood that does not exist today. Nevertheless, I believe it is important for Messianic Jews to comply ceremonially in the universal Jewish way for three reasons: (1) without it, there is no closure regarding the priestly status of firstborn male Israelites beyond their general priestly identity as Jews; (2) without it, there is ambiguity regarding the continuing priestly status of today's descendants of Aaron (i.e. Levitical *cohanim)*; and (3) there is value in our being in solidarity with the rest of the Jewish world on this. I do not, however, believe that failing to comply with this *Mitzvah* in this New Covenant age is sinful.

The ceremony of *Pidyon HaBen* only has meaning when performed within non-Levitical Jewish families since historically, the Levites were not redeemed and did, therefore, serve in the Temple. Although the ceremony is traditionally the responsibility of a firstborn son's Jewish father, in Messianic Judaism it may also be performed by his Jewish mother or by himself when he comes of age. The *Pidyon HaBen* ceremony has no historic or spiritual meaning at all for Gentiles.

Classical Commentators

Meir states that the *Pidyon HaBen* is to be performed after thirty days by Jewish families who are neither *cohanim* nor Levites and, if a firstborn son has no father, he must redeem himself after he comes of age; HaChinuch says this also of a son who has a father, but the father does not redeem him. Maimonides and HaChinuch agree with Meir on all matters, and specifically state that the *Pidyon HaBen* is to be performed by the father—not by the mother.

Meir quotes Scripture that speaks of our need to sanctify the firstborn of *kosher* animals as well, of which we are to say: "This is hereby holy." He says that if we do not consecrate a firstborn *kosher* animal it is, nevertheless, holy. He also says that because there is no Temple, the firstborn animals must be left to graze until they develop a defect, and must then be given to a *cohen*. Both Maimonides and HaChinuch state that the consecration of cattle is to occur only in the Land of Israel, whereas Meir is silent on the matter.

<u>NCLA</u>: JMm (non-*cohen*) JFu KMi KFi GMi GFi

E4. Being a Kingdom of Priests, a Holy Nation, Proclaimers of the Good News and a Light to the Gentiles.

The Jewish people are to be a kingdom of priests, a holy nation, proclaimers of the Good News, and a light to the Gentiles.

This precept is derived from His Word (blessed be He):

Key Scriptures

Genesis 17:4-16 (Maimonides RP215; Meir MP47; Chinuch C2)
"As for me, this is my covenant with you: you will be the father of many nations. Your name will no longer be Avram [exalted father], but your name will be Avraham [father of many], because I have made you the father of many nations. I will cause you to be very fruitful. I will make nations of you, kings will descend from you. I am establishing my covenant between me and you, along with your descendants after you, generation after generation, as an everlasting covenant, to be God for you and for your descendants after you. I will give you and your descendants after you the land in which you are now foreigners, all the land of Kena'an, as a permanent possession; and I will be their God." God said to Avraham, "As for you, you are to keep my covenant, you and your descendants after you, generation after generation. Here is my covenant, which you are to keep, between me and you, along with your descendants after you: every male among you is to be circumcised. You are to be circumcised in the flesh of your foreskin; this will be the sign of the covenant between me and you. Generation after generation, every male among you who is eight days old is to be circumcised, including slaves born within your household and those bought from a foreigner not descended from you. The slave born in your house and the person bought with your money must be circumcised; thus my covenant will be in your flesh as an everlasting covenant. Any uncircumcised male who will not let himself be circumcised in the flesh of his foreskin—that person will be cut off from his people, because he has broken my covenant." God said to Avraham, "As for Sarai your wife, you are not to call her Sarai [mockery]; her name is to be Sarah [princess]. I will bless her; moreover, I will give you a son by her. Truly I will bless her: she will be a mother of nations; kings of peoples will come from her."

Exodus 19:1-8
In the third month after the people of Isra'el had left the land of Egypt, the same day they came to the Sinai Desert. After setting out from Refidim and arriving at the Sinai Desert, they set up camp in the desert; there in front of the mountain, Isra'el set up camp. Moshe went up to God, and ADONAI called to him from the mountain: "Here is what you are to say to the household of Ya'akov, to tell the people of Isra'el: 'You have seen what I did to the Egyptians, and how I carried you on eagles' wings and brought you to myself. Now if you will pay careful attention to what I say and keep my covenant, then you will be my own treasure from among all the peoples, for all the earth is mine; and you will be a kingdom of cohanim for me, a nation set apart [NKJ: "a holy nation"].' These are the words you are to speak to the people of Isra'el." Moshe came, summoned the leaders of the people and presented them with all these words which ADONAI had

ordered him to say. All the people answered as one, "Everything ADONAI has said, we will do." Moshe reported the words of the people to ADONAI.

Leviticus 12:2-3 (Meir MP47)
Tell the people of Isra'el: 'If a woman conceives and gives birth to a boy, she will be unclean for seven days with the same uncleanness as in niddah, when she is having her menstrual period. On the eighth day, the baby's foreskin is to be circumcised.

Deuteronomy 23:8(7)-9(8) (Maimonides RN54-55; Chinuch C563-564)
But you are not to detest an Edomi, because he is your brother; and you are not to detest an Egyptian, because you lived as a foreigner in his land. The third generation of children born to them may enter the assembly of ADONAI.

Isaiah 42:6-7
I, ADONAI, called you righteously, I took hold of you by the hand, I shaped you and made you a covenant for the people, to be a light for the Goyim, so that you can open blind eyes, free the prisoners from confinement, those living in darkness from the dungeon.

Isaiah 49:5-6
So now ADONAI says—he formed me in the womb to be his servant, to bring Ya'akov back to him, to have Isra'el gathered to him, so that I will be honored in the sight of ADONAI, my God having become my strength—he has said, "It is not enough that you are merely my servant to raise up the tribes of Ya'akov and restore the offspring of Isra'el. I will also make you a light to the nations, so my salvation can spread to the ends of the earth.

Isaiah 60:1-3
Arise, shine [Yerushalayim], for your light has come, the glory of ADONAI has risen over you. For although darkness covers the earth and thick darkness the peoples; on you ADONAI will rise; over you will be seen his glory. Nations will go toward your light and kings toward your shining splendor.

Matthew 28:16-20
So the eleven talmidim went to the hill in the Galil where Yeshua had told them to go. When they saw him, they prostrated themselves before him; but some hesitated. Yeshua came and talked with them. He said, "All authority in heaven and on earth has been given to me. Therefore, go and make people from all nations into talmidim, immersing them into the reality of the Father, the Son and the Ruach HaKodesh, and teaching them to obey everything that I have commanded you. And remember! I will be with you always, yes, even until the end of the age.

Mark 16:14-16
Later, Yeshua appeared to the Eleven as they were eating, and he reproached them for their lack of trust and their spiritual insensitivity in not having believed those who had seen him after he had risen. Then he said to them, "As you go throughout the world, proclaim the Good News to all creation. Whoever trusts and is immersed will be saved; whoever does not trust will be condemned.

249

Acts 1:3-8

After his death he showed himself to them and gave many convincing proofs that he was alive. During a period of forty days they saw him, and he spoke with them about the Kingdom of God. At one of these gatherings, he instructed them not to leave Yerushalayim but to wait for "what the Father promised, which you heard about from me. For Yochanan used to immerse people in water; but in a few days, you will be immersed in the Ruach HaKodesh!" When they were together, they asked him, "Lord, are you at this time going to restore self-rule to Isra'el?" He answered, "You don't need to know the dates or the times; the Father has kept these under his own authority. But you will receive power when the Ruach HaKodesh comes upon you; you will be my witnesses both in Yerushalayim and in all Y'hudah and Shomron, indeed to the ends of the earth!"

Acts 13:46-48

However, Sha'ul and Bar-Nabba answered boldly: "It was necessary that God's word be spoken first to you. But since you are rejecting it and are judging yourselves unworthy of eternal life— why, we're turning to the Goyim! For that is what ADONAI has ordered us to do: 'I have set you as a light for the Goyim, to be for deliverance to the ends of the earth.' The Gentiles were very happy to hear this. They honored the message about the Lord, and as many as had been appointed to eternal life came to trust.

Acts 26:19-23

So, King Agrippa, I did not disobey the vision from heaven! On the contrary, I announced first in Dammesek, then in Yerushalayim and throughout Y'hudah, and also to the Goyim, that they should turn from their sins to God and then do deeds consistent with that repentance. It was because of these things that Jews seized me in the Temple and tried to kill me. However, I have had God's help; so to this day, I stand testifying to both small and great, saying nothing but what both the prophets and Moshe said would happen—that the Messiah would die, and that he, as the first to rise from the dead, would proclaim light to both the People and the Goyim.

Romans 3:1-2

Then what advantage has the Jew? What is the value of being circumcised? Much in every way! In the first place, the Jews were entrusted with the very words of God.

Galatians 3:6-9

It was the same with Avraham: "He trusted in God and was faithful to him, and that was credited to his account as righteousness." Be assured, then, that it is those who live by trusting and being faithful who are really children of Avraham. Also the Tanakh, foreseeing that God would consider the Gentiles righteous when they live by trusting and being faithful, told the Good News to Avraham in advance by saying, "In connection with you, all the Goyim will be blessed." So then, those who rely on trusting and being faithful are blessed along with Avraham, who trusted and was faithful.

Supportive Scriptures

Genesis 12:2-3, 13:14-17, 17:1-8, 18-21, 26:1-5, 28:10-15
Leviticus 19:33-34
Isaiah 2:1-4, 19:24-25
Matthew 10:5-8

Commentary

The designation of Israel to be a "kingdom of priests" and a "nation set apart" originated with the covenant that God made with Abraham. It was renewed through Isaac and again through Jacob, and came into fullness with the covenant that God made with the Israelites at Mount Sinai. We call the covenant with Abraham "the Abrahamic Covenant," and the one at Mount Sinai, "the Mosaic Covenant."

Although the Mosaic Covenant was given to Israel, its ultimate purpose was not only to benefit Israel, but rather that, through Israel functioning as a kingdom of priests, the rest of the world (i.e. the Gentile nations) would be blessed. God's plan was (and still is) to bring His Word to the Jew first, and the Jew to bring it to the Gentile. It doesn't always work out that way, but that is the overall plan.

Edom, Assyria, and ancient Egypt have a special role in that plan as being examples of the nations of the world that do not know God. The Israelites of old had reason to despise these three in particular. Esau (the patriarch of the Edomites) showed disdain for his birthright by selling it to his brother Jacob, and he later hated his brother for it (Genesis 27:41). At one point in history, Assyria (Iran today) subjugated Edom (which became an Assyrian vassal state), and captured and subjugated the Israelites of ancient Samaria. Both Edom and Assyria were, therefore, enemies of Israel at one time, and Egypt became an enemy of ancient Israel as well. Although Egypt first sheltered and provided sustenance for the Israelites, it later oppressed and enslaved them.

What is remarkable considering what has transpired, is that the Mosaic Scriptures name all three as blessed nations, and though they (the three nations) and their descendants may hate us and hate God's ways even today, we are, nevertheless, to bring the "Good News" of Yeshua to them with love and with the hope and expectation that some will receive it. In that way and through our prayers and our example of being a servant people devoted to loving God and neighbor, the Jewish people are uniquely commissioned by God to be a light to their own ("the lost sheep of the house of Israel") first, and then to the Gentile nations of the world.

Commentary by Daniel C. Juster

In regard to Assyria and Egypt: Despite the fact that Israel had to struggle with these two empires throughout its history, their people will nevertheless come to embrace the God of Israel and be one with the Jewish people, as the rest of the nations will also come to the knowledge of God (Isaiah 2:1-4, supra).

Classical Commentators

Maimonides and HaChinuch wrote *mitzvot* stating that we are not to exclude the descendants of Esau and of the Egyptians from full membership in our Jewish communities after they have become proselytes; Meir did not write on the subject. All three commentators wrote *mitzvot* requiring *b'rit milah* for Jews.

<u>**NCLA**</u>**: JMm JFm KMm KFm GMu GFu**

E5. Conversion and Receiving Jewish Proselytes and Converts.

We are not to encourage Jewish conversion, but are to receive as Jewish Proselytes or Converts, those who have received conversion under reputable Jewish auspices.

This precept is derived from His Word (blessed is He):

Key Scriptures

Deuteronomy 23:6(5)-9(8) (Maimonides RN54, 55; Chinuch C563, 564)
But ADONAI your God would not listen to Bil'am; rather, ADONAI your God turned the curse into a blessing for you; because ADONAI your God loved you. So you are never to seek their peace or well being, as long as you live. But you are not to detest an Edomi, because he is your brother; and you are not to detest an Egyptian, because you lived as a foreigner in his land. The third generation of children born to them may enter the assembly of ADONAI.

Ezekiel 47:21-23
This is the territory you are to divide among the tribes of Isra'el. You are to divide it by lot as an inheritance both to you and to the foreigners living among you who give birth to children living among you; for you they are to be no different from the native-born among the people of Isra'el—they are to have an inheritance with you among the tribes of Isra'el. You are to give the foreigner an inheritance in the territory of the tribe with whom he is living,' says Adonai ELOHIM.

Ruth 1:16-17
But Rut said, "Don't press me to leave you and stop following you; for wherever you go, I will go; and wherever you stay, I will stay. Your people will be my people and your God will be my God. Where you die, I will die; and there I will be buried. May ADONAI bring terrible curses on me, and worse ones as well, if anything but death separates you and me."

Esther 8:17
In every province and city where the king's order and decree arrived, the Jews had gladness and joy, a feast and a holiday. Many from the peoples of the land became Jews, because fear of the Jews had overcome them.

Esther 9:27
...the Jews resolved and took upon themselves, their descendants and all who might join them that without fail they would observe these two days in accordance with what was written in [this letter] and at the appointed time, every year;

1 Corinthians 7:17-20
Only let each person live the life the Lord has assigned him and live it in the condition he was in when God called him. This is the rule I lay down in all the congregations. Was someone already circumcised when he was called? Then he should not try to remove the marks of his circumcision.

Was someone uncircumcised when he was called? He shouldn't undergo b'rit-milah. Being circumcised means nothing, and being uncircumcised means nothing; what does mean something is keeping God's commandments. Each person should remain in the condition he was in when he was called.

Galatians 5:1-6
What the Messiah has freed us for is freedom! Therefore, stand firm, and don't let yourselves be tied up again to a yoke of slavery. Mark my words—I, Sha'ul, tell you that if you undergo b'rit-milah the Messiah will be of no advantage to you at all! Again, I warn you: any man who undergoes b'rit-milah is obligated to observe the entire Torah! You who are trying to be declared righteous by God through legalism have severed yourselves from the Messiah! You have fallen away from God's grace! For it is by the power of the Spirit, who works in us because we trust and are faithful, that we confidently expect our hope of attaining righteousness to be fulfilled. When we are united with the Messiah Yeshua, neither being circumcised nor being uncircumcised matters; what matters is trusting faithfulness expressing itself through love.

Galatians 5:11-13
And as for me, brothers, if I am still preaching that circumcision is necessary, why am I still being persecuted? If that were the case, my preaching about the execution-stake would cause no offense whatever. I wish the people who are bothering you would go the whole way and castrate themselves! For, brothers, you were called to be free. Only do not let that freedom become an excuse for allowing your old nature to have its way. Instead, serve one another in love.

Supportive Scriptures

Genesis 17:9-14, 23-27
Exodus 12:48-49
Isaiah 56:3-7
Acts 15:13-29

Commentary

The following incorporates excerpts from Tikkun International's[95] *halachic*[96] paper "The Status of Gentiles in Messianic Judaism:"[97]

The word "conversion" has a particularly onerous meaning in the history of Judaism because of its association with persecutions of the Jewish people, and attempts to force Jews to "convert" to Christianity by abandoning their Jewish identity and assimilating into the Christian Church. That notwithstanding, the American Jewish community also uses the term to describe the process

---

95 Tikkun International (a.k.a. "Tikkun") is a Messianic Jewish apostolic network and covenant community of fivefold ministry leaders and congregations.
96 Tikkun's understanding of New Covenant *halachah* is apostolic guidance and, as such, is not binding in the same way as it is understood in historical Judaism. This is principally because New Covenant believers rely on the *Ruach HaKodesh* to direct them individually.
97 "The Status of Gentiles in Messianic Judaism:" Tikkun International, June 12, 2009.

of "receiving Gentiles into the Jewish people by making them Jewish "converts" (proselytes) and, as generally understood, fully Jews. The modern Church and Synagogue have, generally speaking, come to use the term "conversion" as a process by which the "converted" person becomes one of their own flock, rather than as a process whereby one's heart is "converted" from unbelief to one of repentance and faith. This is evident when some Christian denominations do not recognize the baptisms of other Christian denominations, and when groups or denominations within Judaism decline to recognize conversions conducted by other (usually less observant) sectors of the Jewish community.

The word "proselyte," derived from προσήλυτος (proselytos), is used in the Septuagint (LXX) to refer to Gentile "strangers" or "sojourners" in the land of Israel. Gentiles that worshipped the God of Abraham appear very early in the Bible and, by the time of Moses, two categories of "strangers" were recognized. They were those that were subordinate to the Israelites, and those that took on full citizenry that included membership in tribes, and even inheritance of land (see Exodus 12:48-49 and Ezekiel 47:21-23). The practice of receiving Gentiles into Israel continued throughout the centuries and today, the terms "Jewish proselyte" and "Jewish convert" are synonymous, and refer to former Gentiles who have irreversibly taken on covenantal Jewish identity that is subsequently conveyed to their children (through inheritance) *dor l'dor*. From the time of their "conversions," these proselytes or converts are considered, by the Jewish community, to be Jews in every way.

It was inevitable that the matter of "conversion" would make its way into Messianic Judaism. It has always been an issue among us because of desire for unity in mixed marriages, because there are Gentiles within our congregations who perceive that they are called to become Jewish for various reasons (some good and some not so good), and because some Messianic Jewish congregations limit certain aspects of synagogue life to Jews. In tension with it, the biblical legitimacy of conversion has been questioned, principally because of the admonitions of the Apostle Paul to Gentiles in 1 Corinthians 7:17-20 and Galatians 5:1-6, 11-13 that they should not be circumcised, and because of the instruction to Gentiles in Acts 15 that they are exempt from the requirement of full *Torah* observance for salvation.

It is Tikkun's opinion (and the opinion of the authors herein), that the conversion of Gentiles to becoming Jewish proselytes should be discouraged in most cases, but that there are exceptions (illustrated by Ruth 1:16-17 and Esther 8:17b) where it should be allowed. Related to this, it has been noticed there are two categories of Gentiles that populate Messianic Jewish congregations today, analogous to two categories that existed within Israel during the time of Moses. Back then there were those that were genuinely and permanently joined to the nation and the God of Israel (similar to the Gentiles that accompanied the Israelites out of Egypt), and there were those that lived in proximity to the camp of Israel and did business with the Israelites, but remained unaffiliated with the community. Today it is different of course, due to the New Covenant. Today, all Gentiles who receive Yeshua as Lord and Messiah are supernaturally grafted into the "Romans 11 olive tree," and become equal citizens along with all Jewish believers in Yeshua, in what is termed the "commonwealth of Israel" (Ephesians 2:12, NKJ). The Gentiles that are part of this "Commonwealth" of faith comprise the larger circle of Gentile believers. They are joined to the Jewish people by genuine affiliation, but there is an inner circle as well.

Most Gentile citizens of the Commonwealth, while recognizing their grafted-in relationship with the Jewish people, do not consider themselves to be (nor do they want to be) part of the Jewish community per se; these are the believers that we call "Christians." There are, however, some Gentile citizens of the commonwealth who are called by God to have a special and permanent connection to the Jewish community—to live among Jews (Messianic Jews preferably), to maintain a *Torah*-observant New Covenant lifestyle, to marry Messianic Jewish believers or Gentiles similarly called, to raise their children in Messianic Jewish life, and to participate in Messianic Jewish covenantal responsibilities along with their Jewish comrades. Tikkun designates Gentiles who are so called to be known as *K'rovei Yisrael* (singular *K'rov Yisrael*),— "those who are closely related to Israel."[98] We use this term to recognize Gentiles who are a genuine part of the Jewish community, but who have not converted to become Jews.

Because a Jew and Gentile who marry produce Jewish children, for the sake of Jewish continuity we discourage Messianic Jews from marrying those who would raise their family outside of the Messianic Jewish community even if both are believers in Yeshua. Mixed marriages of Messianic Jews and *K'rovei Yisrael* are not-problematic in this way because they both have lifelong callings to the Jewish people, and are therefore certain to bring up their children to understand and embrace their Jewish identities and Jewish covenant obligations. As for two *K'rovei Yisrael* who marry: They will no doubt influence their children to be *K'rovei Yisrael* as well, but they cannot guarantee it because *K'rov Yisrael* Gentiles cannot convey their identities generationally as do Jews. The children of *K'rov Yisrael* parents have a choice, and may not believe that they are called to live among Jewish people or to take on a Messianic Jewish communal way of life.

While we recognize the biblical legitimacy of Jewish conversion, we do not encourage *K'rov Yisrael* Gentiles to convert because Gentile identity (*K'rov Yisrael* identity included) is as important in serving God as is Jewish identity. That notwithstanding, we consider conversion an acceptable option for those *K'rovei Yisrael* Messianic Gentiles who are either married to Jews, betrothed or engaged to Jews, legally adopted by Jews, or who have a Jewish parent or grandparent and wish to acquire, re-acquire, or affirm, Jewish identity.

We discourage conversions under non-Messianic Jewish (i.e. rabbinical) auspices, but are of the opinion that we should receive persons as Jews who are converted by any appropriate and reputable Jewish authority. The procedure of conversion consists essentially of two parts: (1) making a covenant declaration or oath before witnesses (similar to Ruth's declaration to Naomi), and (2) acceptance of the covenant declaration by one or more bona fide representatives of the Jewish community (Ruth was received, and her marriage to Boaz was endorsed by the elders of their Jewish community). For men, conversion also requires *brit milah* (covenant circumcision), and we recommend *tevilah* (ritual immersion) in keeping with the custom of our people.

Classical Commentators

Maimonides and HaChinuch (RN54, RN55; C563, C564) constructed *mitzvot* commanding that we not exclude the descendants of Esau, or of Egyptians from our Jewish communities after they

---

98 See <u>A Place in the Tent; Intermarriage and Conservative Judaism</u>, Oakland: EKS, 2004.

become proselytes, nor refuse to intermarry with them beyond the second generation. While these two nations are singled out as favored, classical Jewish interpretation of <u>Deuteronomy 23:6(5)-9(8)</u> seems to support conversion.

<u>NCLA</u>
Persons Converting: JMi JFi KMn KFn GMp GFp
Persons Receiving Converts: JMm JFm KMm KFm GMm GFm

E6. Tzitzit, Tefillin, and Mezuzot

We are to be reminded of and teach God's Word through tzitzit, tefillin, and mezuzot

This precept is derived from His Word (blessed is He):

Key Scriptures

Exodus 13:9 (Maimonides RP12, 13; Chinuch C421)
Moreover, it will serve you as a sign on your hand and as a reminder between your eyes, so that ADONAI's Torah may be on your lips; because with a strong hand ADONAI brought you out of Egypt.

Exodus 13:16 (Maimonides RP13; Meir MP9; Chinuch C421)
This will serve as a sign on your hand and at the front of a headband around your forehead that with a strong hand *ADONAI* brought us out of Egypt.

Numbers 15:38-40 (Maimonides RP14; Meir MP10; Chinuch C386)
Speak to the people of Isra'el, instructing them to make, through all their generations, tzitziyot on the corners of their garments, and to put with the tzitzit on each corner a blue thread. It is to be a tzitzit for you to look at and thereby remember all of ADONAI's mitzvot and obey them, so that you won't go around wherever your own heart and eyes lead you to prostitute yourselves; but it will help you remember and obey all my mitzvot and be holy for your God.

Deuteronomy 4:9-10 (Meir MP14)
Only be careful, and watch yourselves diligently as long as you live, so that you won't forget what you saw with your own eyes, so that these things won't vanish from your hearts. Rather, make them known to your children and grandchildren—the day you stood before ADONAI your God at Horev, when ADONAI said to me, 'Gather the people to me, and I will make them hear my very words, so that they will learn to hold me in awe as long as they live on earth, and so that they will teach their children.'

Deuteronomy 6:4-9 (Maimonides RP11-13, 15; Meir MP8-9, 12, 14; Chinuch C419, 421-423)
Sh'ma, Yisra'el! ADONAI Eloheinu, ADONAI echad [Hear, Isra'el! ADONAI our God, ADONAI is one]; and you are to love ADONAI your God with all your heart, all your being and all your resources. These words, which I am ordering you today, are to be on your heart; and you are to teach them carefully to your children. You are to talk about them when you sit at home, when you are traveling on the road, when you lie down and when you get up. Tie them on your hand as a sign, put them at the front of a headband around your forehead, and write them on the doorframes of your house and on your gates.

Deuteronomy 11:13-21 (Maimonides RP11, 13, 15; Meir MP12; Chinuch C419, 421 423)
So if you listen carefully to my mitzvot which I am giving you today, to love ADONAI your God and serve him with all your heart and all your being; then, [says ADONAI,] 'I will give your

land its rain at the right seasons, including the early fall rains and the late spring rains; so that you can gather in your wheat, new wine and olive oil; and I will give your fields grass for your livestock; with the result that you will eat and be satisfied.' But be careful not to let yourselves be seduced, so that you turn aside, serving other gods and worshipping them. If you do, the anger of ADONAI will blaze up against you. He will shut up the sky, so that there will be no rain. The ground will not yield its produce, and you will quickly pass away from the good land ADONAI is giving you. Therefore, you are to store up these words of mine in your heart and in all your being; tie them on your hand as a sign; put them at the front of a headband around your forehead; teach them carefully to your children, talking about them when you sit at home, when you are traveling on the road, when you lie down and when you get up; and write them on the door-frames of your house and on your gates—so that you and your children will live long on the land ADONAI swore to your ancestors that he would give them for as long as there is sky above the earth.

Matthew 23:5
Everything they do is done to be seen by others; for they make their t'fillin broad and their tzitziyot long, ...

Mark 6:56
Wherever he went, in towns, cities or country, they laid the sick in the marketplaces. They begged him to let them touch even the tzitzit on his robe, and all who touched it were healed.
(See also, Matthew 9:20, 14:36; Luke 8:44)

Commentary

What is common to *tzitzit, tefillin, and mezuzot,* is that all three are visible reminders of the Word of God, and teaching and remembering God's Word through their use appears to be a Jewish covenant responsibily. The question that must be answered, however, is whether *tefillin* (phylacteries) and *tzitzit* (fringes) must be physically worn (and in what circumstances), and *mezuzot* physically affixed to our doorposts and gates, or whether the Scriptural commandments regarding them are intended to be metaphoric. Orthodox Judaism has concluded that they are all meant to be physically applied, while the Conservative and Reform Jewish community has concluded that the requirement of *mezuzot* is physical, and the others are symbolic or metaphoric. Practical as this latter interpretation seems to be, it is not likely correct because the commandments regarding *tefillin* and *mezuzot* are contained in the very same verses of Scripture, and they should both, therefore, be understood to be either one way or the other. My conclusion is that the *tefillin* and *mezuzot* are meant to be metaphoric but the requirement to wear fringes with a cord of blue is meant to be physical. Putting God's words on our foreheads and tying them to our arms most likely means that God should always be in our thoughts and in what we do, and writing them on our door-frames most likely means that our homes should be dedicated to all that is godly. No harm is done, however, if one elects to apply them all physically, or to physically wear *tzitzit* and display *mezuzot* but decline to wear *tefillin.*

This is one of those calls that (short of God revealing it prophetically) cannot be proven, but I offer several considerations that lean to the literal. First, hanging a *m'zuzah* on the doorpost of a house has the actual effect of reminding those who enter of God's commandments and that only holy thoughts and deeds are welcome within. Second, because displaying *m'zuzot* is entirely a Jewish custom, it has the additional benefit of announcing to all who enter that sons and daughters of the Covenant live there, thus promoting God's primary purpose for Israel, which is to be a nation of priests and a light to the Gentiles.

I cannot help but think of another occasion in the Scriptures where the children of Israel were commanded to put something on the doorposts of their homes—the blood of the *Pesach*—the Passover lamb sacrifice as described in Exodus 12:7, 13:

> *"They are to take some of the blood and smear it on the two sides and top of the door-frame at the entrance of the house in which they eat it. ... The blood will serve you as a sign marking the houses where you are; when I see the blood, I will pass over you—when I strike the land of Egypt, the death blow will not strike you."*

Although one can see how God's instruction to the Israelites could have been interpreted metaphorically (as in the case of the Deuteronomy 6 and 11 *mitzvah*), several things were accomplished by their complying literally. First, it served to identify the houses' occupants as believers in God and trusters in His Word. Second, it served to identify the houses' occupants as probably being Israelites. Third, treating God's commandment metaphorically and failing to physically apply the blood to the doorposts would not have been sufficient and would have resulted in death of the firstborn for that house.

As I have already said, in Orthodox Jewish communities all men wear *tzitziyot,* and there is discussion about whether they are also appropriate for women; Orthodox women normally do not wear them. In communities that have not adopted policies regarding *tzitziyot,* each individual must make his own decision about whether to wear them as described in Scripture, or substitute some other article of clothing or accessory that will accomplish the same thing—reminding anyone seeing it of the commandments of God.

What fringes are is self-evident, so our decisions (other than whether to wear them at all) are what to make them of, whether and how to knot them, what the color and origin of the dye for the blue thread should be, and to what articles of clothing they should be attached. Since the only requirement in Scripture is that they be placed on the corners of garments, unless one's community defines the particulars of acceptable *tzitziyot,* the wearer can use his own judgment on all of these. The orthodox Jewish community has adopted detailed rules for the construction of *tzitziyot,* which their male members attach to a relatively small slip-over four-cornered garment called a *tallit katan,* and wear under their shirts or vests. *Tzitziyot* are also worn on the traditional rectangular prayer shawl, the *tallit gadol.* Both the *tallit katan* and the *tallit gadol* are often intentionally lacking the prescribed blue thread.[99]

It is important to not get so involved in the details of how to make *tzitziyot,* that we forget that of which they are supposed to remind us, which are the commandments of God. We are not only to

---

99 The practice among some to not include the blue thread has its origin in the scarcity of the *chilazon*—a sea creature from which the blue dye was originally extracted.

be reminded, but to be made continually aware of God's commandments as we proceed through each day.

I believe that the commandment to wear *tzitziyot* is applicable for both Jewish men and Jewish women, notwithstanding the prevailing modern practice of their only being worn by men. The principle of wearing *tzitziyot* is also applicable to Gentiles, but there is greater liberty for them and, in fact, it may be preferable that Gentiles (other than *k'rovei Yisrael*) not wear fringes because the wearing of fringes today has become almost completely associated with being a Jew. If that is a concern, some kind of substitution to accomplish the same purpose is easily adaptable.

It is interesting to note that not all references to *tefillin* are for the purpose of remembering God's commandments broadly. Exodus 13:9 connects the *tefillin* to remembering how God brought the Jewish people out of Egypt.

Commentarty by Daniel C. Juster

Whether or not a physical literal application is intended for all times is debatable even if one holds to the literal application as originally intended. Or was this a culturally fitting way of remembering? So for example, wearing the *tzizit* on a four cornered garment fits the culture of the time when such garments were commonly worn. They are not today, so perhaps the general principle to take steps to remember the covenant and its commandments is sufficient.

It is probably a good thing when Messianic Jews do seek ways to apply this *mitzvah* literally— wearing a *tallit gadol* in worship services and wearing fringes daily, because they show covenant loyalty. The same can, of course, be said of putting on *tefillin* for prayer. It is important, however, to remember that we cannot prove that these ways of remembering are required for all times.

Classical Commentators

Maimonides, Meir, and HaChinuch adopt the Orthodox view that *tzitzit, tefillin, and mezuzot* are meant to be applied physically, and they address each one (including the *tefillin* of the arm and head) as a separate *mitzvah*. They also construe the particulars of each (i.e. their shapes, appearances, contents, and how they are applied) according to that which is written in the *Talmud*.

NCLA: JMm JFm KMo KFo GMn GFn

E7. Tithes, Offerings and *Tz'dakah*.

We are to support the Lord's work among men through our tithes, offerings, and charitable giving.

This precept is derived from His Word (blessed be He):

Key Scriptures

Exodus 30:13-14 (Maimonides RP171; Chinuch C105)
Everyone subject to the census is to pay as an offering to ADONAI half a shekel [one-fifth of an ounce of silver]—by the standard of the sanctuary shekel (a shekel equals twenty gerahs). Everyone over twenty years of age who is subject to the census is to give this offering to ADONAI—

Leviticus 27:30-33 (Maimonides RP78, 128, RN109; Chinuch C360-361, 473)
All the tenth given from the land, whether from planted seed or fruit from trees, belongs to ADONAI; it is holy to ADONAI. If someone wants to redeem any of his tenth, he must add to it one-fifth. All the tenth from the herd or the flock, whatever passes under the shepherd's crook, the tenth one will be holy to ADONAI. The owner is not to inquire whether the animal is good or bad, and he cannot exchange it; if he does exchange it, both it and the one he substituted for it will be holy; it cannot be redeemed.

Numbers 18:20-32 (Maimonides RP127, 129; Meir ML12-13; Chinuch C395-396)
ADONAI said to Aharon, "You are not to have any inheritance or portion in their land; I am your portion and inheritance among the people of Isra'el. To the descendants of Levi I have given the entire tenth of the produce collected in Isra'el. It is their inheritance in payment for the service they render in the tent of meeting. From now on, the people of Isra'el are not to approach the tent of meeting, so that they will not bear the consequences of their sin and die. Only the L'vi'im are to perform the service in the tent of meeting, and they will be responsible for whatever they do wrong. This is to be a permanent regulation through all your generations. They are to have no inheritance among the people of Isra'el, because I have given to the L'vi'im as their inheritance the tenths of the produce which the people of Isra'el set aside as a gift for ADONAI. This is why I have said to them that they are to have no inheritance among the people of Isra'el." ADONAI said to Moshe, Tell the L'vi'im, 'When you take from the people of Isra'el the tenth of the produce which I have given you from them as your inheritance, you are to set aside from it a gift for ADONAI, one tenth of the tenth. The gift you set aside will be accounted to you as if it were grain from the threshing-floor and grape juice from the wine vat. In this way you will set aside a gift for ADONAI from all your tenths that you receive from the people of Isra'el, and from these tenths you are to give to Aharon the cohen the gift set aside for ADONAI. From everything given to you, you are to set aside all that is due ADONAI, the best part of it, its holy portion.' Therefore you are to tell them, 'When you set aside from it its best part, it will be accounted to the L'vi'im as if it were grain from the threshing-floor and grape juice from the wine vat. You may eat it anywhere, you and your households; because it is your payment in

return for your service in the tent of meeting. Moreover, because you will have set aside from it its best parts, you will not be committing any sin because of it; for you are not to profane the holy things of the people of Isra'el, or you will die.'

Deuteronomy 14:22-29 (Maimonides RP128, 130; Meir ML14-15; Chinuch C473-474)
Every year you must take one tenth of everything your seed produces in the field, and eat it in the presence of ADONAI your God. In the place where he chooses to have his name live you will eat the tenth of your grain, new wine and olive oil, and the firstborn of your cattle and sheep, so that you will learn to fear ADONAI your God always. But if the distance is too great for you, so that you are unable to transport it, because the place where ADONAI chooses to put his name is too far away from you; then, when ADONAI your God prospers you, you are to convert it into money, take the money with you, go to the place which ADONAI your God will choose, and exchange the money for anything you want—cattle, sheep, wine, other intoxicating liquor, or anything you please—and you are to eat there in the presence of ADONAI your God, and enjoy yourselves, you and your household. But don't neglect the Levi staying with you, because he has no share or inheritance like yours. At the end of every three years you are to take all the tenths of your produce from that year and store it in your towns. Then the Levi, because he has no share or inheritance like yours, along with the foreigner, the orphan and the widow living in your towns, will come, eat and be satisfied—so that ADONAI your God will bless you in everything your hands produce.

Deuteronomy 15:7-11
If someone among you is needy, one of your brothers, in any of your towns in your land which ADONAI your God is giving you, you are not to harden your heart or shut your hand from giving to your needy brother. No, you must open your hand to him and lend him enough to meet his need and enable him to obtain what he wants. Guard yourself against allowing your heart to entertain the mean-spirited thought that because the seventh year, the year of sh'mittah is at hand, you would be stingy toward your needy brother and not give him anything; for then he may cry out to ADONAI against you, and it will be your sin. Rather, you must give to him; and you are not to be grudging when you give to him. If you do this, ADONAI your God will bless you in all your work, in everything you undertake—for there will always be poor people in the land. That is why I am giving you this order, 'You must open your hand to your poor and needy brother in your land.'

Deuteronomy 16:16-17
Three times a year all your men are to appear in the presence of ADONAI your God in the place which he will choose—at the festival of matzah, at the festival of Shavu'ot and at the festival of Sukkot. They are not to show up before ADONAI empty-handed, but every man is to give what he can, in accordance with the blessing ADONAI your God has given you.

Deuteronomy 18:3-5
The cohanim will have the right to receive from the people, from those offering a sacrifice, whether ox or sheep, the shoulder, the jowls and the stomach. You will also give him the firstfruits of your grain, new wine and olive oil, and the first of the fleece of your sheep. For ADONAI your God has chosen him from all your tribes to stand and serve in the name of ADONAI, him and his sons forever.

263

Deuteronomy 26:12-13 (Maimonides RP131; Meir ML17; Chinuch C607)
After you have separated a tenth of the crops yielded in the third year, the year of separating a tenth, and have given it to the Levi, the foreigner, the orphan and the widow, so that they can have enough food to satisfy them while staying with you; you are to say, in the presence of ADONAI your God, 'I have rid my house of the things set aside for God and given them to the Levi, the foreigner, the orphan and the widow, in keeping with every one of the mitzvot you gave me. I haven't disobeyed any of your mitzvot or forgotten them.

Proverbs 3:9-10
Honor ADONAI with your wealth and with the firstfruits of all your income. Then your granaries will be filled and your vats overflow with new wine.

Matthew 23:23
Woe to you hypocritical Torah-teachers and P'rushim! You pay your tithes of mint, dill and cumin; but you have neglected the weightier matters of the Torah—justice, mercy, trust. These are the things you should have attended to—without neglecting the others!

Luke 12:33
Sell what you own and do tzedakah—make for yourselves purses that don't wear out, riches in heaven that never fail, where no burglar comes near, where no moth destroys.

1 Corinthians 16:1-3
Now, in regard to the collection being made for God's people: you are to do the same as I directed the congregations in Galatia to do. Every week, on Motza'ei-Shabbat, each of you should set some money aside, according to his resources, and save it up; so that when I come I won't have to do fundraising. And when I arrive, I will give letters of introduction to the people you have approved, and I will send them to carry your gift to Yerushalayim.

Supportive Scriptures—Tithes

Genesis 14:18-20, 28:13-22
Malachi 3:1-18
Nehemiah 10:36(35)-40(39), 12:43-47
Luke 11:42
Hebrews 7:1-11

Supportive Scriptures—Offerings

Genesis 4:1-8, 28:20-22
Exodus 25:1-2
Psalms 50:7-15
Proverbs 11:24
Matthew 5:23-24
Mark 12:41-44

Luke 6:38, 21:1-4
2 Corinthians 8:8-15, 9:1-7

Supportive Scriptures—Charitable Giving (Tz'dakah)

Psalms 37:21
Proverbs 21:13, 31:9, 20
Matthew 6:1-4, 25:32-46
Acts 11:27-30, 33-35
Romans 12:13
1 Corinthians 9:13-14
Philippians 4:15-18

Commentary

Tithing first appears in the Bible when Abraham gives one-tenth of the increase of his wealth to Melchizedek (Genesis 14:18-20), and it appears again in Genesis 28:13-22, when God promises Jacob blessing and land, and Jacob, in turn, promises to return ten percent of that which he is given by way of provision back to God. This was not, as some construe it, an attempt on Jacob's part to bargain with God, but rather an expression of Jacob's acceptance of the Covenant that had just been passed on to him, and his acknowledgement that all things with which he would be blessed in fulfillment of that Covenant belonged to God.

The tithe appears again as part of the Mosaic Law, in which the Israelites were commanded to give one-tenth of their increase (usually crops and animals) to sustain the Levites who had no inheritance of land. Offerings over and above tithes, used for other purposes, are also prescribed in the Mosaic Law (certain offerings were required and certain ones were voluntary), but a percentage of income was not required of offerings as it was of tithes. Finally, there was *tz'dakah*; giving to the poor and to good causes, though not required, was expected and was considered a matter of moral justice and not mere benevolence.

What survives in the New Covenant of these three today is not a requirement of law, but rather the principle of giving to God's work and to those in need. One sometimes hears that tithing to one's church or synagogue *is required*, and that is not right. One also sometimes hears that tithing to one's church or synagogue today *is no longer appropriate*, and that is not right either. The reason I can espouse these seemingly contradictory things is that, like many things of the Mosaic Law, certain of its principles find their way into the New Covenant, while the particulars and the enforcement mechanisms of the Mosaic Law do not.

There is no true comparison of our congregational sanctuaries today to that of the Tabernacle and Temple, except that they are (as the Tabernacle and Temple were then) places where the believing community goes periodically to meet God in prayer and worship, mediated through priests and a High Priest. Years ago they were the Levitical priests and Aaron was the High Priest, but now we (the priesthood of believers) are the priests, and Yeshua our Messiah is the High Priest. There is another similarity of "then and now" in that both institutions—the

265

Tabernacle (later the Temple) and the synagogue—have expenses of upkeep. In Mosaic times the expenses included maintaining the Levites, and today it includes mortgage payments on our buildings, and the salaries of clergy and other employees.

Whereas tithes and offerings were prescribed by the Mosaic Law for maintaining the Tabernacle (later the Temple) and its priests, we have no such law today but each institution today (synagogues, apostolic networks, etc.) prescribes the way(s) that its members will maintain it.[100] In denominational synagogues, support is usually through membership fees and charging for High Holy Day seats, and in Christian churches and Messianic Synagogues it is usually through members paying ten percent tithes on their income—a logical adaptation of the Mosaic Law. As for special offerings and *tz'dakah,* they are as needed today as much as in the past because membership fees and tithes cannot take care of every need. Messianic communities take up "freewill" offerings to cover such needs, and members of the traditional Jewish community often consider that charitable giving (*tz'dakah*) of ten percent is their minimum moral obligation.

Classical Commentators

The *mitzvot* compiled by Maimonides and Chinuch included the commandments of giving tithes, offerings, and *tz'dakah,* whereas Meir wrote very little on the subjects—a reflection (no doubt) of today's denominational synagogues choosing to not use tithes as their mainstay of support.

NCLA: JMm JFm KMm KFm GMm GFm

---

100 In church history, a justification for enforced tithing by state churches has analogized elders to priests, and *shamashim* (deacons) to Levites.

E8. Being Fruitful and Multiplying in Number and in Fruitfulness.

We are to be fruitful and multiply in number and in fruitfulness.

This precept is derived from His Word (blessed be He):

Key Scriptures

Genesis 1:27-28 (Maimonides RP212; Meir MP43; Chinuch C1)
So God created humankind in his own image; in the image of God he created him: male and female he created them. God blessed them: God said to them, "Be fruitful, multiply, fill the earth and subdue it. Rule over the fish in the sea, the birds in the air and every living creature that crawls on the earth.

Genesis 9:1
God blessed Noach and his sons and said to them, "Be fruitful, multiply and fill the earth.

Genesis 9:7
And you people, be fruitful, multiply, swarm on the earth and multiply on it.

Acts 6:1a
Around this time, when the number of talmidim was growing,

Acts 7:17
As the time drew near for the fulfillment of the promise God had made to Avraham, the number of our people in Egypt increased greatly,

Acts 9:31
Then the Messianic community throughout Y'hudah, the Galil and Shomron enjoyed peace and was built up. They lived in the fear of the Lord, with the counsel of the Ruach HaKodesh; and their numbers kept multiplying.

Acts 12:24
But the word of the Lord went on growing and being multiplied.

Supportive Scriptures

Genesis 35:10-11
Colossians 1:3-6, 9-10
Genesis 1:20-22, 8:16-17

Commentary

The first part of <u>Genesis 1:28</u> states: *"God blessed them: God said to them, "Be fruitful, multiply, fill the earth..."* Notice that the commandment to "be fruitful" in <u>Genesis 1:28</u> comes before the command to "multiply," and that the rest of the verse:

> *"and subdue it. Rule over the fish in the sea, the birds in the air and every living creature that crawls on the earth."*

instructs us that we have an obligation to produce value from our multiplied numbers—in other words, disseminate our fruitfulness.

The agricultural analogy is that fruit comes first and contains the seeds from which reproduction or multiplication of the plant occurs. Then, the more multiplication the more the fruit, so it is an unending cycle.

We see God's expectation that we multiply (increase) in fruitfulness elsewhere in Scripture as well. In <u>Genesis 35:10-11</u>, for example, God repeats his commandment to Israel (Jacob) to multiply, but God also says that a nations and kings will be descended from him, implying that Israel's descendants will have functions to fulfill with their numbers. Of course we know from <u>Exodus 19:6</u> that one of the areas of Israel's fruitfulness is that it is destined to *"be a kingdom of cohanim"*—*"a nation set apart."*

In <u>Acts 9:31</u>, when we are told that the Messianic Community multiplied in number, it is not to inform us of their reproductive fertility, but of the fact that belief in Yeshua spread throughout the area. Similarly, <u>Colossians 1:6</u> speaks of the Good News *"being fruitful and multiplying,"* and <u>Colossians 1:10</u> speaks of *"being fruitful in every good work and multiplying in the full knowledge of God."* It appears clear that God's desire for Israel and for all of mankind is that we multiply (increase) in both number and fruitfulness.

Now a word about reproduction in marriage. The <u>Genesis</u> commandment to multiply was given after man was created to be male and female, but prior to God having made Eve (<u>Genesis 2:18-24</u>). Although reproduction was not mentioned in the context of marriage, after God made Eve, He caused her and Adam to become "one flesh" (<u>verse 24</u>) and, since then, God intended reproduction between man and woman to be only in the context of covenant marriage. Reproduction is so implicitly part of the marriage covenant, that a party who refuses to bear children against the wishes of his or her mate may well be ruled to have abandoned the marriage covenant.

The controversy regarding the use of birth control measures by consenting married persons cannot be resolved within this *Mitzvah*. I do, however, express my opinion that methods of birth control that do not kill or abort fetuses are permitted because (1) Scripture allows unmarried persons to avoid having children by remaining single (<u>Matthew 9:12</u>; <u>1 Corinthians 7:8</u>), and (2) in Paul's warning to married persons that they should not deprive each other of sexual relations (<u>1 Corinthians 7:3-5</u>), the reason he gives is not that deprivation violates a commandment to reproduce, but rather *"because of your lack of self-control, you may succumb to the Adversary's temptation."* [101] Paul then follows up in <u>verse 6</u> with: *"I am giving you this as a suggestion, not as a command."* I deduce from this that since agreed-to abstinence between married persons is not a sin, so neither is preventing conception through other non-lethal means.

Finally, <u>Genesis 1:28</u> requires that mankind, as a species, reproduce, but it does not require that all persons or couples reproduce. Certainly unmarried persons should not, persons with certain medical conditions cannot, and there may be some that God specifically calls to remain unmarried (<u>1 Corinthians 7:8</u>).

Classical Commentators

In his *mitzvah* RP212, Maimonides states that we are to marry in order to multiply, and he cites <u>Yebamoth 65b</u> of the *Talmud* to support his assertion that the duty to be fruitful and multiply applies to men and not women. Meir does not state that it is only the man's duty, but implies it by framing his *mitzvah* MP43 to address only the man. HaChinuch is consistent with Maimonides and Meir and also cites <u>Yebamoth 6</u>. None of the classical commentators treat being fruitful and multiplying as other than marrying and reproducing.

<u>NCLA</u>: **JMm KMm KFm JFm GMm GFm**

---

101 See also, <u>Exodus 21:7-11</u> (Maimonides RN262; Meir MN42; Chinuch C46)

F: Family

F1. Honoring and Revering Our Father and Mother.

We are to honor and revere our father and mother.

This precept is derived from His Word (blessed be He):

Key Scriptures

Exodus 20:12 (Maimonides RP210; Meir MP41; Chinuch C33)
Honor your father and mother, so that you may live long in the land which ADONAI your God is giving you.

Exodus 21:15 (Maimonides RN319; Meir MN44; Chinuch C48)
Whoever attacks his father or mother must be put to death.[102]

Exodus 21:17 (Maimonides RN318; Meir MN46; Chinuch C260)
Whoever curses his father or mother must be put to death.[103]

Leviticus 19:2-3 (Maimonides RP211; Meir MP42; Chinuch C212)
Speak to the entire community of Isra'el; tell them, 'You people are to be holy because I, ADONAI your God, am holy. Every one of you is to revere his father and mother, and you are to keep my Shabbats; I am ADONAI your God.

Leviticus 19:32 (Maimonides RP209; Meir MP17; Chinuch C257)
Stand up in the presence of a person with gray hair, show respect for the old; you are to fear your God; I am ADONAI.

Leviticus 20:9 (Maimonides RN318; Chinuch C260)
A person who curses his father or mother must be put to death; having cursed his father or his mother, his blood is on him.[104]

Mark 10:19
You know the mitzvot—'Don't murder, don't commit adultery, don't steal, don't give false testimony, don't defraud, honor your father and mother…

Ephesians 6:1-3
Children, what you should do in union with the Lord is obey your parents, for this is right. Honor your father and mother"—this is the first commandment that embodies a promise—so that it may go well with you, and you may live long in the Land.

---

102 Death sentences that were statutorily authorized to be carried out by the ancient government of Israel (under the Mosaic Covenant) are no longer authorized in the absence of that government and under the New Covenant.
103 ibid.
104 ibid.

<u>Colossians 3:20</u>
Children, obey your parents in everything; for this pleases the Lord.

<u>1 Timothy 5:1-2</u>
Do not rebuke an older man sharply, but appeal to him as you would to a father; treat younger men like brothers, older women like mothers and younger women like sisters, with absolute purity.

Supportive Scriptures

Proverbs 20:20, 23:22, 30:17
1 Timothy 5:8

Commentary

Honoring our father and mother involves respecting them for their parental position both privately and in public. It also implies obeying them when we are young, but never in a way that disobeys or dishonors God. Although, by promising long life in the land, it is clear that <u>Exodus 20:12</u> and <u>Ephesians 6:1-3</u> are addressing Israelites, the instructions they convey are morally universal and are therefore applicable to Gentiles as well.

The King James Version of the Bible translates *"tira'u"* (derived from *"yara"*) in <u>Leviticus 19:3</u> as *"Ye shall fear,"* whereas other versions translate the word "revere" or "respect." We are not to be frightened by our parents (that is not the kind of "fear" of them we are to have). We are rather to regard them with awesome respect, for God holds them accountable to train us up in righteousness (<u>Proverbs 22:6</u>), and He holds us accountable for how we treat them—how we speak of them, and how we speak to them. We are not to usurp their authority, speak for them (unless asked), contradict them before others in a way that would cause them embarrassment or dishonor and, of course, not curse them or strike them. Our obligation to honor and revere our parents is analogous to our obligation to honor and revere God (<u>Proverbs 3:9</u>; <u>Leviticus 24:15</u>; <u>Deuteronomy 6:13</u>),[105] and it is incumbent upon us, even should they do wrong to us or follow ungodly paths in aspects of their personal lives.

The relevance of <u>1 Timothy 5:8</u> is that providing materially for one's parents, especially when they are at an advanced age, is one way of honoring and revering them, and failing to support them when there is a need to do so is the opposite. It is commonly thought that <u>1 Timothy 5:8</u> is only a reference to husbands supporting their wives and children, but the context in the ancient world (as well as in many places in the world today) included supporting one's parents as well, because aging parents commonly lived with (or close by) their children. This principle is verified in Meir's commentary to his *mitzvah* MP41.

---

105 Similar to the King James Version's translation of *"tira'u"* in <u>Leviticus 19:3</u>, most translators of <u>Deuteronomy 6:13</u> translate *"tira"* (also derived from *"yara"*) as "fear."

Classical Commentators

Maimonides, Meir, and HaChinuch did not combine honoring and revering one's parents into a single *mitzvah.* Instead, they wrote separate *mitzvot* for each, the combination of which agrees with this *Mitzvah.*

In regard to honoring our parents, all three commentators make reference to places in the *Talmud,* most prominently, tractate *Kiddushin,* and also to the *Sifra* (Lev. 19:3).[106] Maimonides adds that we are required to care for our parents when they become old; Meir agrees, and goes into some detail of our obligation to financially support our parents when necessary. He further says that we are to attend our father as a servant would attend his master, but we are not to sin in following our parents' instructions.

In regard to revering our parents, all three commentators link reverence to fear, and instruct against standing or sitting in one's father's place. Meir says that we are not to contradict our father's words or refer to him by his name. HaChinuch is detailed in other ways, and raises the question of how far reverence of parents should go. He indicates that we must be able to suffer indignities and wrongs done to us without putting our parents to shame, and we must be respectful of them even if their minds become unsound in connection with their age. Of course, we are not to curse them or strike them.

NCLA: JMm KMm KFm JFm GMm GFm

---

106 *Halachic midrash* to Leviticus.

F2. The Covenant Laws of Marriage.

We are to obey the biblical laws concerning marriage.

This precept is derived from His Word (blessed be He):

Key Scriptures

The "Creation" Covenant of Marriage

Genesis 2:18-24
ADONAI, God, said, "It isn't good that the person should be alone. I will make for him a companion suitable for helping him." So from the ground ADONAI, God, formed every wild animal and every bird that flies in the air, and he brought them to the person to see what he would call them. Whatever the person would call each living creature, that was to be its name. So the person gave names to all the livestock, to the birds in the air and to every wild animal. But for Adam there was not found a companion suitable for helping him. Then God caused a deep sleep to fall upon the person; and while he was sleeping, he took one of his ribs and closed up the place from which he took it with flesh. The rib which ADONAI, God, had taken from the person, he made a woman-person; and he brought her to the man-person. The man-person said, "At last! This is bone from my bones and flesh from my flesh. She is to be called Woman, because she was taken out of Man." This is why a man is to leave his father and mother and stick with his wife, and they are to be one flesh.

Exodus 21:7-11 (Maimonides RP213; Chinuch 552) [obsolete]
If a man sells his daughter as a slave, she is not to go free like the men-slaves. If her master married her but decides she no longer pleases him, then he is to allow her to be redeemed. He is not allowed to sell her to a foreign people, because he has treated her unfairly. If he has her marry his son, then he is to treat her like a daughter. If he marries another wife, he is not to reduce her food, clothing or marital rights. If he fails to provide her with these three things, she is to be given her freedom without having to pay anything.

Exodus 22:15(16)-16(17) [obsolete]
If a man seduces a virgin who is not engaged to be married and sleeps with her, he must pay the bride-price for her to be his wife. But if her father refuses to give her to him, he must pay a sum equivalent to the bride-price for virgins.

Leviticus 21:13-15 (Maimonides RP38; Chinuch C272) [obsolete]
He [the High Priest] is to marry a virgin; he may not marry a widow, divorcee, profaned woman or prostitute; but he must marry a virgin from among his own people and not disqualify his descendants among his people; because I am ADONAI, who makes him holy.

Deuteronomy 17:17a (Maimonides RN364; Chinuch C501) [obsolete]
Likewise, he is not to acquire many wives for himself, so that his heart will not turn away;

Deuteronomy 21:10-13 (Maimonides RP221; Chinuch C532) [obsolete]
When you go out to war against your enemies, and ADONAI your God hands them over to you, and you take prisoners, and you see among the prisoners a woman who looks good to you, and you feel attracted to her and want her as your wife; you are to bring her home to your house, where she will shave her head, cut her fingernails and remove her prison clothing. She will stay there in your house, mourning her father and mother for a full month; after which you may go in to have sexual relations with her and be her husband, and she will be your wife.

Deuteronomy 21:15-17 [obsolete]
If a man has two wives, the one loved and the other unloved, and both the loved and unloved wives have borne him children, and if the firstborn son is the child of the unloved wife; then, when it comes time for him to pass his inheritance on to his sons, he may not give the inheritance due the firstborn to the son of the loved wife in place of the son of the unloved one, who is in fact the firstborn. No, he must acknowledge as firstborn the son of the unloved wife by giving him a double portion of everything he owns, for he is the firstfruits of his manhood, and the right of the firstborn is his.

Deuteronomy 22:13-21 (Chinuch C552) [obsolete]
If a man marries a woman, has sexual relations with her and then, having come to dislike her, brings false charges against her and defames her character by saying, 'I married this woman, but when I had intercourse with her I did not find evidence that she was a virgin'; then the girl's father and mother are to take the evidence of the girl's virginity to the leaders of the town at the gate. The girl's father will say to the leaders, 'I let my daughter marry this man, but he hates her, so he has brought false charges that he didn't find evidence of her virginity; yet here is the evidence of my daughter's virginity'—and they will lay the cloth before the town leaders. The leaders of that town are to take the man, punish him, and fine him two-and-a-half pounds of silver shekels, which they will give to the girl's father, because he has publicly defamed a virgin of Isra'el. She will remain his wife, and he is forbidden from divorcing her as long as he lives. But if the charge is substantiated that evidence for the girl's virginity could not be found; then they are to lead the girl to the door of her father's house, and the men of her town will stone her to death, because she has committed in Isra'el the disgraceful act of being a prostitute while still in her father's house. In this way you will put an end to such wickedness among you.

Deuteronomy 22:28-29 (Maimonides RP218, RN358; Chinuch 557-558) [partially obsolete]
If a man comes upon a girl who is a virgin but who is not engaged, and he grabs her and has sexual relations with her, and they are caught in the act, then the man who had intercourse with her must give to the girl's father one-and-a-quarter pounds of silver shekels, and she will become his wife, because he humiliated her; he may not divorce her as long as he lives.

Deuteronomy 23:2(1) (Maimonides RN360; Meir MN136; Chinuch C209) [obsolete]
A man with crushed or damaged private parts may not enter the assembly of ADONAI.

Deuteronomy 23:3(2) (Maimonides RN354; Meir MN137; Chinuch C560) [obsolete]
A mamzer may not enter the assembly of ADONAI, nor may his descendants down to the tenth generation enter the assembly of ADONAI.

Deuteronomy 24:1-2 (Maimonides RP213; Meir MP44; Chinuch C552)
Suppose a man marries a woman and consummates the marriage but later finds her displeasing, because he has found her offensive in some respect. He writes her a divorce document, gives it to her and sends her away from his house. She leaves his house, goes and becomes another man's wife…

Deuteronomy 24:5 (Maimonides RP214; Chinuch C582)
If a man has recently married his wife, he is not to be subject to military service; he is to be free of external obligations and left at home for one year to make his new wife happy.

Deuteronomy 25:5-10 (Maimonides RP216-217, RN357; Meir MP45-46, MN135; Chinuch C597-599) [obsolete]
If brothers live together, and one of them dies childless, his widow is not to marry someone unrelated to him; her husband's brother is to go to her and perform the duty of a brother-in-law by marrying her. The first child she bears will succeed to the name of his dead brother, so that his name will not be eliminated from Isra'el. If the man does not wish to marry his brother's widow, then his brother's widow is to go up to the gate, to the leaders, and say, 'My brother-in-law refuses to raise up for his brother a name in Isra'el; he will not perform the duty of a husband's brother for me.' The leaders of his town are to summon him and speak to him. If, on appearing before them, he continues to say, 'I don't want to marry her,' then his brother's widow is to approach him in the presence of the leaders, pull his sandal off his foot, spit in his face and say, 'This is what is done to the man who refuses to build up his brother's family.' From that time on, his family is to be known in Isra'el as 'the family of the man who had his sandal pulled off.'

Marriage in the New Covenant

1 Corinthians 7:36-40
Now if a man thinks he is behaving dishonorably by treating his fiancée this way, and if there is strong sexual desire, so that marriage is what ought to happen; then let him do what he wants—he is not sinning: let them get married. But if a man has firmly made up his mind, being under no compulsion but having complete control over his will, if he has decided within himself to keep his fiancée a virgin, he will be doing well. So the man who marries his fiancée will do well, and the man who doesn't marry will do better. A wife is bound to her husband as long as he lives, but if the husband dies she is free to marry anyone she wishes, provided he is a believer in the Lord. However, in my opinion, she will be happier if she remains unmarried, and in saying this I think I have God's Spirit.

1 Corinthians 11:3
But I want you to understand that the head of every man is the Messiah, and the head of a wife is her husband, and the head of the Messiah is God.

Ephesians 5:22-33
Wives should submit to their husbands as they do to the Lord; because the husband is head of the wife, just as the Messiah, as head of the Messianic Community, is himself the one who keeps the body safe. Just as the Messianic Community submits to the Messiah, so also wives should submit

to their husbands in everything. As for husbands, love your wives, just as the Messiah loved the Messianic Community, indeed, gave himself up on its behalf, in order to set it apart for God, making it clean through immersion in the mikveh, so to speak, in order to present the Messianic Community to himself as a bride to be proud of, without a spot, wrinkle or any such thing, but holy and without defect. This is how husbands ought to love their wives—like their own bodies; for the man who loves his wife is loving himself. Why, no one ever hated his own flesh! On the contrary, he feeds it well and takes care of it, just as the Messiah does the Messianic Community, because we are parts of his Body. Therefore a man will leave his father and mother and remain with his wife, and the two will become one." There is profound truth hidden here, which I say concerns the Messiah and the Messianic Community. However, the text also applies to each of you individually: let each man love his wife as he does himself, and see that the wife respects her husband.

Colossians 3:18-19
Wives, subject yourselves to your husbands, as is appropriate in the Lord. Husbands, love your wives and don't treat them harshly.

Hebrews 13:4a
Marriage is honorable in every respect; and, in particular, sex within marriage is pure.

Prohibited Marriages

Leviticus 18:6-20 (Maimonides RN330-336, 340-345, 353; Meir MN110, 112-113, 115, 119-120, 125-131; Chinuch C188, 190-198, 200-202, 206)
None of you is to approach anyone who is a close relative in order to have sexual relations; I am ADONAI. You are not to have sexual relations with your father, and you are not to have sexual relations with your mother. She is your mother—do not have sexual relations with her. You are not to have sexual relations with your father's wife; that is your father's prerogative. You are not to have sexual relations with your sister, the daughter of your father or the daughter of your mother, whether born at home or elsewhere. Do not have sexual relations with them. You are not to have sexual relations with your son's daughter or with your daughter's daughter. Do not have sexual relations with them, because their sexual disgrace will be your own. You are not to have sexual relations with your father's wife's daughter, born to your father, because she is your sister; do not have sexual relations with her. You are not to have sexual relations with your father's sister, because she is your father's close relative. You are not to have sexual relations with your mother's sister, because she is your mother's close relative. You are not to disgrace your father's brother by having sexual relations with his wife, because she is your aunt. You are not to have sexual relations with your daughter-in-law; because she is your son's wife. Do not have sexual relations with her. You are not to have sexual relations with your brother's wife, because this is your brother's prerogative. You are not to have sexual relations with both a woman and her daughter, nor are you to have sexual relations with her son's daughter or her daughter's daughter; they are close relatives of hers, and it would be shameful. You are not to take a woman to be a rival with her sister and have sexual relations with her while her sister is still alive. You are not to approach a woman in order to have sexual relations with her when she is unclean from her time of niddah. You are not to go to bed with your neighbor's wife and thus become unclean with her.

Leviticus 20:14 (Maimonides RN336; Chinuch C195)
If a man marries a woman and her mother, it is depravity; they are to be put to death by fire, both he and they, so that there will not be depravity among you.

Leviticus 21:7 (Maimonides RN158-160; Meir MN138-140; Chinuch C266-268)
A cohen is not to marry a woman who is a prostitute, who has been profaned or who has been divorced; because he is holy for his God.

2 Corinthians 6:14-15
Do not yoke yourselves together in a team with unbelievers. For how can righteousness and lawlessness be partners? What fellowship does light have with darkness? What harmony can there be between the Messiah and B'liya'al? What does a believer have in common with an unbeliever?

Supportive Scriptures—The "Creation" Covenant of Marriage

Genesis 38:8-10
1 Kings 11:1-6
Jeremiah 29:6
Proverbs 18:22, 19:14, 31:10-31
Matthew 19:3-6
Mark 10:6-8

Supportive Scriptures—Marriage in the New Covenant

Mark 12:25
1 Corinthians 7:1-6, 25-35
2 Corinthians 6:14-15
1 Timothy 3:2, 12
Titus 1:6
Hebrews 13:4a
1 Peter 3:5-7

Supportive Scriptures—Prohibited Marriages

Leviticus 20:17, 19-21, 21:13-14
Deuteronomy 23:1(22:30)-9(8), 24:1-4
Ezra 9:12-14
2 Corinthians 6:14-15

Supportive Scriptures—Singleness

Matthew 19:12
1 Corinthians 7:8, 32-35

Commentary

This *Mitzvah* is derived primarily from <u>Genesis 2:24</u>:

> *"This is why a man is to leave his father and mother and stick with his wife, and they are to be one flesh."* [107]

The resulting "one flesh" is what makes the leaving and cleaving covenantal, and the fact that the commandment appears so early in <u>Genesis</u> is why I call it a "creation" covenant (to distinguish it from other covenants that came later). We commonly call this covenant "marriage."

You will notice that several of the Scriptures from the *Tanakh* cited above are labeled "obsolete." That is because circumstances and conditions today are so different than during the time of Moses. Back then, the Scriptures that are now obsolete made perfect sense and could be implemented, while today they cannot.

Although this *Mitzvah* is expressed as a "man" leaving his parents to join with his wife, the covenant of becoming "one flesh" cannot be fulfilled unless the man's intended wife similarly leaves her parents. The "leaving" of parents in the Scripture is not a reference to where the couple resides. The Scripture is speaking of the controlling influence that parents rightly have over their young unmarried children, but which is improper and interfering if it is allowed to continue once the child (man or woman) becomes married.

I believe the reason <u>Genesis 2:24</u> reads the way it does, is that a man's responsibility to leave his parents is different from a woman's. It is the man's responsibility to take the initiative in leaving, but it is the woman's parents' responsibility to release her to her intended husband. The implication of her parents not doing so is, of course, obvious and, after marriage, problems result when either or both of the marrieds allow improper ties to their parents to continue.

The concept of becoming "one flesh" is not only covenantal, but also mystical and difficult to comprehend. <u>Mark 10:8b</u> attempts to explain it by stating:

> *"Thus they are no longer two, but one."*

<u>Ephesians 5:29-32</u> relates the phenomenon to Messiah and the Body of Believers by stating:

> *"Why, no one ever hated his own flesh! On the contrary, he feeds it well and takes care of it, just as the Messiah does the Messianic Community, because we are parts of his Body. "Therefore a man will leave his father and mother and remain with his wife, and the two will become one." There is profound truth hidden here, which I say concerns the Messiah and the Messianic Community."*

This "oneness" possibly reminds one of the plural unity of the Father, Son, and Holy Spirit.

---

107 Some translations state "cleave" to his wife.

Genesis 2:24 has been interpreted, in some quarters, as requiring everyone to marry. I do not view it that way, especially in light of Paul's remarks in 1 Corinthians 7:8, 32-35. I believe that Scripture teaches that the norm of creation is to marry and procreate, but it allows for not doing so and, in some cases, singleness is God's will for an individual (see Matthew 19:12).

This *Mitzvah* includes Scriptures that prohibit marriage to certain persons. These include family members with whom we cannot have sexual relations, persons with whom we are unequally yoked, Jews marrying persons of certain nations, etc. It also includes persons that a *cohen* cannot marry. Secular law also puts restrictions on marrying family members in order to avoid weakening the human genetic pool and allowing unwanted recessive traits to emerge.

Classical Commentators

Maimonides, Meir, and HaChinuch make no reference to Genesis 2:24 (or any other Scripture) to support leaving one's father and mother and becoming one flesh with one's wife when one marries. Maimonides' RP213, Meir's MP44, and HaChinuch's C552, rely on Deuteronomy 24:1 to support their allegation that marriage must be by *kiddushin* (consecration)—a binding marriage ceremony. The Scripture does not say that, nor does any other Scripture.

Maimonides and HaChinuch refer to Exodus 21:11, and Meir refers to Deuteronomy 24:1 to support their general law of marriage, but I find all three commentators ambiguous as to whether their respective *mitzvot* command marriage or simply describe the *kiddushin* (sanctification), of a marriage ceremony. Apparently, Rabbi Dr. Charles B. Chavel, a prominent translator into English of Maimonides' *"Sefer HaMitzvot"* had the same concern, for he found it necessary to introduce the bracketed word [only] in the first sentence of his *mitzvah* RP213, causing it to read:

> *"By this injunction we are commanded to take a woman to wife [only] by a binding ceremony: either by giving her something [of value],[108] or by handing her a writ of marriage, or by intercourse [accompanied by a declaration of marriage]."*

Meir discusses *kiddushin* through the payment of monetary value, and he also discusses betrothal before *nissuin* (consummation) but not the other ways of consecrating a marriage.

HaChinuch presents the most detail of *kiddushin.* He states that if marriage is consecrated by the giving of monetary value, the groom must say: "You are now consecrated to me by this money (or thing of monetary value)." If the marriage is consecrated by a document, the groom must say: "You are consecrated to me by this document (or whatever it is)." If marriage is consecrated by sexual intercourse, he must say to his bride before witnesses: "You are consecrated to me by this act of intimacy." He then takes his bride into seclusion and is seen doing so by the witnesses.

<u>**NCLA**</u>**: JMm KMm KFm JFm GMm GFm**

---

108 The modern equivalent of paying the bride money is for the groom to give the bride a wedding ring of significant monetary value while stating: "You are hereby consecrated to me with this ring, according to the law of Moses and Israel." It is analogous to a "bride price" practiced in certain other cultures, and opposite to a "dowry" which the bride or the bride's father is expected to pay to the groom.

F3. Divorce and Remarriage.

We are to obey the biblical law concerning divorce and remarriage.

This precept is derived from His Word (blessed be He):

Key Scriptures

God Hates Divorce

Malachi 2:16a
"For I hate divorce," says ADONAI the God of Isra'el...

Mark 10:9
So then, no one should break apart what God has joined together.

The Sinai Covenant's Allowance but Abhorrence of Divorce

Exodus 21:7-11 (Maimonides RP213; Chinuch C552)
If a man sells his daughter as a slave, she is not to go free like the men-slaves. If her master married her but decides she no longer pleases him, then he is to allow her to be redeemed. He is not allowed to sell her to a foreign people, because he has treated her unfairly. If he has her marry his son, then he is to treat her like a daughter. If he marries another wife, he is not to reduce her food, clothing or marital rights. If he fails to provide her with these three things, she is to be given her freedom without having to pay anything.

Deuteronomy 21:10-14
When you go out to war against your enemies, and ADONAI your God hands them over to you, and you take prisoners, and you see among the prisoners a woman who looks good to you, and you feel attracted to her and want her as your wife; you are to bring her home to your house, where she will shave her head, cut her fingernails and remove her prison clothing. She will stay there in your house, mourning her father and mother for a full month; after which you may go in to have sexual relations with her and be her husband, and she will be your wife. In the event that you lose interest in her, you are to let her go wherever she wishes; but you may not sell her for money or treat her like a slave, because you humiliated her.

Matthew 19:7-8
They said to him [Yeshua], "Then why did Moshe give the commandment that a man should hand his wife a get and divorce her?" He answered, "Moshe allowed you to divorce your wives because your hearts are so hardened. But this is not how it was at the beginning.

We Are Not to Break the Covenant of Marriage

Malachi 2:13-16
Here is something else you do: you cover ADONAI's altar with tears, with weeping and with sighing, because he no longer looks at the offering or receives your gift with favor. Nevertheless, you ask, "Why is this?" Because ADONAI is witness between you and the wife of your youth that you have broken faith with her, though she is your companion, your wife by covenant. And hasn't he made [them] one [flesh] in order to have spiritual blood-relatives? For what the one [flesh] seeks is a seed from God. Therefore, take heed to your spirit, and don't break faith with the wife of your youth. "For I hate divorce," says ADONAI the God of Isra'el, "and him who covers his clothing with violence," says ADONAI-Tzva'ot. Therefore take heed to your spirit, and don't break faith.

Matthew 19:3-6
Some P'rushim came and tried to trap him [Yeshua] by asking, "Is it permitted for a man to divorce his wife on any ground whatever?" He replied, "Haven't you read that at the beginning the Creator made them male and female, and that he said, 'For this reason a man should leave his father and mother and be united with his wife, and the two are to become one flesh'? Thus they are no longer two, but one. So then, no one should split apart what God has joined together."

Mark 10:6-9
However, at the beginning of creation, God made them male and female. For this reason, a man should leave his father and mother and be united with his wife, and the two are to become one flesh. Thus they are no longer two, but one. So then, no one should break apart what God has joined together.

Luke 16:18
Every man who divorces his wife and marries another woman commits adultery, and a man who marries a woman divorced by her husband commits adultery.

Abandonment Breaks Covenant and Releases the Innocent Party from Covenant Obligations

Deuteronomy 31:16-17
ADONAI said to Moshe, "You are about to sleep with your ancestors. But this people will get up and offer themselves as prostitutes to the foreign gods of the land where they are going. When they are with those gods, they will abandon me and break my covenant which I have made with them. Then my anger will flare up, and I will abandon them and hide my face from them.

Jeremiah 11:10-11
They [Israelites] have returned to the sins of their ancestors, who refused to hear my words, and they have gone after other gods to serve them. The house of Isra'el and the house of Y'hudah have broken my covenant which I made with their ancestors. Therefore ADONAI says, "I am going to bring on them a disaster which they will not be able to escape; and even if they cry to me, I will not listen to them."

<u>Jeremiah 31:30(31)-31(32)</u>
Here, the days are coming," says ADONAI, "when I will make a new covenant with the house of Isra'el and with the house of Y'hudah. It will not be like the covenant I made with their fathers on the day I took them by their hand and brought them out of the land of Egypt; because they, for their part, violated my covenant, even though I, for my part, was a husband to them," says ADONAI.

A Believer Is Not to Abandon His or Her Spouse

<u>1Corinthians 7:10-11</u>
To those who are married I have a command, and it is not from me but from the Lord: a woman is not to separate herself from her husband. But if she does separate herself, she is to remain single or be reconciled with her husband. Also, a husband is not to leave his wife.

<u>1 Corinthians 7:12-14</u>
To the rest I say—I, not the Lord: if any brother has a wife who is not a believer, and she is satisfied to go on living with him, he should not leave her. Also, if any woman has an unbelieving husband who is satisfied to go on living with her, she is not to leave him. For the unbelieving husband has been set aside for God by the wife, and the unbelieving wife has been set aside for God by the brother—otherwise your children would be "unclean," but as it is, they are set aside for God.

We Are Commanded against Sexual Infidelity in Marriage

<u>Exodus 20:13-14(17)</u>
"Do not murder. "Do not commit adultery. "Do not steal. "Do not give false evidence against your neighbor. "Do not covet your neighbor's house; do not covet your neighbor's wife, his male or female slave, his ox, his donkey or anything that belongs to your neighbor." (see also, <u>Deuteronomy 5:17-18(21)</u>).

<u>Leviticus 18:20</u>
You are not to go to bed with your neighbor's wife and thus become unclean with her.

<u>Deuteronomy 22:22</u>
If a man is found sleeping with a woman who has a husband, both of them must die—the man who went to bed with the woman and the woman too. In this way you will expel such wickedness from Isra'el.

<u>Matthew 5:27-28</u>
You have heard that our fathers were told, 'Do not commit adultery.' But I tell you that a man who even looks at a woman with the purpose of lusting after her has already committed adultery with her in his heart.

<u>Luke 18:20</u>
You know the mitzvot—'Don't commit adultery, don't murder, don't steal, don't give false testimony, honor your father and mother...'

<u>Hebrews 13:4</u>
Marriage is honorable in every respect; and, in particular, sex within marriage is pure. But God will indeed punish fornicators and adulterers.

Sexual Infidelity Is an Abandonment that Breaks the Covenant of Marriage

<u>Malachi 2:13-16</u>
Here is something else you do: you cover ADONAI's altar with tears, with weeping and with sighing, because he no longer looks at the offering or receives your gift with favor. Nevertheless, you ask, "Why is this?" Because ADONAI is witness between you and the wife of your youth that you have broken faith with her, though she is your companion, your wife by covenant. And hasn't he made [them] one [flesh] in order to have spiritual blood-relatives? For what the one [flesh] seeks is a seed from God. Therefore, take heed to your spirit, and don't break faith with the wife of your youth. "For I hate divorce," says ADONAI the God of Isra'el, "and him who covers his clothing with violence," says ADONAI-Tzva'ot. Therefore take heed to your spirit, and don't break faith.

<u>Matthew 5:31-32</u>
It was said, 'Whoever divorces his wife must give her a get.' But I tell you that anyone who divorces his wife, except on the ground of fornication, makes her an adulteress; and that anyone who marries a divorcee commits adultery.

<u>Matthew 19:3-9</u>
Some P'rushim came and tried to trap him by asking, "Is it permitted for a man to divorce his wife on any ground whatever?" He replied, "Haven't you read that at the beginning the Creator made them male and female, and that he said, 'For this reason a man should leave his father and mother and be united with his wife, and the two are to become one flesh'? Thus they are no longer two, but one. So then, no one should split apart what God has joined together." They said to him, "Then why did Moshe give the commandment that a man should hand his wife a get and divorce her?" He answered, "Moshe allowed you to divorce your wives because your hearts are so hardened. But this is not how it was at the beginning. Now what I say to you is that whoever divorces his wife, except on the ground of sexual immorality, and marries another woman commits adultery!"

<u>Mark 10:6-9</u>
However, at the beginning of creation, God made them male and female. For this reason, a man should leave his father and mother and be united with his wife, and the two are to become one flesh. Thus they are no longer two, but one. So then, no one should break apart what God has joined together.

Withholding Sexual Intimacy Is an Abandonment that Breaks the Covenant of Marriage

Genesis 1:28a
God blessed them: God said to them, "Be fruitful, multiply, fill the earth and subdue it.

Exodus 21:10-11 (Maimonides RP213; Chinuch C552)
If he marries another wife, he is not to reduce her [the first wife's] food, clothing or marital rights. If he fails to provide her with these three things, she is to be given her freedom without having to pay anything.

1 Corinthians 7:3-4
The husband should give his wife what she is entitled to in the marriage relationship, and the wife should do the same for her husband. The wife is not in charge of her own body, but her husband is; likewise, the husband is not in charge of his own body, but his wife is.

Hebrews 13:4a
Marriage is honorable in every respect; and, in particular, sex within marriage is pure.

Withholding a Spouse's Basic Provisions Is an Abandonment that Breaks the Covenant of Marriage

Exodus 21:10-11 (Maimonides RP213; Chinuch C552)
If he marries another wife, he is not to reduce her [the first wife's] food, clothing or marital rights. If he fails to provide her with these three things, she is to be given her freedom without having to pay anything.

1 Timothy 5:8
Moreover, anyone who does not provide for his own people, especially for his family, has disowned the faith and is worse than an unbeliever.

If an Unbeliever Abandons His or Her Spouse, the Believing Spouse is Free to Remarry

Two translations:

1 Corinthians 7:15 (CJB)
But if the unbelieving spouse separates himself, let him be separated. In circumstances like these, the brother or sister is not enslaved—God has called you to a life of peace.

1 Corinthians 7:15 (NKJ)
But if the unbeliever departs, let him depart; a brother or a sister is not under bondage in such cases. But God has called us to peace.

Death of a Spouse Ends the Covenant of Marriage

Romans 7:1-3
Surely you know, brothers—for I am speaking to those who understand Torah—that the Torah has authority over a person only so long as he lives? For example, a married woman is bound by Torah to her husband while he is alive; but if the husband dies, she is released from the part of the Torah that deals with husbands. Therefore, while the husband is alive, she will be called an adulteress if she marries another man; but if the husband dies, she is free from that part of the Torah; so that if she marries another man, she is not an adulteress.

1 Corinthians 7:39
A wife is bound to her husband as long as he lives, but if the husband dies she is free to marry anyone she wishes, provided he is a believer in the Lord.

Acquiring a "Get" Does Not Necessarily Break the Covenant of Marriage

Matthew 5:31-32
"It was said, 'Whoever divorces his wife must give her a get.' But I tell you that anyone who divorces his wife, except on the ground of fornication, makes her an adulteress; and that anyone who marries a divorcee commits adultery."

Matthew 19:7-9
They said to him, "Then why did Moshe give the commandment that a man should hand his wife a get and divorce her?" He answered, "Moshe allowed you to divorce your wives because your hearts are so hardened. But this is not how it was at the beginning. Now what I say to you is that whoever divorces his wife, except on the ground of sexual immorality, and marries another woman commits adultery!"

Mark 10:11-12
He [Yeshua] said to them [the P'rushim], "Whoever divorces his wife and marries another woman commits adultery against his wife; and if a wife divorces her husband and marries another man, she too commits adultery."

Divorce Cannot Be Validated Except through a "Get"

Deuteronomy 24:1 (Maimonides RP222; Chinuch C579)
Suppose a man marries a woman and consummates the marriage but later finds her displeasing, because he has found her offensive in some respect. He writes her a divorce document, gives it to her and sends her away from his house.

Matthew 5:31
It was said, 'Whoever divorces his wife must give her a get.'

<u>Matthew 19:7</u>
They said to him, "Then why did Moshe give the commandment that a man should hand his wife a get and divorce her?"

<u>Mark 10:2-4</u>
Some P'rushim came up and tried to trap him by asking him, "Does the Torah permit a man to divorce his wife?" He replied, "What did Moshe command you?" They said, "Moshe allowed a man to hand his wife a get and divorce her."

When a Man May Not Divorce

<u>Deuteronomy 22:13-19</u> (Maimonides RP219; RN359; Chinuch C553, 554)
"If a man marries a woman, has sexual relations with her and then, having come to dislike her, brings false charges against her and defames her character by saying, 'I married this woman, but when I had intercourse with her I did not find evidence that she was a virgin'; then the girl's father and mother are to take the evidence of the girl's virginity to the leaders of the town at the gate. The girl's father will say to the leaders, 'I let my daughter marry this man, but he hates her, so he has brought false charges that he didn't find evidence of her virginity; yet here is the evidence of my daughter's virginity'—and they will lay the cloth before the town leaders. The leaders of that town are to take the man, punish him, and fine him two-and-a-half pounds of silver shekels, which they will give to the girl's father, because he has publicly defamed a virgin of Isra'el. She will remain his wife, and he is forbidden from divorcing her as long as he lives."

<u>Deuteronomy 22:28-29</u> (Maimonides RP218, RN358; Chinuch C557, 558)
"If a man comes upon a girl who is a virgin but who is not engaged, and he grabs her and has sexual relations with her, and they are caught in the act, then the man who had intercourse with her must give to the girl's father one-and-a-quarter pounds of silver shekels, and she will become his wife, because he humiliated her; he may not divorce her as long as he lives."

<u>Mark 10:11-12</u>
He said to them, "Whoever divorces his wife and marries another woman commits adultery against his wife; and if a wife divorces her husband and marries another man, she too commits adultery."

<u>Luke 16:18</u>
Every man who divorces his wife and marries another woman commits adultery, and a man who marries a woman divorced by her husband commits adultery.

When a Man or Woman May Not Remarry

<u>Deuteronomy 24:1-4</u> (Maimonides RN356; Meir MN134; Chinuch C580)
Suppose a man marries a woman and consummates the marriage but later finds her displeasing, because he has found her offensive in some respect. He writes her a divorce document, gives it to her and sends her away from his house. She leaves his house, goes and becomes another man's wife; but the second husband dislikes her and writes her a get, gives it to her and sends her away

from his house; or the second husband whom she married dies. In such a case her first husband, who sent her away, may not take her again as his wife, because she is now defiled. It would be detestable to ADONAI, and you are not to bring about sin in the land ADONAI your God is giving you as your inheritance.

<u>Mark 10:10-12</u>
He said to them, "Whoever divorces his wife and marries another woman commits adultery against his wife; and if a wife divorces her husband and marries another man, she too commits adultery."

<u>Luke 16:18</u>
Every man who divorces his wife and marries another woman commits adultery, and a man who marries a woman divorced by her husband commits adultery.

<u>1Corinthians 7:10-11</u>
To those who are married I have a command, and it is not from me but from the Lord: a woman is not to separate herself from her husband. But if she does separate herself, she is to remain single or be reconciled with her husband. Also, a husband is not to leave his wife.

Commentary

The biblical covenant of marriage consists of one man and one woman joined together to become "one flesh." On one level, "one flesh" is a mystical concept that is difficult to understand but, on a practical level, it defines marriage as being a covenant of exclusive intimacy between lifelong partners, most of whom will produce offspring. We do not profess to know why God allowed men to have multiple wives during the Mosaic and pre-Mosaic periods, but it seems not to have been God's best for us from the beginning (<u>Genesis 2:24</u> and <u>Ephesians 5:31</u>), and it is clearly not his will for us today, as Scripture applies it to elders in <u>1 Timothy 3:2a and 12</u> and <u>Titus 1:6a</u>.

According to <u>Malachi 2:13-16</u>, God hates divorce. He instructed the Israelites to not abandon their marriage covenants through "breaking faith"—a reference to sexual infidelity in marriage. Although sexual infidelity (e.g. adultery) is the only ground for a believer to divorce another believer, it is not the only way to violate one's covenant of marriage; any abandonment or desertion is a violation but, except for the abandonment of adultery, the violation does not release the innocent spouse to seek a decree of divorce from his or her believing spouse. Abandonment most often means physically leaving, but there are other ways to abandon a spouse. Committing adultery is one such abandonment, but so is physical abuse, emotional abuse, child abuse, refusing to engage in sexual intimacy, refusing to provide financial support, exposing one's family to unnecessary danger, etc. Wrongful as these are, they are not—except for adultery—grounds for a believer to seek a divorce from another believer.

Before going further, let us define some terms that are used here. "Violating" one's covenant of marriage means doing something that is contrary to the terms of the covenant, but no violation in itself automatically ends a covenant of marriage. A violation may be of the kind that allows the innocent party to take steps to end the covenant by pursuing a decree of "divorce" (adultery), but the innocent party may choose to overlook or forgive even the most serious transgression and

288

continue in the marriage as before. No violation provides grounds for the guilty party to "create facts of the ground" in order to initiate ending the covenant.

The biblical law of divorce may be (and usually is) different from the secular law of nation states. Indeed, the very meaning of the word "divorce" is subject to a number of interpretations and, rather than discuss each of them, we have set forth our view, and invite the reader to reach his or her own conclusions. There is no single Hebrew or Greek noun in the biblical texts for "divorce" as there is in English. The underlying Hebrew noun for "divorce" is *"sefer k'riytut,"* and the equivalent Greek noun is *"biblion apostasion,"*—both meaning "decree of divorce," "bill of divorcement," or *"get."* The Hebrew and Greek nouns respectively translated "divorce" do not have the same meaning as does the English noun. In English, when one speaks of "a divorce," one is referring to a legal action that terminates a marriage. In the Bible, however, the above Hebrew and Greek words that are typically translated "divorce" do not terminate anything—rather, they formally document that which has occurred, which is that one or both of the spouses have abandoned their marriage covenant through un-covenantal conduct, and the innocent spouse has declared the marriage ended. So for example, a *get* (a Jewish decree of divorce) is legal confirmation that a marriage has ended, but it does not itself end the covenant. The covenant is dissolved the way it was made—through the words of the parties—in this case, by the innocent party. A consequence of this is, therefore, even if an innocent spouse obtains a *get,* if it has been obtained for a biblically unauthorized reason, the *get* is void *ab initio,* the marriage remains intact, and any party that marries or remarries in reliance on the invalid *get* commits adultery.

Whenever a verse of Scripture says that a divorced (and remarried) party is an adulterer or has committed adultery by virtue of the remarriage, such a thing is logically possible only if he or she is still married to the original spouse at the time that the remarriage occurs. Matthew 5:31-32, Matthew 19:9, and Luke 16:18 are examples of this; they state:

> *It was said, 'Whoever divorces his wife must give her a get.' But I tell you that anyone who divorces his wife, except on the ground of fornication, makes her an adulteress; and that anyone who marries a divorcee commits adultery.*[109] (Matthew 5:31-32)

> *"Now what I say to you is that whoever divorces his wife, except on the ground of sexual immorality, and marries another woman commits adultery!"* (Matthew 19:9)

> *"Every man who divorces his wife and marries* [in order to marry] *another woman commits adultery, and a man who marries a woman divorced by her husband commits adultery."* (Luke 16:18).

Matthew 5:31-32 seems to be making an adulteress out of an innocent wife. Although she has not committed adultery, she somehow becomes an adulteress by virtue of her husband having divorced her on an invalid ground. How can that be so? The explanation for this can be deduced from what we have previously said about a decree of divorce—that it does not break a marriage covenant in and of itself. Also, whereas the above Scriptures appear to infer that only husbands can initiate divorce, later Scriptures such as Mark 10:11-12) infer that a wife may do so as well.

---

109 *"anyone who marries a divorcee commits adultery"* refers to a divorcee whose marriage remains valid.

Luke 16:18 and Mark 10:11-12, as commonly translated, appear to be saying that anyone who divorces and re-marries commits adultery. This can only be true if the divorce is invalid so, in what circumstance might the divorce referred to be invalid? I am of the opinion that the Scriptures are speaking of divorces that are obtained for the explicit purpose of marrying another, and so they might rightly read:

> *"Every man who divorces his wife* [in order to marry] *another woman commits adultery, and a man who marries a woman divorced by her husband commits adultery."* (Luke 16:18).

and

> *"He said to them, 'Whoever divorces his wife [in order to marry] another woman commits adultery against his wife; and if a wife divorces her husband [in order to marry] another man, she too commits adultery.'"* (Mark 10:11-12).

As indicated previously, a *get* does not, in and of itself, break the marriage covenant. Therefore, if Spouse A procures a *get* against Spouse B on a ground that is not biblically authorized, their marriage covenant remains intact despite the invalid *get*. If either spouse (let's say Spouse B) then marries another (and presumably has sexual relations with that other) in reliance on the invalid *get*, he or she and the new spouse (Spouse C) are momentarily in adultery, and their attempt at marriage is ineffective because the unauthorized *get* did not end the first marriage. The cohabitation of Spouse B and C therefore comprises adultery and/or fornication, and a new ground is thus created for A to seek a divorce against B—this time on a biblically valid ground. If and when that is done, the impediment to the marriage between B and C is removed, and their marriage becomes legitimized automatically. The lesson in all of this is (1) do not seek to divorce in the first place, and (2) if you find yourself with a court-ordered decree of divorce regardless of who procured it or what court it is from, do not remarry unless the decree was obtained on biblically allowed grounds.

A heavy burden is placed on an innocent marriage partner who has an improper decree of divorce forced on him or her by a spouse that does not remarry or commit adultery in some other way. Under these circumstances, any *get* that is obtained does not end the marriage, and the innocent party, although abandoned and in possession of a *get* is not, at the moment, released to obtain his or her own *get* and remarry.

There is, however, a biblical remedy for this; it is for the innocent spouse to lodge a complaint against the abandoning spouse pursuant to Matthew 18:15-17 which states:

> *Moreover, if your brother [in this case sister in Messiah] commits a sin against you, go and show him his fault—but privately, just between the two of you. If he listens to you, you have won back your brother. If he doesn't listen, take one or two others with you so that every accusation can be supported by the testimony of two or three witnesses. If he refuses to hear them, tell the congregation; and if he refuses to listen even to the congregation, treat him as you would a pagan or a tax-collector [i.e. an unbeliever].*

290

If the complaining spouse follows the aforesaid sequence of steps and, in the midst of it (or after its completion) the abandoning spouse (who has not remarried) repents, remarries his spouse and returns to his spouse to fulfill the marriage covenant by mutual consent, then all is well. If, however, he or she does not repent and a *bet din*[110] rules that he or she should be treated as an unbeliever pursuant to Matthew 18:17, then 1 Corinthians 7:15 can be invoked by the innocent spouse, which said Scripture states:

> *But if the unbelieving spouse separates himself, let him be separated. In circumstances like these, the brother or sister is not enslaved—God has called you to a life of peace.*

This Scripture enables the innocent spouse to petition for a decree of divorce in a public court and, if obtained, to declare the marriage to be over, and that both parties are officially released to remarry. It may seem unfair that the party who is in the wrong is equally free to remarry, but that is, nevertheless, the case.

Although the Scriptures seems to make adultery the only ground for which a believer can sue his or her believing spouse for a *get*, the adjudication of other sins of abandonment using the Matthew 18 process can, nevertheless, result in a *get* being granted provided the offending spouse is found by a *bet din* to be unrepentant and is ordered to be treated as an unbeliever (verse 17). In such a case, 1 Corinthians 7:15 may be invoked by the innocent spouse against the unbelieving spouse that has been adjudicated to be unrepentant:

> *But if the unbeliever departs, let him depart; a brother or a sister is not under bondage [the bond of matrimony has been broken] in such cases. But God has called us to peace.*

The unbelieving spouse's continued lack of repentance justifies the conclusion that the unbeliever has departed.

We would be remiss were we not to remind the reader that 2 Corinthians 6:14-16 warns against a believer covenanting with an unbeliever:

> *"Do not yoke yourselves together in a team with unbelievers. For how can righteousness and lawlessness be partners? What fellowship does light have with darkness? What harmony can there be between the Messiah and B'liya'al? What does a believer have in common with an unbeliever? What agreement can there be between the temple of God and idols? For we are the temple of the*

---

110 A *bet din* is a Jewish ecclesiastical court whose judges generally consist of elders, and where rules of due process apply. There are Christian counterparts of such a court in Roman Catholicism and certain other Christian denominations, and the important thing to keep in mind is that their rulings are often at odds with those of secular courts because, even when both courts have jurisdiction over the subject matter (e.g. divorce) and the litigating parties, they are bound by different laws.

Some hold the position that, anyone that wishes to seek a decree of divorce against his or her spouse, must do so twice (once in each kind of court) in order to fulfill both biblical and secular requirements (see, 1 Corinthians 6:1-8). That is the Orthodox Jewish view. My view is that if one first obtains a *get* from a *bet din*, one must follow it up with a secular divorce in order to be free to remarry in our society. However, if one obtains a secular divorce on a biblical ground (e.g. adultery), because the ground produces the same result in both courts, it is my opinion that one does not need to repeat the process in a *bet din*; the secular court's decree of divorce will suffice.

living God—as God said, "I will house myself in them… and I will walk among you. I will be their God, and they will be my people."

The reason is obvious in that believers and unbelievers (by definition) walk according to different beliefs and values. They will eventually pull against each other causing conflict, or the believer will compromise his or her values in order to keep the peace.

Classical Commentators

Maimonides' and HaChinuch's *mitzvot,* RP222 and C579, respectively, state that a divorce can only be acquired through the issuance of a writ *(get),* and Meir did not write a corresponding *mitzvah* on the subject. All three commentators wrote *mitzvot* acknowledging that Scripture prohibits a man from remarrying his divorced wife if she has remarried in the interim, and all three prohibit a man from divorcing his wife if he subjected her to false accusations that besmirched her character or acquired his wife after stealing her virginity. They also state that a divorce can only be acquired through the issuance of a writ *(get).* They do not discuss or write *mitzvot* about the marriage covenant per se.

Addendum by Daniel C. Juster

Two Evangelical scholars, William Luck (formally a professor at Moody Bible Institute) and David Instone-Brewer, have sought to broaden the biblical grounds for divorce through books each has written. Luck's treatment of divorce expands the meaning of abandoning marriage (re: 1 Corinthians 7) to the idea of the spouse—especially the man—not fulfilling the biblical requirements for basic covenant. Instone-Brewer references Luck's work and expands on it with his vast *Talmudic* knowledge. Luck's basic idea is that Yeshua's exception clause is basically a rejection of the "any-cause" divorce idea, and a reaffirmation of the primary reason for divorce, which is marital unfaithfulness. Instone-Brewer, on the other hand, seeks to show, through much "Second Temple Judaism" scholarship, that unfaithfulness does not only mean adultery, but should be interpreted in terms of four requirements for marriage which first apply to the husband but, by extension, also partially apply to the wife. According to the texts of the *Torah,* the husband is to bring faithfulness to the marriage to not commit adultery (fornicate with another), to give the wife her conjugal rights, to provide sustenance (food and shelter), and lastly to not physically abuse her. Just as a slave goes free who is beaten to the extent of bodily injury, so is physical abuse of a spouse grounds for divorce. Failure to provide any of these four "requirements of marriage" amounts to basic unfaithfulness.

Strangely, after making a strong case for the fourfold meaning of unfaithfulness and grounding it in first century Judaism and more, Brewer misses a central point of Dr. Rudolph's scholarship in this *Mitzvah,* which is the requirement that a *get* (writ of divorce) must be issued by a legitimate court of elders that has the authority over the subject matter and the parties. The depth of Instone-Brewer's Jewish scholarship is very good, so it is astonishing that he misses this, and can see believers acting in accordance with their individual consciences in determining when the lines of fidelity have been sufficiently crossed, so as to allow them a secular divorce. Rather, the biblical

292

teaching is that no such divorce (with the allowance of remarriage) can be validated without a written *get*. Matthew 16 and Matthew 18 provide for this authority to be vested in the leadership of Yeshua's *Kehillah*.

Regarding the fourfold meaning of unfaithfulness and its connection to 1 Corinthians 7, my evaluation of Instone-Brewer is that he makes a convincing case, but that it is not fully proven. While I am loathe to open up greater grounds for divorce in our era of easy divorces and remarriages, I think courts of elders should study evidence that is presented by a complainant seeking to divorce, and decide whether to issue a *get* based upon what they conclude are biblical grounds. Also, the more equal way to judge divorce cases, is to consider that either the husband or the wife can breach the marriage covenant

NCLA: JMm JFm KMm KFm GMm GFm

F4. Withholding Food, Clothing or Marital Rights from Our Wife.

We are forbidden to afflict our wife by withholding food, clothing, or marital rights.

This precept is derived from His Word (blessed be He):

Key Scripture

Exodus 21:7-11 (Maimonides RN262; Meir MN42; Chinuch C46)
If a man sells his daughter as a slave, she is not to go free like the men-slaves. If her master married her but decides she no longer pleases him, then he is to allow her to be redeemed. He is not allowed to sell her to a foreign people, because he has treated her unfairly. If he has her marry his son, then he is to treat her like a daughter. If he marries another wife, he is not to reduce her food, clothing or marital rights. If he fails to provide her with these three things, she is to be given her freedom without having to pay anything.

Ephesians 5:25-33
As for husbands, love your wives, just as the Messiah loved the Messianic Community, indeed, gave himself up on its behalf, in order to set it apart for God, making it clean through immersion in the mikveh, so to speak, in order to present the Messianic Community to himself as a bride to be proud of, without a spot, wrinkle or any such thing, but holy and without defect. This is how husbands ought to love their wives—like their own bodies; for the man who loves his wife is loving himself. Why, no one ever hated his own flesh! On the contrary, he feeds it well and takes care of it, just as the Messiah does the Messianic Community, because we are parts of his Body. Therefore a man will leave his father and mother and remain with his wife, and the two will become one. There is profound truth hidden here, which I say concerns the Messiah and the Messianic Community. However, the text also applies to each of you individually: let each man love his wife as he does himself, and see that the wife respects her husband.

1 Timothy 5:8
Moreover, anyone who does not provide for his own people, especially for his family, has disowned the faith and is worse than an unbeliever.

1 Peter 3:7
You husbands, likewise, conduct your married lives with understanding. Although your wife may be weaker physically, you should respect her as a fellow-heir of the gift of Life. If you don't, your prayers will be blocked.

Commentary

It is clear from the totality of the Scriptures (and especially from the New Covenant Scriptures), that the overarching commandment is for men to love their wives. The particulars of this *Mitzvah* in singling out food, clothing, and marital (conjugal sexual) rights is forced upon us because it is treated that way by the classical commentators, and we felt that we should respond accordingly.

Many Scriptures address men but are clearly applicable to both men and women. We understand that wives are to love their husbands, but the responsibility of this *Mitzvah* is directed specifically to husbands.

Classical Commentators

Maimonides, Meir, and HaChinuch use Exodus 21:9-10 to support their respective *mitzvot* that we must not withhold food, clothing, or marital rights from our wives. The context of the Scripture that they use to support their *mitzvot* is that of a wife who was previously a slave, marries her master, and the master subsequently marries for a second time when his first wife no longer pleases him.

NCLA
Ancient Understanding: JMm JFi KMm KFi GMm GFi
Modern Understanding: JMm JFm KMm KFm GMm GFm

F5. Treatment of Children.

We are to care for and not mistreat children.

This precept is derived from His Word (blessed be He):

Key Scriptures

Proverbs 22:6
Train a child in the way he [should] go; and, even when old, he will not swerve from it.

Matthew 18:5-6
Whoever welcomes one such child in my name welcomes me; and whoever ensnares one of these little ones who trust me, it would be better for him to have a millstone hung around his neck and be drowned in the open sea!

Mathew 18:10
See that you never despise one of these little ones, for I tell you that their angels in heaven are continually seeing the face of my Father in heaven.

Matthew 19:14
However, Yeshua said, "Let the children come to me, don't stop them, for the Kingdom of Heaven belongs to such as these."

Ephesians 6:4
Fathers, don't irritate your children and make them resentful; instead, raise them with the Lord's kind of discipline and guidance.

Supportive Scriptures

Deuteronomy 6:6-7 (see also, Deuteronomy 11:18-19)
Proverbs 13:24, 22:15
1 Timothy 5:8

Commentary

Generally, the statement of the *Mitzvah* speaks for itself, and the only controversy about it has to do with the administration of spankings. The well-known saying "spare the rod and spoil the child" is often mistakenly attributed to Scripture, but its origin is actually a 17th century poem by Samuel Butler titled "Hudibras," which has nothing to do with Scripture. Nevertheless, Proverbs 13:24 and Proverbs 22:15 speak similarly, and have been the subject of law suits and prosecutions promulgated by some in our society who believe that spanking a child for correction is cruel and abusive. In oppositional response to that, much has been written on how to administer a spanking with love that is truly corrective.

Classical Commentators

This *Mitzvah* is not addressed by any of the classical Jewish commentators.

NCLA: JMm JFm KMm KFm GMm GFm

G: Relating to God

G1. Believing in God.

We are to believe in the God of Abraham, Isaac, and Jacob.

This precept is derived from His Word (blessed be He):

Key Scriptures

Exodus 20:2 (Maimonides RP1; Meir MP1; Chinuch C25)
I am ADONAI your God, who brought you out of the land of Egypt, out of the abode of slavery.

Psalms 9:11(10)
Those who know your name put their trust in you, for you have not abandoned those who seek you, ADONAI.

John 14:1
(1) Don't let yourselves be disturbed. Trust in God and trust in me. (CJB)

(2) Let not your heart be troubled; you believe in God, believe also in Me. (NKJ)

Supportive Scriptures

Exodus 4:4-5
Jeremiah 31:32(33)-33(34)
2 Chronicles 20:20
John 3:14-18, 5:24, 6:47, 11:25-27
Hebrews 11:6 (See in the context of Hebrews 11:1-40)

Commentary

Belief in the God of Abraham Isaac and Jacob is not only belief in His existence, but in the fact that He is the God who brought us out of Egypt and is our only God (Exodus 20:2). Also, Scripture teaches that believing in God is connected to trusting God, since one cannot trust in whom one does not believe. In order to emphasize the equivalence of belief and trust, several of the above Scriptures are rendered in two reputable translations—the NKJ that speaks of belief, and the CJB that speaks of trust in their handling the same Scriptures.

Classical Commentators

Maimonides, Meir, and HaChinuch concur that Exodus 20:2 is a Scripture that, by implication, commands that we believe in God. The rationale for this is God's own statement that He is our God, and the supreme means of our having been brought out of the slavery of Egypt. To believe, therefore, that God is God, one has to trust His Word that He is whom He says He is, thereby illustrating the inseparability of belief and trust. Meir makes another cogent point by stating that belief in God is the foundation of Jewish faith, and anyone who does not believe in God has no place among the Jewish people.

NCLA: JMm JFm KMm KFm GMm GFm

G2. Acknowledging Our Belief in God and in Yeshua the Messiah.

We are to acknowledge and never deny our belief in God and in Yeshua the Messiah.

This precept is derived from His Word (blessed be He):

Key Scriptures

Numbers 15:38-40 (Maimonides RP14; Meir MP10; Chinuch C386)
Speak to the people of Isra'el, instructing them to make, through all their generations, tzitziyot on the corners of their garments, and to put with the tzitzit on each corner a blue thread. It is to be a tzitzit for you to look at and thereby remember all of ADONAI's mitzvot and obey them, so that you won't go around wherever your own heart and eyes lead you to prostitute yourselves; but it will help you remember and obey all my mitzvot and be holy for your God.

Deuteronomy 6:4-9 (Maimonides RP12-13, 15; Meir MP8-9, 12; Chinuch C421-423)
Sh'ma, Yisra'el! ADONAI Eloheinu, ADONAI echad [Hear, Isra'el! ADONAI our God, ADONAI is one]; and you are to love ADONAI your God with all your heart, all your being and all your resources. These words, which I am ordering you today, are to be on your heart; and you are to teach them carefully to your children. You are to talk about them when you sit at home, when you are traveling on the road, when you lie down and when you get up. Tie them on your hand as a sign, put them at the front of a headband around your forehead, and write them on the doorframes of your house and on your gates.

Deuteronomy 10: 20 (Maimonides RP6; Meir MP16; Chinuch C434)
You are to fear ADONAI your God, serve him, cling to him and swear by his name.

Deuteronomy 11:18-20 (Maimonides RP13, 15; Meir MP12; Chinuch C421, 423)
Therefore, you are to store up these words of mine in your heart and in all your being; tie them on your hand as a sign; put them at the front of a headband around your forehead; teach them carefully to your children, talking about them when you sit at home, when you are traveling on the road, when you lie down and when you get up; and write them on the door-frames of your house and on your gates —

Deuteronomy 11:22-23 (Maimonides RP6; Chinuch C434)
For if you will take care to obey all these mitzvot I am giving you, to do them, to love ADONAI your God, to follow all his ways and to cling to him, then ADONAI will expel all these nations ahead of you; and you will dispossess nations bigger and stronger than you are.

Job 1:13-22
One day when Iyov's sons and daughters were eating and drinking in their oldest brother's house, a messenger came to him and said, "The oxen were plowing, with the donkeys grazing near them, when a raiding party from Sh'va came and carried them off; they put the servants to the sword too, and I'm the only one who escaped to tell you." While he was still speaking,

another one came and said, "Fire from God fell from the sky and burned up the sheep and the servants; it completely destroyed them, and I'm the only one who escaped to tell you." While he was still speaking, another one came and said, "The Kasdim, three bands of them, fell on the camels and carried them off; they put the servants to the sword too, and I'm the only one who escaped to tell you." While he was still speaking, another one came and said, "Your sons and daughters were eating and drinking wine in their oldest brother's house, when suddenly a strong wind blew in from over the desert. It struck the four corners of the house, so that it fell on the young people; they are dead, and I'm the only one who escaped to tell you." Iyov got up, tore his coat, shaved his head, fell down on the ground and worshipped; he said, "Naked I came from my mother's womb, and naked I will return there. ADONAI gave; ADONAI took; blessed be the name of ADONAI." In all this Iyov neither committed a sin nor put blame on God.

Daniel 3:13-18
In a raging fury N'vukhadnetzar ordered that Shadrakh, Meishakh and 'Aved-N'go be brought. When the men had been brought before the king, N'vukhadnetzar said to them, "Shadrakh! Meishakh! 'Aved-N'go! Is it true that you neither serve my gods nor worship the gold statue I set up? All right, then. If you are prepared, when you hear the sound of the horn, pipe, harp, zither, lute, bagpipe and the rest of the musical instruments, to fall down and worship the gold statue, very well. But if you won't worship, you will immediately be thrown into a blazing hot furnace—and what god will save you from my power then?" Shadrakh, Meishakh and 'Aved-N'go answered the king, "Your question doesn't require an answer from us. Your majesty, if our God, whom we serve, is able to save us, he will save us from the blazing hot furnace and from your power. But even if he doesn't, we want you to know, your majesty, that we will neither serve your gods nor worship the gold statue which you have set up."

Matthew 10:32-33
"Whoever acknowledges me in the presence of others I will also acknowledge in the presence of my Father in heaven. But whoever disowns me before others I will disown before my Father in heaven."

1 John 2:23
Everyone who denies the Son is also without the Father, but the person who acknowledges the Son has the Father as well.

1 John 4:2-3
Here is how you recognize the Spirit of God: every spirit which acknowledges that Yeshua the Messiah came as a human being is from God, and every spirit which does not acknowledge Yeshua is not from God—in fact, this is the spirit of the Anti-Messiah.

1 John 4:15
If someone acknowledges that Yeshua is the Son of God, God remains united with him, and he with God.

Supportive Scriptures

Matthew 28:16-20
Mark 6:56
Luke 22:31-34
Philippians 2:9-11
Hebrews 13:15
2 Peter 2:1

Commentary

The undeniable weight of Scripture is that we are to always acknowledge our belief in God and in Yeshua the Messiah, and never deny it. Denial can be by lying or through silence that is misleading. The most common reasons that men deny their faith in God or Messiah are fear or to gain some advantage.

Temptations to deny our faith predate the *Torah* itself. Consider how Job was consistently urged to curse God, but he did not. That book was preserved for us in Scripture, that we might follow Job's example when hard times, danger, or even benefit befall us where logic and common expectation tells us that we will fare better and safer if we lie or mislead someone about our Messianic faith. The story of Job is one of success. Centuries later, the story of Peter is one of failure, as he denied that he knew Yeshua and that he was one of Yeshua's disciples—not once, but three times.

The temptation to deny the Lord can be subtle, and can come in many forms. Usually it comes from someone we want to please or someone we do not want to anger. It can occur when a co-worker blasphemes the name of the Lord and we do not (at the very least) walk away. It can occur when our employer makes a rude remark about the Lord's chosen people and we do not correct him or admit that we are one of them. It can occur when we go along with a joke that mocks marriage, sex, or other things that the Lord gave us and cares about deeply. It can occur when we hold back from witnessing to our parents, or when, as Jews, we acquiesce to eating *treyf* in order to be social. It can occur when we mislead another about our belief in Yeshua in our attempt to pursue Jewish conversion or apply for *aliyah* to Israel.

The Scriptures cannot be clearer, from the earliest in the *Tanakh* to the most recent in the *B'rit Chadasha*. The *mitzvot* to wear fringes (and by traditional understanding phylacteries) for all to see, to display *m'zuzot* on one's doorposts (again for all to see), and to cleave to God and love Him with all of our heart, being, and resources, are the antithesis of denying Him.

Regarding Yeshua, the New Covenant Scriptures make it very clear that our responsibility is to preach the Good News of His Messiahship, and that there are dire consequences if we hide it or deny it.

Classical Commentators

In their respective *mitzvot,* Maimonides, Meir, and HaChinuch interpret "clinging" or "cleaving" to God in <u>Deuteronomy 10:20</u> and <u>Deuteronomy 11:22</u> as "associating" with wise men. Although in his 12th Article of Faith, Maimonides warns against not believing in Messiah's coming or denying Messiah's greatness, he makes no reference to them in his *Sefer HaMitzvot.*

<u>NCLA</u>: **JMm JFm KMm KFm GMm GFm**

G3. Knowing that God is Echad and Triune

We are to know that God is echad and Triune.

This precept is derived from His Word (blessed be He):

Key Scriptures

God is Echad

Deuteronomy 6:4 (Maimonides RP2; Meir MP2; Chinuch C417)

שְׁמַע יִשְׂרָאֵל יְהוָה אֱלֹהֵינוּ יְהוָה| אֶחָד:

Sh'ma, Yisra'el! ADONAI Eloheinu, ADONAI echad
[Hear, Isra'el! *ADONAI* our God, *ADONAI* is one]

Mark 12:28-29
One of the Torah-teachers came up and heard them engaged in this discussion. Seeing that Yeshua answered them well, he asked him, "Which is the most important mitzvah of them all?" Yeshua answered, "The most important is, 'Sh'ma Yisra'el, ADONAI Eloheinu, ADONAI echad [Hear, O Isra'el, the LORD our God, the LORD is one],...

John 16: 13-15
However, when the Spirit of Truth comes, he will guide you into all the truth; for he will not speak on his own initiative but will say only what he hears. He will also announce to you the events of the future. He will glorify me, because he will receive from what is mine and announce it to you. Everything the Father has is mine; this is why I said that he receives from what is mine and will announce it to you.

1 Corinthians 8:4
So, as for eating food sacrificed to idols, we "know" that, as you say, "An idol has no real existence in the world, and there is only one God."

1 Corinthians 8:6
...yet for us there is one God, the Father, from whom all things come and for whom we exist; and one Lord, Yeshua the Messiah, through whom were created all things and through whom we have our being.

Galatians 3:20
Now a mediator implies more than one, but God is one.

<u>1 Timothy 2:5</u>
For God is one; and there is but one Mediator between God and humanity, Yeshua the Messiah, himself human, who gave himself as a ransom on behalf of all, thus providing testimony to God's purpose at just the right time.

God Is Triune

<u>Genesis 1:26</u>
Then God said, "Let us make humankind in our image, in the likeness of ourselves; and let them rule over the fish in the sea, the birds in the air, the animals, and over all the earth, and over every crawling creature that crawls on the earth."

<u>Genesis 3:22</u>
ADONAI, God, said, "See, the man has become like one of us, knowing good and evil. Now, to prevent his putting out his hand and taking also from the tree of life, eating, and living forever-"

<u>Genesis 11:7</u>
Come, let's go down and confuse their language, so that they won't understand each other's speech.

<u>2 Samuel 7:28</u>
Now, Adonai ELOHIM, you alone are God; your words are truth; and you have made this wonderful promise to your servant.

<u>Isaiah 6:8</u>
Then I heard the voice of Adonai saying, "Whom should I send? Who will go for us?" I answered, "I'm here, send me!"

<u>Isaiah 48:16</u>
Come close to me, and listen to this: since the beginning I have not spoken in secret, since the time things began to be, I have been there; and now Adonai ELOHIM has sent me and his Spirit.

<u>Isaiah 61:1</u>
The Spirit of Adonai ELOHIM is upon me, because ADONAI has anointed me to announce good news to the poor. He has sent me to heal the brokenhearted; to proclaim freedom to the captives, to let out into light those bound in the dark;

<u>Matthew 3:16-17</u>
As soon as Yeshua had been immersed, he came up out of the water. At that moment heaven was opened, he saw the Spirit of God coming down upon him like a dove, and a voice from heaven said, "This is my Son, whom I love; I am well pleased with him."

<u>Matthew 28:18-19</u>
Yeshua came and talked with them. He said, "All authority in heaven and on earth has been given to me. Therefore, go and make people from all nations into talmidim, immersing them into the reality of the Father, the Son and the Ruach HaKodesh...

Mark 1:10-11

Immediately upon coming up out of the water, he saw heaven torn open and the Spirit descending upon him like a dove; then a voice came from heaven, "You are my Son, whom I love; I am well pleased with you." Immediately the Spirit drove him out into the wilderness...

2 Corinthians 13:14

The grace of the Lord Yeshua the Messiah, the love of God and the fellowship of the Ruach HaKodesh be with you all.

Hebrews 1:1-5

In days gone by, God spoke in many and varied ways to the Fathers through the prophets. But now, in the acharit-hayamim, he has spoken to us through his Son, to whom he has given ownership of everything and through whom he created the universe. This Son is the radiance of the Sh'khinah, the very expression of God's essence, upholding all that exists by his powerful word; and after he had, through himself, made purification for sins, he sat down at the right hand of HaG'dulah BaM'romim. So he has become much better than angels, and the name God has given him is superior to theirs. For to which of the angels did God ever say, "You are my Son; today I have become your Father"? Also, God never said of any angel, "I will be his Father, and he will be my Son."

1 Peter 1:1-2

From: Kefa, an emissary of Yeshua the Messiah To: God's chosen people, living as aliens in the Diaspora—in Pontus, Galatia, Cappadocia, the province of Asia, and Bythinia—chosen according to the foreknowledge of God the Father and set apart by the Spirit for obeying Yeshua the Messiah and for sprinkling with his blood: Grace and shalom be yours in full measure.

Commentary

The Hebrew Scripture (Deuteronomy 6:4) tells us that God is *echad*, a word that is universally translated into English as "one." Consequently, all English translations of the New Covenant Scriptures tell us that God is "one," while at the same time telling us that He also exists as the "Father, Son, and Holy Spirit." This appears to be a contradiction until we understand that *echad* does not mean "one" in number, but rather "one" in plural unity, such as in Genesis 2:24:

עַל־כֵּ֞ן יַֽעֲזָב־אִ֗ישׁ אֶת־אָבִ֖יו וְאֶת־אִמּ֑וֹ וְדָבַ֣ק בְּאִשְׁתּ֔וֹ וְהָי֖וּ לְבָשָׂ֥ר אֶחָֽד׃

"This is why a man is to leave his father and mother and stick with his wife, and they are to be one (echad) flesh."

So, my wife and I are "one," in the sense that we share life together, and often think, believe, and respond to things as if we were one person rather than two. In the case of the *echad* of God being the Father, Son, and Holy Spirit sharing deity, He is three rather than two such as my wife and I but there are, nevertheless, similarities.

Now most analogies of this kind, while helpful to a degree, break down at some point. Although my wife and I were made in the image of God, we are not God, so our *echad* nature does not result in our being connected in the amazing way that God connects to himself. If my wife is in a separate room from me I cannot see, smell, or experience what she is experiencing, nor can I know what she is thinking. God's *echad* nature does not have those limitations in that the Father, Son, and Holy Spirit experience together and communicate as if they were *yachid* (a numerical one) instead of *echad* (an implied plurality). This three-in-one nature of God is what we mean by His triunity.

There are other biblical evidences for God being plural while at the same time "one," but I will mention only two here. First, Genesis 1:26a states:

"Then God said, "Let us make humankind in our image, in the likeness of ourselves..."

Notice the plurality of to whom God was speaking ("us"), yet the oneness of "image" as distinguished from "images." Second, the Hebrew word for "our God" in Deuteronomy 6:4 is *"Eloheynu,"* which is the first person plural possessive of *"Elohim"*—a word which, despite its plurality, all translators of Genesis 1:1 agree means "God."

So, while our God is plural in nature, He is one God, and not many gods combined into one. This is a great mystery for which we have no natural example to aid us in our understanding.

Classical Commentators

Maimonides, Meir, and HaChinuch express this *mitzvah* as "knowing that God is a unity." They emphasize the singleness of the unity by adding that God has no partner or associate, and they are in agreement that the unity of God is a core belief of the Jewish faith. None of the commentators acknowledge or discuss the composite nature of *"echad,"* or the plural nature of *"Elohim."*

NCLA: JMm JFm KMm KFm GMm GFm

G4. Loving God.

We are to love God with all of our heart, soul, strength, and mind.

This precept is derived from His Word (blessed be He):

Key Scripture

Deuteronomy 6:5-9 (Maimonides RP3; Meir MP3; Chinuch C418)
...and you are to love ADONAI your God with all your heart, all your being and all your resources. These words, which I am ordering you today, are to be on your heart; and you are to teach them carefully to your children. You are to talk about them when you sit at home, when you are traveling on the road, when you lie down and when you get up. Tie them on your hand as a sign, put them at the front of a headband around your forehead, and write them on the doorframes of your house and on your gates.

Matthew 22:33-38
When the crowds heard how he taught, they were astounded; but when the P'rushim learned that he had silenced the Tz'dukim, they got together, and one of them who was a Torah expert asked a sh'eilah to trap him: "Rabbi, which of the mitzvot in the Torah is the most important?" He told him, "'You are to love ADONAI your God with all your heart and with all your soul and with all your strength.' This is the greatest and most important mitzvah.

Mark 12:28-30
One of the Torah-teachers came up and heard them engaged in this discussion. Seeing that Yeshua answered them well, he asked him, "Which is the most important mitzvah of them all?" Yeshua answered, "The most important is, 'Sh'ma Yisra'el, ADONAI Eloheinu, ADONAI echad [Hear, O Isra'el, the LORD our God, the LORD is one], and you are to love ADONAI your God with all your heart, with all your soul, with all your understanding and with all your strength.

Luke 10:25-28
An expert in Torah stood up to try and trap him by asking, "Rabbi, what should I do to obtain eternal life?" But Yeshua said to him, "What is written in the Torah? How do you read it?" He answered, "You are to love ADONAI your God with all your heart, with all your soul, with all your strength and with all your understanding; and your neighbor as yourself." "That's the right answer," Yeshua said. "Do this, and you will have life."

John 14:21-24
Whoever has my commands and keeps them is the one who loves me, and the one who loves me will be loved by my Father, and I will love him and reveal myself to him." Y'hudah (not the one from K'riot) said to him, "What has happened, Lord, that you are about to reveal yourself to us and not to the world?" Yeshua answered him, "If someone loves me, he will keep my word; and my Father will love him, and we will come to him and make our home with him. Someone who doesn't love me doesn't keep my words—and the word you are hearing is not my own but that of the Father who sent me.

<u>1 John 4:20-21</u>
If anyone says, "I love God," and hates his brother, he is a liar. For if a person does not love his brother, whom he has seen, then he cannot love God, whom he has not seen. Yes, this is the command we have from him: whoever loves God must love his brother too.

Commentary

This *Mitzvah* is recited by Jews the world over several times a day in a portion of the *Torah* known as the "*Sh'ma*" (<u>Deuteronomy 6:4-9</u>). It is so foundational to Jewish faith, that when Yeshua was asked in <u>Matthew 22:36</u>: *"Rabbi, which of the mitzvot in the Torah is the most important?"* he replied by quoting <u>Deuteronomy 6:5</u>: *"...you are to love ADONAI your God with all your heart, all your being and all your resources."* (see also <u>Mark 12:30</u> and <u>Luke 10:27</u>).'

Loving God is a covenant commitment to Him that is proven though our obedience (<u>John 14:21-24</u>) and our willingness and sincere desire to put His agenda before our own (<u>Matthew 6:33, 16:24-25</u>; <u>Luke 9:23</u>). That notwithstanding, love (including love of God) has an emotional component to it, a passion, that must be guided by that covenant commitment; the two go together. Also, perceiving God's nature, character, majesty, and faithfulness, causes us to recognize His love of us, and stimulates our love of Him in return (<u>1 John 4:19</u>).

Loving God is also connected to our loving one another in two prominent Scriptures. <u>1 John 4:20-21</u> makes it clear that, despite any claim we may make to the contrary, we cannot love God if we do not also love our brother. The other Scripture is a continuation of Yeshua's statement that loving God is the most important commandment; in <u>Matthew 22:39</u> he also said: *"And a second is similar to it, 'You are to love your neighbor as yourself.'"* (See also, <u>Mark 12:31</u> and <u>Luke 10:27</u>).

Classical Commentators

Maimonides analogizes loving God with meditating upon and contemplating His *mitzvot;* he says that by so doing, we get to know Him and receive joy. Also, because the words of the *Sh'ma* speak of teaching God's *mitzvot,* Maimonides associates the commandment to love God with our obligation to teach the people of the world that they must have faith in Him and serve Him.

Meir agrees with Maimonides, and adds the component of having affection for God. He refers to Abraham's relationship with God as an example of there being "love" between them, and he quotes <u>Genesis 12:5</u> as an example of Abraham's love through obedience, and <u>Isaiah 41:8</u> as an example of God considering Abraham to be His friend (see reference to this in <u>James 2:23</u>).

HaChinuch adds an interesting perspective by stating that a man cannot fully obey God's Commandments unless he loves Him. This is the reverse of (but not inconsistent with) the Scriptures cited above that infer that one way to love God is by obeying His Commandments.

HaChinuch also cites God's relationship with Abraham, and says that our love of God should cause us to encourage others to serve and worship Him as well.

<u>NCLA</u>: JMm JFm GMm GFm KMm KFm

G5. Testing God's Promises and Warnings.

We are not to test God's promises and warnings.

This precept is derived from His Word (blessed be He):

Key Scriptures

Exodus 17:3-7
However, the people were thirsty for water there and grumbled against Moshe, "For what did you bring us up from Egypt? To kill us, our children and our livestock with thirst?" Moshe cried out to ADONAI, "What am I to do with these people? They're ready to stone me!" ADONAI answered Moshe, "Go on ahead of the people, and bring with you the leaders of Isra'el. Take your staff in your hand, the one you used to strike the river; and go. I will stand in front of you there on the rock in Horev. You are to strike the rock, and water will come out of it, so the people can drink." Moshe did this in the sight of the leaders of Isra'el. The place was named Massah [testing] and M'rivah [quarreling] because of the quarreling of the people of Isra'el and because they tested ADONAI by asking, "Is ADONAI with us or not?"

Deuteronomy 6:16 (Maimonides RN64; Chinuch C424)
Do not put ADONAI your God to the test, as you tested him at Massah.

Matthew 4:5-7 (see also, Luke 4:9-12)
Then the Adversary took him to the holy city and set him on the highest point of the Temple. "If you are the Son of God," he said, "jump! For the Tanakh says, 'He will order his angels to be responsible for you… . They will support you with their hands, so that you will not hurt your feet on the stones.'" Yeshua replied to him, "But it also says, 'Do not put ADONAI your God to the test.'"

Supportive Scriptures

Judges 6:36-40
Malachi 3:10

Commentary

We are commanded by Deuteronomy 6:16 not to put God to the test. What this means is that we must believe God in that whatever He says He will do, and not intentionally act in such a way as to force His hand and provoke Him to prove it. The bottom line is that we must trust and not doubt God's warnings and promises. In Matthew 4:5-7, we read how Yeshua Himself demonstrated the principle by refusing to jump from the Temple in order to prove His identity by forcing His Father to save Him supernaturally.

There are two instances in Scripture where God seems to be saying the opposite. One of them is in Judges 6:36-40, where Gid'on asks God for supernatural signs of His Word. But Gid'on was not testing God; he believed God. On the contrary, he was doubting the accuracy with which he was hearing God, and was testing himself. The other instance is in Malachi 3:10, in which God says, in part: *"Bring the whole tenth into the storehouse, so that there will be food in my house, and put me to the test…"* This is not a contradiction of the Deuteronomy 6:16 commandment either, because here God is not asking doubters or unbelievers to put Him to test Him in order to prove His truthfulness. He is lovingly beseeching Israelite believers to follow His instructions so that they can have and enjoy His promised blessings.

Classical Commentators

Maimonides does not command against testing the promises and warnings contained in Scripture, but rather against those voiced by God's prophets. HaChinuch interprets Deuteronomy 6:16 somewhat differently by saying that we should not test true prophets excessively. Meir does not have a *mitzvah* on this subject at all.

NCLA: JMm JFm KMm KFm GMm GFm

G6. Fearing God.

We are to reverently and lovingly fear God.

This precept is derived from His Word (blessed be He):

Key Scriptures

Leviticus 24:16 (Maimonides RP4; Chinuch C432)[111]
...and whoever blasphemes the name of ADONAI must be put to death; the entire community must stone him. The foreigner as well as the citizen is to be put to death if he blasphemes the Name.

Numbers 1:17 (Maimonides RP4; Chinuch C432)[112]
So Moshe and Aharon took these men who had been designated by name...

Deuteronomy 6:13 (Maimonides RP4; Meir MP4)
You are to fear ADONAI your God, serve him and swear by his name.

Deuteronomy 10:20 (Maimonides RP4; Meir MP4; Chinuch C432)
You are to fear ADONAI your God, serve him, cling to him and swear by his name.

Matthew 10:28 (see also, Luke 12:5)
Do not fear those who kill the body but are powerless to kill the soul. Rather, fear him who can destroy both soul and body in Gei-Hinnom.

Acts 9:31
Then the Messianic community throughout Y'hudah, the Galil and Shomron enjoyed peace and was built up. They lived in the fear of the Lord, with the counsel of the Ruach HaKodesh; and their numbers kept multiplying.

Ephesians 5:21
Submit to one another in fear of the Messiah.

1 Peter 2:17
Be respectful to all—keep loving the brotherhood, fearing God and honoring the emperor.

Supportive Scriptures

Isaiah 8:11-13, 11:3, 66:1-2
Psalms 19:10(9), 36:2(1), 89:7-8(6-7), 103:17-18
Proverbs 1:7, 8:13, 10:27, 14:26-27, 16:6, 19:23, 22:4
2 Corinthians 5:11
Philippians 2:12

---

111 The relevance of this Scripture to the subject of fearing God is not immediately evident, but it is listed here because it is referenced by Maimonides and HaChinuch in their respective *mitzvah* compilations.
112 Ibid.

Hebrews 12:28-29
1 Peter 1:17

Commentary

Scripture tells us that God is our Heavenly Father, that we are His created children, and that He wants us to have a loving relationship with Him. At the same time, we are not to approach Him with the same kind of comfortable familiarity as we would a peer, but with awesome respect, having full knowledge of His power.

This is easier to understand for those of us who have (or had) godly and loving parents here on earth, because we have experienced, in the natural, what good fathers and mothers are like, and we are able to transfer our understanding to our relationship with God. It is more difficult (and even counter-intuitive) for those of us who have not had good parental experiences, so we must glean our understanding from the words of Scripture, and from what others tell us and teach us.

The attributes of God disclosed in Scripture are many, and often seem contradictory. God is compassionate, yet He executes judgment. God loves, yet He punishes. So when we read in Deuteronomy 6:5 *"...you are to love ADONAI your God with all your heart..,"* and then read in Scriptures like Deuteronomy 6:13 *"...You are to fear ADONAI your God...,"* we may not know what to think.

The problem is partially that our English language Bibles tend to use the word "fear" to translate different underlying Hebrew and Greek words used in different kinds of situations. So, for example, the derivative of יָרֵא *(yarei)* that is applied to God in Deuteronomy 6:13 means "reverend fear"—the kind that holds God in awe, deference, and honor. Yes, the word can also mean to be afraid of God but, when it is used that way, it is meant as a warning to sinners who ought to be afraid.

It is a different kind of fear that is referred to in 2 Timothy 1:7, which the NKJ version translates:

"For God has not given us a spirit of fear, but of power and of love and of a sound mind."

Here, the Greek word for "fear" is δειλία *(deiliah),* which has a different connotation than יָרֵא *(yarei)* in that it means a lack of courage, cowardice, or timidity. Other Greek words such as φόβος *(phabas)* and φοβέω *(phabei-oh)* in 2 Corinthians 5:11 and 1 Peter 2:17 respectively, have connotations similar to יָרֵא *(yarei).*

In addition to the lexical evidence that fearing God (for an obedient believer) should not mean being afraid of Him, we also have textual evidence for the same premise. A Scripture that strongly implies this is Proverbs 22:4; it informs us that "fear of God" ("fear" being derived from יָרֵא) is a reward that results from our being humble. In other words, it is a good thing—not something to be dreaded. Another Scripture that implies something similar is Ephesians 5:21 that tells us to *"submit to one another in fear of the Messiah"* ("fear" here is φόβος). There is no other place in the New Covenant Scriptures that suggests that we should be afraid of Messiah Yeshua and, in fact, everything we read about Him suggests the opposite. Therefore "fear of the

313

Messiah" (and therefore φόβος in this context) could not mean being afraid and must, instead, be referring to a character virtue.

Classical Commentators

Maimonides does not say that we are to fear God, but rather that we are to believe in the fear of God, and be expectant of his punishment at all times. He then launches into a discussion of blaspheming, and pronouncing the Name of God in vain as it is related to fearing Him.

Meir states that we must fear God, and that the path to fear and love are the same. He also refers to "reverend fear" that requires that we not pronounce God's Holy Name in vain or without purpose.

HaChinuch also uses the term "reverend fear," and warns us to fear God's punishment if we sin. Like Maimonides (and to a lesser extent Meir), HaChinuch spends a considerable proportion of his writing on our not blaspheming or speaking the Lord's Name in vain. The connection that both he and Maimonides make to fearing God is that, doing either, results in our losing the kind of reverend fear of God that God requires.

Maimonides and HaChinuch emphasize an expectation and fear of God's punishment, whereas this *Mitzvah* emphasizes a reverend and loving fear of God, with the hope and expectation of our not sinning. Maimonides also speaks of not speaking God's Name in vain.

Although all three commentators state that we are not to speak God's Name in vain, none of them make reference to the third of the Ten Commandments, Exodus 20:7.[113] Also, even though it is a reality that if one sins, punishment is likely to follow, I do not believe it is the intended meaning of the Commandment to fear God. Perhaps the difference in my approach has to do with my belief that we are exclusively in and subject to the New Covenant. The New Covenant acknowledges the possibility that a believer in God and Messiah will sin, but it does not assume it. This is unambiguously taught in 1 John 2:1:

> *My children, I am writing you these things so that you won't sin. But if anyone does sin, we have Yeshua the Messiah, the Tzaddik, who pleads our cause with the Father.*

NCLA: JMm JFm KMm KFm GMm GFm

---

113 For a discussion of Exodus 20:7, see *Mitzvah* #A6 of this compilation.

G7. Treating God as Holy by Proclaiming Him Holy and by Not Profaning His Name.

We are to treat God as holy by proclaiming Him holy, by being holy, and by not profaning His Name.

This precept is derived from His Word (blessed be He):

Key Scriptures

Exodus 20:7
You are not to use lightly the name of ADONAI your God, because ADONAI will not leave unpunished someone who uses his name lightly.

Exodus 22:27(28) (Maimonides RN60)
You are not to curse God, and you are not to curse a leader of your people.

Leviticus 11:44-45
For I am ADONAI your God; therefore, consecrate yourselves and be holy, for I am holy; and do not defile yourselves with any kind of swarming creature that moves along the ground. For I am ADONAI, who brought you up out of the land of Egypt to be your God. Therefore you are to be holy, because I am holy.

Leviticus 18:21 (Maimonides RN63; Chinuch C295)
You are not to let any of your children be sacrificed to Molekh, thereby profaning the name of your God; I am ADONAI.

Leviticus 19:2
Speak to the entire community of Isra'el; tell them, 'You people are to be holy because I, ADONAI your God, am holy.

Leviticus 19:12 (Maimonides RN63; Chinuch C295)
Do not swear by my name falsely, which would be profaning the name of your God; I am ADONAI.

Leviticus 22:32-33 (Maimonides RP9, RN63; Meir MP5, MN155; Chinuch C295, 296)
You are not to profane my holy name; on the contrary, I am to be regarded as holy among the people of Isra'el; I am ADONAI, who makes you holy, who brought you out of the land of Egypt to be your God; I am ADONAI.

Leviticus 24:10-16 (Maimonides RN60; Chinuch C70)
There was a man who was the son of a woman of Isra'el and an Egyptian father. He went out among the people of Isra'el, and this son of a woman of Isra'el had a fight in the camp with a man of Isra'el, in the course of which the son of the woman of Isra'el uttered the Name

[Yud-Heh-Vav-Heh] in a curse. So they brought him to Moshe. (His mother's name was Shlomit the daughter of Dibri, of the tribe of Dan.) They put him under guard until ADONAI would tell them what to do. ADONAI said to Moshe, "Take the man who cursed outside the camp, have everyone who heard him lay their hands on his head, and have the entire community stone him. Then tell the people of Isra'el, 'Whoever curses his God will bear the consequences of his sin; and whoever blasphemes the name of ADONAI must be put to death; the entire community must stone him. The foreigner as well as the citizen is to be put to death if he blasphemes the Name."

Matthew 6:9
You, therefore, pray like this: 'Our Father in heaven! May your Name be kept holy.'"

Matthew 12:31-32
Because of this, I tell you that people will be forgiven any sin and blasphemy, but blaspheming the Ruach HaKodesh will not be forgiven. One can say something against the Son of Man and be forgiven; but whoever keeps on speaking against the Ruach HaKodesh will never be forgiven, neither in the 'olam hazeh nor in the 'olam haba.

Luke 11:2a
He [Yeshua] said to them, "When you pray, say: 'Father, May your name be kept holy...'"

Supportive Scriptures

Isaiah 6:1-3
Psalms 99:9
1 Peter 1:15-16
Revelation 4:8, 15:4

Commentary

This *Mitzvah* re-formulates two of the traditional *taryag mitzvot* into a *mitzvah* having three components. The traditional *mitzvot* direct us to (1) sanctify God's Name, and (2) not profane God's Name. The components of this re-formulated *mitzvah* direct us to (1) treat God as holy, (2) proclaim God's holiness, and (3) not profane God's Name. There is logic to linking them in this way. God proclaims His own holiness, and requires that we acknowledge it by being obedient to these three directives. God's holiness encompasses His entire nature that includes His integrity, purity, trustworthiness, goodness, righteousness, justice, compassion, love, and all His other attributes.

There are other ways (in addition to these three) of acknowledging God's holiness, but the key to them all is holding God holy in our hearts and thoughts and reminding ourselves of it regularly. That is the purpose of the third benediction of the *Amidah* and of the *Kedushah*—prayers that are a part of most synagogue services.

The third benediction of the *Amidah* states:[114]

> *"You are holy and Your Name is holy, and holy ones praise You every day, forever. Blessed are You, Hashem, the Holy God."*

And the *Kedushah* (quoting Isaiah 6:3) states:[115]

> *"We shall sanctify Your Name in this world, just as they sanctify It in heaven above, as it is written by Your prophet, "And one [angel] will call to another and say: 'Holy, holy, holy is Hashem, Master of Legions, the whole world is filled with His glory.'"*

And it ends with:[116]

> *"From generation to generation we shall relate Your greatness and for infinite eternities we shall proclaim Your holiness. Your praise, our God, shall not leave our mouth forever and ever, for You O God, are a great and holy King. Blessed are You Hashem, the holy God."*

Classical Commentators

Maimonides', Meir's, and HaChinuch's positive *mitzvot* RP9, MP5, and C296, respectively, all draw, from Leviticus 22:32, the commandment that we are to sanctify God (or God's Name). Their negative *mitzvot* RN63, MN155, and C295, respectively, draw from the same Scripture, the commandment that we are not to profane (or desecrate) God's Name. All three commentators say, of their positive *mitzvot,* that we are to proclaim God to the world and never deny Him— even at the risk of injury or death. We are also to refrain from committing sin (especially sins connected to idolatry), since sin dishonors God and, by inference, denies His holiness.

NCLA: *JMm JFm KMm KFm GMm GFm*

---

114 Translation: The ArtScroll Siddur, Third Edition, (Brooklyn, New York: *Mesorah* Publications, Ltd., Sept. 2006).
115 Ibid.
116 Ibid.

G8. Serving, Worshiping, Praising, and Praying to God.

We are to serve, worship, praise, and pray to God.

This precept is derived from His Word (blessed be He):

Key Scriptures

Serving God

Exodus 23:25 (Maimonides RP5; Chinuch C433)
You are to serve ADONAI your God; and he will bless your food and water. I will take sickness away from among you.

Deuteronomy 6:13 (Maimonides RP5; Meir MP7; Chinuch C433)
You are to fear ADONAI your God, serve him and swear by his name.

Deuteronomy 10:20 (Chinuch 433)
You are to fear ADONAI your God, serve him, cling to him and swear by his name.

Deuteronomy 11:13-14 (Maimonides RP5; Meir MP7; Chinuch C433)
So if you listen carefully to my mitzvot which I am giving you today, to love ADONAI your God and serve him with all your heart and all your being; then, [says ADONAI,] 'I will give your land its rain at the right seasons, including the early fall rains and the late spring rains; so that you can gather in your wheat, new wine and olive oil...'

Deuteronomy 13:5(4)
You are to follow ADONAI your God, fear him, obey his mitzvot, listen to what he says, serve to him...

Luke 4 :8
Yeshua answered him, "The Tanakh says, 'Worship ADONAI your God and serve him only.'"

Romans 12:11
Don't be lazy when hard work is needed, but serve the Lord with spiritual fervor.

Hebrews 12:28
Therefore, since we have received an unshakeable Kingdom, let us have grace, through which we may offer service that will please God, with reverence and fear.

Worshipping God

Exodus 7:26(8:1)
ADONAI said to Moshe, "Go in to Pharaoh and say to him, 'Here is what ADONAI says: "Let my people go, so that they can worship me.

Psalms 29:2
...give ADONAI the glory due his name; worship ADONAI in holy splendor.

Psalms 95:5-6
The sea is his—he made it—and his hands shaped the dry land. Come, let's bow down and worship; let's kneel before ADONAI who made us.

Psalms 117:1
Praise ADONAI, all you nations! Worship him, all you peoples!

Matthew 4:8-10 (see also, Luke 4:5-8)
Once more, the Adversary took him up to the summit of a very high mountain, showed him all the kingdoms of the world in all their glory, and said to him, "All this I will give you if you will bow down and worship me." "Away with you, Satan!" Yeshua told him, "For the Tanakh says, 'Worship ADONAI your God, and serve only him.'"

John 4:21-24
Yeshua said, "Lady, believe me, the time is coming when you will worship the Father neither on this mountain nor in Yerushalayim. You people don't know what you are worshipping; we worship what we do know, because salvation comes from the Jews. But the time is coming—indeed, it's here now—when the true worshippers will worship the Father spiritually and truly, for these are the kind of people the Father wants worshipping him. God is spirit; and worshippers must worship him spiritually and truly."

Romans 14:11
...since it is written in the Tanakh, "As I live, says ADONAI, every knee will bend before me, and every tongue will publicly acknowledge God."

Praising God

Deuteronomy 10:21-22
He is your praise, and he is your God, who has done for you these great and awesome things, which you have seen with your own eyes. Your ancestors went down into Egypt with only seventy people, but now ADONAI your God has made your numbers as many as the stars in the sky!

Psalms 20:8(7)
Some trust in chariots and some in horses, but we praise the name of ADONAI our God.

<u>Psalms 30:5(4)</u>
Sing praise to ADONAI, you faithful of his; and give thanks on recalling his holiness.

<u>Psalms 34:2(1)</u>
I will bless ADONAI at all times; his praise will always be in my mouth.

<u>Matthew 5:15-16</u>
Likewise, when people light a lamp, they don't cover it with a bowl but put it on a lampstand, so that it shines for everyone in the house. In the same way, let your light shine before people, so that they may see the good things you do and praise your Father in heaven.

<u>Romans 15:11</u>
And again, "Praise ADONAI, all Gentiles! Let all peoples praise him!"

<u>Hebrews 13:15</u>
Through him, therefore, let us offer God a sacrifice of praise continually. For this is the natural product of lips that acknowledge his name.

<u>James 5:13b</u>
Is someone feeling good? He should sing songs of praise.

Praying to God

<u>Psalms 122:6a</u>
Pray for shalom in Yerushalayim;

<u>Matthew 5:44</u>
But I tell you, love your enemies! Pray for those who persecute you!

<u>Matthew 6:9</u>
You, therefore, pray like this: 'Our Father in heaven! May your Name be kept holy...'

<u>Matthew 21:13a</u>
He said to them, "It has been written, 'My house will be called a house of prayer.'...

<u>Mark 11:24</u>
Therefore, I tell you, whatever you ask for in prayer, trust that you are receiving it, and it will be yours.

<u>Romans 12:12</u>
Rejoice in your hope, be patient in your troubles, and continue steadfastly in prayer.

<u>Philippians 4:6</u>
Don't worry about anything; on the contrary, make your requests known to God by prayer and petition, with thanksgiving.

<u>Colossians 4:2</u>
Keep persisting in prayer, staying alert in it and being thankful.

<u>James 5:13a</u>
Is someone among you in trouble? He should pray.

Supportive Scriptures—Worshiping God

Isaiah 45:22-25
Psalms 5:8(7)
Philippians 2:9-11, 3:3a
Revelation 4:9-11, 5:14

Supportive Scriptures—Praising God

Psalms 95:2, 135:1, 150:1-6
Revelation 5:13, 19:5

Supportive Scriptures—Praying to God

Genesis 20:17, 25:21
Numbers 11:2, 21:7
Deuteronomy 9:26b
Psalms 5:3(2)
Luke 6:12
James 5:14-16

Supportive Scriptures—Serving God

Deuteronomy 28:47-48
Joshua 22:5, 24:14-15
1 Samuel 12:24
Malachi 3:18
Psalms 2:11
Matthew 6:24, 20:27
John 12:26
Ephesians 6:7
Colossians 3:23-24
Hebrews 9:13-14

Commentary

Despite the numerous Scriptures in both the *Tanakh* and the *Kitvey B'rit Chadasha* that exemplify and exhort to worship, praise, and prayer, there is no explicit commandment in the *Torah* that requires any of them. The overall message of Scripture embracing them is unmistakable, however, so the early Rabbis and codifiers of the Law decided to list (in their *mitzvah* compilations) Scriptures that command giving service to God, and to treat "service" as encompassing prayer. I chose to do something similar in this *Mitzvah* by joining worship, praise, prayer, and service, and letting "worship" be the umbrella that encompasses the other three. Scripture (in particular Zechariah 4:6, Romans 8:26-27, and Philippians 3:3) is clear that true worship and its components can only be entered into with the power and assistance of the Holy Spirit.

If one understands worship as being a complete giving over of oneself to another, it is easy to see how praise, prayer, and service can be components of worship. It is not always the case, however; whether they are part of, and contribute to worship, depends upon the degree of "giving over," and their intensity. For example, merely complementing someone (praising him) does not constitute worship, and neither does asking an ordinary favor of someone (old English usage of praying), or serving someone as an employee. That notwithstanding, requesting something of a person while continuously praising him, showering him with unsolicited service, and pursuing him with an attitude of submission and adulation, may very constitute worship.

In common modern usage, the word "prayer" is generally limited to petitioning God but, as I have indicated, in "old English" usage, it was a request made to anyone. For example, in Job 33:1 (rendered in the King James Version of the Bible) we read of God saying:

> *"Wherefore, Job, I pray thee, hear my speeches, and hearken to all my words."*

God was certainly not "praying" to Job as we understand Job to have prayed to God.

Serving another is similar, in that whether or not it constitutes worship depends upon the degree to which the service is rendered and the attitude that accompanies it. We read in 1 Peter 4:10:

> *"As each one has received some spiritual gift, he should use it to serve others, like good managers of God's many-sided grace."*

This exhortation to serve others is clearly not an invitation to worship them, whereas Yeshua's answer to Satan in Luke 4:8:

> *"The Tanakh says, 'Worship ADONAI your God and serve him only."*

illustrates how giving service to God does (and should) rise to the level of worship. Serving another with abandon (as a willing slave) is what constitutes worship, and it is only appropriate in our rendering service to God.

An additional word concerning prayer: It has been taught, in certain circles, that Mark 11:24 (and similar Scriptures) can be used as a way of getting God to give us what we want, the theory being that, if we believe for something enough, God will give it to us. It is called "faith" by those who advance this view, but it is a mistake because true faith requires first hearing from God, and then believing and praying for what God wants—not for what we want unless the two coincide. A Scripture that must be applied when interpreting Mark 11:24 is Jude 1:20:

322

> *"But you, dear friends, build yourselves up in your most holy faith, and pray in union with the Ruach HaKodesh."*

Praying in union with the Holy Spirit is the key (See also, <u>Hebrews 11:1</u>).

Classical Commentators

Whereas Maimonides, Meir, and HaChinuch express themselves somewhat differently, they essentially agree that prayer is linked to service. Because they cannot find anything in the *Torah* explicitly commanding prayer, they treat praying to God and rendering service to God as being essentially the same and only quote Scriptures that command service.

The only reference to worship is found in the caption of Maimonides' Commandment #RP5, as translated by Charles B. Chavel in his two-volume work, "The Commandments."[117] Meir captions his Commandment #MP7 as "Praying Every Day to God," and HaChinuch captions his Commandment #C433 as "The Precept of Prayer to the Almighty." Despite Chavel's caption, Maimonides does not discuss worshiping God at all, but rather exhorts us only to serving Him and to prayer.

Of the three, Meir is the only one of the commentators that connects praising God to prayer and service. He states that the commandment requires a sequence in addressing God: (1) praising Him; (2) petitioning Him; and (3) both praising and thanking Him. He also says that, in praying to God, it is necessary to do so with "focused intention of the heart." This is known as praying with *kavanah.*

HaChinuch begins his *mitzvah* #C433 by referring to the Scriptures commanding that we give service to God, and then quotes Maimonides: *"Now, R. Moses b. Maimon of blessed memory wrote: Although this mitzvah is one of the all-inclusive precepts—in other words, those which include the entire Torah, since the service of God includes all the mitzvot—it likewise contains a specific detail: namely, that God commanded us to pray to Him..."* HaChinuch then proceeds to explain our responsibility to pray three times a day, corresponding to the times when sacrifices were conducted in the Temple. He uses the term "prayer services," which links prayer with service, and expresses that predominant Jewish understanding that "prayer services" are meant to give "service" to God. As in the case of the other commentators, HaChinuch does not refer to worship even once.

All three of the commentators, Maimonides, Meir, and HaChinuch, rely on *Talmud Bavli Ta'anith 2a* as their authority for linking prayer to the Scriptures commanding service to God.

<u>NCLA</u>: **JMm JFm KMm KFm GMm GFm**

---

117 Charles B. Chavel, <u>The Commandments</u>, vol. 1, (London: The Soncino Press, 1967).

G9. Clinging to God.

We are to cling to God.

This precept is derived from His Word (blessed be He):

Key Scriptures

Genesis 32:25(24)-31(30)
Then some man wrestled with him [Jacob] until daybreak. When he saw that he did not defeat Ya'akov, he struck Ya'akov's hip socket, so that his hip was dislocated while wrestling with him. The man said, "Let me go, because it's daybreak." But Ya'akov replied, "I won't let you go unless you bless me." The man asked, "What is your name?" and he answered, "Ya'akov." Then the man said, "From now on, you will no longer be called Ya'akov, but Isra'el; because you have shown your strength to both God and men and have prevailed." Ya'akov asked him, "Please tell me your name." But he answered, "Why are you asking about my name?" and blessed him there. Ya'akov called the place P'ni-El [face of God], "Because I have seen God face to face, yet my life is spared."

Deuteronomy 10:20 (Maimonides RP6, Meir MP16; Chinuch C434)
You are to fear ADONAI your God, serve him, cling to him and swear by his name.

Deuteronomy 11:22 (Maimonides RP6; Chinuch C434)
For if you will take care to obey all these mitzvot I am giving you, to do them, to love ADONAI your God, to follow all his ways and to cling to him...

Deuteronomy 13:5(4)
You are to follow ADONAI your God, fear him, obey his mitzvot, listen to what he says, serve him and cling to him;

Jeremiah 13:11
For just as a loincloth clings to a man's body, I made the whole house of Isra'el and the whole house of Y'hudah cling to me,' says ADONAI, 'so that they could be my people, building me a name and becoming for me a source of praise and honor.

John 15:1-5
Stay united with me, as I will with you—for just as the branch can't put forth fruit by itself apart from the vine, so you can't bear fruit apart from me. I am the vine and you are the branches. Those who stay united with me, and I with them, are the ones who bear much fruit; because apart from me you can't do a thing.

Commentary

Clinging to God means that we are to tenaciously grab hold of Him and not let go. We are to derive our strength from God, trust Him, and allow nothing to separate us from Him or entice us away from Him. This becomes most meaningful during times when we are tempted us to abandon God and follow the path of self or sin. <u>James 4:7-8a</u> teaches that, during such times, we must

> *"submit to God. Moreover, take a stand against the Adversary, and he will flee from you [us]. Come close to God, and he will come close to you [us]."*

We do this by remembering God's Word in <u>2 Timothy 2:26</u>:

> *"that [we] may come to [our] senses and escape the snare of the devil, having been taken captive by him to do his will."*

Yeshua addresses this in <u>Matthew 6:13a</u>, in the prayer he recommends to His disciples:

> *"And do not lead us into hard testing, but keep us safe from the Evil One."*

Classical Commentators

Maimonides states his *mitzvah* as our being commanded to cleave (or cling) to God, and he goes on to say that the cleaving or clinging to God is accomplished through associating with wise men. Meir's and HaChinuch's *mitzvot* do not even mention clinging to God in the way they are stated (although <u>Deuteronomy 10:20</u> is quoted as the operative Scripture); instead, they command us to attach ourselves to *Torah* scholars and their disciples. They then say that if we do so, it is as though we are attaching ourselves to the *Shechinah*. It is ironic that all three commentators choose to redirect Scripture's clear message of clinging to God, to a different message—that of clinging to men. They derive this equivalence from *Talmud*.

<u>NCLA</u>: JMm JFm KMm KFm GMm GFm

G10. Approaching God while Unrepentant.

We are not to approach God in prayer or worship while we are unrepentant of our sins.

This precept is derived from His Word (blessed be He):

Key Scriptures

Genesis 4:3-7
In the course of time Kayin [Cain] brought an offering to ADONAI from the produce of the soil; and Hevel [Abel] too brought from the firstborn of his sheep, including their fat. ADONAI accepted Hevel and his offering but did not accept Kayin and his offering. Kayin was very angry, and his face fell. ADONAI said to Kayin, "Why are you angry? Why so downcast? If you are doing what is good, shouldn't you hold your head high? And if you don't do what is good, sin is crouching at the door—it wants you, but you can rule over it."

Leviticus 16:11
Aharon is to present the bull of the sin offering for himself; he will make atonement for himself and his household; he is to slaughter the bull of the sin offering which is for himself.

Psalms 66:16-18
Come and listen, all you who fear God, and I will tell what he has done for me. I cried out to him with my mouth, his praise was on my tongue. Had I cherished evil thoughts, Adonai would not have listened.

Matthew 5:23-24
So if you are offering your gift at the Temple altar and you remember there that your brother has something against you, leave your gift where it is by the altar, and go, make peace with your brother. Then come back and offer your gift.

1 Corinthians 11:27-29
Therefore, whoever eats the Lord's bread or drinks the Lord's cup in an unworthy manner will be guilty of desecrating the body and blood of the Lord! So let a person examine himself first, and then he may eat of the bread and drink from the cup; for a person who eats and drinks without recognizing the body eats and drinks judgment upon himself.

1 John 1:9
If we acknowledge our sins, then, since he is trustworthy and just, he will forgive them and purify us from all wrongdoing.

Supportive Scriptures

Isaiah 1:15-19, 59:1-2
Proverbs 15:29

1 Corinthians 3:16-17, 6:19-20
James 5:16

Commentary

In the Mosaic Covenant, an Israelite would bring his animal sacrifice to the Temple (or the Tabernacle), and a Levitical *cohen* would assist him by slaying it, placing it on an altar, and offering it up to God in his behalf. The Israelite had to be ceremonially clean (i.e. ritually pure) to even enter the Temple's sanctuary, but whether or not he was actually repentant (i.e. the condition of his heart was right) when he offered his sacrifice was known only to God. There is another Mosaic Covenant example of the need to approach God only when repentant, and that is Leviticus 16:11's requirement that the High Priest sacrifice a bull for himself prior to sacrificing a goat for the sins of Israel on *Yom Kippur.* We also assume that the ten days between *Yom T'ruah* and *Yom Kippur* was for the purpose of all Israelites examining themselves and repenting of their sins (committed during the previous year) prior to their coming before the Lord on *Yom Kippur.*

The various commandments requiring that the worshiper be ceremonially clean in order to enter the Holy Temple were, no doubt, given in order to remind him of God's holiness, and that the house in which God chose to put His Name (i.e. where the *Sh'khinah* dwelt) must not be defiled. One thing is certain however—the worshipper's sacrifice was only acceptable if his heart was repentant before God (Genesis 4:3-7; Isaiah 1:15-19, 59:1-2; Matthew 5:23-24).

The Temple that stood in Jerusalem was built of brick and mortar but, in this era of the New Covenant, God's presence (The Holy Spirit) lives in Temples made of flesh (the "bodies" of believers) and, therefore, in the "bodies" of each and every one of us who will have Him (1 Corinthians 3:16-17, 6:19-20). That gives new meaning to the requirement that God's Temple be undefiled. Today, the commandment has not to do with entering a physical Temple while in an unclean state; rather, it is allowing the Temple of our bodies to fall into a spiritually unclean state, thereby making it uninhabitable by the Holy Spirit. Spiritual uncleanliness is caused by sin, and it persists if there is no repentance.

Our need for spiritual cleanness and repentance is illustrated by several Scriptures (listed above) that essentially state that God does not have fellowship with, nor does He even hear, those who are unrepentant of their sin (see Proverbs 15:29; Isaiah 59:1-2; 1 Corinthians 11:27-29 and James 5:16).

Classical Commentators

Maimonides and HaChinuch wrote *mitzvot* #RN77 and #C363 respectively, which state that no person who is ceremonially unclean is to enter the Sanctuary. Maimonides and HaChinuch do not offer *mitzvot* on spiritual cleanness broadly or of approaching God while unrepentant, and Meir is silent on both subjects.

NCLA: JMm JFm KMm KFm GMm GFm

G11. Being Thankful to God and Blessing Him in All Things.

We are to be thankful to God and bless Him in all things.

This precept is derived from His Word (blessed be He):

Key Scriptures

Being Thankful to God

Deuteronomy 8:6-18 (Maimonides RP19; Meir MP13; Chinuch C430)
So obey the mitzvot of ADONAI your God, living as he directs and fearing him. For ADONAI your God is bringing you into a good land, a land with streams, springs and water welling up from the depths in valleys and on hillsides. It is a land of wheat and barley, grapevines, fig trees and pomegranates; a land of olive oil and honey; a land where you will eat food in abundance and lack nothing in it; a land where the stones contain iron and the hills can be mined for copper. So you will eat and be satisfied, and you will bless ADONAI your God for the good land he has given you. [(NKJ): *"When you have eaten and are full, then you shall bless the LORD your God for the good land which He has given you."*] *Be careful not to forget ADONAI your God by not obeying his mitzvot, rulings and regulations that I am giving you today. Otherwise, after you have eaten and are satisfied, built fine houses and lived in them, and increased your herds, flocks, silver, gold and everything else you own, you will become proud-hearted. Forgetting ADONAI your God—who brought you out of the land of Egypt, where you lived as slaves; who led you through the vast and fearsome desert, with its poisonous snakes, scorpions and waterless, thirsty ground; who brought water out of flint rock for you; who fed you in the desert with man, unknown to your ancestors; all the while humbling and testing you in order to do you good in the end—you will think to yourself, 'My own power and the strength of my own hand have gotten me this wealth.' No, you are to remember ADONAI your God, because it is he who is giving you the power to get wealth, in order to confirm his covenant, which he swore to your ancestors, as is happening even today.*

Psalms 50:23
Whoever offers thanksgiving as his sacrifice honors me; and to him who goes the right way I will show the salvation of God.

Psalms 100:4
Enter his gates with thanksgiving, enter his courtyards with praise; give thanks to him, and bless his name.

Ephesians 5:20:
...always give thanks for everything to God the Father in the name of our Lord Yeshua the Messiah.

Colossians 1:3
Whenever we pray, we always give thanks for you to God, the Father of our Lord Yeshua the Messiah.

Blessing God in All Things

Deuteronomy 10:8
At that time ADONAI set apart the tribe of Levi to carry the ark for the covenant of ADONAI and to stand before ADONAI to serve him and to bless in his name, as they still do today.

Psalms 34:2(1)
I will bless ADONAI at all times; his praise will always be in my mouth.

Psalms 100:4
Enter his gates with thanksgiving, enter his courtyards with praise; give thanks to him, and bless his name.

Matthew 23:39
For I tell you, from now on, you will not see me again until you say, 'Blessed is he who comes in the name of ADONAI.'"

Supportive Scriptures—Being Thankful to God

Psalms 9:1-2(9:1), 50:14, 92:2(1), 95:2, 97:12, 100:1-5, 105:1, 118:1, 28-29, 136:1-3, 26
Romans 1:20b-21a
2 Corinthians 2:14
Philippians 4:6
Colossians 2:6-7, 3:15b-17
1 Thessalonians 5:18
2 Timothy 1:3

Supportive Scriptures—Blessing God in All Things

Genesis 9:26
Exodus 18:10
Judges 5:2-3
Psalms 16:7, 28:6, 41:14(13), 63:5(4), 68:20(19), 72:18-19, 96:2, 103:1-2, 104:1-2, 115:18, 134:1-2, 135:19-21, 145:21
Ruth 4:14
Daniel 2:19-20
1 Chronicles 29:20
Matthew 26:26-27
Mark 14:22-23
Luke 22:17-20

1 Co 11:23-24).
James 3:7-10

Commentary

It should be apparent from the many Scriptures quoted above, that both the *Tanakh* and the *Kitvey B'rit Chadasha* enjoin us to be thankful to God, giving thanks to Him who created all and who continues to provide for our every need. There exists, however, only one place in the *Torah* that specifically commands thankfulness—Deuteronomy 8:6-18, verse 10, which is the basis for the traditional Grace after Meals, the *Birkat Hamazon.* Notwithstanding that single occurrence, being thankful and giving thanks to God are deeply ingrained in Judaism and in Jewish practice. They are addressed in various places in the *Talmud* (e.g. in B'rakhot and Avot), and appear in the *Siddur* as the first blessing that is said upon awakening *(Modeh Ani),* as the next-to-last benediction of the *Sh'moneh Esreh ("Modim anachnu lach...")*, and as the central theme of the *Aleinu* prayer *("Va'anachnu korim umishtachavim umodim").* They are also implicit in the multitude of blessings that begin *"Baruch atah adonai, eloheynu melech ha-olam..."* ("Blessed are you Lord, our God, King of the universe, who...").

There are essentially two ways in which we can bless God. The first is by expressing thankful praise to Him for the blessings He bestows on us. It may be emoted spontaneously or recited ritually in what is termed a *"b'rakhah."* The second way is by loving Him as our Heavenly Father, Messiah savior, and Holy Spirit, and by fulfilling His highest expectation of us, which is to be unswervingly obedient to His Word and to walk in His ways.

The totality of Scripture makes it plain that our being thankful to God and our blessing Him should not be only for His provision of food, but for all of His provisions and blessings that He bestows upon us, not the least of which is His unconditional love. There is therefore a deeper way to understand and employ the *Birkat Hamazon* than as merely "grace after meals." It is that, in the fullness of our having eaten, we should allow its words to permeate our soul while contemplating our blessings, and thankfully remembering that God is our provider and sustainer, and not we ourselves.

Classical Commentators

None of the commentators (Maimonides, Meir, or HaChinuch) wrote general *mitzvot* commanding that we be thankful to God. That is no doubt because they only sought to codify commandments they found in the *Torah,* and concluded that Deuteronomy 8:10 is the only Scripture in the *Torah* that commands thankfulness.

Two English translations for Deuteronomy 8:10 are included in the Scripture list above. None of the commentators worked in the English language, of course, but the way the New King James Version translates Deuteronomy 8:10 must have been close to how all three of them understood the Hebrew. I conclude this because all three of their *mitzvot* command that we bless God after we have eaten a meal (i.e. say Grace). Although the context of the Scripture is the Israelites having come into the Promised Land, Maimonides, Meir, HaChinuch and all of Judaism interpret it broadly to mean that, after we have eaten and are satisfied, we are to remember God who brought us out of Egypt. That is the purpose of the *Birkat Hamazon.* Meir states that we are also to bless God before eating. Using the logic of *kal va-chomer* (less to more), he states that if we are to bless God when we are satisfied, how much more is our obligation to bless him when we are hungry. The logic seems a little backwards, but that is his logic.

As with thanking God, none of the commentators wrote *mitzvot* on "blessing God" either.

<u>NCLA</u>: JMm JFm KMm KFm GMm GFm

G12. Having Faith in God and Trusting Him for All Things.

We are to have faith in God and trust Him for all things—for our protection, for those we love, for our worldly needs, and for our very lives.

This precept is derived from His Word (blessed be He):

Key Scriptures

Trusting God in the Sabbatical Year

Exodus 23:10-11 (Maimonides RP134; Meir ML20; Chinuch C84)
For six years, you are to sow your land with seed and gather in its harvest. But the seventh year, you are to let it rest and lie fallow, so that the poor among your people can eat; and what they leave, the wild animals in the countryside can eat. Do the same with your vineyard and olive grove.

Exodus 34:21 (Maimonides RP135)
Six days you will work, but on the seventh day you are to rest—even in plowing time and harvest season you are to rest.

Leviticus 25:1-2 (Maimonides RP135; Meir ML21; Chinuch C112)
ADONAI spoke to Moshe on Mount Sinai; he said, "Tell the people of Isra'el, 'When you enter the land I am giving you, the land itself is to observe a Shabbat rest for ADONAI."

Leviticus 25:3-4 (Maimonides RN220-221; Meir ML22-23; Chinuch C326-327)
Six years you will sow your field; six years you will prune your grapevines and gather their produce. But in the seventh year is to be a Shabbat of complete rest for the land, a Shabbat for ADONAI; you will neither sow your field nor prune your grapevines.

Leviticus 25:5-7 (Maimonides RP134, RN222-223; Meir ML24-25; Chinuch C84, 328-329)
You are not to harvest what grows by itself from the seeds left by your previous harvest, and you are not to gather the grapes of your untended vine; it is to be a year of complete rest for the land. But what the land produces during the year of Shabbat will be food for all of you—you, your servant, your maid, your employee, anyone living near you, your livestock and the wild animals on your land; everything the land produces may be used for food.

Leviticus 25:20-22
If you ask, "If we aren't allowed to sow seed or harvest what our land produces, what are we going to eat the seventh year?" then I will order my blessing on you during the sixth year, so that the land brings forth enough produce for all three years. The eighth year you will sow seed but eat the old, stored produce until the ninth year; that is, until the produce of the eighth year comes in, you will eat the old, stored food.

Deuteronomy 15:1
At the end of every seven years you are to have a sh'mittah.

Deuteronomy 15:2 (Maimonides RN230; Meir MN57, MP64; Chinuch C475)
Here is how the sh'mittah is to be done: every creditor is to give up what he has loaned to his fellow member of the community—he is not to force his neighbor or relative to repay it, because ADONAI's time of remission has been proclaimed.

Deuteronomy 15:3 (Maimonides RP141-142; Chinuch 476-477)
You may demand that a foreigner repay his debt, but you are to release your claim on whatever your brother owes you.

Deuteronomy 15:4-6
In spite of this [releasing debts owed to you] there will be no one needy among you; because ADONAI will certainly bless you in the land which ADONAI your God is giving you as an inheritance to possess—if only you will listen carefully to what ADONAI your God says and take care to obey all these mitzvot I am giving you today. Yes, ADONAI your God will bless you, as he promised you—you will lend money to many nations without having to borrow, and you will rule over many nations without their ruling over you.

Deuteronomy 15:7-11 (Maimonides RN231; Meir MN56; Chinuch C480)
If someone among you is needy, one of your brothers, in any of your towns in your land which ADONAI your God is giving you, you are not to harden your heart or shut your hand from giving to your needy brother. No, you must open your hand to him and lend him enough to meet his need and enable him to obtain what he wants. Guard yourself against allowing your heart to entertain the mean-spirited thought that because the seventh year, the year of sh'mittah is at hand, you would be stingy toward your needy brother and not give him anything; for then he may cry out to ADONAI against you, and it will be your sin. Rather, you must give to him; and you are not to be grudging when you give to him. If you do this, ADONAI your God will bless you in all your work, in everything you undertake—for there will always be poor people in the land. That is why I am giving you this order, 'You must open your hand to your poor and needy brother in your land.'

Trusting God in the Jubillee Year

Exodus 13:12 (Maimonides RP140)
you are to set apart for ADONAI everything that is first from the womb. Every firstborn male animal will belong to ADONAI.

Exodus 34:19 (Maimonides RP140)
Everything that is first from the womb is mine. Of all your livestock, you are to set aside for me the males, the firstborn of cattle and flock.

Leviticus 25:4-5 (Chinuch C334)
But in the seventh year is to be a Shabbat of complete rest for the land, a Shabbat for ADONAI; you will neither sow your field nor prune your grapevines. You are not to harvest what grows by

itself from the seeds left by your previous harvest, and you are not to gather the grapes of your untended vine; it is to be a year of complete rest for the land.

Leviticus 25:8 (Maimonides RP140; Chinuch C330)
You are to count seven Shabbats of years, seven times seven years, that is, forty-nine years.

Leviticus 25:9 (Maimonides RP137; Chinuch C331)
Then, on the tenth day of the seventh month, on Yom-Kippur, you are to sound a blast on the shofar; you are to sound the shofar all through your land...

Leviticus 25:10 (Maimonides RP136-137; Chinuch C331-332)
and you are to consecrate the fiftieth year, proclaiming freedom throughout the land to all its inhabitants. It will be a yovel for you; you will return everyone to the land he owns, and everyone is to return to his family.

Leviticus 25:11 (Maimonides RN224-226; Chinuch C333, 335)
That fiftieth year will be a yovel for you; in that year you are not to sow, harvest what grows by itself or gather the grapes of untended vines...

Leviticus 25:12 (Maimonides RP136)
because it is a yovel. It will be holy for you; whatever the fields produce will be food for all of you.

Leviticus 25:13-17
In this year of yovel, every one of you is to return to the land he owns. If you sell anything to your neighbor or buy anything from him, neither of you is to exploit the other. Rather, you are to take into account the number of years after the yovel when you buy land from your neighbor, and he is to sell to you according to the number of years crops will be raised. If the number of years remaining is large, you will raise the price; if few years remain, you will lower it; because what he is really selling you is the number of crops to be produced. Thus you are not to take advantage of each other, but you are to fear your God; for I am ADONAI your God.

Leviticus 25:23 (Maimonides RN227; Chinuch C339)
The land is not to be sold in perpetuity, because the land belongs to me—you are only foreigners and temporary residents with me.

Leviticus 25:24-28 (Maimonides RP138; Chinuch C340)
Therefore, when you sell your property, you must include the right of redemption. That is, if one of you becomes poor and sells some of his property, his next-of-kin can come and buy back what his relative sold. If the seller has no one to redeem it but becomes rich enough to redeem it himself, he will calculate the number of years the land was sold for, refund the excess to its buyer, and return to his property. If he hasn't sufficient means to get it back himself, then what he sold will remain in the hands of the buyer until the year of yovel; in the yovel the buyer will vacate it and the seller return to his property.

Leviticus 25:29-31 (Maimonides RP139; Chinuch C341)
If someone sells a dwelling in a walled city, he has one year after the date of sale in which to redeem it. For a full year he will have the right of redemption; but if he has not redeemed the dwelling in the walled city within the year, then title in perpetuity passes to the buyer through all his generations; it will not revert in the yovel. However, houses in villages not surrounded by walls are to be dealt with like the fields in the countryside—they may be redeemed [before the yovel], and they revert in the yovel.

Trusting God by Resting on the Weekly and Annual Sabbaths

Exodus 12:16 (Maimonides RP159; Meir MP25; Chunuch C297)
On the first and seventh days, you are to have an assembly set aside for God. On these days no work is to be done, except what each must do to prepare his food; you may do only that.

Exodus 20:8-11(Maimonides RP155; Meir MP19; Chinuch C31)
Remember the day, Shabbat, to set it apart for God. You have six days to labor and do all your work, but the seventh day is a Shabbat for ADONAI your God. On it, you are not to do any kind of work—not you, your son or your daughter, not your male or female slave, not your livestock, and not the foreigner staying with you inside the gates to your property. For in six days, ADONAI made heaven and earth, the sea and everything in them; but on the seventh day he rested. This is why ADONAI blessed the day, Shabbat, and separated it for himself.

Exodus 23:12 (Meir MP20; Chinuch C85)
For six days, you are to work. But on the seventh day, you are to rest, so that your ox and donkey can rest, and your slave-girl's son and the foreigner be renewed.

Exodus 34:21 (Maimonides RP154)
Six days you will work, but on the seventh day you are to rest—even in plowing time and harvest season you are to rest.

Leviticus 16:29-31 (Maimonides RP165)
It is to be a permanent regulation for you that on the tenth day of the seventh month you are to deny yourselves and not do any kind of work, both the citizen and the foreigner living with you. For on this day, atonement will be made for you to purify you; you will be clean before ADONAI from all your sins. It is a Shabbat of complete rest for you, and you are to deny yourselves. "This is a permanent regulation.

Leviticus 23:3 (Maimonides RP154)
Work is to be done on six days; but the seventh day is a Shabbat of complete rest, a holy convocation; you are not to do any kind of work; it is a Shabbat for ADONAI, even in your homes.

Leviticus 23:7 (Maimonides RP159; Meir MP25; Chinuch C297)
On the fifteenth day of the same month is the festival of matzah; for seven days you are to eat matzah. On the first day you are to have a holy convocation; don't do any kind of ordinary work.

Leviticus 23:8 (Maimonides RP160; Meir MP27; Chinuch C300)
On the seventh day [of Matzah] is a holy convocation; do not do any kind of ordinary work.

Leviticus 23:21 (Maimonides RP162; Meir MP28; Chinuch C308)
On the same day [Shavu'ot], you are to call a holy convocation; do not do any kind of ordinary work; this is a permanent regulation through all your generations, no matter where you live.

Leviticus 23:24-25 (Maimonides RP163; Meir MP29; Chinuch C310)
Tell the people of Isra'el, 'In the seventh month, the first of the month is to be for you a day of complete rest for remembering, a holy convocation announced with blasts on the shofar. Do not do any kind of ordinary work, and bring an offering made by fire to ADONAI.

Leviticus 23:27-32 (Meir MP31; C317)
The tenth day of this seventh month is Yom-Kippur; you are to have a holy convocation, you are to deny yourselves, and you are to bring an offering made by fire to ADONAI. You are not to do any kind of work on that day, because it is Yom-Kippur, to make atonement for you before ADONAI your God. Anyone who does not deny himself on that day is to be cut off from his people; and anyone who does any kind of work on that day, I will destroy from among his people. You are not to do any kind of work; it is a permanent regulation through all your generations, no matter where you live. It will be for you a Shabbat of complete rest, and you are to deny yourselves; you are to rest on your Shabbat from evening the ninth day of the month until the following evening.

Leviticus 23:34-35 (Maimonides RP166; Meir MP34; Chinuch C318)
Tell the people of Isra'el, 'On the fifteenth day of this seventh month is the feast of Sukkot for seven days to ADONAI. On the first day there is to be a holy convocation; do not do any kind of ordinary work.

Leviticus 23:36 (Maimonides RP167; Meir MP37; Chinuch C321)
For seven days you are to bring an offering made by fire to ADONAI; on the eighth day you are to have a holy convocation and bring an offering made by fire to ADONAI; it is a day of public assembly; do not do any kind of ordinary work.

Luke 4:16-19
Now when he [Yeshua] went to Natzeret, where he had been brought up, on Shabbat he went to the synagogue as usual. He stood up to read, and he was given the scroll of the prophet Yesha'yahu. Unrolling the scroll, he found the place where it was written, "The Spirit of ADONAI is upon me; therefore he has anointed me to announce Good News to the poor; he has sent me to proclaim freedom for the imprisoned and renewed sight for the blind, to release those who have been crushed, to proclaim a year of the favor of ADONAI."

Having Faith in God and Trusting Him at All Other Times

Genesis 15:6
He [Avram] believed in ADONAI, and he credited it to him as righteousness.

336

Deuteronomy 7:6-15

For you are a people set apart as holy for ADONAI your God. ADONAI your God has chosen you out of all the peoples on the face of the earth to be his own unique treasure. ADONAI didn't set his heart on you or choose you because you numbered more than any other people—on the contrary, you were the fewest of all peoples. Rather, it was because ADONAI loved you, and because he wanted to keep the oath which he had sworn to your ancestors, that ADONAI brought you out with a strong hand and redeemed you from a life of slavery under the hand of Pharaoh king of Egypt. From this you can know that ADONAI your God is indeed God, the faithful God, who keeps his covenant and extends grace to those who love him and observe his mitzvot, to a thousand generations. But he repays those who hate him to their face and destroys them. He will not be slow to deal with someone who hates him; he will repay him to his face. Therefore, you are to keep the mitzvot, laws and rulings which I am giving you today, and obey them. Because you are listening to these rulings, keeping and obeying them, ADONAI your God will keep with you the covenant and mercy that he swore to your ancestors. He will love you, bless you and increase your numbers; he will also bless the fruit of your body and the fruit of your ground—your grain, wine, olive oil and the young of your cattle and sheep—in the land he swore to your ancestors that he would give you. You will be blessed more than all other peoples; there will not be a sterile male or female among you, and the same with your livestock. ADONAI will remove all illness from you—he will not afflict you with any of Egypt's dreadful diseases, which you have known; instead, he will lay them on those who hate you.

Deuteronomy 28:1-14

If you listen closely to what ADONAI your God says, observing and obeying all his mitzvot which I am giving you today, ADONAI your God will raise you high above all the nations on earth; and all the following blessings will be yours in abundance—if you will do what ADONAI your God says: A blessing on you in the city, and a blessing on you in the countryside. A blessing on the fruit of your body, the fruit of your land and the fruit of your livestock—the young of your cattle and flocks. A blessing on your grain-basket and kneading-bowl. A blessing on you when you go out, and a blessing on you when you come in. ADONAI will cause your enemies attacking you to be defeated before you; they will advance on you one way and flee before you seven ways. ADONAI will order a blessing to be with you in your barns and in everything you undertake; he will bless you in the land ADONAI your God is giving you. ADONAI will establish you as a people separated out for himself, as he has sworn to you—if you will observe the mitzvot of ADONAI your God and follow his ways. Then all the peoples on earth will see that ADONAI's name, his presence, is with you; so that they will be afraid of you.

ADONAI will give you great abundance of good things—of the fruit of your body, the fruit of your livestock and the fruit of your land in the land ADONAI swore to your ancestors to give you. ADONAI will open for you his good treasure, the sky, to give your land its rain at the right seasons and to bless everything you undertake. You will lend to many nations and not borrow; ADONAI will make you the head and not the tail; and you will be only above, never below—if you will listen to, observe and obey the mitzvot of ADONAI your God and not turn away from any of the words I am ordering you today, neither to the right nor to the left, to follow after other gods and serve them.

337

Psalms 62:7(6)-9(8)

He alone is my rock and salvation, my stronghold; I won't be moved. My safety and honor rest on God. My strong rock and refuge are in God. Trust in him, people, at all times; pour out your heart before him; God is a refuge for us.

Psalms 118:6-9

With ADONAI on my side, I fear nothing—what can human beings do to me? With ADONAI on my side as my help, I will look with triumph at those who hate me. It is better to take refuge in ADONAI than to trust in human beings; better to take refuge in ADONAI than to put one's trust in princes.

Proverbs 3:5-6

Trust in ADONAI with all your heart; do not rely on your own understanding. In all your ways acknowledge him; then he will level your paths.

Proverbs 16:20

He who has skill in a matter will succeed; he who trusts in ADONAI will be happy.

Proverbs 29:25

Fearing human beings is a snare; but he who trusts in ADONAI will be raised high [above danger].

Matthew 6:25-34

Therefore, I tell you, don't worry about your life—what you will eat or drink; or about your body—what you will wear. Isn't life more than food and the body more than clothing? Look at the birds flying about! They neither plant nor harvest, nor do they gather food into barns; yet your heavenly Father feeds them. Aren't you worth more than they are? Can any of you by worrying add a single hour to his life? And why be anxious about clothing? Think about the fields of wild irises, and how they grow. They neither work nor spin thread, yet I tell you that not even Shlomo in all his glory was clothed as beautifully as one of these. If this is how God clothes grass in the field—which is here today and gone tomorrow, thrown in an oven—won't he much more clothe you? What little trust you have! So don't be anxious, asking, 'What will we eat?,' 'What will we drink?' or 'How will we be clothed?' For it is the pagans who set their hearts on all these things. Your heavenly Father knows you need them all. But seek first his Kingdom and his righteousness, and all these things will be given to you as well. Don't worry about tomorrow—tomorrow will worry about itself! Today has enough tsuris already!

John 5:24

Yes, indeed! I tell you that whoever hears what I am saying and trusts the One who sent me has eternal life—that is, he will not come up for judgment but has already crossed over from death to life!

John 14:1

Don't let yourselves be disturbed. Trust in God and trust in me.

338

Romans 5:1-2

So, since we have come to be considered righteous by God because of our trust, let us continue to have shalom with God through our Lord, Yeshua the Messiah. Also through him and on the ground of our trust, we have gained access to this grace in which we stand; so let us boast about the hope of experiencing God's glory.

Supportive Scriptures—Trusting God in the Sabbatical Year

Proverbs 11:24-25
Matthew 6:25-34
Luke 12:22-32
2 Corinthians 9:10-12

Supportive Scriptures—Trusting God in the Jubilee Year

Isaiah 61:1-2
Proverbs 11:24-25
Matthew 6:25-34
Luke 12:22-32

Supportive Scriptures—Trusting God by Resting on the Weekly and Annual Sabbaths

Mark 2:27
Hebrews 4:9

Supportive Scriptures—Having Faith in God and Trusting Him at All Other Times

2 Samuel 22:31-33
Isaiah 12:2, 26:3-4, 43:2
Jeremiah 17:7-8
Nahum 1:7
Psalms 4:6(5), 7:2(1), 9:9(8)-11(10), 18 30(29),
    20:8(7), 27:5, 32:10, 37:3-6, 40:2(1)-18(17),
    46:2(1), 56:3(2)-12(11), 71:5-6, 91:1-7,
    112:7, 121:2-8, 143:8-9, 145:18-20
Proverbs 30:5
Job 13:15
Daniel 3:16-18
2 Chronicles 20:20
Matthew 8:23-26

Mark 10:46-52, 11:20-22, 16:16
Luke 12:4-7
John 3:16-18, 6:35, 47, 11:25-26, 40
Romans 3:28-30, 4:4-5, 10:8-13, 15:13
2 Corinthians 5:5-7
Galatians 2:15-16, 3:5-14, 21-26
Ephesians 2:8
Philippians 3:8-9
1 Timothy 4:9-10
Hebrews 11:1-34
James 1:2-8
1 Peter 1:8-9
1 John 3:21-23, 4:16, 5:3-5, 13-14

Commentary

This *Mitzvah* commands us to have faith in God and trust Him for all things. Faith and trust are at the very heart of our relationship with God, so it is no wonder that there are so many Scriptures in the Bible that speak to it. Many Scriptures address it directly, and it is also built into the Jewish life experience through the *Sh'mitah,* the Year of Jubilee, and the various Sabbaths that require that we rest ourselves and/or our land, cancel debts, and return our land to its original owners every fifty years. All of these require that we put ourselves in God's hands and trust Him to provide for us and protect us.

Scripturally, there is no difference between faith and trust as we may see from the following two translations of Hebrews 11:1:

CJB: *"Trusting is being confident of what we hope for, convinced about things we do not see."*
NKJ: *"Now faith is the substance of things hoped for, the evidence of things not seen."*

This connection of trust and faith to our not seeing is vitally important. When we exercise faith, it is not only that we do not see God; that is always the case. It is that we do not see or understand the circumstance or the issue for which we trust Him, and we must therefore make ourselves vulnerable to Him and rely solely on Him. The extent to which we do that betrays how discipled we are. If we are new in the Lord, we likely give ourselves over to Him periodically and on a case by case basis. The ideal, however, is that our walk with God is one of continuous reliance and continuous trust as it appears was the case with Enoch in Genesis 5:24:

"Hanokh [Enoch] walked with God, and then he wasn't there, because God took him."

Classical Commentators

Despite the plethora of Scriptures on trust and faith, Maimonides, Meir and HaChinuch did not construct any *mitzvot* specifically on the subject. Nevertheless, Maimonides separately wrote his famous "Thirteen Basic Principles of Faith" that list what we are to believe about God apart from our having natural evidence:

1. God exists.
2. God is one.
3. God is incorporeal.
4. God is eternal.
5. Only God may be worshipped.
6. Prophets exist who hear God's voice.
7. Moses was the chief of the prophets.
8. The entire *Torah* was given to Moses from heaven.
9. The *Torah* is perfect and we must therefore not add nor subtract from it.
10. God is omniscient.

11. God rewards and punishes.

12. The Messiah will come, and we should not try to predict when

13. There is a resurrection from the dead

NCLA: JMm JFm KMm KFm GMm GFm

G13. Dedicating Ourselves to God.

We are to dedicate ourselves to God through Messiah.

This precept is derived from His Word (blessed be He):

Key Scriptures

Nazirite Dedication

Numbers 6:1-3 (Maimonides RN202-204; Chinuch C368-370)
ADONAI said to Moshe, "Tell the people of Isra'el, 'When either a man or a woman makes a special kind of vow, the vow of a nazir, consecrating himself to ADONAI; he is to abstain from wine and other intoxicating liquor, he is not to drink vinegar from either source, he is not to drink grape juice, and he is not to eat grapes or raisins."

Numbers 6:4 (Maimonides RN205-206; Chinuch C371-372)
As long as he remains a nazir he is to eat nothing derived from the grapevine, not even the grape-skins or the seeds.

Numbers 6:5 (Maimonides RP92, RN209; Chinuch C373-374)
Throughout the period of his vow as a nazir, he is not to shave his head. Until the end of the time for which he has consecrated himself to ADONAI he is to be holy: he is to let the hair on his head grow long.

Numbers 6:6-8 (Maimonides RP93, RN207-208; Chinuch C375-376)
Throughout the period for which he has consecrated himself to ADONAI, he is not to approach a corpse. He is not to make himself unclean for his father, mother, brother or sister when they die, since his consecration to God is on his head. Throughout the time of his being a nazir he is holy for ADONAI.

Numbers 6:9-15 (Maimonides RP93; Chinuch C377)
If someone next to him dies very suddenly, so that he defiles his consecrated head, then he is to shave his head on the day of his purification; he is to shave it on the seventh day. On the eighth day he is to bring two doves or two young pigeons to the cohen at the entrance to the tent of meeting. The cohen is to prepare one as a sin offering and the other as a burnt offering and thus make atonement for him, inasmuch as he sinned because of the dead person. That same day he is to re-consecrate his head; he is to consecrate to ADONAI the full period of his being a nazir by bringing a male lamb in its first year as a guilt offering. The previous days will not be counted, because his consecration became defiled. 'This is the law for the nazir when his period of consecration is over: he is to be brought to the entrance of the tent of meeting, where he will present his offering to ADONAI—one male lamb in its first year without defect as a burnt offering, one female lamb in its first year without defect as a sin offering, one ram without defect

as peace offerings, a basket of matzah, loaves made of fine flour mixed with olive oil, unleavened wafers spread with olive oil, their grain offering and their drink offerings.

<u>Numbers 6:16-18</u> (Chinuch C377)
The cohen is to bring them before ADONAI, offer his sin offering, his burnt offering, and his ram as a sacrifice of peace offerings to ADONAI, with the basket of matzah. The cohen will also offer the grain offering and drink offering that go with the peace offering. The nazir will shave his consecrated head at the entrance to the tent of meeting, take the hair removed from his consecrated head and put it on the fire under the sacrifice of peace offerings.

<u>Numbers 6:19-21</u>
When the ram has been boiled, the cohen is to take its shoulder, one loaf of matzah from the basket and one unleavened wafer, and place them in the hands of the nazir, after he has shaved his consecrated head. The cohen is to wave them as a wave offering before ADONAI; this is set aside for the cohen, along with the breast for waving and the raised-up thigh. Following that, the nazir may drink wine. This is the law for the nazir who makes a vow and for his offering to ADONAI for his being a nazir—in addition to anything more for which he has sufficient means. In keeping with whatever vow he makes, he must do it according to the law for the nazir.

<u>Numbers 8:5-7</u> (Maimonides RP93; Chinuch C377)[118]
ADONAI said to Moshe, "Take the L'vi'im from among the people of Isra'el and cleanse them. Here is how you are to cleanse them: sprinkle the purification water on them, have them shave their whole body with a razor, and have them wash their clothes and cleanse themselves.

<u>Acts 18:18</u>
Sha'ul remained for some time, then said good-bye to the brothers and sailed off to Syria, after having his hair cut short in Cenchrea, because he had taken a vow; with him were Priscilla and Aquila.

Non-Nazirite and New Covenant Dedication

<u>Joshua 3:5</u>
Y'hoshua said to the people, "Consecrate yourselves, because tomorrow ADONAI is going to work wonders among you.

<u>Matthew 16:24</u>
Then Yeshua told his talmidim, "If anyone wants to come after me, let him say 'No' to himself, take up his execution-stake, and keep following me. (see also, <u>Mark 8:34</u>; <u>Luke 9:23</u>)

<u>2 Corinthians 6:17-18</u>
Therefore ADONAI says, " 'Go out from their midst; separate yourselves; don't even touch what is unclean. Then I myself will receive you. In fact, I will be your Father, and you will be my sons and daughters.' says ADONAI-Tzva'ot."

---

118 The text does not mention anything connected to the Nazirite dedication but it is referred to by Maimonides in his RP93 *mitzvah* that requires the Nazirite to shave his head upon completion of his vow.

<u>1 Peter 2:5</u>
...you yourselves, as living stones, are being built into a spiritual house to be cohanim set apart for God to offer spiritual sacrifices acceptable to him through Yeshua the Messiah.

Supportive Scriptures—Non-Nazirite Dedications

Romans 6:19, 10:8, 12:1, 13:14
2 Corinthians 8:5
Ephesians 5:18
Philippians 2:9-11
Colossians 3:17

Supportive Scriptures—Samson Dedicated to God as a Nazirite from Birth

Judges 13:1-25

Supportive Scripture—Samuel Dedicated to God as a Nazirite from Birth[119]

1 Samuel 1:10-28

Supportive Scriptures—Abraham and His Descendants (Israel) Dedicated to God

Genesis 17:9-14
Exodus 13:1-2, 19:4-6, 28:1
Numbers 3:9-13, 45
Deuteronomy 7:6-8
Isaiah 61:6a
Romans 3:1-2

Supportive Scriptures—The Body of Believers in Yeshua Dedicated to God through Their Faith

Isaiah 66:16-23
1 Peter 2:9-10
Revelation 1:4-6, 5:9-10, 20:6

Commentary

God has always required that mankind worship and obey Him, which is a form of dedication. Nevertheless, from very early times, God chose certain men to dedicate[120] their lives to Him in a special way. Sometimes God imposed it on them and sometimes it was voluntary. Sometimes they were referred to as priests, but not always. Let's start with God's covenant with Abraham. The Scriptures show that there was a voluntary relationship between Abraham and God, but there came a time when God gave Abraham a covenant that was not voluntary on Abraham's part. The

---

119 Whether Samuel was a Nazirite is controversial among scholars.
120 "Dedicate" and "Consecrate" are interchangeable.

covenant had several components to it, but the bottom line was that Abraham and his descendants were to be dedicated to God for special service. We know this because, by the time of Moses, God was referring to the children of Israel (Israelites) as a *"kingdom of cohanim for me, a nation set apart"* (Exodus 19:6). But God went further than that, and commanded that the firstborn of every Israelite and every animal within the camp of Israel must be dedicated to His service:

> Exodus 13:1-2: *"ADONAI said to Moshe, "Set aside for me all the firstborn. Whatever is first from the womb among the people of Isra'el, both of humans and of animals, belongs to me."*

Then God reversed Himself. He ordered that all the firstborn of the Israelites be redeemed from their service, and that Aaron and his sons (from the tribe of Levi) be dedicated to His service instead:

> Numbers 3:10a: *"You are to appoint Aharon and his sons to carry out the duties of cohanim;"*

And He dedicated the rest of the Levites to serve Aaron and his sons in carrying out their priestly functions:

> Numbers 3:9: *"Assign the L'vi'im to Aharon and his sons; their one responsibility in regard to the people of Isra'el is to serve him."*

> Numbers 3:11-12: *"ADONAI said to Moshe, "I have taken the L'vi'im from among the people of Isra'el in lieu of every firstborn male that is first from the womb among the people of Isra'el; the L'vi'im are to be mine."*

All of the dedications referred to up to now were imposed dedications; they were not voluntary. But there came a time when God allowed a very special kind of dedication that could be either imposed or volunteered for, and those who were so dedicated were called "Nazirites." The voluntary Nazirite vow of dedication was normally for a specified season, after which the person who took the vow was released. The law of the Nazirite is partially as follows:

> Numbers 6:2-8: *"Tell the people of Isra'el, 'When either a man or a woman makes a special kind of vow, the vow of a nazir, consecrating himself to ADONAI; he is to abstain from wine and other intoxicating liquor, he is not to drink vinegar from either source, he is not to drink grape juice, and he is not to eat grapes or raisins. As long as he remains a nazir he is to eat nothing derived from the grapevine, not even the grape-skins or the seeds. Throughout the period of his vow as a nazir, he is not to shave his head. Until the end of the time for which he has consecrated himself to ADONAI he is to be holy: he is to let the hair on his head grow long. Throughout the period for which he has consecrated himself to ADONAI, he is not to approach a corpse. He is not to make himself unclean for his father, mother, brother or sister when they die, since his consecration to God is on his head. Throughout the time of his being a nazir he is holy for ADONAI."*

Because there are other requirements for the Nazirite that require the Temple and the Levitical priests, it is not possible to become a Nazirite today and, by the grace of God it is not needed any longer. The reason it is not needed is that today, our vow of dedication to Yeshua as Lord of our lives is the New Covenant equivalent of the Nazirite vow and more:

Romans 10:8 and 12:1 *"that if you acknowledge publicly with your mouth that Yeshua is Lord and trust in your heart that God raised him from the dead, you will be delivered."* … *"I exhort you, therefore, brothers, in view of God's mercies, to offer yourselves as a sacrifice, living and set apart for God. This will please him; it is the logical "Temple worship" for you."*

In the New Covenant, this new way of dedicating ourselves to God is available to everyone and required of everyone.

Commentary by Daniel C. Juster

Notwithstanding the Nazirite vow's obsolescence, we do occasionally find people who believe that God is asking them to give themselves to Him for a period of special consecration, prayer or other purpose. Sometimes they believe that they are led, as part of that, to emulate the Nazirite vow by giving up wine and other foods such as meat, and to a time of partial liquid (e.g. water) fasting. If done with balance, there should be no objection to special seasons of dedication done in that way.

Classical Commentators

Maimonides and HaChinuch wrote several *mitzvot* pertaining to Nazirite vows but wrote none pertaining to any other kind of personal dedication to God. Meir did not address Nazirite vows or matters of dedication at all.

NCLA: JMm JFm KMm KFm GMm GFm

G14. Knowing God by Observing His Creation.

We are to know that God exists and Who God is by observing His creation.

This precept is derived from His Word (blessed be He):

Key Scripture

Romans 1:18-32
What is revealed is God's anger from heaven against all the godlessness and wickedness of people who in their wickedness keep suppressing the truth; because what is known about God is plain to them, since God has made it plain to them. For ever since the creation of the universe his invisible qualities—both his eternal power and his divine nature—have been clearly seen, because they can be understood from what he has made. Therefore, they have no excuse; because, although they know who God is, they do not glorify him as God or thank him. On the contrary, they have become futile in their thinking; and their undiscerning hearts have become darkened. Claiming to be wise, they have become fools! In fact, they have exchanged the glory of the immortal God for mere images, like a mortal human being, or like birds, animals or reptiles! This is why God has given them up to the vileness of their hearts' lusts, to the shameful misuse of each other's bodies. They have exchanged the truth of God for falsehood, by worshipping and serving created things, rather than the Creator—praised be he forever. Amen. This is why God has given them up to degrading passions; so that their women exchange natural sexual relations for unnatural; and likewise the men, giving up natural relations with the opposite sex, burn with passion for one another, men committing shameful acts with other men and receiving in their own persons the penalty appropriate to their perversion. In other words, since they have not considered God worth knowing, God has given them up to worthless ways of thinking; so that they do improper things. They are filled with every kind of wickedness, evil, greed and vice; stuffed with jealousy, murder, quarrelling, dishonesty and ill-will; they are gossips, slanderers, haters of God; they are insolent, arrogant and boastful; they plan evil schemes; they disobey their parents; they are brainless, faithless, heartless and ruthless. They know well enough God's righteous decree that people who do such things deserve to die; yet not only do they keep doing them, but they applaud others who do the same.

Supportive Scriptures—God is Good.

Nahum 1:7
Psalms 25:8-9, 86:5, 100:5, 106:1, 119:68
Matthew 19:17b
Luke 18:19

Supportive Scriptures—God Saw That His Creation was Good.

Genesis 1:1
1 Timothy 4:4-5
James 1:17-18

Commentary

Romans 1:19-20 says that godless and wicked people are without excuse for not knowing God because God's qualities (His eternal power and divine nature) are clearly seen in "what He has made." What He has made is another way of saying His creation. I am assuming that no one reading this *Mitzvah* is in the category of being godless and wicked or he would not very likely be reading it, so I will address my following remarks to those who are not yet convinced about God's existence, and to the rest of us who already know Him, want more of Him, and aspire to His virtues.

Since what can be known about God (His existence and His nature) are there for all to see by observing His creation, then we are remiss if we do not seek to observe His creation at every opportunity. But how can Romans 1:19-20 make such a sweeping statement—that everyone, everywhere, can know about God merely by observing His creation? If we were to point to some item of God's creation and ask a typical unbeliever to explain how it could have come about without God, he would very likely respond with the Darwinism he had been taught—that it came about from organic compounds in the oceans that combined and, through natural selection, evolved to its present state. Now to me, the logic of that happening is so implausible as to defy imagination, but not to a person who has been taught that, and that has not yet had a personal encounter with God.

I would fare no better were I to show the unbeliever what the Bible says about God because unbelievers do not believe the Bible either. Now the negative picture I have painted does not mean that I should not try, because (1) it is my obligation under the instruction of Matthew 28:16-20, and (2) the Holy Spirit might anoint my words and make Himself known to the unbeliever at that moment or thereafter, and that, of course, will make all the difference. But whether I see it happen or not, I have an obligation to bring the truth of God (including the salvation brought by Yeshua) to the unbeliever at every opportunity. Although I cannot predict when God will come to him, I can nevertheless bring him face-to-face with God through speaking the words of Scripture, and through an effective presentation of God's creation.

But what is an effective presentation? I previously hypothesized an unbeliever who rejected the idea of God's existence even after I showed him something of God's creation and challenged him to explain by logic how it could have come about without God. So, that is not the approach I recommend. The approach I recommend is to show Him God's creation in nature, and draw his attention to its goodness and beauty. Ask him: "Do you see beauty in this tree?" "Do you see beauty in this other tree?" "Do you see beauty in all of these trees?" How come? They are all shaped differently, yet they are all picture-beautiful, and there is nothing about their beauty that has anything to do with their survivability. The unbeliever will admit to seeing beauty in the trees I show him because we, being part of God's creation and having been made in His image, have an instinctive understanding of goodness and beauty. There is no logic to it and there is no usefulness to it. Trees would be just as functional in adding oxygen to the environment, just as useful to nesting birds, and just as survivable in a forest crowded by other trees, if they were ugly instead of beautiful. Darwin's theory of evolution through natural selection does not explain why the natural world is filled with beauty, and the truth of that will not be lost on the unbeliever.

But we ought not to consider this *Mitzvah* to be only for the unbeliever, because the rest of us (who already know Him) want to (and have a need to) regularly encounter Him, and one of the ways is to observe and contemplate what He has made—His creation, that God Himself said was very good.

You have no doubt noticed that, in speaking of God's creation, I have associated goodness with beauty, and have shown you how relying on the beauty of God's creation can impress an unbeliever and bring him to the place of considering the existence of God and Messiah. Genesis 1:1-31 says that God saw, on five of the six days of creation, that what He had made was "good," and the Hebrew words used for "good" in all five are *"ki-tov."* Now although *"tov"* is very often translated as "good," it is not the only possibility and, in fact the word (and concept of) "good" is quite hard to define. What, for example comprises that which is good? The way something looks? The way it feels? The way it tastes? The way it works? When we consult the prestigious "Brown-Driver-Briggs-Gesenius Hebrew Lexicon"[121] for the definition of *"tov,"* we get all of these possibilities: (1) good; (2) pleasing; (3) delightful; (4) delicious; sweet or savory; (5) pure and clean; (6) cheerful; (7) happy; (8) glad; (9) joyful; (10) kind; (11) acceptable; (12) vigorous; (13) excellent; (14) fair; and (15) beautiful. It is this last definition—"beautiful"—that I suggest is a better translation of *"tov"* in Genesis 1:1-31, because then the verses of Genesis read:

On day 1 God created light, and *"God saw that the light was beautiful."*

On day 2 God separated sky from water, and on day 3 He created land, the seas, grass, plants, fruit trees and seed-bearing fruit, and *"God saw that it was beautiful."*

On day 4 God created day and night, seasons, days, years, the sun, the moon and the stars, and *"God saw that it was beautiful."*

On day 5 God created swimming creatures, birds, sea creatures and creeping creatures, all of which could reproduce, and *"God saw that it was beautiful."*

On day 6 God created other living creatures, livestock, crawling animals, wild beasts, and man, and *"God saw that it was beautiful."*

Finally, at the end of day 6, just before He rested on the *Shabbat, "God saw everything that he had made, and indeed it was very beautiful."*

Now perhaps you are thinking that substituting "beautiful" for "good" as a translation of *"tov"* is forcing the translation in order to suit the purposes of this *Mitzvah.* Not so! Here are three occurrences in Genesis where a derivative of *"tov"* is translated as "beautiful" or "attractive" in the NKJ, NIV, NAS, and yes, even in the Jewish Publication Society's TNK![122] In the CJB:

---

121 "New Brown-Driver-Briggs-Gesenius Hebrew and English Lexicon of the Old Testament," pp. 373-376, (Peabody, Mass: Hendrickson Publishers 1979).

122 1985 JPS *Tanakh.*

Genesis 6:2: *"...the sons of God saw that the daughters of men were attractive;"* The Hebrew word used for "attractive" is *"ki-tovat."*

Genesis 24:16: *"The girl was very beautiful,"* The Hebrew word used for "beautiful" is *"tovat."*

Genesis 26:7: *"After all, she is a beautiful woman."* The Hebrew word used for "beautiful" is *"ki-tovat."*

It is similar in many other Scriptures; for example, in Esther 1:11, the word for "beautiful" is *"ki-tovat."* In Daniel 1:4, it is *"v'tovei,"* in 1 Samuel 9:2 its first occurrence is *"v'tov,"* further in the verse it is *"tov,"* and in 2 Samuel 11:2 the Hebrew word is *"tovat."* All are variations of *"tov,"* and all are translated "beautiful." If we use it in Psalms 106:1, we get:

Give thanks to ADONAI; for he is beautiful, for his grace continues forever.

Not bad—in fact, beautiful!

Classical Commentators

This *Mitzvah* is not addressed by any of the classical commentators.

NCLA: JMm JFm KMm KFm GMm GFm

G15. Blaspheming God vs. Receiving Messiah and the Holy Spirit.

We are not to blaspheme God; instead we are to receive Him via Messiah and the Holy Spirit.

This precept is derived from His Word (blessed be He):

Key Scriptures

Cursing God

Exodus 22:27(28) (Maimonides RN60)
You are not to curse God, and you are not to curse a leader of your people.

Leviticus 24:14-15 (Maimonides RN60; Chinuch C70)
Take the man who cursed [God] outside the camp, have everyone who heard him lay their hands on his head, and have the entire community stone him. Then tell the people of Isra'el, 'Whoever curses his God will bear the consequences of his sin...

Blaspheming God

Leviticus 24:16
...and whoever blasphemes the name of ADONAI must be put to death; the entire community must stone him. The foreigner as well as the citizen is to be put to death if he blasphemes the Name.

1Timothy 1:12-13
...and I thank the one who has given me strength, the Messiah Yeshua, our Lord, that he considered me trustworthy enough to put me in his service, even though I used to be a man who blasphemed and persecuted and was arrogant! But I received mercy because I had acted in unbelief, not understanding what I was doing.

Revelation 13:4-6
They worshipped the dragon, because he had given his authority to the beast; and they worshipped the beast, saying, "Who is like the beast? Who can fight against it?" It was given a mouth speaking arrogant blasphemies; and it was given authority to act for forty-two months. So it opened its mouth in blasphemies against God to insult his name and his Sh'khinah, and those living in heaven...

Blaspheming, Cursing, or Opposing the Holy Spirit

Matthew 12:30-32
Those who are not with me are against me, and those who do not gather with me are scattering. Because of this, I tell you that people will be forgiven any sin and blasphemy, but blaspheming the Ruach HaKodesh will not be forgiven. One can say something against the Son of Man and

be forgiven; but whoever keeps on speaking against the Ruach HaKodesh will never be forgiven, neither in the 'olam hazeh nor in the 'olam haba.

<u>Mark 3:28-30</u>
Yes! I tell you that people will be forgiven all sins and whatever blasphemies they utter; however, someone who blasphemes against the Ruach HaKodesh never has forgiveness but is guilty of an eternal sin. For they had been saying, "He has an unclean spirit in him.

<u>Luke 12:8-10</u>
Moreover, I tell you, whoever acknowledges me in the presence of others, the Son of Man will also acknowledge in the presence of God's angels. But whoever disowns me before others will be disowned before God's angels. Also, everyone who says something against the Son of Man will have it forgiven him; but whoever has blasphemed the Ruach HaKodesh will not be forgiven.

Receiving Yeshua and His Ministry

<u>John 1:1-14</u>
In the beginning was the Word, and the Word was with God, and the Word was God. He was with God in the beginning. All things came to be through him, and without him nothing made had being. In him was life, and the life was the light of mankind. The light shines in the darkness, and the darkness has not suppressed it. There was a man sent from God whose name was Yochanan. He came to be a testimony, to bear witness concerning the light; so that through him, everyone might put his trust in God and be faithful to him. He himself was not that light; no, he came to bear witness concerning the light. This was the true light, which gives light to everyone entering the world. He was in the world—the world came to be through him—yet the world did not know him. He came to his own homeland, yet his own people did not receive him.

But to as many as did receive him, to those who put their trust in his person and power, he gave the right to become children of God, not because of bloodline, physical impulse or human intention, but because of God. The Word became a human being and lived with us, and we saw his Sh'khinah, the Sh'khinah of the Father's only Son, full of grace and truth.

<u>John 3:14-16</u>
Just as Moshe lifted up the serpent in the desert, so must the Son of Man be lifted up; so that everyone who trusts in him may have eternal life. For God so loved the world that he gave his only and unique Son, so that everyone who trusts in him may have eternal life, instead of being utterly destroyed.

<u>John 3:36</u>
Whoever trusts in the Son has eternal life. But whoever disobeys the Son will not see that life but remains subject to God's wrath.

<u>John 14:6</u>
Yeshua said, "I AM the Way—and the Truth and the Life; no one comes to the Father except through me.

Acts 4:12
There is salvation in no one else! For there is no other name under heaven given to mankind by whom we must be saved!

Acts 16:30-31
Then, leading them outside, he [the jailer] said, "Men, what must I do to be saved?" They said, "Trust in the Lord Yeshua, and you will be saved—you and your household!"

2 Corinthians 5:17-19
Therefore, if anyone is united with the Messiah, he is a new creation—the old has passed; look, what has come is fresh and new! And it is all from God, who through the Messiah has reconciled us to himself and has given us the work of that reconciliation, which is that God in the Messiah was reconciling mankind to himself, not counting their sins against them, and entrusting to us the message of reconciliation.

1 John 2:23-25
Everyone who denies the Son is also without the Father, but the person who acknowledges the Son has the Father as well. Let what you heard from the beginning remain in you. If what you heard from the beginning remains in you, you will also remain in union with both the Son and the Father. And this is what he has promised us: eternal life.

Receiving the Holy Spirit

Joel 3:1(2:28)-2(2:29)
After this, I will pour out my Spirit on all humanity. Your sons and daughters will prophesy, your old men will dream dreams, your young men will see visions; and also on male and female slaves in those days I will pour out my Spirit.

John 7:39
(Now he said this about the Spirit, whom those who trusted in him were to receive later—the Spirit had not yet been given, because Yeshua had not yet been glorified.)

John 14:16-17
..and I will ask the Father, and he will give you another comforting Counselor like me, the Spirit of Truth, to be with you forever. The world cannot receive him, because it neither sees nor knows him. You know him, because he is staying with you and will be united with you.

John 20:21-22
"Shalom aleikhem!" Yeshua repeated. "Just as the Father sent me, I myself am also sending you." Having said this, he breathed on them and said to them, "Receive the Ruach HaKodesh!

Acts 2:1-4
The festival of Shavu'ot arrived, and the believers all gathered together in one place. Suddenly there came a sound from the sky like the roar of a violent wind, and it filled the whole house where they were sitting. Then they saw what looked like tongues of fire, which separated and

came to rest on each one of them. They were all filled with the Ruach HaKodesh and began to talk in different languages, as the Spirit enabled them to speak.

Supportive Scriptures—Cursing God

Revelation 16:9-11, 1-21

Supportive Scriptures—Blaspheming God

Isaiah 37:23, 52:5, 65:6-7
Ezekiel 20:27
Hosea 7:13-14
Malachi 3:13-14
Psalms 139:19-20
Romans 2:23-24

Supportive Scriptures—More Examples of Speaking Against God

Isaiah 40:27
Jeremiah 4:10, 20:7-8
Ezekiel 8:12, 9:9, 18:25, 33:17
Psalms 10:13, 73:9-11. 78:19, 94:6-7
Job 15:13, 25-26, 19:6-7, 21:14, 22:12-14, 17; 30:21, 34:5-9, 35-37

Supportive Scriptures—Blaspheming, Cursing or Opposing the Holy Spirit

Acts 7:51

Supportive Scriptures—Yeshua Accused of Blasphemy

Matthew 26:62-66
Mark 2:1-7
John 10:31-33

Supportive Scriptures—Receiving Yeshua and His Ministry

Isaiah 53:4-8
Matthew 7:21-23, 16:16
Mark 1:8, 2:28, 16:15-16
Luke 1:32-33, 24:45-47, 49
John 1:33, 3:3-8, 5:24-30, 6:44-45, 14:12-27
Acts 1:6-8, 2:16-21, 38, 8:12, 35-38, 10:47-48, 11:15-18
Romans 5:1-2, 8, 6:3-8, 22-23, 8:3-4, 10:8-13
Galatians 2:15-16, 3:26-28
Ephesians 1:13, 2:8-9, 3:14-17

Colossians 2:6-7, 11-13
1 Thessalonians 5:23
2 Timothy 1:8-10
Titus 3:4-5
Hebrews 4:15
1 Peter 1:3-4, 3:21-22
Revelation 20:4

Supportive Scriptures—Receiving the Holy Spirit

Judges 3:9-10
Luke 11:13, 24:49
John 3:5-8, 14:25-26
Acts 1:8, 4:31, 8:38a-39, 10:44, 47-48, 11:15-18, 15:7-9

Supportive Scriptures—Ministry and Gifts of the Holy Spirit

Judges 3:9-10
Joel 3:1(2:28)-2(2:29)
Micah 3:8
Mark 16:17-18
Luke 24:49
John 3:5-6, 14:25-26
Acts 1:8
Acts 2:1-4, 4:31, 10:45-46, 19:6
Romans 5:4-5, 8:1-2, 5-6, 26-27, 12:6-8
1 Corinthians 12:3, 7-11, 14:1-3
Ephesians 1:13, 3:14-16, 6:17-18
Titus 3:4-5
1 Peter 4:10-11
Jude 1:20

Supportive Scriptures—Baptism and Filling of the Holy Spirit

Matthew 3:11, 28:19
Mark 1:8
Luke 3:16
Acts 1:5, 8, 2:1-4, 38, 4:8, 31, 7:55, 11:15-18, 13:9, 19:6
1 Corinthians 12:13
Ephesians 5:18

Commentary

Blasphemy is communicating disrespect for something that is sacred or someone who is holy. Among believers, we often hear doctrinal statements espoused as though they have nothing or little to do with each other. For example:

355

1. Blaspheming God is a forgivable sin, whereas blaspheming the Holy Spirit is an unpardonable sin (Leviticus 24:15-16; Matthew 12:32).

2. If we believe in our heart and confess with our mouth that Yeshua was raised from the dead we will be saved (Romans 10:8-9).

3. It is necessary that we receive the Holy Spirit in order to receive power and spiritual gifts from on high (Acts 1:8; 1 Corinthians 14:1).

These sayings are correct, but have we sufficiently considered how they are related to each other, and why they are correct in view of their raising perplexing questions? For example, statement #1 raises the question: "Why is blaspheming the Holy Spirit unforgivable, whereas blaspheming Yeshua or the Father forgivable?" And as to statement #2: "What is special about believing in Yeshua as compared to God the Father and the Holy Spirit? Is it not sufficient to believe in God broadly? After all, there are those in the world that have never heard of Yeshua." And a question that may arise regarding statement #3 is: "Why does God single out the Holy Spirit as the conveyer of His power and gifts? Can we not receive God's power and gifts directly from the Father and Yeshua without the Holy Spirit's intervention?"

The answers to these questions become clearer when we stop thinking of biblical doctrines such as these as standing on their own, and begin to appreciate them as interrelated. As a matter of fact, despite the prominence given in some quarter to sayings #1, #2, and #3, none of them are primary. What is primary and the umbrella for all of them is what is known as the "*Sh'ma*"—Deuteronomy 6:4-6 as explained by Yeshua in Matthew 22:34-40:

> "*...but when the P'rushim learned that he had silenced the Tz'dukim, they got together, and one of them who was a Torah expert asked a sh'eilah to trap him: "Rabbi, which of the mitzvot in the Torah is the most important?' He told him, 'You are to love ADONAI your God with all your heart and with all your soul and with all your strength.' This is the greatest and most important mitzvah. And a second is similar to it, You are to love your neighbor as yourself. All of the Torah and the Prophets are dependent on these two mitzvot.'*"

We cannot love God with all of our heart, soul and strength unless we know Him intimately, and we cannot know Him intimately unless God reveals Yeshua to us through the Holy Spirit (John 6:44). We cannot know Him by our own knowledge and virtue—even by the Words of Scripture if the Holy Spirit does not first soften our hearts and give us understanding (Ephesians 2:8-9). Then, once God and His nature are revealed to us, we have the choice of whether or not to receive Him. If we do, the Holy Spirit takes up residence in us, we are given a new spirit, our hearts become softened, and we become open to more of God. If we do not, we keep our old spirit, our hearts become hardened, and God becomes more distant to us over time.

But you say: "How do sayings #1, #2, and #3 fit into this? What about #1 for example? What about trusting in Yeshua to be saved?" Consider the totality of what John 3:14-18 says:

> "*Just as Moshe lifted up the serpent in the desert, so must the Son of Man be lifted up; so that everyone who trusts in him may have eternal life. For God so loved the world that he gave his only*

and unique Son, so that everyone who trusts in him [some translations say "believes in Him"] *may have eternal life, instead of being utterly destroyed. For God did not send the Son into the world to judge the world, but rather so that through him, the world might be saved. Those who trust in him are not judged; those who do not trust have been judged already, in that they have not trusted in the one who is God's only and unique Son."*

For anyone to believe and trust in Yeshua we must be brought to that belief and trust by the Holy Spirit, i.e. by God Himself who draws us near through the Holy Spirit (John 6:44). Man cannot perceive the invisible God by his natural senses so, without the Holy Spirit, there is no natural way to know Him, and therefore no reason to believe in Him since we (presumably) do not believe what the Bible says of Him either.

So, the Holy Spirit is needed in order for statement #1 above to be true. And the Holy Spirit is likewise needed for statement #2 but, as valuable as receiving power and spiritual gifts are, they are not as primary as knowing God for Who He Is; that knowledge can only be brought to us by the Holy Spirit. As for statement #3, if we blaspheme and therefore reject the Holy Spirit, we cannot be brought to the place of knowing either God the son or God the Father, and we therefore cannot be saved. On the other hand, if we blaspheme the Father or Yeshua (sinful to be sure) but do not reject the Holy Spirit, the Holy Spirit can eventually lead us to repentance and salvation. That is why Scripture refers to blaspheming the Holy Spirit (and not the Father nor the Son) as an eternal sin.[123]

Thus far, I have spoken of receiving Messiah and the Holy Spirit and of their respective ministries, but Scripture also speaks of an "immersion" or "baptism" (Matthew 3:11), and a "filling" (Ephesians 5:18) of the Holy Spirit as well. I believe that they are essentially the same, but perhaps the baptism is an initial filling. Apparently, the Holy Spirit is like a fluid, and we can have more of less of Him depending upon our willingness to receive Him, and our repentant condition. We can have a minimal amount of Him—just enough to bring us to the place of salvation, and we can also be filled with Him, the result being that He can give us spiritual power and spiritual gifts (1 Corinthians 12:8-10). Oppositely, we can lose a portion of the Holy Spirit (drip-by-drip) as a result of sin, and can be re-filled with the Holy Spirit if and when we repent (Ephesians 5:18).

This *Mitzvah* and its accompanying Scriptures clearly show that the triune persons of God work together, and that the Holy Spirit, along with Messiah, is key to our relationship with God and to our salvation.

Classical Commentators

This *Mitzvah* is not addressed by any of the classical commentators.

NCLA: JMm JFm KMm KFm GMm GFm

---

123 I do not believe that Scripture teaches that a momentary blasphemous remark against the Holy Spirit leads to eternal unforgiveness. I believe that Stern translates Matthew 12:32 correctly in saying: "...*but whoever keeps on speaking against the Ruach HaKodesh will never be forgiven...*"

G16. Putting God First.

We are to put God first in our priorities.

This precept is derived from His Word (blessed be He):

Key Scriptures

Exodus 20:3 (Maimonides RN1; Meir MN8; Chinuch C26)
You are to have no other gods before me.

Deuteronomy 6:5
...and you are to love ADONAI your God with all your heart, all your being and all your resources.

Luke 14:26
If anyone comes to me and does not hate his father, his mother, his wife, his children, his brothers and his sisters, yes, and his own life besides, he cannot be my talmid.

Luke 14:33
So every one of you who doesn't renounce all that he has cannot be my talmid.

Acts 5:29
Kefa and the other emissaries answered, "We must obey God, not men.

Colossians 3:23
Whatever work you do, put yourself into it, as those who are serving not merely other people, but the Lord.

Supportive Scriptures

Matthew 6:31-33, 22:35-38
Luke 12:28-31
Romans 12:1
2 Corinthians 8:1-5
Colossians 3:2

Commentary

If we understand that the "gods" in Exodus 20:3 are not only false deities, but rather all persons, matters, and things to which we "bow down" (i.e. put ahead of God and allow to control our lives), we understand how it is the quintessential Scripture that supports this *Mitzvah*. After that, Matthew 6:33 calls us to faith by exhorting us to *"..seek first his Kingdom and his righteousness, and all these things will be given to you as well."* It is telling us that, despite our perceived needs and natural inclination to dwell on them, if we put our attention on God instead of ourselves, He will see to it that our needs are met.

Classical Commentators

Maimonides, Meir, and HaChinuch interpret Exodus 20:3 as referring only to false deities. This *Mitzvah* is not, therefore, addressed by any of the Jewish classical commentators in the broader sense of putting God ahead of all other persons, matters, and things.

NCLA: JMm JFm KMm KFm GMm GFm

G17. Being Continuous, Persistent, and Fervent in Prayer.

We are to be continuous, persistent, and fervent in our prayers of petition.

This precept is derived from His Word (blessed be He):

Key Scriptures

Romans 12:11-12
Don't be lazy when hard work is needed, but serve the Lord with spiritual fervor. Rejoice in your hope, be patient in your troubles, and continue steadfastly in prayer.

Ephesisans 6:18
...as you pray at all times, with all kinds of prayers and requests, in the Spirit, vigilantly and persistently, for all God's people.

1 Thessalonians 5:17
Pray regularly. [NKJ: Pray without ceasing].

James 5:16
Therefore, openly acknowledge your sins to one another, and pray for each other, so that you may be healed. The [NKJ: effective fervent] prayer of a righteous person is powerful and effective.

Supportive Scriptures

Genesis 18: 23-33, 32:25(24)-29(28)
Deuteronomy 9:25-29
Psalms 116:1-2, 119:147
1 Chronicles 16:11
Matthew 7:7-11
Luke 11:9-13, 18:1-7, 22:42-44
Acts 1:13-14, 2:41-42
2 Corinthians 12:7-9

Commentary

The Scriptures that support this *Mitzvah* speak for themselves and, for the most part, require little embellishment. I will, however, comment on one of them that is often misunderstood. In 1 Thessalonians 5:17 (according to many translations) the Apostle Paul exhorts us to:

> *"Pray without ceasing."*

If looked at the Scripture wrongly, it seems impossible to do and still conduct the other affairs of life. Therefore, I believe that Paul is referring, not to formal prayer where we stop everything and speak with God, but rather to the continuous dialogue that believers are able to have with God as we walk with Him (and He with us) throughout the day.

Classical Commentators

This *Mitzvah* is not addressed by any of the classical commentators.

<u>NCLA</u>: JMm JFm KMm KFm GMm GFm

G18. Waiting on God.

We are to be patient and wait for God to act.

This precept is derived from His Word (blessed be He):

Key Scriptures

Micah 7:7
But as for me, I will look to ADONAI, I will wait for the God of my salvation; my God will hear me.

Lamentations 3:25-26
ADONAI is good to those waiting for him, to those who are seeking him out. It is good to wait patiently for the saving help of ADONAI.

Romans 8:25
But if we continue hoping for something we don't see, then we still wait eagerly for it, with perseverance.

James 5:7-8
So, brothers, be patient until the Lord returns. See how the farmer waits for the precious "fruit of the earth"—he is patient over it until it receives the fall and spring rains. You too, be patient; keep up your courage; for the Lord's return is near.

Supportive Scriptures—Waiting on God

Isaiah 30:18, 40:31
Psalms 37:7, 40:2(1)
Acts 1:3-4
Romans 12:12
Galatians : 6:9

Supportive Scriptures—Having Patience

Isaiah 8:17
Habakkuk 2:3
Psalms 25:5, 27:14, 33:20, 37:7-9, 40:2(1), 62:6(5), 69:7(6), 130:5-6
Job 14:14
Ecclesiastes 7:8
Luke 8:15
Romans 2:7, 12:12
1 Corinthians 13:4
2 Corinthians 6:6-7
Galatians 5:22

Ephesians 4:2-3
Colossians 1:11
Colossians 3:12
1 Thessalonians 5:14
Hebrews 6:11-12
Hebrews 6:15
James 5:7-8
Revelations 2:19

Commentary

Waiting on God and having patience are obviously connected. As a matter of fact, according to Galatians 5:22, patience is a fruit of the Spirit. So why is exercising patience to wait on God sufficiently problematic so as to warrant a *mitzvah* devoted to it? It is because natural man's way is to be impatient and to seek immediate gratification, so that when natural man petitions God for something in prayer, he judges whether or not God has answered or will answer his prayer by whether or not he sees immediate results.

This *Mitzvah* calls us to exercise faith for God's timeframe which is not the same as ours; consider the following Scriptures:

2 Peter 3:8-9: *"Moreover, dear friends, do not ignore this: with the Lord, one day is like a thousand years and a thousand years like one day. The Lord is not slow in keeping his promise, as some people think of slowness; on the contrary, he is patient with you; for it is not his purpose that anyone should be destroyed, but that everyone should turn from his sins."*

Ecclesiastes 3:1: *"For everything there is a season, a right time for every intention under heaven-"*

Acts 1:6-7: *"When they [Yeshua and his disciples] were together, they asked him, "Lord, are you at this time going to restore self-rule to Isra'el?" He answered, "You don't need to know the dates or the times; the Father has kept these under his own authority.""*

Waiting on God builds our faith and our dependence on Him, which are good things. Proverbs 3:5-6 expresses it well:

"Trust in ADONAI with all your heart; do not rely on your own understanding. In all your ways acknowledge him; then he will level your paths."

Classical Commentators

This *Mitzvah* is not addressed by any of the classical commentators.

NCLA: JMm JFm KMm KFm GMm GFm

G19. Praying in Faith and Having Faith for That Which We Pray.

We are to pray in faith, and have faith for the things for which we pray.

This precept is derived from His Word (blessed be He):

Key Scriptures

Mark 11:23-24
Yes! I tell you that whoever does not doubt in his heart but trusts that what he says will happen can say to this mountain, 'Go and throw yourself into the sea!' and it will be done for him. Therefore, I tell you, whatever you ask for in prayer, trust that you are receiving it, and it will be yours.

James 1:5-8
Now if any of you lacks wisdom, let him ask God, who gives to all generously and without reproach; and it will be given to him. But let him ask in trust, doubting nothing; for the doubter is like a wave in the sea being tossed and driven by the wind. Indeed that person should not think that he will receive anything from the Lord, because he is double-minded, unstable in all his ways.

James 5:14-16
Is someone among you ill? He should call for the elders of the congregation. They will pray for him and rub olive oil on him in the name of the Lord. The prayer offered with trust will heal the one who is ill—the Lord will restore his health; and if he has committed sins, he will be forgiven. Therefore, openly acknowledge your sins to one another, and pray for each other, so that you may be healed. The prayer of a righteous person is powerful and effective.

Supportive Scriptures

Matthew 9:27-29, 21:18-22
Hebrews 11:1-6

Commentary

First, we should understand that "faith" and "trust" as it applies to God are identical, and merely a translator's choice of words. Some interpret Mark 11:23-24 as assuring us that if we strongly believe for anything, God has obligated Himself to make it happen. But that is not at all what the Scripture says or implies. The Scripture says *"whoever does not doubt in his heart but trusts that what he says will happen..."* There is only one way for us to not doubt in our heart for something, and that is for God to have placed it there. Then, having recognized what God's will is, if we trust Him and speak it, it will happen.

God is not calling us to what is often called "positive confession," because in "positive confession" the presumption is that we have the power to control God and cause Him to do what we want him to do. Do we want a new car? The proponents of positive confession would say that all we must do is believe strongly enough for it and we will have it. No! God is calling us to first discern His will, and then trust Him enough to speak it aloud. If we properly hear God's will and speak it in faith, we can be assured that it will come to pass.

Classical Commentators

This *Mitzvah* is not addressed by any of the classical commentators.

NCLA: JMm JFm KMm KFm GMm GFm

G20. Knowing God and Who He Is.

We are to know God and who He Is.

This precept is derived from His Word (blessed be He):

Key Scriptures

Isaiah 43:10
"You are my witnesses," says ADONAI, "and my servant whom I have chosen, so that you can know and trust me and understand that I am he—no god was produced before me, nor will any be after me.

Jeremiah 31:32(33):33(34) (see also, Hebrews 8:11)
For this is the covenant I will make with the house of Isra'el after those days," says ADONAI: "I will put my Torah within them and write it on their hearts; I will be their God, and they will be my people. No longer will any of them teach his fellow community member or his brother, 'Know ADONAI'; for all will know me, from the least of them to the greatest; because I will forgive their wickednesses and remember their sins no more.

John 17:3
And eternal life is this: to know you, the one true God, and him whom you sent, Yeshua the Messiah.

Galatians 4:8-9
In the past, when you did not know God, you served as slaves beings which in reality are non-gods. But now you do know God, and, more than that, you are known by God. So how is it that you turn back again to those weak and miserable elemental spirits? Do you want to enslave yourselves to them once more?

Supportive Scriptures—Knowing God In General

Jeremiah 9:22(23)-23(24)
Ezekiel 38:16 (God known through Israel's enemy)
Hosea 2:22(20), 6:3, 8:2
Daniel 11:32
1 Chronicles 28:9
1Corinthians 1:21
Philippians 3:10-11
Hebrews 8:11

Supportive Scriptures—Not Knowing God

Isaiah 45:4-5
Jeremiah 2:8, 4:22, 9:5(6)

Hosea 5:4
Job 18:21
Galatians 4:8
1 Thessalonians 4:3-5
2 Thessalonians 1:6-8
Titus 1:16
1 John 4:8

Supportive Scriptures—
Persons that Knew God
(A partial list)

Adam and Eve Knew God
Genesis 3:8-10

Enoch Knew God
Genesis 5:22-24

Noah Knew God
Genesis 6:9

Abraham Knew God
Isaiah 41:8
James 2:23

Moses Knew God
Exodus 33:11, 19-23
Numbers 12:6-8

David Knew God
1 Samuel 13:14
Acts 13:22

Yeshua Knew God
John 5:19-20, 10:30, 14:10-11

Yeshua's disciples Knew God
(The disciples knew God through
knowing Yeshua)
Luke 22:34
John 14:7-9

Supportive Scriptures—
Knowing Who God Is
(A partial list of virtues and
confirming Scriptures)

God Is a blesser of men
Genesis 22:16-18
Exodus 23:25
Numbers 6:23-27
Deuteronomy 7:13-14
Malachi 3:10
Matthew 5:1-11
James 1:12

God Is a Comforter
Isaiah 41:13
Psalms 147:3
John 14:15-16
2 Corinthians 1:3

God Is Compassionate
Exodus 34:6
Isaiah 30:18
Psalms 86:15, 103:13
Nehemiah 9:31
Romans 9:15
2 Corinthians 1:3

God Is a Creator
Genesis 1:27, 2:3
Deuteronomy 32:6
Malachi 2:10
Psalms 124:8
1 Corinthians 8:6

God Is our Deliverer and Savior
Isaiah 33:22, 43:11, 49:26, 60:16
Jeremiah 17:14

Psalms 25:5, 79:9, 103:2-4, 107:19-20
1John 4:14
1 Peter 1:3

God Is an Encourager
Joshua 1:9
John 16:33
Acts 23:11
Romans 15:4-6
2 Corinthians 1:3-5

God Is Eternal
Isaiah 57:15
Psalms 90:1-2, 93:2, 102:13(12)
Lamentations 5:19
Matthew 6:13
1 Timothy 1:17, 6:15-16

God Is Faithful
Deuteronomy 7:9
Isaiah 25:1
Psalms 89:2(1)-3(2)

God Is the Father of Yeshua
Mark 1:10-11
John 1:14, 3:16
Romans 15:5-6
2 Corinthians 1:3
1 Peter 1:3

God Is our Father
Deuteronomy 32:6
Isaiah 64:7(8)
Malachi 2:10
Matthew 23:9
1 Corinthians 8:6
Ephesians 4:5-6

God Is Fearsome
Genesis 31:42
Deuteronomy 6:24
Psalms 103:13, 111:10, 115:12-13, 130:4
Proverbs 1:7
Job 25:2, 28:28
Nehemiah 1:5

God Is a Forgiver of Sin
Micah 7:18-19
Psalms 103:3, 130:4
Daniel 9:9
Matthew 6:14
Mark 11:25
Luke 6:37
Ephesians 1:7-8
Colossians 3:13
1 John 1:9

God Is a Giver of Gifts
Matthew 7:11
Romans 6:23, 12:6-8
Ephesians 2:8
James 1:17

God Is Glorious
Exodus 24:16
Numbers 14:21-23
1 Kings 8:10-11
Isaiah 6:3, 49:3
Ezekiel 9:3, 10:19
Habakkuk 2:14
Psalms 19:2(1), 79:9
Revelation 19:1

God Is God of All
Deuteronomy 4:39
Jeremiah 32:27
Ephesians 4:6

God Is Good
Psalms 25:7-8, 34:9(8), 106:48 (107:1), 119:68, 145:9
Matthew 19:16-17
1 Timothy 4:4
2 Peter 1:3

God Is Gracious
Exodus 34:6
Isaiah 30:19
Psalms 89:2(1)-3(2), 145:17
Romans 1:5, 3:24
Hebrews 4:16

God Is Great
1 Kings 8:41-42
Jeremiah 10:6, 32:18
Ezekiel 38:23
Psalms 86:10, 95:3, 96:4, 104:1, 135:5
Nehemiah 1:5
1 Chronicles 16:25

God Is Our Healer
Exodus 15:26, 23:25
Jeremiah 17:14
Psalms 30:3(2), 103:2-3, 107:19-20
James 5:14-15

God Is our Helper and Counselor
Isaiah 9:5(6), 41:13
Psalms 32:8, 46:2(1), 54:6(4), 124:8
John 14:15-16, 26
Hebrews 13:6

God Is Holy
Exodus 15:11
Leviticus 20:26
1 Samuel 2:2
Isaiah 6:3
Ezekiel 38:23
Psalms 99:2-3
1 Peter 1:16
Revelation 4:8

God Is Immutable
(unchangeable)
Numbers 23:19
1 Samuel 15:29
Malachi 3:6
Psalms 102:27(26)-28(27)
Job 23:13
Hebrews 1:11-12, 6:17
James 1:17

God Is Incomparable
Exodus 15:11
Psalms 89:7(6), 113:5

God Is Invisible
John 1:18
1 Timothy 1:17, 6:15-16
1 John 4:12, 20

God Is Jealous
Exodus 20:4-5, 34:13-14
Nahum 1:2

God Is our Judge
Genesis 18:25
Isaiah 33:22
Jeremiah 9:23(24)
Romans 2:16, 11:33
1 Peter 1:17

God Is Just
Genesis 18:24-25
Isaiah 30:18
Jeremiah 9:23(24)
Psalms 99:4, 140:13(12)
Nehemiah 9:32-33
Romans 2:2
1 Peter 1:17
1 John 1:9

God Is Kind
1 Samuel 20:14
1 Kings 3:5-6
Romans 2:4
Titus 3:4

God Is a Law-Giver
Exodus 13:8-9, 16:4, 24:12
Deuteronomy 4:8
Isaiah 33:22
James 4:12

God Is our Leader
Psalms 5:9(8), 23:2, 25:4-5, 27:11,
    31:4(3), 143:10
Romans 2:4
2 Corinthians 2:14

God Is Lord
Isaiah 42:8, 43:11, 44:24
Jeremiah 9:23(24), 32:27

God Is Love
1 John 4:8, 16

God Is Loving
John 3:16
Romans 5:5, 8
1 John 4:16, 19

God Is Merciful
Exodus 34:6-7
2 Samuel 22:26
Psalms 25:6-7, 86:15, 103:8
Nehemiah 9:31
Romans 9:15-16, 23, 12:1
Ephesians 2:4
Hebrews 4:16
1 Peter 1:3-4

God Is Near
Deuteronomy 4:7
Jeremiah 23:23-24
Acts 17:27-28

God Is Omnipotent
Exodus 15:6
Jeremiah 32:17
Matthew 6:13, 19:26
Mark 14:36
Romans 1:20
1 Corinthians 2:3-5
Ephesians 6:10
Hebrews 1:3
Revelation 19:1

God Is Omnipresent
1 Kings 8:27
Jeremiah 23:23-24
Psalms 139:7-10

God Is Omniscient
(all knowing, wise and seeing)
Ezekiel 11:5

Psalms 139:1-5, 147:5
Job 11:7-11
Act 15:18
Romans 2:16, 11:33
Hebrews 4:13
1 John 3:20

God is One
Deuteronomy 6:4
Mark 12:28-29
John 16: 13-15
1 Corinthians 8:4
Galatians 3:20
1 Timothy 2:5

God Is One with Yeshua
John 10:30, 14:9-11
1 John 4:15

God Is Patient
Isaiah 48:9
Jeremiah 15:15
Romans 2:4
2 Peter 3:9, 3:15

God Is Praiseworthy
Exodus 15:2, 11
Deuteronomy 10:21
Isaiah 25:1, 63:7
Jeremiah 20:13
Psalms 47:7(6), 48:2(1), 68:5(4), 145:3-4
Ephesians 1:5-6

God Is our Protector
Exodus 14:14
Deuteronomy 31:6
Isaiah 54:17
Psalms 3:2(1)-4(3), 18:31(30), 32:7, 118:6,
    119:114, 121:7
Ephesians 6:11

God Is our Provider
Genesis 22:8, 13-14
Psalms 107:9, 147:8
Matthew 6:26, 7:7-11
Acts 14:17

2 Corinthians 9:8-9
Philippians 4:13, 19

God Is Righteous
Jeremiah 9:22(23)-23(24)
Psalms 145:17
Romans 1:32

God Is Self-Existent / Self-Defining
Exodus 3:14
Isaiah 41:4
John 5:26
Revelation 1:8

God Is a Server
Matthew 20:28
John 3:16, 13:3-8
1 Peter 1:18-19

God Is Slow to Anger
Exodus 34:6
Numbers 14:18
Joel 2:13
Psalms 86:15, 103:8, 145:8

God Is Sovereign / King
Exodus 29:46, 31:13, 33:19b
2 Samuel 7:22
Isaiah 33:22, 46:9-11
Psalms 24:10, 47:7(6)-9(8), 59:14(13),
    93:1-2, 115:3
Matthew 10:29
Ephesians 1:11
1 Timothy 6:15-16

God Is a Spirit
Genesis 1:1-2
Zechariah 4:6
John 4:24
Romans 8:26-27
1 John 4:13

God Is a Teacher
Exodus 4:15
Isaiah 2:3, 54:13
Micah 4:2
Psalms 25:8-9, 32:8, 71:17, 119:102, 143:10

God Is Transcendent
(beyond our understanding)
Isaiah 55:8-9
Psalms 139:6
Job 36:26
Ecclesiastes 11:5
Romans 11:33-34
Philippians 4:7

God Is Triune
Genesis 1:26, 3:22, 11:7
2 Samuel 7:28
Isaiah 6:8, 48:16, 61:1
Matthew 3:16-17, 28:19
Mark 1:10-11
2 Corinthians 13:14

God Is Trustworthy
Psalms 9:10(9)-11(10), 13:6(5), 20:8(7),
    31:15(14), 56:4(3)-5(4), 84:13(12)
Proverbs 3:5-6
1 Corinthians 1:9
1 John 1:9

God Is Truthful
Numbers 23:19
Psalms 25:5, 31:5(4), 43:3, 86:11
John 16:13

God Is Vengeful
Deuteronomy 32:35
Ezekiel 25:17
Nahum 1:2
Psalms 94:1
Romans 12:19
Hebrews 10:30

God Is Wise
Isaiah 40:28
Proverbs 3:19
Romans 16:25-27
1 Corinthians 1:23-24
Ephesians 1:7-8
James 3:17

Commentary

Scripture commands us to know God, but we cannot know Him without knowing something about who He is. It is true of humans as well. We can know everything about a person and still not know him because knowing a person requires that there be a relationship; if there is none, then we do not really know him. Scripture exhorts us to know God by having an intimate and personal relationship with Him; for example:

> John 17:3: *"And eternal life is this: to know you, the one true God, and him whom you sent, Yeshua the Messiah."*

> 1 John 4:8: *"Those who do not love do not know God; because God is love."*

Indeed, Scripture tells us that God is our heavenly father; but, do we relate to Him as a father? One test is whether we relate to Him as we do (or should do) our earthly father. We talk to our earthly father. Do we talk to God? We listen when our earthly father speaks. Do we hear God when He talks to us? Ideally, we love our earthly father (and mother) because they gave birth to us and first loved us. God gave birth to us through His creation and 1 John 4:19 says:

> *"We ourselves love now because he loved us first."*

Loving God is foundational to our having a personal relationship with Him, and we cannot love God without knowing Him, and cannot know Him without knowing who He is. How do we know who God (in fact any person) is? We have to spend time with a person to know who he or she is, and it is no less true of God. If this *Mitzvah* causes us to evaluate whether we spend enough time with God to know who God is, then it has done its job.

It is important that we know how to spend time with a God whom we cannot see. First, we can converse with God. If we are a believer, we know that God hears us when we speak to Him, but what is sometimes more challenging is hearing Him when He speaks to us. For those of us that confess that we rarely hear God or do not hear God at all, I would say that the first step in our hearing Him is our believing that we can.

Our ability to know God through conversing with Him is a foundational attribute and empowerment of the New Covenant; we read in Jeremiah 31:32(33)-33(34):

> *"'For this is the covenant I will make with the house of Isra'el after those days,' says ADONAI: 'I will put my Torah within them and write it on their hearts; I will be their God, and they will be my people. No longer will any of them teach his fellow community member or his brother [to] "Know ADONAI"; for all will know me, from the least of them to the greatest; because I will forgive their wickednesses and remember their sins no more.'"*

God says that the New Covenant he will make with the Israelites will result in everyone who is party to it knowing Him as Lord and, to achieve it, He will put the *Torah* within each of us, and write it on each of our hearts. I have no doubt that the Israelites of old who heard Jeremiah speak his prophesy did not have a clear understanding of how God would bring it to pass, but we now know that He did it by sending the Holy Spirit to indwell those of us who receive him. For that reason, knowing God must involve the Holy Spirit for, without the Holy Spirit, we are out of communication with both Yeshua and the Father, and therefore out of communication with God.

God has graciously provided us with help for our getting to know Him, and that help is the Bible that tell us about Him—*ergo*, the Scriptures quoted in this *Mitzvah* about knowing Him. We must keep in mind, however, that knowing God (which is the goal) is different from knowing about Him, but knowing about Him helps us to know Him. Here are two Scriptures that exhort us to have knowledge about Him:

> Ephesians 1:16-17: *"I have not stopped giving thanks for you. In my prayers I keep asking the God of our Lord Yeshua the Messiah, the glorious Father, to give you a spirit of wisdom and revelation, so that you will have full knowledge of him."*

> Colossians 1:9-10: *"Therefore, from the day we heard of it, we have not stopped praying for you, asking God to fill you with the knowledge of his will in all the wisdom and understanding which the Spirit gives; so that you may live lives worthy of the Lord and entirely pleasing to him, being fruitful in every good work and multiplying in the full knowledge of God."*

While these Scriptures exhort us to have knowledge of God, they do not themselves give us that knowledge. I therefore refer the reader of this *Mitzvah* to the above list of God's many attributes. The list tells us who God is and, interestingly, most of the items on it tell us who we should be as well. We achieve those attributes by putting off our old selves and modeling our new selves after Yeshua (Ephesians 4:22-24).

Classical Commentators

The m*itzvot* compiled by Maimonides, Meir, and HaChinuch command us to believe in God, to love Him, worship Him, fear Him, cleave to Him and relate to Him in other ways, but they do not address knowing Him.

NCLA: JMm JFm KMm KFm GMm GFm

H: Holiness and God's Order

H1. Having Reverence for God's Sanctuary.

We are to have reverence for God's sanctuary.

This precept is derived from His Word (blessed be He):

Key Scriptures

Leviticus 19:30 (Maimonides RP21; Meir MP18; C254)
Keep my Shabbats, and revere my sanctuary; I am ADONAI.

Leviticus 26:2 (Maimonides RP21; Meir MP18)
Keep my Shabbats, and revere my sanctuary; I am ADONAI.

1 Corinthians 3:16-17
Don't you know that you people are God's temple and that God's Spirit lives in you? So if anyone destroys God's temple, God will destroy him. For God's temple is holy, and you yourselves are that temple.

1 Corinthians 6:19-20
Or don't you know that your body is a temple for the Ruach HaKodesh who lives inside you, whom you received from God? The fact is, you don't belong to yourselves; for you were bought at a price. So use your bodies to glorify God.

Supportive Scripture

2 Corinthians 6:16-17

Commentary

This *Mitzvah* historically applies to having reverence for the Tabernacle of God and later for the Temple, for these were, according to Scripture, most holy. Today, we may apply this *Mitzvah* to any biblically authorized sanctuary in which God dwells or in which we worship Him. This includes edifices such as synagogues, churches and chapels, and may be extended to their furnishings and accoutrements that are set aside as holy objects used in worship. We must treat even the space of these sanctuaries with respect and not conduct ourselves in ways that demean their purpose.

Some synagogue and church sanctuaries are temporary or convertible spaces that are used for other things besides worship. In such cases, the space ought to be ceremonially commissioned when it is about to be used as a sanctuary, and decommissioned, and its holy objects put away, when its use as a sanctuary is concluded.

The 1 Corinthians 6:19-20 Scripture is interesting in that it applies to our personal bodies and also to our corporate body, the body of believers. Having reverence for these bodies is not very different from how we are to treat sanctuaries of brick and mortar, in that we are to care for them and not subject them to, or use them for, unholy purposes.

Classical Commentators

Maimonides and HaChinuch treat their respective *mitzvot* as only applying to the historical sanctuary of the Temple, whereas Meir applies it in a more contemporary way. He refers to synagogues and places where *Torah* is studied as "little sanctuaries" and states that we must not do ordinary and frivolous things in them like sleep and engage in laughter and idle conversation.

<u>**NCLA**</u>**: JMm JFm KMm KFm GMm GFm**

H2. Modeling God's Holiness by Our Appearance and by What We Wear.

We are to model God's Holiness by our appearance and by what we wear.

This precept is derived from His Word (blessed is He):

Key Scriptures

Leviticus 10:6 (Maimonides RN163, 164; Chinuch C149, 150)
Then Moshe told Aharon and his sons El'azar and Itamar, "Don't unbind your hair or tear your clothes in mourning, so that you won't die and so that ADONAI won't be angry with the entire community. Rather, let your kinsmen—the whole house of Isra'el—mourn, because of the destruction ADONAI brought about with his fire.

Leviticus 19:19 (Maimonides RN215, 217; Meir MN107, 142; Chinuch C244, 245)
Observe my regulations. "'Don't let your livestock mate with those of another kind, don't sow your field with two different kinds of grain, and don't wear a garment of cloth made with two different kinds of thread.

Leviticus 19:27 (Maimonides RN43-44; Meir MN176-177; Chinuch C251-252)
Don't round your hair at the temples or mar the edges of your beard.

Leviticus 19:28 (Maimonides RN41, 45; Meir MN163; Chinuch C253, 467)
Don't cut gashes in your flesh when someone dies or tattoo yourselves; I am ADONAI.

Leviticus 21:5-6 (Maimonides RN171; Chinuch C468)
Cohanim are not to make bald spots on their heads, mar the edges of their beards or cut gashes in their flesh. Rather, they are to be holy for their God and not profane the name of their God.

Leviticus 22:24 (Maimonides RN361; Meir MN143; Chinuch C291)
An animal with bruised, crushed, torn or cut genitals you are not to offer to ADONAI. You are not to do these things in your land, ...

Deuteronomy 14:1-2 (Maimonides RN45, 171; Meir MN28, 164; Chinuch C467, 468)
You are the people of ADONAI your God. You are not to gash yourselves or shave the hair above your foreheads in mourning for the dead, because you are a people set apart as holy for ADONAI your God.

Deuteronomy 22:5 (Maimonides RN39, 40; Meir MN178, 179; Chinuch 542, 543)
A woman is not to wear men's clothing, and a man is not to put on women's clothing, for whoever does these things is detestable to ADONAI your God.

Deuteronomy 22:11 (Maimonides RN42; Meir MN181; Chinuch C551)
You are not to wear clothing woven with two kinds of thread, wool and linen together.

1Corinthians 11:4-16
Every man who prays or prophesies wearing something down over his head brings shame to his head, but every woman who prays or prophesies with her head unveiled brings shame to her head—there is no difference between her and a woman who has had her head shaved. For if a woman is not veiled, let her also have her hair cut short; but if it is shameful for a woman to wear her hair cut short or to have her head shaved, then let her be veiled. For a man indeed should not have his head veiled, because he is the image and glory of God, and the woman is the glory of man. For man was not made from woman, but woman from man; and indeed man was not created for the sake of the woman but woman for the sake of the man. The reason a woman should show by veiling her head that she is under authority has to do with the angels. Nevertheless, in union with the Lord neither is woman independent of man nor is man independent of woman; for as the woman was made from the man, so also the man is now born through the woman. But everything is from God. Decide for yourselves: is it appropriate for a woman to pray to God when she is unveiled? Doesn't the nature of things itself teach you that a man who wears his hair long degrades himself? But a woman who wears her hair long enhances her appearance, because her hair has been given to her as a covering. However, if anyone wants to argue about it, the fact remains that we have no such custom, nor do the Messianic communities of God.

1 Timothy 2:9
Likewise, the women, when they pray, should be dressed modestly and sensibly in respectable attire, not with elaborate hairstyles and gold jewelry, or pearls, or expensive clothes.

Commentary

A common feature of the Scriptures supporting this *Mitzvah* is that they speak against conduct that detracts from some aspect of God's holy order. By "holy order" I mean the natural order of things from the creation, before the "Fall," that reflects God's will and perfection. One would hope that the Scriptures cited are self-evident and that man would want to obey them. Sadly, however, there are many perversions rampant in today's society, and ungodly forces agitating to hold them out as acceptable.

The Scriptures that teach against wearing two species of thread (animal wool and vegetable linen) or sowing two species of seeds are symbolic of not mating two species of animals. With modern manufactured clothing such as we wear, it is not possible to know what kinds of threads have been used to make our clothing, but modern clothing is not known to combine wool and linen.

Today there is no universal standard of what constitutes a male or female garment. It is defined by the culture in which the garment is worn, and tends to change over time. For example, women in the western countries wear slacks, whereas in years gone by they did not because slacks were then thought to be for men only.

The prohibitions against marking one's skin, cutting one's flesh, and trimming one's hair and beard in certain styles deserve special mention because tattooing, body piercing, and bizarre hair styles have become increasingly popular. The commandments prohibiting them were given at a time when each of them was a recognized heathen practice, and anyone who exhibited any one of them was, essentially, declaring himself to be an idolater. Castration also mars the body, but its affect is more profound and will be dealt with separately elsewhere.

It is still the case that permanent markings, disfigurements, extreme hair styles, and cross-dressing are with us today. Idol worship in its classical sense is no longer the issue, but rebellion against godly norms is, as is illustrated by "Punk" and "Goth" appearances that emphasize darkness over light. In addition, tattooing, cutting, and gross piercing permanently disfigures the body that God gave us and, for that reason, should be understood to not be God's will despite any religious theme (e.g. a cross) that a tattoo or item of jewelry attached to piercings may have. A believer who receives one of these knowing beforehand that Scripture prohibits them commits sin; one who receives a tattoo innocently has not committed sin, but he or she should refrain from making it visibly obvious because of what it implies. Once a tattoo has been received it is permanent, and if the wearer repents in Yeshua, any sin that may have been committed concerning it is over and done with. In my opinion, there is no continuing responsibility to attempt to remove a tattoo surgically.

Classical Commentators

Maimonides, Meir, and HaChinuch treat the Scriptures cited herein similarly and literally, and connect them to the practices of idol worshippers. Gashing and balding the head (tearing out hair) over the dead are illustrative of those practices. HaChinuch refers to God's evaluation of the creation in Genesis 1:31: *"God saw everything that he had made, and indeed it was very good."* To attempt to alter what God made is therefore very bad, and is sin.

NCLA: JMm JFm KMm KFm GMm GFm

H3. Preserving Things That Belong to God and That Are Holy.

We are to preserve and not destroy things that belong to God and that are holy.

This precept is derived from His Word (blessed be He):

Key Scriptures

Deuteronomy 12:2-4 (Maimonides RN65; Meir MN157; Chinuch C437)
You must destroy all the places where the nations you are dispossessing served their gods, whether on high mountains, on hills, or under some leafy tree. Break down their altars, smash their standing-stones to pieces, burn up their sacred poles completely and cut down the carved images of their gods. Exterminate their name from that place. But you are not to treat ADONAI your God this way.

Deuteronomy 20:19-20 (Maimonides RN57; Meir MN191; Chinuch C529)
When, in making war against a town in order to capture it, you lay siege to it for a long time, you are not to destroy its trees, cutting them down with an axe. You can eat their fruit, so don't cut them down. After all, are the trees in the field human beings, so that you have to besiege them too? However, if you know that certain trees provide no food, you may destroy them and cut them down, in order to build siege-works against the town making war with you, until it falls.

John 2:13-16
It was almost time for the festival of Pesach in Y'hudah, so Yeshua went up to Yerushalayim. In the Temple grounds he found those who were selling cattle, sheep and pigeons, and others who were sitting at tables exchanging money. He made a whip from cords and drove them all out of the Temple grounds, the sheep and cattle as well. He knocked over the money-changers' tables, scattering their coins; and to the pigeon-sellers he said, "Get these things out of here! How dare you turn my Father's house into a market?"

Romans 3:1-2
Then what advantage has the Jew? What is the value of being circumcised? Much in every way! In the first place, the Jews were entrusted with the very words of God.

2 Timothy 1:14
Keep safe the great treasure that has been entrusted to you, with the help of the Ruach HaKodesh, who lives in us.

Revelation 22:18-19
I warn everyone hearing the words of the prophecy in this book that if anyone adds to them, God will add to him the plagues written in this book. And if anyone takes anything away from the words in the book of this prophecy, God will take away his share in the Tree of Life and the holy city, as described in this book.

Commentary

This *Mitzvah* brings together two Scriptures that, at first glance, have little in common. Deuteronomy 12:2-4 commands the Israelites to destroy all the places and objects used for idol-worship that they find among the heathen nations they are dispossessing; however, if in the process of doing so they come across places of worship and things belonging to *HaShem*—those they must not destroy. Eight chapters later, Deuteronomy 20:19-20 forbids the Israelites from destroying fruit trees while laying siege to a city.

The connection between these seemingly unrelated Scriptures is the attribute of "holiness" as applied to the trees. God indeed wants places where idolatry is practiced and implements used there to be destroyed, but He does not want His holy places and things—things that belong to Him or that He provides as a blessing for men (like the fruit trees) to be destroyed in the process. Even when they have fallen into the hands of an enemy—holy things of God retain their holiness and must not be destroyed.

Ephesians 4:29 illustrates this *Mitzvah* in a less tangible form:

> *Let no harmful language come from your mouth, only good words that are helpful in meeting the need, words that will benefit those who hear them.*

Here the holy item of God that we must not harm or destroy is our neighbor. The Scripture warns us that our words can be harmful to those who hear them, so we must speak only good and helpful words in order to not bring destruction to our neighbor who is God's holy creation.

Jewish *halachah* and tradition have long recognized the principle of preserving, and not destroying, things that belong to God and that are holy. An example is that we do not "trash" or tear up old Bibles, *Torah* scrolls or *siddurim*. Instead, there is a procedure whereby we ceremonially bury them in a way that is analogous to the way we bury a deceased person.[124] I am also reminded of the way in which Leviticus 19:23-24 commands our holy respect for fruit-bearing trees. We do not eat their fruit during the first three years of their planting; the fourth year fruit is considered holy, and all of it must be used for praising God. It is only from the fifth year on that we may eat the fruit with an expectation of receiving its blessing year after year. Consider also, our "practical" respect for trees in Israel where we seek to plant them and not destroy them (e.g. *Tu B'shvat*). By contrast, the Israel Defense Forces came under severe criticism for destroying olive trees in the process of clearing land for Israeli settlements.

This *Mitzvah* is mandated for both Jews and *K'rovei Yisrael* and is highly recommended for believing Gentiles as well. The particulars of how to accomplish it need prayer—especially in these modern times when text that includes God's Name can be deleted from a computer or from cyberspace at the touch of a button.

---

124 In Orthodox Jewish practice the list is greater, and includes such things as *t'filin, tzitzit, m'zuzot, bima* covers, personal writings that contain God's Name, etc.

Classical Commentators

Maimonides, Meir, and HaChinuch treat this *Mitzvah* as two distinct *mitzvot* as follows:

Regarding <u>Deuteronomy 12:3-4</u>: All three commentators generalize the circumstances alluded to in this Scripture to include anything that is overtly holy (including one of the seven Names of God) and anything that is generally useful. Meir would carry this even to the point of not melting down a piece of metal upon which has been written one of God's Names. HaChinuch emphasizes that we must not erase any holy writing, or destroy a temple or altar established for the worship of God. Both he and Maimonides state that if Scripture is written down by an Israelite, it must not be erased or destroyed. If it is written by an heretical Israelite, it is not holy and must be destroyed (even if it contains God's Name) because the heretic did not believe in the holiness of the Name when he wrote it. HaChinuch says that if it is written by a heathen, it should not be destroyed, but rather hidden and stored out of sight. Maimonides agrees with Meir and HaChinuch, that we must not break down houses where the Lord is worshiped.

Regarding <u>Deuteronomy 20:19</u>: All three commentators interpret this Scripture broadly to include destruction of all kinds. Maimonides and Meir first deal with the Scripture literally as prohibiting our destroying fruit trees in the process of setting siege to a town, and Maimonides adds: "in order to cause distress."[125] Meir goes on to say that we must not cut down any fruit tree destructively, nor break a useful object, nor tear a garment, nor ruin food, nor demolish a sound structure. HaChinuch states that we must not destroy fruit trees in order to cause damage or loss, nor should we needlessly set fires, tear clothing, or break vessels. He says that the reason for these restrictions is in order to fulfill the *mitzvah* of loving others (presumably he means our enemies), and to bring out the love that is inherent in godly people. We are to love that which is good and beneficial, be saddened when a valuable thing is broken or destroyed, and never destroy anything in anger.

<u>NCLA</u>: **JMm JFm KMm KFm GMr GFr**

---

125 See also, *Mishneh Torah, Shoftim, Hilchot Melachim VI, 10.*

H4. Using Our Speech, Minds, Hearts and Actions for That which Is Good and Holy.

We are to use our speech, minds, hearts and actions for that which is good and holy.

This precept is derived from His Word (blessed be He):

Key Scriptures

Our Speech

Psalms 34:2(1)-3(2)
I will bless ADONAI at all times; his praise will always be in my mouth. When I boast, it will be about ADONAI; the humble will hear of it and be glad.

Proverbs 10:11a:
The speech of the righteous is a fountain of life…

Proverbs 12:17a:
He who tells the truth furthers justice…

Matthew 15:18-20
But what comes out of your mouth is actually coming from your heart, and that is what makes a person unclean. For out of the heart come forth wicked thoughts, murder, adultery and other kinds of sexual immorality, theft, lies, slanders… . These are what really make a person unclean, but eating without doing n'tilat-yadayim does not make a person unclean.

Ephesians 4:29
Let no harmful language come from your mouth, only good words that are helpful in meeting the need, words that will benefit those who hear them.

Colossians 3:17
That is, everything you do or say, do in the name of the Lord Yeshua, giving thanks through him to God the Father.

Titus 2:7b-8
When you are teaching, have integrity and be serious; let everything you say be so wholesome that an opponent will be put to shame because he will have nothing bad to say about us.

Our Minds and Hearts

Deuteronomy 6:5
…and you are to love ADONAI your God with all your heart, all your being and all your resources…

<u>Romans 12:2</u>
In other words, do not let yourselves be conformed to the standards of the 'olam hazeh. Instead, keep letting yourselves be transformed by the renewing of your minds; so that you will know what God wants and will agree that what he wants is good, satisfying and able to succeed.

<u>Philippians 4:8</u>
In conclusion, brothers, focus your thoughts on what is true, noble, righteous, pure, lovable or admirable, on some virtue or on something praiseworthy.

<u>Colossians 3:2-3</u>
Focus your minds on the things above, not on things here on earth. For you have died, and your life is hidden with the Messiah in God.

<u>1 Peter 1:13</u>
Therefore, get your minds ready for work, keep yourselves under control, and fix your hopes fully on the gift you will receive when Yeshua the Messiah is revealed.

Our Actions

<u>Exodus 20:1-12</u>
Then God said all these words: "I am ADONAI your God, who brought you out of the land of Egypt, out of the abode of slavery. You are to have no other gods before me. You are not to make for yourselves a carved image or any kind of representation of anything in heaven above, on the earth beneath or in the water below the shoreline. You are not to bow down to them or serve them; for I, ADONAI your God, am a jealous God, punishing the children for the sins of the parents to the third and fourth generation of those who hate me, but displaying grace to the thousandth generation of those who love me and obey my mitzvot. You are not to use lightly the name of ADONAI your God, because ADONAI will not leave unpunished someone who uses his name lightly. Remember the day, Shabbat, to set it apart for God. You have six days to labor and do all your work, but the seventh day is a Shabbat for ADONAI your God. On it, you are not to do any kind of work—not you, your son or your daughter, not your male or female slave, not your livestock, and not the foreigner staying with you inside the gates to your property. For in six days, ADONAI made heaven and earth, the sea and everything in them; but on the seventh day he rested. This is why ADONAI blessed the day, Shabbat, and separated it for himself. Honor your father and mother, so that you may live long in the land which ADONAI your God is giving you.

<u>Isaiah 1:17</u>
Learn to do good! Seek justice, relieve the oppressed, defend orphans, plead for the widow.

<u>Psalms 37:3-4</u>
Trust in ADONAI, and do good; settle in the land, and feed on faithfulness. Then you will delight yourself in ADONAI, and he will give you your heart's desire.

Psalms 37:27
If you turn from evil and do good, you will live safely forever.

Matthew 5:16
In the same way, let your light shine before people, so that they may see the good things you do and praise your Father in heaven.

1 Corinthians 16:14
Let everything you do be done in love.

Galatians 5:14
For the whole of the Torah is summed up in this one sentence: "Love your neighbor as yourself";

Supportive Scriptures—Our Speech

Ecclesiastes 7:21-22
Matthew 6:9
Mark 7:15-23
Romans 10:8-9
Colossians 4:2
1 Peter 2:9

Supportive Scriptures—Our Minds and Hearts

2 Corinthians 10:4b-5
Philippians 2:5

Supportive Scriptures—Our Actions

Proverbs 3:27
Luke 10:26-28
Romans 2:7
2 Corinthians 5:9-10
Galatians 6:9
Ephesians 2:10
Colossians 3:17
2 Thessalonians 3:13
2 Timothy 3:16-17
Titus 2:6-7
Hebrews 10:24, 13:16
James 2:14-17 and 26

Commentary

This "positive" *Mitzvah* on "directing our speech, thoughts and actions to that which is good and holy" is a companion to a "negative" *Mitzvah* that "we are not to wrong one another through our speech." While the compilations of rabbinical commentators list many of the positive and negative elements of this *Mitzvah,* the weight of Scripture (that we should use every aspect of our being for good) suggests that this *Mitzvah* be written to combine them.

This *Mitzvah* quotes a goodly number of Scriptures that reference how we are to use (and not use) speech and actions, but I want to also address what might seem (at first) to be opposite, which is holding back on speech, or remaining silent. Proverbs 18:21 says that speech has power, but silence also has power, as we read in Isaiah 53:7, a prophecy of Yeshua's use of silence in the final hours of his life:

> "*He was oppressed and He was afflicted, Yet He opened not His mouth; He was led as a lamb to the slaughter, and as a sheep before its shearers is silent, So He opened not His mouth.*"

Here are some other Scriptures that suggest times when there is wisdom and virtue in being slow to speak or in remaining silent:

Exodus 14:14 (NIV): "*The LORD will fight for you; you need only to be still.*"

Psalms 37:7a: "*Be still before ADONAI; wait patiently till he comes.*"

Proverbs 11:12: "*He who belittles another lacks good sense, whereas a person of discernment stays silent.*"

Proverbs 13:3: "*He who guards his mouth preserves his life, but one who talks too much comes to ruin.*"

Proverbs 17:28" "*Even a fool, if he stays silent, is thought wise; he who keeps his mouth shut can pass for smart.*"

James 1:19: "*Therefore, my dear brothers, let every person be quick to listen but slow to speak, slow to get angry;*"

Classical Commentators

Maimonides, Meir, and HaChinuch list *mitzvot* that include the components of this one, such as their *mitzvot* to love God (RP3, MP3, C418), not murder (RN289, MN32, C34), and not to steal (RN244, MN34, C224).

NCLA: JMm JFm KMm KFm GMm GFm

H5. Conducting Sacrifices Apart from the Holy Temple.

We are not to conduct sacrifices of any kind apart from the Holy Temple.

This precept is derived from His Word (blessed be He):

Key Scriptures

Leviticus 17:3-9 (Maimonides RN90; Chinuch C186)
When someone from the community of Isra'el slaughters an ox, lamb or goat inside or outside the camp without bringing it to the entrance of the tent of meeting to present it as an offering to ADONAI before the tabernacle of ADONAI, he is to be charged with blood—he has shed blood, and that person is to be cut off from his people. The reason for this is so that the people of Isra'el will bring their sacrifices that they sacrifice out in the field—so that they will bring them to ADONAI, to the entrance of the tent of meeting, to the cohen, and sacrifice them as peace offerings to ADONAI. The cohen will splash the blood against the altar of ADONAI at the entrance to the tent of meeting and make the fat go up in smoke as a pleasing aroma for ADONAI. No longer will they offer sacrifices to the goat-demons, before whom they prostitute themselves! This is a permanent regulation for them through all their generations.' Also tell them, 'When someone from the community of Isra'el or one of the foreigners living with you offers a burnt offering or sacrifice without bringing it to the entrance of the tent of meeting to sacrifice it to ADONAI, that person is to be cut off from his people.

Deuteronomy 12:2-5
You must destroy all the places where the nations you are dispossessing served their gods, whether on high mountains, on hills, or under some leafy tree. Break down their altars, smash their standing-stones to pieces, burn up their sacred poles completely and cut down the carved images of their gods. Exterminate their name from that place. But you are not to treat ADONAI your God this way. Rather, you are to come to the place where ADONAI your God will put his name. He will choose it from all your tribes; and you will seek out that place, which is where he will live, and go there.

Deuteronomy 12:13-14 (Maimonides RN89-90; Chinuch C186, 439)
Be careful not to offer your burnt offerings just anywhere you see, but do it in the place ADONAI will choose in one of your tribal territories; there is where you are to offer your burnt offerings and do everything I order you to do.

Hebrews 9:11-12
But when the Messiah appeared as cohen gadol of the good things that are happening already, then, through the greater and more perfect Tent which is not man-made (that is, it is not of this created world), he entered the Holiest Place once and for all. And he entered not by means of the blood of goats and calves, but by means of his own blood, thus setting people free forever.

<u>Hebrews 10:12-14</u>
But this one, after he had offered for all time a single sacrifice for sins, sat down at the right hand of God, from then on to wait until his enemies be made a footstool for his feet. For by a single offering he has brought to the goal for all time those who are being set apart for God and made holy.

<u>1 John 2:2</u>
Also, he is the kapparah for our sins—and not only for ours, but also for those of the whole world.

Supportive Scriptures

Deuteronomy 12:29-31
2 Chronicles 23:16-17

Commentary

This *Mitzvah* is based on ones that Maimonides and HaChinuch wrote, limiting sacrifices to within the Sanctuary court. Their reason for highlighting this limitation was that the Israelites were to be reminded to not sacrifice to (or in the manner of) foreign Gods. This instruction is especially relevant in precluding our conducting sacrifices today at a time when there is no Holy Temple, but it gives no hint of whether sacrifices might be resumed if (and at such time as) the Temple is rebuilt, nor what kind of sacrifices they might be if it is. Clearly, with the sacrifice of Yeshua having occurred, they cannot be sacrifices for sin.

The few Scriptures included herein that prohibit the use of unauthorized altars for sacrifice are but a sampling of many others that are in the Bible.

Classical Commentators

Maimonides and HaChinuch paraphrase closely the Scriptures upon which they rely, and Meir chose not to write a *mitzvah* on the subject.

<u>NCLA</u>: **JMm JFm KMm KFm GMm GFm**

H6. Appointing a Ruler Whom God Chooses.

If we appoint a ruler over us, he is to be one whom God chooses—one who rules according to the Word of God, and does not prefer himself over his people.

This precept is derived from His Word (blessed be He):

Key Scriptures

Deuteronomy 17:14-20 (Maimonides RN365; Chinuch C502)
When you have entered the land ADONAI your God is giving you, have taken possession of it and are living there, you may say, 'I want to have a king over me, like all the other nations around me.' In that event, you must appoint as king the one whom ADONAI your God will choose. He must be one of your kinsmen, this king you appoint over you—you are forbidden to appoint a foreigner over you who is not your kinsman. However, he is not to acquire many horses for himself or have the people return to Egypt to obtain more horses, inasmuch as ADONAI told you never to go back that way again. Likewise, he is not to acquire many wives for himself, so that his heart will not turn away; and he is not to acquire excessive quantities of silver and gold. When he has come to occupy the throne of his kingdom, he is to write a copy of this Torah for himself in a scroll, from the one the cohanim and L'vi'im use. It is to remain with him, and he is to read in it every day, as long as he lives; so that he will learn to fear ADONAI his God and keep all the words of this Torah and these laws and obey them; so that he will not think he is better than his kinsmen; and so that he will not turn aside either to the right or to the left from the mitzvah. In this way he will prolong his own reign and that of his children in Isra'el.

Romans 13:1-6
Everyone is to obey the governing authorities. For there is no authority that is not from God, and the existing authorities have been placed where they are by God. Therefore, whoever resists the authorities is resisting what God has instituted; and those who resist will bring judgment on themselves. For rulers are no terror to good conduct, but to bad. Would you like to be unafraid of the person in authority? Then simply do what is good, and you will win his approval; for he is God's servant, there for your benefit. But if you do what is wrong, be afraid! Because it is not for nothing that he holds the power of the sword; for he is God's servant, there as an avenger to punish wrongdoers. Another reason to obey, besides fear of punishment, is for the sake of conscience. This is also why you pay taxes; for the authorities are God's public officials, constantly attending to these duties.

Supportive Scriptures

Acts 5:26-29
Hebrews 13:17
1 Peter 2:13-17
Revelation 13:11-18, 20:4

Commentary

How can Romans 13:1-6 say:

> *"For there is no authority that is not from God, and the existing authorities have been placed where they are by God."*

And how can Hebrews 13:17 say without qualification:

> *"Obey your leaders and submit to them."*

Are there not evil rulers that would command us to do ungodly things and yet we must obey them? It is indeed a conundrum unless we consider that the leaders spoken of are those referred to in Deuteronomy 17:14-20—leaders approved by God, and governing with knowledge of *Torah,* and with intent to do God's will. These rulers may be of our secular governments or they may be the elders of our congregations but, if we do what we ought to do—choose rulers that are approved by God and accountable to Him, all will be well. This requires that we be involved in the appointing process of our leaders, in order to make sure that whether king, or president, or governor, or congregational elder—our rulers will be of the mind and character to govern in godly ways. Yes, things go awry in this fallen world and, when they do, we must take our instruction from God (through the Holy Spirit) and rely on Him to set things right. And until things are set right, if we are commanded against God's *Torah*, must obey God and not man (see Acts 5:26-29 and Revelation 13: 6-10).

Classical Commentators

Maimonides and HaChinuch refer to Deuteronomy 17:16-17 to support their *mitzvot* stating only that a king must not amass great personal wealth. The quintessential example of a king that did amass great wealth is King Solomon who, according to 2 Chronicles 9:13-29, received twenty-two tons of gold each year in addition to other items of worth, and according to 1 Kings 11:3, had seven hundred wives and three hundred concubines who eventually turned his heart away from God. Meir wrote no *mitzvah* on the subject.

NCLA: JMm JFm KMm KFm GMm GFm

H7. Castration.

We are not to castrate a male human being other than for medical necessity.

This precept is derived from His Word (blessed is He):

Key Scripture

Leviticus 22:24 (Maimonides RN361; Meir MN143; Chinuch C291)
An animal with bruised, crushed, torn or cut genitals you are not to offer to ADONAI. You are not to do these things in your land...

Matthew 19:12
For there are different reasons why men do not marry—some because they were born without the desire, some because they have been castrated, and some because they have renounced marriage for the sake of the Kingdom of Heaven. Whoever can grasp this, let him do so.

Supportive Scriptures

Leviticus 21:17-23
Deuteronomy 23:2

Commentary

Castration is removing or doing irreparable damage to a male's testicles. There is no specific commandment in Scripture prohibiting the castration of human beings or animals, but we surmise it with regard to men from the Scriptures cited that impute holiness-connected disabilities to castrated men and beasts. Castrated men were prohibited from entering the assembly of the Lord and could not serve as priests, and castrated animals could not be used for sacrifice in the Temple.

So far as I am aware, men-slaves are no longer castrated to produce eunuchs for guarding harams or young boys castrated to preserve their soprano, mezzo-soprano or contralto voices. Nevertheless, our society does neuter male animals to change their behavior, their size, or their tenderness when used for food. For example, steer meat comes from a castrated bull, a capon "chicken" is a castrated rooster, and an ox is a steer that has been bred for work. Castrating animals or fowls does not appear to prohibit their being considered kosher for food.

Castration of men is occasionally done for medical reasons (e.g. cancer), and our various societies have, on occasion, castrated especially sex offenders as part of a punitive process.

Classical Commentators

Maimonides, Meir, and HaChinuch state that <u>Leviticus 22:24</u> (despite it not saying so) prohibits castrating a male of any species whatsoever. Also, Maimonides and HaChinuch (not Meir) reference <u>Leviticus 2:11</u> and <u>Leviticus 6:10(17)</u>, neither of which seem to have relevance to the subject of castration.

<u>NCLA</u>: JMm JFm KMm KFm GMm GFm

H8. Dying to Self.

We are to forgo self-interest when appropriate.

This precept is derived from His Word (blessed is He):

Key Scriptures

Matthew 16:24-25
Then Yeshua told his talmidim, "If anyone wants to come after me, let him say 'No' to himself, take up his execution-stake, and keep following me. For whoever wants to save his own life will destroy it, but whoever destroys his life for my sake will find it. (See also Mark 8:34-35 and Luke 9:23-24).

Luke 14:27
Whoever does not carry his own execution-stake and come after me cannot be my talmid.

Romans 6:8
Now since we died with the Messiah, we trust that we will also live with him.

Romans 8:13
For if you live according to your old nature, you will certainly die; but if, by the Spirit, you keep putting to death the practices of the body, you will live.

Romans 12:1
I exhort you, therefore, brothers, in view of God's mercies, to offer yourselves as a sacrifice, living and set apart for God. This will please him; it is the logical "Temple worship" for you.

Romans 12:10 (NKJ)
Be kindly affectionate to one another with brotherly love, in honor giving preference to one another;

Galatians 2:20 (NKJ)
I have been crucified with Christ [Messiah]; it is no longer I who live, but Christ [Messiah] lives in me; and the life which I now live in the flesh I live by faith in the Son of God, who loved me and gave Himself for me.

Galatians 5:24
Moreover, those who belong to the Messiah Yeshua have put their old nature to death on the stake, along with its passions and desires.

Philippians 2:3
Do nothing out of rivalry or vanity; but, in humility, regard each other as better than yourselves.

Colossians 3:5
Therefore, put to death the earthly parts of your nature—sexual immorality, impurity, lust, evil desires and greed (which is a form of idolatry)...

1 Peter 2:24
He himself bore our sins in his body on the stake, so that we might die to sins and live for righteousness—by his wounds you were healed.

Supportive Scriptures—Dying to Self-Interest

Psalms 44:23(22)
Matthew 10:38-39
Mark 10:24-30
Luke 9:23-24, 17:33
John 12:25, 15:13
Romans 6:3-13, 12:1a
1 Corinthians 11:33, 15:31
2 Corinthians 2:20, 4:10-11, 5:17
Galatians 2:20, 6:14
Ephesians 4:22, 5:25
Colossians 3:3
2 Timothy 2:11
1 John 3:16

Supportive Scriptures—Properly Responding to Self-Interest

Leviticus 19:18, 34
Proverbs 19:8, 26:15
Matthew 11:28-29, 19:19, 22:37-39
Ephesians 5:29-30
Philippians 2:4
Galatians 5:14
James 2:8

Commentary

The plethora of Scriptures that exhort us to die to our self-interests are due to the inclination of fallen man to dwell on himself and to put his interests above those of others. Still, we cannot completely ignore aspects of our welfare or we cannot live. We have to eat, clothe and shelter ourselves, keep from things unhealthy, and petition God to meet our needs (yes, petitioning God is most certainly a choice that is in our self-interest). Several of the Scriptures cited above speak of "loving ourselves," so "dying to self—interest" cannot be an absolute, and we therefore need the wisdom of the Holy Spirit to determine when and how much each is needed.

We encounter problems when we step out of God's will by being legalistic in either extreme—(1) putting others before ourselves in inappropriate circumstances, or (2) putting ourselves before others in equally inappropriate circumstances. A ludicrous example of the first extreme (putting another's need before our own) would be our stopping to feed a homeless man in the midst of our being severely injured and in need of emergency treatment. An equally ludicrous example of the second extreme (putting our self before another), would be our passing by an injured person lying in the street because we are hungry and late for dinner. Although neither of these examples are realistic, they do point to our need for God to cleanse us of unholy self-interest that is common to fallen man, and also to our need for Holy Spirit imparted wisdom in balancing our personal needs against those of others in the various situations that we encounter.

Classical Commentators

This *Mitzvah* is not addressed by any of the Jewish classical commentators.

NCLA: JMm JFm KMm KFm GMm GFm

I: Idolatry, Heathens and the Occult

11. Practicing Idolatry.

We are not to practice idolatry.

This precept is derived from His Word (blessed be He):

Key Scriptures

Exodus 20:3 (Maimonides RN1; Meir MN8; Chinuch C26)
You are to have no other gods before me.

Exodus 20:4 (Maimonides RN2; Meir MN9; Chinuch C27)
You are not to make for yourselves a carved image or any kind of representation of anything in heaven above, on the earth beneath or in the water below the shoreline.

Exodus 20:5 (Maimonides RN5, 6; Meir MN11, 12; Chinuch C28, 29)
You are not to bow down to them or serve them; for I, ADONAI your God, am a jealous God, punishing the children for the sins of the parents to the third and fourth generation of those who hate me...

Exodus 23:13 (Maimonides RN14, RN26; Meir MN13, MN27; Chinuch C86, C518)
Pay attention to everything I have said to you; do not invoke the names of other gods or even let them be heard crossing your lips.

Exodus 23:23-24
When my angel goes ahead of you and brings you to the Emori, Hitti, P'rizi, Kena'ani, Hivi and Y'vusi, I will make an end of them. You are not to worship their gods, serve them or follow their practices; rather, you are to demolish them completely and smash their standing-stones to pieces.

Exodus 34:14 (Chinuch C28)
...because you are not to bow down to any other god; since ADONAI—whose very name is Jealous—is a jealous God.

Leviticus 17:7 (Maimonides RN5)
No longer will they offer sacrifices to the goat-demons, before whom they prostitute themselves! This is a permanent regulation for them through all their generations.

Leviticus 18:21 (Maimonides RN7; Chinuch C208)
You are not to let any of your children be sacrificed to Molekh, thereby profaning the name of your God; I am ADONAI.

Leviticus 19:4 (Maimonides RN10; Meir MN16; Chinuch C213)
Do not turn to idols, and do not cast metal gods for yourselves; I am ADONAI your God.

Leviticus 26:1 (Maimonides RN12; Meir MN161; Chinuch C349)
You are not to make yourselves any idols, erect a carved statue or a standing-stone, or place any carved stone anywhere in your land in order to bow down to it. I am ADONAI your God.

Deuteronomy 4:15-19 (Maimonides RN10; Chinuch C213)
Therefore, watch out for yourselves! Since you did not see a shape of any kind on the day ADONAI spoke to you in Horev from the fire, do not become corrupt and make yourselves a carved image having the shape of any figure—not a representation of a human being, male or female, or a representation of any animal on earth, or a representation of any bird that flies in the air, or a representation of anything that creeps along on the ground, or a representation of any fish in the water below the shoreline. For the same reason, do not look up at the sky, at the sun, moon, stars and everything in the sky, and be drawn away to worship and serve them; ADONAI your God has allotted these to all the peoples under the entire sky.

Deuteronomy 4:23-28
Watch out for yourselves, so that you won't forget the covenant of ADONAI your God, which he made with you, and make yourself a carved image, a representation of anything forbidden to you by ADONAI your God. For ADONAI your God is a consuming fire, a jealous God. When you have had children and grandchildren, lived a long time in the land, become corrupt and made a carved image, a representation of something, and thus done what is evil in the sight of ADONAI your God and provoked him; I call on the sky and the earth to witness against you today that you will quickly disappear from the land that you are crossing the Yarden to possess. You will not prolong your days there but will be completely destroyed. ADONAI will scatter you among the peoples; and among the nations to which ADONAI will lead you away, you will be left few in number. There you will serve gods which are the product of human hands, made of wood and stone, which can't see, hear, eat or smell.

Deuteronomy 8:19
If you forget ADONAI your God, follow other gods and serve and worship them, I am warning you in advance today that you will certainly perish.

Deuteronomy 11:16 (Maimonides RN10; Chinuch 213)
But be careful not to let yourselves be seduced, so that you turn aside, serving other gods and worshipping them.

Deuteronomy 12:29-31 (Maimonides RN10; Chinuch C213)
When ADONAI your God has cut off ahead of you the nations you are entering in order to dispossess, and when you have dispossessed them and are living in their land; be careful, after they have been destroyed ahead of you, not to be trapped into following them; so that you inquire after their gods and ask, 'How did these nations serve their gods? I want to do the same.' You must not do this to ADONAI your God! For they have done to their gods all the abominations that ADONAI hates! They even burn up their sons and daughters in the fire for their gods!

Deuteronomy 16:21-22 (Maimonides RN13; Chinuch C492)
You are not to plant any sort of tree as a sacred pole beside the altar of ADONAI your God that you will make for yourselves. Likewise, do not set up a standing-stone; ADONAI your God hates such things.

Deuteronomy 18:10-11 (Maimonides RN7; Chinuch C208)
There must not be found among you anyone who makes his son or daughter pass through fire, a diviner, a soothsayer, an enchanter, a sorcerer, a spell-caster, a consulter of ghosts or spirits, or a necromancer.

Deuteronomy 30:15-18
Look! I am presenting you today with, on the one hand, life and good; and on the other, death and evil—in that I am ordering you today to love ADONAI your God, to follow his ways, and to obey his mitzvot, regulations and rulings; for if you do, you will live and increase your numbers; and ADONAI your God will bless you in the land you are entering in order to take possession of it. But if your heart turns away, if you refuse to listen, if you are drawn away to prostrate yourselves before other gods and serve them; I am announcing to you today that you will certainly perish; you will not live long in the land you are crossing the Yarden to enter and possess.

Joshua 23:6-8
Therefore be very firm about keeping and doing everything written in the book of the Torah of Moshe and not turning aside from it either to the right or to the left. Then you won't become like those nations remaining among you. Don't even mention the name of their gods, let alone have people swear by them, serve them or worship them; but cling to ADONAI your God, as you have done to this day.

Jeremiah 16:10-11
When you tell this people all that I have said, and they ask you, 'Why has ADONAI decreed all this terrible disaster against us? What is our iniquity, what is our sin, that we have committed against ADONAI our God?' then you are to say to them, 'It is because your ancestors abandoned me, says ADONAI, and went after other gods, serving and worshipping them, but abandoned me and did not keep my Torah.

Ezekiel 20:7
I told them, "Each of you is to throw away the detestable things that draw your eyes. Do not defile yourselves with the idols of Egypt. I am ADONAI your God."

Jonah 2:9(8)
Those who worship vain idols give up their source of mercy...

Psalms 16:4
Those who run after another god multiply their sorrows; To such gods I will not offer drink offerings of blood or take their names on my lips.

Psalms 97:7
All who worship images will be put to shame, those who make their boast in worthless idols. Bow down to him, all you gods!

Romans 1:22-25
Claiming to be wise, they have become fools! In fact, they have exchanged the glory of the immortal God for mere images, like a mortal human being, or like birds, animals or reptiles! This is why God has given them up to the vileness of their hearts' lusts, to the shameful misuse of each other's bodies. They have exchanged the truth of God for falsehood, by worshipping and serving created things, rather than the Creator—praised be he forever. Amen.

1 Corinthians 6:9-10
Don't you know that unrighteous people will have no share in the Kingdom of God? Don't delude yourselves—people who engage in sex before marriage, who worship idols, who engage in sex after marriage with someone other than their spouse, who engage in active or passive homosexuality, who steal, who are greedy, who get drunk, who assail people with contemptuous language, who rob—none of them will share in the Kingdom of God.

1 Corinthians 10:14
Therefore, my dear friends, run from idolatry!

1 Corinthians 10:19-20
So, what am I saying? That food sacrificed to idols has any significance in itself? Or that an idol has significance in itself? No, what I am saying is that the things which pagans sacrifice, they sacrifice not to God but to demons; and I don't want you to become sharers of the demons!

2 Corinthians 6:16-17
What agreement can there be between the temple of God and idols? For we are the temple of the living God—as God said, "I will house myself in them...and I will walk among you. I will be their God, and they will be my people." Therefore ADONAI says, "'Go out from their midst; separate yourselves; don't even touch what is unclean. Then I myself will receive you.

1 John 5:21
Children, guard yourselves against false gods!

Supportive Scriptures

Matthew 6:19-21, 24
Luke 12:16-21
1 Corinthians 12:2

Commentary

Most of the *mitzvot* promulgated in the Mosaic era appear to command against worshiping foreign gods of the supernatural kind—sometimes attributed to animals and natural objects (e.g.

the Nile river god and the frog god of the Egyptians), and sometimes man-made objects (e.g. heathen carved statues and the golden calf). While not spoken of directly in the Mosaic Law, Satan and satanic influence is at the core of all idolatry and of all gods other than the God of Abraham, Isaac, and Jacob. It was the archangel Lucifer (later named Satan) who first rebelled against God, and who was cast out of heaven and allowed to become the god of the earth to the extent that man would allow him. Satan's first attempt at seducing man away from God was successful (i.e. Adam and Eve), and the rest of the earth's history has been his war against God for the heart of mankind.

There were (and still are) pagans who were/are susceptible to worshiping foreign gods, such as the Canaanites and Egyptians of old, and the Hindus and Satanists of today. The religions of the Canaanites and Egyptians severely impacted the Israelites in years gone by but, today, Satan's attack on God's people is more subtle. We get a hint of the kinds of idols that impact us most today from the following Scriptures:

> 1 Samuel 15:23: *"For rebellion is like the sin of sorcery, stubbornness like the crime of idolatry. Because you have rejected the word of* ADONAI, *he too has rejected you as king."*

> Ephesians 5:5: *"For of this you can be sure: every sexually immoral, impure or greedy person—that is, every idol-worshipper—has no share in the Kingdom of the Messiah and of God."*

> Colossians 3:5: *"Therefore, put to death the earthly parts of your nature—sexual immorality, impurity, lust, evil desires and greed (which is a form of idolatry);"*

> 1 Timothy 6:10: *"For the love of money is a root of all the evils; because of this craving, some people have wandered away from the faith and pierced themselves to the heart with many pains."*

These Scriptures indicate that stubbornness, sexual immorality, impurity, lust, evil desires and greed for money and property are all idols. Other common idols are money, property, power, and security. An idol is therefore anything (or anyone) that we desire more strongly than we desire God, and idolatry is any giving-in to such a desire, such that we put that thing or person ahead of God. This *Mitzvah* commands us to put away all idolatry, both the worship of foreign gods, as well as those other idols that draw us away from the God of Abraham, Isaac, and Jacob. Anyone who allows such things to dominate his or her life is guilty of idolatry.

Classical Commentators

Maimonides, Meir, and HaChinuch each wrote nine *mitzvot* that collectively express the principle of this one *Mitzvah*. Most of the commentators' *mitzvot* are self-explanatory, but there is one that bears special mention. In his *mitzvah* C27, HaChinuch criticizes Maimonides for making no distinction of culpability between making an idol with one's own hands, and commissioning one's agent to make an idol for him. HaChinuch writes that there should be such a distinction because of an established Talmudic rule *(TB Kidushin 42b)* that a person who commissions another to commit a wrong is not himself guilty of the wrong. In saying this, HaChinuch may be referring to Maimonides' RN3 and not RN2 which is described in this *Mitzvah*.

Maimonides, Meir, and HaChinuch wrote separate *mitzvot* for bowing down to an idol (Maimonides RN5; Meir MN11; HaChinuch C28), and for worshiping an idol (Maimonides RN6; Meir MN 12; HaChinuch C29), which seems to me to be splitting hairs.

In their *mitzvot* RN14, MN13, and C86 respectively, Maimonides, Meir, and HaChinuch interpret Exodus 23:13 narrowly to mean that we are not to swear in the name of idols, and in their *mitzvot* RN26, MN27, and C518 respectively, they interpret it to mean that we are not to prophesy in the name of an idol.

In his *mitzvah* RN10, Maimonides admonishes the reader to not study or pay attention to idolatry, whereas Meir and HaChinuch (MN16 and C213 respectively) command the reader to not turn toward idolatry. While there is, indeed, the possibility that a spiritually weak person could become attracted to idolatry through learning about it, I do not believe that the Scriptures cited support such a broad restriction. Deuteronomy 12:30 is clear that the prohibition is against inquiring about foreign gods for the purpose of following them.

NCLA: JMm JFm KMm KFm GMm GFm

12. Pursuing the Occult

We are not to pursue, engage in, or utilize anything that is occult.

This precept is derived from His Word (blessed be He):

Key Scriptures

Exodus 22:17(18)
You are not to permit a sorceress to live.

Leviticus 19:26 (Maimonides RN32, RN33; Meir MN165, MN 166; Chinuch C249, C250)
Do not eat anything with blood. Do not practice divination or fortune-telling.

Leviticus 19:31 (Maimonides RN8, 9; Meir MN170, 171; Chinuch C255, 256)
Do not turn to spirit-mediums or sorcerers; don't seek them out, to be defiled by them; I am ADONAI your God.

Leviticus 20:6
The person who turns to spirit-mediums and sorcerers to go fornicating after them—I will set myself against him and cut him off from his people.

Leviticus 20:27 (Maimonides RN9; Chinuch C256)
A man or woman who is a spirit-medium or sorcerer must be put to death; they are to stone them to death; their blood will be on them.

Deuteronomy 4:19
For the same reason, do not look up at the sky, at the sun, moon, stars and everything in the sky, and be drawn away to worship and serve them; ADONAI your God has allotted these to all the peoples under the entire sky.

Deuteronomy 18:9-12 (Maimonides RN31-38; MN167-169, 172-174; Chinuch C249, 250, 510-513, 515)
When you enter the land ADONAI your God is giving you, you are not to learn how to follow the abominable practices of those nations. There must not be found among you anyone who makes his son or daughter pass through fire, a diviner, a soothsayer, an enchanter, a sorcerer, a spell-caster, a consulter of ghosts or spirits, or a necromancer. For whoever does these things is detestable to ADONAI, and because of these abominations ADONAI your God is driving them out ahead of you.

*Job 5:23 (Chinuch C514) (There is no *Torah* reference for C514; see Classical Commentators section below)
...for you will be in league with the stones in the field, and the wild animals will be at peace with you.

403

Acts 13:8-12

...but the sorcerer Elymas (for that is how his name is translated) opposed them, doing his best to turn the governor away from the faith. Then Sha'ul, also known as Paul, filled with the Ruach HaKodesh, stared straight at him and said, "You son of Satan, full of fraud and evil! You enemy of everything good! Won't you ever stop making crooked the straight paths of the Lord? So now, look! The hand of the Lord is upon you; and for a while you will be blind, unable to see the sun." Immediately mist and darkness came over Elymas; and he groped about, trying to find someone to lead him by the hand. Then, on seeing what had happened, the governor trusted, astounded by the teaching about the Lord.

Acts 19:18-19

Many of those who had earlier made professions of faith now came and admitted publicly their evil deeds; and a considerable number of those who had engaged in occult practices threw their scrolls in a pile and burned them in public. When they calculated the value of the scrolls, it came to fifty thousand drachmas.

Galatians 5:19-21

And it is perfectly evident what the old nature does. It expresses itself in sexual immorality, impurity and indecency; involvement with the occult and with drugs; in feuding, fighting, becoming jealous and getting angry; in selfish ambition, factionalism, intrigue and envy; in drunkenness, orgies and things like these. I warn you now as I have warned you before: those who do such things will have no share in the Kingdom of God!

Supportive Scriptures

1 Samuel 15:23, 28:3
2 Kings 17:17b-18, 21:6, 23:24
Isaiah 2:6, 8:19-20, 19:3, 47:12-15
Jeremiah 10:2, 27:9-10
Ezekiel 13:18a
Micah 5:11(12)
Malachi 3:5
1 Chronicles 10:13-14
2 Chronicles 33:6
Acts 8:9-23, 16:16-18
Revelation 9:20-21, 18:22-23, 21:8, 22:14-15

Commentary

This *Mitzvah* commands against seeking, engaging in, or utilizing occult supernatural powers. The term "occult" covers a wide range of prohibited activities that include (but are not limited to) divining, fortune-telling, sorcery, astrology, magic, wizardry, witchcraft, enchanting, soothsaying, spell-casting, or consulting the dead or communicating with spirits other than the Spirit of God. This *Mitzvah* is relevant today because many (if not all) of the occult practices mentioned in Scriptures are still practiced in certain quarters. Some more recent occult activities that are not mentioned in Scripture are hexing, water witching, numerology, *Kabbalah,* voodoo, new age spiritism, mindreading, channeling, energy healing (and there are others). It is not necessary to know the definitions of each of these or how each is different from the others. All that one needs to know is that it is a serious sin to attempt to communicate with any spirit other than the Holy Spirit, or to seek power from any source other than from God.

Classical Commentators

Maimonides, Meir, and HaChinuch each wrote ten *mitzvot* that collectively express the principle of this *Mitzvah.* Curiously and uncharacteristically, HaChinuch's *mitzvah* C514 (having to do with a kind of wizardry) that is analogous to Maimonides' *mitzvah* RN37 and Meir's *mitzvah* MN173, does not reference a Scripture from the *Torah,* but only tractate *Kil'ayim* (viii, 4) of the Jerusalem Talmud, and <u>Job 5:23</u> (see * above) that seemingly speaks to an unrelated subject.

<u>NCLA</u>: JMm JFm KMm KFm GMm GFm

13. Benefitting from Idolatry.

We are not to derive any benefit from idolatry.

This precept is derived from His Word (blessed be He):

Key Scriptures

Exodus 34:12 (Meir MN15; Chinuch C111)
Be careful not to make a covenant with the people living in the land where you are going, so that they won't become a snare within your own borders.

Exodus 34:13-16 (Maimonides RN194; Meir MN15; Chinuch C111)
Rather, you are to demolish their altars, smash their standing-stones and cut down their sacred poles; because you are not to bow down to any other god; since ADONAI—whose very name is Jealous—is a jealous God. Do not make a covenant with the people living in the land. It will cause you to go astray after their gods and sacrifice to their gods. Then they will invite you to join them in eating their sacrifices, and you will take their daughters as wives for your sons. Their daughters will prostitute themselves to their own gods and make your sons do the same!

Numbers 25:1 (Maimonides RN194)
Isra'el stayed at Sheetim, and there the people began whoring with the women of Mo'av.

Deuteronomy 7:25 (Maimonides RN22; Meir MN17; Chinuch C428)
You are to burn up completely the carved statues of their gods. Don't be greedy for the silver or gold on them; don't take it with you, or you will be trapped by it; for it is abhorrent to ADONAI your God.

Deuteronomy 7:26 (Maimonides RN25; Meir MN18; Chinuch C429)
Don't bring something abhorrent into your house, or you will share in the curse that is on it; instead, you are to detest it completely, loathe it utterly; for it is set apart for destruction.

Deuteronomy 13:16(15)-18(17) (Maimonides RN24, 25; Meir MN18; Chinuch C429, 466)
...you must put the inhabitants of that city to death with the sword, destroying it completely with the sword, everything in it, including its livestock. Heap all its spoils in an open space, and burn the city with its spoils to the ground for ADONAI your God; it will remain a tel forever and not be built again—none of what has been set apart for destruction is to stay in your hands. Then ADONAI will turn from his fierce anger and show you mercy, have compassion on you and increase your numbers, as he swore to your ancestors-

Deuteronomy 32:17
They sacrificed to demons, non-gods, gods that they had never known, new gods that had come up lately, which your ancestors had not feared.

Deuteronomy 32:38 (Maimonides RN194; Chinuch C111)
Who ate the fat of their sacrifices and drank the wine of their drink offering? Let him get up and help you, let him protect you!

Acts 15:28-29
For it seemed good to the Ruach HaKodesh and to us not to lay any heavier burden on you than the following requirements: to abstain from what has been sacrificed to idols, from blood, from things strangled, and from fornication. If you keep yourselves from these, you will be doing the right thing. Shalom!

1 Corinthians 10:19-21
So, what am I saying? That food sacrificed to idols has any significance in itself? or that an idol has significance in itself? No, what I am saying is that the things which pagans sacrifice, they sacrifice not to God but to demons; and I don't want you to become sharers of the demons! You can't drink both a cup of the Lord and a cup of demons, you can't partake in both a meal of the Lord and a meal of demons.

2 Corinthians 6:16-17
What agreement can there be between the temple of God and idols? For we are the temple of the living God—as God said, "I will house myself in them...and I will walk among you. I will be their God, and they will be my people. Therefore ADONAI says, "'Go out from their midst; separate yourselves; don't even touch what is unclean. Then I myself will receive you."

1 John 5:21
Children, guard yourselves against false gods (NkJ: idols)!

Supportive Scriptures

Psalms 106:36-37
Colossians 3:5
Revelation 9:20

Commentary

This *Mitzvah* prohibits us from deriving any benefit from idolatry. This includes deriving benefit from objects of idolatry, from idolatry as a practice, and from those who engage in it. We are prohibited from selling or even possessing objects of idolatrous worship, and thereby benefitting from their value and the intrinsic value of their material components. We are also prohibited from benefitting in less obvious ways such as (I would argue) employing idolaters to do for us on the *Shabbat,* that which we are commanded to not do ourselves. It also prohibits us from benefitting from idols that are not of the physical kind, but rather idols of the heart and flesh such as pride, lust, self before God (and others), etc. There are numerous ways that we might be able to (but must not) derive benefit from such idols; an example would be compromising a moral biblical precept in order to not lose a business opportunity (see Matthew 6:24 and Colossians 3:5).

407

Idols of all kinds (including things of the occult) are associated with demons and curses (see Deuteronomy 7:26), and we must therefore not possess them, take them into our homes, or even touch them. It is a matter of discernment, however, as to how direct the receiving of benefit from an idol or idolatry must be, in order for it to be considered a violation of Scripture. For example, is it permissible to eat food prepared by one you suspect of being an idol worshiper? Suppose the restaurant one enters exhibits a statue of Buddha or displays food sacrificed to the proprietor's ancestors? Interestingly, Scripture allows Israelites to receive commercial benefit from foreigners (most likely idolaters during the time of Moses) that they cannot receive from fellow Jews. One such example is that all debts are cancelled during the *sh'mittah* (sabbatical year) as to fellow Jews but not as to foreigners (Deuteronomy 15:1-3). Therefore, if you loan to a foreigner and the *sh'mittah* arrives, you can continue to collect what you have loaned, whereas if you loan to a Jew, you cannot. Another example is that, according to Deuteronomy 23:21(20), a Jew can lend at interest to an outsider (presumably even an idolater), whereas a loan to a fellow Jew has to be interest-free.

Finally, note the similarity of Acts 15:28-29 and Deuteronomy 32:38 in their instruction to not eat or drink foods connected to idol worship. They both prohibit the physical eating of such foods, but one might perceive a broader and higher meaning from them, which is to abstain from nourishing ourselves with anything related to idolatry.

Classical Commentators

Maimonides, Meir, and HaChinuch treat the subject of not benefiting from idolatry as several *mitzvot*. They anticipate that some of the prohibited benefits of idolatry could be (1) covenanting with idolaters for any gainful purpose; (2) wearing items that have adorned an idol; (3) obtaining an idolater wife for one's son; and (4) profiting from the precious materials of carved statues.

NCLA: JMm JFm KMm KFm GMm GFm

14. Enticing Others to Idolatry.

We are not to entice others to idolatry.

This precept is derived from His Word (blessed be He):

Key Scriptures

Exodus 23:13 (Maimonides RN15; Meir MN14; Chinuch C87)
Pay attention to everything I have said to you; do not invoke the names of other gods or even let them be heard crossing your lips.

Deuteronomy 13:7(6)-16(15) (Maimonides RN15, 16; Meir MN23; Chinuch C462)
If your brother the son of your mother, or your son, or your daughter, or your wife whom you love, or your friend who means as much to you as yourself, secretly tries to entice you to go and serve other gods, which you haven't known, neither you nor your ancestors—gods of the peoples surrounding you, whether near or far away from you, anywhere in the world—you are not to consent, and you are not to listen to him; and you must not pity him or spare him; and you may not conceal him. Rather, you must kill him! Your own hand must be the first one on him in putting him to death, and afterwards the hands of all the people. You are to stone him to death; because he has tried to draw you away from ADONAI your God, who brought you out of the land of Egypt, out of a life of slavery. Then all Isra'el will hear about it and be afraid, so that they will stop doing such wickedness as this among themselves. If you hear it told that in one of your cities which ADONAI your God is giving you to live in, certain scoundrels have sprung up among you and have drawn away the inhabitants of their city by saying, 'Let's go and serve other gods, which you haven't known,' then you are to investigate the matter, inquiring and searching diligently. If the rumor is true, if it is confirmed that such detestable things are being done among you, you must put the inhabitants of that city to death with the sword, destroying it completely with the sword, everything in it, including its livestock.

1 Corinthians 12:2
You know that when you were pagans, no matter how you felt you were being led, you were being led astray to idols, which can't speak at all.

Revelation 2:14
Nevertheless, I have a few things against you: you have some people who hold to the teaching of Bil'am, who taught Balak to set a trap for the people of Isra'el, so that they would eat food that had been sacrificed to idols and commit sexual sin.

Commentary

The Scriptures are clear that we are not to entice anyone into idolatry. Although they refer to physical idols and false gods, Matthew 6:24 and Colossians 3:5 consider anything to be a "god" or an idol that competes with the one true God by becoming man's master, or that we put ahead of the one true God in any other way. Such idols can be money, sexual immorality, impurity, lust, evil desires, property, power, security, greed, and others. Consequently, anyone who entices others to pursue such things is guilty of violating the Scriptures that underlie this *Mitzvah*.

Classical Commentators

Maimonides, Meir, and HaChinuch published similar *mitzvot* on the subject of this *Mitzvah*. Maimonides' RN15, Meir's MN14, and HaChinuch's C87 declare that we must not call any person to idolatry, and Maimonides' RN16, Meir's MN23, and HaChinuch's C462 state that we must not persuade an Israelite to engage in idolatry. Maimonides supports the Scripture's prescribed death penalty for leading an Israelite into idolatry, and states that the victim—the one who was persuaded—should be the one to put the enticer to death. Capital punishment by the governing authorities is not authorized in the New Covenant but, where there is unrepentance, excommunication and expulsion from the community of believers is authorized (see Proverbs 22:10, Matthew 18:15-17, Romans 16:17, 1 Corinthians 5:11, 2 Thessalonians 3:6, and Titus 3:10-11).

NCLA: JMm JFm KMm KFm GMm GFm

15. Enabling Idolatry.

We are not to enable others to idolatry.

This precept is derived from His Word (blessed be He):

Key Scriptures

Exodus 17:8-13 (Maimonides RN59)
Then 'Amalek came and fought with Isra'el at Refidim. Moshe said to Y'hoshua, "Choose men for us, go out, and fight with 'Amalek. Tomorrow I will stand on top of the hill with God's staff in my hand." Y'hoshua did as Moshe had told him and fought with 'Amalek. Then Moshe, Aharon and Hur went up to the top of the hill. When Moshe raised his hand, Isra'el prevailed; but when he let it down, 'Amalek prevailed. However, Moshe's hands grew heavy; so they took a stone and put it under him, and he sat on it. Aharon and Hur held up his hands, the one on the one side and the other on the other; so that his hands stayed steady until sunset. Thus Y'hoshua defeated 'Amalek, putting their people to the sword.

Exodus 20:20 (Maimonides RN4; Meir MN144; Chinuch C39)
You are not to make with me gods of silver, nor are you to make gods of gold for yourselves.

Exodus 23:27-33 (Maimonides RN51; Meir ML26; Chinuch C94)
I will send terror of me ahead of you, throwing into confusion all the people to whom you come; and I will make all your enemies turn their backs on you. I will send hornets ahead of you to drive out the Hivi, Kena'ani and Hitti from before you. I will not drive them out from before you in one year, which would cause the land to become desolate and the wild animals too many for you. I will drive them out from before you gradually, until you have grown in number and can take possession of the land. I will set your boundaries from the Sea of Suf to the sea of the P'lishtim and from the desert to the [Euphrates] River, for I will hand the inhabitants of the land over to you, and you will drive them out from before you. You are not to make a covenant with them or with their gods. They are not to live in your land; otherwise they will make you sin against me by ensnaring you to serve their gods.

Leviticus 19:4 (Maimonides RN3; Meir MN10; Chinuch C214)
Do not turn to idols, and do not cast metal gods for yourselves; I am ADONAI your God.

Deuteronomy 7:1-2 (Maimonides RN50; Meir MN20; Chinuch C426)
ADONAI your God is going to bring you into the land you will enter in order to take possession of it, and he will expel many nations ahead of you—the Hitti, Girgashi, Emori, Kena'ani, P'rizi, Hivi and Y'vusi, seven nations bigger and stronger than you. When he does this, when ADONAI your God hands them over ahead of you, and you defeat them, you are to destroy them completely! Do not make any covenant with them. Show them no mercy.

Deuteronomy 13:7(6)-9(8) (Maimonides RN17-21; Meir MN24-26; Chinuch 457-461)
If your brother the son of your mother, or your son, or your daughter, or your wife whom you love, or your friend who means as much to you as yourself, secretly tries to entice you to go and serve other gods, which you haven't known, neither you nor your ancestors—gods of the peoples surrounding you, whether near or far away from you, anywhere in the world—you are not to consent, and you are not to listen to him; and you must not pity him or spare him; and you may not conceal him.

Deuteronomy 13:13-17 (Maimonides RN23; Chinuch C465)
If you hear it told that in one of your cities which ADONAI your God is giving you to live in, certain scoundrels have sprung up among you and have drawn away the inhabitants of their city by saying, 'Let's go and serve other gods, which you haven't known,' then you are to investigate the matter, inquiring and searching diligently. If the rumor is true, if it is confirmed that such detestable things are being done among you, you must put the inhabitants of that city to death with the sword, destroying it completely with the sword, everything in it, including its livestock. Heap all its spoils in an open space, and burn the city with its spoils to the ground for ADONAI your God; it will remain a tel forever and not be built again-

Deuteronomy 16:21-22 (Maimonides RN11; Meir MN162; Chinuch C493)
You are not to plant any sort of tree as a sacred pole beside the altar of ADONAI your God that you will make for yourselves. Likewise, do not set up a standing-stone; ADONAI your God hates such things.

Deuteronomy 20:10-11 (Maimonides RN56; Chinuch C562)
When you advance on a town to attack it, first offer it terms for peace. If it accepts the terms for peace and opens its gates to you, then all the people there are to be put to forced labor and work for you.

Deuteronomy 23:4(3)-7(6) (Maimonides RN56; Chinuch C562)
No 'Amoni or Mo'avi may enter the assembly of ADONAI, nor may any of his descendants down to the tenth generation ever enter the assembly of ADONAI, because they did not supply you with food and water when you were on the road after leaving Egypt, and because they hired Bil'am the son of B'or from P'tor in Aram-Naharayim to put a curse on you. But ADONAI your God would not listen to Bil'am; rather, ADONAI your God turned the curse into a blessing for you; because ADONAI your God loved you. So you are never to seek their peace or well being, as long as you live.

Deuteronomy 25:17-19 (Maimonides RN59; Meir MN194; Chinuch C605)
Remember what 'Amalek did to you on the road as you were coming out of Egypt, how he met you by the road, attacked those in the rear, those who were exhausted and straggling behind when you were tired and weary. He did not fear God. Therefore, when ADONAI your God has given you rest from all your surrounding enemies in the land ADONAI your God is giving you as your inheritance to possess, you are to blot out all memory of 'Amalek from under heaven. Don't forget!

412

<u>1 Corinthians 10:14</u>
Therefore, my dear friends, run from idolatry!

<u>Ephesians 5:11</u>
Have nothing to do with the deeds produced by darkness, but instead expose them…

Supportive Scriptures

Isaiah 44:9-11
Psalms 115:3-8
Proverbs 3:27
Romans 1:32
2 Thessalonians 3:10-15
1 Timothy 5:22b
2 Timothy 2:25
2 John 1:9-11

Commentary

<u>Matthew 6:24</u> and <u>Colossians 3:5</u> make it clear that Idolatry is broader than just worshiping physical idols and foreign gods. An idol is anything (or anyone) that we desire more strongly than we desire God, and idolatry is any giving-in to such a desire, and putting that thing or person ahead of God. Given that definition, what it means to practice idolatry or entice others to idolatry is clear but, what is not as clear is what it means to enable idolatry. That is more subtle and often goes unrecognized. We know that a family member is addicted to alcohol, yet we allow him to store liquor in the house. We have a listless son who will not work, yet we house him, feed him, and lend him our car. Consciously enabling another to commit sin (including idolatrous sin) makes us a participant, and as culpable as the one who actually commits it.

The commandment in <u>Deuteronomy 7:2</u> to kill the heathen and show no mercy was given in the context of Israel first entering the promised land and God delivering the heathen of the land into their hands for destruction. Even today, we should show limited mercy to the opponents of God if the mercy will further their idolatry. To give a trivial opinion example, if a person drops a stack of pamphlets that teach unbiblical practices, we should not assist him in gathering them up. We cannot apply the Scripture to justify destroying all heathens in these New Covenant times because that would be in violation of <u>Leviticus 19:18</u> and <u>Matthew 22:39</u>, which require that we love our neighbor, in violation of <u>Matthew 5:44</u>, which commands us to love our enemies, and in violation of <u>1 Peter 2:13-14</u>, which commands us to submit to human authorities. To destroy all idolaters today would also be contrary to our New Covenant commission to carry God's Word to the sinners of the world (<u>Mark 16:15</u>; <u>Luke 15:10</u>; <u>Romans 5:8</u>; <u>1 Timothy 1:15</u>).

Now a word about <u>Exodus 23:33</u> that prohibits us from allowing idolaters to dwell in our land lest their sin be a snare for us. As individuals, we cannot control what is allowed in the Land of Israel, but we do have control over who we allow to live in our houses and congregations. This is not to say that we should not invite idolatrous sinners into our dwelling places as guests for a time, for how else can we minister the Word of God to them? Still, such persons should not be invited for an extended period of time, or allowed to share occupancy with us as co-owners or co-tenants.

Classical Commentators

This *Mitzvah* consolidates several *mitzvot* that were codified separately by Maimonides, Meir, and HaChinuch. In his *mitzvah* to show no mercy to idol-worshippers, Meir takes an exceptionally severe position by saying that if we see an idol-worshipper drowning, we are not to save him, and if we find him ill, we are not to cure him. He does not, however, advocate precipitating a person's death merely because he is an idol-worshipper. Maimonides treats this *mitzvah* in another way—as a prohibition against extending grace to an idolater. He says, for example, that we must not complement an idolater as being good-looking. A strange example, but it makes the point.

Note: Leviticus 19:16 that is cited by Maimonides' RN19, and Exodus 23:5 that is cited in Maimonides' RN18 and HaChinuch's C458, do not appear to have relevance to the subject of this *Mitzvah*.

NCLA: JMm JFm KMm KFm GMm GFm

16. Destroying Idolatry.

We are to destroy idolatry-related objects and places that are within our domain and control.

This precept is derived from His Word (blessed be He):

Key Scriptures

Destroying Objects and Places of Idolatry

Exodus 23:23-24
When my angel goes ahead of you and brings you to the Emori, Hitti, P'rizi, Kena'ani, Hivi and Y'vusi, I will make an end of them. You are not to worship their gods, serve them or follow their practices; rather, you are to demolish them completely and smash their standing-stones to pieces.

Leviticus 26:30
I will destroy your high places, cut down your pillars for sun-worship, and throw your carcasses on the carcasses of your idols; and I will detest you.

Numbers 33:50-53
ADONAI spoke to Moshe in the plains of Mo'av by the Yarden, across from Yericho. He said to tell the people of Isra'el, "When you cross the Yarden into the land of Kena'an, you are to expel all the people living in the land from in front of you. Destroy all their stone figures, destroy all their metal statues and demolish all their high places. Drive out the inhabitants of the land, and live in it, for I have given the land to you to possess.

Deuteronomy 7:5 (Maimonides RP185; Chinuch 436)
No, treat them this way: break down their altars, smash their standing-stones to pieces, cut down their sacred poles and burn up their carved images completely.

Deuteronomy 7:25-26
You are to burn up completely the carved statues of their gods. Don't be greedy for the silver or gold on them; don't take it with you, or you will be trapped by it; for it is abhorrent to ADONAI your God. Don't bring something abhorrent into your house, or you will share in the curse that is on it; instead, you are to detest it completely, loathe it utterly; for it is set apart for destruction.

Deuteronomy 12:1-3 (Maimonides RP185; Chinuch C436)
Here are the laws and rulings you are to observe and obey in the land ADONAI, the God of your ancestors, has given you to possess as long as you live on earth. You must destroy all the places where the nations you are dispossessing served their gods, whether on high mountains, on hills, or under some leafy tree. Break down their altars, smash their standing-stones to pieces, burn up their sacred poles completely and cut down the carved images of their gods. Exterminate their name from that place.

415

Deuteronomy 13:17(16)-19(18) (Maimonides RP186; Chinuch C464)
Heap all its spoils in an open space, and burn the city with its spoils to the ground for ADONAI your God; it will remain a tel forever and not be built again—none of what has been set apart for destruction is to stay in your hands. Then ADONAI will turn from his fierce anger and show you mercy, have compassion on you and increase your numbers, as he swore to your ancestors— provided you listen to what ADONAI says and obey all his mitzvot that I am giving you today, thus doing what ADONAI your God sees as right.

Destroying Persons Who Are Idolaters (Not authorized in the New Covenant)

Exodus 22:19(20)
Anyone who sacrifices to any god other than ADONAI alone is to be completely destroyed.

Numbers 24:12-20 (Chinuch C603)
Bil'am answered Balak, "Didn't I tell the messengers you sent me that even if Balak would give me his palace full of silver and gold, I could not of my own accord go beyond the word of ADONAI to do either good or bad? that what ADONAI said is what I would say? But now that I am going back to my own people, come, I will warn you what this people will do to your people in the acharit-hayamim. So he made his pronouncement: "This is the speech of Bil'am, son of B'or; the speech of the man whose eyes have been opened; the speech of him who hears God's words; who knows what 'Elyon knows, who sees what Shaddai sees, who has fallen, yet has open eyes: "I see him, but not now; I behold him, but not soon—a star will step forth from Ya'akov, a scepter will arise from Isra'el, to crush the corners of Mo'av and destroy all descendants of Shet. His enemies will be his possessions—Edom and Se'ir, possessions. Isra'el will do valiantly, From Ya'akov will come someone who will rule, and he will destroy what is left of the city." He saw 'Amalek and made this pronouncement: "First among nations was 'Amalek, but destruction will be its end."

Deuteronomy 3:21-22 (Maimonides RN58; Chinuch C525)
Also at that time I gave this order to Y'hoshua: 'Your eyes have seen everything that ADONAI your God has done to these two kings. ADONAI will do the same to all the kingdoms you encounter when you cross over. Don't be afraid of them, because ADONAI your God will fight on your behalf.'

Deuteronomy 7:1-4 (Chinuch C425)
ADONAI your God is going to bring you into the land you will enter in order to take possession of it, and he will expel many nations ahead of you—the Hitti, Girgashi, Emori, Kena'ani, P'rizi, Hivi and Y'vusi, seven nations bigger and stronger than you. When he does this, when ADONAI your God hands them over ahead of you, and you defeat them, you are to destroy them completely! Do not make any covenant with them. Show them no mercy. Don't intermarry with them—don't give your daughter to his son, and don't take his daughter for your son. For he will turn your children away from following me in order to serve other gods. If this happens, the anger of ADONAI will flare up against you, and he will quickly destroy you.

Deuteronomy 7:16-21 (Maimonides RN58; Chinuch C525)
You are to devour all the peoples that ADONAI your God hands over to you—show them no pity, and do not serve their gods, because that will become a trap for you. If you think to yourselves, 'These nations outnumber us; how can we dispossess them?' nevertheless, you are not to be afraid of them; you are to remember well what ADONAI your God did to Pharaoh and all of Egypt—the great ordeals which you yourself saw, and the signs, wonders, strong hand and outstretched arm by which ADONAI your God brought you out. ADONAI will do the same to all the peoples of whom you are afraid. Moreover, ADONAI your God will send the hornet among them until those who are left and those who hide themselves perish ahead of you. You are not to be frightened of them, because ADONAI your God is there with you, a God great and fearsome.

Deuteronomy 13:7(6)-16(15)
If your brother the son of your mother, or your son, or your daughter, or your wife whom you love, or your friend who means as much to you as yourself, secretly tries to entice you to go and serve other gods, which you haven't known, neither you nor your ancestors—gods of the peoples surrounding you, whether near or far away from you, anywhere in the world—you are not to consent, and you are not to listen to him; and you must not pity him or spare him; and you may not conceal him. Rather, you must kill him! Your own hand must be the first one on him in putting him to death, and afterwards the hands of all the people. You are to stone him to death; because he has tried to draw you away from ADONAI your God, who brought you out of the land of Egypt, out of a life of slavery. Then all Isra'el will hear about it and be afraid, so that they will stop doing such wickedness as this among themselves. If you hear it told that in one of your cities which ADONAI your God is giving you to live in, certain scoundrels have sprung up among you and have drawn away the inhabitants of their city by saying, 'Let's go and serve other gods, which you haven't known,' then you are to investigate the matter, inquiring and searching diligently. If the rumor is true, if it is confirmed that such detestable things are being done among you, you must put the inhabitants of that city to death with the sword, destroying it completely with the sword, everything in it, including its livestock.

Deuteronomy 17:2-5
If there is found among you, within any of your gates [in any city] that ADONAI your God gives you, a man or woman who does what ADONAI your God sees as wicked, transgressing his covenant by going and serving other gods and worshipping them, the sun, the moon, or anything in the sky—something I have forbidden—and it is told to you, or you hear about it; then you are to investigate the matter diligently. If it is true, if it is confirmed that such detestable things are being done in Isra'el; then you are to bring the man or woman who has done this wicked thing to your city gates, and stone that man or woman to death.

Deuteronomy 18:20
But if a prophet presumptuously speaks a word in my name which I didn't order him to say, or if he speaks in the name of other gods, then that prophet must die.

Deuteronomy 20:16-18 (Maimonides RP187; Chinuch C425)
As for the towns of these peoples, which ADONAI your God is giving you as your inheritance, you are not to allow anything that breathes to live. Rather you must destroy them completely—

the Hitti, the Emori, the Kena'ani, the P'rizi, the Hivi and the Y'vusi—as ADONAI your God has ordered you; so that they won't teach you to follow their abominable practices, which they do for their gods, thus causing you to sin against ADONAI your God.

Deuteronomy 25:17-19 (Maimonides RP188-189; Meir MP76-77; Chinuch C603-604)
Remember what 'Amalek did to you on the road as you were coming out of Egypt, how he met you by the road, attacked those in the rear, those who were exhausted and straggling behind when you were tired and weary. He did not fear God. Therefore, when ADONAI your God has given you rest from all your surrounding enemies in the land ADONAI your God is giving you as your inheritance to possess, you are to blot out all memory of 'Amalek from under heaven. Don't forget!

Jeremiah 48:10 (Chinuch C525)
A curse on him who does the work of ADONAI carelessly! A curse on him who withholds his sword from blood!

Colossians 3:5
Therefore, put to death the earthly parts of your nature—sexual immorality, impurity, lust, evil desires and greed (which is a form of idolatry)...

Idolatry Dealt with in the New Covenant

Acts 17:22-24
Sha'ul stood up in the Council meeting and said, "Men of Athens: I see how very religious you are in every way! For as I was walking around, looking at your shrines, I even found an altar which had been inscribed, 'To An Unknown God.' So, the one whom you are already worshipping in ignorance—this is the one I proclaim to you. The God who made the universe and everything in it, and who is Lord of heaven and earth, does not live in man-made temples...

1 Corinthians 10:19-21
So, what am I saying? That food sacrificed to idols has any significance in itself? or that an idol has significance in itself? No, what I am saying is that the things which pagans sacrifice, they sacrifice not to God but to demons; and I don't want you to become sharers of the demons! You can't drink both a cup of the Lord and a cup of demons, you can't partake in both a meal of the Lord and a meal of demons.

2 Corinthians 10:3-5
For although we do live in the world, we do not wage war in a worldly way; because the weapons we use to wage war are not worldly. On the contrary, they have God's power for demolishing strongholds. We demolish arguments and every arrogance that raises itself up against the knowledge of God; we take every thought captive and make it obey the Messiah.

Ephesians 6:11-13
Use all the armor and weaponry that God provides, so that you will be able to stand against the deceptive tactics of the Adversary. For we are not struggling against human beings, but against the rulers, authorities and cosmic powers governing this darkness, against the spiritual forces of

evil in the heavenly realm. So take up every piece of war equipment God provides; so that when the evil day comes, you will be able to resist; and when the battle is won, you will still be standing.

Supportive Scriptures—The High Places Were Initially Not Destroyed

1 Kings 22:42-45
2 Kings 14:1-4, 15:1-5, 32-35
2 Chronicles 33:15-17

Supportive Scriptures—The High Places Were Finally Destroyed

2 Kings 18:1-5, 23:4-16

Commentary

The Mosaic Law calls for a complete destruction of idolatry including, in many cases, killing idolaters themselves. During the time of Moses, the Israelites lived under a theocracy that was governed directly by God that made these practices reasonable, but today we live under (and are subject to) governments that are secular. The laws under which we live today do not allow us to apply many of the Mosaic Laws literally, and they should not allow it, because the governments under which we now live are not ruled by God. That notwithstanding, God's extremely negative attitude toward idolatry should be adopted as our own, and we should seek the Holy Spirit for how to bring destruction to idolatry in every way that is permissible in our individual circumstances.

Idolatry, in its broadest terms, comprises not only the worship of false deities, but anything that we allow to displace God in ruling our lives. Colossians 3:5 lists some of them and, although slaying idolatrous people is not authorized in the New Covenant, we are called to put to death instead, things such as sexual immorality, impurity, evil desires, and greed (see also, Matthew 6:24).

Because today we live under secular laws and governments, we cannot do away with objects and places of idolatry that are owned by others. We cannot, for example, smash the statue of Buddha in our neighborhood Chinese restaurant, nor burn down the Hindu temple across town. We can, however, destroy and remove from our own houses and domains under our control, idolatry-connected art, jewelry, books, videos, and other such items that are owned by us, and we should. Similarly, we should not play games or view videos that depict idolatrous or occult practices, and should not show approval of those that do. As for the broader definition of idols, i.e. associations, things and practices that draw us toward unholy thoughts or deeds or that exercise power over us that is not from God—these we must renounce and do away with, and help others to do so as well.

Classical Commentators

The *mitzvot* of Maimonides and HaChinuch ascribe credibility to a literal interpretation of the Mosaic Scriptures, whereas Meir does not. For example, in his RN186 and RN187, Maimonides states[126] that we must "slay all the people of an apostate city," and "exterminate the seven Nations that inhabited the Land of Canaan." Meir simply does not write *mitzvot* that correspond to these.

<u>NCLA</u>: **JMm JFm KMm KFm GMm GFm**

---

126 Maimonides, <u>Sefer Ha-Mitzvot of Maimonides</u>, v. 1, pp. 199-202 (London: The Soncino Press Ltd, 1967).

17. Listening to Those Who Would Lead Us toward Idolatry.

We are not to listen to those who would lead us toward idolatry.

This precept is derived from His Word (blessed be He):

Key Scriptures

Exodus 14:10-14 (Maimonides RN46; Chinuch C500)
As Pharaoh approached, the people of Isra'el looked up and saw the Egyptians right there, coming after them. In great fear the people of Isra'el cried out to ADONAI and said to Moshe, "Was it because there weren't enough graves in Egypt that you brought us out to die in the desert? Why have you done this to us, bringing us out of Egypt? Didn't we tell you in Egypt to let us alone, we'll just go on being slaves for the Egyptians? It would be better for us to be the Egyptians' slaves than to die in the desert!" Moshe answered the people, "Stop being so fearful! Remain steady, and you will see how ADONAI is going to save you. He will do it today—today you have seen the Egyptians, but you will never see them again! ADONAI will do battle for you. Just calm yourselves down!"

Deuteronomy 13:2(1)-4(3) (Maimonides RN28; Meir MN22; Chinuch C456)
If a prophet or someone who gets messages while dreaming arises among you and he gives you a sign or wonder, and the sign or wonder comes about as he predicted when he said, 'Let's follow other gods, which you have not known; and let us serve them,' you are not to listen to what that prophet or dreamer says. For ADONAI your God is testing you, in order to find out whether you really do love ADONAI your God with all your heart and being.

Deuteronomy 13:7(6)-12(11)
If your brother the son of your mother, or your son, or your daughter, or your wife whom you love, or your friend who means as much to you as yourself, secretly tries to entice you to go and serve other gods, which you haven't known, neither you nor your ancestors—gods of the peoples surrounding you, whether near or far away from you, anywhere in the world—you are not to consent, and you are not to listen to him; and you must not pity him or spare him; and you may not conceal him. Rather, you must kill him! Your own hand must be the first one on him in putting him to death, and afterwards the hands of all the people. You are to stone him to death; because he has tried to draw you away from ADONAI your God, who brought you out of the land of Egypt, out of a life of slavery. Then all Isra'el will hear about it and be afraid, so that they will stop doing such wickedness as this among themselves.

Deuteronomy 17:14-16 (Maimonides RN46; Meir MN192; Chinuch C500)
When you have entered the land ADONAI your God is giving you, have taken possession of it and are living there, you may say, 'I want to have a king over me, like all the other nations around me.' In that event, you must appoint as king the one whom ADONAI your God will choose. He must be one of your kinsmen, this king you appoint over you—you are forbidden to

appoint a foreigner over you who is not your kinsman. However, he is not to acquire many horses for himself or have the people return to Egypt to obtain more horses, inasmuch as ADONAI told you never to go back that way again.

Deuteronomy 18:9-14
When you enter the land ADONAI your God is giving you, you are not to learn how to follow the abominable practices of those nations. There must not be found among you anyone who makes his son or daughter pass through fire, a diviner, a soothsayer, an enchanter, a sorcerer, a spell-caster, a consulter of ghosts or spirits, or a necromancer. For whoever does these things is detestable to ADONAI, and because of these abominations ADONAI your God is driving them out ahead of you. You must be wholehearted with ADONAI your God. For these nations, which you are about to dispossess, listen to soothsayers and diviners; but you, ADONAI your God does not allow you to do this.

Deuteronomy 18:20
But if a prophet presumptuously speaks a word in my name which I didn't order him to say, or if he speaks in the name of other gods, then that prophet must die.

Deuteronomy 28:63-68 (Maimonides RN46; Chinuch C500)
Thus it will come about that just as once ADONAI took joy in seeking to do you good and increase your numbers, so now ADONAI will take joy in causing you to perish and be destroyed, and you will be plucked off the land you are entering in order to take possession of it. ADONAI will scatter you among all peoples from one end of the earth to the other, and there you will serve other gods, made of wood and stone, which neither you nor your ancestors have known. Among these nations you will not find repose, and there will be no rest for the sole of your foot; rather ADONAI will give you there anguish of heart, dimness of eyes and apathy of spirit. Your life will hang in doubt before you; you will be afraid night and day and have no assurance that you will stay alive. In the morning you will say, 'Oh, how I wish it were evening!' and in the evening you will say, 'Oh, how I wish it were morning!'—because of the fear overwhelming your heart and the sights your eyes will see. Finally, ADONAI will bring you back in ships to Egypt, the place of which I said to you, 'You will never ever see it again'; and there you will try to sell yourselves as slaves to your enemies, but no one will buy you.

Galatians 1:8-9
But even if we—or, for that matter, an angel from heaven!—were to announce to you some so-called "Good News" contrary to the Good News we did announce to you, let him be under a curse forever! We said it before, and I say it again: if anyone announces "Good News" contrary to what you received, let him be under a curse forever!

Supportive Scriptures

1 Corinthians 10:14, 12:1-2
2 Corinthians 6:16-17
1 John 5:21

Commentary

The Scriptures are clear that we are not to listen to those who would lead us toward idolatry. Although they refer to physical idols and false gods, Matthew 6:24 and Colossians 3:5 consider anything to be a "god" or an idol that competes with the one true God by becoming man's master, or that we put ahead of the one true God. Such idols can be money, sexual immorality, impurity, lust, evil desires, property, power, security, greed, and others. Consequently, anyone who listens to persons who lead others toward such things violates this *Mitzvah*.

Classical Commentators

This *Mitzvah* incorporates two of the classical commentators' *mitzvot*—to not listen to one who prophesies in the name of an idol, and to not make one's home in the land of Egypt where one can be influenced by Egypt's heresies and idolatrous customs.

NCLA: **JMm JFm KMm KFm GMm GFm**

18. Covenanting with Idolaters and Unbelievers.

We are not to enter into covenants with idolaters and unbelievers.

This precept is derived from His Word (blessed be He):

Key Scriptures

Exodus 23:28-33 (Maimonides RN48; Chinuch C93)
I will send hornets ahead of you to drive out the Hivi, Kena'ani and Hitti from before you. I will not drive them out from before you in one year, which would cause the land to become desolate and the wild animals too many for you. I will drive them out from before you gradually, until you have grown in number and can take possession of the land. I will set your boundaries from the Sea of Suf to the sea of the P'lishtim and from the desert to the [Euphrates] River, for I will hand the inhabitants of the land over to you, and you will drive them out from before you. You are not to make a covenant with them or with their gods. They are not to live in your land; otherwise they will make you sin against me by ensnaring you to serve their gods.

Exodus 34:11-16
Observe what I am ordering you to do today. Here! I am driving out ahead of you the Emori, Kena'ani, Hitti, P'rizi, Hivi and Y'vusi. Be careful not to make a covenant with the people living in the land where you are going, so that they won't become a snare within your own borders. Rather, you are to demolish their altars, smash their standing-stones and cut down their sacred poles; because you are not to bow down to any other god; since ADONAI—whose very name is Jealous—is a jealous God. Do not make a covenant with the people living in the land. It will cause you to go astray after their gods and sacrifice to their gods. Then they will invite you to join them in eating their sacrifices, and you will take their daughters as wives for your sons. Their daughters will prostitute themselves to their own gods and make your sons do the same!

Numbers 25:3-15 (Maimonides RN52; Chinuch C427)
With Isra'el thus joined to Ba'al-P'or, the anger of ADONAI blazed up against Isra'el. ADONAI said to Moshe, "Take all the chiefs of the people, and hang them facing the sun before ADONAI, so that the raging fury of ADONAI will turn away from Isra'el." Moshe said to the judges of Isra'el, "Each of you is to put to death those in his tribe who have joined themselves to Ba'al-P'or." Just then, in the sight of Moshe and the whole community of Isra'el, as they were weeping at the entrance to the tent of meeting, a man from Isra'el came by, bringing to his family a woman from Midyan. When Pinchas the son of El'azar, the son of Aharon the cohen, saw it, he got up from the middle of the crowd, took a spear in his hand, and pursued the man from Isra'el right into the inner part of the tent, where he thrust his spear through both of them—the man from Isra'el and the woman through her stomach. Thus was the plague among the people of Isra'el stopped; nevertheless, 24,000 died in the plague. ADONAI said to Moshe, "Pinchas the son of El'azar, the son of Aharon the cohen, has deflected my anger from the people of Isra'el by being as zealous as I am, so that I didn't destroy them in my own zeal. Therefore say, 'I am giving him my covenant of shalom, making a covenant with him and his descendants after him that the

office of cohen will be theirs forever.' This is because he was zealous on behalf of his God and made atonement for the people of Isra'el." The name of the man from Isra'el who was killed, put to death with the woman from Midyan, was Zimri the son of Salu, leader of one of the clans from the tribe of Shim'on. The name of the woman from Midyan who was killed was Kozbi the daughter of Tzur, and he was head of the people in one of the clans of Midyan.

Deuteronomy 7:1-6 (Maimonides RN48, 52; Meir MN19; Chinuch C93, 427)
ADONAI your God is going to bring you into the land you will enter in order to take possession of it, and he will expel many nations ahead of you—the Hitti, Girgashi, Emori, Kena'ani, P'rizi, Hivi and Y'vusi, seven nations bigger and stronger than you. When he does this, when ADONAI your God hands them over ahead of you, and you defeat them, you are to destroy them completely! Do not make any covenant with them. Show them no mercy. Don't intermarry with them—don't give your daughter to his son, and don't take his daughter for your son. For he will turn your children away from following me in order to serve other gods. If this happens, the anger of ADONAI will flare up against you, and he will quickly destroy you. No, treat them this way: break down their altars, smash their standing-stones to pieces, cut down their sacred poles and burn up their carved images completely. For you are a people set apart as holy for ADONAI your God. ADONAI your God has chosen you out of all the peoples on the face of the earth to be his own unique treasure.

Deuteronomy 20:16-18 (Maimonides RN49; Chinuch C528)
As for the towns of these peoples, which ADONAI your God is giving you as your inheritance, you are not to allow anything that breathes to live. Rather you must destroy them completely—the Hitti, the Emori, the Kena'ani, the P'rizi, the Hivi and the Y'vusi—as ADONAI your God has ordered you; so that they won't teach you to follow their abominable practices, which they do for their gods, thus causing you to sin against ADONAI your God.

Deuteronomy 23:4(3)-7(6) (Maimonides RN53; Chinuch C561)
No 'Amoni or Mo'avi may enter the assembly of ADONAI, nor may any of his descendants down to the tenth generation ever enter the assembly of ADONAI, because they did not supply you with food and water when you were on the road after leaving Egypt, and because they hired Bil'am the son of B'or from P'tor in Aram-Naharayim to put a curse on you. But ADONAI your God would not listen to Bil'am; rather, ADONAI your God turned the curse into a blessing for you, because ADONAI your God loved you. So you are never to seek their peace or well being, as long as you live.

2 Corinthians 6:14-16
Do not yoke yourselves together in a team with unbelievers. For how can righteousness and lawlessness be partners? What fellowship does light have with darkness? What harmony can there be between the Messiah and B'liya'al? What does a believer have in common with an unbeliever? What agreement can there be between the temple of God and idols? For we are the temple of the living God—as God said, "I will house myself in them...and I will walk among you. I will be their God, and they will be my people."

425

Supportive Scripture

Deuteronomy 22:10

Commentary

The Scriptures are plain in commanding that we are not to enter into covenants with idolaters and unbelievers in God, Yeshua, or the Bible. The kinds of covenants prohibited are not trivial agreements, but rather the kind that yoke individuals in causes for which the covenanting parties' understanding of God, morality, and ethics is material. Likewise, the kinds of idolaters contemplated are not those with minor personal bondages, but rather those whose idolatries render them unbelievers or persons whose judgments are likely to adversely affect the covenants into which they enter. The result of a believer entering into covenant with such a person can be disastrous because a believer's basis for conduct is God's Law, whereas an unbeliever recognizes no such authority.

The prohibition of this *Mitzvah* does not usually apply to contracts such as those to buy or sell a described item at a defined price, because the terms of such agreements are not vague and are usually not dependent on the moral and ethical values of the parties. On the other hand, partnerships of most kinds (especially marriage) by believers and unbelievers are prohibited because, in the course of continuously dealing with one another, partners must be biblically in accord in handling situations as they arise. In cases of unequal yoking, the covenanting parties hold different values and respond to different authorities for their conduct; the result is that, sooner or later, they will either dissolve their covenant and part ways, or the believing party will be persuaded by the unbelieving party to compromise his or her biblical principles. Many a marriage and business partnership has been shattered through unequal yoking.

Classical Commentators

Maimonides, Meir, and HaChinuch limit their *mitzvot* to the kinds of idolatries that are prevalent in the *Tanakh*—the kinds that involve unbelief in the God of Abraham, Isaac, and Jacob, and the consequent worship of heathen gods and physical idols. The people groups they include are the seven nations of Canaan and the Ammonites, Moabites, and heretics in general. They do not address idolatries of the heart and flesh.

<u>**NCLA:**</u> **JMm JFm KMm KFm GMm GFm**

19. Adopting Heathen Practices.

We are not to adopt the customs and practices of heathens.

This precept is derived from His Word (blessed be He):

Key Scriptures

Leviticus 18:3 (Maimonides RN30; Meir MN21; Chinuch C262)
You are not to engage in the activities found in the land of Egypt, where you used to live; and you are not to engage in the activities found in the land of Kena'an, where I am bringing you; nor are you to live by their laws.

Leviticus 19:27 (Maimonides RN43-44; Mei MN176-177; Chinuch C251-252)
Don't round your hair at the temples or mar the edges of your beard.

Leviticus 19:28 (Maimonides RN41, 45; Meir MN163; Chinuch C253, 467)
Don't cut gashes in your flesh when someone dies or tattoo yourselves; I am ADONAI.

Leviticus 20:23 (Maimonides RN30; Chinuch C262)
Do not live by the regulations of the nation which I am expelling ahead of you; because they did all these things, which is why I detested them.

Leviticus 26:1 (Maimonides RN12; Meir MN161; Chinuch C349)
You are not to make yourselves any idols, erect a carved statue or a standing-stone, or place any carved stone anywhere in your land in order to bow down to it. I am ADONAI your God.

Deuteronomy 12:29-31 (Maimonides RN30; Chinuch C262)
When ADONAI your God has cut off ahead of you the nations you are entering in order to dispossess, and when you have dispossessed them and are living in their land; be careful, after they have been destroyed ahead of you, not to be trapped into following them; so that you inquire after their gods and ask, 'How did these nations serve their gods? I want to do the same.' You must not do this to ADONAI your God! For they have done to their gods all the abominations that ADONAI hates! They even burn up their sons and daughters in the fire for their gods!

Deuteronomy 14:1-2 (Maimonides RN45; Meir MN28; Chinuch C467)
You are the people of ADONAI your God. You are not to gash yourselves or shave the hair above your foreheads in mourning for the dead, because you are a people set apart as holy for ADONAI your God. ADONAI your God has chosen you to be his own unique treasure out of all the peoples on the face of the earth.

Deuteronomy 22:5 (Maimonides RN39-40; Meir MN178-179; Chinuch C542-543)
A woman is not to wear men's clothing, and a man is not to put on women's clothing, for whoever does these things is detestable to ADONAI your God.

Deuteronomy 22:9-11 (Maimonides RN42; Meir MN181; Chinuch C551)
You are not to sow two kinds of seed between your rows of vines; if you do, both the two harvested crops and the yield from the vines must be forfeited. You are not to plow with an ox

and a donkey together. You are not to wear clothing woven with two kinds of thread, wool and linen together.

Zephaniah 1:8 (Maimonides RN30)
When the time comes for ADONAI's sacrifice—"I will punish the leaders and the sons of the king, also those who dress in foreign clothes.

Matthew 6:7-13
And when you pray, don't babble on and on like the pagans, who think God will hear them better if they talk a lot. Don't be like them, because your Father knows what you need before you ask him. You, therefore, pray like this: 'Our Father in heaven! May your Name be kept holy. May your Kingdom come, your will be done on earth as in heaven. Give us the food we need today. Forgive us what we have done wrong, as we too have forgiven those who have wronged us. And do not lead us into hard testing, but keep us safe from the Evil One. For kingship, power and glory are yours forever. Amen.'

Ephesians 4:17
Therefore I say this—indeed, in union with the Lord I insist on it: do not live any longer as the pagans live, with their sterile ways of thinking.

Colossians 2:8
Watch out, so that no one will take you captive by means of philosophy and empty deceit, following human tradition which accords with the elemental spirits of the world but does not accord with the Messiah.

1 Peter 4:1-5
Therefore, since the Messiah suffered physically, you too are to arm yourselves with the same attitude. For whoever has suffered physically is finished with sin, with the result that he lives the rest of his earthly life no longer controlled by human desires, but by God's will. For you have spent enough time already living the way the pagans want you to live—in debauchery, lust, drunkenness, orgies, wild parties and forbidden idol-worship. They think it strange that you don't plunge with them into the same flood of dissoluteness, and so they heap insults on you. But they will have to give an account to him who stands ready to judge the living and the dead.

Supportive Scriptures

Leviticus 19:19, 26
Deuteronomy 12:2-4
Ezekiel 36:16-19
Luke 11:2-4
Romans 12:1-2

Commentary

The Scriptures quoted herein prohibit the ancient Israelites and later New Covenant believers from adopting the customs and practices of heathens. Typical of these practices are eating blood, fortune-telling, practicing divination, rounding one's hair, cutting the edge of one's beard, tattooing or cutting one's flesh, wearing heathen-style of clothing, wearing garments of the opposite sex, worshiping idols, practicing debauchery, becoming drunk, and participating in wild parties and orgies.

Of special interest are Deuteronomy 12:2-4 and Deuteronomy 12:29-31 that enumerate ways in which heathens served their gods, and forbid Israelites from serving the one true God in similar ways. These two Scriptures have been the source of much debate as to whether customs and practices that were once used in idolatrous ways but are no longer used in those ways can be redeemed. Can a church not have a steeple because ancient heathen temples most probably had pointed roofs? Can we not light candles on *Shabbat* because the ancient heathen used candles and torches as part of their idolatrous worship? My opinion is that some such things can be used and some cannot, and we need to consult the Holy Spirit to know which are which.[127]

Other Scriptures that are related to this *Mitzvah* are those that prohibit wearing clothing made of wool and linen, and clothing of the opposite sex. I see them as related. Deuteronomy 22:9-11 prohibits our sowing two different kinds of seeds, plowing with two kinds of animals, and wear clothing made of two kinds of thread (wool and Linen). Leviticus 19:19 prohibits our mating two kinds of animals, sowing two kinds of grain, and wearing clothing made of two kinds of זְנַעַטְשֵׁ *(shatneiz),* which means "stuff." Deuteronomy 22:5 prohibits our wearing clothing of the opposite sex, which presumably means mixing two kinds of clothing—those of our own sex, and those of the opposite sex. The theme that is common to all of these is mixing things that do not naturally go together, and reminds one of 2 Corinthians 6:14 that states:

> *"Do not yoke yourselves together in a team with unbelievers. For how can righteousness and lawlessness be partners? What fellowship does light have with darkness?"*

Mixing things that do not belong together was (and still is) a perverted heathen practice (for example, mixing temple worship with prostitution), and we are prohibited from adopting heathen practices as our own.

Classical Commentators

Maimonides, Meir, and HaChinuch address each Scriptural prohibition separately; they do not connect them in a common theme. For example, Maimonides' RN30 deals with adopting the habits and customs of unbelievers generally, RN43 deals with shaving our temples, RN44 with shaving our beards, RN41 with receiving tattoos, etc.

According to Meir, examples of heathen customs that we must not follow are distinctive heathen dress, growing locks of hair, shaving the sides of the head, and leaving a crest of hair in the middle of the head (Mohawk hair style). Curiously, Meir exempts from such restrictions, those who are close to government rulers and, for whatever reason, must emulate their appearance. Maimonides likewise prohibits our wearing heathen dress, emulating heathens in their appearance, and participating in their social gatherings.

NCLA: JMm JFm KMm KFm GMm GFm

---

127 In view of this prohibition, one might consider the inappropriateness of Christians adopting heathen practices such as displaying images of deceased persons, erecting Christmas trees, and coloring Easter eggs.

J: Justice

J1. Applying the Mosaic Law in a Manner Consistent with New Covenant Realities.

We are to apply the Mosaic Law in a manner that is consistent with New Covenant realities.

This precept is derived from His Word (blessed be He):

Key Scriptures

Jeremiah 31:30(31)-33(34)
"Here, the days are coming," says ADONAI, "when I will make a new covenant with the house of Isra'el and with the house of Y'hudah. It will not be like the covenant I made with their fathers on the day I took them by their hand and brought them out of the land of Egypt; because they, for their part, violated my covenant, even though I, for my part, was a husband to them," says ADONAI. "For this is the covenant I will make with the house of Isra'el after those days," says ADONAI: "I will put my Torah within them and write it on their hearts; I will be their God, and they will be my people. No longer will any of them teach his fellow community member or his brother, 'Know ADONAI'; for all will know me, from the least of them to the greatest; because I will forgive their wickednesses and remember their sins no more."

Matthew 5:17-20
Don't think that I have come to abolish the Torah or the Prophets. I have come not to abolish but to complete. Yes indeed! I tell you that until heaven and earth pass away, not so much as a yud or a stroke will pass from the Torah—not until everything that must happen has happened. So whoever disobeys the least of these mitzvot and teaches others to do so will be called the least in the Kingdom of Heaven. But whoever obeys them and so teaches will be called great in the Kingdom of Heaven. For I tell you that unless your righteousness is far greater than that of the Torah-teachers and P'rushim, you will certainly not enter the Kingdom of Heaven!

Matthew 22:36-40
"Rabbi, which of the mitzvot in the Torah is the most important?" He [Yeshua] told him, 'You are to love ADONAI your God with all your heart and with all your soul and with all your strength.' This is the greatest and most important mitzvah. And a second is similar to it, 'You are to love your neighbor as yourself.' All of the Torah and the Prophets are dependent on these two mitzvot."

Romans 2:13-16
For it is not merely the hearers of Torah whom God considers righteous; rather, it is the doers of what Torah says who will be made righteous in God's sight. For whenever Gentiles, who have no Torah, do naturally what the Torah requires, then these, even though they don't have Torah, for themselves are Torah! For their lives show that the conduct the Torah dictates is written in their hearts. Their consciences also bear witness to this, for their conflicting thoughts sometimes accuse them and sometimes defend them on a day when God passes judgment on people's inmost secrets. (According to the Good News as I proclaim it, he does this through the Messiah Yeshua.)

431

Romans 3:19-23

Moreover, we know that whatever the Torah says, it says to those living within the framework of the Torah, in order that every mouth may be stopped and the whole world be shown to deserve God's adverse judgment. For in his sight no one alive will be considered righteous on the ground of legalistic observance of Torah commands, because what Torah really does is show people how sinful they are. But now, quite apart from Torah, God's way of making people righteous in his sight has been made clear—although the Torah and the Prophets give their witness to it as well— and it is a righteousness that comes from God, through the faithfulness of Yeshua the Messiah, to all who continue trusting. For it makes no difference whether one is a Jew or a Gentile, since all have sinned and come short of earning God's praise.

Romans 7:6-7

But now we have been released from this aspect of the Torah, because we have died to that which had us in its clutches, so that we are serving in the new way provided by the Spirit and not in the old way of outwardly following the letter of the law. Therefore, what are we to say? That the Torah is sinful? Heaven forbid! Rather, the function of the Torah was that without it, I would not have known what sin is. For example, I would not have become conscious of what greed is if the Torah had not said, "Thou shalt not covet."

Romans 8:1-5

Therefore, there is no longer any condemnation awaiting those who are in union with the Messiah Yeshua. Why? Because the Torah of the Spirit, which produces this life in union with Messiah Yeshua, has set me free from the "Torah" of sin and death. For what the Torah could not do by itself, because it lacked the power to make the old nature cooperate, God did by sending his own Son as a human being with a nature like our own sinful one [but without sin]. God did this in order to deal with sin, and in so doing he executed the punishment against sin in human nature, so that the just requirement of the Torah might be fulfilled in us who do not run our lives according to what our old nature wants but according to what the Spirit wants. For those who identify with their old nature set their minds on the things of the old nature, but those who identify with the Spirit set their minds on the things of the Spirit.

Galatians 3:19-25

So then, why the legal part of the Torah? It was added in order to create transgressions, until the coming of the seed about whom the promise had been made. Moreover, it was handed down through angels and a mediator. Now a mediator implies more than one, but God is one. Does this mean that the legal part of the Torah stands in opposition to God's promises? Heaven forbid! For if the legal part of the Torah which God gave had had in itself the power to give life, then righteousness really would have come by legalistically following such a Torah. But instead, the Tanakh shuts up everything under sin; so that what had been promised might be given, on the basis of Yeshua the Messiah's trusting faithfulness, to those who continue to be trustingly faithful. Now before the time for this trusting faithfulness came, we were imprisoned in subjection to the system which results from perverting the Torah into legalism, kept under guard until this yet-to-come trusting faithfulness would be revealed. Accordingly, the Torah functioned as a custodian until the Messiah came, so that we might be declared righteous on the ground of trusting and being faithful. But now that the time for this trusting faithfulness has come, we are no longer under a custodian.

2 Timothy 3:16-17

All Scripture is God-breathed and is valuable for teaching the truth, convicting of sin, correcting faults and training in right living; thus anyone who belongs to God may be fully equipped for every good work.

Hebrews 7:14-22

...for everyone knows that our Lord arose out of Y'hudah, and that Moshe said nothing about this tribe when he spoke about cohanim. It becomes even clearer if a "different kind of cohen," one like Malki-Tzedek, arises, one who became a cohen not by virtue of a rule in the Torah concerning physical descent, but by virtue of the power of an indestructible life. For it is stated, "You are a cohen FOREVER, to be compared with Malki-Tzedek." Thus, on the one hand, the earlier rule is set aside because of its weakness and inefficacy (for the Torah did not bring anything to the goal); and, on the other hand, a hope of something better is introduced, through which we are drawing near to God. What is more, God swore an oath. For no oath was sworn in connection with those who become cohanim now; but Yeshua became a cohen by the oath which God swore when he said to him, "ADONAI has sworn and will not change his mind, 'You are a cohen forever.'" Also this shows how much better is the covenant of which Yeshua has become guarantor.

Hebrews 8:6-13

But now the work Yeshua has been given to do is far superior to theirs, just as the covenant he mediates is better. For this covenant has been given as Torah on the basis of better promises. Indeed, if the first covenant had not given ground for faultfinding, there would have been no need for a second one. For God does find fault with the people when he says, 'See! The days are coming,' says ADONAI, 'when I will establish over the house of Isra'el and over the house of Y'hudah a new covenant. It will not be like the covenant which I made with their fathers on the day when I took them by their hand and led them forth out of the land of Egypt; because they, for their part, did not remain faithful to my covenant; so I, for my part, stopped concerning myself with them,' says ADONAI. 'For this is the covenant which I will make with the house of Isra'el after those days,' says ADONAI: ' I will put my Torah in their minds and write it on their hearts; I will be their God, and they will be my people. None of them will teach his fellow-citizen or his brother, saying, "Know ADONAI!" For all will know me, from the least of them to the greatest, because I will be merciful toward their wickednesses and remember their sins no more.' By using the term, "new," he has made the first covenant "old"; and something being made old, something in the process of aging, is on its way to vanishing altogether.

Hebrews 10:1

For the Torah has in it a shadow of the good things to come, but not the actual manifestation of the originals. Therefore, it can never, by means of the same sacrifices repeated endlessly year after year, bring to the goal those who approach the Holy Place to offer them.

Commentary

This *Mitzvah* was written to explain God's expectation of us in the New Covenant, and how to apply His commandments today that were given under the Mosaic Covenant. Although many Mosaic commandments are impossible or imprudent to comply with literally today, 2 Timothy 3:16 assures us that all of them are valuable in some way:

"All Scripture is God-breathed and is valuable for teaching the truth, convicting of sin, correcting faults and training in right living..."

The reason that some of the commandments given under Moses cannot be complied with today is that they were constructed for a covenant that has been replaced (or has almost been replaced) by a New Covenant that is very different:

Jeremiah 31:30(31)-31(32): *"'Here, the days are coming,' says ADONAI, "when I will make a new covenant with the house of Isra'el and with the house of Y'hudah. It will not be like the covenant I made with their fathers on the day I took them by their hand and brought them out of the land of Egypt; because they, for their part, violated my covenant, even though I, for my part, was a husband to them," says ADONAI. "*

Hebrews 8:13: *"By using the term, "new," he has made the first covenant "old"; and something being made old, something in the process of aging, is on its way to vanishing altogether."*

Today's conditions are changed. We no longer have the Tabernacle or Temple, there is no longer a functioning Levitical priesthood or Levitical High Priest and, even if we rebuilt the Temple and reinstalled Levitical priests, most of the sacrifices required by the Mosaic Law would be unauthorized because Yeshua is now our sacrifice for sin and our High Priest:

Hebrews 10:10-13: *"It is in connection with this will that we have been separated for God and made holy, once and for all, through the offering of Yeshua the Messiah's body. Now every cohen stands every day doing his service, offering over and over the same sacrifices, which can never take away sins. But this one, after he had offered for all time a single sacrifice for sins, sat down at the right hand of God, from then on to wait until his enemies be made a footstool for his feet."*

Hebrews 4:14: *"Therefore, since we have a great cohen gadol who has passed through to the highest heaven, Yeshua, the Son of God, let us hold firmly to what we acknowledge as true."*

Hebrews 7:17-27: *"For it is stated, "You are a cohen FOREVER, to be compared with Malki-Tzedek." Thus, on the one hand, the earlier rule is set aside because of its weakness and inefficacy (for the Torah did not bring anything to the goal); and, on the other hand, a hope of something better is introduced, through which we are drawing near to God. What is more, God swore an oath. For no oath was sworn in connection with those who become cohanim now; but Yeshua became a cohen by the oath which God swore when he said to him, "ADONAI has sworn and will not change his mind, 'You are a cohen forever.'"*

Also this shows how much better is the covenant of which Yeshua has become guarantor. Moreover, the present cohanim are many in number, because they are prevented by death from continuing in office. But because he lives forever, his position as cohen does not pass on to someone else; and consequently, he is totally able to deliver those who approach God through him; since he is alive forever and thus forever able to intercede on their behalf. This is the kind of cohen gadol that meets our need—holy, without evil, without stain, set apart from sinners and raised higher than the heavens; one who does not have the daily necessity, like the other cohanim g'dolim, of offering up sacrifices first for their own sins and only then for those of the people; because he offered one sacrifice, once and for all, by offering up himself."

Attempting to apply statutory laws in a literal way when the result is improper or does not make sense is what is called "legalism," and it is warned against in Scripture:

<u>Romans 6:14-15</u>: *"For sin will not have authority over you; because you are not under legalism but under grace. Therefore, what conclusion should we reach? "Let's go on sinning, because we're not under legalism but under grace"? Heaven forbid!"*

<u>Galatians 3:10-12</u>: *"For everyone who depends on legalistic observance of Torah commands lives under a curse, since it is written, "Cursed is everyone who does not keep on doing everything written in the Scroll of the Torah." Now it is evident that no one comes to be declared righteous by God through legalism, since "The person who is righteous will attain life by trusting and being faithful." Furthermore, legalism is not based on trusting and being faithful, but on [a misuse of] the text that says, 'Anyone who does these things will attain life through them.'"*

So, the question remains: How do we apply the Scriptural commandments of the *Torah* that seem undoable today? The answer is different for every commandment and for every situation in which we find ourselves, and the New Covenant Scriptures tells us how; it is to consult and be led by the Holy Spirit:

<u>John 14:26</u>: *"But the Counselor, the Ruach HaKodesh, whom the Father will send in my name, will teach you everything; that is, he will remind you of everything I have said to you."*

<u>Romans 7:6</u>: *"But now we have been released from this aspect of the Torah, because we have died to that which had us in its clutches, so that we are serving in the new way provided by the Spirit and not in the old way of outwardly following the letter of the law."*

<u>Romans 8:1-2</u>: *"Therefore, there is no longer any condemnation awaiting those who are in union with the Messiah Yeshua. Why? Because the Torah of the Spirit, which produces this life in union with Messiah Yeshua, has set me free from the "Torah" of sin and death."*

<u>Romans 8:14</u>: *"All who are led by God's Spirit are God's sons."*

Notwithstanding the importance of being led by the Spirit, it is sometimes helpful to group literally undoable commandments by subject category and consider their significance and application collectively. What follows is a list of such subject categories along with suggested applications, and one or two Scripture examples for each:

Scriptures that Require the Holy Tabernacle, Temple, or Other Place that God Chooses

Exodus 25:8: *"They are to make me a sanctuary, so that I may live among them."*

Deuteronomy 12:21: *"If the place which ADONAI your God chooses to place his name is too far away from you; then you are to slaughter animals from your cattle or sheep, which ADONAI has given you; and eat on your own property, as much as you want."*

The Holy Tabernacle, the Temple, and other special places designated by God were not only places in which to conduct sacrifices, but also where the glory of God dwelt on earth, and where men (who were authorized) could encounter God intimately and powerfully. Chapters 40 to 48 of Ezekiel prophesy the detailed rebuilding of a Temple that is mysterious as to its identity, function, and when it is to happen (or has happened). Some scholars believe that the passage is a commandment for the Jewish people to rebuild God's Temple. Most significant, however, is that the place where God chooses to place his name is a foreshadowing of the New Covenant's visitation of the Holy Spirit who has come to live within all men that are willing to receive Him:

1 Corinthians 6:19a: *"Or don't you know that your body is a temple for the Ruach HaKodesh who lives inside you, whom you received from God?"*

Also, 1 Corinthians 3:16 shows that the corporate body of Messiah is also a Temple of the Spirit today:

Don't you know that you people are God's temple and that God's Spirit lives in you?

This is anticipated by John 4:23-24 where worship in spirit and in truth transcends a particular temple location:

"But the time is coming—indeed, it's here now—when the true worshippers will worship the Father spiritually and truly, for these are the kind of people the Father wants worshipping him. God is spirit; and worshippers must worship him spiritually and truly."

Scriptures that Assume an Operative Levitical Priesthood

Leviticus 8:1-4: *"ADONAI said to Moshe, "Take Aharon and his sons with him, the garments, the anointing oil, the bull for the sin offering, the two rams and the basket of matzah; and assemble the entire community at the entrance to the tent of meeting." Moshe did as ADONAI ordered him, and the community was assembled at the entrance to the tent of meeting."*

The above Scripture speaks of the ordination of Aaron and his sons as Levitical priests, and Aaron as High Priest. A significant value of the Scriptures concerning Levitical priests, is that they teach us what the functions of a priest and priesthood should be and, although the Levitical priesthood is no longer operative, other priesthoods are. The people of Israel are said, in Scripture, to be a kingdom of priests (Exodus 19:6). Also, 1 Peter 2:4-5 defines a priesthood of believers in Yeshua, and Hebrews 4:14-16 establishes Yeshua as the New Covenant's High Priest. God has New Covenant priestly expectations of Israelites (today referred to as Jews) and of all believers in Yeshua—not to conduct sacrifices—but to prayerfully intercede for others, teach, counsel, and otherwise serve our fellow man.

Scriptures that Call for Punishment

Exodus 22:2b(3b)-3(4): *"A thief must make restitution; so if he has nothing, he himself is to be sold to make good the loss from the theft. If what he stole is found alive in his possession, he is to pay double, no matter whether it is an ox, a donkey or a sheep."*

Exodus 31:13-15: *"Tell the people of Isra'el, 'You are to observe my Shabbats; for this is a sign between me and you through all your generations; so that you will know that I am ADONAI, who sets you apart for me. Therefore you are to keep my Shabbat, because it is set apart for you. Everyone who treats it as ordinary must be put to death; for whoever does any work on it is to be cut off from his people. On six days work will get done; but the seventh day is Shabbat, for complete rest, set apart for ADONAI. Whoever does any work on the day of Shabbat must be put to death."*

Leviticus 24:19-20: *"If someone injures his neighbor, what he did is to be done to him—break for break, eye for eye, tooth for tooth—whatever injury he has caused the other person is to be rendered to him in return."*

Deuteronomy 21:18-21: *" If a man has a stubborn, rebellious son who will not obey what his father or mother says, and even after they discipline him he still refuses to pay attention to them; then his father and mother are to take hold of him and bring him out to the leaders of his town, at the gate of that place, and say to the leaders of his town, 'This son of ours is stubborn and rebellious, he doesn't pay attention to us, lives wildly, gets drunk.' Then all the men of his town are to stone him to death; in this way you will put an end to such wickedness among you, and all Isra'el will hear about it and be afraid."*

Leviticus 24:19-20 declares that "eye for eye, tooth for tooth" is the Mosaic standard of punishment for causing personal injury to another. Expanding the principle to other kinds of infractions, one is reminded of a quote from W.S. Gilbert's The Mikado: "Let the punishment fit the crime." Sensible as these standards for punishment may seem, they are rarely employed by today's secular governments that tend to not allow creative discretion to judges.

The Scriptures requiring execution and other extreme punishments of those who violate certain biblical commandments are often shocking because, by today's standards, many of the offenses that called for death and other severe punishments during the time of Moses are not even considered crimes today. We no longer stone our rebellious and drunkard sons, nor do we put to death those who violate the Sabbath and, should we attempt to do so, we would be in violation of the laws of the secular governments under which we live.

During the time of Moses, the Israelites lived under a theocracy that was governed directly by God and today, we do not. *Torah* for us today, is ancient law that we read about in the Bible in order to understand its principles. For the Israelites under Moses, however, it was contemporary law that was spoken by God directly to them from Mount Sinai. For the Israelites to disobey that which God commanded them in so personal a way would have been a direct "slap in the face" of God, and worthy of the severe punishments that we read about.

There are also offenses in the *Torah* for which punishments are not severe by today's standards, but which, nevertheless, cannot be applied without transgressing today's secular laws. For example, Exodus 22:2b(3b)-3(4) directs that a thief must pay double restitution for what he has stolen, and he must be sold as a laborer (a slave) if he cannot afford to pay. On the surface, double restitution seems fair and doable, but it is not enforceable because the secular laws under which we live do not allow for it, and slave labor is, of course, a violation of the secular law.

For us, the main value of the various punishments we read about in the Scriptures is that they give us an understanding of the seriousness with which God considers certain kinds of wrongful conduct. In today's world, capital punishment of a rebellious son would not be allowed. Yet, God considers rebellion and stubbornness so serious a sin that we read in 1 Samuel 15:23:

> *"For rebellion is like the sin of sorcery, stubbornness like the crime of idolatry. Because you have rejected the word of ADONAI, he too has rejected you as king."*

It is also of interest to note that, except for captives in war, nothing in the Mosaic Law authorizes imprisonment as a punishment; yet, imprisonment is the principle form of punishment employed by secular governments today. Really, imprisonment as a punishment is a blunt instrument because it does not promote heart-felt repentance. For non-capital offenses, restoration through community service and paying back offended persons (and then some) is much more redemptive. What is more, being imprisoned with other offenders often brings greater criminality that is acted out upon the prisoner's release—the opposite of that which is intended. Societies should take this into account in constructing their systems of law.

Scriptures that Pertain to the Government of Ancient Israel

> Exodus 30:13-14: *"Everyone subject to the census is to pay as an offering to ADONAI half a shekel [one-fifth of an ounce of silver]—by the standard of the sanctuary shekel (a shekel equals twenty gerahs). Everyone over twenty years of age who is subject to the census is to give this offering to ADONAI..."*

> Deuteronomy 1:17: *"You are not to show favoritism when judging, but give equal attention to the small and to the great. No matter how a person presents himself, don't be afraid of him; because the decision is God's. The case that is too hard for you, bring to me and I will hear it."*

The Scriptures quoted could be complied with if one were a citizen of Israel under Moses, but could not (and cannot) be complied with under other governments. Still, they have teaching value. For example, the Exodus Scripture teaches us that there is a government's need to know how many residents occupy its country, and the Deuteronomy Scripture establishes standards for judging legal cases, except that today, cases that are removed from a lower court are sent to a higher court—not to Moses.

Note by Daniel C. Juster

These standards are crucial for all societies. In addition, the idea of witnesses, the rejection of trial by ordeal, and more, have informed Western legal systems. That judges must not take bribes, but be scrupulously honest and judge on the basis of at least two or three witnesses is also foundational to courts. The rabbinic tradition also teaches that the Noachide laws require Gentiles to establish fair courts in order to have a positive destiny in the age to come. Finally, the idea that rulers are subject to God's laws and are not a law unto themselves is a great principle of Scripture that is enshrined in western law. The king can be called to account by the prophet and is to make a copy of the Law and be subject to it:

> Deuteronomy 17:18-20: *"When he has come to occupy the throne of his kingdom, he is to write a copy of this Torah for himself in a scroll, from the one the cohanim and L'vi'im use. It is to remain with him, and he is to read in it every day, as long as he lives; so that he will learn to fear ADONAI his God and keep all the words of this Torah and these laws and obey them; so that he will not think he is better than his kinsmen; and so that he will not turn aside either to the right or to the left from the mitzvah. In this way he will prolong his own reign and that of his children in Isra'el."*

The law is above the king or, as quoted by the famous Puritan writer Samuel Rutherford: *"Lex Rex"*—Law is King.

Scriptures that Pertain to the Land of Ancient Israel

> Leviticus 25:1-13: *"ADONAI spoke to Moshe on Mount Sinai; he said, "Tell the people of Isra'el, 'When you enter the land I am giving you, the land itself is to observe a Shabbat rest for ADONAI. Six years you will sow your field; six years you will prune your grapevines and gather their produce. But in the seventh year is to be a Shabbat of complete rest for the land, a Shabbat for ADONAI; you will neither sow your field nor prune your grapevines. You are not to harvest what grows by itself from the seeds left by your previous harvest, and you are not to gather the grapes of your untended vine; it is to be a year of complete rest for the land. But what the land produces during the year of Shabbat will be food for all of you—you, your servant, your maid, your employee, anyone living near you, your livestock and the wild animals on your land; everything the land produces may be used for food. You are to count seven Shabbats of years, seven times seven years, that is, forty-nine years. Then, on the tenth day of the seventh month, on Yom-Kippur, you are to sound a blast on the shofar; you are to sound the shofar all through your land; and you are to consecrate the fiftieth year, proclaiming freedom throughout the land to all its inhabitants. It will be a yovel for you; you will return everyone to the land he owns, and everyone is to return to his family. That fiftieth year will be a yovel for you; in that year you are not to sow, harvest what grows by itself or gather the grapes of untended vines; because it is a yovel. It will be holy for you; whatever the fields produce will be food for all of you. In this year of yovel, every one of you is to return to the land he owns."*

> Deuteronomy 26:1-3: *"When you have come to the land ADONAI your God is giving you as your inheritance, taken possession of it and settled there; you are to take the firstfruits of all the crops the ground yields, which you will harvest from your land that ADONAI your God is giving you, put them in a basket and go to the place where ADONAI your God will choose to have his name live. You will approach the cohen holding office at the time and say to him, 'Today I declare to ADONAI your God that I have come to the land ADONAI swore to our ancestors that he would give us.'"*

439

This category "The Land of Ancient Israel" and the previously listed category "The Government of Ancient Israel" are closely related, and many of the Scriptures that pertain to one of them also pertain to the other. The modern land of Israel (and its government) does not operate with a functioning Levitical priesthood or Temple as in the past, and therefore certain Scriptures (including those above) cannot be complied with literally. Nevertheless, the principles they teach are valuable today both in the Land and in the diaspora, but they have to be applied utilizing the wisdom of the Holy Spirit that is available to us through the New Covenant. Examples of how we apply and practice such Scriptures today are found in the ways that Jews of today keep the *Shabbat* and celebrate the feasts and other appointed times wherever in the world they may happen to be.

Scriptures that Pertain to Specific Wars

Deuteronomy 7:1-2: *"ADONAI your God is going to bring you into the land you will enter in order to take possession of it, and he will expel many nations ahead of you—the Hitti, Girgashi, Emori, Kena'ani, P'rizi, Hivi and Y'vusi, seven nations bigger and stronger than you. When he does this, when ADONAI your God hands them over ahead of you, and you defeat them, you are to destroy them completely! Do not make any covenant with them. Show them no mercy."*

There are a number of Scriptures in the *Torah* in which God Instructs the Israelites about how they are to conduct themselves in specific wars (mainly against heathen nations). Some of the Scriptures order destruction of the enemy's idols, while some go further and order the annihilation of all men, women, and children of the enemy, which would be considered a war crime today. The severity of such Scriptures reminds us that destroying idolatry and heathen worship is vitally important to God—so much so, that He commanded the Israelites to not make covenants with them.

Exodus 34:12-14: *"Be careful not to make a covenant with the people living in the land where you are going, so that they won't become a snare within your own borders. Rather, you are to demolish their altars, smash their standing-stones and cut down their sacred poles; because you are not to bow down to any other god; since ADONAI—whose very name is Jealous—is a jealous God."*

It is a principle that today's diplomats would do well to remember

Scriptures that Pertain to Sacrificing Animals

Leviticus 16:3-10: *"Here is how Aharon is to enter the Holy Place: with a young bull as a sin offering and a ram as a burnt offering. He is to put on the holy linen tunic, have the linen shorts next to his bare flesh, have the linen sash wrapped around him, and be wearing the linen turban—they are the holy garments. He is to bathe his body in water and put them on. He is to take from the community of the people of Isra'el two male goats for a sin offering and one ram for a burnt offering. Aharon is to present the bull for the sin offering which is for himself and make atonement for himself and his household. He is to take the two goats and place them before ADONAI at the entrance to the tent of meeting. Then Aharon is to cast lots for the two goats, one lot for ADONAI and the other for 'Az'azel. Aharon is to present the goat whose lot fell to ADONAI and offer it as a sin offering. But the goat whose lot fell to 'Az'azel is to be presented alive to ADONAI to be used for making atonement over it by sending it away into the desert for 'Az'azel."*

There are many animal sacrifices commanded in Scripture. The <u>Leviticus</u> Scripture quoted above is associated with *Yom Kippur*—the Day of Atonement. We know that the commanded animal sacrifices cannot be complied with today due to their being no Tabernacle or Temple. There is, however, a more significant reason, and that is because Yeshua has become our once and for all-time sacrifice for sin:

> <u>Hebrews 10:11-18</u>: " *Now every cohen stands every day doing his service, offering over and over the same sacrifices, which can never take away sins. But this one, after he had offered for all time a single sacrifice for sins, sat down at the right hand of God, from then on to wait until his enemies be made a footstool for his feet. For by a single offering he has brought to the goal for all time those who are being set apart for God and made holy. And the Ruach HaKodesh too bears witness to us; for after saying, 'This is the covenant which I will make with them after those days,' says ADONAI: 'I will put my Torah on their hearts, and write it on their minds...'" he then adds, " 'And their sins and their wickednesses I will remember no more.'" Now where there is forgiveness for these, an offering for sins is no longer needed.*"

Scriptures that Pertain to Bloodless Offerings

> <u>Leviticus 7:9-13</u>: *"Every grain offering baked in the oven, cooked in a pot or fried on a griddle will belong to the cohen who offers it. But every grain offering which is mixed with olive oil or is dry will belong to all the sons of Aharon equally. This is the law for sacrificing peace offerings offered to ADONAI: If a person offers it for giving thanks, he is to offer it with the thanksgiving sacrifice of unleavened cakes mixed with olive oil, matzah spread with olive oil, and cakes made of fine flour mixed with olive oil and fried. With cakes of leavened bread he is to present his offering together with the sacrifice of his peace offerings for giving thanks."*

Bloodless offerings—sacrifices such as grain offerings—are many, and they are typically associated with animal sacrifices that are performed at the same time. As with animal sacrifices, most bloodless offerings require the Tabernacle or Temple and the Levitical priesthood, so they cannot be performed today as commanded. Nevertheless, there are two bloodless sacrifice that can be conducted:

> <u>Hebrews 13:12-15</u>: *"So too Yeshua suffered death outside the gate, in order to make the people holy through his own blood. Therefore, let us go out to him who is outside the camp and share his disgrace. For we have no permanent city here; on the contrary, we seek the one to come. Through him, therefore, let us offer God a sacrifice of praise continually. For this is the natural product of lips that acknowledge his name."*

> <u>1 Peter 2:3-5</u>: *"For you have tasted that ADONAI is good. As you come to him, the living stone, rejected by people but chosen by God and precious to him, you yourselves, as living stones, are being built into a spiritual house to be cohanim set apart for God to offer spiritual sacrifices acceptable to him through Yeshua the Messiah."*

Scriptures that Pertain to Holy Places and Things

> <u>Leviticus 16:3-4</u>: *"Here is how Aharon is to enter the Holy Place: with a young bull as a sin offering and a ram as a burnt offering. He is to put on the holy linen tunic, have the linen shorts next to his*

bare flesh, have the linen sash wrapped around him, and be wearing the linen turban—they are the holy garments. He is to bathe his body in water and put them on."

Numbers 4:18-20: *"Do not cut off the clan of K'hat from among the L'vi'im; rather, do this for them, so that they will live and not die: when they approach the especially holy things, Aharon and his sons are to go in—and you are to assign each one his task; but the descendants of K'hat are not to go in and look at the holy things as they are being covered; if they do, they will die."*

Although we cannot comply literally with Scriptures pertaining to holy places and holy things that no longer exist, they give us food for thought as to the holy things and places that do exist today. We know that Jerusalem is a holy city (Isaiah 52:1) and the mountain in Jerusalem is a holy mountain (Isaiah 27:13); but where else? We no longer have the Holy Place of the Tabernacle and Temple; is the sanctuary of a modern synagogue holy by analogy? We no longer have the Holy Ark; is a synagogue's *"Aron Hakodesh"* holy by analogy? The characteristic of anything holy is that it is set apart to God, or for a godly purpose. The original holy places and things we read about in Scripture were made holy by God, but God commanded us:

Leviticus 11:45: *"For I am the LORD who brings you up out of the land of Egypt, to be your God. You shall therefore be holy, for I am holy."*

With that understanding, it seems to me that we, as holy people, can designate places and things as holy, so yes, the synagogue's sanctuary is holy and so is its *Aron Hokodesh.*

Scriptures that Pertain to Consecrations, Dedications, and Redemptions

Exodus 13:13: *"Every firstborn from a donkey, you are to redeem with a lamb; but if you choose not to redeem it, you must break its neck. But from people, you are to redeem every firstborn son."*

Exodus 29:37: *"Seven days you will make atonement on the altar and consecrate it; thus the altar will be especially holy, and whatever touches the altar will become holy."*

Numbers 7:11: *"...and ADONAI said to Moshe, "They are to present their offerings to dedicate the altar, each leader on his own day.""*

Consecrations, dedications, and redemptions of various kinds are performed today, but the persons, objects, and places dedicated, etc. are typically not the same as in the past. The rabbinical ceremony of *pidyon ha-ben* (buying back one's firstborn son from a *cohen*) is an adaptation of the Exodus 13:13 commandment to redeem one's firstborn son from serving in the Tabernacle / Temple, and an example of a New Covenant dedication and consecration is found in Romans 12:1:

"I exhort you, therefore, brothers, in view of God's mercies, to offer yourselves as a sacrifice, living and set apart for God. This will please him; it is the logical "Temple worship" for you."

Scriptures that Pertain to Ritual Purity

> Leviticus 15:19-24: *"If a woman has a discharge, and the discharge from her body is blood, she will be in her state of niddah for seven days. Whoever touches her will be unclean until evening. Everything she lies on or sits on in her state of niddah will be unclean. Whoever touches her bed is to wash his clothes and bathe himself in water; he will be unclean until evening. Whoever touches anything she sits on is to wash his clothes and bathe himself in water; he will be unclean until evening. Whether he is on the bed or on something she sits on, when he touches it, he will be unclean until evening. If a man goes to bed with her, and her menstrual flow touches him, he will be unclean seven days; and every bed he lies on will be unclean."*

> Numbers 5:2-4: *"'Order the people of Isra'el to expel from the camp everyone with tzara'at, everyone with a discharge and whoever is unclean because of touching a corpse. Both male and female you must expel; put them outside the camp; so that they won't defile their camp, where I live among you.' The people of Isra'el did this and put them outside the camp—the people of Isra'el did what ADONAI had said to Moshe."*

At the time of Moses, the commandments that pertained to ritual purity had to do with being "clean" or "unclean"—not in the sense of being sanitary, but for the purposes of being able to touch or be in the proximity of holy objects or places. The cleanness of Human beings was the assumed norm, but there were conditions and things that could render persons unclean and unable to serve in the Tabernacle (later the Temple) and sometimes even unable to be within the camp of Israel. Touching dead bodies, possessing weeping sores (and other contagious conditions), giving birth, and a woman's menses are some of the conditions.

Scholars disagree on the expectation of everyone living in ritual purity. For example, a farmer is always touching dead animals and animal excrements. In our opinion, being unclean for such reasons was expected and was not a problem unless the unclean person was planning to go up to the Temple while in that state.

Note also, that violating some of the laws of purity (e.g. disregarding the holiness of blood and having sex during a woman's period) are beyond matters of ritual purity, and required being cut off from one's people. Such standards (without the penalty of being cut off) should be observed today.

In the New Covenant, being unclean always has to do with being in sin. For example:

> Matthew 5:23-24: *"So if you are offering your gift at the Temple altar and you remember there that your brother has something against you [i.e. you sinned against your brother], leave your gift where it is by the altar, and go, make peace with your brother. Then come back and offer your gift."*

The assumption here is that you who are about to offer your gift at God's altar, have committed sin against your brother, and need to repent to him in order to be ritually clean. A similar requirement that one must be repentant in order to be ritually clean is found in 1 Corinthians 11:26-29; referring to the *Shulchan Adonai* (Table of the Lord), we read:

443

"For as often as you eat this bread and drink the cup, you proclaim the death of the Lord, until he comes. Therefore, whoever eats the Lord's bread or drinks the Lord's cup in an unworthy manner will be guilty of desecrating the body and blood of the Lord! So let a person examine himself first, and then he may eat of the bread and drink from the cup; for a person who eats and drinks without recognizing the body eats and drinks judgment upon himself."

Scriptures that Pertain to Health and Sanitation

Leviticus 13:32-34: *"On the seventh day the cohen is to examine the sore, and if he sees that the crusted area hasn't spread, that it has no yellow hair in it, and that the crusted area is not deeper than the skin around it; then the person is to be shaved, except for the crusted area itself, and the cohen is to isolate him for seven more days. On the seventh day the cohen is to examine the crusted area; and if he sees that the crusted area has not spread on the skin and does not appear to be deeper than the skin around it, then the cohen is to declare him clean; he is to wash his clothes and be clean."*

Deuteronomy 23:13(12)-14(13): *"Also you are to have an area outside the camp to use as a latrine. You must include a trowel with your equipment, and when you relieve yourself, you are to dig a hole first and afterwards cover your excrement."*

Health-related Scriptures such as those exemplified above are self-explanatory. In both the *Tanakh* and the New Testament, physical disease is associated with men's sinful condition; in fact, in the Mosaic Covenant, some of the functions of the Levitical *cohanim* were similar to those of physicians and public health officers. Good hygiene and reasonable care to keep disease from spreading should be (and often is) an obvious application of the Mosaic Law today. This is the way that Jewish communities were preserved in times of plague in numbers that greatly exceeded their Gentile counterparts.

Supernatural healing appears in the *Tanakh* as well as in the New Testament—for example in Deuteronomy 7:15, where God refers to Himself as the Israelites' healer (see also, Exodus 15:26). Nevertheless, it is in the New Covenant Scriptures that we find supernatural healing emphasized to its fullest, and with the power and authority to summon God's healing delegated to men:

Matthew 10:1: *"Yeshua called his twelve talmidim and gave them authority to drive out unclean spirits and to heal every kind of disease and weakness."*

Matthew 10:7-8: *"As you go, proclaim, 'The Kingdom of Heaven is near,' heal the sick, raise the dead, cleanse those afflicted with tzara'at, expel demons. You have received without paying, so give without asking payment."*

James 5:14-16: *"Is someone among you ill? He should call for the elders of the congregation. They will pray for him and rub olive oil on him in the name of the Lord. The prayer offered with trust will heal the one who is ill—the Lord will restore his health; and if he has committed sins, he will be forgiven. Therefore, openly acknowledge your sins to one another, and pray for each other, so that you may be healed. The prayer of a righteous person is powerful and effective."*

Scriptures that Pertain to Slavery and Indenture

(a) <u>Slavery Resulting from Debt</u>:

<u>Exodus 22:2b(3b)</u>: *"A thief must make restitution; so if he has nothing, he himself is to be sold to make good the loss from the theft."*

<u>2 Kings 4:1</u>: *"The wife of one of the guild prophets complained to Elisha. 'Your servant my husband died," she said, "and you know that he feared ADONAI. Now a creditor has come to take my two children as his slaves.'"*

(b) <u>Slaves Bought, Sold, and Bequeathed</u>

<u>Exodus 21:7-8</u>: *"If a man sells his daughter as a slave, she is not to go free like the men-slaves. If her master married her but decides she no longer pleases him, then he is to allow her to be redeemed. He is not allowed to sell her to a foreign people, because he has treated her unfairly."*

<u>Leviticus 25:44-46</u>: *"Concerning the men and women you may have as slaves: you are to buy men— and women-slaves from the nations surrounding you. You may also buy the children of foreigners living with you and members of their families born in your land; you may own these. You may also bequeath them to your children to own; from these groups you may take your slaves forever. But as far as your brothers the people of Isra'el are concerned, you are not to treat each other harshly."*

(c) <u>Captives of War Enslaved</u>

<u>Deuteronomy 20:10-11</u>: *"When you advance on a town to attack it, first offer it terms for peace. If it accepts the terms for peace and opens its gates to you, then all the people there are to be put to forced labor and work for you."*

(d) <u>Voluntary Slavery and Indenture</u>

<u>Exodus 21:5-6</u>: *"Nevertheless, if the slave declares, 'I love my master, my wife and my children, so I don't want to go free,' then his master is to bring him before God; and there at the door or doorpost, his master is to pierce his ear with an awl; and the man will be his slave for life.*

<u>Leviticus 25:47-48</u>: *If a foreigner living with you has grown rich, and a member of your people has become poor and sells himself to this foreigner living with you or to a member of the foreigner's family, he may be redeemed after he has been sold. One of his brothers may redeem him…"*

<u>Deuteronomy 15:12-17</u>: *"If your kinsman, a Hebrew man or woman, is sold to you, he is to serve you for six years; but in the seventh year, you are to set him free. Moreover, when you set him free, don't let him leave empty-handed; but supply him generously from your flock, threshing-floor and winepress; from what ADONAI your God has blessed you with, you are to give to him. Remember that you were a slave in the land of Egypt, and ADONAI your God redeemed you; that is why I am giving you this order today. But if he says to you, 'I don't want to leave you,' because he loves you and your household, and because his life with you is a good one; then take an awl, and pierce his ear through, right into the door; and he will be your slave forever. Do the same with your female slave."*

The Mosaic Law not only permitted slavery—it regulated it. Slavery in Scripture is not, however, the same as typically occurs in some secular societies today, where certain people, for no fault of their own, are kidnaped and enslaved or sold as slaves for personal gain:

Exodus 21:16: *"Whoever kidnaps someone must be put to death, regardless of whether he has already sold him or the person is found still in his possession."*

Deuteronomy 24:7: *"If a man kidnaps any of his brothers, fellow members of the community of Isra'el, and makes him his slave or sells him, that kidnapper must die; in this way you will put an end to such wickedness among you."*

An Israelite or non-Israelite might become a slave for a number of reasons. In the examples above, slavery that was procured by kidnaping was illegal and was punishable by death, but slavery was also a means by which a person could pay off a personal debt that he could not pay otherwise (2 Kings 4:1 supra). Slavery was also imposed on idolaters whose land was conquered by Israel at God's command (Deuteronomy 20:10-11 supra). Also, an Israelite who burglarized and could not afford to pay back double could be sold into slavery, and the value of his labor used to pay his debt (Exodus 22:2b(3b) supra). Israelite slaves would work for six years and be freed automatically on the *Sh'mitah,* at which time his debt would be forgiven (Exodus 21:2; Deuteronomy 15:1-3 supra);[128] Slavery was, therefore, an ancient means of debt-collection that had an escape clause for Israelites. Indentured servanthood was a kind of slavery that was voluntarily entered into for a season, and there was another kind of voluntary slavery that was permanent (see Exodus 21:5-6 supra).

Unlike the Scriptures of the Mosaic Covenant, those of the New Covenant do not seek to regulate slavery. They do, however, recognize its existence, and instruct those who are subjugated by it how to cope by bringing glory to God by maintaining a servant's heart.

Colossians 3:22-25: *"Slaves, obey your human masters in everything, not serving only when they are watching you, to win their favor, but single-heartedly, fearing the Lord. Whatever work you do, put yourself into it, as those who are serving not merely other people, but the Lord. Remember that as your reward, you will receive the inheritance from the Lord. You are slaving for the Lord, for the Messiah. Don't worry—whoever is doing wrong will be paid in kind for his wrong, and there is no favoritism shown."*

Ephesians 6:5-9: *"Slaves, obey your human masters with the same fear, trembling and single-heartedness with which you obey the Messiah. Don't obey just to win their favor, serving only when they are watching you; but serve as slaves of the Messiah, doing what God wants with all your heart. Work willingly as slaves, as people do who are serving not merely human beings but the Lord. Remember that whoever does good work, whether he be a slave or a free man, will be rewarded by the Lord. And masters, treat your slaves the same way. Don't threaten them. Remember that in heaven both you and they have the same Master, and he has no favorites."*

1 Timothy 6:1: *"Those who are under the yoke of slavery should regard their masters as worthy of full respect, so that the name of God and the teaching will not be brought into disrepute."*

---

128 Gentile slaves were not freed on the *Sh'mitah.*

<u>Titus 2:9-10</u>: *"Tell slaves to submit to their masters in everything, to give satisfaction without talking back or pilfering. On the contrary, they should demonstrate complete faithfulness always, so that in every way they will make the teaching about God our Deliverer more attractive."*

<u>1 Peter 2:18-19</u>: *"Household servants, submit yourselves to your masters, showing them full respect— and not only those who are kind and considerate, but also those who are harsh. For it is a grace when someone, because he is mindful of God, bears up under the pain of undeserved punishment."*

Paul's letter to <u>Philemon</u> urges the New Covenant's position that one who is a slave is not less of a person before God. In his epistle, Paul (who is in prison) appeals to Philemon to receive back his runaway slave Onesimus as a brother in the Lord and as an equal because he had received Messiah and been "born again." Also, <u>1 Corinthians 7:21-23</u> teaches:

"Were you a slave when you were called? Well, don't let it bother you; although if you can gain your freedom, take advantage of the opportunity. For a person who was a slave when he was called is the Lord's freedman; likewise, someone who was a free man when he was called is a slave of the Messiah. You were bought at a price, so do not become slaves of other human beings."

The thrust of the New Covenant whereby the slave is considered equal in value as his master who is to treat him as a brother, eventually led to the perception among believers in Yeshua, that slavery was incompatible with there being a brotherhood of believers. Thus slavery fell into disuse in the believing communities of the first century. Today, slavery is outlawed in the western countries, but the Scriptures about slavery are, nevertheless, still useful in teaching us how to selflessly serve God, how to give godly service to others, and how to compassionately treat and respect those who give service to us.

Scriptures that Pertain to the Sh'mitah and the Jubilee

<u>Leviticus 25:1-24</u>: *"ADONAI spoke to Moshe on Mount Sinai; he said, "Tell the people of Isra'el, 'When you enter the land I am giving you, the land itself is to observe a Shabbat rest for ADONAI. Six years you will sow your field; six years you will prune your grapevines and gather their produce. But in the seventh year is to be a Shabbat of complete rest for the land, a Shabbat for ADONAI; you will neither sow your field nor prune your grapevines. You are not to harvest what grows by itself from the seeds left by your previous harvest, and you are not to gather the grapes of your untended vine; it is to be a year of complete rest for the land. But what the land produces during the year of Shabbat will be food for all of you—you, your servant, your maid, your employee, anyone living near you, your livestock and the wild animals on your land; everything the land produces may be used for food. You are to count seven Shabbats of years, seven times seven years, that is, forty-nine years. Then, on the tenth day of the seventh month, on Yom-Kippur, you are to sound a blast on the shofar; you are to sound the shofar all through your land; and you are to consecrate the fiftieth year, proclaiming freedom throughout the land to all its inhabitants. It will be a yovel for you; you will return everyone to the land he owns, and everyone is to return to his family. That fiftieth year will be a yovel for you; in that year you are not to sow, harvest what grows by itself or gather the grapes of untended vines; because it is a yovel. It will be holy for you; whatever the fields produce will be food for all of you. In this year of yovel, every one of you is to return to the land he owns. If you sell anything to your neighbor or buy anything from him, neither of you is to exploit the other. Rather, you are to take into account the number of years after the yovel when you buy land from your neighbor, and he is to sell to you according to the number of years crops will be raised. If the number of years remaining is large,*

you will raise the price; if few years remain, you will lower it; because what he is really selling you is the number of crops to be produced. Thus you are not to take advantage of each other, but you are to fear your God; for I am ADONAI your God. Rather, you are to keep my regulations and rulings and act accordingly. If you do, you will live securely in the land. The land will yield its produce, you will eat until you have enough, and you will live there securely. If you ask, "If we aren't allowed to sow seed or harvest what our land produces, what are we going to eat the seventh year?" then I will order my blessing on you during the sixth year, so that the land brings forth enough produce for all three years. The eighth year you will sow seed but eat the the old, stored produce until the ninth year; that is, until the produce of the eighth year comes in, you will eat the old, stored food. The land is not to be sold in perpetuity, because the land belongs to me—you are only foreigners and temporary residents with me. Therefore, when you sell your property, you must include the right of redemption."

Clearly, that which the *sh'mitah* and the *yovel* (jubilee) require of us is not enforceable by modern secular law but it is, nevertheless, possible for individuals to comply with some aspects of the Mosaic commandments regarding them voluntarily. We can forgive debts owed to us in the sabbatical year *(sh'mitah)* by others, but we cannot require that our debts to others be forgiven us. We can give rest to land that we own or control in the *sh'mitah* or the *yovel*, but we cannot (especially in the diaspora) return our land to its original owners in the *yovel*.

The *sh'mitah* and the *yovel* were provided by God as a hedge against the social and economic injustice to persons who have become indebted in a society that does not provide them the opportunity to extricate themselves. The forgiveness of debts, the freeing of slaves, and the return of land to its original owners, are a great equalizer of men, a promoter of social and economic justice, and a reminder that it is God and not we who ultimately owns all.

The biblical principle of forgiveness of debts in the sabbatical year slowly found their way into Anglo-American law. In the middle ages in England, debtors were bonded to their creditors similar to indenture in the Bible, but with no escape in the seventh year. Imprisonment for debtors was also employed as a means of coercing family members to pay for a debtor's release. Then, in 1705, the "Bankrupts Act" was enacted in England, that empowered the Lord Chancellor to release debtors from their financial obligations once their assets were accounted for and appropriately distributed to their creditors. This eventually developed into modern bankruptcy law that, in the United States today, allows insolvent debtors to be discharged from their debts every six years, analogous to the biblical discharge every sabbatical year.

The godliness of social and economic justice pervades throughout the Bible, and comes to its highest expression in the Scriptures of the New Covenant; here are some examples from the *Tanakh* and the New Testament:

Isaiah 1:17: *"...learn to do good! Seek justice, relieve the oppressed, defend orphans, plead for the widow."*

Proverbs 14:31: *"The oppressor of the poor insults his maker, but he who is kind to the needy honors him."*

Proverbs 31:8-9: *"Speak up for those who can't speak for themselves, for the rights of all who need an advocate. Speak up, judge righteously, defend the cause of the poor and the needy."*

Matthew 7:7-10: *"Keep asking, and it will be given to you; keep seeking, and you will find; keep knocking, and the door will be opened to you. For everyone who keeps asking receives; he who keeps seeking finds; and to him who keeps knocking, the door will be opened. Is there anyone here who, if his son asks him for a loaf of bread, will give him a stone? or if he asks for a fish, will give him a snake?"*

Matthew 7:12: *"Always treat others as you would like them to treat you; that sums up the teaching of the Torah and the Prophets."*

Matthew 11:28-30: *"Come to me, all of you who are struggling and burdened, and I will give you rest. Take my yoke upon you and learn from me, because I am gentle and humble in heart, and you will find rest for your souls. For my yoke is easy, and my burden is light."*

Matthew 19:21: *"Yeshua said to him, 'If you are serious about reaching the goal, go and sell your possessions, give to the poor, and you will have riches in heaven. Then come, follow me!'"*

Matthew 25:35-40: *"For I was hungry and you gave me food, I was thirsty and you gave me something to drink, I was a stranger and you made me your guest, I needed clothes and you provided them, I was sick and you took care of me, I was in prison and you visited me.' Then the people who have done what God wants will reply, 'Lord, when did we see you hungry and feed you, or thirsty and give you something to drink? When did we see you a stranger and make you our guest, or needing clothes and provide them? When did we see you sick or in prison, and visit you?' The King will say to them, 'Yes! I tell you that whenever you did these things for one of the least important of these brothers of mine, you did them for me!'"*

Acts 2:44-45: *"All those trusting in Yeshua stayed together and had everything in common; in fact, they sold their property and possessions and distributed the proceeds to all who were in need."*

Galatians 3:28: *"...there is neither Jew nor Gentile, neither slave nor freeman, neither male nor female; for in union with the Messiah Yeshua, you are all one."*

James 1:27: *"The religious observance that God the Father considers pure and faultless is this: to care for orphans and widows in their distress and to keep oneself from being contaminated by the world."*

James 2:1-7: *"My brothers, practice the faith of our Lord Yeshua, the glorious Messiah, without showing favoritism. Suppose a man comes into your synagogue wearing gold rings and fancy clothes, and also a poor man comes in dressed in rags. If you show more respect to the man wearing the fancy clothes and say to him, "Have this good seat here," while to the poor man you say, "You, stand over there," or, "Sit down on the floor by my feet," then aren't you creating distinctions among yourselves, and haven't you made yourselves into judges with evil motives? Listen, my dear brothers, hasn't God chosen the poor of the world to be rich in faith and to receive the Kingdom which he promised to those who love him? But you despise the poor! Aren't the rich the ones who oppress you and drag you into court? Aren't they the ones who insult the good name of Him to whom you belong?"*

James 2:14-18: *"What good is it, my brothers, if someone claims to have faith but has no actions to prove it? Is such "faith" able to save him? Suppose a brother or sister is without clothes and daily food, and someone says to him, "Shalom! Keep warm and eat hearty!" without giving him what he needs, what good does it do? Thus, faith by itself, unaccompanied by actions, is dead. But someone will say that you have faith and I have actions. Show me this faith of yours without the actions, and I will show you my faith by my actions!"*

<u>1 John 3:17-18</u>: *"If someone has worldly possessions and sees his brother in need, yet closes his heart against him, how can he be loving God? Children, let us love not with words and talk, but with actions and in reality!"*

Throughout the Bible, God's laws concerning indebtedness disclose that the heart of God is that those who fall into debt should have an opportunity to recover. It is vitally important that this principle guide our contemporary societies.

Note by Daniel C. Juster

The jubilee year anticipates equal financial opportunity, and a society that finds ways to prevent monetary wealth from being concentrated in a wealthy class of persons generation after generation. This shows the heart of God for those of limited means, and most scholars see Yeshua announcing His ministry in the context of liberty being proclaimed in the jubilee year.

Scriptures that Pertain to Criminal Justice

<u>Exodus 21:12</u>: *"Whoever attacks a person and causes his death must be put to death."*

<u>Leviticus 24:19-20</u>: *"If someone injures his neighbor, what he did is to be done to him—break for break, eye for eye, tooth for tooth—whatever injury he has caused the other person is to be rendered to him in return."*

<u>Deuteronomy 17:2-7</u>: *"If there is found among you, within any of your gates [in any city] that ADONAI your God gives you, a man or woman who does what ADONAI your God sees as wicked, transgressing his covenant by going and serving other gods and worshipping them, the sun, the moon, or anything in the sky—something I have forbidden—and it is told to you, or you hear about it; then you are to investigate the matter diligently. If it is true, if it is confirmed that such detestable things are being done in Isra'el; then you are to bring the man or woman who has done this wicked thing to your city gates, and stone that man or woman to death. The death sentence is to be carried out only if there was testimony from two or three witnesses; he may not be sentenced to death on the testimony of only one witness. The witnesses are to be the first to stone him to death; afterwards, all the people are to stone him. Thus you will put an end to this wickedness among you."*

The section "Scriptures that pertain to criminal justice" overlaps the section "Scriptures that call for punishment." There are behaviors considered criminal under Mosaic Law and not by our contemporary laws, and vice-versa. There are also behaviors that are considered criminal under both but, even when it is criminal under both, the law it offends is not the same because the governments behind the laws are not the same. The way that we of the New Covenant should view the Mosaic criminal law, is that it gives us God's view of the seriousness of certain criminal offences and the punishments that should be applied to them. We read in <u>Romans 13:1-5</u>:

"Everyone is to obey the governing authorities. For there is no authority that is not from God, and the existing authorities have been placed where they are by God. Therefore, whoever resists

the authorities is resisting what God has instituted; and those who resist will bring judgment on themselves. For rulers are no terror to good conduct, but to bad. Would you like to be unafraid of the person in authority? Then simply do what is good, and you will win his approval; for he is God's servant, there for your benefit. But if you do what is wrong, be afraid! Because it is not for nothing that he holds the power of the sword; for he is God's servant, there as an avenger to punish wrongdoers. Another reason to obey, besides fear of punishment, is for the sake of conscience."

Note by Daniel C. Juster

The Puritans applied Mosaic criminal law literally, and so would Rushdoony.[129] The Anglicans, on the other hand, argued that the New Testament, with the power of Yeshua, gives us an ability to apply the law with greater flexibility and more compassion.

Scriptures that Pertain to Civil Justice

Exodus 22:4(5)-14(15): *"If a person causes a field or vineyard to be grazed over or lets his animal loose to graze in someone else's field, he is to make restitution from the best produce of his own field and vineyard. If a fire is started and spreads to thorns, so that stacked grain, standing grain or a field is destroyed, the person who lit it must make restitution. If a person entrusts a neighbor with money or goods, and they are stolen from the trustee's house, then, if the thief is found, he must pay double. But if the thief is not found, then the trustee must state before God that he did not take the person's goods himself. In every case of dispute over ownership, whether of an ox, a donkey, a sheep, clothing, or any missing property, where one person says, 'This is mine,' both parties are to come before God; and the one whom God condemns must pay the other one double. If a person trusts a neighbor to look after a donkey, ox, sheep or any animal, and it dies, is injured or is driven away unseen, then the neighbor's oath before ADONAI that he has not taken the goods will settle the matter between them—the owner is to accept it without the neighbor's making restitution. But if it was stolen from the neighbor, he must make restitution to the owner. If it was torn to pieces by an animal, the neighbor must bring it as evidence, and then he doesn't need to make good the loss. If someone borrows something from his neighbor, and it gets injured or dies with the owner not present, he must make restitution. If the owner was present, he need not make good the loss. If the owner hired it out, the loss is covered by the hiring fee."*

Much that has been said regarding the Mosaic criminal law is the same for the Mosaic civil law in that they are both promulgated by, and enforced pursuant to, the ancient government of Israel that no longer exists. By the term "civil law," we do not mean law promulgated by civil authorities since that is true of criminal law as well. The difference between criminal and civil law is that offenses of civil law are against individuals, whereas violations of criminal law are deemed to be against society as a whole. We normally associate violations of criminal law with punishment, and violations of civil law with restitution, and damages having to be paid to individuals who have been harmed. Sometimes the same wrongful act violates both a criminal and a civil statute, such as in the case of an unjustified physical assault. An assault against an individual is a breach of the peace against society as a whole, but it also causes injury to the person who is assaulted; consequently, both punishment and monetary damages to the injured party is commonly required. As has been said regarding the Mosaic criminal law, the way that we of the New Covenant should view it, is that it gives us God's view of the seriousness of certain kinds of wrongful behaviors, and the kinds of restitution that should be required for transgressing. Romans 13:7-10 expresses the New Covenant concept of civil law best; it states:

---

129 Rousas J. Rushdoony, "The Institutes of Biblical Law," vols. 1-3, 1973.

"Pay everyone what he is owed: if you owe the tax-collector, pay your taxes; if you owe the revenue-collector, pay revenue; if you owe someone respect, pay him respect; if you owe someone honor, pay him honor. Don't owe anyone anything—except to love one another; for whoever loves his fellow human being has fulfilled Torah. For the commandments, "Don't commit adultery," "Don't murder," "Don't steal," "Don't covet," and any others are summed up in this one rule: "Love your neighbor as yourself." Love does not do harm to a neighbor; therefore love is the fullness of Torah."

Scriptures that Pertain to Mosaic Jurisprudence

<u>Exodus 18:13-24</u>: *"The following day Moshe sat to settle disputes for the people, while the people stood around Moshe from morning till evening. When Moshe's father-in-law saw all that he was doing to the people, he said, "What is this that you are doing to the people? Why do you sit there alone, with all the people standing around you from morning till evening?" Moshe answered his father-in-law, "It's because the people come to me seeking God's guidance. Whenever they have a dispute, it comes to me; I judge between one person and another, and I explain to them God's laws and teachings." Moshe's father-in-law said to him, "What you are doing isn't good. You will certainly wear yourself out—and not only yourself, but these people here with you as well. It's too much for you—you can't do it alone, by yourself. So listen now to what I have to say. I will give you some advice, and God will be with you. You should represent the people before God, and you should bring their cases to God. You should also teach them the laws and the teachings, and show them how to live their lives and what work they should do. But you should choose from among all the people competent men who are God-fearing, honest and incorruptible to be their leaders, in charge of thousands, hundreds, fifties and tens. Normally, they will settle the people's disputes. They should bring you the difficult cases; but ordinary matters they should decide themselves. In this way, they will make it easier for you and share the load with you. If you do this—and God is directing you to do it—you will be able to endure; and all these people too will arrive at their destination peacefully." Moshe paid attention to his father-in-law's counsel and did everything he said."*

<u>Numbers 35:10-12</u>: *"Tell the people of Isra'el, 'When you cross the Yarden into the land of Kena'an, you are to designate for yourselves cities that will be cities of refuge for you, to which anyone who kills someone by mistake can flee. These cities are to be a refuge for you from the dead person's next-of-kin, who might otherwise avenge his kinsman's death by slaying the killer prior to his standing trial before the community."*

<u>Deuteronomy 17:6-10</u>: *"The death sentence is to be carried out only if there was testimony from two or three witnesses; he may not be sentenced to death on the testimony of only one witness. The witnesses are to be the first to stone him to death; afterwards, all the people are to stone him. Thus you will put an end to this wickedness among you. If a case comes before you at your city gate which is too difficult for you to judge, concerning bloodshed, civil suit, personal injury or any other controversial issue; you are to get up, go to the place which ADONAI your God will choose, and appear before the cohanim, who are L'vi'im, and the judge in office at the time. Seek their opinion, and they will render a verdict for you. You will then act according to what they have told you there in that place which ADONAI will choose; you are to take care to act according to all their instructions."*

<u>Deuteronomy 19:15-21</u>: *"One witness alone will not be sufficient to convict a person of any offense or sin of any kind; the matter will be established only if there are two or three witnesses testifying against him. If a malicious witness comes forward and gives false testimony against someone, then both the men involved in the controversy are to stand before ADONAI, before the cohanim and the judges in office at the time. The judges are to investigate carefully. If they find that the witness is lying*

and has given false testimony against his brother, you are to do to him what he intended to do to his brother. In this way, you will put an end to such wickedness among you. Those who remain will hear about it, be afraid and no longer commit such wickedness among you. Show no pity: life for life, eye for eye, tooth for tooth, hand for hand, foot for foot."

Jurisprudence is the manner (including the rules) by which violations and disputes of law are adjudicated. Modern Anglo-American jurisprudence draws heavily from Scriptural concepts but there are significant differences as well. An example of a difference is that we no longer have cities of refuge to where persons accused of murder can go to escape capture.

Many aspects of jurisprudence are, however, the same or similar. The delegation of judicial authority to a panel of judges is often the same. Also, one witness alone is not generally sufficient to convict a person of a crime but, by today's standards, one witness plus circumstantial or DNA evidence may very well be. The *Torah's* requirement that there be more than one witness to convict of a crime is reflected in 2 Corinthians 13:1:

"This will be the third time that I have come to visit you. Any charge must be established by the testimony of two or three witnesses."

And also, in 1 Timothy 5:19 we read:

"Never listen to any accusation against a leader unless it is supported by two or three witnesses."

Today as in the days of Moses, giving false testimony is considered a serious crime, but a difference from during the time of Moses is that today, maximum punishments for crimes are prescribed by statute and are not individually tailored to each crime (e.g. an eye for eye, etc.).[130] Today, judgments for restitution in civil cases are generally established according to the extent of injury to the victim, and restitution is usually in money, and not in causing injury to the perpetrator as was often the case during the days of Moses.

In general, Scripture discourages adjudication and, instead, encourages the avoidance of disputes:

Proverbs 17:14: *"Starting a fight is like letting water through [a dike]—better stop the quarrel before it gets worse."*

Proverbs 20:3: *"Avoiding quarrels brings a person honor; for any fool can explode in anger."*

Proverbs 25:7b-8: *"What your eyes have seen, don't rush to present in a dispute. For what will you do later on, if your neighbor puts you to shame?"*

Matthew 5:40: *"If someone wants to sue you for your shirt, let him have your coat as well!"*

---

130 "Eye for eye and tooth for tooth" is an expression referring to Exodus 21:22-25 that is often quoted out of context to justify personal acts of vengeance. Yeshua responded to this wrong application of the Scripture in Matthew 5:38-45.

If an offense has already occurred and a dispute cannot be avoided, Scripture recommends settling out of court rather than litigating:

> Matthew 5:25: *"If someone sues you, come to terms with him quickly, while you and he are on the way to court; or he may hand you over to the judge, and the judge to the officer of the court, and you may be thrown in jail!"*

In the New Covenant, we are instructed to not bring complaints against brother believers to the public courts, but rather to bring them to *betei din* of the Messianic community:

> 1 Corinthians 6:1-7: *"How dare one of you with a complaint against another go to court before pagan judges and not before God's people? Don't you know that God's people are going to judge the universe? If you are going to judge the universe, are you incompetent to judge these minor matters? Don't you know that we will judge angels, not to mention affairs of everyday life? So if you require judgments about matters of everyday life, why do you put them in front of men who have no standing in the Messianic Community? I say, shame on you! Can it be that there isn't one person among you wise enough to be able to settle a dispute between brothers? Instead, a brother brings a lawsuit against another brother, and that before unbelievers! Actually, if you are bringing lawsuits against each other, it is already a defeat for you. Why not rather be wronged? Why not rather be cheated?"*

When we do bring complaints against brother believers in the New Covenant, there is a pre-scribed way of going about it.

1. Deciding Whether to Overlook an Offense

Even when we are authorized to seek redress for a sin committed against us, we need not do so.

> Proverbs 19:11: *"People with good sense are slow to anger, and it is their glory to overlook an offense."*

Some offenses are easily overlooked—especially those that are unintentional, have done no great harm, and are unlikely to be repeated. Although it may seem that overlooking an offense is always the loving thing to do, it is not necessarily so. One's decision should always be based upon what is best for the offender, and what is best for others against whom the offender may sin if he is not made accountable. If, however, the offense is overlooked, it must not be brought up again unless the offense is repeated.

2. Bringing Correction to an Offending Brother

If our decision is to not overlook the offense, we must confront the offending brother privately:

> Matthew 18:15: *"Moreover, if your brother commits a sin against you, go and show him his fault—but privately, just between the two of you. If he listens to you, you have won back your brother."*

> Galatians 6:1-2: *"Brothers, suppose someone is caught doing something wrong. You who have the Spirit should set him right, but in a spirit of humility, keeping an eye on yourselves so that you won't be tempted too. Bear one another's burdens—in this way you will be fulfilling the Torah's true meaning, which the Messiah upholds."*

454

There are three things in the foregoing Scriptures which stand out. First, when we go to our brother to tell him his fault, our attitude must be pure and our demeanor proper. The operative expression in the <u>Galatians</u> Scripture is "a spirit of gentleness."

Second, we are to go to our brother alone. That means we are not to share our complaint with others before first giving our brother the opportunity to repent and make things right. This principle assumes two things: (1) The parties are relatively equal in their ability to deal with one another, and (2) There is no impropriety in the parties meeting privately. An example of inequality would be a child having to confront an adult; an example of improper privacy would be a male and female meeting alone to confront one another concerning sexual sin. In these and similar cases, the Scriptures should be interpreted broadly enough to permit chaperoning and for allowing the weaker of the two adversaries to be accompanied by a suitable protector but not an advocate or spokesperson.

Third, our purpose for confronting our brother must be to restore him to righteousness, and our hope must be for reconciliation.

3. Returning with Witnesses

If the offending brother agrees with our complaint and repents, the matter is, of course, concluded, and we forgive him. If he does not agree or refuses to meet privately, we must then elect whether to pursue the matter further, or to belatedly overlook his sin (<u>Proverbs 19:11</u>) while being content that we have complied with <u>Galatians 6:1-2</u>. Although overlooking the sin at this point is possible, its appropriateness is unlikely. If there remains un-reconciliation, we are obligated to go to our brother again, and this time, with one or two witnesses:

> <u>Matthew 18:16</u>: *"If he doesn't listen, take one or two others with you so that every accusation can be supported by the testimony of two or three witnesses."*

These need not be witnesses to the original offense complained of (although they may be), but rather to this second meeting with our brother.[131] Our usual concept of witnesses is that they are silent observers. In this case, however, the verse of Scripture that follows (<u>Matthew 18:17</u>), infers that these witnesses determine which of the parties to the dispute is wrong, and urges that person to listen to reason and repent. These verses of Scripture are constructed with the assumption that the brother receiving the visit is the one who is in the wrong but, in our interpretation, we allow for the possibility that, after hearing the dialog between the brothers, the witnesses conclude that the brother bringing the complaint is the one who is in the wrong.

As before, if the parties come to agreement during the visit or the offending brother repents, the matter is concluded. If however, the attempt at reconciliation is unsuccessful, the matter must not be allowed to fester, and must therefore be brought for adjudication to the *ekklesia*.

---

131 Although not addressed in Scripture, fairness probably allows the offending brother to invite his own witnesses to observe the meeting as well.

455

4. Bringing the Dispute to the Ekklesia

> Matthew 18:17: *"If he refuses to hear them, tell the congregation; and if he refuses to listen even to the congregation, treat him as you would a pagan or a tax-collector."*

The word "congregation" in the CJB (translated "church" in the NKJ) is ἐκκλησία *(ekklesia)*, in the Greek text, which means "a gathering," "an assembly (for worship)," "a deliberative council." According to Matthew 18:17, if the complainant and the witnesses are unsuccessful in convincing the offender to repent, the matter is to be brought to the *ekklesia* for adjudication.

Since the entire *ekklesia* (the body of believers or even the membership of a single congregation) is too large a group to assemble in order to hear and judge disputes, it is the prevailing view that a *bet din* (ecclesiastical court) of assembled elders acts for the *ekklesia* and rules on the complaint brought before it. If, after announcing its judgment, the person ruled to be in the wrong does not repent, we are to treat him as we would *"a pagan or a tax-collector"* (Matthew 18:17). This is sometimes referred to as a decree of "disfellowship" or "excommunication."

It is a common misunderstanding that when a brother is excommunicated pursuant to Matthew 18:17, he must necessarily be ejected from the congregation. On the contrary, after a judgment of excommunication, the brother must be treated as an unbeliever in every way. Therefore, although he must be refused holy communion *(Shulchan Adonai)* with the brethren, unless he is also a violator of 1 Corinthians 5:9-13 (walking in immorality while calling himself a believer) or Titus 3:10-11 (divisive or otherwise harmful to the body), he should be encouraged to attend congregational services and other events where he is likely to hear the Word of God and be encouraged to repent.

One interesting consequence of a Matthew 18:17 excommunication, is that the innocent complainant is released from the constraint of 1 Corinthians 6:1-7, and is free to sue the unrepentant "former" brother in a secular court. This has special ramifications for persons seeking to divorce an excommunicated spouse.

Another common misunderstanding is that a decree of excommunication applies only to the excommunicating congregation or religious denomination in which the excommunication occurs. Biblically, that is not so. Judgments arising from Matthew 18 proceedings apply across the entire body of believers and, so long as correct biblical doctrine has been applied and due process afforded, congregations of all stripes are biblically required to recognize the judgment. What is more, God Himself recognizes and honors the judgment, for we read in Matthew 18:18:

> *"Yes! I tell you people that whatever you prohibit on earth will be prohibited in heaven, and whatever you permit on earth will be permitted in heaven."*

We note that sins without repentance that would lead to capital punishment in the Mosaic order generally require disfellowship in the New Covenant order.

5. Restoring a Brother to Fellowship

A <u>Matthew 18</u> judgment of "disfellowship" is reversible in the same way as the status of being an unbeliever is reversible. What is required is that the sanctioned brother repent of his former sin, comply with all orders of the convicting *bet din*, and receive Yeshua again as his Lord and savior. Ideally, the same *bet din* that ruled previously is convened to judge the repentance and, if the repentance is deemed genuine, the tribunal should set aside its prior judgment, and publish a decree of restoration. This restoration which is bound on earth, is also bound in heaven (<u>Matthew 18:18</u>).

6. When the Offender is Us!

> <u>Matthew 5:23-24</u>: *"So if you are offering your gift at the Temple altar and you remember there that your brother has something against you, leave your gift where it is by the altar, and go, make peace with your brother. Then come back and offer your gift."*

This is the reciprocal of the situation dealt with in <u>Matthew 18</u>. If we know or suspect that we have sinned against a brother, we are not to wait until the brother comes to us—we are to go to him. A noted author, Jay Adams, has written that, because of <u>Matthew 5:23-24</u> and <u>Matthew 18:15</u>, the offender and the offended should be meeting in the street between their respective homes, each on his way to seek reconciliation with the other.

Scriptures that Pertain to Idols and Idolatry

> <u>Exodus 20:3-6</u>: *"You are to have no other gods before me. You are not to make for yourselves a carved image or any kind of representation of anything in heaven above, on the earth beneath or in the water below the shoreline. You are not to bow down to them or serve them; for I, ADONAI your God, am a jealous God, punishing the children for the sins of the parents to the third and fourth generation of those who hate me, but displaying grace to the thousandth generation of those who love me and obey my mitzvot."*

> <u>Exodus 22:19(20)</u>: *"Anyone who sacrifices to any god other than ADONAI alone is to be completely destroyed."*

> <u>Deuteronomy 7:1-5</u>: *"ADONAI your God is going to bring you into the land you will enter in order to take possession of it, and he will expel many nations ahead of you—the Hitti, Girgashi, Emori, Kena'ani, P'rizi, Hivi and Y'vusi, seven nations bigger and stronger than you. When he does this, when ADONAI your God hands them over ahead of you, and you defeat them, you are to destroy them completely! Do not make any covenant with them. Show them no mercy. Don't intermarry with them— don't give your daughter to his son, and don't take his daughter for your son. For he will turn your children away from following me in order to serve other gods. If this happens, the anger of ADONAI will flare up against you, and he will quickly destroy you. No, treat them this way: break down their altars, smash their standing-stones to pieces, cut down their sacred poles and burn up their carved images completely."*

We see from the examples cited above that idolatry (worshiping gods other than the Lord our God) is punishable by death under Mosaic Law, and all objects of idolatrous worship are to be torn down and destroyed. Upon the New Covenant's arrival, pagan worship of physical idols and foreign gods was still rampant among the Romans, Greeks and others, and so a significant number of New Testament Scriptures speak against it; for example:

Acts 15:28-29: *"For it seemed good to the Ruach HaKodesh and to us not to lay any heavier burden on you than the following requirements: to abstain from what has been sacrificed to idols, from blood, from things strangled, and from fornication. If you keep yourselves from these, you will be doing the right thing. Shalom!"*

Acts 17:29: *"So, since we are children of God, we shouldn't suppose that God's essence resembles gold, silver or stone shaped by human technique and imagination."*

1 Corinthians 10:7: *"Don't be idolaters, as some of them were—as the Tanakh puts it, 'The people sat down to eat and drink, then got up to indulge in revelry.'"*

1 Corinthians 10:14: *"Therefore, my dear friends, run from idolatry!"*

1 Corinthians 12:2: *"You know that when you were pagans, no matter how you felt you were being led, you were being led astray to idols, which can't speak at all."*

1 John 5:21: *"Children, guard yourselves against false gods!"*

Also, the Mosaic Law that required death for idolaters and destruction of their idols is carried forward into the New Covenant—not that we execute idolaters any longer, but that God dispatches them by denying them eternal life:

1 Corinthians 6:9-10: *"Don't you know that unrighteous people will have no share in the Kingdom of God? Don't delude yourselves—people who engage in sex before marriage, who worship idols, who engage in sex after marriage with someone other than their spouse, who engage in active or passive homosexuality, who steal, who are greedy, who get drunk, who assail people with contemptuous language, who rob—none of them will share in the Kingdom of God."*

Revelation 21:8: *"But as for the cowardly, the untrustworthy, the vile, the murderers, the sexually immoral, those involved with the occult and with drugs, idol-worshippers, and all liars—their destiny is the lake burning with fire and sulfur, the second death."*

Apart from the New Testament's warnings against worshiping foreign gods and physical idols, the New Covenant expands the meaning of idolatry to giving ourselves to satanic temptations and sinful temptations of the flesh: Of course, explicitly worshipping idols is grounds for disfellowshipping in the New Covenant.

1 Corinthians 10:13-14: *"No temptation has seized you beyond what people normally experience, and God can be trusted not to allow you to be tempted beyond what you can bear. On the contrary, along with the temptation he will also provide the way out, so that you will be able to endure. Therefore, my dear friends, run from idolatry!"*

1 Corinthians 10:19-20: *"So, what am I saying? That food sacrificed to idols has any significance in itself? or that an idol has significance in itself? No, what I am saying is that the things which pagans*

sacrifice, they sacrifice not to God but to demons; and I don't want you to become sharers of the demons!"

Galatians 4:7-9: *"So through God you are no longer a slave but a son, and if you are a son you are also an heir. In the past, when you did not know God, you served as slaves beings which in reality are non-gods. But now you do know God, and, more than that, you are known by God. So how is it that you turn back again to those weak and miserable elemental spirits? Do you want to enslave yourselves to them once more?"*

Colossians 3:5: *"Therefore, put to death the earthly parts of your nature—sexual immorality, impurity, lust, evil desires and greed (which is a form of idolatry)..."*

James 4:7 commands us:

"Therefore, submit to God. Moreover, take a stand against the Adversary, and he will flee from you."

The NKJ translates James 4:7: *"Therefore submit to God. Resist the devil and he will flee from you."* The New Covenant has given us the Holy Spirit to dwell within each of us, and He empowers us to be able to *"resist the devil"* and keep God's *Torah.* Nevertheless, the responsibility of inviting the Holy Spirit to help us in resisting is ours and ours alone.

Scriptures that Pertain to Family Matters

Deuteronomy 22:13-19: *"If a man marries a woman, has sexual relations with her and then, having come to dislike her, brings false charges against her and defames her character by saying, 'I married this woman, but when I had intercourse with her I did not find evidence that she was a virgin'; then the girl's father and mother are to take the evidence of the girl's virginity to the leaders of the town at the gate. The girl's father will say to the leaders, 'I let my daughter marry this man, but he hates her, so he has brought false charges that he didn't find evidence of her virginity; yet here is the evidence of my daughter's virginity'—and they will lay the cloth before the town leaders. The leaders of that town are to take the man, punish him, and fine him two-and-a-half pounds of silver shekels, which they will give to the girl's father, because he has publicly defamed a virgin of Isra'el. She will remain his wife, and he is forbidden from divorcing her as long as he lives."*

Scriptures of the Mosaic Law pertaining to family matters (typical of the above Scripture) are not enforceable in the New Covenant because they infringe on, and conflict with, the laws of the secular governments under which we live. Still, there is teaching value in each of them. So, for example, the Deuteronomy 22:13-19 Scripture instructs us (1) to uphold the value of premarital virginity; (2) to value the permanence of marriage and not seek divorce for unsubstantial reasons such as dislike; (3) to not bring false charges against our spouse; and (4) to not impugn our spouse's reputation. We might also weigh the issue of marriage as required in the Bible for believers who become sexually involved. It is a difficult issue that requires more reflection and discussion. Would it be only with a virgin woman as in the Bible? At the date of this writing, eight states and the District of Columbia recognize common-law marriage, which is a legally recognized state of marriage (despite their being no marriage license or ceremony) by couples who cohabit openly with the intention of being married. Intent is the key. Even in common-law marriage states, sexual cohabitation without the intent of being considered married does not create a marriage and is simply fornication.

Commentary by Daniel C. Juster

Romans 7 makes it clear that we are in the New Covenant Order and not the Mosaic when it refers to the widow and indicates that she is now freed from her covenant bond. That would not have been the case were we still under the Mosaic Covenant. We who are believers have died and been raised in the Messiah and, although we have been released from the Mosaic Covenant, we are, nevertheless, expected to apply its teaching in a manner that is applicable in the New Covenant.

Contrary to the idea of secular society, the Bible enjoins all nations to acknowledge God and to embrace the principles of God's Law for the governing of the society. In classical Protestant thought first defined by John Calvin, this was called the second use of the Law. God's Law (both Mosaic and New Covenant) provides the framework for society's civil law, so followers of Yeshua should work toward bringing their civil society into conformity with its principles. The ideal of all nations acknowledging the Lordship of God and His Law is repeated throughout the Prophets and the Writings.

Classical Commentators

The 613 *mitzvot* listed by Maimonides and HaChinuch include several that cannot be literally complied with today. Meir's compilation leaves out many of them, which is why his compilation lists fewer. None of the classical Jewish commentators recognize the existence of a New Covenant, and their interpretations of the *Torah* Scriptures reflect that view.

NCLA: JMm JFm KMm KFm GMm GFm

J2. God's Law of Justice.
We are to administer justice both in and out of our courts.

This precept is derived from His Word (blessed be He):

Key Scriptures

We Are to Obey the Decisions pf a Court

Deuteronomy 17:8-12 (Maimonides RP174, RN312; Meir MN158; Chinuch C495-496)
If a case comes before you at your city gate which is too difficult for you to judge, concerning bloodshed, civil suit, personal injury or any other controversial issue; you are to get up, go to the place which ADONAI your God will choose, and appear before the cohanim, who are L'vi'im, and the judge in office at the time. Seek their opinion, and they will render a verdict for you. You will then act according to what they have told you there in that place which ADONAI will choose; you are to take care to act according to all their instructions. In accordance with the Torah they teach you, you are to carry out the judgment they render, not turning aside to the right or the left from the verdict they declare to you. Anyone presumptuous enough not to pay attention to the cohen appointed there to serve ADONAI your God or to the judge—that person must die. Thus you will exterminate such wickedness from Isra'el-

Hebrews 13:17
Obey those who rule over you, and be submissive, for they watch out for your souls, as those who must give account. Let them do so with joy and not with grief, for that would be unprofitable for you.

1 Peter 2:13-14
Therefore submit yourselves to every ordinance of man for the Lord's sake, whether to the king as supreme, or to governors, as to those who are sent by him for the punishment of evildoers and for the praise of those who do good.

We Are to Adhere to the Majority Decisions of a Court

Exodus 23:2 (Maimonides RP175; Chinuch 78)
Do not follow the crowd when it does what is wrong; and don't allow the popular view to sway you into offering testimony for any cause if the effect will be to pervert justice.
(see notes under "Classical Commentators" below)

Believers Are Not to Sue Each Other in Secular Courts

1 Corinthians 6:1-7
How dare one of you with a complaint against another go to court before pagan judges and not before God's people? Don't you know that God's people are going to judge the universe? If you are going to judge the universe, are you incompetent to judge these minor matters? Don't

461

you know that we will judge angels, not to mention affairs of everyday life? So if you require judgments about matters of everyday life, why do you put them in front of men who have no standing in the Messianic Community? I say, shame on you! Can it be that there isn't one person among you wise enough to be able to settle a dispute between brothers? Instead, a brother brings a lawsuit against another brother, and that before unbelievers! Actually, if you are bringing lawsuits against each other, it is already a defeat for you. Why not rather be wronged? Why not rather be cheated?

Believers Are to Resolve their Disputes via Mediation or in an Ecclesiastical Court

Matthew 18:15-17
Moreover, if your brother commits a sin against you, go and show him his fault—but privately, just between the two of you. If he listens to you, you have won back your brother. If he doesn't listen, take one or two others with you so that every accusation can be supported by the testimony of two or three witnesses. If he refuses to hear them, tell the congregation; and if he refuses to listen even to the congregation, treat him as you would a pagan or a tax-collector.

1 Corinthians 6:1-5
How dare one of you with a complaint against another go to court before pagan judges and not before God's people? Don't you know that God's people are going to judge the universe? If you are going to judge the universe, are you incompetent to judge these minor matters? Don't you know that we will judge angels, not to mention affairs of everyday life? So if you require judgments about matters of everyday life, why do you put them in front of men who have no standing in the Messianic Community? I say, shame on you! Can it be that there isn't one person among you wise enough to be able to settle a dispute between brothers?

We Are Not to Curse a Judge

Exodus 22:27(28) (Maimonides RN315; Meir MN63; Chinuch C69)
You are not to curse God, and you are not to curse a leader of your people.

We Are Not to Add or Subtract from the Commandments of God

Deuteronomy 13:1(12:32) (Maimonides RN313-314; Meir MN159-160; Chinuch C454-455)
Everything I am commanding you, you are to take care to do. Do not add to it or subtract from it.

Judges Are Not to Take Gifts from Litigants

Exodus 23:8 (Maimonides RN274; Chinuch C83)
You are not to receive a bribe, for a bribe blinds the clearsighted and subverts the cause of the righteous.

Leviticus 19:14 (Meir MN71)
Do not speak a curse against a deaf person or place an obstacle in the way of a blind person; rather, fear your God; I am ADONAI.

Deuteronomy 16:19-20 (Maimonides RN274; Chinuch C83)
You are not to distort justice or show favoritism, and you are not to accept a bribe, for a gift blinds the eyes of the wise and twists the words of even the upright. Justice, only justice, you must pursue; so that you will live and inherit the land ADONAI your God is giving you.

Judges Are to Treat Litigants Equally

Exodus 23:3 (Maimonides RN277; Meir MN66; Chinuch C79)
On the other hand, don't favor a person's lawsuit simply because he is poor.

Exodus 23:6 (Maimonides RN278; Meir MN67; Chinuch 81)
Do not deny anyone justice in his lawsuit simply because he is poor.

Leviticus 19:15 (Maimonides RP177, RN273, 275, 277, 280; Meir MN68-70; Chinuch C79, 233-235, 590)
Do not be unjust in judging—show neither partiality to the poor nor deference to the mighty, but with justice judge your neighbor.

Luke 18:1-7
Then Yeshua told his talmidim a parable, in order to impress on them that they must always keep praying and not lose heart. "In a certain town, there was a judge who neither feared God nor respected other people. There was also in that town a widow who kept coming to him and saying, 'Give me a judgment against the man who is trying to ruin me.' For a long time he refused; but after awhile, he said to himself, 'I don't fear God, and I don't respect other people; but because this widow is such a nudnik, I will see to it that she gets justice—otherwise, she'll keep coming and pestering me till she wears me out!'" Then the Lord commented, "Notice what this corrupt judge says. Now won't God grant justice to his chosen people who cry out to him day and night? Is he delaying long over them?

Judges Are Not to Pervert Justice

Exodus 23:1-2 (Maimonides RN281, 283; Meir MN65, 77; Chinuch C74)
You are not to repeat false rumors; do not join hands with the wicked by offering perjured testimony. Do not follow the crowd when it does what is wrong; and don't allow the popular view to sway you into offering testimony for any cause if the effect will be to pervert justice.

Deuteronomy 1:16-17 (Maimonides RN276; Meir MN72; Chinuch C415)
At that time I commissioned your judges, 'Hear the cases that arise between your brothers; and judge fairly between a man and his brother, and the foreigner who is with him. You are not to show favoritism when judging, but give equal attention to the small and to the great. No matter

how a person presents himself, don't be afraid of him; because the decision is God's. The case that is too hard for you, bring to me and I will hear it.

<u>Deuteronomy 19:11-13</u> Maimonides RN279; Chinuch C521)
However, if someone hates his fellow member of the community, lies in wait for him, attacks him, strikes him a death blow, and then flees into one of these cities; then the leaders of his own town are to send and bring him back from there and hand him over to the next-of-kin avenger, to be put to death. You are not to pity him. Rather, you must put an end to the shedding of innocent blood in Isra'el. Then things will go well with you.

<u>Deuteronomy 19:21</u> (Maimonides RN279; Chinuch C521)
Show no pity: life for life, eye for eye, tooth for tooth, hand for hand, foot for foot.

<u>Deuteronomy 24:17a</u> (Maimonides RN280; Meir MN68; Chinuch C590)
You are not to deprive the foreigner or the orphan of the justice which is his due...

Appointing Judges

<u>Numbers 11:16-17</u> (Maimonides RP176; Chinuch C491)
ADONAI said to Moshe, "Bring me seventy of the leaders of Isra'el, people you recognize as leaders of the people and officers of theirs. Bring them to the tent of meeting, and have them stand there with you. I will come down and speak with you there, and I will take some of the Spirit which rests on you and put it on them. Then they will carry the burden of the people along with you, so that you won't carry it yourself alone.

<u>Deuteronomy 1:16-17</u> (Maimonides RN284; Meir MN64; Chinuch C414)
At that time I commissioned your judges, 'Hear the cases that arise between your brothers; and judge fairly between a man and his brother, and the foreigner who is with him. You are not to show favoritism when judging, but give equal attention to the small and to the great. No matter how a person presents himself, don't be afraid of him; because the decision is God's. The case that is too hard for you, bring to me and I will hear it.

<u>Deuteronomy 16:18</u> (Maimonides RP176; Chinuch C491)
You are to appoint judges and officers for all your gates [in the cities] ADONAI your God is giving you, tribe by tribe; and they are to judge the people with righteous judgment.

No Conviction or Punishment unless More than One Witness Testifies at a Trial

<u>Numbers 35:12</u> (Maimonides RN292; Chinuch C409)
These cities are to be a refuge for you from the dead person's next-of-kin, who might otherwise avenge his kinsman's death by slaying the killer prior to his standing trial before the community.

<u>Numbers 35:30</u> (Maimonides RN291; Chinuch C411)
If anyone kills someone, the murderer is to be put to death upon the testimony of witnesses; but the testimony of only one witness will not suffice to cause a person to be put to death.

Deuteronomy 19:15 (Maimonides RN288; Meir MN73; Chinuch C523)
One witness alone will not be sufficient to convict a person of any offense or sin of any kind; the matter will be established only if there are two or three witnesses testifying against him.

A Trial Must Allow for the Examination of Witnesses

Deuteronomy 13:15 (Maimonides RP179; Chinuch C463)
If you hear it told that in one of your cities which ADONAI your God is giving you to live in, certain scoundrels have sprung up among you and have drawn away the inhabitants of their city by saying, 'Let's go and serve other gods, which you haven't known, then you are to investigate the matter, inquiring and searching diligently. If the rumor is true, if it is confirmed that such detestable things are being done among you, you must put the inhabitants of that city to death with the sword, destroying it completely with the sword, everything in it, including its livestock.

Witnesses Must Testify Truthfully

Exodus 20:13b (Maimonides RN285; Meir MN39; Chinuch C37)
Do not give false evidence against your neighbor.

Exodus 23:1b-2 (Maimonides RN282, 286; Meir MN75; Chinuch 75-76)
...do not join hands with the wicked by offering perjured testimony. Do not follow the crowd when it does what is wrong; and don't allow the popular view to sway you into offering testimony for any cause if the effect will be to pervert justice.

Deuteronomy 5:17b (Maimonides RN285; Meir MN39; Chinuch C37)
Do not give false evidence against your neighbor. (Deu 5:17 CJB)

Deuteronomy 19:18-19 (Maimonides RP180, RN285; Meir MN39; Chinuch C37, 524)
The judges are to investigate carefully. If they find that the witness is lying and has given false testimony against his brother, you are to do to him what he intended to do to his brother. In this way, you will put an end to such wickedness among you.

Refusing to Testify

Leviticus 5:1 (Maimonides RP178; Chinuch C122)
If a person who is a witness, sworn to testify, sins by refusing to tell what he has seen or heard about the matter, he must bear the consequences.

No Excessive Corporal Punishment

Deuteronomy 25:1-3 (Maimonides RN300; Meir MN43; Chinuch C595)
If people have a dispute, seek its resolution in court, and the judges render a decision in favor of the righteous one and condemning the wicked one; then, if the wicked one deserves to be flogged, the judge is to have him lie down and be flogged in his presence. The number of strokes is to be proportionate to his offense; but the maximum number is forty. He is not to exceed this; if he goes over this limit and beats him more than this, your brother will be humiliated before your eyes.

465

No Punishment for Sin Committed while under Duress

Deuteronomy 22:25-27 (Maimonides RN294; Chinuch C556)
But if the man comes upon the engaged girl out in the countryside, and the man grabs her and has sexual relations with her, then only the man who had intercourse with her is to die. You will do nothing to the girl, because she has done nothing deserving of death. The situation is like the case of the man who attacks his neighbor and kills him. For he found her in the countryside, and the engaged girl cried out, but there was no one to save her.

No Capital Punishment if Circumstantial Evidence or any Chance of Fraud

Exodus 23:7 (Maimonides RN290; Chinuch C82)
Keep away from fraud, and do not cause the death of the innocent and righteous; for I will not justify the wicked.

No Capital Punishment for the Sins of One's Relatives

Deuteronomy 24:16 (Maimonides RN287; Meir MN74; Chinuch C589)
Fathers are not to be executed for the children, nor are children to be executed for the fathers; every person will be executed for his own sin.

No Ransom from Punishment for Committing Murder [obsolete]

Numbers 35:31-32 (Maimonides RN295-296; Chinuch C412-413)
Also, you are not to accept a ransom in lieu of the life of a murderer condemned to death; rather, he must be put to death. Likewise, you are not to accept for someone who has fled to his city of refuge a ransom that would allow him to return to his land before the death of the cohen.

Justice in Everyday Life

Deuteronomy 10:18
He secures justice for the orphan and the widow; he loves the foreigner, giving him food and clothing.

Isaiah 1:16-17
Wash yourselves clean! Get your evil deeds out of my sight! Stop doing evil, learn to do good! Seek justice, relieve the oppressed, defend orphans, plead for the widow.

Isaiah 30:18
Yet ADONAI is just waiting to show you favor, he will have pity on you from on high; for ADONAI is a God of justice; happy are all who wait for him!

Isaiah 56:1-7
Here is what ADONAI says: "Observe justice, do what is right, for my salvation is close to coming, my righteousness to being revealed. Happy is the person who does this, anyone who

grasps it firmly, who keeps Shabbat and does not profane it, and keeps himself from doing any evil. A foreigner joining ADONAI should not say, "ADONAI will separate me from his people"; likewise the eunuch should not say, "I am only a dried-up tree." For here is what ADONAI says: "As for the eunuchs who keep my Shabbats, who choose what pleases me and hold fast to my covenant: in my house, within my walls, I will give them power and a name greater than sons and daughters; I will give him an everlasting name that will not be cut off. And the foreigners who join themselves to ADONAI to serve him, to love the name of ADONAI, and to be his workers, all who keep Shabbat and do not profane it, and hold fast to my covenant, I will bring them to my holy mountain and make them joyful in my house of prayer; their burnt offerings and sacrifices will be accepted on my altar; for my house will be called a house of prayer for all peoples."

Isaiah 61:8-9
For I, ADONAI, love justice; I hate robbery for burnt offerings. So I will be faithful to reward them and make an eternal covenant with them. Their descendants will be known among the nations, their offspring among the peoples; all who see them will acknowledge that they are the seed ADONAI has blessed.

Jeremiah 9:22(23)-23(24)
Here is what ADONAI says: "The wise man should not boast of his wisdom, the powerful should not boast of his power, the wealthy should not boast of his wealth; instead, let the boaster boast about this: that he understands and knows me—that I am ADONAI, practicing grace, justice and righteousness in the land; for in these things I take pleasure," says ADONAI.

Hosea 12:6(5)-7(6)
Adonai ELOHEI-Tzva'ot; ADONAI is his name! So you, return to your God; hold fast to grace and justice; and always put your hope in your God.

Amos 5:15
Hate evil, love good; Establish justice in the gate. It may be that the LORD God of hosts Will be gracious to the remnant of Joseph.

Amos 5:23-24
*Spare me the noise of your songs! I don't want to hear the strumming of your lutes!
Instead, let justice well up like water, and righteousness like an ever-flowing stream.*

Micah 6:8
*Human being, you have already been told what is good, what ADONAI demands of you—
no more than to act justly, love grace and walk in purity with your God.*

Zechariah 7:9-11
In the past ADONAI-Tzva'ot said, 'Administer true justice. Let everyone show mercy and compassion to his brother. Don't oppress widows, orphans, foreigners or poor people. Don't plot evil against each other.' But they wouldn't listen, they stubbornly turned their shoulder away and stopped up their ears, so that they wouldn't have to hear it.

Psalms 37:27-29
If you turn from evil and do good, you will live safely forever. For ADONAI loves justice and will not abandon his faithful; they are preserved forever. But the descendants of the wicked will be cut off. The righteous will inherit the land and live in it forever.

Psalms 101:1-2
I am singing of grace and justice; I am singing to you, ADONAI. I will follow the path of integrity; when will you come to me? I will run my life with a sincere heart inside my own house.

Psalms 106:3
How happy are those who act justly, who always do what is right!

Proverbs 21:2-3
All a person's ways are right in his own view, but ADONAI weighs the heart. To do what is right and just is more pleasing to ADONAI than sacrifice.

Proverbs 21:15
Acting justly is a joy for the righteous but it terrifies evildoers.

Proverbs 28:5
Evil people don't understand justice, but those who seek ADONAI understand everything.

Job 8:3
Does God distort judgment? Does Shaddai pervert justice?

Matthew 5:38-42
You have heard that our fathers were told, 'Eye for eye and tooth for tooth.' But I tell you not to stand up against someone who does you wrong. On the contrary, if someone hits you on the right cheek, let him hit you on the left cheek too! If someone wants to sue you for your shirt, let him have your coat as well! And if a soldier forces you to carry his pack for one mile, carry it for two! When someone asks you for something, give it to him; when someone wants to borrow something from you, lend it to him.

Romans 12:19
Never seek revenge, my friends; instead, leave that to God's anger; for in the Tanakh it is written, "ADONAI says, 'Vengeance is my responsibility; I will repay.'

Hebrews 10:30
For the One we know is the One who said, "Vengeance is my responsibility; I will repay," and then said, "ADONAI will judge his people."

Statutes Pertaining to Justice that Are of Varying Contemporary Applicability

Exodus 21:1—22:26
"These are the rulings you are to present to them: If you purchase a Hebrew slave, he is to work six years; but in the seventh, he is to be given his freedom without having to pay anything. If he came single, he is to leave single; if he was married when he came, his wife is to go with him

when he leaves. But if his master gave him a wife, and she bore him sons or daughters, then the wife and her children will belong to her master, and he will leave by himself. Nevertheless, if the slave declares, 'I love my master, my wife and my children, so I don't want to go free,' then his master is to bring him before God; and there at the door or doorpost, his master is to pierce his ear with an awl; and the man will be his slave for life. If a man sells his daughter as a slave, she is not to go free like the men-slaves. If her master married her but decides she no longer pleases him, then he is to allow her to be redeemed. He is not allowed to sell her to a foreign people, because he has treated her unfairly. If he has her marry his son, then he is to treat her like a daughter. If he marries another wife, he is not to reduce her food, clothing or marital rights. If he fails to provide her with these three things, she is to be given her freedom without having to pay anything. Whoever attacks a person and causes his death must be put to death.

If it was not premeditated but an act of God, then I will designate for you a place to which he can flee. But if someone willfully kills another after deliberate planning, you are to take him even from my altar and put him to death. Whoever attacks his father or mother must be put to death.

Whoever kidnaps someone must be put to death, regardless of whether he has already sold him or the person is found still in his possession. Whoever curses his father or mother must be put to death. If two people fight, and one hits the other with a stone or with his fist, and the injured party doesn't die but is confined to his bed; then, if he recovers enough to be able to walk around outside, even if with a cane, the attacker will be free of liability, except to compensate him for his loss of time and take responsibility for his care until his recovery is complete. If a person beats his male or female slave with a stick so severely that he dies, he is to be punished; except that if the slave lives for a day or two, he is not to be punished, since the slave is his property.

If people are fighting with each other and happen to hurt a pregnant woman so badly that her unborn child dies, then, even if no other harm follows, he must be fined. He must pay the amount set by the woman's husband and confirmed by judges. But if any harm follows, then you are to give life for life, eye for eye, tooth for tooth, hand for hand, foot for foot, burn for burn, wound for wound and bruise for bruise. If a person hits his male or female slave's eye and destroys it, he must let him go free in compensation for his eye. If he knocks out his male or female slave's tooth, he must let him go free in compensation for his tooth. If an ox gores a man or a woman to death, the ox is to be stoned and its flesh not eaten, but the owner of the ox will have no further liability. However, if the ox was in the habit of goring in the past, and the owner was warned but did not confine it, so that it ended up killing a man or a woman; then the ox is to be stoned, and its owner too is to be put to death. However, a ransom may be imposed on him; and the death penalty will be commuted if he pays the amount imposed. If the ox gores a son or daughter, the same rule applies. If the ox gores a male or female slave, its owner must give their master twelve ounces of silver; and the ox is to be stoned to death. If someone removes the cover from a cistern or digs one and fails to cover it, and an ox or donkey falls in, the owner of the cistern must make good the loss by compensating the animal's owner; but the dead animal will be his.

If one person's ox hurts another's, so that it dies, they are to sell the live ox and divide the revenue from the sale; and they are also to divide the dead animal. But if it is known that the ox was in the habit of goring in the past, and the owner did not confine it; he must pay ox for ox, but the dead animal will be his. If someone steals an ox or a sheep and slaughters or sells it, he is to pay five oxen for an ox and four sheep for a sheep. pens after sunrise, in which case it is murder. A thief must make restitution; so if he has nothing, he himself is to be sold to make good the loss from the theft. If what he stole is found alive in his possession, he is to pay double, no matter whether it is an ox, a donkey or a sheep. If a person causes a field or vineyard to be grazed over or lets his animal loose to graze in someone else's field, he is to make restitution from the best produce of his own field and vineyard.If a fire is started and spreads to thorns, so that stacked grain, standing grain or a field is destroyed, the person who lit it must make restitution. If a person entrusts a neighbor with money or goods, and they are stolen from the trustee's house, then, if the thief is found, he must pay double. But if the thief is not found, then the trustee must state before God that he did not take the person's goods himself. In every case of dispute over ownership, whether of an ox, a donkey, a sheep, clothing, or any missing property, where one person says, 'This is mine,' both parties are to come before God; and the one whom God condemns must pay the other one double. If a person trusts a neighbor to look after a donkey, ox, sheep or any animal, and it dies, is injured or is driven away unseen, then the neighbor's oath before ADONAI that he has not taken the goods will settle the matter between them—the owner is to accept it without the neighbor's making restitution. But if it was stolen from the neighbor, he must make restitution to the owner. If it was torn to pieces by an animal, the neighbor must bring it as evidence, and then he doesn't need to make good the loss. If someone borrows something from his neighbor, and it gets injured or dies with the owner not present, he must make restitution. If the owner was present, he need not make good the loss. If the owner hired it out, the loss is covered by the hiring fee. If a man seduces a virgin who is not engaged to be married and sleeps with her, he must pay the bride-price for her to be his wife. But if her father refuses to give her to him, he must pay a sum equivalent to the bride-price for virgins. You are not to permit a sorceress to live. Whoever has sexual relations with an animal must be put to death. Anyone who sacrifices to any god other than ADONAI alone is to be completely destroyed. "You must neither wrong nor oppress a foreigner living among you, for you yourselves were foreigners in the land of Egypt. You are not to abuse any widow or orphan.

If you do abuse them in any way, and they cry to me, I will certainly heed their cry.[23] My anger will burn, and I will kill you with the sword—your own wives will be widows and your own children fatherless. If you loan money to one of my people who is poor, you are not to deal with him as would a creditor; and you are not to charge him interest. If you take your neighbor's coat as collateral, you are to restore it to him by sundown, because it is his only garment—he needs it to wrap his body; what else does he have in which to sleep? Moreover, if he cries out to me, I will listen; because I am compassionate.

Commentary

The following is Merriam-Webster's definition of "Justice:"

> *1a. The Maintenance of administration of what is just especially by the impartial adjustment of conflicting claims or the assignment of merited rewards or punishments.*

> *1b. The administration of law; especially the establishment or determination of rights according to the rules of law or equity.*

2a. The quality of being just, impartial, or fair.

(1) The principle or ideal of just dealing or right action
(2) Conformity to righteousness and law.

3. Conformity to truth, fact, or reason—correctness

It is a helpful definition but not dispositive because it self-defines by using the word "just." "Justice" is hard to define. I think of it as fairness that is somehow connected to authority. It has the connotation of a person receiving that which is due him or that which he deserves.

In reviewing the Scriptures with the purpose of listing those having to do with justice, it becomes apparent that one would have to list just about the entire Bible. The Scriptures listed in support of this *Mitzvah* are therefore only a representative sample of those that can be listed, and the Bible's emphasis on justice is evidence of how important justice is to God.

Justice (or the lack of it) exists in all of society, and can broadly be put into one of two categories. First, there is justice that is connected to a court of law or other governmental authority, where what is considered "just" is defined by a rule or statute. The other category is justice that is informal, and has to do with how individuals or groups of individuals treat each other in their daily encounters.

There is also a term known as "social justice," that can involve either or both of the aforementioned categories. Exactly what "social justice" comprises is controversial, but it refers to the equality (or lack thereof) of individuals within society, regarding their opportunities, privileges, and the distribution of wealth. It is too great a subject to be dealt with in this *Mitzvah*.

As with all of the Mosaic era commandments, many of those having to do with justice are no longer directly applicable in today's world in which we live. Examples are the commandment establishing sanctuary cities and commandments prescribing punishments for infractions of law—capital punishment in particular. Whereas, capital punishment was the ultimate penalty under the Mosaic Law and still is today under many systems of secular law, it no longer exists under the New Covenant, for which the ultimate penalty is expulsion from the body of believers (see Matthew 18:17). We understand that today's legal matters pertaining to persons and things outside of the body of believers are under the exclusive jurisdiction of the secular governments to which we are subject, but we consider the Mosaic Law still relevant in guiding us as to the principles of punishment, restitution, restoration, and God's will in general.

In order for a court to have the capacity to adjudicate a case, it must have three kinds of jurisdiction—personal, territorial, and subject-matter. This applies to ecclesiastical courts as well as to secular courts, except that the territorial jurisdictions of ecclesiastical courts are considered to be the entire world. Secular courts get their subject-matter jurisdiction from civil laws (e.g. statutes, ordinances, case law, etc.), whereas ecclesiastical courts usually get their subject-matter jurisdiction from the Bible.[132] Personal jurisdiction is acquired in various ways in each of the court systems. In the secular courts it is sometimes connected to the defendant's domicile, sometimes to where damages sued for have occurred, and sometimes it is defined by

---

132 Sometimes also from extra-biblical writings such as the Talmud.

471

statute. Personal jurisdiction in an ecclesiastical court is a debated matter. It should be over all believers—Jews (Messianic and non-Messianic) if it is a rabbinical court *(beit din)* and over all Messianic Jews and Gentile believers in Yeshua if it is a court convened by a Christian church or Messianic synagogue. Sometimes, personal jurisdiction is acquired by the defendant being a member of a congregation, denomination, network of congregations, or organization; plaintiffs are automatically subject to the jurisdiction of the court to which they apply for relief.

Classical Commentators

Maimonides' *mitzvah* RP175 and Chinuch's C78 are worthy of special mention because of how Maimonides and HaChinuch translate <u>Exodus 23:2</u>. Both of their *mitzvot* follow TB <u>Hullin 112</u>[133] in declaring that the majority should rule in a legal case when there is a dispute among judges. Not contrary but different, the Complete Jewish Bible (in basic agreement with Christian translations) states:

> *"Do not follow the crowd when it does what is wrong; and don't allow the popular view to sway you into offering testimony for any cause if the effect will be to pervert justice."*

That notwithstanding, the following English translation of the *Tanakh*[134] supports Maimonides and HaChinuch by translating <u>Exodus 23:2</u>:

> *"Thou shalt not follow a multitude to do evil; neither shalt thou speak in a cause to decline after many to wrest judgment."*

Clearly, this second translation is quite opposite in that its phrase "to decline after many to wrest judgment" supports Maimonides' and HaChinuch's *mitzvot* RP175 and C78 respectively, whereas the CJB translation does not.

It is important to note that even when a *mitzvah* of Mosaic vintage appears to have application today, the application may have to be adjusted. An example would be the *mitzvah* to not convict a person on the testimony of only one witness. The caution is still observed, but today's forensic technologies (e.g. ballistic and DNA testing, photographs, voice recordings, etc.) allow very great certainty in connecting suspects to crimes without their being even a single eyewitness.

A word is needed regarding Maimonides' departure from Meir and HaChinuch concerning the meaning of <u>Deuteronomy 17:11</u>. Meir and HaChinuch interpret *"the place which ADONAI your God will choose"* as the *Sanhedrin.* Maimonides, on the other hand, in his RN312, interprets the Scripture to mean that we are not to disagree with the authorized conveyors of tradition.

<u>**NCLA: JMm JFm KMm KFm GMm GFm**</u>

---

133 This reference is to tractate *Hullin* of the Babylonian Talmud.
134 "The Holy Scriptures: Hebrew and English," The Society for Distributing Hebrew Scriptures (no publishing date).

J3. Injury and Damages.

We are not to injure or cause damages but, should we do so, we must make restitution and pay penalties prescribed by law.

This precept is derived from His Word (blessed be He):

Key Scriptures

Injury to Combatants and Bystanders

Exodus 21:18-19 (Maimonides RP236; Chinuch C49)
If two people fight, and one hits the other with a stone or with his fist, and the injured party doesn't die but is confined to his bed; then, if he recovers enough to be able to walk around outside, even if with a cane, the attacker will be free of liability, except to compensate him for his loss of time and take responsibility for his care until his recovery is complete.

Exodus 21:20-21
If a person beats his male or female slave with a stick so severely that he dies, he is to be punished; except that if the slave lives for a day or two, he is not to be punished, since the slave is his property.

Exodus 21:22-25
If people are fighting with each other and happen to hurt a pregnant woman so badly that her unborn child dies, then, even if no other harm follows, he must be fined. He must pay the amount set by the woman's husband and confirmed by judges. But if any harm follows, then you are to give life for life, eye for eye, tooth for tooth, hand for hand, foot for foot, burn for burn, wound for wound and bruise for bruise.

Exodus 21:26-27
If a person hits his male or female slave's eye and destroys it, he must let him go free in compensation for his eye. If he knocks out his male or female slave's tooth, he must let him go free in compensation for his tooth.

Leviticus 24:19-20 (Maimonides RP236; Chinuch C49)
If someone injures his neighbor, what he did is to be done to him—break for break, eye for eye, tooth for tooth—whatever injury he has caused the other person is to be rendered to him in return.

Injury Caused by an Ox

Exodus 21:28-32 (Maimonides RP237; Chinuch C51)
If an ox gores a man or a woman to death, the ox is to be stoned and its flesh not eaten, but the owner of the ox will have no further liability. However, if the ox was in the habit of goring in

the past, and the owner was warned but did not confine it, so that it ended up killing a man or a woman; then the ox is to be stoned, and its owner too is to be put to death. However, a ransom may be imposed on him; and the death penalty will be commuted if he pays the amount imposed. If the ox gores a son or daughter, the same rule applies. If the ox gores a male or female slave, its owner must give their master twelve ounces of silver; and the ox is to be stoned to death.

Exodus 21:35-36 (Maimonides RP237; Chinuch C51)
If one person's ox hurts another's, so that it dies, they are to sell the live ox and divide the revenue from the sale; and they are also to divide the dead animal. But if it is known that the ox was in the habit of goring in the past, and the owner did not confine it; he must pay ox for ox, but the dead animal will be his.

Injury Caused by an Open Pit

Exodus 21:33-34 (Maimonides RP238; Chinuch C53)
If someone removes the cover from a cistern or digs one and fails to cover it, and an ox or donkey falls in, the owner of the cistern must make good the loss by compensating the animal's owner; but the dead animal will be his.

Damges Caused by a Grazing Animal

Exodus 22:4(5) (Maimonides RP240; Chinuch C55)
If a person causes a field or vineyard to be grazed over or lets his animal loose to graze in someone else's field, he is to make restitution from the best produce of his own field and vineyard.

Damages Caused by Theft or Robbery

Exodus 22:1(2)-3(4)
If a thief caught in the act of breaking in is beaten to death, it is not murder; unless it happens after sunrise, in which case it is murder. A thief must make restitution; so if he has nothing, he himself is to be sold to make good the loss from the theft. If what he stole is found alive in his possession, he is to pay double, no matter whether it is an ox, a donkey or a sheep.

Leviticus 5:21(6:2)-24 (6:5) (Maimonides RN245; Chinuch C229)
If someone sins and acts perversely against ADONAI by dealing falsely with his neighbor in regard to a deposit or security entrusted to him, by stealing from him, by extorting him, or by dealing falsely in regard to a lost object he has found, or by swearing to a lie—if a person commits any of these sins, then, if he sinned and is guilty, he is to restore whatever it was he stole or obtained by extortion, or whatever was deposited with him, or the lost object which he found, or anything about which he has sworn falsely. He is to restore it in full plus an additional one-fifth; he must return it to the person who owns it, on the day when he presents his guilt offering.

Leviticus 19:11 (Maimonides RN244; Meir MN34; Chinuch C224)
Do not steal from, defraud or lie to each other.

Leviticus 19:13 (Maimonides RN245; Meir MN35; Chinuch C229)
Do not oppress or rob your neighbor; specifically, you are not to keep back the wages of a hired worker all night until morning.

Damages Caused by Delaying the Payment of Wages

Leviticus 19:13 (Maimonides RN238; Meir MN38; Chinuch C230)
Do not oppress or rob your neighbor; specifically, you are not to keep back the wages of a hired worker all night until morning.

Deuteronomy 24:14-15 (Maimonides RN238; Meir MN38; Chinuch C230)
You are not to exploit a hired worker who is poor and needy, whether one of your brothers or a foreigner living in your land in your town. You are to pay him his wages the day he earns them, before sunset; for he is poor and looks forward to being paid. Otherwise he will cry out against you to ADONAI, and it will be your sin.

Damages Caused by Refusing to Pay Our Debts

Leviticus 19:13 (Maimonides RN247; Meir MN37; Chinuch C228)
Do not oppress or rob your neighbor; specifically, you are not to keep back the wages of a hired worker all night until morning.

Damages Caused by Repudiating Our Debts

Leviticus 5:21(6:2)-24 (6:5) (Maimonides RN248; Chinuch C225)
If someone sins and acts perversely against ADONAI by dealing falsely with his neighbor in regard to a deposit or security entrusted to him, by stealing from him, by extorting him, or by dealing falsely in regard to a lost object he has found, or by swearing to a lie—if a person commits any of these sins, then, if he sinned and is guilty, he is to restore whatever it was he stole or obtained by extortion, or whatever was deposited with him, or the lost object which he found, or anything about which he has sworn falsely. He is to restore it in full plus an additional one-fifth; he must return it to the person who owns it, on the day when he presents his guilt offering.

Leviticus 19:11 (Maimonides RN248; Meir MN36; Chinuch C225)
Do not steal from, defraud or lie to each other.

Damages Caused by Swearing Falsely in Repudiating Our Debts

Leviticus 5:21(6:2)-24 (6:5) (Maimonides RN249; Chinuch C226)
If someone sins and acts perversely against ADONAI by dealing falsely with his neighbor in regard to a deposit or security entrusted to him, by stealing from him, by extorting him, or by dealing falsely in regard to a lost object he has found, or by swearing to a lie—if a person commits any of these sins, then, if he sinned and is guilty, he is to restore whatever it was he stole or obtained by extortion, or whatever was deposited with him, or the lost object which he found,

or anything about which he has sworn falsely. He is to restore it in full plus an additional one-fifth; he must return it to the person who owns it, on the day when he presents his guilt offering.

Leviticus 19:11-12 (Maimonides RN249; Meir MN30; Chinuch C226)
Do not steal from, defraud or lie to each other. Do not swear by my name falsely, which would be profaning the name of your God; I am ADONAI.

Damages Caused by Wronging One Another with Words

Leviticus 25:17[135] (Maimonides RN251; Meir MN48; Chinuch C338)
Thus you are not to take advantage of each other, but you are to fear your God; for I am ADONAI your God.

Proverbs 11:9
With his mouth the hypocrite can ruin his neighbor, but by knowledge the righteous are delivered.

Proverbs 16:28
A deceitful person stirs up strife, and a slanderer can separate even close friends.

Proverbs 17:9
He who conceals an offense promotes love, but he who harps on it can separate even close friends.

Proverbs 18:21
The tongue has power over life and death; those who indulge it must eat its fruit.

Proverbs 26:28
A lying tongue hates its victims, and a flattering mouth causes ruin.

Ephesians 4:29
Let no harmful language come from your mouth, only good words that are helpful in meeting the need, words that will benefit those who hear them.

Damages Caused by Fire

Exodus 22:5(6) (Maimonides RP241; Chinuch C56)
If a fire is started and spreads to thorns, so that stacked grain, standing grain or a field is destroyed, the person who lit it must make restitution.

Damages involving Bailments

Exodus 22:6(7)-14(15) (Maimonides RP242; Chinuch C57)
If a person entrusts a neighbor with money or goods, and they are stolen from the trustee's house, then, if the thief is found, he must pay double. But if the thief is not found, then the trustee must state before God that he did not take the person's goods himself. In every case of dispute over ownership, whether of an ox, a donkey, a sheep, clothing, or any missing property, where

---

135 Referenced by classical commentators but off the subject of the *mitzvah.*

one person says, 'This is mine,' both parties are to come before God; and the one whom God condemns must pay the other one double. If a person trusts a neighbor to look after a donkey, ox, sheep or any animal, and it dies, is injured or is driven away unseen, then the neighbor's oath before ADONAI that he has not taken the goods will settle the matter between them—the owner is to accept it without the neighbor's making restitution. But if it was stolen from the neighbor, he must make restitution to the owner. If it was torn to pieces by an animal, the neighbor must bring it as evidence, and then he doesn't need to make good the loss. If someone borrows something from his neighbor, and it gets injured or dies with the owner not present, he must make restitution. If the owner was present, he need not make good the loss. If the owner hired it out, the loss is covered by the hiring fee.

Exodus 22:9(10)-12(13) (Maimonides RP243; Chinuch C59)
If a person trusts a neighbor to look after a donkey, ox, sheep or any animal, and it dies, is injured or is driven away unseen, then the neighbor's oath before ADONAI that he has not taken the goods will settle the matter between them—the owner is to accept it without the neighbor's making restitution. But if it was stolen from the neighbor, he must make restitution to the owner. If it was torn to pieces by an animal, the neighbor must bring it as evidence, and then he doesn't need to make good the loss.

Damages involving Disputed Ownership

Exodus 22:8(9) (Maimonides RP246; Chinuch C58)
In every case of dispute over ownership, whether of an ox, a donkey, a sheep, clothing, or any missing property, where one person says, 'This is mine,' both parties are to come before God; and the one whom God condemns must pay the other one double.

Damages involving a Borrower

Exodus 22:13(14)-14(15) (Maimonides RP244; Chinuch C60)
If someone borrows something from his neighbor, and it gets injured or dies with the owner not present, he must make restitution. If the owner was present, he need not make good the loss. If the owner hired it out, the loss is covered by the hiring fee.

Commentary

"Damages" is that aspect of law that has to do with loss. If damage is to a person, we call it "injury." Damages that are actionable (recoverable from another) originate in either "tort" or "contract." A tort is a wrongful act (intentional or unintentional) that infringes the rights of another and leads to damages. An example of an intentional tort is assault, and of an unintentional tort is negligence that causes damages. A contract is an agreement between parties, and damages can result from a party either intentionally or unintentionally failing to fulfill his or her part of the agreement. An intentional bailment is usually a contract to place one's property in the custody and care of another. A bailment can, however, come about unintentionally, such as when one finds and takes temporary possession lost property.

Depending on the circumstance of what causes damage or injury, appropriate remedies can be restitution, paying compensatory money damages, paying punitive damages (in the case of an intentional or reckless tort or gross negligence), specific performance of a contract (a court order to perform a contract as agreed), etc. What we are speaking of here are infractions of civil law as distinguished from criminal law, but they sometimes overlap. An example of overlap is theft. Theft is a civil offense to the victim who incurs financial damage, and it is simultaneously a criminal offense to society at large because of damage to the peace of the community. Bringing a thief to justice can, therefore, involve making restitution to the person from whom he stole, paying a fine to society, and also possibly a jail sentence.

The Scriptures listed above each speak to circumstances and conduct that can and often do cause damages. The torts, contracts, and remedies illustrated by the Scriptures are mere examples of others that exist, but they serve to make the point. Some of them are geared more to the time of Moses than to today, but similarities to modern situations can easily be seen, which is why our contemporary laws have largely been derived from these ancient examples. In today's urban society I do not have an ox to be gored by my neighbor's ox, but I do have a car that could conceivably be gored by his car; it is the same principle.

In order for a civil court to have the capacity to adjudicate a claim for damages, it must have three kinds of jurisdiction—personal, territorial, and subject matter. An ecclesiastical court (a Jewish court is called a *bet din*) must have these as well, except that its territorial jurisdiction is considered the entire world. Civil courts get their subject matter jurisdiction from civil law (e.g. statutes, ordinances, case law, etc.) and ecclesiastical courts get their subject matter jurisdiction from the Bible. Personal jurisdiction is acquired in various ways. In the civil courts it is sometimes acquired by the defendant's domicile, sometimes to where the damages sued for occurred, and sometimes it is defined by statute. Personal jurisdiction in an ecclesiastical court is a debated matter. It should be over all believers in Yeshua if it is a church court, and over Jews (Messianic or not Messianic) if it is a *bet din*. Sometimes, personal jurisdiction is acquired by the defendant being a member of a congregation, denomination, network of congregations, or organization. Plaintiffs are automatically subject to the jurisdiction of whatever court they apply to for relief.

Classical Commentators

Maimonides, Meir, and HaChinuch limit their respective *mitzvot* to the specific torts and contracts referred to in the *Torah*; they do not discuss modern applications or adaptations.

<u>**NCLA:**</u> **JMm JFm KMm KFm GMm GFm**

J4. Law of Inheritance.

We are to receive inheritance according to established law and to that which is approved by God.

This precept is derived from His Word (blessed be He):

Key Scriptures

Financial Inheritance

<u>Numbers 27:1-11</u> (Maimonides RP248; Meir MP73; Chinuch C400)
Then the daughters of Tz'lof'chad the son of Hefer, the son of Gil'ad, the son of Machir, the son of M'nasheh, of the families of M'nasheh, the son of Yosef, approached. These were the names of his daughters: Machlah, No'ah, Hoglah, Milkah and Tirtzah. They stood in front of Moshe, El'azar the cohen, the leaders and the whole community at the entrance to the tent of meeting and said, "Our father died in the desert. He wasn't part of the group who assembled themselves to rebel against ADONAI in Korach's group, but he died in his own sin, and he had no sons. Why should the name of our father be eliminated from his family just because he didn't have a son? Give us property to possess along with the brothers of our father." Moshe brought their cause before ADONAI. ADONAI answered Moshe, "The daughters of Tz'lof'chad are right in what they say. You must give them property to be inherited along with that of their father's brothers; have what their father would have inherited pass to them. Moreover, say to the people of Isra'el, 'If a man dies and does not have a son, you are to have his inheritance pass to his daughter. If he doesn't have a daughter, give his inheritance to his brothers. If he has no brothers, give his inheritance to his father's brothers. If his father doesn't have brothers, give his inheritance to the closest relative in his family, and he will possess it. This will be the standard for judgment to be used by the people of Isra'el, as ADONAI ordered Moshe.'"

<u>Numbers 36:6-9</u>
Here is what ADONAI has ordered concerning the daughters of Tz'lof'chad: 'Let them be married to whomever they think best, but they must marry only into a family from their father's tribe. In this way no inheritance of the people of Isra'el will move from one tribe to another; for each of the people of Isra'el is to hold on to the land for inheritance belonging to his father's tribe. Every daughter who possesses an inheritance in any tribe of the people of Isra'el is to become the wife of someone from the family of her father's tribe, so that every one of the people of Isra'el will stay in possession of his ancestors' inheritance. Thus no inheritance will move from one tribe to another, for each of the tribes of the people of Isra'el will hold on to its own inheritance."

<u>Deuteronomy 21:15-17</u> (Maimonides RP248; Chinuch C400)
If a man has two wives, the one loved and the other unloved, and both the loved and unloved wives have borne him children, and if the firstborn son is the child of the unloved wife; then, when it comes time for him to pass his inheritance on to his sons, he may not give the inheritance due the firstborn to the son of the loved wife in place of the son of the unloved one, who is in fact

the firstborn. No, he must acknowledge as firstborn the son of the unloved wife by giving him a double portion of everything he owns, for he is the firstfruits of his manhood, and the right of the firstborn is his.

<u>Joshua 1:6</u>
Be strong, be bold; for you will cause this people to inherit the land I swore to their fathers I would give them.

<u>Ezekiel 46:16-18</u>
Adonai ELOHIM says this: 'If the prince turns over part of his hereditary property to one of his sons, it is his inheritance; it will belong to his sons; it is their possession by inheritance. But if he gives part of his hereditary property to one of his slaves, it will be his until the year of freedom, at which time it will revert to the prince, so that the prince's heritage will go to his sons. The prince is not to take over any of the people's inheritance, thereby evicting them wrongfully from their property; he is to give his sons an inheritance out of his own property, so that none of my people will be driven off their property.'

<u>Luke 15:11-13</u>
Again Yeshua said, "A man had two sons. The younger of them said to his father, 'Father, give me the share of the estate that will be mine.' So the father divided the property between them. As soon as he could convert his share into cash, the younger son left home and went off to a distant country, where he squandered his money in reckless living.

Royal Inheritance

<u>1 Kings 9:2-9</u>
ADONAI appeared to Shlomo a second time, as he had appeared to him in Giv'on. ADONAI said to him, "I have heard your prayer and your plea that you made before me: I am consecrating this house which you built and placing my name there forever; my eyes and heart will always be there. As for you, if you will live in my presence, as did David your father, in pureness of heart and uprightness, doing everything I have ordered you to do, and observing my laws and rulings; then I will establish the throne of your rulership over Isra'el forever, just as I promised David your father when I said, 'You will never lack a man on the throne of Isra'el.' But if you turn away from following me, you or your children, and do not observe my mitzvot and regulations which I have set before you, and go and serve other gods, worshipping them; then I will cut off Isra'el from the land I have given them. This house, which I consecrated for my name, I will eject from my sight; and Isra'el will become an example to avoid and an object of scorn among all peoples. This house, now so exalted—everyone passing by will gasp in shock at the sight of it and will ask, 'Why has ADONAI done this to this land and to this house?' But the answer will be, 'It's because they abandoned ADONAI their God, who brought their ancestors out of the land of Egypt, and took hold of other gods, worshipping and serving them; this is why ADONAI brought all these calamities on them.'

480

Moral Inheritance

Proverbs 13:22
A good man leaves an inheritance to his grandchildren, but the wealth of a sinner is stored up for the righteous.

Proverbs 22:6
Train a child in the way he [should] go; and, even when old, he will not swerve from it.

Abraham and His Seed Inherited through God's Will and Promise

Romans 4:13-15
For the promise to Avraham and his seed that he would inherit the world did not come through legalism but through the righteousness that trust produces. For if the heirs are produced by legalism, then trust is pointless and the promise worthless. For what law brings is punishment. But where there is no law, there is also no violation.

Galatians 3:18
For if the inheritance comes from the legal part of the Torah, it no longer comes from a promise. But God gave it to Avraham through a promise.

We Are Heirs of Our Father Abraham

Romans 4:16-17
The reason the promise is based on trusting is so that it may come as God's free gift, a promise that can be relied on by all the seed, not only those who live within the framework of the Torah, but also those with the kind of trust Avraham had—Avraham avinu for all of us. This accords with the Tanakh, where it says, "I have appointed you to be a father to many nations." Avraham is our father in God's sight because he trusted God as the one who gives life to the dead and calls nonexistent things into existence.

Galatians 3:29
Also, if you belong to the Messiah, you are seed of Avraham and heirs according to the promise.

Yeshua Inherited Ownership of All from God his Father

Hebrews 1:2
But now, in the acharit-hayamim, he has spoken to us through his Son, to whom he has given ownership of everything and through whom he created the universe.

We Have Inherited Holiness and the New Covenant from Yeshua

Acts 20:32
And now I [Yeshua] entrust you to the care of the Lord and to the message of his love and kindness, for it can build you up and give you an inheritance among all those who have been set apart for God.

Hebrews 9:15
It is because of this death that he is mediator of a new covenant [or will]. Because a death has occurred which sets people free from the transgressions committed under the first covenant, those who have been called may receive the promised eternal inheritance.

We Are Children of God and Joint Heirs with Yeshua of Deliverance, Glorification, and Eternal Life

Romans 8:16-17
The Spirit himself bears witness with our own spirits that we are children of God; and if we are children, then we are also heirs, heirs of God and joint-heirs with the Messiah—provided we are suffering with him in order also to be glorified with him.

Ephesians 1:11-14
Also in union with him we were given an inheritance, we who were picked in advance according to the purpose of the One who effects everything in keeping with the decision of his will, so that we who earlier had put our hope in the Messiah would bring him praise commensurate with his glory. Furthermore, you who heard the message of the truth, the Good News offering you deliverance, and put your trust in the Messiah were sealed by him with the promised Ruach HaKodesh, who guarantees our inheritance until we come into possession of it and thus bring him praise commensurate with his glory.

Titus 3:4-7
But when the kindness and love for mankind of God our Deliverer was revealed, he delivered us. It was not on the ground of any righteous deeds we had done, but on the ground of his own mercy. He did it by means of the mikveh of rebirth and the renewal brought about by the Ruach HaKodesh, whom he poured out on us generously through Yeshua the Messiah, our Deliverer. He did it so that by his grace we might come to be considered righteous by God and become heirs, with the certain hope of eternal life.

1 Peter 1:3-4
Praised be God, Father of our Lord Yeshua the Messiah, who, in keeping with his great mercy, has caused us, through the resurrection of Yeshua the Messiah from the dead, to be born again to a living hope, to an inheritance that cannot decay, spoil or fade, kept safe for you in heaven.

The Gentiles are Joint Heirs with the Jews of God's Promises

Ephesians 3:5-6
In past generations it was not made known to mankind, as the Spirit is now revealing it to his emissaries and prophets, that in union with the Messiah and through the Good News the Gentiles were to be joint heirs, a joint body and joint sharers with the Jews in what God has promised.

We All Share in the Inheritance of God's People Who Are in the Light

Colossians 1:11-12
We pray that you will be continually strengthened with all the power that comes from his glorious might; so that you will be able to persevere and be patient in any situation, joyfully giving thanks to the Father for having made you fit to share in the inheritance of his people in the light.

Those Who Follow the Lord and Are Righteous Will Inherit; Sinners Will Not

Joshua 14:9
On that day Moshe swore, 'Surely the land where your foot has been will be the inheritance for you and your descendants forever, because you have followed ADONAI my God completely.'

Psalms 37:29
The righteous will inherit the land and live in it forever.

1 Corinthians 6:9-10
Don't you know that unrighteous people will have no share in the Kingdom of God? Don't delude yourselves—people who engage in sex before marriage, who worship idols, who engage in sex after marriage with someone other than their spouse, who engage in active or passive homosexuality, who steal, who are greedy, who get drunk, who assail people with contemptuous language, who rob—none of them will share in the Kingdom of God.

Galatians 3:19-21
So then, why the legal part of the Torah? It was added in order to create transgressions, until the coming of the seed about whom the promise had been made. Moreover, it was handed down through angels and a mediator. Now a mediator implies more than one, but God is one. Does this mean that the legal part of the Torah stands in opposition to God's promises? Heaven forbid! For if the legal part of the Torah which God gave had had in itself the power to give life, then righteousness really would have come by legalistically following such a Torah.

Ephesians 5:5-7
For of this you can be sure: every sexually immoral, impure or greedy person—that is, every idol-worshipper—has no share in the Kingdom of the Messiah and of God. Let no one deceive you with empty talk; for it is because of these things that God's judgment is coming on those who disobey him. So don't become partners with them!

Colossians 3:23-24
Whatever work you do, put yourself into it, as those who are serving not merely other people, but the Lord. Remember that as your reward, you will receive the inheritance from the Lord. You are slaving for the Lord, for the Messiah.

The Meek Shall Inherit the Earth

Psalms 37:11
But the meek will inherit the land and delight themselves in abundant peace.

Matthew 5:5
How blessed are the meek! for they will inherit the Land!

Last Will and Testament

Hebrews 9:13-17
For if sprinkling ceremonially unclean persons with the blood of goats and bulls and the ashes of a heifer restores their outward purity; then how much more the blood of the Messiah, who, through the eternal Spirit, offered himself to God as a sacrifice without blemish, will purify our conscience from works that lead to death, so that we can serve the living God! It is because of this death that he is mediator of a new covenant [or will]. Because a death has occurred which sets people free from the transgressions committed under the first covenant, those who have been called may receive the promised eternal inheritance. For where there is a will, there must necessarily be produced evidence of its maker's death, since a will goes into effect only upon death; it never has force while its maker is still alive.

Commentary

There are three kinds of inheritance referred to in Scripture; they are (1) financial inheritance (money, personal property and land), (2) royal inheritance (e.g. kingship passing from father to son), and (3) moral inheritance (i.e. non-tangible assets such as character traits and ethical values. In addition, there are two mechanisms that govern inheritance—(1) last wills and testaments, and (2) statutes of intestacy (i.e. rules that govern inheritance in the absence of a last will and testament). All of these date back to the time of Moses and before but, because today we live under secular governments (not the theocracy of ancient Israel), today's laws of inheritance are what govern.

Financial inheritance under Moses and today are the same in that they were and are controlled by statute, albeit statutes that are different. The system of financial inheritance under and prior to Moses was what we call "primogeniture." It is where all the financial assets of a deceased person are inherited by the person's firstborn or eldest son (sometimes firstborn daughters inherited as well), who then become the family's patriarch and is expected to use his inheritance to care for his siblings and their families. Primogeniture still exists in places, but has been largely eliminated in the western world where it has been replaced by laws of intestacy and "last wills and testaments." Wills that are duly made and executed govern (within limits) and, in the absence of a will, a person's financial assets usually go to his spouse and children according to a statutorily defined plan.

Royal inheritance, where it exists in kingdoms today, is similar to how it was at times in the past, in that it normally goes to the firstborn child (sometimes the firstborn son) by law. In that way it is similar to primogeniture in that the firstborn has responsibility to provide for his siblings as kings have responsibility to provide for their subjects. King David was succeeded by his son Solomon in what is sometimes referred to as the Davidic Dynasty, and the kingship passed from father to son) until the Babylonian exile in 586 BCE.

Moral inheritance is different from the other two in that through it, moral, ethical, and religious values are conveyed through God's influence rather than through law, but the result of conveyance is just as real. Within the Jewish community (and some other communities) there exists what is sometimes referred to as a *zava'ah* or "ethical will," which is a document designed to pass wisdom and ethical and moral values from one generation to the next. The idea of the ethical will is inspired by Genesis 49:1-33, where Jacob prophesies over, and seeks to convey blessings to, his gathered sons.

Classical Commentators

Maimonides, Meir, and HaChinuch, wrote only one *mitzvah* each on inheritance. They were on financial inheritance, supported by Numbers 27:8-9 and Deuteronomy 21:17.

NCLA: JMm JFm KMm KFm GMm GFm

J5. Appointing Elders to Lead, Pray, Teach, Judge, and Make *Halachah*.

We are to appoint elders in our communities to lead, pray, judge, teach, and make halachah.

This precept is derived from His Word (blessed be He):

Key Scriptures

Appointing Elders

Exodus 18:21-22
But you should choose from among all the people competent men who are God-fearing, honest and incorruptible to be their leaders, in charge of thousands, hundreds, fifties and tens. Normally, they will settle the people's disputes. They should bring you the difficult cases; but ordinary matters they should decide themselves. In this way, they will make it easier for you and share the load with you.

Deuteronomy 1:11-13
May ADONAI, the God of your ancestors, increase you yet a thousandfold and bless you, as he has promised you! But you are burdensome, bothersome and quarrelsome! How can I bear it by myself alone? Pick for yourselves from each of your tribes men who are wise, understanding and knowledgeable; and I will make them heads over you.'

Deuteronomy 16:18
You are to appoint judges and officers for all your gates [in the cities] ADONAI your God is giving you, tribe by tribe; and they are to judge the people with righteous judgment.

Acts 14:23
After appointing elders for them in every congregation, Sha'ul and Bar-Nabba, with prayer and fasting, committed them to the Lord in whom they had put their trust.

1 Timothy 3:1-7
Here is a statement you can trust: anyone aspiring to be a congregation leader is seeking worthwhile work. A congregation leader must be above reproach, he must be faithful to his wife, temperate, self-controlled, orderly, hospitable and able to teach. He must not drink excessively or get into fights; rather, he must be kind and gentle. He must not be a lover of money. He must manage his own household well, having children who obey him with all proper respect; for if a man can't manage his own household, how will he be able to care for God's Messianic Community? He must not be a new believer, because he might become puffed up with pride and thus fall under the same judgment as did the Adversary. Furthermore, he must be well regarded by outsiders, so that he won't fall into disgrace and into the Adversary's trap.

<u>Titus 1:4-5</u>
To: Titus, a true son in the faith we share: Grace and shalom from God the Father and from the Messiah Yeshua, our Deliverer. The reason I left you in Crete was so that you might attend to the matters still not in order and appoint congregation leaders in each city—those were my instructions.

Elders Are to Lead

<u>Proverbs 31:23</u>
Her husband is known at the city gates when he sits with the leaders of the land.

<u>Acts 20:28-31</u>
Watch out for yourselves, and for all the flock in which the Ruach HaKodesh has placed you as leaders, to shepherd God's Messianic community, which he won for himself at the cost of his own Son's blood. I know that after I leave, savage wolves will come in among you; and they won't spare the flock. Even from among your own number, men will arise and teach perversions of the truth, in order to drag away the talmidim after themselves. So stay alert! Remember that for three years, night and day, with tears in my eyes, I never stopped warning you!

<u>Titus 1:7-14</u>
For an overseer, as someone entrusted with God's affairs, must be blameless—he must not be self-willed or quick-tempered, he must not drink excessively, get into fights or be greedy for dishonest gain. On the contrary, he must be hospitable, devoted to good, sober-mindedness, uprightness, holiness and self-control. He must hold firmly to the trustworthy Message that agrees with the doctrine; so that by his sound teaching he will be able to exhort and encourage, and also to refute those who speak against it. For there are many, especially from the Circumcision faction, who are rebellious, who delude people's minds with their worthless and misleading talk. They must be silenced; because they are upsetting entire households by teaching what they have no business teaching, and doing it for the sake of dishonest gain. Even one of the Cretans' own prophets has said, "Cretans are always liars, evil brutes, lazy gluttons"- and it's true! For this reason, you must be severe when you rebuke those who have followed this false teaching, so that they will come to be sound in their trust and no longer pay attention to Judaistic myths or to the commands of people who reject the truth.

<u>Hebrews 13:17</u>
Obey your leaders and submit to them, for they keep watch over your lives, as people who will have to render an account. So make it a task of joy for them, not one of groaning; for that is of no advantage to you.

<u>1 Peter 5:1-3</u>
Therefore, I urge the congregation leaders among you, as a fellow-leader and witness to the Messiah's sufferings, as well as a sharer in the glory to be revealed: shepherd the flock of God that is in your care, exercising oversight not out of constraint, but willingly, as God wants; and not out of a desire for dishonest gain, but with enthusiasm; also not as machers domineering over those in your care, but as people who become examples to the flock.

Elders Are to Pray

<u>James 5:14</u>
Therefore, I urge the congregation leaders among you, as a fellow-leader and witness to the Messiah's sufferings, as well as a sharer in the glory to be revealed: shepherd the flock of God that is in your care, exercising oversight not out of constraint, but willingly, as God wants; and not out of a desire for dishonest gain, but with enthusiasm; also not as machers domineering over those in your care, but as people who become examples to the flock.

<u>Revelation 4:10-11</u>
the twenty-four elders fall down before the One sitting on the throne, who lives forever and ever, and worship him. They throw their crowns in front of the throne and say, "You are worthy, ADONAI Eloheinu, to have glory, honor and power, because you created all things—yes, because of your will they were created and came into being!"

Elders Are to Teach

<u>1 Timothy 3:2</u>
A congregation leader must be above reproach, he must be faithful to his wife, temperate, self-controlled, orderly, hospitable and able to teach.

<u>1 Timothy 5:17</u>
The leaders who lead well should be considered worthy of double honor, especially those working hard at communicating the Word and at teaching.

Elders Are to Judge

<u>Exodus 18:13-26</u>
The following day Moshe sat to settle disputes for the people, while the people stood around Moshe from morning till evening. When Moshe's father-in-law saw all that he was doing to the people, he said, "What is this that you are doing to the people? Why do you sit there alone, with all the people standing around you from morning till evening?" Moshe answered his father-in-law, "It's because the people come to me seeking God's guidance. Whenever they have a dispute, it comes to me; I judge between one person and another, and I explain to them God's laws and teachings." Moshe's father-in-law said to him, "What you are doing isn't good. You will certainly wear yourself out—and not only yourself, but these people here with you as well. It's too much for you—you can't do it alone, by yourself. So listen now to what I have to say. I will give you some advice, and God will be with you. You should represent the people before God, and you should bring their cases to God. You should also teach them the laws and the teachings, and show them how to live their lives and what work they should do. But you should choose from among all the people competent men who are God-fearing, honest and incorruptible to be their leaders, in charge of thousands, hundreds, fifties and tens. Normally, they will settle the people's disputes. They should bring you the difficult cases; but ordinary matters they should decide themselves. In this way, they will make it easier for you and share the load with you. If you do this—and God is directing you to do it—you will be able to endure; and all these people too will arrive at their destination peacefully." Moshe paid attention to his father-in-law's counsel

488

and did everything he said. Moshe chose competent men from all Isra'el and made them heads over the people, in charge of thousands, hundreds, fifties and tens. As a general rule, they settled the people's disputes—the difficult cases they brought to Moshe, but every simple matter they decided themselves.

Deuteronomy 1:9-18 (Moses speaking)
At that time I told you, 'You are too heavy a burden for me to carry alone. ADONAI your God has multiplied your numbers, so that there are as many of you today as there are stars in the sky. May ADONAI, the God of your ancestors, increase you yet a thousandfold and bless you, as he has promised you! But you are burdensome, bothersome and quarrelsome! How can I bear it by myself alone? Pick for yourselves from each of your tribes men who are wise, understanding and knowledgeable; and I will make them heads over you.' You answered me, 'What you have said would be a good thing for us to do.' So I took the heads of your tribes, men wise and knowledgeable, and made them heads over you—leaders in charge of thousands, of hundreds, of fifties and of tens, and officers, tribe by tribe. At that time I commissioned your judges, 'Hear the cases that arise between your brothers; and judge fairly between a man and his brother, and the foreigner who is with him. You are not to show favoritism when judging, but give equal attention to the small and to the great. No matter how a person presents himself, don't be afraid of him; because the decision is God's. The case that is too hard for you, bring to me and I will hear it.' I also gave you orders at that time concerning all the things you were to do.

Deuteronomy 16:18-20
You are to appoint judges and officers for all your gates [in the cities] ADONAI your God is giving you, tribe by tribe; and they are to judge the people with righteous judgment. You are not to distort justice or show favoritism, and you are not to accept a bribe, for a gift blinds the eyes of the wise and twists the words of even the upright. Justice, only justice, you must pursue; so that you will live and inherit the land ADONAI your God is giving you.

Deuteronomy 17:8-12
If a case comes before you at your city gate which is too difficult for you to judge, concerning bloodshed, civil suit, personal injury or any other controversial issue; you are to get up, go to the place which ADONAI your God will choose, and appear before the cohanim, who are L'vi'im, and the judge in office at the time. Seek their opinion, and they will render a verdict for you. You will then act according to what they have told you there in that place which ADONAI will choose; you are to take care to act according to all their instructions. In accordance with the Torah they teach you, you are to carry out the judgment they render, not turning aside to the right or the left from the verdict they declare to you. Anyone presumptuous enough not to pay attention to the cohen appointed there to serve ADONAI your God or to the judge—that person must die. Thus you will exterminate such wickedness from Isra'el-

Ruth 4:1-2
Meanwhile, Bo'az had gone up to the gate and had sat down there, when the redeemer of whom Bo'az had spoken passed by. "Such-and-such," he said, "come over, and sit down"; so he came over and sat down. He took ten of the city's leaders and said, "Sit down here"; and they sat down.

1 Corinthians 6:1-5

How dare one of you with a complaint against another go to court before pagan judges and not before God's people? Don't you know that God's people are going to judge the universe? If you are going to judge the universe, are you incompetent to judge these minor matters? Don't you know that we will judge angels, not to mention affairs of everyday life? So if you require judgments about matters of everyday life, why do you put them in front of men who have no standing in the Messianic Community? I say, shame on you! Can it be that there isn't one person among you wise enough to be able to settle a dispute between brothers?

Elders Are to Make Halachah

Acts 15:1-31

But some men came down from Y'hudah to Antioch and began teaching the brothers, "You can't be saved unless you undergo b'rit-milah in the manner prescribed by Moshe." This brought them into no small measure of discord and dispute with Sha'ul and Bar-Nabba. So the congregation assigned Sha'ul, Bar-Nabba and some of themselves to go and put this sh'eilah before the emissaries and the elders up in Yerushalayim. After being sent off by the congregation, they made their way through Phoenicia and Shomron, recounting in detail how the Gentiles had turned to God; and this news brought great joy to all the brothers. On arrival in Yerushalayim, they were welcomed by the Messianic community, including the emissaries and the elders; and they reported what God had done through them. But some of those who had come to trust were from the party of the P'rushim; and they stood up and said, "It is necessary to circumcise them and direct them to observe the Torah of Moshe." The emissaries and the elders met to look into this matter. After lengthy debate, Kefa got up and said to them, "Brothers, you yourselves know that a good while back, God chose me from among you to be the one by whose mouth the Goyim should hear the message of the Good News and come to trust. And God, who knows the heart, bore them witness by giving the Ruach HaKodesh to them, just as he did to us; that is, he made no distinction between us and them, but cleansed their heart by trust. So why are you putting God to the test now by placing a yoke on the neck of the talmidim which neither our fathers nor we have had the strength to bear? No, it is through the love and kindness of the Lord Yeshua that we trust and are delivered—and it's the same with them." Then the whole assembly kept still as they listened to Bar-Nabba and Sha'ul tell what signs and miracles God had done through them among the Gentiles. Ya'akov broke the silence to reply. "Brothers," he said, "hear what I have to say. Shim'on has told in detail what God did when he first began to show his concern for taking from among the Goyim a people to bear his name. And the words of the Prophets are in complete harmony with this for it is written, '"After this, I will return; and I will rebuild the fallen tent of David. I will rebuild its ruins, I will restore it, so that the rest of mankind may seek the Lord, that is, all the Goyim who have been called by my name," says ADONAI, who is doing these things.' All this has been known for ages. Therefore, my opinion is that we should not put obstacles in the way of the Goyim who are turning to God. Instead, we should write them a letter telling them to abstain from things polluted by idols, from fornication, from what is strangled and from blood. For from the earliest times, Moshe has had in every city those who proclaim him, with his words being read in the synagogues every Shabbat." Then the emissaries and the elders, together with the whole Messianic community, decided to select men from among themselves to send to Antioch with Sha'ul and Bar-Nabba. They sent Y'hudah, called Bar-Sabba, and Sila, both leading men among the brothers, with the following letter: From: The emissaries and the elders, your brothers To: The brothers from among the Gentiles throughout Antioch, Syria and Cilicia: Greetings! We have heard that some people went out from among us without our authorization, and that they have upset you with their talk, unsettling your minds. So we have decided unanimously to select men and send them to you with our dear friends Bar-Nabba and Sha'ul, who have dedicated their lives to upholding the name of our Lord, Yeshua the Messiah. So we have sent Y'hudah and Sila, and they will confirm in person what we are writing. For it seemed good to the Ruach HaKodesh and to us not to lay any heavier burden on you than the following requirements: to abstain from what has been sacrificed to idols, from blood, from things strangled, and from fornication. If you keep yourselves from these, you will be doing the right thing. Shalom! The messengers were sent off and went to Antioch, where they gathered the group together and delivered the letter. After reading it, the people were delighted by its encouragement.

Acts 16:3-4
Sha'ul wanted Timothy to accompany him; so he took him and did a b'rit-milah, because of the Jews living in those areas; for they all knew that his father had been a Greek. As they went on through the towns, they delivered to the people the decisions reached by the emissaries and the elders in Yerushalayim for them to observe.

Commentary.

This *Mitzvah* presents Scriptures supporting the statement: "We are to appoint elders in our communities to lead, pray, judge, teach, and make *halachah*." The Scriptures on appointing, leading, praying, and teaching are self-explanatory, so this commentary is limited to discussing the role of elders making *halachah.*

Halachot are rules that have the force of law in a Jewish community. Elders of a Messianic Jewish congregational (or network of congregations) community can declare *halachah* (law) for their congregation or network if their community acknowledges that they have been given the authority to do so by Scripture. Examples of common *halachic* rules for congregations are (a) membership in the congregation requires tithing; (b) membership in the congregation requires attendance at services; (c) pork products are not allowed to be served at congregational meals; and (d) men that assist in a *Shabbat Torah* service must wear a *tallit gadol.*

During the Mosaic era, elders were appointed to sit at the gates of the Israelites' cities and judge cases that were brought to them (e.g. Deuteronomy 21:18-21; Ruth 4:1-2). With one exception, the cases decided by elders that we read about in the Bible are those in which a person lodges a complaint against another person. The exception, the one in which *halachah* is made, is Acts 15:1-31. In that Scripture, elders and apostles gathered in Jerusalem to consider and rule upon how much of *Torah* (Mosaic Law) is required of the Gentiles.

It is an inescapable necessity that elders of a community interpret God's Law (both Mosaic and New Covenant) for their respective communities, and make decisions as to the Law's application. If they do not, the practices of individuals and families within each community will be out of step with one another, confusion will result, and the community will not be able to function. Here is a Scripture from the Mosaic era that will illustrate my point; it is the familiar commandment to keep the *Shabbat:*

> Exodus 20:8-10: *"Remember the day, Shabbat, to set it apart for God. You have six days to labor and do all your work, but the seventh day is a Shabbat for ADONAI your God. On it, you are not to do any kind of work—not you, your son or your daughter, not your male or female slave, not your livestock, and not the foreigner staying with you inside the gates to your property."*

But, what constitutes work? Continuing in one's income-producing occupation is obviously the kind of work that is prohibited by the Scripture, but what about an elderly or disabled person walking three miles to a synagogue? That is obviously hard work for them, so is it allowed? If the elders of the synagogue community determine that it is, or is not, and make their ruling a standard for that community, they are making *halachah,* and such decisions are absolutely necessary for a community of individuals to be able to function together.

There are hundreds if not thousands of such examples, but I will present just one more for clarity; referring to the Feast of Unleavened bread, we read:

> Exodus 12:15: *"For seven days you are to eat matzah—on the first day remove the leaven from your houses. For whoever eats hametz [leavened bread] from the first to the seventh day is to be cut off from Isra'el."*

But what does it mean to eat *matzah* for seven days? Does it mean to eat it every day for seven days, or does it only mean to not eat leavened bread for seven days? And what constitutes *chametz?* Clearly, bread risen with yeast is *chametz,* but is it also other foods that have yeast in them? And if we let a piece of *matzah* be exposed to the air long enough for yeast spores from the air to fall on it, does the *matzah* become *chametz* and therefore unacceptable to be eaten during *Pesach* and the week following? These are the kinds of decisions that are best made by the Jewish community in which we live, and when the elders of our community declare the answers to these and similar questions, they are making *halachah* for their community.

The concept of *halachah* is not the same in the Messianic Jewish community as in the wider Jewish community. In the wider Jewish community, *halachah* is inextricably connected to certain ancient rabbis whose rulings on Mosaic Law (both written and oral) are recorded in the *Talmud. Responsa* are modern (and not-so-modern) era decisions and rulings made by respected Jewish scholars in response to questions of Jewish law put to them—also involving the written and (what they consider) oral Mosaic law. Messianic Jewish *halachah,* however, is fundamentally different in that it does not acknowledge an oral *Torah,* and looks to the Scriptures (Old and New Testaments) as the only divine authority. It does, from time to time, consider teachings in the *Talmud*—not for their authority, but for information about what is considered to be Jewish in the wider Jewish community, and occasionally for interpretive wisdom and cultural application.

There is another way in which Messianic and "wider-Jewish-world" *halachah* are different, and that is that Messianic Judaism seeks God's interpretation of His Law, whereas Orthodox Judaism believes that it has the authority to interpret it themselves and even change God's *Torah;* the origin of this belief can be found in *TB Bava Metziah 59b*, in which one translation states:[136]

> *"It has been taught: On that day R. Eliezer brought forward every imaginable argument, 3 but they did not accept them. Said he to them: 'If the halachah agrees with me, let this carob-tree prove it!' Thereupon the carob-tree was torn a hundred cubits out of its place—others affirm, four hundred cubits. 'No proof can be brought from a carob-tree,' they retorted. Again he said to them: 'If the halachah agrees with me, let the stream of water prove it!' Whereupon the stream of water flowed backwards—'No proof can be brought from a stream of water,' they rejoined. Again he urged: 'If the halachah agrees with me, let the walls of the schoolhouse prove it,' whereupon the walls inclined to fall. But R. Joshua rebuked them, saying: 'When scholars are engaged in a halachic dispute, what have ye to interfere?' Hence they did not fall, in honor of R. Joshua, nor did they resume the upright, in honor of R. Eliezer; and they are still standing thus inclined. Again he said to them: 'If the halachah agrees with me, let it be proved from Heaven!' Whereupon a Heavenly Voice cried out: 'Why do ye dispute with R. Eliezer, seeing that in all matters the halachah agrees with him!' But R. Joshua arose and exclaimed: 'It is not in heaven.'4 What did he mean by this?—Said R. Jeremiah: That the Torah had already been given at Mount Sinai; we pay no attention to a Heavenly Voice, because Thou hast long since written in the Torah at Mount Sinai, After the majority must one incline."*

The *Mitzvot* presented in this book are my and Dr. Juster's offered suggestions for Messianic Jewish (New Covenant) *halachah,* but can only become *halachah* if and when they are received as such by a Messianic Jewish community.

Classical Commentators

This *Mitzvah* is not addressed by any of the classical commentators.

NCLA: JMm JFm KMm KFm GMm GFm

---

136 Online Soncino Babylonian Talmud Translation, Rabbi Dr. I. Epstein, editor, 2015.